Lecture Notes in Computer Science 7517

Commenced Publication in 1973
Founding and Former Series Editors:
Gerhard Goos, Juris Hartmanis, and Jan van Leeuwen

Jacques Blanc-Talon   Wilfried Philips
Dan Popescu   Paul Scheunders
Pavel Zemčík (Eds.)

Advanced Concepts for Intelligent Vision Systems

14th International Conference, ACIVS 2012
Brno, Czech Republic, September 4-7, 2012
Proceedings

 Springer

Volume Editors

Jacques Blanc-Talon
DGA, 92 221 Bagneux, France
E-mail: jacques.blanc-talon@dga.defense.gouv.fr

Wilfried Philips
Ghent University
Telecommunications and Information Processing (TELIN)
9000 Ghent, Belgium
E-mail: wilfried.philips@telin.ugent.be

Dan Popescu
CSIRO ICT Centre, Epping, NSW 1710, Australia
E-mail: dan.popescu@csiro.au

Paul Scheunders
University of Antwerp, 2610 Wilrijk, Belgium
E-mail: paul.scheunders@ua.ac.be

Pavel Zemčík
Brno University of Technology, Faculty of Information Technology
61266 Brno, Czech Republic.
E-mail: zemcik@fit.vutbr.cz

ISSN 0302-9743   e-ISSN 1611-3349
ISBN 978-3-642-33139-8   e-ISBN 978-3-642-33140-4
DOI 10.1007/978-3-642-33140-4
Springer Heidelberg Dordrecht London New York

Library of Congress Control Number: 2012945428

CR Subject Classification (1998): I.4, I.5, C.2, I.2, I.2.10, H.3-4

LNCS Sublibrary: SL 6 – Image Processing, Computer Vision,
Pattern Recognition, and Graphics

Typesetting: Camera-ready by author, data conversion by Scientific Publishing Services, Chennai, India

Printed on acid-free paper

Springer is part of Springer Science+Business Media (www.springer.com)

Preface

This volume collects the papers accepted for presentation at the 14th International Conference on "Advanced Concepts for Intelligent Vision Systems" (ACIVS 2012), which was organized in Brno University of Technology, in the Czech Republic. Following the first meeting in Baden-Baden (Germany) in 1999, which was part of a large multiconference, the ACIVS conference has since then developed into an independent scientific event and has maintained the tradition of being a single-track conference. ACIVS 2012 attracted scientists from 21 different countries, mostly from Europe, but also from Australia, Japan, Korea, China, Algeria, the United Arab Emirates, Canada, and the USA.

Although ACIVS is a conference on all areas of image and video processing, submissions tend to gather within some major fields of interest. This year, most of the papers dealt with image analysis and computer vision, with a focus on detection, recognition, tracking, and identification.

We would like to thank the invited speakers Heikki Kälviäinen (Lappeenranta University of Technology), Brian Barsky (University of California, Berkeley), and Josef Kittler (University of Surrey) for enhancing the technical program with their presentations.

A conference like ACIVS would not be feasible without the concerted effort of many people and the support of various institutions. The paper submission and review procedure was carried out electronically and a minimum of three reviewers was assigned to each paper. From 81 submissions, 37 were selected for oral presentation and nine as posters. A large and energetic Program Committee, helped by additional referees (about 70 people in total) – listed on the following pages – completed the long and demanding reviewing process. We would like to thank all of them for their timely and high-quality reviews. Also, we would like to thank our sponsors, Camea, Ghent University, Honeywell, Redhat, Unis, and Zoner for their valuable support.

Last but not least, we would like to thank all the participants who trusted in our ability to organize this conference for the 14th time. We hope they attended a stimulating scientific event and enjoyed the atmosphere of the ACIVS social events in the city of Brno.

July 2012

J. Blanc-Talon
D. Popescu
W. Philips
R. Kleihorst
P. Scheunders
P. Zemcik

Organization

Acivs 2012 was organized by Brno University of Technology, Czech Republic.

Steering Committee

Jacques Blanc-Talon   DGA, France
Wilfried Philips   Ghent University - IBBT, Belgium
Dan Popescu   CSIRO, Australia
Paul Scheunders   University of Antwerp, Belgium
Pavel Zemcik   Brno University of Technology, Czech Republic

Organizing Committee

Roman Juranek   Brno University of Technology, Czech Republic
Lukáš Maršík   Brno University of Technology, Czech Republic
Jozef Mlích   Brno University of Technology, Czch Republic
Jan Navrátil   Brno University of Technology, Czech Republic
Ondřej Nečas   Brno University of Technology, Czech Republic
Marek Šolony   Brno University of Technology, Czech Republic

Sponsors

Acivs 2012 was sponsored by the following organizations:

- Camea
- Ghent University
- Honeywell
- Redhat
- Unis
- Zoner

Program Committee

Hamid Aghajan   Stanford University, USA
Marc Antonini   Université de Nice Sophia Antipolis, France
Philippe Bolon   University of Savoie, France
Don Bone   Cannon Information Systems Research, Australia
Salah Bourennane   Ecole Centrale de Marseille, France
Toby Breckon   Cranfield University, UK
Dumitru Burdescu   University of Craiova, Romania

Nicole Vincent   Université Paris Descartes, France
Gerald Zauner   Fachhochschule Ober Osterreich, Austria
Djemel Ziou   Sherbrooke University, Canada

Reviewers

Hamid Aghajan   Stanford University, USA
Marc Antonini   Université de Nice Sophia Antipolis, France
Sileye Ba   Telecom Bretagne, FR
Jacques Blanc-Talon   DGA, France
Philippe Bolon   University of Savoie, France
Don Bone   Cannon Information Systems Research,
                                      Australia
Salah Bourennane   Ecole Centrale de Marseille, France
Patrick Bouthemy   IRISA/INRIA, France
Toby Breckon   Cranfield University, UK
Dumitru Burdescu   University of Craiova, Romania
Vicent Caselles   Universitat Pompeu Fabra, Spain
Jocelyn Chanussot   Grenoble Institute of Technology, France
Pamela Cosman   University of California at San Diego, USA
Jennifer Davidson   Iowa State University, USA
Arturo de la Escalera Hueso   Universidad Carlos III de Madrid, Spain
Bjorn De Sutter   Ghent University, Belgium
Francis Deboeverie   Ghent University College, Belgium
Severine Dubuisson   Laboratoire d'Informatique de Paris 6, France
Marc Ebner   Eberhard Karls Universität Tübingen,
                                      Germany
David Filliat   ENSTA ParisTech, France
Gilles Foulon   ONERA Palaiseau, France
Don Fraser   Australian Defence Force Academy, Australia
Jérôme Gilles   UCLA, USA
Georgy Gimel'farb   The University of Auckland, New Zealand
Dongfeng Han   University of Iowa
Markku Hauta-Kasari   University of Eastern Finland, Finland
Monson Hayes   Georgia Institute of Technology, USA
Adam Herout   Brno University of Technology, Faculty of
                                      Information Technology, Czech Republic
Mark Holden   Australia
Dimitris Iakovidis   Technological Educational Institute of Lamia,
                                      Greece
Ljubomir Jovanov   Ghent University - IBBT, Belgium
Arto Kaarna   Lappeenranta University of Technology,
                                      Finland
Andrzej Kasinski   Poznan University of Technology, Poland
Richard Kleihorst   VITO and Ghent University, Belgium
Nikos Komodakis   University of Crete, Greece

Table of Contents

3D, Optics, and Light

Hardware Mapping

Quality and Documents

Segmentation, Decomposition and Surface

Feature Extraction and Classification

Geometry and Shape

Detection, Recognition and Retrieval

Object Tracking and Identification

System Identification: 3D Measurement Using Structured Light System

Deokwoo Lee and Hamid Krim

Department of Electrical and Computer Engineering
North Carolina State University
Raleigh NC 27606, USA
{dlee4,ahk}@ncsu.edu
http://www.vissta.ncsu.edu/

Abstract. The problem of 3D reconstruction from 2D captured images is solved using a set of cocentric circular light patterns. Once the number of light sources and cameras, their location and the orientations, and the sampling density (the number of circular patterns) are determined, we propose a novel approach to representation of the reconstruction problem as system identification. Akin to system identification using the relationship between input and output, to develop an efficient 3D functional camera system, we identify the reconstruction system by choosing / defining input and output signals appropriately. One algorithm states that an input and an output are defined as projected circular patterns and 2D captured image (overlaid with deformed circular patterns) respectively. Another one is that a 3D target and the captured 2D image are defined as the input and the output respectively, leading to a problem of input estimation by demodulating an output (received) signal. The former approach identifies the system from the ratio of output to input, and is akin to a modulation-demodulation theory, the latter identifies the reconstruction system by estimating the input signal. This paper proposes the approach to identification of reconstruction system, and also substantiates the algorithm by showing results using inexpensive and simple experimental setup.

Keywords: 3D reconstruction, Structured light system, Circular patterns, System identification, Ratio of the output to input, Modulation-demodulation theory.

1 Introduction

Structured light systems have been extensively used to efficiently measure 3D object information (e.g. geometric / photometric information) from 2D observed scenes (e.g. captured image in a camera) ([8], [9], [10]). Jason Geng [11] has reviewed the previous 3D reconstruction algorithms using the deformation of light patterns, phase differences of projected light patterns or codes (e.g. binary, color, etc.) assigned to the patterns. Deokwoo Lee [1] has proposed a simple and efficient reconstruction algorithm using circular light patterns. By establishing a

J. Blanc-Talon et al. (Eds.): ACIVS 2012, LNCS 7517, pp. 1–11, 2012.

relationship between the original circular patterns and the deformed ones due to the surface shape, 3D real world coordinates are recovered. To achieve high quality reconstruction results, we can increase the sampling density (i.e. increase the number of circular patterns to be projected onto the target object.), but the higher reconstruction accuracy may result in complex and high-cost reconstruction system. Akin to sampling rate determination based on the *Shannon-Nyquist Sampling Theorem* [12], maximal spatial frequency component is estimated using specific geometric information (e.g. the highest curvature). The optimal sampling rate, *the minimum number of circular patterns*, for a reconstruction, is determined by the maximum spatial frequency component [13]. In the areas of object recognition or of classification, extremely accurate reconstruction may be inefficient, therefore, approximate reconstruction is sufficient to uniquely characterize the target object and this leads to employing a concept of *system identification*. In the field of system identification, the system is uniquely represented by the interrelationship of the input and the output signal(s) (Fig. 1). The system can be determined efficiently by appropriately selecting input signals, for instance, a *dirac delta function*, a *step function*, a *pseudorandom binary sequence*, a *sinusoidal function*, etc. These are widely used input signals for system representation [14]. The reconstruction problem can be considered a *system identification problem*. Since it is very difficult and inefficient to recover entire 3D object information, efficient 3D reconstruction (approximate reconstruction) may be achieved by simply characterizing the target object, such that recognition or classification is possible. One of the most widely used methods for characterizing a system is representing it using the ratio of output to input. For example, *Fourier transform, Laplace Transform or Z-transform* enables us to represent a system as the ratio of output to input. In the reconstruction work using circular patterns, to employ the concept of *system identification*, the 3D object is defined as the system, and we need to select an appropriate input signal rather than the ideal signals shown above. Therefore, this paper defines the system as the 3D object, and the reconstruction problem is then restated as the system identification problem. The reconstructed object can be represented as the ratio of output to input, where the output includes the information of deformed patterns and the input includes the information of the original patterns. Instead of using ideal input signals, a single circular pattern is projected and the deformed pattern is captured in a 2D image plane. This paper establishes the ratio of the output to input in object space domain, and the characteristics of the object are represented based on the *Thales Theorem* [6].

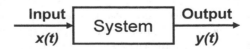

Fig. 1. A system (generally, static or dynamic) with input $x(t)$ and output $y(t)$ is defined as the ratio of the output to input in frequency, Laplace or Z domain

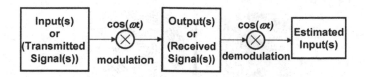

Fig. 2. In communication system, the *modulation-demodulation theory* is used to detect the user(s) or transmitted signals from the output signal(s) using carrier signal, $\cos \omega t$

Another method to achieve an efficient reconstruction system is employing communication systems. In communication systems, modulation-demodulation theory [7] is used to detect / estimate a transmitted signal (input signal). Carrier frequency is used for modulation and demodulation processes (Fig. 2). The *modulation-demodulation theory* can be applied to the reconstruction system by defining the input and output signal as the 3D object which is to be reconstructed and the observed scene in a 2D image plane, respectively. Although we do not actually use the carrier signal, in the reconstruction system, circular patterns play the role of a carrier signal (Section 3.2). This paper provides method to represent 3D reconstruction results, especially in a multiple-projector(input)-viewpoints(output) system, using a modulation-demodulation theory, called *MIMO-MODEM reconstruction*. There have been no contributions relating the reconstruction problem to system identification, by representing the reconstruction system using a *the ratio of output to input* or a *modulation-demodulation theory*, and we can achieve a very efficient reconstruction system leading to the development of an efficient and low-cost 3D functional camera. In addition the proposed approaches can be applied to many areas of 3D imaging.

The organization of the rest of the paper is as follows : The next section will briefly explains a geometric 3D reconstruction algorithm which is designed on the basis of structured circular light patterns. Section 3 is the most important contribution of this paper, where the reconstruction problem is represented as the *system identification* problem ; *the ratio of output to input* and a *modulation-demodulation theory*. Using a *system identification*, the ratio of the output to input in a space domain represents the *system function* of the reconstruction work, and the output and input correspond to the characteristics of the deformed and the original circular patterns, respectively (Section 3.1). *Modulation-demodulation theory* is employed to represent the reconstruction problem by estimating input signal(s) (the target object(s)) (Section 3.2). We substantiate the proposed algorithms in Section 4 prior to the conclusion.

2 Geometric 3D Recovery Algorithm

The problem of 3D reconstruction from 2D captured images is solved using a set of cocentric circular patterns each of which has a different radius. Without any prior information about a target, the reconstruction problem can be solved by the active method. The patterns projected onto the object surface are deformed due

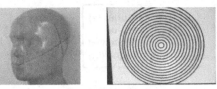

Face Model and Circular Patterns

Projected Circular Patterns

Geometrical Representation

Fig. 3. A face model is illuminated by a set of cocentric circular patterns. Given the information of the original circular patterns, deformed circular patterns provides sufficient information to recover 3D real world coordinates of the face model.

to its shape. Comparison between the original circular patterns and the deformed ones provides sufficient information to recover complete 3D coordinates of the target (Fig 3). The structure of circular patterns (i.e. radii and the location of the center of circles, and the location of the light source are known), the location of the arbitrary reference plane and optical center of the camera are also known as assumed in Deokwoo's work [1]. Although the calibration of a camera and projector is also an independent research topic in 3D imaging, this paper is focused on the geometric reconstruction algorithm ([2], [3], [4]). In [1], mathematical modeling and simulation results are presented, and this paper uses the principle of the reconstruction algorithm using circular patterns to represent the reconstruction algorithm as a system identification.

3   System Identification

This section details the approaches to representing the reconstruction problem using a *system identification*. In general, a system is composed of input and output. The reconstruction problem is restated as the relationship between input and output signals in Section 3.1. Alternatively, the reconstruction problem may be restated as an input estimation problem. In communication systems, the transmitted signal is estimated using a *carrier signal* when we use a *modulation-demodulation theory*. The object to be reconstructed is considered an estimated input and the *carrier signal* is considered a set circular patterns each of which has a different radius. To avoid confusion, the input, output and system are denoted by $A(t)$, $B(t)$ and $H(t)$, respectively, and t, the position of a circular pattern, is sometimes omitted.

3.1   The Ratio of Output to Input

Let us define A, H and B as an inputs, system and output respectively. In the reconstruction problem, the target object $(H \subset \mathbb{R}^3)$ is projected on a set of circular patterns $(A \subset \mathbb{R}^3)$. The observed scene $(B \subset \mathbb{R}^2)$ is in a 2D image plane, and is an object overlaid with circular patterns. In general, a very well known method to identify a system is by estimating or measuring an output signal as a response to *dirac delta function* as an input signal. In our image reconstruction problem, since generating such an input signal is not possible in practice, we use a single circular pattern to identify a system (i.e. a target object). Our goal in this section is to acquire a system function, H, using A and B. Let $M \subset \mathbb{R}^3$ and $m \subset \mathbb{R}^2$ be real points of an object and imaged points, respectively. According to the *Thales' Theorem* [6], the relationship between M and m is the following (or see Fig. 4):

$$x = z\frac{u}{f}, \ y = z\frac{v}{f}, \tag{1}$$

$$x^2 + y^2 = R^2, \tag{2}$$

$$z = \frac{fR}{\sqrt{u^2 + v^2}}, \tag{3}$$

where f is the *focal length* of a camera, and R is a radius of a circular pattern, respectively (See Fig.4). The depth value, z characterizes the target object because it deforms the projected circular patterns, and we define the *system function* as *the ratio of the output to input*,

$$H(t) = \frac{B(t)}{A(t)}, \tag{4}$$

$$A(t) = \frac{1}{f(t)R(t)}, \tag{5}$$

$$B(t) = \frac{1}{\sqrt{u(t)^2 + v(t)^2}}, \tag{6}$$

where the domain of input and output is defined as the positions of projected curves (Fig. 5) and the *focal length* is assumed to be invariant (i.e. $f(t) = f$). Alternatively, the ratio of neighboring depths can be considered a system function (i.e. $H(t) = \frac{z(t)}{z(t+1)}$). Another approach to the system identification is the ratio of a curve velocity. The velocity of a curve $(\alpha(t) = (x(t), y(t)))$ is $\sqrt{x'(t)^2 + y'(t)^2}$, and let V_I and V_O be a velocity of an original circle and a deformed circle, respectively. The system function $H = \frac{V_O}{V_I}$ is represented as

$$V_I = \sqrt{x_I'(t)^2 + y_I'(t)^2} = R(t)\omega(t), \tag{7}$$

$$V_O = \sqrt{x_O'(t)^2 + y_O'(t)^2} = \sqrt{\left(\frac{dr(t)}{dt}\right)^2 + \theta'(t)^2 r^2(t)}, \tag{8}$$

$$x_I'(t) = \frac{dx_I(t)}{dt}, \ y_I'(t) = \frac{dy_I(t)}{dt},$$

$$x_O'(t) = \frac{dx_O(t)}{dt}, \ y_O'(t) = \frac{dy_O(t)}{dt},$$

$$H = \frac{V_O}{V_I}, \tag{9}$$

where $\theta(t) = \arctan(y_O'(t)/x_O'(t))$, $\alpha_I(t) = (x_I(t), y_I(t))$ and $\alpha_O(t) = (x_O(t), y_O(t))$ represent the original circular patterns and the deformed patterns, respectively, and $\omega(t)$ is an angular frequency. Using a *Fourier Descriptor* [5], we

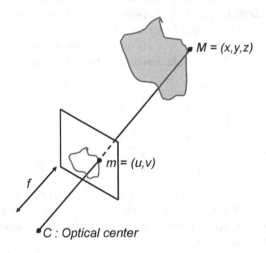

Fig. 4. According to *Thales' Theorem*, and using circular patterns, the relationship between 3D and 2D points is established

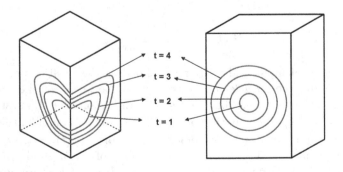

Fig. 5. Instead of *Fourier, Laplace* or *Z domain*, our system is defined in the domain of the position of a circular pattern

also can obtain a ratio of fourier coefficients of original and deformed circles to identify a system. The system function may be acquired using intensity values of illuminated light patterns on an object. Assuming that the distance between an arbitrary reference plane of an object and a light source is invariant, the light intensity of illuminated light patterns on the object depends only on the depth of the object (by *the Inverse-Square Law*) [15]. This idea leads to the reconstruction system using a shape from shading algorithm ([16]).

3.2 MIMO MODEM Theoretic Algorithm

This section formulates the reconstruction problem using concepts of the *multiple input-multiple output* communication system and *modulation-demodulation* theory. In communication systems, once signals are transmitted with a carrier signal, called *modulation*, transmitted signals are estimated / detected by demodulating received signals (*demodulation*) (Fig. 2). When the signal is transmitted and reconstructed, a *Nyquist Sampling Rate* is used. A low-pass filter is used to complete the transmitted signal estimation and the cutoff frequency is determined by the bandwidth of the transmitted signal. Akin to the principle of modulation and demodulation, our reconstruction problem may be stated using the same system notions. The transmitted signals and the received ones correspond to the target object(s) and the captured image(s) of the object(s) overlaid with projected circular light patterns. Once the transmitted and received signals are defined, we need to define the *carrier frequency component* to complete a reconstruction system (we call this a *MODEM reconstruction system*). Since the target(s) are overlaid with the projected circular patterns, and the solution of the depth recovery problem is closely related to the radius of the pattern (Eq. (3)), the *carrier frequency component* may associated to the radius of the pattern. Let $\mathbf{A} = [A_1, A_2, ..., A_N]$ be a set of target objects (or a single object composed of N subsets, A_1, A_2, ..., A_N), and $\mathbf{B} = [B_1, B_2, ..., B_N]$ be a set of observed scenes, using the previously derived reconstruction algorithm, the carrier frequency for a demodulation corresponds to $\frac{1}{f\mathbf{R}}$, where $\mathbf{R} = [R_1, R_2, ..., R_N]$ is a set of radii of circular patterns. Modulation process corresponds to projecting a circular pattern whose radius is $\mathbf{R}$. Note that $f\mathbf{R}$ is defined as the carrier frequency component of a reconstruction system (Fig. 6). Let $\mathbf{A}' = [A'_1, A'_2, ..., A'_N]$ be the estimated / detected transmitted signal(s), we can then write,

$$\mathbf{B} = \mathbf{A} \otimes_{mod} f\mathbf{R}, \tag{10}$$

$$\mathbf{A}' = \mathbf{B} \otimes_{demod} f\mathbf{R}, \tag{11}$$

where $\otimes_{mod}$ and $\otimes_{demod}$ are our modulation and demodulation operation, using a projection of circular patterns with radii R_i, and f is the *focal length* of a camera (assumed to be invariant). In Fig. 6, Obj_i is the input signal which is to be reconstructed, and the input is illuminated by a circular pattern. Projection of light patterns is referred to as *circular modulation*. Modulated input signals are represented as (u_i, v_i), captured image points in a 2D image plane. Using

Eq. 3, the depth of the object is recovered (to avoid confusion, $\otimes_{demod}$ is referred to as a *circular demodulation*). Akin to determining the sampling rate based on the *Shannon-Nyquist Sampling Theorem*, Deokwoo [13] presented an algorithm for a sampling rate determination to recover a surface coordinates, which is the minimum number of circular patterns (i.e. the minimum number of components $[R_1, R_2, \ldots, R_N]$). The reconstruction problem using circular light patterns with an arbitrary sized object or any number of objects may hence be restated as a multiple input-multiple output(MIMO) theoretic problem with an associated solution.

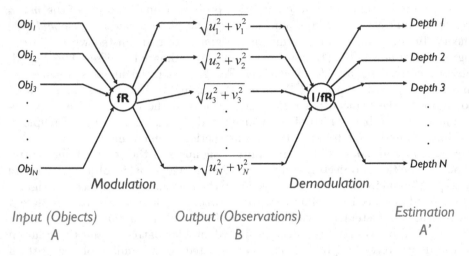

Fig. 6. Radius of a projected circular pattern is used to estimate the depth of an object and the reconstruction system can be represented using a communication system

4   Experimental Results

This section substantiates the proposed algorithm using simple experimental setup. To acquire clear projected light patterns on the object, we used a projector, but from a practical perspective, low-cost LED light source and a light modulator may be used instead of a projector. The experimental system includes projectors, cameras and a generic 3D object. A single-projector-viewpoint (SPV) and Multiple-projector-viewpoints (MPV) system requires a single projector and a camera (Fig. 7), and two or more projectors and cameras (Fig.s 8 and 9). Each projector, connected to a laptop computer, generates circular patterns, and is located approximately 1 meter away from the object. Regular (simple commercial digital) cameras fixed on tripods are used to capture the object overlaid with the projected circular patterns. These are also located approximately 1 meter away from the object. We used the following projectors and cameras ; 1024 × 768 resolution COMPAQ MP1600, 1024 × 768 resolution LCD EPSON POWERLITE 76C, and 1280 × 720 pixel resolution Canon camera [17]. The camera calibration

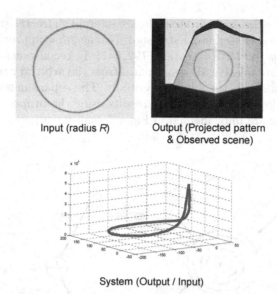

Fig. 7. Reconstruction of a terrain model Input : A, Output : B and System : $H = B/A$

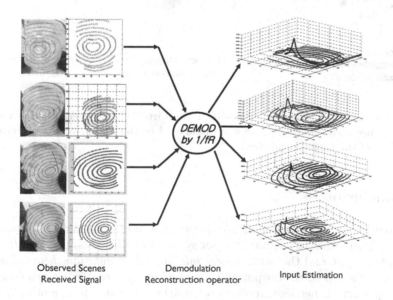

Fig. 8. The observed scene is composed of the target object overlaid with circular patterns. Akin to demodulation of communication system for estimating transmitted signals, the input, 3D object from each viewpoint, is estimated using projected circular patterns.

is performed using a checkerboard to estimate internal characteristics such as the *focal length*, an *image center*, etc. Estimated *focal length* is approximately 2480.3 pixels and an *image center*, (u_o, v_o), is $(792, 547)$. In reconstruction work, since we intend to measure relative 3D coordinates from the arbitrary reference plane, we deal with a scaling factor only tangentially. These parameters constitute a *projection matrix* [6]. The experimental results using the proposed algorithm in Section 3.1 and 3.2 are implemented in Fig.s 7, and 9, respectively.

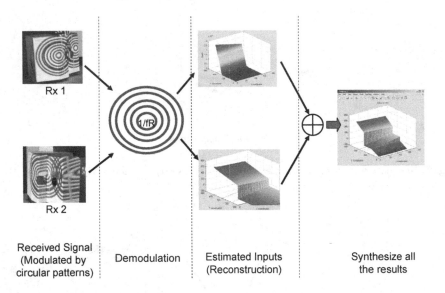

Fig. 9. The observed scene is composed of the target object overlaid with circular patterns. Once each observed scene is demodulated by the same circular patterns, 3D coordinates of the target is achieved.

5   Conclusion

In this paper, we have proposed a novel approach to reconstruction system identification. There were two approaches for system identification, one uses *the ratio of output to input*, and the other *the modulation - demodulation theory*. The former defines the input, the output and the system as a circular pattern (single or multiple patterns if needed), reconstructed 3D coordinates (i.e. depth), and the captured image of deformed patterns, respectively. By establishing the relationship between the parameters of the original and deformed circular patterns, the *system function* is determined in the spatial domain. The latter defines the input and the output as the target object and captured image, respectively. The input, the target, is estimated using a modulation-demodulation theory and this algorithm can be successfully applied to the case of multiple target objects (MIMO theoretic algorithm). Since this paper has presented novel approaches for 3D reconstruction systems related to the *system identification*, there is much future work to improve the proposed algorithm as well as to apply to other research areas, especially in vision, 3D imaging, etc. 3D reconstruction using structured light systems, requires accurate experimental setup for high quality reconstruction results. From a practical perspective, an experimental setup, such as camera calibration, preprocessing of object data to capture accurate 2D data points and a processing of noise effect (e.g. ambient light, specular component of an object, etc) should be carefully handled in future work.

References

1. Lee, D., Krim, H.: 3D Surface Reconstruction Using Structured Circular Light Patterns. In: Blanc-Talon, J., Bone, D., Philips, W., Popescu, D., Scheunders, P. (eds.) ACIVS 2010, Part I. LNCS, vol. 6474, pp. 279–289. Springer, Heidelberg (2010)
2. Hor, M.-K., Tang, C.-Y., Wu, Y.-L., Chan, K.-H., Tsai, J.-J.: Robust refinement methods for camera calibration and 3D reconstruction from multiple images. Pattern Recognition Letters 32(8), 1210–1221 (2011)
3. Li, T., Hu, F., Geng, Z.: Geometric Calibration of a Camera-Projector 3D Imaging System. In: Proceedings of the 10th International Conference on Virtual Reality Continuum and Its Applications in Industry, VRCAI 2011, pp. 187–194 (2011)
4. Wong, K.-Y.K., Zhang, G., Chen, Z.: A Stratified Approach for Camera Calibration Using Spheres. IEEE Transactions on Image Processing 20(2), 305–316 (2011)
5. Zahn, C.T., Roskies, R.Z.: Fourier Descriptors for Plane Closed Curves. IEEE Transactions on Computers C-21(3), 269–281 (1972)
6. Faugeras, O., Luong, Q.-T.: The Geometry of Multiple Images. The MIT Press Cambridge, Massachusetts
7. Proakis, J.G.: Digital Communications, 4th edn. McGraw Hill
8. Bruno, F., Bianco, G., Muzzupappa, M., Barone, S., Razionale, A.V.: Experimentation of structured light and stereo vision for underwater 3D reconstruction. Journal of Photogrammetry and Remote Sensing 66, 508–518 (2011)
9. Salvi, J., Batlle, J., Mouaddib, E.: A robust-coded pattern projection for dynamic 3D scene measurement. Pattern Recognition Letters 19(11), 1055–1065 (1998)
10. Fang, Y.-H., Chou, H.-L., Chen, Z.: 3D shape recovery of complex objects from multiple silhouette images. Pattern Recognition Letters 24(9-10), 1279–1293 (2003)
11. Geng, J.: Structured-light 3D surface imaging: a tutorial. Advances in Optics and Photonics 3(2), 128–160 (2011)
12. Papoulis, A.: Signal Analysis. McGraw-Hill (1977)
13. Lee, D., Krim, H.: A Sampling Theorem for a 2D Surface. In: Bruckstein, A.M., ter Haar Romeny, B.M., Bronstein, A.M., Bronstein, M.M. (eds.) SSVM 2011. LNCS, vol. 6667, pp. 556–567. Springer, Heidelberg (2012)
14. Söderström, T., Stoica, P.: System Identification. Prentice Hall (1989)
15. Iwahori, Y., Sugie, H., Ishii, N.: Reconstructing shape from shading images under point light source illumination. In: 10th International Conference on Pattern Recognition (1990)
16. Zhang, R., Tsai, P.-S., Cryer, J.E., Shah, M.: Shape-from-shading: a survey. Pattern Analysis and Machine Intelligence. IEEE Transactions on Pattern Analysis and Machine Intelligence 21(8), 690–706
17. Lee, D., Krim, H.: Surface Reconstruction: Multiple-View-Projector System. In: International Conference on Image Processing (submitted, 2012)

Gradual Iris Code Construction
from Close-Up Eye Video

Valérian Némesin[1], Stéphane Derrode[1], and Amel Benazza-Benyahia[2]

[1] Univ. Paul Cézanne, Institut Fresnel (CNRS UMR 7249), Domaine Univ. Saint Jérôme, av. Escadrille Normandie-Niémen, 13397 Marseille Cedex 20, France
{vnemesin,sderrode}@fresnel.fr
[2] COSIM Lab., Univ. de Carthage, SUP'COM, Cité Technologique des Communications, Route de Raoued, 2083 El Ghazala, Tunisia
benazza.amel@supcom.rnu.tn

Abstract. This work deals with dynamic iris biometry using video, which is increasingly gaining interest for its flexibility in the framework of biometric portals. We propose several improvements for "real-time" dynamic iris biometry in order to build gradually an iris code of high quality by selecting on-the-fly the best iris images as they appear during acquisition. In particular, tracking is performed using an optimally-tuned Kalman's filter, *i.e.* a Kalman's filter with state and observation matrices specifically learned to follow the movement of a pupil. Experiments on four videos acquired with an IR-sensitive low-cost webcam show reduced computation time with a slight but significant gain in accuracy when compared to the classical Kalman tracker.

The second main contribution is to combine iris codes of images within the video stream providing the "best quality" iris texture. The so-obtained fuzzy iris codes clearly exhibit areas with high confidence and areas with low one due to eyelashes and eyelids. Hence, these areas involve an imprecision in detecting iris and pupil. Such uncertainty can be further exploited for identification.

1 Introduction

The use of close-up eye video for iris biometry has many advantages when compared with conventional type photographic acquisitions. Indeed, still image systems are not easy to use and they require a strict cooperation of the user during acquisition. In general, more acquisitions are needed to obtain an operational image of the iris for recognition purpose.

Close-up eye video can make iris recognition systems more friendly, flexible and so, open to large public applications. Since the pioneering work by W. Ketchantang [7], video-based iris biometry has attracted increasing attention [9,1,8], particular thanks to the deployment of biometric portals. Despite the first published results, video-based iris identification still requires the development of robust algorithms to fully exploit the very rich information conveyed by video for identification.

J. Blanc-Talon et al. (Eds.): ACIVS 2012, LNCS 7517, pp. 12–23, 2012.

Indeed, the video modality poses new problems with respect to still iris images. First the spatial resolution is generally low (*e.g.* 640 × 480) pixels resolution is generally lower and the quality of images is additionally degraded by eye motion blur, especially when using low-cost cameras such as the webcams we consider in this work. Also, to locate pupil and iris with the precision required for identification and with a complexity compatible with on-line processing of the video stream, a very performing pupil tracking algorithm should be implemented.

The work presented in this paper proposes several improvements for "real-time" dynamic iris biometry in order to build an iris code of high quality by selecting on-the-fly the best operational images as they appear during acquisition. In particular, tracking is performed using an optimally-tuned Kalman's filter, *i.e.* a Kalman's filter with state and observation matrices specifically learned to follow the pupil movement. The second contribution is to combine iris codes of images within the video stream providing the "best quality" iris texture, resulting in a fuzzy iris code showing confidence areas that can be taken into account for identification.

The remaining of the paper is organized as follows. Section 2 describes how the optimal Kalman-based tracking is combined with processing methods for robust pupil detection at a low computational cost in close-up eye video. Then, Section 3 deals with external iris border detection that is able to cope partially with eyelids, in a way to select on-the-fly images with exploitable iris texture. We also discuss how to combine iris of selected images in order to construct a fuzzy iris-code that show confidence measure. Section 4 draws conclusion and proposes some perspectives for this work.

2   Optimal Pupil Tracking and Detection

This section is intended to describe how the optimal Kalman-based tracking is combined with some image processing methods for detecting pupil in close-up eye video. The entire algorithm for this task is sketched in flowchart 1.

2.1   Pupil Detection

The following pupil detection algorithm is applied either on a Region Of Interest (ROI) or on the full image (Figure 2a), depending on the success of previous pupil detection. Classically, the pupil is assumed to be a dark and convex region. Before any processing, image histogram is stretched to $[0, 255]$. Let us briefly present the different steps in Figure 1 to extract pupil.

1. Following [10], darkest regions are selected by detecting modes of the ROI smoothed histogram (Figure 2b), and binarizing using the dynamically tuned threshold T_t^{pupil}. Actually, the threshold is set to be the mean value of the ten previous thresholds (Figure 2c).

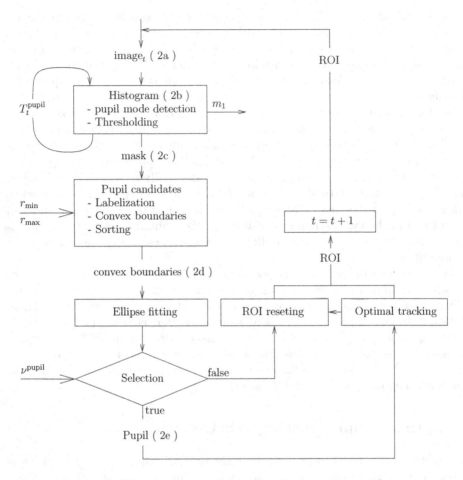

Fig. 1. Flowchart for pupil detection in close-up eye video

2. Then, after applying a closing operator with a disk to the ROI, all candidate regions are first labeled, and their external convex boundary is extracted (Figure 2d). A first selection is operated based on the shape of candidates, according to their compactness (elongated areas which can be found in the ciliary region are eliminated).

3. Finally, for each pre-selected region, the optimal fitting ellipse with parameters x^{pupil}, y^{pupil}, a and b is computed using the method described in [4]. The final candidate if any, is the one that minimizes the following criterion, $|\frac{S_{\text{Ellipse}}}{S_{\text{Connex}}} - \frac{S_{\text{Connex}}}{S_{\text{Ellipse}}}|$ which depends on surface S (Figure 2e). If the criterion is above $\nu^{\text{pupil}} = 0.5$, the pupil is considered lost and the ROI is reset in the next frame. Otherwise, the predicted ROI for the next frame is optimally tuned using the Kalman filter described below.

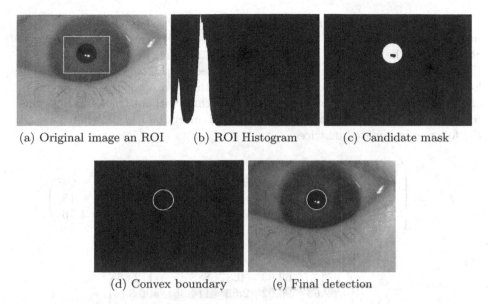

(a) Original image an ROI   (b) ROI Histogram   (c) Candidate mask

(d) Convex boundary   (e) Final detection

Fig. 2. Steps for pupil detection illustrated through an example

2.2 Pupil Tracking

The motion of a pupil is characterized by its position and velocity. Let $(x_t^{\text{pupil}},$ $y_t^{\text{pupil}}, r_t^{\text{pupil}} = \sqrt{a_t^2 + b_t^2})$ represent the instantaneous parameters of pupil circle and (v_t^x, v_t^y) its instant velocity at time t. The hidden state vector can therefore be represented as $\boldsymbol{x}_t = (x_t^P, y_t^P, r_t^P, v_t^x, v_t^y)^T$ and the observed state vector as $\boldsymbol{y}_t = (x_t^{\text{pupil}}, y_t^{\text{pupil}}, r_t^{\text{pupil}})^T$. Let us consider the following dynamic state-space system

$$\boldsymbol{x}_t = \boldsymbol{F}^{x,x} \boldsymbol{x}_{t-1} + \boldsymbol{\omega}_t^x$$
$$\boldsymbol{y}_{t-1} = \boldsymbol{F}^{y,x} \boldsymbol{x}_{t-1} + \boldsymbol{\omega}_t^y$$

where $\boldsymbol{\omega}_t^x \sim \mathcal{N}(0, \boldsymbol{Q}^{x,x})$ and $\boldsymbol{\omega}_t^y \sim \mathcal{N}(0, \boldsymbol{Q}^{y,y})$, two zero-mean and independent Gaussian noise with covariance matrices $\boldsymbol{Q}^{x,x}$ and $\boldsymbol{Q}^{y,y}$. The ROI is updated using Kalman-predicted mean and covariance matrix.

Most of the time, pupil motion is assumed to be a Brownian motion, so that matrices are classically defined by

$$\boldsymbol{F}^{x,x} = \begin{pmatrix} 1 & 0 & 0 & dT & 0 \\ 0 & 1 & 0 & 0 & dT \\ 0 & 0 & 1 & 0 & 0 \\ 0 & 0 & 0 & 0 & 0 \\ 0 & 0 & 0 & 0 & 0 \end{pmatrix} \text{ and } \boldsymbol{F}^{y,x} = \begin{pmatrix} 1 & 0 & 0 & 0 & 0 \\ 0 & 1 & 0 & 0 & 0 \\ 0 & 0 & 1 & 0 & 0 \end{pmatrix},$$

with dT is the temporal sampling period (in our simulation $dT = 0.04$).

The structure of these matrices is not specifically adapted to the real eye motion and we propose to replace them by optimally learned matrix entries, according to the maximum likelihood rule. To this end, we use the robust EM (Expectation Maximization) algorithm proposed in [11] according to the following procedure. Parameters were learned with video named A (451 frames), observation being given by the detection algorithm (without tracking). Parameters were initialized with classical matrices and, after 200 EM iterations, we get the following estimated matrices

$$\hat{F}^{x,x} = \begin{pmatrix} 0.95 & 0.08 & 0.05 & 0.04 & 0.00 \\ -0.01 & 0.95 & 0.02 & 0.00 & 0.04 \\ 0.00 & -0.00 & 1.00 & 0.00 & 0.00 \\ -0.24 & 0.06 & 0.24 & 0.00 & 0.00 \\ 0.16 & -0.66 & -0.14 & 0.00 & 0.00 \end{pmatrix}, \hat{Q}^{y,y} = \begin{pmatrix} 0.79 & 0.09 & -0.67 \\ 0.09 & 0.31 & 0.18 \\ -0.67 & 0.18 & 1.76 \end{pmatrix}$$

and

$$\hat{Q}^{x,x} = \begin{pmatrix} 274.87 & 62.63 & -0.87 & 888.35 & -112.66 \\ 62.63 & 96.02 & 2.53 & 114.56 & 496.33 \\ -0.87 & 2.53 & 0.42 & -3.81 & 21.59 \\ 888.35 & 114.56 & -3.81 & 3080.31 & -903.77 \\ -112.66 & 496.33 & 21.59 & -903.77 & 3513.55 \end{pmatrix}.$$

One interesting point to note is that the upper 3×3 sub-matrices in $\hat{F}^{x,x}$ is almost diagonal as $F^{x,x}$. However, new dependencies, which are not taken into account in the classical model appear (see for instance the last two rows in $\hat{F}^{x,x}$ corresponding to pupil celerity) and, two first diagonal terms of $\hat{F}^{x,x}$ are 0.95 instead of 1.00 for $F^{x,x}$. They indicate that the subject trended to look to the center of the camera. From $\hat{Q}^{x,x}$ one can also note the low variance of radius variable, which can be explained by the low dilatation of the pupil in that video. The noise covariance matrix $\hat{Q}^{y,y}$ shows that the segmentation algorithm was performing on that video.

To account for the influence of the optimal tracking with respect to the classical one, we conducted the following experiment on 4 close-up eye videos. These videos have been acquired with a webcam-type camera sensitive to near infrared in order to reduce specular spots in the eye. For all the 4 sequences, the pupil was detected using the algorithm described in Section 2.1 using either (i) no specific tracking (and working with the whole images), (ii) classic Kalman tracking or (iii) optimal Kalman tracking. The number of frames lost during tracking and the processing time in frames per second are reported in Table 1. In all cases, the number of lost frames is greatly reduced with Kalman tracking (failure cases is reduced by 20 to 50%) ; small improvements can also be achieved with optimal tracking when compared to the classical one. The second point to note concerns the Frame Per Second (FPS) which is multiplied by 1.5 when Kalman tracking is used. Again, a small improvement is observed when optimal tracking is used in place of classical one. All processed videos are available at url http://www.fresnel.fr/nemesin/index.php?url=demo.php&demo=IT.php.

Table 1. Number of lost frames and processing rates (in Frames Per Second) during the pupil tracking for several video sequences. Lost frames account for the failing detection but also for frames with no pupil in the field of view. The FPS has be measured on a single thread with a 3.0 GHz processor running linux OS.

		FPS	Lost Frames
Video A	Without tracking	43	42 (9.3%)
	Classical Kalman tracking	60	31 (6.9%)
(451 frames)	Optimal Kalman Tracking	64	26 (5.8%)
Video B	Without tracking	44	29 (6.4%)
	Classical Kalman tracking	64	22 (4.9%)
(451 frames)	Optimal Kalman Tracking	68	15 (3.3%)
Video C	Without tracking	41	42 (9.3%)
	Classical Kalman tracking	56	25 (6.9%)
(268 frames)	Optimal Kalman Tracking	65	17 (5.8%)
Video D	Without tracking	42	63 (14.0%)
	Classical Kalman tracking	54	58 (12.9%)
(242 frames)	Optimal Kalman Tracking	58	45 (10.0%)

Figure 3 shows the detection of iris in a test frame with classical Kalman tracking and with optimal Kalman tracking. It is important to note that the ROI size is significantly reduced with optimal filter.

3   Iris Segmentation

This section is concerned with iris border detection from an image where a pupil has been detected (otherwise iris detection is no sense). The entire algorithm for this task is described in flowchart 4a. It is essentially based on the well-known Daugman's algorithm [3], which we combined to an original algorithm described in [5] for refining edge detection.

3.1   Iris Localization

Let us give some brief comments to the steps in flowchart 4a, which are illustrated in 5.

1. An approximate circle for the iris is first computed by the following method (Figure 5a). The rough iris detection is based on the search for external borders along the horizontal line passing through the pupil center. To that goal, the radius is estimated using Bayesian decision on the mixture model made of two equiprobable Gaussian laws $\mathcal{N}(m_1, \sigma_1^2)$ and $\mathcal{N}(m_2, \sigma_2^2)$. Parameters σ_1, m_2 and σ_2 are manually adjusted whereas m_1 is computed as the first local maximum found in the ROI histogram after T^{pupil}. This rough iris detection helps to reduce the size of the search region for the Daugman's algorithm.

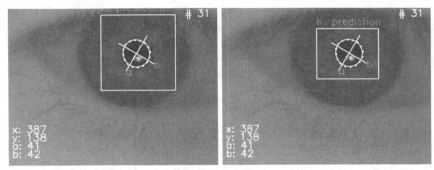

(a) With classical Kalman tracking   (b) With optimal Kalman tracking

Fig. 3. An example of pupil detection for the two strategies mentioned in Table 1. The white box represents the ROI estimated by Kalman filters to predict pupil localization in current frames from previous observations.

2. Then, Daugman's integro-differential [3] operator is used for circle parameter refining (Figure 5b). We can note small differences for estimated parameters.
3. Afterward, the algorithm developed in [5] is used as an eyelid detector. Iris edge is modeled by means of a "one-dimensional Markov field". Pixels inside and outside the iris are assumed to be statistically independent Gaussian random variables. This algorithm determines if a pixel is in the iris area or in the background. In this respect, pixels are characterized by its polar coordinates (r, θ) from the iris center. Iris boundary is parameterized by a radius r_k for all $p = 32$ angular directions θ_k, $k = 1, \ldots, p$. Assuming the intensity of a pixel $I_{\theta_k, r}$ to follow gaussian laws with different parameters for the iris and the background. The related probability density functions (pdfs) can be written:

$$p(I_{\theta_k, r} | r_k) = \frac{\exp\left(-\frac{(I_{\theta_k, r} - m_1)^2}{2\sigma_1^2}\right)}{\sqrt{2\pi}\sigma_1} \text{ if } r \in [\alpha r^{\text{pupil}} : r_k]$$

$$p(I_{\theta_k, r} | r_k) = \frac{\exp\left(-\frac{(I_{\theta_k, r} - m_2)^2}{2\sigma_2^2}\right)}{\sqrt{2\pi}\sigma_2} \text{ if } r \in [r_k + 1 : \beta r^{\text{pupil}}]$$

with parameters α and β are respectively set to 2 and 5 in our experiment. Random variables for radii r_k are assumed to follow a Gaussian Markov random field structure, whose local conditional law is given by

$$p(r_i | r_{i-1}, r_{i+1}) \propto \exp\left(\delta\left((r_i - r_{i-1})^2 + (r_{i+1} - r_i)^2\right)\right),$$

where δ is the regularity parameter.
To find optimal radii, and according to [5], the algorithm decomposes into 2 iterated steps, from an initial position given by Daugman's iris circle:

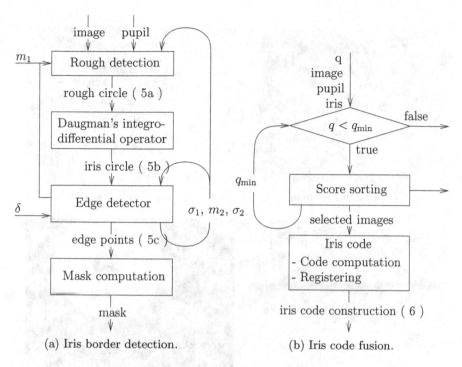

Fig. 4. Flowchart for iris border detection (a) and code construction (b) in close-up video

- Update of m_1, m_2, σ_1 and σ_2: from r_k, Gaussian parameters are updated using empirical formulas.
- Update of radii r_k: optimization is performed by mean of an ICM (Iterated Conditional Mode) algorithm which approximates MAP (Maximum A Posteriori) Bayesian restoration for Markov random fields [2].

For our experiment, convergence of the algorithm is assumed after 10 iterations.

3.2 Focus Score

Not all images for which pupil and iris have been found are employed to construct the iris code. We only take into account images for which the focus score proposed in [6] is above a given threshold (set to 50 in our experiments). The focus score q is computed by following formula

$$q = 100 \times \frac{x}{x+c}, \quad \text{with } x = \frac{\text{energy(Filtered signal)}}{\text{energy(Signal)}}$$

In our experiments, c was set to 0.2. The filtered signal is calculated by convolving the image with Park's filter defined by the kernel:

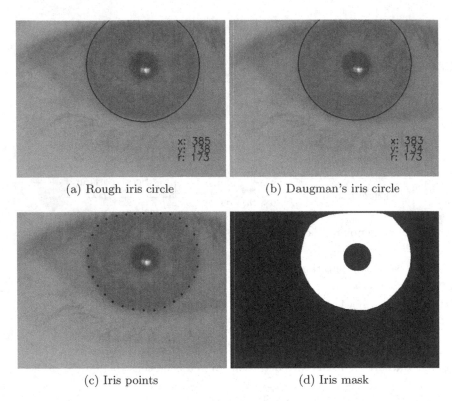

(a) Rough iris circle   (b) Daugman's iris circle

(c) Iris points   (d) Iris mask

Fig. 5. Steps for iris localization illustrated thought an example

$$\begin{vmatrix} -1 & -1 & -1 & -1 & -1 \\ -1 & -1 & +4 & -1 & -1 \\ -1 & +4 & +4 & +4 & -1 \\ -1 & -1 & +4 & -1 & -1 \\ -1 & -1 & -1 & -1 & -1 \end{vmatrix}.$$

3.3   Gradual Iris Code Construction

This section describes how an iris code can be constructed gradually from a video stream. Let us briefly present the different steps sketched in flowchart 4b.

Iris Code Computation. At this stage, we only consider an image at frame t whose focus score is above the threshold q_{min}. Note that this score is evolving during video processing to keep only the N "best quality" images. So, from iris boundaries and pupil parameters, we set (i) an iris mask M_t (Figure 5d), (ii) an iris code I_t from Daugman's work [3], and (iii) a polar occlusion mask. In our algorithm, 360 directions and 160 samples per radius are used for iris code computation.

Iris Code Fusion. At this stage, we considered we have the N "best quality" images from the beginning of the video to the actual time t. Their focus score are denoted q_n, $n \in [1, N]$.

In [8], authors propose to fuse the polar representation of selected iris texture before computing the iris code. Here, we propose to fuse the iris code computed separately for all selected frames.

1. All iris codes are co-registered in rotation according to the minimum Hamming distance from the image with the higher focus score (the registration is tested from $-10°$ to $+10°$).

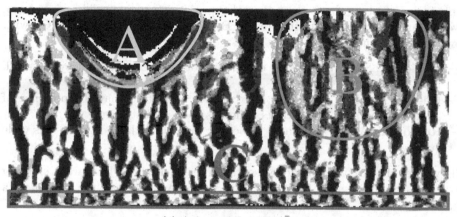

(a) A fuzzy iris code ($\bar{I}$)

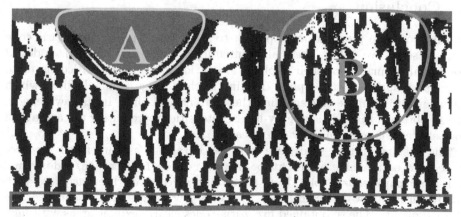

(b) Binarized iris code ($\hat{I}$)

Fig. 6. Example of iris code construction from close-up eye video

2. Then, the following weighted mean between the N iris codes is computed according to

$$\bar{I}(\theta, r) = \frac{\displaystyle\sum_{n=1}^{N} q_n M_n(\theta, r) I_n(\theta, r)}{\displaystyle\sum_{n=1}^{N} q_n M_n(\theta, r)}.$$

An example of fuzzy iris code is shown in Figure 6a.

3. It is possible to get a "hard" copy $\hat{I}$ of the fuzzy iris code by thresholding $\bar{I}$ with respect to 0.5. An example is given in Figure 6b, where the area in red $\hat{M}$ shows the intersection of masks M_n, $n \in [1, N]$.

This fusion strategy shows three typical types of areas –an eyelid region **A**, an eyelash and an eyelash reflection region **B**, and a pupil and iris region **C**– with low levels of confidence:

- **Region A:** Some pixels of the eyelid are not taken into account by the mask $\hat{M}$.
- **Region B:** Many pixels are gray-valued, indicating that the presence of eyelashes degrades the quality of the iris code in that area.
- **Region C:** A lack of data at the outer pupil boundary degrades iris code quality.

Elsewhere, the fuzzy iris code presents large black and white areas showing structures of interest for identification ; transitions between the two show a gradient.

4   Conclusion

In this work, we proposed an approach to compute progressively an iris code from close-up eye video. The main contribution was to combine iris codes of good-quality images for their exploitation in identification. This led us to to develop an optimally-tuned pupil tracking method using Kalman's filter, which has shown to be more efficient than the conventional filter. In its raw version, the so-obtained iris code is in gray-levels, intensities representing the average of the selected iris codes in the video stream.

The results of this study are very encouraging, as illustrated by processed videos available at url http://www.fresnel.fr/nemesin/index.php?url=demo.php&demo=IT.php. Note that these videos have been acquired with an IR-sensitive low-cost camera, so that only few images in the sequences are of good quality. The so-obtained fuzzy iris codes clearly exhibit areas with high confidence and areas with low one. These areas can be related to eyelashes, eyelid and unavoidable imprecision in detecting iris and pupil. The overall processing time –which includes pupil tracking, iris detection and iris code computation–, is "real-time" since FPS is always above 15 when using a single thread with a 3.0GHz processor running linux OS.

We now plan to compare our performances with those obtained with the VASIR project[1] [9] by means of the publicly available MBGC dataset[2], which is made of near infrared image sequences and high definition video sequences of people going through a portal. It will then be possible to measure the impact of spatial and angular resolutions of iris codes for identification and to study several distances to compare gray-level iris codes taking into account the fuzziness of the proposed solution.

Acknowledgment. Authors would like to thank DGA (French *Direction Générale de l'Armement*) and CNRS (*Centre National de la Recherche Scientifique*) for financial support.

References

1. Benletaief, N., Benazza-Benyahia, A., Derrode, S.: Pupil localization and tracking for video-based iris biometrics. In: Proc. of the 10th Int. Conf. on Information Sciences, Signal Processing and their Applications (ISSPA 2010), Kuala Lumpur, Malaysia, pp. 650–653 (2010)
2. Besag, J.: On the statistical analysis of dirty pictures (with discussion). J. of Royal Statistical Society 48(3), 259–302 (1986)
3. Daugman, J.: How iris recognition works. IEEE Trans. on Circuits and Systems for Video Technology 14, 21–30 (2004)
4. Gander, W., Golub, G.H., Strebel, R.: Least-squares fitting of circles and ellipses. BIT Numerical Mathematics 34, 558–578 (1994)
5. Haddouche, A., Adel, M., Rasigni, M., Conrath, J., Bourennane, S.: Detection of the foveal avascular zone on retinal angiograms using Markov random fields. Digital Signal Processing 20, 149–154 (2010)
6. Kang, B.J., Park, K.R.: A Study on Iris Image Restoration. In: Kanade, T., Jain, A., Ratha, N.K. (eds.) AVBPA 2005. LNCS, vol. 3546, pp. 31–40. Springer, Heidelberg (2005)
7. Ketchantang, W., Derrode, S., Bourennane, S., Martin, L.: Video Pupil Tracking for Iris Based Identification. In: Blanc-Talon, J., Philips, W., Popescu, D.C., Scheunders, P. (eds.) ACIVS 2005. LNCS, vol. 3708, pp. 1–8. Springer, Heidelberg (2005)
8. Kien, N., Fookes, C., Sridharan, S., Denman, S.: Quality-driven super-resolution for less constrained iris recognition at a distance and on the move. IEEE Trans. on Information Forensics and Security 6, 1248–1258 (2011)
9. Lee, Y., Phillips, P.J., Micheals, R.J.: An automated video-based system for iris recognition. In: Proc. of the 3rd IAPR-IEEE Int. Conf. on Biometrics, Sassari, Italy (2009)
10. Li, P., Liu, X., Xiao, L., Song, Q.: Robust and accurate iris segmentation in very noisy iris images. Image and Vision Computing 28, 246–253 (2010)
11. Shumway, R.H., Stoffer, D.S.: An approach to time series smoothing and forecasting using the EM algorithm. J. of Time Series Analysis 3(4), 253–264 (1982)

---

[1] Video-based Automated System for Iris Recognition: http://www.nist.gov/itl/iad/ig/vasir.cfm

[2] Multiple Biometric Grand Challenge: http://www.nist.gov/itl/iad/ig/mbgc.cfm

Depth from Vergence and Active Calibration for Humanoid Robots

Xin Wang, Boris Lenseigne, and Pieter Jonker

Delft Bio-robotics Lab, Delft University of Technology,
Mekelweg 2, 2628 CD Delft, The Netherlands
{xin.wang,b.a.j.lenseigne,p.p.jonker}@tudelft.nl

Abstract. In human eyes, many clues are used to perceive depth. For nearby tasks involving eye-hand coordination, depth from vergence is a strong cue. In our research on humanoid robots we study binocular robotic eyes that can pan and tilt and perceive depth from stereo, as well as depth from vergence by fixing both eyes on a nearby object. In this paper, we report on a convergent robot vision set-up: Firstly, we describe the mathematical model for convergent vision system. Secondly, we introduce an algorithm to estimate the depth of an object under focus. Thirdly, as the centers of rotation of the eye motors do not align with the center of image planes, we develop an active calibration algorithm to overcome this problem. Finally, we examine the factors that have impact on the depth error. The results of experiments and tests show the good performance of our system and provide insight into depth from vergence.

Keywords: eye-hand coordination, humanoid robots, depth from vergence, active calibration.

1 Introduction

The human visual system obeys Listing's law, which means that the cyclorotation of the eyes can be predicted from the direction of a fixed point, which is also called vergence. The first to employ the principle of foveated vision is in[1]. Listing's law can be expressed in terms of suitable rotation matrices, which provides the foundation for the model construction of a convergent eyes system[2]. Based on these, We want to develop the human being's vergent vision system for humanoid robots.

Vergence in robotic vision system has been widely investigated over the past decades. The previous researches mainly focus on: design of space variant sensors and models to make the vision system with higher resolution concentrated at foveation[3][4][5]; use of log-polar map to generate foveated image from viewpoint of software[6]; implementation of the control mechanism to maintain the object in the foveation[7][8]; use of PTZ camera to mimic the way of foveated vision system[9]; use of two pair of cameras, one of which is used for object following to make it in the center of the view, one of which is used for standard stereo vision system to derive the depth information[10]; research of the error in depth perception for convergent eyes[11].

J. Blanc-Talon et al. (Eds.): ACIVS 2012, LNCS 7517, pp. 24–35, 2012.

For all above researches they did not give the description of the depth calculation method and they did not concern about the calibration part. In our work we extend previous research and use a pair of motors carrying cameras that can move. We first describe stereopsis for convergent vision system, i.e. both eyes can move(pan and tilt) to track a nearby object in the center view of left and right image. Instead of using disparity between stereo rig to estimate the depth information with respect to stanard stereo system[12], we obtain the depth information by measuring the angles of the axes of left and right eye motors. [13]employs the eye-hand calibration method to calibrate active stereo system which requires high precision motor. We propose a new robust active calibration method which is inspired by standard image rectification method. Comparing with the standard image rectification method that transforms each image plane such that pairs of conjugate epipolar lines become collinear and parallel to one of the image axis (usually the horizontal one)[14], our calibration method makes use of it to transform the image planes such that they become virtually orthogonal to the eye axes. The differences lie in that the main goal of image rectification is to reduce the stereo searching problem from 2D to 1D and it is for fixed set-up. Our calibration method extends the idea of image rectification and it does not involve a stereo matching concern, and it is used for active vision system. In this case, we name it active calibration instead of image rectification to make it more clear and use it to derive more accurate depth calculation performance.

The main contribution in this paper is that we built up a model of a system for convergent robot eyes. Based on this model, we described a simple algorithm for depth estimation and developed a novel active calibration algorithm to improve accuracy of depth calculation.

This paper is organized as follows: in section 2, the model of our convergent eyes system is constructed and described; in section 3, the basic idea of vergence is illustrated and the depth calculation algorithm is presented; in section 4, the active calibration algorithm is proposed and explained; in section 5, the related experimental results are shown; finally, a conclusion with discussion of planned future work is given in section 6.

2   Model of a Convergent Vision System

In this section, we construct and describe a kinematic model of a robot eyes system, which can be easily incorporated into a standard camera model of a stereo vision system. From now on we use the word eye as abbreviation for the robot eye motor system. Fig. 1 shows the geometric configuration of such a system. The system has 4-DOFs: both eyes can pan and tilt around the eye axes. The assumption is that the pan and tilt axes intersect with and are orthogonal to each other and that the joints connecting eyes and cameras are fixed.

2.1   Standard Stereo Camera System

First we introduce some mathematical notations: $P_w = \begin{bmatrix} x_w\ y_w\ z_w \end{bmatrix}^T$ is a point in our 3D world (reference) frame. $P_e = \begin{bmatrix} x_e\ y_e\ z_e \end{bmatrix}^T$ indicates the 3D coordinates

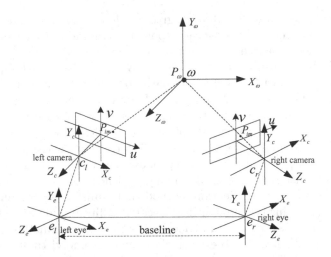

Fig. 1. Kinematic model of the eye-camera system

of an eye, in which we use e_l and e_r to indicate the rotation centers for left and right eye. $P_c = \begin{bmatrix} x_c\ y_c\ z_c \end{bmatrix}^T$ indicates the 3D coordinates of a camera, in which we use c_l and c_r to indicate the optic centers for left and right camera. $P_{im} = \begin{bmatrix} u\ v \end{bmatrix}^T$ indicates the 2D coordinates of an image. Let $\tilde{P}_{im} = \begin{bmatrix} u\ v\ 1 \end{bmatrix}^T$ and $\tilde{P}_w = \begin{bmatrix} x_w\ y_w\ z_w\ 1 \end{bmatrix}^T$ be the homogeneous coordinates of P_{im} and P_w. Then the mapping from 3D world reference coordinates to 2D image coordinates is given by:

$$\lambda \tilde{P}_{im} = H \tilde{P}_w \tag{1}$$

where λ is the scale factor, and H is a projection matrix with the form $H = A\,[R|T]$. H depends on intrinsic and extrinsic parameters. Note that a prerequisite for this model are fixed cameras.

2.2   Kinematics of Eyes Vergence

In contrast with a standard stereo-vision set-up, in our system the eye motors are fixed and the cameras are mounted on a joint on the eye motors. Hence there is a projection relationship between camera frame and eye frame in world coordinates. Consequently, for the kinematic model of our set up we extended the standard stereo camera system. Let rotation matrix R_e and translation vector T_e be the extrinsic parameters specifying the transformation from world coordinates to eye coordinates, let rotation matrix R_c and translation vector T_c be the extrinsic parameters specifying the transformation from eye coordinates to camera coordinates. Then the transformations are:

$$P_e = [R_e|T_e]\,P_\omega \tag{2}$$
$$P_c = [R_c|T_c]\,P_e \tag{3}$$

Define that an initial eye axes at start-up position are orthogonal to $e_r - e_l$. Then define the eye rotation matrices around the initial left eye axis and right eye axis as $R_x^t(\varphi)$ and $R_y^t(\theta)$ at time t from start-up. $R_x^t(\varphi)$ is pan (left and right) rotation matrix which affects the v pixels in image coordinates and $R_y^t(\theta)$ is the tilt (up and down) rotation matrix which affects the u pixels in image coordinates. $R_x^t(\varphi)$ and $R_y^t(\theta)$ are the anticlockwise rotations around angles φ and angle θ:

$$R_x(\varphi) = \begin{bmatrix} 1 & 0 & 0 \\ 0 & \cos(\varphi) & -\sin(\varphi) \\ 0 & \sin(\varphi) & \cos(\varphi) \end{bmatrix} \tag{4}$$

$$R_y(\theta) = \begin{bmatrix} \cos(\theta) & 0 & \sin(\theta) \\ 0 & 1 & 0 \\ -\sin(\theta) & 0 & \cos(\theta) \end{bmatrix} \tag{5}$$

With regard to a initial eye axes, the rotation transformation of that eye axes at time t is represented as:

$$P_e^t = R_x^t(\varphi)R_y^t(\theta)P_e^0 \tag{6}$$

where P_e^0 and P_e^t denote the eye coordinates at times 0 and t.

Rewrite (2) and (3) as:

$$P_e^0 = [R_e|T_e]\, P_\omega \tag{7}$$
$$P_c^t = [R_c|T_c]\, P_e^t \tag{8}$$

and by using (6) we can derive the new projection matrix for converging eyes:

$$\tilde{P}_{im} = H^t \tilde{P}_\omega \tag{9}$$

with:

$$H^t = A\,[R_c|T_c]\, R_x^t(\varphi)R_y^t(\theta)\,[R_e|T_e] \tag{10}$$

This forms the kinematic model of our convergent eyes system and the transformation from world coordinates to image coordinates is known at any time t.

3   Depth Calculation from Vergence

3.1   Basic Idea of Convergent Eyes

In standard stereo systems, the depth is calculated by estimating the disparity of correspondences in image pairs. This can be either dense matching or sparse matching. Based on the disparity, a depth map can be derived[15].

We try to simulate the human eyes in a way that both robot eyes can move with different angles and hence the system can track object of interest in the center of the image planes by individual pan and tilt rotations; the angles of the eyes with respect to the initial axes are used to obtain the depth of the object. As such we generate a sparse depth map.

It is worth noting that the baseline for the depth calculation should be chosen with care. In a standard stereo camera the baseline is the line from left to right camera. In a convergent vision system there are two choices of baseline; one is from the left to the right eye while the other is from the left to the right camera. The latter choice of baseline is not constant, resulting in a more complicated computation model for the reason that the lengths between rotation centers and optical centers are less easy to estimate.

3.2   Depth Calculation

We use a simplified model for the depth calculation as shown in Fig. 2

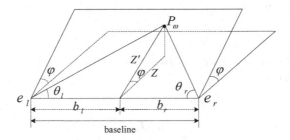

Fig. 2. Depth calculation model

Assuming that the left and right sight line from the rotation center to the object is a straight line, i.e. eye, camera and object are aligned without rotation and translation, we can easily derive the following equations:

$$\tan(\theta_l) = \frac{Z'}{b_l} \tag{11}$$

$$\tan(\theta_r) = \frac{Z'}{b_r} \tag{12}$$

$$b = b_l + b_r \tag{13}$$

From (11), (12) and (13), we have:

$$Z' = \frac{b}{1/\tan(\theta_l) + 1/\tan(\theta_r)} \tag{14}$$

where $b = e_r - e_l$ is the baseline, θ_l and θ_r are the left angle of the left eye axis and the right angle of the right eye axis, respectively. According to Fig. 2, Z is the ground depth instead of Z'. Z is affected by the tilt rotation angle φ, indicated by equation $Z = Z' \cos(\varphi)$. For now, the tilt rotation angle φ_l of the left eye equals the tilt rotation angle φ_r of the right eye. That is, $\varphi = \varphi_l = \varphi_r$. Note that e.g. for a humanoid robot φ_l and φ_r are generally equal, but if the robot rolls its head aside both will vary in tilt.

The equation for the depth calculation is now given by:

$$Z = \frac{b}{1/\tan(\theta_l) + 1/\tan(\theta_r)} \cos(\varphi) \tag{15}$$

4   Active Calibration

The purpose of standard image rectification lies in reducing the computation cost by changing the 2D stereo correspondences problem into a 1D search problem along the horizontal lines of the rectified images. Its basic idea is transforming each image plane such that pairs of conjugate epipolar lines become collinear and parallel to one of the image axes.

The purpose of our active calibration is to correct the left and right angle of the eye axes to reduce the depth error. The basics of this method is transforming each image plane to be orthogonal to each eye axis.

Let us assume that the stereo rig is calibrated, i.e., the intrinsic parameters A and extrinsic parameters: R_e, T_e, R_c and T_c are known. The intrinsic parameters can be calibrated by using various algorithms in which Zhang's method [16] is widely used. Also, the rotation matrices $R_x^t(\varphi)$ and $R_y^t(\theta)$ are known. In real applications, these two parameters can be read from motor encoders. Due to the existence of extrinsic parameters, the sight line from eye to object is not straight, which is one of the main factors that accounts for the depth error. Our method transforms each image plane to be orthogonal to each eye axis, which produces a straight virtual line, at which eyes, cameras and image centers are aligned. By doing this, updated projection matrices and rectified images are obtained. Afterwards, we track the object of interest so that it is in the center of the rectified images. In other words, the angles of the eye axes are renewed. Repeating this procedure, the image points which are projected by the object will converge to the image centers, until the final depth is obtained. The details are as follows:

First we write H into another form:

$$H = \begin{bmatrix} h_1^T & h_{14} \\ h_2^T & h_{24} \\ h_3^T & h_{34} \end{bmatrix} = \begin{bmatrix} h & \hat{h} \end{bmatrix} \tag{16}$$

In Cartesian coordinates, the projection matrix can be written into:

$$u = \frac{h_1^T P_w + h_{14}}{h_3^T P_w + h_{34}} \tag{17}$$

$$v = \frac{h_2^T P_w + h_{24}}{h_3^T P_w + h_{34}} \tag{18}$$

The focal plane is the plane parallel to the retinal plane that contains the optical center C. The coordinatec of C is given by:

$$c = -h^{-1}\hat{h} \tag{19}$$

therefore, we can write H as:

$$H = [h\,|-hc] \tag{20}$$

then, we have:

$$\lambda \begin{bmatrix} u \\ v \\ 1 \end{bmatrix} = [h| - hc] \begin{bmatrix} x_w \\ y_w \\ z_w \\ 1 \end{bmatrix} \tag{21}$$

Consequently, the transformation from homogeneous world coordinates to homogeneous image coordinates converts to a transformation from homogeneous image coordinates to world coordinates:

$$P_w = c + \lambda h^{-1}\tilde{P}_{im} \tag{22}$$

The main point behind active calibration is the generation of new left and right projection matrices according to time t. They can be obtained by rotating the image planes to be orthogonal to the eye axes instead of the camera axes. The positions, i.e., the optical centers of the new projection matrices are the same as the old ones, and also the intrinsic parameters are the same, whereas the new rotation matrices differ from the old ones by a rotation. Given time t, define the old projection matrices as:

$$H_0^t = A[R_0^t| - R_0^t c^t] \tag{23}$$

and new projection matrices as:

$$H_n^t = A[R_n^t| - R_n^t c^t] \tag{24}$$

In a 3D perspective, we can write

$$\lambda_0 \tilde{P}^t_{im0} = H_0^t \tilde{P}_w \tag{25}$$

$$\lambda_n \tilde{P}^t_{imn} = H_n^t \tilde{P}_w \tag{26}$$

There is only a very small difference between λ_0 and λ_n; so we can ignore it and assume $\lambda = \lambda_0 = \lambda_n$. Hence, we have the equation:

$$P_w = c^t + \lambda(h_0^t)^{-1}\tilde{P}^t_{im0} \tag{27}$$

$$P_w = c^t + \lambda(h_n^t)^{-1}\tilde{P}^t_{imn} \tag{28}$$

From (27) and (28) we obtain rectified image coordinates at given time t:

$$\tilde{P}^t_{imn} = h_n^t(h_0^t)^{-1}\tilde{P}^t_{im0} \tag{29}$$

where $T_{0n}^t = h_n^t (h_0^t)^{-1}$ is the final transformation matrix which can generate a rectified image at time t.

According to T_{0n}^t, h_0^t can be calculated using knowledge on the intrinsic and extrinsic parameters. h_n^t can be constructed by the row vector:

$$h_n^t = \begin{bmatrix} (h_{n1}^t)^T \\ (h_{n2}^t)^T \\ (h_{n3}^t)^T \end{bmatrix} \tag{30}$$

where $(h_{n1}^t)^T$, $(h_{n2}^t)^T$, and $(h_{n3}^t)^T$ are X, Y and Z axes, respectively.

h_n^t is deduced following the procedure:

In step 1, we can deduce the coordinates of the rotation centers e_l and e_r from the coordinates of c_l^0 and c_r^0 at the initial positions which are derived by equation (19). Here, the rotation centers are fixed, which means $e_l^0 = e_l^t$ and $e_r^0 = e_r^t$.

In step 2, the baseline is calculated by $e_r - e_l$.

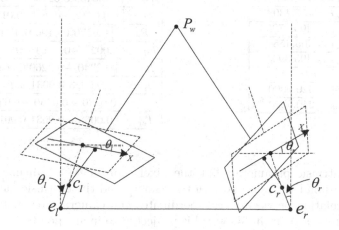

Fig. 3. Active calibration model

In step 3, take the left eye-camera as an example, as shown in Fig. 3, the new left X axis is parallel to the baseline rotated to the angle θ_l. Thus, the new left X axis is $h_{ln1}^t = R_y^t(\theta_l)(e_r - e_l)/\|R_y^t(\theta_l)(e_r - e_l)\|$ and the new right X axis is $h_{rn1}^t = R_y^t(\theta_r)(e_r - e_l)/\|R_y^t(\theta_r)(e_r - e_l)\|$

In step 4, the new Y axes are obtained by rotating the axes which are orthogonal to the new X axes with the angle φ. The new left and right Y axes are:

$$h_{ln2}^t = R_x^t(\varphi_l)(h_{ln1}^t \wedge k_l)/\|R_x^t(\varphi_l)(h_{ln1}^t \wedge k_l)\|$$
$$h_{rn2}^t = R_x^t(\varphi_r)(h_{rn1}^t \wedge k_r)/\|R_x^t(\varphi_r)(h_{rn1}^t \wedge k_r)\|$$

where $\wedge$ is the out product of vectors.

Here, we take k_l equal to the Z unit vector of the old left projection matrix and k_r equal to the Z unit vector of the old right projection matrix.

In step 5, the new Z axes are orthogonal to X-Y(mandatory): $h_{n3}^t = h_{n1}^t \wedge h_{n2}^t$.

Hence, with the knowledge on h_n^t, we can calculate a rectified image at any time t.

5   Experimental Results

The algorithms are realized and tested using MATLAB on a simulated convergent eyes system. In general, the setting of the test bed has the following properties shown in Table. 1. The image resolution is 640×480. Unless otherwise noted, the length unit is meter, and the angle unit is radian.

Table 1. Parameters setting

Intrinsic Parameters		Extrinsic Parameters
$f_{ul} = 405.4392$		$R_{cl} = \begin{bmatrix} -0.0400\ 0.0210\ -0.0540 \end{bmatrix}^T$
$f_{ur} = 405.3726$		$T_{cl} = \begin{bmatrix} -0.0012\ -0.0067\ 0.0110 \end{bmatrix}^T$
$f_{vl} = 405.4556$		$R_{el} = \begin{bmatrix} 0.0270\ 0.0190\ 0.0700 \end{bmatrix}^T$
$f_{vr} = 405.3945$		$T_{el} = \begin{bmatrix} 0.0026\ -0.0019\ -0.0019 \end{bmatrix}^T$
$\gamma = 0$		$R_{cr} = \begin{bmatrix} 0.0340\ -0.0260\ 0.0610 \end{bmatrix}^T$
$u_0 = 320.0000$		$T_{cr} = \begin{bmatrix} -0.0023\ 0.0031\ 0.0100 \end{bmatrix}^T$
$v_0 = 240.0000$		$R_{er} = \begin{bmatrix} 0.0180\ -0.0250\ -0.0360 \end{bmatrix}^T$
		$T_{er} = \begin{bmatrix} 0.0065\ -0.0031\ 0.0018 \end{bmatrix}^T$

Here the intrinsic parameters link the pixel coordinates of an image point with the corresponding coordinates in the camera and the extrinsic parameters describe the relation between world coordinates and camera coordinates. With these parameters, a point in 3D world is projected to image points.

For the experiments we followed this procedure: Apply the projective matrices to transform the 3D world reference coordinates to image coordinates in the retinal plane. Then rotate the eye axes to track the object in the center of the image pair; making it possible to calculate the depth before active calibration. Finally apply active calibration to correct the angles of the eye axes and obtain the rectified depth.

It is worthy noting that in our paper we focus on geometry of the convergent vision system model while the effects of acquisition conditions are not our main concern.

In our experiments, not only we tested the validity of the depth calculation and active calibration algorithms, but we also investigated which factors that contribute to the depth error.

Experiment 1 examines how the baseline and ground truth depth affect the depth error. The result according to (14) is given in Fig. 4. It can be seen in

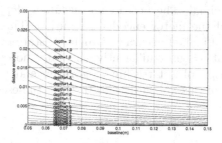

Fig. 4. Depth error vs. baseline and ground depth based on (14)

Fig. 4, that with an increase of the baseline, the depth error decreases inversely, whereas the depth error increases with an increase of the ground truth depth. That is, the depth accuracy depends on the ground truth depth and the baseline. Note that, the increase of the baseline is at the cost of computation time. Also, in real robotic applications, the baseline determines the size of the robot's head, which can not be increased without limitation.

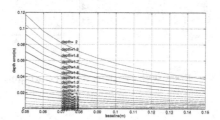

Fig. 5. Depth error vs. baseline and ground depth based on our model

5.1   Experiment 1

The results of our convergent eyes model are given in Fig. 5, in which the extrinsic parameters are considered. By comparing Fig. 5 with Fig. 4, the validity of our model as well as the depth calculation algorithm is shown.

5.2   Experiment 2

Experiment 2 investigates the influence of the object positioning accuracy on the depth error. First, we introduce the definition of positioning accuracy. Given the image center, we track the projected image point of an object inside a window of the size ε around the image center. We call ε the positioning accuracy. The smaller ε, the more accurate the positioning.

As shown in Fig. 6, the depth error drops significantly when the positioning accuracy increases 10 times, whereas after this threshold, the improvement of the performance is minimal. The positioning accuracy depends on the object tracking algorithm and the motor encoder resolution. This experiment shows that we can achieve a 0.1 pixel accuracy, which is "state of art" in perceiving depth. We assume that we use sufficiently accurate motor encoders, a good enough saliency detection/object tracking algorithm and images with enough resolution. The details of this are subject to further studies.

5.3   Experiment 3

Experiment 3 evaluates the performance of the proposed active calibration algorithm compared with the one without active calibration. The results are given in Fig. 7. We add noise with standard normal distribution to the projected image points.

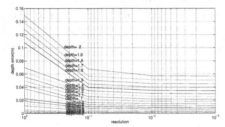

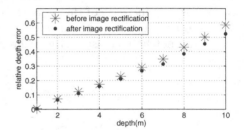

Fig. 6. Depth error vs. positioning accuracy

Fig. 7. Performance comparison with noise

According to Fig. 7, in general, our active calibration algorithm improves the depth accuracy with respect to no active calibration. Especially with the increase of depth, our active calibration algorithm performs much better.

6   Conclusion

In this paper, we adopted a stereo vision system by using convergent eyes. We have set-up and investigated a model and developed a novel depth calculation and active calibration algorithm, and tested them using our model. Experimental results showed the precision and effectiveness of our algorithms.

In the near future we will put these algorithms into a real system. The influence of the accuracy of low cost motor and motor encoders on the depth will then be studied.

References

1. Bandera, C., Scott, P.D.: Foveal Machine Vision System. In: IEEE International Conference on System, Man and Cybernetics, USA, vol. 2, pp. 596–599 (1989)

2. Hansard, M., Horaud, R.: Cyclorotation Models for Eyes and Cameras. IEEE Transactions on Systems, Man, and Cybernetics 40(1), 151–161 (2010)
3. Wodnicki, R., Roberts, G.W., Levine, M.D.: A foveated image sensor in standard CMOS technology. In: Proceedings of the IEEE Custom Integrated Circuits Conference, USA, pp. 357–360 (1995)
4. Wang, Z., Member, S., Bovik, A.C.: Embedded Foveation Image Coding. IEEE Transactions on Image Processing 10, 1397–1410 (2000)
5. Weber, C., Triesch, J.: Implementations and Implications of Foveated Vision. Recent Patents on Computer Science 2(1), 75–85 (2009)
6. Bernardino, A., Santos-Victor, J.: A Binocular Stereo Algorithm for Log-Polar Foveated Systems. In: Bülthoff, H.H., Lee, S.-W., Poggio, T., Wallraven, C. (eds.) BMCV 2002. LNCS, vol. 2525, pp. 127–136. Springer, Heidelberg (2002)
7. Ude, A., Gaskett, C., Cheng, G.: Foveated Vision Systems with two Cameras per Eye. In: International Conference on Robotics and Automation, FL, pp. 3457–3462 (2006)
8. Olson, T.J., Coombs, D.J.: Coombs: Real-Time Vergence Control for Binocular Robots. International Journal of Computer Vision 7(1), 67–89 (1991)
9. Gould, S., Arfvidsson, J., Kaehler, A., Sapp, B., Messner, M., Bradski, G., Baumstarck, P., Chung, S., Ng, A.Y.: Peripheral-foveal vision for real-time object recognition and tracking in video. In: Proceedings of the 20th International Joint Conference on Artifical Intelligence, USA, pp. 2115–2121 (2007)
10. Björkman, M., Eklundh, J.-O.: Foveated Figure-Ground Segmentation and Its Role in Recognition. In: British Machine Vision Conference, pp. 57–88 (2005)
11. Sahabi, H., Basu, A.: Analysis of Error in Depth Perception with Vergence and Spatially Varing Sensing. Computer Vision and Image Understanding 63(3), 447–461 (1996)
12. Scharstein, D., Szeliski, R.: A Taxonomy and Evaluation of Dense Two-Frame Stereo Correspondence Algorithms 47(1-3), 7–42 (2002)
13. Li, M.: Kinematic calibration of an active head-eye system. IEEE Transactions on Robotics and Automation 14(1), 153–158 (1998)
14. Fusiello, A., Trucco, E., Verri, A.: A compact algorithm for rectification of stereo pairs. Machine Vision and Applications 12(1), 16–22 (2000)
15. Trucco, E., Verri, A.: Introduction Techniques for 3-D Computer Vision. Prentice Hall, Upper Saddle River (1998)
16. Zhang, Z.: A flexible new technique for camera calibration. IEEE Transactions on Pattern Analysis and Machine Intelligence 22(11), 1330–1334 (2000)

Information-Gain View Planning for Free-Form Object Reconstruction with a 3D ToF Camera

Sergi Foix[1], Simon Kriegel[2], Stefan Fuchs[2], Guillem Alenyà[1], and Carme Torras[1]

[1] Institut de Robòtica i Informàtica Industrial, CSIC-UPC,
Llorens i Artigas 4-6, 08028 Barcelona, Spain
{sfoix,galenya,torras}@iri.upc.edu
[2] Institute of Robotics and Mechatronics, German Aerospace Center (DLR),
82234 Oberpfaffenhofen, Germany
{simon.kriegel,stefan.fuchs}@dlr.de

Abstract. Active view planning for gathering data from an unexplored 3D complex scenario is a hard and still open problem in the computer vision community. In this paper, we present a general task-oriented approach based on an information-gain maximization that easily deals with such a problem. Our approach consists of ranking a given set of possible actions, based on their task-related gains, and then executing the best-ranked action to move the required sensor.

An example of how our approach behaves is demonstrated by applying it over 3D raw data for real-time volume modelling of complex-shaped objects. Our setting includes a calibrated 3D time-of-flight (ToF) camera mounted on a 7 degrees of freedom (DoF) robotic arm. Noise in the sensor data acquisition, which is too often ignored, is here explicitly taken into account by computing an uncertainty matrix for each point, and refining this matrix each time the point is seen again. Results show that, by always choosing the most informative view, a complete model of a 3D free-form object is acquired and also that our method achieves a good compromise between speed and precision.

1 Introduction

Viewpoint planning tries to exploit the process of modifying the pose of a sensor to acquire a new view of the scene. All tasks requiring different views (modelling, recognition, feature discovery...) can be interpreted as an information gain process, since an increment of information is expected with every new view. This information is classically used for geometrical modelling, but should not be limited to it, and also may include other characteristics such as leaf contours for plant segmentation [6] or wrinkles on clothes for grasping [14]. Specially when dealing with unknown scenarios, the system should decide actions based only on the available information and the expected reward of executing the selected action. In such scenarios, the ability to explicitly measure the gain of each action is crucial, and it is closely related to the internal representation used.

Active view planning becomes a space characterization task whose goal is to answer the question: *where should the sensor be placed for locating specific characteristics?*

J. Blanc-Talon et al. (Eds.): ACIVS 2012, LNCS 7517, pp. 36–47, 2012.

Because it involves spatial characteristics (or at least located in space), the proposed approach uses a voxelized space where each voxel contains a complete 3×3 covariance matrix. This representation allows to account not only for exploration (unknown areas) but also for refinement, that is, the information gain of seeing characteristics again from a different point of view.

In summary, this paper brings the following contributions: A) an algorithm to select the most informative action from a given set for general view planning tasks; B) a convenient representation of the informative characteristics and their position on the space using a 3×3 covariance matrix for each one, and an efficient implementation using a multiresolution octree; C) an efficient method to compute the expected gain of a new data acquisition fusing information from exploration and from refinement, that accounts explicitly for the orientation of the sensor and for the acquisition covariance matrix.

This paper is organized as follows: Sec. 2 summarizes related work; in Sec. 3 ToF sensors and their acquisition uncertainty are introduced; Sec. 4 presents the overall algorithm structure; the procedure used in the experiments to obtain the list of viewpoint candidates is presented in Sec. 5; Sec. 6 introduces the proposed view planning method based on information-gain, while Sec. 7 presents some results using real data; and finally, Sec. 8 discusses the main conclusions.

2 Related Work

Sensor view planning has been commonly used for the tasks of precise geometrical model construction and object recognition (see the reviews [18] and [15]), and to a lesser extent for the optimal segmentation of particular object characteristics [11,16] and to exploit sensor features to easily detect occlusions, formerly using a laser [12] and more recently with a ToF sensor [6]. These algorithms can be classified according to the constraints they impose, on the type of objects that can handle, the sensors they use, the restrictions of the sensor positioning system, and more important, the decision-making strategy and the symbolic object representation they used.

In [17] objects are represented statistically by multidimensional receptive field histograms, and the camera is controlled by making hypotheses on the salient points of the previously learned objects and then moving to the most discriminative viewpoint. In [3] reinforcement learning is used to associate the current state with camera actions and their corresponding reward. Here the model is a particle representation, and it is updated with new sensor readings with the Condensation algorithm. More recently, a boost-based algorithm to combine different appearance estimators [9] has been proposed to compute the next view in a rotating object framework.

All the previous algorithms require some degree of training. When training is not applicable or too expensive, approaches using information-gain measures are a good alternative. In such approaches, two steps can be distinguished: the generation of a set of viewpoint candidates and the ranking of such candidates by evaluating the expected information gain of each action. Again, for viewpoint generation, the internal representation of the environment model plays an important role. Surface-based methods provide a set of viewpoints based on the location of jump edges [13], the trend

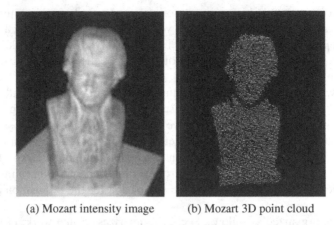

(a) Mozart intensity image   (b) Mozart 3D point cloud

Fig. 1. Typical intensity image and matched point cloud acquired by a Swissranger SR4000

of a contour [10] or the fitting of a parametric surface representation [1]. Volumetric methods provide viewpoints using the information of visited and non-visited portions of the workspace, and generally encode this space using voxel representations (or, more efficiently, octrees).

Information gain has been used before as viewpoint selection criterion in classical object modelling, where the sensor uncertainty is modelled using only the viewing direction and is considered uniform for all the acquired points. While some approaches require some degree of overlap to match consecutive sensor readings, other methods do not and consider this to be a positive feature (see [2] for a review). This is true for precise sensors, and for precise positioning systems, but it is not so when considering noisy sensors, specially when sensor readings have different uncertainties depending on their position on the image, as it is here the case with 3D ToF cameras.

This paper proposes a different approach for viewpoint evaluation. Independently of the viewpoint generation algorithm used, it relies on a volumetric space representation to encode the complete covariance matrix of the observed characteristics. The (possibly non-uniform) uncertainty in the acquisition process is explicitly used to compute the information gain produced by revisiting characteristics with large uncertainties (herein, overlapping is encouraged). This is combined with the information gain produced by exploring new areas to produce the total information gain for each different action.

3   3D ToF Camera

Depth measurements for the modelling task are captured by a 3D ToF camera. 3D ToF cameras have several advantageous features that make them more suitable for short-range applications than other range measurement technologies, such as laser scanners, stereo camera systems or the Kinect sensor. First, a 3D ToF camera provides registered depth and intensity images at frame-rates of up to 50 Hz (see Fig. 1a and 1b). Thus, they perform faster than sequentially measuring laser scanners. Second, a 3D

ToF camera features an illumination unit, which makes it independent from external light sources. Unlike stereo camera systems, a 3D ToF camera does not depend on textures. Finally, the minimal depth measuring range can get as close as 0.2 m [1]. This is necessary, because the sensor is attached to the tool-center point (TCP) of an articulated robot. There is thus only a small working range where the robot's TCP can reach all the poses required to capture the desired object spherically. Consequently, the sensor has to approach the object as close as possible. In contrast, a Kinect sensor can only measure ranges from 0.6 m with the current specifications. The Kinect sensor is thus not suited for such modelling tasks.

However, 3D ToF camera data lacks accuracy and precision due to systematic errors and noise. There are two types of measurement noise: noise generated by the electronics and the so-called "jumping edges". The former is limited by appropriately adjusting the integration time. The latter is caused by large depth-jumps within the scene, which are measured by the very same pixel. The resulting spurious measurement is handled by a specialized edge filter [13].

The systematic errors can be classified into intrinsic and extrinsic ones. The intrinsic systematic errors comprise the widely known distance- and amplitude-related errors. These errors are highly reduced by calibration procedures as proposed by [7]. The extrinsic systematic errors are generated by multiple light reception. On the one hand, there is light scattering, caused by imperfect optics and inter-reflections within the camera. This phenomenon is significant in case that there are large amplitude differences in the image, whereby the distance measurements with low amplitudes are affected by distance measurements with stronger amplitudes. The reasons are either large distances between foreground and background objects or large viewing angles. Both cases are negligible in our modelling task, because the desired object is always at the nearest distance in the sensor's field of view and consequently the most illuminated. For a more detailed and broad classification and explanation of the different error sources, advantages and limitations of 3D ToF cameras, please refer to [5].

4 View Planning Procedure

The initial configuration of the system consists of placing the sensor at a certain distance in such a way that its field-of-view covers part of the scene and it remains in its focused range. Once the initial configuration is reached, the proposed method can be synthesized by four iterative steps (see some details in algorithm 1). First, data is acquired by means of a sensor (e.g. a 3D ToF camera). In the second step, two representations of the scene, one for the view generator and one for the information gain estimator (i.e. a 3D occupancy grid for active view planning), are updated with the new sensor measurements. During the third step, a set of candidate viewpoints is computed using the viewpoint generator. see Sec. 5. Finally, the view with the highest information gain is selected after simulating each candidate viewpoint, see Sec. 6.

---

[1] Measures extracted with a Swissranger SR4000 camera decreasing its integration time to 1.0 ms.

Algorithm 1. Autonomous active view planning

$\mathcal{M} \leftarrow$ ACTIVEVIEWPLANNING($\mathbf{x}_0$, $\mathbf{\Sigma}_s$, $\mathcal{O}$, $\mathcal{S}$)

    INPUTS:

        $\mathbf{x}_0$:   Initial sensor pose in global coordinates.

        $\mathbf{\Sigma}_s$:   Sensor measurement covariance matrix.

        $\mathcal{O}$:   3D occupancy grid.

        $\mathcal{S}$:   A set of n measurements.

    OUTPUT:

        $\mathcal{M}$:   Task-based representation.

1: $i = 0$

2: **repeat**

3:     $\mathcal{S}_i \leftarrow$ DATAACQUISITION($\mathbf{x}_i$)

4:     $(\mathcal{M}, \mathcal{O}) \leftarrow$ UPDATEREPRESENTATIONS($\mathcal{S}$)

5:     $\mathbf{c}_m \leftarrow$ VIEWPOINTSGENERATION($\mathbf{x}_i$, $\mathcal{M}$)

6:     $\mathbf{x}_{i+1} \leftarrow$ DECISIONMAKER($\mathbf{c}_m$, $\mathcal{O}$, $\mathbf{\Sigma}_s$)

7:     $i = i + 1$

8: **until** task completed

9: **return** $\mathcal{M}$

---

5   Viewpoint Generation

In order to determine the following viewpoint accordingly to the information gain, a search space consisting of multiple viewpoints (possible sensor positions and orientations) is required as input. Since the workspace around an object features an infinite number of views, many authors reduce the search space by sampling candidate views around an approximate sphere or cylinder. Their candidate views always point to the center of their figures and, consequently, the sensor can not be positioned in a way that achieves optimal modelling results.

In this work, the *Viewpoint Estimator* [10] algorithm will be used. This algorithm that generates viewpoints by detecting boundary trends in a triangular mesh. It works as follows. Once new 3D data are acquired, a triangular mesh is reconstructed in a real-time stream. A quadratic patch is then fitted to each boundary region and new viewpoints, perpendicular to those patches, are then generated. Therefore, the search space is not limited to a set of pre-defined poses over a sphere or cylinder but it allows for any position and orientation. Depending on their position, relative to the sensor, the detected boundaries are classified as left, right, top and bottom. In their work, the next viewpoint was chosen heuristically by first going through the left, then right, top and bottom boundaries. Figure 2 shows an example of two boundaries classified as left and the subsequent region growing, which is used to fit a quadratic patch.

6   View Planning: Information Gain Ranking Criterion

In Information Theory, *information gain* is a probabilistic measure of how significant a new state estimate of the environment is. The concept of information gain is equivalent

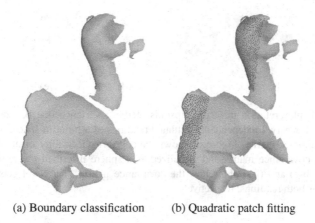

(a) Boundary classification   (b) Quadratic patch fitting

Fig. 2. Example of two boundaries obtained from a partial camel mesh, which are classified as left boundaries. A region growing is performed in order to fit a quadratic patch.

to the one of uncertainty or entropy reduction. Entropy, as defined by [19], is computed as:

$$H(x) = -\sum_X p(x) \log p(x), \qquad (1)$$

where X is a finite set of values of a discrete random variable x that has $p(x)$ as probability distribution function. For a n multivariate Gaussian distribution with covariance matrix Σ, entropy can be computed as:

$$H(x) = \frac{1}{2} \log((2\pi)^n |\Sigma|). \qquad (2)$$

As [20] already pointed out, using the determinant over all possible measurements for computing the information gain is computationally expensive. Based on his work, our approach uses the trace of the covariance matrix instead of its determinant and, therefore, efficiently computing the overall gain. This is possible thanks to having the same representation units for all the observable features and, consequently, avoiding scalability problems. Finally, and despising the constants, the entropy of a discrete random variable can be efficiently computed as:

$$H(x) = \sum_{i=0}^{3n} \log(\Sigma_{ii}). \qquad (3)$$

6.1   Scene Representation: 3D Occupancy Grid

A 3D occupancy grid is a map of a 3D space represented by a set of random variables, which are uniformly distributed on a discrete grid. These random variables are binary and specify whether each of the grid cells is occupied or free. Usually occupancy grid maps are used for building a consistent map after solving the SLAM problem, since they assume exact robot's pose information. In a different way, our approach does not

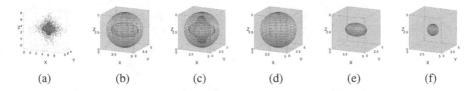

(a)   (b)   (c)   (d)   (e)   (f)

Fig. 3. Graphical interpretation through ellipsoids of the covariance matrix reduction inside a voxel. Figure a) shows two independent simulated readings of a point in space, which are taken to be perpendicular for clarity. Figure d) shows the a priori uncertainty of an unknown voxel represented as a covariance matrix and visualized as a sphere inscribed inside the voxel cube. Pairs of figures (b-e) and (c-f) show how the covariance matrix of a voxel gets updated after combining one or both readings, respectively.

use the occupancy grid map as a final result but as a tool to evaluate the information gain of multiple possible view poses.

Our 3D occupancy grid map is based on a probabilistic voxel space defined by a multiresolution octree structure. All 3D grid cells, also called voxels, have associated a covariance matrix depending on all the history of measurements. At the same time, each voxel is defined by three possible occupancy types: *occupied*, *free* or *unknown*. By using the covariance matrix as an uncertainty voxel-related measurement, our approach can optimally obtain the information gain taking into account the orientation of the sensor. This is an important feature when using a noisy sensor such as a 3D ToF camera, since the error is usually bigger on one component.

6.2 Expected Gain Using an Occupancy Grid

Initially, all voxel states are set to *unknown*, state with the highest uncertainty. Once new sensor data are obtained, the states of all voxels intersected by a ray are updated. Depending on whether a voxel is crossed by a ray-trace or whether it encloses a new measurement, the voxel state is set to *free* or to *occupied*, respectively. Also, each *occupied* voxel is assigned its measurement covariance matrix Σ_i in order to posteriorly compute the information gain of new viewpoints. If the voxel was previously defined *occupied*, both the new covariance matrix and the former are combined as shown in Fig. 3 by

$$(\Sigma_i)^{-1} = (\Sigma_i^{t-1})^{-1} + (\Sigma_i^t)^{-1}. \tag{4}$$

Only voxels with *unknown* and *occupied* states would be considered for estimating the information gain, since *free* voxels do not provide any information. The reason for this behaviour is to minimize the effect of non-filtered noise and possible miss-readings due to non-systematic 3D ToF camera errors. Once the viewpoint estimator recommends a set of n viewpoints, their expected information gain (IG) is computed. Every viewpoint is simulated by ray-tracing from the sensor's pose to the occupancy

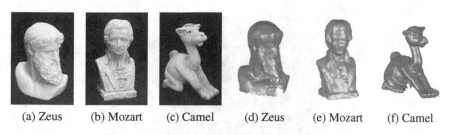

| (a) Zeus | (b) Mozart | (c) Camel | (d) Zeus | (e) Mozart | (f) Camel |

Fig. 4. a), b) and c) are the original object figures. d), e) and f), final triangle mesh of the modeled objects. Note that some details of the objects can not be captured due to the low resolution of the 3D ToF camera.

grid. Each colliding ray updates the corresponding voxel's covariance matrix and a copy is kept in memory as a sparse matrix

$$A = \begin{pmatrix} \Sigma_0 & 0 & \cdots & 0 \\ 0 & \Sigma_1 & \ddots & \vdots \\ \vdots & \ddots & \ddots & 0 \\ 0 & \cdots & 0 & \Sigma_n \end{pmatrix}. \tag{5}$$

Finally, the overal expected information gain is computed as

$$IG = \sum_{i=0}^{3n} \log(A_{ii}). \tag{6}$$

7 Experimentation

In order to be evaluated, the proposed active view planning has been applied to the task of modelling three free-form objects (see Fig. 4). Although all objects have similar sizes, each of them has its own degree of complexity, mainly based on the number of concavities. The most complex object is the Camel, followed by the Zeus and the Mozart bust. On the Mozart bust the only influential concavity is the one at its neck. The Zeus bust shows a higher complexity by having a big concavity under its beard. Finally, the Camel has a big concavity under its legs and a very heterogeneous structure due to its neck and head.

7.1 Setup

The current approach has been tested using a 7 DoF manipulator robot type Kuka KR16 and a 3D ToF camera type Swissranger SR4000 attached to its flange. The 3D ToF camera is attached in a 90 degree angle with respect to the tool-center-point (TCP). During the experiments, the objects were placed on a fixed and static platform at a height of approximately 670 mm. At this height, and due to its wide workspace, the Kuka KR16 manipulator is able to cover comfortably the surrounding volume of a medium-sized

Fig. 5. Experimental setup. A SR4000 3D ToF camera is attached to the end effector of a Kuka KR16 industrial robot.

object at a distance of 40 cm (see Fig. 5). The high accuracy of Kuka KR16 is required since the approach only takes into account the uncertainty of the measurements and not the one of the sensor's pose. Alternatively, if a high accuracy arm it is not available consecutive point clouds can be put in correspondence with a minimisation proces, as is done a.e. in [4]. The 3D ToF camera is intrinsically and extrinsically calibrated. Moreover, depth calibration is applied to improve 3D ToF camera measurements following the methodology of [7]. All together helps to get more accurate point clouds and to correctly register them in order to make the model grow.

7.2 Results

The Zeus, Mozart and Camel objects are appropriate for the evaluation because they have been used previously in other works. Moreover, the obtained results can be compared with two previous approaches used at DLR in the past (Fig. 6). Although a straightforward comparison between them is not an easy task because each approach used different sensors, some interesting conclusions can be extracted.

First, [8] used two different 3D ToF cameras, a Swissranger SR-3000 and IFM O3D100, for modelling the Camel. Their approach consisted in building a surface mesh by registering a pre-defined human-driven set of measurements and merging the views using Iterative-Closest-Point (ICP) without possibly refine their result. Their resulting models are reproduced in Fig. 6a and 6b. Later, Kriegel [10] used a laser scanner for modelling both the Camel and Mozart objects, providing a very precise model at the expense of a time consuming process. Fig. 6d shows the final model of the Camel.

Alternatively, our proposed algorithm (Fig. 6c) presents a good model compromise between model precision and time acquisition for most robotic tasks. Our approach takes explicit advantage of the noisy and low resolution data obtained from a 3D ToF camera. Images are obtained at a high frame rate (20 fps.) and with less complexity in the setup. Note that with this algorithm an explicit uncertainty measure of each point of the model is maintained, and therefore it is easy to define measures of the overall quality on the model. One natural consequence of the algorithm is that for complex objects with concavities and details, a higher number of view points for completing the

(a) Pre-defined trajectory with SR3000 3D ToF camera.

(b) Pre-defined trajectory with O3D100 3D ToF camera.

(c) Current approach with SR4000 3D ToF camera.

(d) Boundary trend approach with laser scanner

Fig. 6. a) and b) from [8]. c) is our current approach and d) from [10].

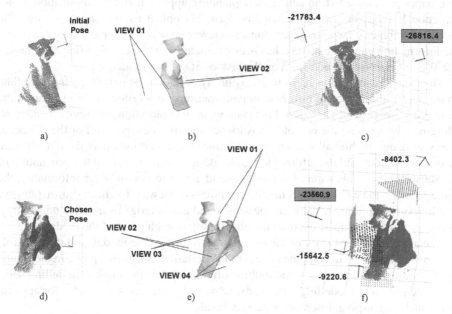

Fig. 7. Graphical representation of the steps carried out to compute consecutive viewpoints. a) shows the initial acquired point cloud. b) shows the corresponding mesh and the two candidate viewpoints on the basis of the detected edge-trends. c) simulates the measurements from the previous viewpoint candidates and the one with maximum information gain is chosen (marked on green). d) shows how the new point cloud is integrated into the previous one. e) shows the new corresponding mesh and the four new candidates. Finally, f) shows the new simulated ray-tracing measurements. Observed how part of the simulated ray-tracings on VIEW 03 do not impact on the not-sensed bounding box but into areas already seen.

model is required and automatically computed. On the contrary, the simpler the object, the fewer number of views. But more important, the algorithm can intrinsically refine the model to a desired precision, always limited by the sensor's resolution, by defining a threshold on the overall amount of information gain.

Figure 7 shows a graphical example of how candidate views are computed and how the model is incrementally updated. Step by step, the algorithm adds new measurements to the model based on the maximum information gain. Those new measurements are previously forced to belong to a contiguous area. By applying these two constraints, the algorithm succeeds to model almost completely any free-form objects. It can be seen that the Zeus bust and the Camel have a hole on their surfaces. These holes are a consequence of the sensor's configuration and the impossibility of the robot arm to attain the required poses. Figure 4 shows the final result of each of the objects used in three of our experiments.

8   Conclusions and Future Research

The paper presents a hybrid active view planning approach and its application to autonomously modelling an unknown free-form 3D object using a noisy sensor. The method combines viewpoint generation and viewpoint selection based on evaluation of the information gain. The method has been evaluated experimentally using a calibrated 3D ToF camera and a robotic arm on the task of 3D object modelling.

The proposed algorithm keeps track explicitly of the uncertainty in each point of the space. Using the proposed information gain measure as a criterion for evaluating the different views provides a trade-off between vicinity exploration and model refinement. Moreover, by keeping the complete covariance matrix in every voxel of the 3D occupancy grid, our method allows not only to reduce the uncertainty over the already seen voxels but to compute the information gain taking also into account the orientation of the sensor's pose. This naturally encodes the idea that to obtain better information the same point has to be observed from different points of view, as has been shown. Observe that it is very important to calibrate the sensor and characterize its inherent uncertainty, as this is a lower bound measure of the uncertainty in each point of the model.

The algorithm keeps track of the overall uncertainty of the model, and it is possible also to envisage ways to compute the overall uncertainty of selected parts. In the future, this algorithm can be used to build multiresolution models by roughly modelling some parts and precisely modelling other parts. Obviously this would be useful for applications, such as grasping, insertion or part removal.

Acknowledgedments.   This work has been partially supported by the EU IntellAct project FP7-ICT2009-6-269959, the Spanish Ministry of Science and Innovation under the project DPI2011-27510, and by KUKA Roboter GmbH. S. Foix is supported by PhD fellowship from CSIC's JAE program. The authors gratefully acknowledge the suggestions and deep insight of Michael Suppa and Tim Bodenmüeller.

References

1. Alenyà, G., Dellen, B., Torras, C.: 3D modelling of leaves from color and tof data for robotized plant measuring. In: Proc. IEEE Int. Conf. Robot. Automat., Shanghai, pp. 3408–3414 (May 2011)

2. Chen, S., Li, Y., Zhang, J., Wang, W.: Active sensor planning for multiview vision tasks. Springer, Heidelberg (2008)
3. Deinzer, F., Derichs, C., Niemann, H.: A framework for actively selecting viewpoints in object recognition. Int. J. Pattern Recogn. Artif. Intell. 23(4), 765–799 (2009)
4. Foix, S., Alenyà, G., Andrade-Cetto, J., Torras, C.: Object modeling using a ToF camera under an uncertainty reduction approach. In: Proc. IEEE Int. Conf. Robot. Automat., Anchorage, pp. 1306–1312 (May 2010)
5. Foix, S., Alenyà, G., Torras, C.: Lock-in Time-of-Flight (ToF) cameras: a survey. IEEE Sensors J. 11(9), 1917–1926 (2011)
6. Foix, S., Alenyà, G., Torras, C.: Towards plant monitoring through next best view. In: Proc. 14th Int. Conf. Cat. Assoc. Artificial Intelligence, Lleida (October 2011)
7. Fuchs, S., Hirzinger, G.: Extrinsic and depth calibration of ToF-cameras. In: Proc. 22nd IEEE Conf. Comput. Vision Pattern Recog., Anchorage, vol. 1-12, pp. 3777–3782 (June 2008)
8. Fuchs, S., May, S.: Calibration and registration for precise surface reconstruction with time of flight cameras. Int. J. Int. Syst. Tech. App. 5(3-4), 274–284 (2008)
9. Jia, Z., Chang, Y., Chen, T.: A general boosting-based framework for active object recognition. In: Proc. British Machine Vision Conf., pp. 46.1–46.11. BMVA Press (September 2010)
10. Kriegel, S., Bodenmüller, T., Suppa, M., Hirzinger, G.: A surface-based next-best-view approach for automated 3D model completion of unknown objects. In: Proc. IEEE Int. Conf. Robot. Automat., Shanghai, pp. 4869–4874 (May 2011)
11. Madsen, C., Christensen, H.: A viewpoint planning strategy for determining true angles on polyhedral objects by camera alignment. IEEE Trans. Pattern Anal. Machine Intell. 19(2), 158–163 (1997)
12. Maver, J., Bajcsy, R.: Occlusions as a guide for planning the next view. IEEE Trans. Pattern Anal. Machine Intell. 15(5), 417–433 (1993)
13. May, S., Droeschel, D., Holz, D., Fuchs, S., Malis, E., Nuchter, A., Hertzberg, J.: Three-dimensional mapping with time-of-flight cameras. J. Field Robotics 26(11-12), 934–965 (2009)
14. Ramisa, A., Alenyà, G., Moreno-Noguer, F., Torras, C.: Determining where to grasp cloth using depth information. In: Proc. 14th Int. Conf. Cat. Assoc. Artificial Intelligence, Lleida (October 2011)
15. Roy, S.D., Chaudhury, S., Banerjee, S.: Active recognition through next view planning: A survey. Pattern Recogn. 37(3), 429–446 (2004)
16. Saxena, A., Sun, M., Ng, A.Y.: Make3d: Depth perception from a single still image. In: Proc. 23th AAAI Conf. on Artificial Intelligence, Chicago, pp. 1571–1576 (July 2008)
17. Schiele, B., Crowley, J.: Transinformation for active object recognition. In: Proc. IEEE Int. Conf. Comput. Vision, Bombay, pp. 249–254 (January 1998)
18. Scott, W.R., Roth, G.: View planning for automated three-dimensional object reconstruction and inspection. ACM Computing Surveys 35(1), 64–96 (2003)
19. Shannon, C.E.: A mathematical theory of communication. Bell Syst. Tech. J. 27, 379–423 (1948)
20. Sim, R.: Stable exploration for bearings-only SLAM. In: Proc. IEEE Int. Conf. Robot. Automat., Barcelona, pp. 2422–2427 (April 2005)

DSP Embedded Smart Surveillance Sensor with Robust SWAD-Based Tracker

Gaetano Di Caterina[1], Iain Hunter[2], and John J. Soraghan[1]

[1] Department of Electronic and Electrical Engineering, University of Strathclyde,
204 George Street, Glasgow, G1 1XW, UK
[2] Texas Instruments Limited, 800 Pavilion Drive, Northampton, NN4 7YL, UK

Abstract. Smart video analytics algorithms can be embedded within surveillance sensors for fast in-camera processing. This paper presents a DSP embedded video analytics system for object and people tracking, using a PTZ camera. The tracking algorithm is based on adaptive template matching and it employs a novel Sum of Weighted Absolute Differences. The video analytics is implemented on the DSP board DM6437 EVM and it automatically controls the PTZ camera, to keep the target central to the field of view. The EVM is connected to the network and the tracking algorithm can be remotely activated, so that the PTZ enhanced with the DSP embedded video analytics becomes a smart surveillance sensor. The system runs in real-time and simulation results demonstrate that the described SWAD outperforms other template matching measures in terms of efficiency and accuracy.

1 Introduction

Modern digital video surveillance has made possible the semantic analysis of video data via software, on computer systems, using Video Analytics [1, 2]. As digital circuits become smaller and faster, video surveillance sensor systems can be equipped with processing functionalities and DSPs, so that smart video analytics algorithms can be embedded within the surveillance sensors, for fast in-camera processing. Such sensors are referred to as smart cameras and they can exchange information with each other, to form a collaborative network of smart surveillance sensors, where the human intervention is reduced to the minimum.

Starting from the work described in [3], in this paper we present a DSP embedded implementation of an adaptive template matching algorithm for object and people tracking, in the context of a smart surveillance sensor including a pan-tilt-zoom (PTZ) camera. The novel Sum of Weighted Absolute Differences (SWAD) proposed in [4] for robust target tracking is implemented in real-time on the single core DSP board DM6437 Evaluation Module (EVM) from Spectrum Digital. When compared to other tracking methods, such as Sum of Absolute Difference (SAD), Normalized Cross-Correlation (NCC) and Mean Shift tracker (MS), the SWAD-based algorithm shows better performance in the context of an embedded implementation, as it exploits the DM6437 fixed-point architecture.

J. Blanc-Talon et al. (Eds.): ACIVS 2012, LNCS 7517, pp. 48–58, 2012.

The video analytics algorithm on the EVM automatically controls the PTZ camera to follow the target and keep it central to the field of view, when it moves towards the frame boundaries. The EVM is connected to the network and, differently from the system in [3], the tracker can be activated and deactivated from remote, through on/off TCP-based messages. The contribution of this paper is therefore threefold: first, a real-time DSP embedded implementation of the SWAD-based tracker described in [4] is presented; second, extended performance evaluation of the SWAD-based tracker compared with SAD, NCC and MS is provided; third, the smart surveillance system in [3] is improved with remote activation, faster processing and better tracking performance, to create, in conjunction with the PTZ camera, an embedded smart surveillance sensor.

The remainder of the paper is organized as follows. Section 2 reviews related work in the field of tracking algorithms and embedded surveillance applications. An overview of the DSP embedded system described in this paper is given in section 3, while section 4 describes the video analytics implemented on the DSP, including tracking algorithm and camera controller. Section 5 provides a quantitative performance evaluation of the system, while section 6 concludes the paper.

2   Related Work

The implementation of image processing algorithms on embedded platforms poses challenges due to hardware limitations and time constraints. However, a number of implementation techniques were introduced to overcome these issues [5–7]. Previous work using static cameras [8–10] describe the implementation of smart surveillance sensors, for example for object detection and tracking.

The usage of active cameras for tracking applications is described in [11–14], but these mainly focus on the algorithm itself, rather than on creating an actual embedded smart sensor, as in the case of the work presented in this paper. To the best of the authors' knowledge, only the work in [15] has implemented a tracking algorithm [16] to control an active camera on an embedded device, namely an FPGA. However, performance evaluation and comparison with other algorithms or systems are missing from both [15] and [16]. Moreover, the work in [15] comprises an implementation exercise of a given tracking algorithm: the implementation choices on the FPGA are driven by the characteristics of the selected algorithm, rather than the algorithm itself being tailored for specific hardware requirements. In contrast, the video analytics system presented in this paper is embedded on a single core DSP board and such real-time implementation serves more as a proof of concept, i.e. prove that the described SWAD-based tracker achieves better performance compared with other algorithms, when implemented on devices with limited capabilities. As there exist automatic code generation tools and integrated development environments (IDE) for the DM6437 EVM as explained in [3], an initial working prototype has been obtained using Simulink and the Target Support Package. Such prototype has then been manually optimized and used as a test bench to implement and evaluate the SWAD-based tracker proposed in [4], as reported in section 5. Clearly, a reasonable follow-up for the work

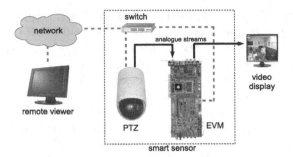

Fig. 1. Overview of the DSP embedded system, with the EVM and PTZ coupled together to form a smart surveillance sensor

presented in this paper would be to implement the same video analytics algorithm on an FPGA, for further performance evaluation.

The migration from a computer-based implementation of a tracking algorithm, like those described in [17], to a DSP embedded one is not straightforward. In such a context, the hardware available plays a fundamental part in the choice of the actual algorithm to implement. In this work, a PTZ camera is used, so that algorithms which rely strictly on the position of the target in the previous frames do not represent an ideal choice. For example, the Mean-Shift tracker (MS) [18] requires target overlapping in consecutive frames, within the so-called basin of attraction. However, this condition cannot be guaranteed with a moving camera.

On the other hand, DSP boards have limited resources, such as memory, bandwidth and word-length for number representation, so that not every tracking algorithm is suitable for an embedded implementation. In the proposed system, the hardware available is a DM6437 EVM equipped with a single core fixed-point DSP, that can perform integer operations on groups of 4–8 bytes in parallel. Therefore, on such DSP, algorithms working with floating point numbers would not take advantage of the architecture of the processor. Also in this case, the MS is not an ideal choice, as it heavily relies on floating point operations. Instead, two algorithms that can exploit such architecture are Normalized Cross-Correlation (NCC) and Sum of Absolute Differences (SAD) template matching [19]. As we will shown in section 5, the SAD algorithm gives better performance than NCC in terms of efficiency, since additions are performed much faster than multiplications. However, SAD fails in many cases when occlusion or noise pixels exist. In this paper the new Sum of Weighted Absolute Differences proposed in [4] is implemented, as it can deal with partial occlusions, offering better tracking performance than SAD, as demonstrated in section 5.

3   DSP Embedded System

An illustration of the DSP embedded video analytics system described in this paper is shown in Fig. 1. The system hardware comprises two main components:

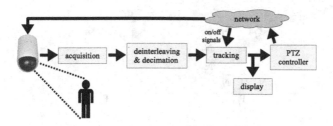

Fig. 2. Block diagram of the video analytics system

a Spectrum Digital DM6437 Evaluation Module (EVM) equipped with a Texas Instruments TMS320DM6437 fixed-point DSP; and an ACTi IP Speed Dome CAM-6510, which is a pan-tilt-zoom (PTZ) camera with 360° panning range, 180° tilting range and a maximum angular speed of 400° per second. A composite analogue video signal is also available as output from the PTZ and is fed into the EVM's video-in port. Both PTZ and EVM are connected to a local area network (LAN) through their Ethernet interfaces, so that they can communicate with each other via TCP/IP. For display purposes only, the EVM's video-out port is connected to a video display.

The system software is implemented in C and runs in real-time at more than 30 frames per second on the EVM. The PTZ camera hosts a proprietary web server and hence no software has been developed for it. Commands for the PTZ are encoded in HTTP requests to the camera web server. The video analytics algorithm on the EVM controls the PTZ by issuing such HTTP-based commands over the network. The EVM also runs a simple TCP server, so that remote on/off signals can be sent to the EVM, to activate the tracking algorithm.

When in stand-by mode, the system does not track any target and the PTZ can be moved freely. When the algorithm is activated, it starts tracking what is in the middle of the field of view at that exact moment. It is straightforward to integrate the proposed DSP embedded smart sensor with other event-based surveillance systems: for example an external smart system [20] can detect an event, compute the 3D position of the target, control the PTZ to point on the target, and then activate the SWAD-based tracking algorithm on the EVM, to follow the designated target.

4   Embedded Video Analytics

This section describes the video analytics implemented in our embedded system. A block diagram of it is shown in Fig. 2. Following the acquisition, deinterleaving and decimation processes, the output from the tracking block is the position of the target in the current frame. This information is used by the display block to highlight the target on the video display. The PTZ controller block uses the target position to decide whether to pan/tilt the PTZ camera. The tracking block also receives its own activation signals from the network.

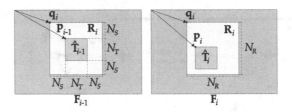

Fig. 3. Layout of the current frame $\mathbf{F}_i$ showing the best match $\hat{\mathbf{T}}_i$, the region of interest $\mathbf{R}_i$ and their positions within $\mathbf{F}_i$

4.1   Acquisition, Deinterleaving and Decimation

The composite analogue video output from the PTZ is fed into the EVM's video-in port. This video stream is digitized into 8-bit interleaved YCbCr 4:2:2 frames of 576×1440 pixels, with CbYCrY packed format and video resolution of 576×720 pixels, by the video decoder present on the EVM board. A deinterleaving operation separates individual YCbCr 4:2:2 frames into luminance ($\mathbf{Y}$), blue ($\mathbf{C_b}$) and red ($\mathbf{C_r}$) chrominance components, of which the tracking algorithm requires only $\mathbf{Y}$ to perform its task. The luminance component is then downsampled by a factor of 2 both vertically and horizontally, achieving a frame size of 288×360 pixels.

For speed optimization on the EVM, deinterleaving and decimation are performed at the same time, by simply extracting only the required samples from the 4:2:2 YCbCr frames. If $\mathbf{J}_i$ is the ith interleaved YCbCr 4:2:2 frame of 576×1440 pixels, the corresponding decimated luminance component $\mathbf{F}_i$ of 288×360 pixels is computed as:

$$F_i(x, y) = J_i(2x, 4y + 1) : x \in [0, H - 1], y \in [0, W - 1] \tag{1}$$

where $H = 288$ and $W = 360$ are height and width of $\mathbf{F}_i$.

4.2   Adaptive Template Matching Target Tracking

The tracking algorithm implemented on the DM6437 EVM is the adaptive template matching with minimization of a Sum of Weighted Absolute Differences (SWAD) described in [4]. The target model is represented by a template $\mathbf{T}_i$ of $N_T \times N_T$ pixels. As illustrated in Fig. 3, in the current frame $\mathbf{F}_i$ a region of interest $\mathbf{R}_i$ of $N_R \times N_R$ pixels, with $N_R = N_T + 2N_S$, is selected around the target position $\mathbf{p}_{i-1}$ in the previous frame $\mathbf{F}_{i-1}$. The best match $\hat{\mathbf{T}}_i$ in $\mathbf{F}_i$ for the target template $\mathbf{T}_i$ is found within the region of interest $\mathbf{R}_i$, by minimizing the SWAD coefficient $\psi(x, y)$ computed as:

$$\psi(x, y) = \sum_{m=0}^{N_T-1} \sum_{n=0}^{N_T-1} K(m, n) \Delta(x, y, m, n) \tag{2}$$

with pixel difference $\Delta(x, y, m, n)$:

$$\Delta(x, y, m, n) = |R_i(x + m, y + n) - T_i(m, n)| \tag{3}$$

The kernel $\mathbf{K}$ in (2) is:

$$K(x,y) = \left\lfloor 255 \cdot \frac{g(x,y)}{g(\lfloor\mu\rfloor,\lfloor\mu\rfloor)} \right\rfloor \tag{4}$$

where $x, y \in [0, N_T - 1]$ and $g(x,y)$ is a 2-dimensional Gaussian function with mean $\mu = (N_T - 1)/2$ and standard deviation $\sigma = N_T/5$, defined as:

$$g(x,y) = \exp\left(-\frac{(x-\mu)^2}{2\sigma^2} - \frac{(y-\mu)^2}{2\sigma^2}\right) \tag{5}$$

Such kernel is used to assign high weights to central pixels and low weights to peripheral ones, as these pixels might belong to background or even occluding objects. In our DSP-based implementation, the values in $\mathbf{K}$ and the absolute differences in the SWAD metric are integers in the range $[0, 255]$. The kernel values are computed offline once and stored in a look-up table. Using 8-bit integers allows us to optimally exploit the fixed-point architecture of the DM6437 DSP.

To take into account possible rescaling, rotation and target changes in general, the target template is updated using an infinite impulse response filter approach. Therefore the new target template $\mathbf{T}_{i+1}$ is computed as:

$$\mathbf{T}_{i+1} = (1 - \alpha)\mathbf{T}_i + \alpha\hat{\mathbf{T}}_i \tag{6}$$

where $\alpha \in [0, 1]$ is a blending factor. In our implementation it is $\alpha = 0.5$. The position $\mathbf{p}_i$ in $\mathbf{F}_i$ of the best match $\mathbf{T}_i$ represent the position of the target in the current frame. This information is passed to the PTZ control block, to decide whether to pan/tilt the camera.

4.3 PTZ Controller

The commands for the PTZ camera are hexadecimal sequences of 6 bytes included as parameters within standard HTTP requests, sent from the algorithm on the EVM to the web server running on the PTZ camera. The tracking algorithm establishes a TCP connection and sends the appropriate commands to the PTZ when the target approaches the frame boundaries. This situation is handled as follows. The current frame $\mathbf{F}_i$ is divided into horizontal and vertical regions, as shown in Fig. 4: horizontal-left (HL), horizontal-centre (HC) and horizontal-right (HR); vertical-top (VT), vertical-centre (VC) and vertical-bottom (VB). For a given best match $\hat{\mathbf{T}}_i$ in $\mathbf{F}_i$, the PTZ pans to the left if $\hat{\mathbf{T}}_i$ overlaps the HL region, or to the right if $\hat{\mathbf{T}}_i$ overlaps HR; otherwise the camera does not move horizontally. Similarly, the PTZ tilts up if $\hat{\mathbf{T}}_i$ overlaps VT, or tilts down if $\hat{\mathbf{T}}_i$ overlaps VB; otherwise the camera does not move vertically. This simple procedure allows the PTZ to follow the target, preventing it from going out of the field of view.

4.4 Video Display

The high resolution digital video output from the PTZ can be accessed over the network. For display purposes only, an analogue video signal is available from

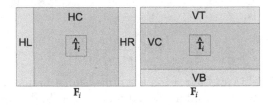

Fig. 4. Horizontal and vertical regions in the frame $\mathbf{F}_i$

Fig. 5. Four images from the tracking algorithm running on the EVM

the EVM's video-out port. This signal contains the interleaved 4:2:2 YCbCr version $\mathbf{S}_i$ of the frame $\mathbf{F}_i$, with the values of the chrominance pixels set to 127. The interleaved frame $\mathbf{S}_i$ is therefore a single plane matrix, with size equal to $H \times 2W = 288 \times 720$ pixels. The interleaving process is performed similarly to the deinterleaving process described in section 4.1. For every new incoming frame $\mathbf{F}_i$, only the pixels of $\mathbf{S}_i$ corresponding to the luminance component are modified and set equal to $\mathbf{F}_i$, while all the other pixels remains set to 127, as:

$$S_i(x,y) = \begin{cases} F_i(x,m), & y = 2m+1 \\ 127, & otherwise \end{cases} \quad (7)$$

where $x \in [0, H-1]$, $y \in [0, 2W-1]$ and $m \in [0, W-1]$. Four frames from the video analytics algorithm running on the EVM are shown in Fig. 5. For display purpose, the best match $\hat{\mathbf{T}}_i$, the region of interest $\mathbf{R}_i$ and the vertical and horizontal regions described in section 4.3 are all highlighted on the display. Note that the current template $\mathbf{T}_i$ is shown on the top-left corner of each video frame.

5 System Performance Evaluation

In this section, a quantitative evaluation of the embedded system is given.

5.1 Accuracy and Precision

A comparison of PC-based Matlab implementations of SWAD, SAD, NCC and MS has been carried out to assess the relative tracking capability of the SWAD-based adaptive template matching tracker, as shown in Fig. 6. Four publicly

Table 1. Mean value μ_ϵ and standard deviation σ_ϵ of error ϵ_i in pixels, and percentage λ_ϵ of frames with lowest error, for each tracker

	SAD			NCC			MS			SWAD		
	μ_ϵ	σ_ϵ	λ_ϵ	μ_ϵ	σ_ϵ	λ_ϵ	μ_ϵ	σ_ϵ	λ_ϵ	μ_ϵ	σ_ϵ	λ_ϵ
Dudek	4.25	2.54	7%	4.29	2.36	24%	–	–	–	3.67	2.13	34%
PETS2006	30.99	22.56	0%	34.13	24.21	0%	14.19	4.44	7%	10.91	4.14	93%
PETS2007	6.67	6.22	15%	9.93	9.24	11%	7.34	1.35	7%	3.89	1.50	53%
PETS2009	4.27	3.25	37%	27.38	47.80	7%	81.95	97.72	0%	2.26	1.42	48%

available test sequences have been used: Dudek face sequence [21], S1-T1-C/3 from PETS2006 dataset [22], S06_2/1 from PETS2007 dataset [23], and S3-multi-12.43/8 from PETS2009 dataset [24]. As the Dudek sequence is in grey scale, the MS has not been applied to it. The ground truth for the Dudek sequence is already available, while the three PETS sequences have been manually labelled. For each frame $\mathbf{F}_i$, an error ϵ_i is computed in terms of Euclidean distance between the ground truth and the target position returned by the trackers. The accuracy in pixels of a tracker is therefore obtained as mean value μ_ϵ of the error ϵ_i over a sequence, while the precision is computed as the standard deviation σ_ϵ. With λ_ϵ we define the percentage of frames in a sequence in which a given tracker has the lowest error compared with the other trackers. In the left column of Fig. 6 the first frames with initial target positions for each sequence are shown, while in the right column graphs of the error ϵ_i are illustrated. Numerical values of μ_ϵ, σ_ϵ and λ_ϵ are reported in Table 1. It can be seen that in general the error for SWAD is significantly lower, with better accuracy and precision, i.e. the lowest mean error μ_ϵ and standard deviation σ_ϵ. Moreover the SWAD-based tracker has also the lowest error for most of the frames, i.e. highest λ_ϵ.

5.2 Execution Time

After manual profiling and code optimization, the total running time of the DSP embedded SWAD-based adaptive template matching target tracking algorithm described in section 4 is of 15 ms per frame, giving a processing frame rate comfortably higher than the real-time requirement of $25 - 30$ fps. The SWAD matching block in (2) and (3) with $N_T = 32$ and $N_S = 50$ takes 7 ms. Optimization for the SWAD matching is achieved by exploiting the C code "intrinsics", which are specific functions for the C6000 architecture of the DM6437 DSP [25]. Each C-level intrinsic function is mapped to a single assembly instruction and it executes additions, multiplications and absolute subtractions on groups of four 8-bit integers. For example, the intrinsic function _MEM4 reads 4 pixel values from memory; _SUBABS4 computes the absolute difference between two groups of 4 pixels; and _DOTPU4 computes the dot product between two vectors of 4 pixels. This approach reduces the number of operations for each row of pixels in the template $\mathbf{T}_i$ by a factor of 4. A plain implementation of the SWAD matching without intrinsics takes 63 ms, so being 9 times slower than optimized SWAD.

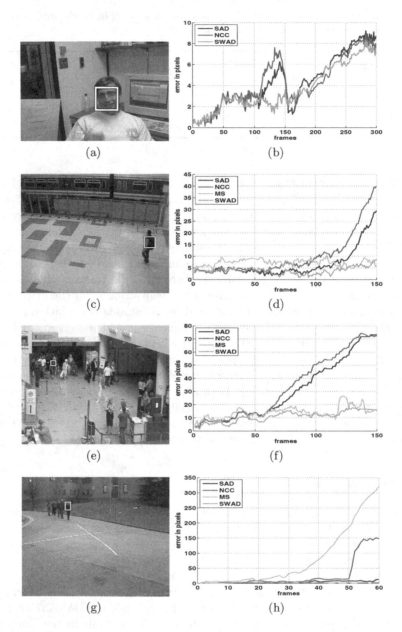

Fig. 6. Accuracy and precision test. (a-b) Dudek face sequence; (c-d) PETS2006; (e-f) PETS2007; (g-h) PETS2009. (a-c-e-g) Initialization frames; (b-d-f-h) error distance from ground truth in pixels.

This demonstrates that the presented SWAD-based adaptive template matching algorithm exploits the fixed-point architecture of the DSP on the EVM.

An optimized version of the SAD matching using intrinsic functions takes 5 ms. Nonetheless, even though SWAD is slightly slower than SAD, its better tracking performance reported in section 5.1 entirely justifies its usage over conventional SAD. Concerning an implementation of NCC on the DM6437, it can be said that extra care must be taken to simulate floating point operations, as for example square root, in integer arithmetic. It takes about 9 ms just to compute the mean values of the template $\mathbf{T}_i$ and of each $N_T \times N_T$ subregion in the ROI $\mathbf{R}_i$. Thus it is clear that the execution of a complete implementation of NCC matching on the DM6437 DSP would definitely take longer than 7 ms, and therefore NCC would be slower than SWAD.

6 Conclusion

In this paper we have presented a DSP embedded smart surveillance tracking sensor, using a PTZ camera to follow a target and always keep it central to the field of view. The system runs in real-time and it is implemented on the fixed-point single core DSP DM6437 Evaluation Module. The adaptive template matching tracking algorithm employs a robust Sum of Weighted Absolute Differences (SWAD) to maintain high accuracy under noise and partial occlusion when conventional SAD fails. The system can be used as a working framework to develop new real-time matching techniques for tracking and video analytics. The system can also be easily integrated with other surveillance systems, to create a collaborative network of smart surveillance sensors.

Currently the speed of the active camera is fixed and therefore the system might fail in case of (very) fast moving targets. It is planned to set the panning and tilting angular speed of the camera proportional to the speed of the target. In such a way, the system should be able to follow very fast moving targets. Also, a zooming capability is going to be incorporated in the smart sensor. Finally, a strategy for handling severe and complete occlusion will be also added.

References

1. Valera, A., Velastin, S.A.: Intelligent distributed surveillance systems: a review. IEE Proc. - Vision, Image and Signal Processing 152(2), 192–204 (2005)
2. Dee, H., Velastin, S.A.: How close are we to solving the problem of automated visual surveillance? A review of real-world surveillance, scientific progress and evaluative mechanisms. Machine Vision and Applications 19(5-6), 329–343 (2008)
3. Di Caterina, G., Hunter, I., Soraghan, J.: An embedded smart surveillance system for target tracking using a PTZ camera. In: European DSP Education and Research Conference, pp. 165–169 (2010)
4. Di Caterina, G., Soraghan, J.J.: Adaptive template matching algorithm based on swad for robust target tracking. IET Electronics Letters 48(5), 261–262 (2012)
5. Hunter, I.: Overview of embedded DSP design. In: European Signal Processing Conference, pp. 475–479 (2009)

6. Kisacanin, B.: Examples of low-level computer vision on media processors. In: IEEE Conf. on Computer Vision and Pattern Recognition, pp. 135–140 (2005)
7. Kisacanin, B., Nikolic, Z.: Algorithmic and software techniques for embedded vision on programmable processors. Signal Processing: Image Communication 25(5), 352–362 (2010)
8. Wang, Y., Velipasalar, S., Casares, M.: Cooperative object tracking and composite event detection with wireless embedded smart cameras. IEEE Trans. on Image Processing 19(10), 2614–2633 (2010)
9. Magno, M., Tombari, F., Brunelli, D., Di Stefano, L., Benini, L.: Multimodal abandoned/removed object detection for low power video surveillance systems. In: IEEE Int. Conf. on Advanced Video and Signal Based Surveillance, pp. 188–193 (2009)
10. Arth, C., Bischof, H.: Real-time object recognition using local features on a DSP-based embedded system. Journal of Real-Time Image Processing 3(4), 233–253 (2008)
11. Yang, C.S., Chen, R.H., Lee, C.Y., Lin, S.J.: PTZ camera based position tracking in IP surveillance system. In: Int. Conf. on Sensing Technology, pp. 142–146 (2008)
12. Kumar, P., Dick, A., Sheng, T.S.: Real time target tracking with pan tilt zoom camera. In: Digital Image Computing: Techniques and Applications, pp. 492–497 (2009)
13. Chang, F., Zhang, G., Wang, X., Chen, Z.: PTZ camera target tracking in large complex scenes. In: World Congress on Intelligent Control and Automation, pp. 2914–2918 (2010)
14. Micheloni, C., Rinner, B., Foresti, G.L.: Video analysis in pan-tilt-zoom camera networks. IEEE Signal Processing Magazine 27(5), 78–90 (2010)
15. McErlean, M.: An FPGA implementation of hierarchical motion estimation for embedded object tracking. In: IEEE Int. Symposium on Signal Processing and Information Technology, pp. 242–247 (2006)
16. McErlean, M.: Hierarchical motion estimation for embedded object tracking. In: IEEE Int. Symposium on Signal Processing and Information Technology, pp. 797–802 (2006)
17. Yilmaz, A., Javed, O., Shah, M.: Object tracking: a survey. ACM Computing Surveys 38(4), 1–45 (2006)
18. Comaniciu, D., Ramesh, V., Meer, P.: Kernel-based object tracking. IEEE Trans. on Pattern Analysis and Machine Intelligence 25(5), 564–577 (2003)
19. Tombari, F., Di Stefano, L., Mattoccia, S.: A robust measure for visual correspondence. In: Int. Conf. on Image Analysis and Processing, pp. 376–381 (2007)
20. Manap, N.A., Di Caterina, G., Ibrahim, M.M., Soraghan, J.J.: Co-operative surveillance cameras for high quality face acquisition in a real-time door monitoring system. In: European Workshop on Visual Information Processing, pp. 99–104 (2011)
21. Visual Tracking Benchmark: Dudek face sequence (2003), http://www.cs.toronto.edu/vis/projects/adaptiveAppearance.html
22. PETS 2006: Benchmark Data (2006), http://www.cvg.rdg.ac.uk/PETS2006/data.html
23. PETS 2007: Benchmark Data (2007), http://www.cvg.rdg.ac.uk/PETS2007/data.html
24. PETS 2009: Benchmark Data (2009), http://www.cvg.rdg.ac.uk/PETS2009/a.html
25. Texas Instruments: TMS320C6000 Programmer's Guide – SPRU198I (March 2006)

GPU Optimization of Convolution
for Large 3-D Real Images

Pavel Karas[1], David Svoboda[1], and Pavel Zemčík[2]

[1] Centre for Biomedical Image Analysis, Faculty of Informatics, Masaryk University,
Botanická 68a, Brno, CZ
{xkaras1,svoboda}@fi.muni.cz
[2] Dept. of Computer Graphics and Multimedia, Faculty of Information Technology,
Brno University of Technology, Božetěchova 2, Brno, CZ
zemcik@fit.vutbr.cz

Abstract. In this paper, we propose a method for computing convolution of large 3-D images with respect to real signals. The convolution is performed in a frequency domain using a convolution theorem. Due to properties of real signals, the algorithm can be optimized so that both time and the memory consumption are halved when compared to complex signals of the same size. Convolution is decomposed in a frequency domain using the decimation in frequency (DIF) algorithm. The algorithm is accelerated on a graphics hardware by means of the CUDA parallel computing model, achieving up to 10× speedup with a single GPU over an optimized implementation on a quad-core CPU.

1 Introduction

Convolution is one of the essential operations in both image and signal processing. In some applications, it can be also viewed as a *filter* of a signal f, parametrized by g, so-called *filter kernel*. A kernel is given by so-called point spread function (PSF), a function that describes the impulse response of an imaging system to a point source [14]. The PSF can be a simple function; for example, Gaussian is a typical representative of common convolution kernel. In some applications, such as optical microscopy, the PSF can be a non-analytic function, obtained e.g. from empirical measurements of an optical system. An example of the convolution is shown in Fig. 1.

The convolution can be employed for blurring images, edge detection, noise suppression, image registration, and in many other applications [8,14,26]. It can be used to simulate image formation in optical systems, such as optical microscopes [32], as shown in Fig. 1. In image restoration, it is employed as an essential part of deconvolution algorithms [24,29,34].

The convolution can be time-demanding. A naïve convolution of two discrete signals f and g, according to the definition, has the computational complexity of $\mathcal{O}(M_f M_g)$ where M_f and M_g are number of samples of f and g, respectively. In some applications, this is sufficient since the kernel is usually small (hundreds or

J. Blanc-Talon et al. (Eds.): ACIVS 2012, LNCS 7517, pp. 59–71, 2012.
© Springer-Verlag Berlin Heidelberg 2012

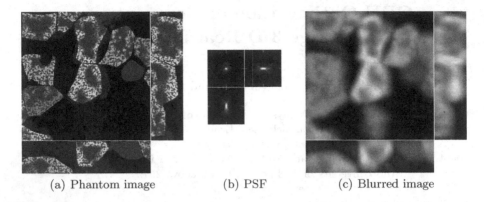

(a) Phantom image   (b) PSF   (c) Blurred image

Fig. 1. Example of a 3-D convolution. The images show an artificial (phantom) image of a tissue, a PSF of an optical microscope, and blurred image, computed by the convolution of the two images. Each 3-D image is represented by three 2-D views (XY, YZ, and XZ).

thousands of samples in maximum) or it is separable [2]. In other applications—such as optical microscopy—one deals with millions of samples. In this case, it is advisable to compute the convolution in the frequency domain, according to the so-called convolution theorem [2]. This approach allows to decrease the computational complexity to $\mathcal{O}(M \log M)$ where $M = M_f + M_g$ [35]. In practice, this means that the computation can take seconds or minutes instead of hours or days. The comparison of convolution in the spatial and the frequency domain was made e.g. in [5]. Further speed-up can be achieved using graphics cards.

At present, graphics processing units (GPU) are used not only for visualisation purposes but also to accelerate general computations. This phenomenon is often referred to as general-purpose computing on graphics processing units (GPGPU) [23]. Recently, two programming frameworks are widely used among the GPGPU community, namely CUDA [21] and OpenCL [10].

The GPU implementations of a naïve convolution and a convolution with separable kernel can be found in [25]. These algorithms can be used in many applications, such as fast computation of Canny edge detection [16,22]. As for the convolution in the frequency domain, the essential part of this approach is the Fourier transform. Recently, the CUFFT library [19] by NVIDIA offers a framework for implementing convolution in a straightforward manner. Besides CUFFT, other FFT libraries for GPU were developed, such as [9,18]. GPU acceleration of FFT and convolution in practical applications have been well described in literature [4,5].

Relatively small global memory of the GPU architecture poses a significant problem in applications where one deals with huge images. Several approaches exist to decompose the convolution into sub-problems, such as the partition in the spatial domain described in [33] and succesfully adopted in [1,31]. In [15], authors proposed a new method, based on the decimation in frequency (DIF) algorithm and specifically designed for the GPU architecture. This approach allows efficient computation of the convolution on GPU that is not limited by the size of the GPU memory. The main drawback is that it is designed for complex input data, hence it is relatively inefficient when processing real signals.

In this paper, we propose an optimized method for convolution of huge images on GPU which consists of two concepts: (i) the decomposition of the problem, as proposed in [15], (ii) the optimization for real input data (i.e. data with zero imaginary part) which are of interest in most practical applications. In Section 2, we recall the convolution, some of its properties, and the decomposition concept. In Section 3, we recall approaches to optimize the convolution for real data. We consider which one is the most suitable to be combined with the decomposition. In Section 4, we test the performance and the precision of the GPU implementation. Finally, the conclusions summarize the main contributions of our work.

2   Convolution

A 1-D convolution of two discrete finite signals f, g is defined by following:

$$[f * g](m') \equiv \sum_{m=0}^{M_g-1} f(m' - m)g(m), \quad m' = 0, \ldots, M - 1, \tag{1}$$

where M_f and M_g is the number of samples of f and g, respectively. The convolution then produces a signal of size $M = M_f + M_g - 1$. The convolution can be extended to any number of dimensions. For details, refer to [2,11].

2.1   Convolution Theorem

An efficient approach to compute a convolution is given by so-called convolution theorem. Having two periodic signals f, g, it can be proved that

$$f * g = \mathcal{F}^{-1} \left[\mathcal{F}[f] \mathcal{F}[g] \right], \tag{2}$$

where $\mathcal{F}$ denotes a discrete Fourier transform (DFT).

2.2   Decimation in Frequency (DIF) Algorithm

FFT algorithms are based on the divide-and-conquer approach. To perform the data division, two algorithms can be used: decimation in time (DIT) and decimation in frequency (DIF) [3]. We will introduce the idea of the DIF algorithm for the 1-D case. Let us have a function $f(m)$ and its Fourier transform $F(\mu)$, $m, \mu = 0, \ldots, M-1$. Supposing that M is even we introduce new functions $r(m')$ and $s(m')$, $m' = 0, \ldots, M/2 - 1$ as follows [28,12]:

$$r(m') \equiv f(m') + f(m' + M/2), \tag{3a}$$

$$s(m') \equiv [f(m') - f(m' + M/2)] W_M^{-m'}, \tag{3b}$$

where $W_M = e^{i\frac{2\pi}{M}}$. Vice versa, it is simple to deduce

$$f(m') = \left[r(m') + s(m')W_M^{m'}\right]/2, \tag{4a}$$

$$f(m' + M/2) = \left[r(m') - s(m')W_M^{m'}\right]/2. \tag{4b}$$

Then it can be proved that the Fourier transforms $R(\mu')$ and $S(\mu')$ of the functions $r(m')$ and $s(m')$ fulfil the following property:

$$R(\mu') = F(2\mu'), \tag{5a}$$

$$S(\mu') = F(2\mu' + 1). \tag{5b}$$

2.3   GPU Accelerated Convolution

In [15], authors proposed the efficient GPU implementation of convolution of large 3-D images. The algorithm has three phases: (i) both signal and kernel are decomposed into $\mathcal{P}$ parts on CPU, using the DIF algorithm; (ii) the convolution is computed piecewise in the frequency domain on GPU; (iii) the result is composed from the subparts on CPU. The scheme of the algorithm is shown in Fig. 2.

The most important contribution of this approach is that the computation is not limited by the size of GPU memory which is usually significantly smaller than CPU memory. The main drawback is that the algorithm is designed for complex input data; therefore, it is sub-optimal in most applications. In this paper, we will describe how this algorithm can be further optimized for real input data. We will show that a significant improvement can be achieved in means of both the time and the memory complexity.

The method specified in the following section consists basically of two concepts. One, already described in [15], will be referred to as *data decomposition*. The new concept, introduced in the section 3.1, will be reffered to as *real data optimization*.

3   Method

3.1   Fourier Transform of a Real Signal

The (discrete) Fourier transform of a real signal keeps some specific properties, which can be used for further optimization, when processing real images. Many of these properties were described in the literature [2,13,27]. In particular, if the input signal $f(m)$, $m = 0, 1, \ldots, M - 1$ is real, then the following property is held:

$$F(m) = F^*(M - m). \tag{6}$$

As a result, one half of the output data is redundant. It is reasonable not to compute redundant data in order to reduce computation complexity as well as memory requirements.

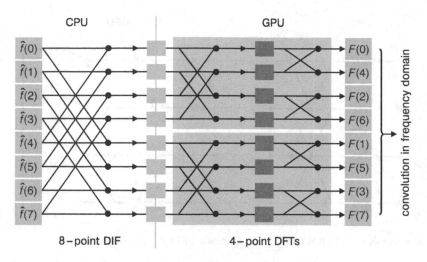

Fig. 2. A scheme description of the convolution algorithm with a decomposition in a frequency domain proposed in [15]. An input signal is decomposed into 2 parts by the declination in frequency (DIF) algorithms, i.e. $\mathcal{P} = 2$. The parts are subsequently processed independently on GPU, using the discrete Fourier transform (DFT). Moving the border line between CPU and GPU to the right is equivalent to setting $\mathcal{P} = 4, 8, \ldots$

When optimizing computation of DFT of the aforementioned input signal $f(m)$, several approaches can be considered. In the first—used by most popular implementations of DFT, including the FFTW [7] and the CUFFT [19] libraries—only the half transform $F(m')$, $m' = 0, 1, \ldots, M/2$ is computed. Yet it is difficult to combine this approach with our decomposition method. Firstly, it requires padding the input signal (for details, refer to [7]) that leads to reallocating of the whole memory block. Secondly, the "R2C"[1] method implemented in CUFFT, according to our experiments, is less efficient than a "classic C2C"[2] method applied to a complex signal of half size.

In the second approach, two real input signals $f(m)$, $g(m)$ of the same size are combined into one complex signal $h(m) = f(m) + ig(m)$ of the same length. Unfortunately, this combination requires creating an additional buffer of at least the size of f. This places higher demands on CPU memory.

Our method is based on the third approach which uses the following idea: A real input signal $f(m)$, $m = 0, \ldots, M - 1$ is processed as a complex signal $\hat{f}(m')$, $m' = 0, \ldots, M/2 - 1$ of the half size (provided that the size of the input signal is even):

$$\hat{f}(m') \equiv f(2m') + if(2m' + 1). \tag{7}$$

Using the common representation of real and complex numbers in the C language, this means that a real signal can be turned into a complex one by simply over-casting the data type, avoiding any data transfers. The relationship between

---

[1] Real-to-complex.

[2] Complex-to-complex.

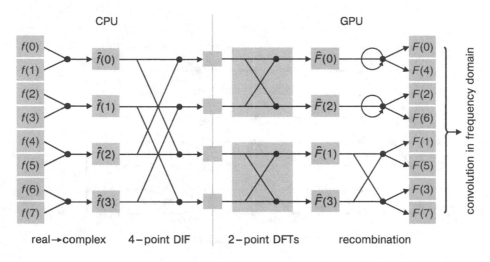

Fig. 3. A scheme description of the modified algorithm, $\mathcal{P} = 2$. For a comparison with original algorithm, refer to Fig. 2.

the Fourier transform $F(m)$ of the real signal $f(m)$ and the Fourier transform $\hat{F}(m')$ of the complex signal $\hat{f}(m')$ is given by following [12]:

$$F(m') = \frac{1}{2}\left(\alpha_+(m') - iW_M^{-m'}\alpha_-(m')\right), \tag{8a}$$

$$F(m' + M/2) = \frac{1}{2}\left(\alpha_+(m') + iW_M^{-m'}\alpha_-(m')\right), \tag{8b}$$

where
$$\alpha_\pm(m') \equiv \hat{F}(m') \pm \hat{F}^*(M/2 - m'). \tag{9}$$

3.2   Optimization of the Decomposition Algorithm

The real data optimization, described above, can be seamlessly combined with the data decomposition method, proposed in [15]. The optimization basically requires no modifications to the composition and decomposition functions. Some changes must be made to the CUDA kernel which computes the point-wise multiplication so that it incorporates the recombination described in Eq. (8a) and (8b). The scheme of the modified algorithm is shown in Fig. 3.

It can be noted that the algorithms for both decimation and array permutation were originally introduced in 1970s not only to reduce the time complexity of FT but also to allow efficient use of memory spaces available [6]. In this context, our approach can be viewed as a revival of such techniques.

3.3   Getting Further

One has to take into account more dimensions when processing d-dimensional data. For implementation reasons, described in the previous section, it is reasonable to perform real data optimization in the last (usually x) axis. On the other hand, to achieve maximum data transfer efficiency, it is advisable to perform the decomposition in the first (y for $d = 2$ or z for $d = 3$) axis, as explained in [15]. For example, in 2-D space, Eq. (8a) and (8b) can be extended as follows:

$$F(m', n) = \frac{1}{2} \left(\alpha_+(m', n) - iW_M^{-m'} \alpha_-(m', n) \right), \tag{10a}$$

$$F(m' + M/2, n) = \frac{1}{2} \left(\alpha_+(m', n) + iW_M^{-m'} \alpha_-(m', n) \right), \tag{10b}$$

where $m' = 0, 1, \ldots, M/2 - 1$, $n = 0, 1, \ldots, N - 1$, and

$$\alpha_\pm(m', n) \equiv \hat{F}(m', n) \pm \hat{F}^*(M/2 - m', N - n). \tag{11}$$

The real data optimization can be combined with data decomposition for any number of parts $\mathcal{P}$ that the data are decomposed into. It should be noted that due to the recombination phase, memory requirements change for $\mathcal{P} > 2$. Whereas first two parts recombine with themselves, the others recombine in pairs. Therefore, the GPU memory requirements are no longer $(M_f + M_g)/\mathcal{P}$ but $2(M_f + M_g)/\mathcal{P}$. For a practical example, refer to the following section.

4   Experimental Results

Experiments were conducted on a machine described in Table 1. The CPU implementation uses the multi-threaded FFTW library while the GPU implementation uses our algorithm along with the CUFFT library. The decomposition and the composition functions are performed on CPU and improved with SSE intrinsics for a better performance.

Table 1. Machine used for experiments

CPU/GPU	# of cores	Clock speed	RAM size	Bandwidth
Intel Core i7 950	4	3.07 GHz	6 GB	12.8 GB/s
NVIDIA GeForce GTX 480	480	1.40 GHz	1.5 GB	88.7 GB/s

In the experiments, we used randomly generated images of certain sizes. Two datasets were created. In the first dataset, the image dimensions were powers of 2 which allows most efficient computation of FFT. In the second dataset, the images were arbitrarily sized except that in the z dimension the padded size is kept so that the decomposition can be performed without the need of additional image padding. We refer to the images from the two datasets as *specifically* and *arbitrarily* sized, respectively. For details, refer to Table 2.

In the first experiment, we compared CPU and GPU implementations for a single value of $\mathcal{P}$, various image sizes, and both real and complex input data. The parameter $\mathcal{P}$ was chosen the smallest possible in all cases, allowing the best GPU performance. As shown in the following experiment, and described in [15], the

Table 2. Sizes of the images used in experiments

Image size [Mpx]	1st dataset	2nd dataset
34	$512 \times 512 \times 128$	$514 \times 514 \times 128$
67	$1024 \times 512 \times 128$	$1028 \times 514 \times 128$
134	$1024 \times 1024 \times 128$	$1028 \times 1028 \times 128$
268	$1024 \times 1024 \times 256$	$1028 \times 1028 \times 256$

GPU performance slightly decreases when increasing $\mathcal{P}$. The results are shown in Fig. 4(a),(b). For better visual comparison of implementations in plots, the performance P is computed as $P = s/t$, where s is the output image size and t is the computation time including data transfers between CPU and GPU.

The results clearly show that the real data optimization not only increases the performance significantly, it also allows processing images that could not be processed without the optimization, due to insufficient CPU memory. The GPU performance slightly decreases as the image size increases. This is in fact due to increase of the $\mathcal{P}$ parameter. Still, the speed-up over the CPU implementation is approx. 4× for the 1st dataset and up to 10× for the 2nd dataset.

In the second experiment, we measured the performance of CPU and GPU implementations for various values of $\mathcal{P}$, fixed image size, and real input data. We also evaluated the GPU memory requirements. The results are shown in Fig. 5(a),(b). The experiment confirmed that the GPU performance decreases with the increase of the $\mathcal{P}$ parameter. On the other hand, the amount of the GPU memory required decreases except the step between $\mathcal{P} = 2$ and $\mathcal{P} = 4$. This is due to algorithm properties, explained in Section 3.3.

4.1 Multi-GPU Performance

As described in [15], the decomposition algorithm can be adopted for multi-GPU systems, allowing further speed-up. However, bandwidth of data transfers is limited by the PCI-Express bus data processing [30]. This has negative impact on GPU performance and can cause even its decrease. In the third experiment, we measured performance of 2 GPUs computing simultaneously, using the same system with an additional graphics card, namely the NVIDIA GeForce GTX 285. Again, we measured the performance for various values of $\mathcal{P}$ and fixed image size.

The results, shown in Table 3, indicate that in the case of a specifically-sized image (columns 2 and 3), the data transfer overhead is crucial. Hence, adding the second GPU brings no speed-up. In case of an arbitrarily-sized image (columns 3 and 4), the computation of FFT is the most time-demanding phase of the algorithm so with 2 GPUs, a significant speed-up can be achieved. In general, the contribution of the multi-GPU implementation increases with the increase of $\mathcal{P}$.

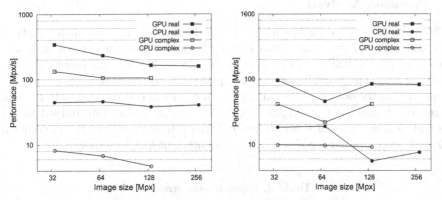

(a) 1st dataset (specifically sized images) (b) 2nd dataset (arbitrarily sized images)

Fig. 4. Comparison of CPU and GPU implementations for a single value of $\mathcal{P}$ (best choice), various image sizes, and both real and complex input data

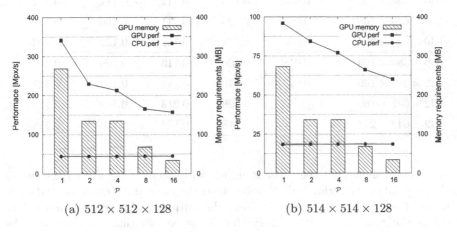

(a) $512 \times 512 \times 128$ (b) $514 \times 514 \times 128$

Fig. 5. Comparison of CPU and GPU implementations for various values of $\mathcal{P}$, fixed image size, and real input data. Plots also show GPU memory requirements.

Table 3. Computing time of the GPU implementation: 1 GPU vs 2 GPUs

Image size	$512 \times 512 \times 128$		$514 \times 514 \times 128$	
$\mathcal{P}$	1 GPU [ms]	2 GPUs [ms]	1 GPU [ms]	2 GPUs [ms]
2	146.4	176.7	403.7	293.6
4	157.9	175.8	442.5	274.6
8	203.0	192.4	515.9	275.9
16	213.9	201.2	568.4	298.6

4.2   Precision Analysis

In this experiment, we evaluated the error of the output data in a practical application. The tissue image from Fig. 1(a) was cropped to various sizes and convolved with the PSF from Fig. 1(b) of size $128 \times 128 \times 96$. The input data was 16-bit integers. The convolution was computed on GPU in the single precision and on CPU in the double precision. The error δ_{max} was computed as a maximum difference between the two output images. The results for various output image sizes and various values of $\mathcal{P}$ are shown in Table 4. In some cases, the convolution could not be computed for $\mathcal{P} = 1$, due to insufficient GPU memory.

Table 4. Computation error

Image size	δ_{max}				
$x \times y \times z$	$\mathcal{P} = 1$	$\mathcal{P} = 2$	$\mathcal{P} = 4$	$\mathcal{P} = 8$	$\mathcal{P} = 16$
$384 \times 384 \times 160$	0.006	0.097	0.112	0.105	0.105
$640 \times 384 \times 160$	0.007	0.143	0.112	0.117	0.122
$640 \times 640 \times 160$	0.008	0.225	0.211	0.166	0.121
$640 \times 640 \times 224$	0.009	0.177	0.162	0.132	0.103
$386 \times 386 \times 160$	0.018	0.100	0.113	0.106	0.107
$642 \times 386 \times 160$	0.017	0.146	0.112	0.122	0.125
$642 \times 642 \times 160$	—	0.226	0.213	0.169	0.125
$642 \times 642 \times 224$	—	0.178	0.164	0.133	0.113

The results show that the error is significantly smaller for $\mathcal{P} = 1$, i.e. when no decomposition is performed. Nevertheless, the error does not grow with the increase of $\mathcal{P}$. As $\delta_{max} < 1$ in all cases, the output 16-bit integer images are virtually the same. Still, it is likely that in some practical applications, the single precision will not be enough. Fortunately, the recent GPU architecture allows efficient computation in the double precision [17,20].

5   Conclusions

We have reviewed efficient approaches to compute convolution of large 3-D images, with special regard to the currently popular GPU architecture. At present, the GPU architecture achieves significantly higher performance than the common multi-core CPU architecture. The main drawback of GPU is relatively small memory which can impose limitations on practical applications, such as optical microscopy, where huge images are of interest. In this paper, we have recalled our GPU implementation of convolution which allows to decompose the problem into sub-parts in an efficient way.

The main contribution of this paper is the optimization of the aforementioned method for the real data which are of interest in most practical applications. Thanks to the optimization, the GPU implementation achieves up to 10× speed-up—including data transfers—over the multi-core CPU implementation, namely the one in the FFTW library which is widely used and considered the state of the art. The GPU implementation is able to compute the convolution of two 270 Mpx images within less than 2 s.

Our experiments proved the GPU implementation to be not only efficient but also precise enough for the optical microscopy images. In applications where the precision is crucial, double precision can be used.

Both concepts, the decomposition and the optimization, are designed to be performed in-place in the CPU memory which allows the maximum exploitation of resources. However, in some applications, the images can even exceed the CPU memory. Here, our method can potentially be combined with the approach described in [31] so that the convolution can be decomposed on multiple levels. Furthermore, the proposed method is not strictly dependent on CUDA nor on the GPU architecture. It can be implemented also in OpenCL and other languages. Other parallel architectures can be taken into account as well. Generally, it can be implemented on a heterogeneous cluster of computers allowing both CPU and GPU to take part in the computation.

Acknowledgements. This work has been supported by the Ministry of Education of the Czech Republic (Project No. 2B06052) and the Grant Agency of the Czech Republic (Grant No. P302/12/G157).

References

1. Boden, A.F., Redding, D.C., Hanisch, R.J., Mo, J.: Massively parallel spatially variant maximum-likelihood restoration of Hubble Space Telescope imagery. J. Opt. Soc. Am. A 13(7), 1537–1545 (1996)
2. Bracewell, R.N.: The Fourier Transform and Its Applications, 3rd edn. McGraw-Hill (2000)
3. Brigham, E.: Fast Fourier Transform and Its Applications, 1st edn. Prentice-Hall (1988)
4. Domanski, L., Vallotton, P., Wang, D.: Two and Three-Dimensional Image Deconvolution on Graphics Hardware. In: Proceedings of the 18th World IMACS/MODSIM Congress, Cairns, Australia, July 13-17, pp. 1010–1016 (2009)
5. Fialka, O., Cadik, M.: FFT and Convolution Performance in Image Filtering on GPU. In: Tenth International Conference on Information Visualization, IV 2006, pp. 609–614 (2006)
6. Fraser, D.: Array permutation by index-digit permutation. J. ACM 23(2), 298–309 (1976), http://doi.acm.org/10.1145/321941.321949
7. Frigo, M., Johnson, S.G.: FFTW 3.2.2. Massachusetts Institute of Technology (July 2009), http://www.fftw.org/fftw3.pdf
8. Gonzales, R.C., Woods, R.E.: Digital Image Processing, 2nd edn. Prentice-Hall (2002)

9. Govindaraju, N.K., Lloyd, B., Dotsenko, Y., Smith, B., Manferdelli, J.: High performance discrete Fourier transforms on graphics processors. In: SC 2008: Proceedings of the 2008 ACM/IEEE Conference on Supercomputing, pp. 1–12. IEEE Press, Piscataway (2008)

10. Group, K.: OpenCL (2011), http://www.khronos.org/opencl/

11. Hanna, J.R., Rowland, J.H.: Fourier Series, Transforms, and Boundary Value Problems, 2nd edn. John Wiley & Sons (1990)

12. Hey, A.: The FFT Demystified. Engineering Productivity Tools Ltd., 21 Leaveden Road, Watford, Hertfordshire, UK (1999), http://www.engineeringproductivitytools.com/stuff/T0001/PT10.HTM

13. Ifeachor, E.C., Jervis, B.W.: Digital Signal Processing: A Practical Approach, 2nd edn. Pearson Education (2002)

14. Jähne, B.: Digital Image Processing, 6th edn. Springer (2005)

15. Karas, P., Svoboda, D.: Convolution of large 3D images on GPU and its decomposition. EURASIP Journal on Advances in Signal Processing (120), 1–12 (2011), http://asp.eurasipjournals.com/content/2011/1/120

16. Luo, Y., Duraiswami, R.: Canny edge detection on NVIDIA CUDA. In: Computer Vision and Pattern Recognition Workshop, pp. 1–8 (2008)

17. Nickolls, J., Dally, W.: The GPU Computing Era. IEEE Micro 30, 56–69 (2010), http://dx.doi.org/10.1109/MM.2010.41

18. Nukada, A., Ogata, Y., Endo, T., Matsuoka, S.: Bandwidth intensive 3-D FFT kernel for GPUs using CUDA. In: SC 2008: Proceedings of the 2008 ACM/IEEE Conference on Supercomputing, pp. 1–11. IEEE Press, Piscataway (2008)

19. NVIDIA Corporation: CUDA^{TM} CUFFT Library 2.3 (June 2009), http://developer.nvidia.com/object/cuda_2_3_downloads.html

20. NVIDIA Corporation: FERMI Tuning Guide (August 2010), http://developer.download.nvidia.com/compute/cuda/3_2_prod/toolkit/docs/Fermi_Tuning_Guide.pdf

21. NVIDIA Corporation, 2701 San Tomas Expressway, Santa Clara, USA: NVIDIA GPU Computing Developer Home Page (June 2011), http://developer.nvidia.com/category/zone/cuda-zone

22. Ogawa, K., Ito, Y., Nakano, K.: Efficient canny edge detection using a GPU. In: International Conference on Natural Computation, pp. 279–280 (2010)

23. Owens, J.D., Luebke, D., Govindaraju, N., Harris, M., Krüger, J., Lefohn, A.E., Purcell, T.J.: A Survey of General-Purpose Computation on Graphics Hardware, pp. 21–51 (August 2005)

24. Pankajakshan, P.: Blind Deconvolution for Confocal Laser Scanning Microscopy. Ph.D. thesis, Universite de Nice Sophia Antipolis (December 2009), http://tel.archives-ouvertes.fr/tel-00474264/fr/

25. Podlozhnyuk, V.: Image Convolution with CUDA (June 2007), http://developer.download.nvidia.com/compute/cuda/1.1-Beta/x86_64_website/projects/convolutionSeparable/doc/convolutionSeparable.pdf

26. Pratt, W.K.: Digital Image Processing, 3rd edn. John Wiley & Sons (2001)

27. Rabiner, L.R.: On the use of symmetry in fft computation. IEEE Transactions on Acoustics, Speech, and Signal Processing 27, 233–239 (1979)

28. Saidi, A.: Generalized FFT Algorithm. In: IEEE International Conference on Communications 93: Technical program, conference record. In: IEEE International Conference on Communications, Geneva, Switzerland, May 23-26, vols. 1-3, pp. 227–231 (1993)

29. Sarder, P., Nehorai, A.: Deconvolution methods for 3-D fluorescence microscopy images. IEEE Signal Processing Magazine 23(3), 32–45 (2006)

30. Schaa, D., Kaeli, D.: Exploring the multiple-GPU design space. In: Proceedings of the 2009 IEEE International Symposium on Parallel & Distributed Processing, IPDPS 2009, pp. 1–12. IEEE Computer Society, Washington, DC (2009)
31. Svoboda, D.: Efficient Computation of Convolution of Huge Images. In: Maino, G., Foresti, G.L. (eds.) ICIAP 2011, Part I. LNCS, vol. 6978, pp. 453–462. Springer, Heidelberg (2011)
32. Svoboda, D., Kozubek, M., Stejskal, S.: Generation of Digital Phantoms of Cell Nuclei and Simulation of Image Formation in 3D Image Cytometry. Cytometry Part A 75A(6), 494–509 (2009)
33. Trussell, H., Hunt, B.: Image restoration of space variant blurs by sectioned methods. In: IEEE International Conference on Acoustics, Speech, and Signal Processing, ICASSP 1978, vol. 3, pp. 196–198 (1978)
34. Verveer, P.J.: Computational and optical methods for improving resolution and signal quality in fluorescence microscopy. Ph.D. thesis, Technische Universiteit Te Delft (1998)
35. Press, W.H., Teukolsky, S.A., Vettrling, W.T., Flannery, B.P.: Numerical Recipes in C, 2nd edn., ch. 7. Cambridge University Press (1992)

Modified Bilateral Filter for the Restoration of Noisy Color Images

Krystyna Malik and Bogdan Smolka

Silesian University of Technology, Department of Automatic Control,
Akademicka 16 Str, 44-100 Gliwice, Poland
krystyna.malik@polsl.pl, smolka@ieee.org

Abstract. In the paper a novel technique of noise removal in color images is presented. The proposed filter design is a modification of the bilateral denosing scheme, which considers the similarity of color pixels and their spatial distance. However, instead of direct calculation of the dissimilarity measure, the cost of a connection through a digital path joining the central pixel of the filtering window and its neighbors is determined. The filter output, like in the standard bilateral filter, is calculated as a weighted average of the pixels which are in the neighborhood relation with the center of the filtering window, and the weights are functions of the minimal connection costs. Experimental results prove that the new denoising method yields significantly better results than the bilateral filter in case of color images contaminated by strong mixed Gaussian and impulsive noise.

1 Introduction

Visual information processing is increasingly becoming widespread as multimedia becomes common in everyday life. With the expanding use of color images in various multimedia applications and the proliferation of color capturing and display units, the interest in color image enhancement is rapidly growing.

Quite often color images are corrupted by various types of noise introduced by malfunctioning sensors in the image formation pipeline, electronic instability of the image signal, faulty memory locations in hardware, aging of the storage material, transmission errors and electromagnetic interferences due to natural or man-made sources [1–4]. Therefore, noise reduction is one of the most frequently performed image processing operation, as the enhancement of images or video streams degraded by noise is indispensable to facilitate subsequent image processing steps.

In this work, we focus on the restoration of color images corrupted by mixed Gaussian and impulsive noise. The reduction of such kind of noise is quite a challenging task, as the techniques capable of reducing efficiently the Gaussian noise, fail in the presence of impulses and the methods suited for the removal of impulsive noise are mostly ineffective when restoring images distorted by other noise types [5–10].

J. Blanc-Talon et al. (Eds.): ACIVS 2012, LNCS 7517, pp. 72–83, 2012.
© Springer-Verlag Berlin Heidelberg 2012

The most widely used filtering designs are based on the concept of the *Vector Median Filter* (VMF), whose output is computed using the concept of *vector ordering* of a set of pixels from the filtering window. The vector ordering scheme is defined through the sorting of the cumulated distances from a given pixel to all other pixels from the filtering window. Then the scalar sum of distances are sorted and the associated vectors can be correspondingly ordered [1, 11, 12]. The vector median filter is very effective at reducing impulsive noise, however its efficiency is decreased when the image is distorted by Gaussian noise and therefore in such a case the VMF is usually combined with other filtering solutions.

Many noise reducing designs are based on the concept of adaptive weighted averaging, where the weights are assigned to pixels from a filtering window according to some rules which downweight the influence of outliers [13–19].

An efficient scheme proposed in [20, 21] divides the pixels of the filtering window into two sets. The first one consists of the pixels similar to the central pixel of the local window and the other one is composed of those pixels, which diverge greatly from the central pixel. The output is computed as a weighted average of the peer-group members.

Similar concept is utilized by the technique proposed in [22], which calculates the distances between the central pixel in a local window and its neighbors. If the number of pixels classified as close to the central pixel is higher than a predefined threshold then the pixel is treated as uncorrupted, otherwise it is replaced by a vector median of all pixels from W or an average of the uncorrupted pixels in W. In [23] the peer-group members were found using a technique based on the evaluation of the statistical properties of a sorted sequence of accumulated distances used for the calculation of the vector median. The peer-group concept has been also successfully extended to the fuzzy context, so that the proposed technique is able to remove mixed noise by combining a statistical method for impulse noise detection and a replacement scheme utilizing an averaging operation aimed at smoothing out the Gaussian noise component [24, 25].

An efficient method of image denoising called *Non-Local Means* (NLM) was proposed in [26, 27]. This method is based on a non-local averaging of the image pixels in such a way that the new pixel value of the restored image is estimated as a weighted average of the pixels, whose local neighborhood is similar to the local neighborhood of the pixel which is currently being processed. The NLM filter is extremely efficient when restoring images corrupted by Gaussian noise, but fails in the presence of distortions introduced by impulsive noise.

2 Bilateral Filter

Another powerful nonlinear noise reducing filtering design, whose aim is to smooth images while preserving their edges, called *Bilateral Filter* (BF) was proposed in [28] and discussed in [29–32].

In this method, the intensity value at each image pixel is being replaced by a weighted average of the grayscale values of pixels belonging to the local neighborhood. The weight function depends on the spatial distance between the central pixel of the local filtering window and the neighboring pixels as well as on the difference of their intensities. The bilateral filter output $J(\boldsymbol{x})$ at image domain location $\boldsymbol{x}$ is defined as

$$J(\boldsymbol{x}) = \frac{1}{Z} \sum_{\boldsymbol{y} \in \mathcal{N}_{\boldsymbol{x}}} w(\boldsymbol{x}, \boldsymbol{y}) \cdot I(\boldsymbol{y}), \quad Z = \sum_{\boldsymbol{y} \in \mathcal{N}_{\boldsymbol{x}}} w(\boldsymbol{x}, \boldsymbol{y}), \tag{1}$$

where $\mathcal{N}_{\boldsymbol{x}}$ is the local neighborhood of $\boldsymbol{x}$ and $w(\boldsymbol{x}, \boldsymbol{y})$ is the weight assigned to pixel at location $\boldsymbol{y}$ which belongs to $\mathcal{N}_{\boldsymbol{x}}$. The weight assigned to pixel at $\boldsymbol{y} \in \mathcal{N}_{\boldsymbol{x}}$ is defined as

$$w(\boldsymbol{x}, \boldsymbol{y}) = w_S(\boldsymbol{x}, \boldsymbol{y}) \cdot w_I(\boldsymbol{x}, \boldsymbol{y}). \tag{2}$$

This weight is a result of multiplication of two components

$$w_S(\boldsymbol{x}, \boldsymbol{y}) = \exp\left(-\frac{\|\boldsymbol{x} - \boldsymbol{y}\|^2}{2\sigma_S^2}\right), \quad w_I(\boldsymbol{x}, \boldsymbol{y}) = \exp\left(-\frac{|I(\boldsymbol{x}) - I(\boldsymbol{y})|^2}{2\sigma_I^2}\right), \tag{3}$$

where $\|\cdot\|$ denotes the Euclidean distance between $\boldsymbol{x}$ and $\boldsymbol{y}$, σ_S and σ_I are weighting parameters in the *spatial* and *intensity* domains respectively.

The w_S weighting function decreases with the spatial distance and the pixels which are far away from the center of the processing window has low influence on the weighted average expressed by (1). The w_I weighting function is a decreasing function of the absolute difference of pixel intensities. Thus, the weight w_I operating in the intensity domain reduces the influence of pixels with significantly different intensities, which ensures the preservation of sharp image edges.

Figure 1 explains the construction of the bilateral filter. It depicts an exemplary filtering window (a), the array of Euclidean distances (b) between the central pixel and all other pixels of the window and the array of the absolute differences of intensities (c).

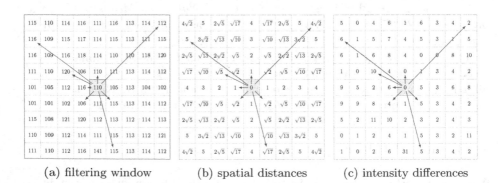

(a) filtering window   (b) spatial distances   (c) intensity differences

Fig. 1. Illustration of the bilateral filter construction

For color images, the difference of the intensity is replaced by the distance between color pixels in the RGB color space

$$\|\boldsymbol{I}(\boldsymbol{x}) - \boldsymbol{I}(\boldsymbol{y})\|^2 = \sum_{k=1}^{3} \left(I_k\left(\boldsymbol{x}\right) - I_k\left(\boldsymbol{y}\right)\right)^2, \tag{4}$$

where $\|\boldsymbol{I}(\boldsymbol{x}) - \boldsymbol{I}(\boldsymbol{y})\|$ is the Euclidean distance between the color pixels $\boldsymbol{I}(\boldsymbol{x})$ and $\boldsymbol{I}(\boldsymbol{y})$ and the index represents the k-th color channel (Red, Green or Blue). Therefore, for color images the scheme given in (3) can be modified and the weight w_I can be expressed as

$$w_I(\boldsymbol{x}, \boldsymbol{y}) = \exp\left(-\frac{\|\boldsymbol{I}(\boldsymbol{x}) - \boldsymbol{I}(\boldsymbol{y})\|^2}{2\sigma_I^2}\right). \tag{5}$$

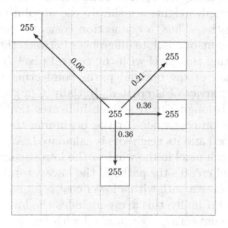

Fig. 2. Illustration of the BF inability to suppress impulsive noise

The bilateral filter is a highly efficient noise reducing scheme, however it has severe problems to remove the pixels introduced by impulsive noise process. Assuming that the central pixel of the local filtering window is an impulse and some of the pixels in the window are also injected by the noise and possess similar intensities or colors as the central pixel, then the weights expressed by (5) are relatively high, which leads to the preservation of the corrupted pixel.

This undesired effect is illustrated by the situation depicted in Fig. 2. The filtering window contains pixels whose intensities are equal to 128 and some white impulses. The weights assigned to gray pixels are very close to 0 for $\sigma_I = 20$, $\sigma_S = 2$ and the weights assigned to white pixels are depicted near the arrows. As a result the white impulse in the center of the filtering window will be preserved.

So, if in the close neighborhood of a noisy central pixel, another similar pixels corrupted by noise are present, then while calculating the new pixel value, the noisy pixel will be included with large weights and as a result the impulses will be preserved. Therefore, in this paper we propose a modification of the bilateral filter, which alleviates the described above drawback.

3   Modified Bilateral Filter

The concept of the proposed modification of the bilateral filter is based on assigning the pixels from the filtering window W a minimum connection cost of
a digital path which joins them with the central pixel. In this way, each pixel
is connected with the central pixel through a digital path with minimum cost
function value. The cost of a connection is used to calculate a weight assigned
to each pixel from W and the filter output is the weighted average of the local
neighborhood.

For the calculation of the weights we treat the image as a graph and utilize the
Dijkstra algorithm for finding the optimal connections between the pixels (graph
vertices), where the graph weights are simply the absolute differences between
adjacent pixels intensities. Thus, a connection cost of a pixel at position y is
defined as a minimum sum of absolute differences between the pixels constituting
a digital path connecting this pixel with the central pixel $I(x)$ [33].

For the computation of the optimal paths connecting the pixels with the
central pixel x a cost array C is created. Initially $C(x) = 0$ and $C(y) = \infty$
for all other pixels y belonging to W, which indicates that the pixels were not
yet assigned a connection cost value. At the beginning the cost of the crossing
between the central pixel and its neighbors is calculated. Afterwards the Dijkstra
algorithm assigns to each pixel in the window the lowest connection cost relative
to the central pixel and creates the paths of the lowest total cost. Every pixel of
W is visited and whenever a path with a lower cost is found, the current value in
the array C is updated. Finally, this array includes the lowest costs and enables
to find optimal paths connecting a given pixel with the starting point as shown
in Fig. 3.

The connection costs can be treated as similarity measures between the central pixel of W and the pixels of the local neighborhood and in this way the

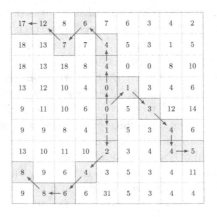

Fig. 3. Connection costs with some exemplary optimal paths

proposed filtering scheme is simply a weighted average of the pixels y which are in neighborhood relation with the central pixel x. The weights are defined as

$$w(x, y) = \exp\left(-\frac{C(x, y)^2}{h^2}\right), \tag{6}$$

where h is a tuning parameter and $C(x, y)$ is a cost function of the optimal path connecting x and y.

The cost function is the sum of the connection costs of the pixels creating the optimal optimal paths:

$$C(x, y) = \sum_{j=1}^{m} |I(x_j) - I(x_{j-1})|, \tag{7}$$

where $x_0 = x$ is the starting point of a path, $x_m = y$ and m is the number of path segments.

For color images the connection costs are calculated using the Euclidean distance in RGB color space between neighboring pixels. Thus, the structure of filter output is the same as in the case of the bilateral filter

$$J(x) = \frac{1}{Z} \sum_{y \in \mathcal{N}_x} w(x, y) \cdot I(y), \quad Z = \sum_{y \in \mathcal{N}_x} w(x, y). \tag{8}$$

4 Experimental Results

In this section we compare the bilateral filter with the proposed modification in terms of the visual quality of the restored image and also in terms of objective quality measures.

First, the relationship between the control parameters of the filters and the noise level was analyzed. The effectiveness of the new filter was tested on the standard color test images LENA, PEPPERS and GOLDHILL corrupted with Gaussian and mixed Gaussian and impulse noise.

We used two kinds of impulsive noise. In the first model, which will be denoted by I, the noisy signal is modeled as $x_i = \{x_{i1}, x_{i2}, x_{i3}\}$, with $x_{ik} = \rho$ with probability π, and o_{ik} with probability $1 - \pi$. The original, uncorrupted image pixel is denoted by o_i and the contamination component ρ is a random variable, which takes the value 0 or 255 with the same probability. In this noise model the contamination of the color image components is uncorrelated and the overall contamination rate is $p = 1 - (1 - \pi)^3$.

The second type of impulsive noise, called random-valued or uniform noise denoted as U is modeled as $x_i = \rho_i$ with probability p, and o_i with probability $1 - p$, where ρ_i is a noisy pixel with all channels corrupted by noise of uniform distribution in the range $[0, 255]$. In the first model the noise can corrupt one, two or all three channels. In the second model all channels are contaminated by random values within the range $[0, 255]$.

The test images were contaminated by: Gaussian noise of $\sigma = 10$, $\sigma = 20$, $\sigma = 30$, and mixed Gaussian and impulsive noise of $\sigma = 10$ and $p = 0.1$, $\sigma = 20$ and $p = 0.2$, $\sigma = 30$ and $p = 0.3$, where p denotes the contamination probability.

The noise removal capabilities of the modified bilateral filter were extensively tested. To quantitatively evaluate the denoising methods we used the Peak Signal to Noise Ratio (PSNR) measure [2].

As can be derived from (3) the properties of the bilateral filter are controlled by the parameters σ_S and σ_I. Figure 4 shows the dependence of the PSNR on the σ_I and σ_S values for the noisy images restored by the bilateral filter.

The values of PSNR depend mainly on σ_I parameter, however σ_S has strong influence on the PSNR value in the range $[1, 3]$. Examining the plots, it can be observed that the optimal value of σ_S is relatively insensitive to noise level in the case of mixed noise but has to be tuned when restoring images polluted by Gaussian noise.

The color images contaminated by mixed Gaussian and impulsive noise were also restored by the modified bilateral filter. This filter was applied for different values of the parameters h in (6) and the dependence of PSNR measure on the parameter h is depicted in Fig. 5.

As can be observed, for test images contaminated by Gaussian noise of increasing intensity, the optimal results depend significantly on the tuning parameter h. Similarly, as in the case of the bilateral filter, the value of h increases with the

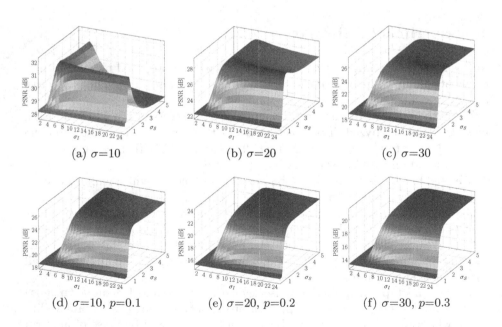

Fig. 4. Dependence of PSNR on σ_S and σ_I parameters for the bilateral filter operating in 5×5 window. The color image GOLDHILL was corrupted by Gaussian (a, b, c) and mixed Gaussian and impulsive, uniform noise U (d, e, f).

Table 1. Comparison of PSNR values obtained when restoring the color test images with the proposed algorithm and other denoising techniques

IMAGE	NOISE	FILTER								
		NLM	VMF	ANNMF	FVMF	VDF	$BF_{5\times5}$	$MBF_{5\times5}$	$BF_{9\times9}$	$MBF_{9\times9}$
LENA	$G(10)$	34.76	27.09	31.46	31.55	31.01	32.86	32.26	32.92	31.93
	$G(20)$	31.93	26.53	28.18	28.21	27.77	29.38	29.78	29.68	29.48
	$G(30)$	30.39	25.84	25.51	25.53	25.12	27.27	28.06	27.90	27.98
	$M(10)_I$	19.51	26.75	31.02	31.16	30.23	27.50	28.28	28.27	27.48
	$M(20)_I$	20.22	25.15	26.97	27.19	25.41	24.81	26.41	26.22	26.89
	$M(30)_I$	21.09	23.11	23.29	23.70	21.03	22.66	24.55	24.34	25.98
	$M(10)_U$	19.11	28.57	29.38	30.45	29.53	26.87	28.67	27.52	28.47
	$M(20)_U$	16.93	23.3	24.45	25.29	24.23	23.32	25.25	24.23	26.11
	$M(30)_U$	15.41	19.4	20.65	21.07	20.08	20.57	21.99	21.46	23.00
GOLDHILL	$G(10)$	33.40	25.31	29.47	29.55	28.71	31.90	30.91	31.90	30.74
	$G(20)$	30.21	24.94	27.04	27.11	26.18	28.56	28.30	28.74	27.98
	$G(30)$	28.19	24.47	24.74	24.85	23.70	26.47	26.79	26.84	26.55
	$M(10)_I$	17.92	25.00	29.13	29.11	23.24	25.52	25.99	26.16	25.13
	$M(20)_I$	19.68	23.92	25.81	26.11	20.36	23.91	24.95	25.06	25.15
	$M(30)_I$	20.63	22.29	21.61	22.93	17.31	21.97	23.50	23.51	24.70
	$M(10)_U$	19.34	27.25	27.98	28.70	27.84	26.33	27.32	26.7	26.94
	$M(20)_U$	17.53	22.89	23.44	24.67	22.92	23.36	24.84	24.08	25.33
	$M(30)_U$	15.48	19.42	19.69	21.03	19.02	20.93	22.16	21.74	22.98
PEPPERS	$G(10)$	33.71	26.54	30.85	31.13	30.32	32.15	31.74	32.29	31.55
	$G(20)$	31.31	25.97	27.86	28.07	27.23	28.73	29.51	28.92	29.39
	$G(30)$	29.81	25.27	25.23	25.47	24.55	26.70	27.61	27.13	27.75
	$M(10)_I$	18.54	26.01	30.27	30.66	29.22	26.37	26.95	27.07	26.46
	$M(20)_I$	19.48	24.50	26.11	26.86	24.17	23.46	24.87	24.69	25.61
	$M(30)_I$	19.68	22.96	21.84	23.29	19.56	21.18	22.82	22.57	24.37
	$M(10)_U$	18.49	28.13	28.47	29.91	28.33	26.04	27.96	26.68	28.02
	$M(20)_U$	16.62	22.93	23.20	24.84	23.16	22.35	24.24	23.14	25.18
	$M(30)_U$	14.36	19.05	19.35	20.66	19.07	19.61	21.03	20.36	21.98

noise magnitude. The obtained results also show that the optimal h parameter does not depend significantly on the image structure. For images contaminated by mixed Gaussian and impulse noise the optimal value of h is not considerably sensitive to the noise level. The range of of the h parameter, for which the optimal PSNR values can be obtained, is about $[200, 250]$.

The effectiveness of the new filtering design was compared with some of the existing methods:

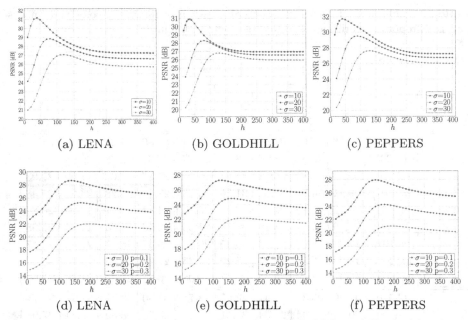

(a) LENA   (b) GOLDHILL   (c) PEPPERS

(d) LENA   (e) GOLDHILL   (f) PEPPERS

Fig. 5. Dependence of PSNR when applying the modified bilateral filter using a 5× 5 window on the h parameter for the color image PEPPERS corrupted with Gaussian (a, b, c) and mixed Gaussian and impulsive, uniform noise U (d, e, f)

- Non-Local Means filter (NLM) [26, 27],
- Vector Median Filter (VMF) [12],
- ANNMF - Adaptive Nearest-Neighbor Multichannel Filter [15],
- FVMF - Fuzzy Vector Median Filter [16–18],
- VDF - Vector Directional Filter [19] .

The *Bilateral Filter* (BF) and the proposed *Modified Bilateral Filter* (MBF) were tested for windows of size 5×5 and 9×9. The control parameters were selected experimentally to obtain optimal results in terms of the PSNR quality coefficient. The comparison of the efficiency of the proposed MBF with the mentioned above filters are summarized in Tab. 1.

As can be observed, for images contaminated by Gaussian noise, the best results are obtained by the NLM algorithm and the results of the modified bilateral are quite similar to those obtained using the bilateral filter. However, the results for images contaminated by mixed Gaussian and impulse noise obtained using the new filter are significantly better especially for images contaminated by high and medium mixed noise levels.

Figure 6 exhibits the restoration results of the modified and standard bilateral filter. As can be observed the image is smoothed, edges and details are better preserved and the filtering output is visually more pleasing. Unfortunately, as can be noticed in the images contaminated by a mixed Gaussian and impulse noise, small clusters consisting of two or more pixels distorted by impulsive

(a)   (b)   (c)

(d)   (e)   (f)

Fig. 6. Comparison of the efficiency of the bilateral filter with the proposed approach: (a) GOLDHILL image corrupted by mixed noise ($\sigma=20$, $p=0.2$, impulsive noise I), (b) BF output , (c) MBF output, (d) GOLDHILL image corrupted by mixed noise ($\sigma=20$, $p=0.2$, impulsive noise U), (e) BF output, (f) MBF output, (filtering window 5×5)

(a) PSNR=24.93 dB (b) PSNR=26.16 dB(c) PSNR=24.21 dB (d) PSNR=25.49 dB

Fig. 7. Results of the restoration of the test color image GOLDHILL corrupted by mixed noise ($\sigma=20$, $p=0.2$, impulsive noise U) using a 5×5 filtering window: (a) BF output , (b) MBF output, (c) BF with additional denoising of impulses using the method described in [22], (d) MBF with the same impulsive noise removal technique

noise are preserved. However, for images processed with the modified bilateral, this artifact can be easily removed using a switching filter with good impulse detection mechanism [9, 34].

For images processed with the standard bilateral filter, the removal of the remaining impulse noise is more difficult, because the impulses are blurred by the image restoration technique. The restoration results with additional impulsive noise reduction, using the method described in [22], are presented in Fig. 7.

5 Conclusions

In the paper a novel filtering scheme has been presented and analyzed. The results of the performed experiment indicate that very good restoration quality has been achieved for color images contaminated by strong mixed Gaussian and impulsive noise. The new filtering method yields significantly better results in comparison with other denoising methods both in terms of subjective quality and objective restoration measures. The beneficial feature of the proposed method is the removal of mixed noise with preservation of edges and image details.

References

1. Lukac, R., Smolka, B., Martin, K., Plataniotis, K., Venetsanopoulos, A.: Vector filtering for color imaging. IEEE Signal Processing Magazine 22(1), 74–86 (2005)
2. Plataniotis, K., Venetsanopoulos, A.: Color Image Processing and Applications. Springer (2000)
3. Boncelet, C.G.: Image noise models. In: Bovik, A. (ed.) Handbook of Image and Video Processing. Communications, Networking and Multimedia, pp. 397–410. Elsevier Academic Press (2005)
4. Zheng, J., Valavanis, K., Gauch, J.: Noise removal from color images. Journal of Intelligent and Robotic Systems 7(3), 257–285 (1993)
5. Peng, S., Lucke, L.: Multi-level adaptive fuzzy filter for mixed noise removal. In: IEEE International Symposium on Circuits and Systems, ISCAS 1995, vol. 2, pp. 1524–1527 (1995)
6. Wang, C., L.-F. Sun, Yang, B., Liu, Y.M., Yang, S.Q.: Video enhancement using adaptive spatio-temporal connective filter and piecewise mapping. EURASIP J. Adv. Sig. Proc (2008)
7. Garnett, R., Huegerich, T., Chui, C., Wenjie, H.: A universal noise removal algorithm with an impulse detector. IEEE Transactions on Image Processing 14(11), 1747–1754 (2005)
8. Tang, K., Astola, J., Neuvo, Y.: Nonlinear multivariate image filtering techniques. IEEE Transactions on Image Processing 4(6), 788–798 (1995)
9. Lukac, R.: Adaptive vector median filtering. Pattern Recognition Letters 24(12), 1889–1899 (2003)
10. Lukac, R., Smolka, B., Plataniotis, K., Venetsanopoulos, A.: Vector sigma filters for noise detection and removal in color images. Journal of Visual Communication and Image Representation 17(1), 1–26 (2006)
11. Pitas, I., Tsakalides, P.: Multivariate ordering in color image filtering. IEEE Trans. on Circuits and Systems for Video Technology 1(3), 247–259, 295-296 (1991)
12. Astola, J., Haavisto, P., Neuvo, Y.: Vector median filters. Proceedings of the IEEE 78(4), 678–689 (1990)
13. Plataniotis, K., Androutsos, D., Venetsanopoulos, A.: Multichannel filters for image processing. Signal Processing: Image Communication 9(2), 143–158 (1997)

14. Lukac, R., Plataniotis, K., Venetsanopoulos, A., Smolka, B.: A statistically-switched adaptive vector median filter. Journal of Intelligent and Robotic Systems 42(4), 361–391 (2005)
15. Plataniotis, K., Sri, V., Androutsos, D., Venetsanopoulos, A.: An adaptive nearest neighbor multichannel filter. IEEE Transactions on Circuits and Systems for Video Technology 6(6), 699–703 (1996)
16. Plataniotis, K.N., Androutsos, D., Venetsanopoulos, A.N.: Fuzzy adaptive filters for multichannel image processing. Signal Processing 55(1), 93–106 (1996)
17. Plataniotis, K., Androutsos, D., Venetsanopoulos, A.: Adaptive fuzzy systems for multichannel signal processing. Proceedings of the IEEE 87(9), 1601–1622 (1999)
18. Chatzis, V., Pitas, I.: Fuzzy scalar and vector median filters based on fuzzy distances. IEEE Transactions on Image Processing 8(5), 731–734 (1999)
19. Trahanias, P., Venetsanopoulos, A.: Vector directional filters-a new class of multichannel image processing filters. IEEE Transactions on Image Processing 2(4), 528–534 (1993)
20. Kenney, C., Deng, Y., Manjunath, B.S., Hewer, G.: Peer group image enhancement. IEEE Transactions on Image Processing 10(2), 326–334 (2001)
21. Deng, Y., Kenney, C., Moore, M., Manjunath, B.S.: Peer group filtering and perceptual color image quantization. In: Proceedings of the 1999 IEEE International Symposium on Circuits and Systems, ISCAS 1999, pp. 21–24 (1999)
22. Smolka, B., Chydzinski, A.: Fast detection and impulsive noise removal in color images. Real-Time Imaging 11(5-6), 389–402 (2005)
23. Smolka, B.: Peer group switching filter for impulse noise reduction in color images. Pattern Recognition Letters 31(6), 484–495 (2010)
24. Morillas, S., Gregori, V., Peris-Fajarnes, G., Sapena, A.: New adaptive vector filter using fuzzy metrics. Journal of Electronic Imaging 16(3), 033007 (2007)
25. Morillas, S., Gregori, V., Hervas, A.: Fuzzy peer groups for reducing mixed Gaussian-impulse noise from color images. IEEE Transactions on Image Processing 18(7), 1452–1466 (2009)
26. Buades, A., Coll, B., Morel, J.M.: A non-local algorithm for image denoising. In: IEEE Conf. on Computer Vision and Pattern Recognition, CVPR 2005, vol. 2, pp. 60–65. Washington, DC (2005)
27. Buades, A., Coll, B., Morel, J.M.: A review of image denoising algorithms, with a new one. Multiscale Modeling and Simulation 4(2) (2006)
28. Tomasi, C., Manduchi, R.: Bilateral filtering for gray and color images. In: Proceedings of the IEEE Int. Conf. on Computer Vision, pp. 839–846 (1998)
29. Paris, S., Durand, F.: A fast approximation of the bilateral filter using a signal processing approach. Int. J. Comput. Vision 81(1), 24–52 (2009)
30. Barash, D.: Bilateral Filtering and Anisotropic Diffusion: Towards a Unified Viewpoint. In: Kerckhove, M. (ed.) Scale-Space 2001. LNCS, vol. 2106, pp. 273–280. Springer, Heidelberg (2001)
31. Barash, D.: Fundamental relationship between bilateral filtering, adaptive smoothing, and the nonlinear diffusion equation. IEEE Transactions on Pattern Analysis and Machine Intelligence 24(6), 844–847 (2002)
32. Elad, M.: On the origin of the bilateral filter and ways to improve it. IEEE Transactions on Image Processing 11(10), 1141–1151 (2002)
33. Falcao, A., Stolfi, J., de Alencar Lotufo, R.: The image foresting transform: theory, algorithms, and applications. IEEE Transactions on Pattern Analysis and Machine Intelligence 26(1), 19–29
34. Smolka, B., Plataniotis, K.N., Chydzinski, A., Szczepanski, M., Venetsanopoulos, A.N., Wojciechowski, K.: Self-adaptive algorithm of impulsive noise reduction in color images. Pattern Recognition 35(8), 1771–1784 (2002)

Correction, Stitching and Blur Estimation of Micro-graphs Obtained at High Speed

Seyfollah Soleimani[1,3,*], Jacob Premkumar Sukumaran[2], Koen Douterloigne[1],
Filip Rooms[1], Wilfried Philips[1,4], and Patrick De Baets[2]

[1] Ghent University IBBT-Telin-IPI St-Pietersnieuwstraat 41, B-9000 Gent, Belgium
[2] Ghent University, Laboratory Soete,
Technologiepark Zwijnaarde 903, B-9052 Gent, Belgium
[3] Department of Computer Engineering, Faculty of Engineering,
Arak University, Arak 38156-8-8349, Iran
[4] Senior member of IEEE
Seyfollah.Soleimani@telin.ugent.be

Abstract. Micro-structures of surface are considered to be effective in identifying the damage mechanisms. The industry uses computer vision to auto detect misalignment of the components as it is a contactless tool. However, in scientific investigations micro structures obtained online at high-speed has to be analyzed. In this work the change detection of a specimen rotating at a high speed studied online using image processing techniques in micro graphs which provides a clear insight about the dimensional changes. The specimen under study is made from polymer composite which has contact with a steel wheel and rotates at a high speed. The blur as a measure of dimensional change of the polymer composite can be identified due to the change in focus. The micro-structure images were dark and span a very small region of the surface due to high speed image acquisition, short shutter time and magnification of the microscope. Thus, pre-processing procedures like image enhancement, stitching and registration are performed. Then 15 blur estimation methods are applied to the stitched images. The results of three methods present a good correlation with dimensional change provided by a stylus instrument.

Keywords: Micro-graph, Blur estimation, Registration, Stitching, Change detection.

1 Introduction

Image processing techniques have been used a lot in different fields of engineering. In the current industrial practice it is used to identify the faulty components or to segregate the unmatched parts automatically. Such technique uses surface morphologies of components and textures of manufactured surface. Micro-graphs which is the micro structure of the material surface is very limitedly worked using

---

* Corresponding author.

J. Blanc-Talon et al. (Eds.): ACIVS 2012, LNCS 7517, pp. 84–95, 2012.
© Springer-Verlag Berlin Heidelberg 2012

image processing techniques for surface characterization. Micro-graphs serve as evidence in characterizing the surface modification undergone by the material as a consequence of damage. In some case the postmortem image of the damaged surface has been used to study the condition and the kind of process the material has undergone. Optical techniques are often used in the investigation of material surfaces for identifying the involved wear mechanisms. Research by Sukumaran et al illustrated the benefits of optical methods for online monitoring system in identifying surface changes in the wear process [15]. Even though different types of techniques are readily available for image processing in engineering applications a combination of methods is required to adopt efficient analysis of surfaces.

In this work we study the possibility of using image processing techniques for overall change detection of the fast moving specimen in micro level. Micrograph images reflect only a small area (few microns squared) from which analysis and conclusions are rather difficult. Nevertheless, techniques like stitching of multiple images can provide a significant surface area for micro level investigation which increases the efficiency of analyzing the modification gone through by the material. The stitching can be done if there is some overlapping between successive images. After stitching, we use blur estimation for measuring the dimension change of the specimen during the experiment. To be able to use blur as an evident of change detection, at the beginning of the experiment the imaging system should be focused carefully on the surface of the specimen. By starting the wear process, the diameter of the specimen starts to change which results in de-focussing of the imaging system. So the images will be blurry and the amount of blur can be used as an overall evidence of wear. Although our observations show that the surface of the specimen damages locally, we can assume that these small changes do not have considerable effect on overall amount of blur. Because firstly, the changes are small in a long period of the experiment and secondly we compare a large area of the surface. Anyway, as a limitation, blur estimation can be used as long as the damages are not considerable. In addition when the images become completely blurry and they contain no meaningful signal (due to considerable damage), the blur estimation cannot be applied anymore. In such a situation, the solution is to focus again on the surface and take into account the amount of focus changing.

The paper is organized as follows: In section 2, we explain briefly the materials in the experiments and also the imaging system and its parameters. In section 3, the needed pre-processing procedures for enhancing, registration and stitching of frames are explained. The output of the pre-processing step is a stitched image of a large area of the surface of the specimen for every sampling time. In section 4, the used blur estimation methods are introduced and results will be presented in section 5. A conclusion is drawn in section 6.

2   Materials and Methods

The chosen model for testing is a twin-disc which is used to characterise the surface properties of applications such as gears, cam and rollers. In the used model, the specimen geometry is described in the earlier research [14] which is of a cylindrical profile and it which rotates at a relatively high speed of 250RPM (Rotation Per Minute). Out of the two discs, one (specimen) is made from a polymer composite and other one from alloy steel. We are interested in the wear and change detection of the polymer. So, micro-graphs were obtained from polymer surface. Specific details about the materials such as material properties are not considered in this paper since it is beyond the scope of image processing. The digital image of the test setup is shown in figure 1. A detailed description of the test set-up, materials and the schematics of the test and image acquisition methods was previously reported in [15,14,13]. Online images were acquired using the developed computer vision. The microscope is focused on the surface of the specimen at the beginning of the experiment manually and subjectively. The dimensional changes which are a consequence of material damage is collected using a linear velocity displacement transducer (LVDT) as the stylus instrument.

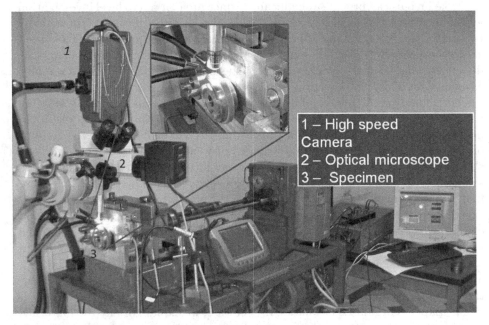

Fig. 1. Figure shows the high speed camera in conjunction with a microscope for Ultra high-speed online microscopy in a twin-disc model [15]

3 Preprocessing

3.1 Enhancing and Cropping

The rotating specimen is recorded with a high speed camera by a frame rate of 3000 frames per second while the shutter time was set to $66\mu s$ to reduce motion blur. The videos are taken every two hours and every video includes

1000 frames. A high power external light source was used to have enough light. However, due to short shutter time, the images became dark. One of the frames is shown in figure 2(a). To enhance images, we increased the brightness, contrast and saturation of the images (using an avisynth script). Furthermore, the sides of the image are not illuminated at all, so there is no useful information there and we cropped them out.

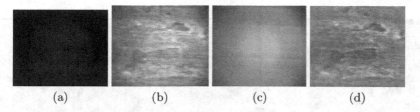

(a)   (b)   (c)   (d)

Fig. 2. Finding and removing the vignette from a frame

3.2   Vignette Removal

Even with the cropping, the external light source creates severe vignetting. The corners of the image are dark, while the center is too bright (see figure 2(b)). This has to be removed, otherwise the registration gets distracted by this vignette, as it is the same in both images (in every step of registration two successive images are considered) and what will happen is that the matching will perform on the static vignette instead of on the surface of the specimen. To remove the vignette we first have to measure it. This is done by taking the average of all input frames (figure 2(c)). Finally we subtract every frame with this average, and add a value of 128 to every pixel to avoid too much clipping. Values greater than 128 are clipped anyway. One of the resulting images is shown in figure 2(d). Some static noise remains, but the vignetting is gone as well as the effect of some dust in the lens. However the motion blur is also still present. It shows that we need shorter shutter time which in turn requires a more powerful and more expensive light source.

3.3   Registration

The next step is registration [19]. This is done on a frame by frame basis, every time registering one frame with the next and so on. Mutual information [16] gives a clear peak, enabling us to optimize the process for speed. We also know that there can be only translation, vastly simplifying the job. However also ignoring the vertical translation would simplify the work even more, as a significant vertical translation is present beside the (much bigger) horizontal translation.

With these two considerations, we get a speed of around 10 registrations per second. We might further increase the speed or accuracy by noting that the rotation is at a constant speed, so every transformation will be roughly the same as the previous one.

3.4 Stitching

With a transformation for every image pair, we can do the stitching. We prefer that the resulting mosaic has as little dark areas as possible, so we search for the orientation of the first image that achieves this. We find an orientation of about 0.04 radians. This is probably because the camera itself was rotated a bit while looking at the specimen (see figure 3).

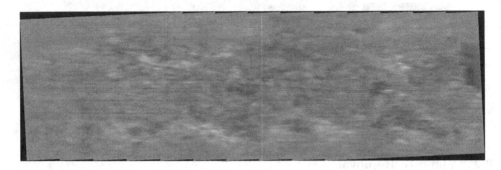

Fig. 3. Stitch of the 10 frames of a video. The motion blur is clearly visible, as well as some extra blur caused by the stitching. The initial frame was rotated a little to fit the entire mosaic.

3.5 Intra- and Inter-video Matching

The next challenge is to match video captures taken at different times (videos are taken every 2 hours). Because the specimen keeps rotating, the first frame of one video will not match the first frame of another video necessarily. So we will try to match the first frame of one video with every frame of another video. One such registration gives us a certain transformation, along with a certain value of the mutual information for that transformation. Even when the images do not overlap and there is no registration possible, the algorithm will still find a registration, corresponding to the maximum of the mutual information over all translations. Of course this registration will be wrong, but the automated matching can not know this based on two frames alone. We can fix this by comparing the optimal values of the mutual information for all the images. This is shown in figure 4. The maximum mutual information over all images (the peak in the graph) corresponds to frames that have the same image content, i.e. frames taken at the same part of the surface of the specimen. For instance, the frame 585 of the second video matches best with frame 1 of the first video. We can also check this within the video itself. At rotation speed of 200 RPM, 3000 fps, we theoretically should get the same image content after 900 frames. Matching the first frame of a video with the 1000 next, gives the plot of figure 4(b). We see that the first few frames match fine to frame 1, as well as a group of frames around number 908, indicating that they have the same content. We also see that there is not just one frame that matches, but a group of frames. This enables us to speed up the process by only comparing to one in every four (or so) frames. For 1000 frames, with a skip of 4 and at 10 registrations per seconds, this takes 25 seconds to find the correspondence between two videos. With this offset in frames, we can compare stitches of different videos. An example of one stitched image is shown in figure 5.

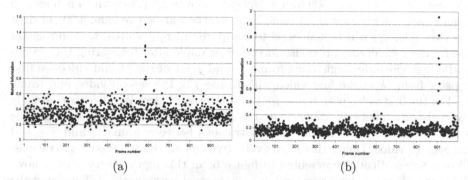

(a) (b)

Fig. 4. Maximum mutual information between the first frame of video 1 and every frame of (a) video 2 and (b) video 1

3.6 Wrapping

To compare the full video with another full video, we have to keep in mind that we are dealing with a rotating object. Basically, the frames wrap around, so that frame 1 is more or less equal to frame 900 or so. Suppose the first frame of the first video matches the frame 500 of the second video. To create comparable mosaics, we have to stitch frame 1 to 900 of the first video , and 500 to 1400 modulo 900 of the second video.

The frame where the video of the rotating band wraps can be computed theoretically, giving 900, but in practice it was found to be a bit higher, being around frame 908. This indicates that either the rotation was slower than 200 rpm or the camera was faster than 3000 fps.

Fig. 5. a stitch of frames 0 to 20 in the first video

3.7   Dealing with Drift

Every registration has a small error. These errors add up, causing noticeable deviations after a while. When registering the first video, or 908 frames, the found transformations will be a little bit different than the transformations found in the second video. It is important to keep this in mind in case blind comparisons have to be made between the two resulting mosaics from two videos. For a 0.1 average pixel error, after 500 frames the error can be 50 pixels which is huge. To ensure that the errors will be same between the videos (we cannot avoid drift error completely) which enables us to compare different videos, we can register the frames considering previous video. For example after registering the frames of the first video, for registering frames j and $j + 1$ of the second video we first register frame k of the first video with frame j of the second video and frame $k+1$ of the first video with frame $j+1$ of the second video. We also know already the registration between frames k and $k + 1$ of the first video. Considering these 3 registrations, we determine the registrations between frames j and $j + 1$ of the second video. Doing this recursively gives us all the required registrations. This is schematically represented in figure 6. In this figure, every arrow shows the pair of frames which registration is performed between them. For doing the registration between frames j and $j + 1$ of video i (which is shown by $*$), we use the registration information of ones which are shown by $1, 2$ and 3.

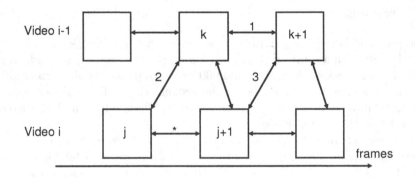

Fig. 6. Registering two video streams with each other

4   Blur Estimation

By pre-processing explained in previous section, now we have a stitched image for every 2 hours.

Every stitched image spans 10 successive frames from same region of the surface of the specimen.

In total we have 8 stitched images from the first experiment and 7 for the second experiment. We applied 15 no-reference blur estimation methods to the stitched images. The codes are taken from [9]. The using methods are listed below. For every method we term an acronym in parentheses to simplify referring:

- Natural Scene Statistics for JPEG2K (NSS) [12]: In this method authors proposed to use natural scene statistics for quality assessment based on this reasoning that those statistics and image quality are related. They presented an algorithm for quantifying the change in natural behavior of the image before and after compression and calibrated this metric against subjective scores.
- No reference JPEG (NRJPEG) [17]: In this method first the absolute value of differences between two successive pixels are calculated for any row of the image. Then the blockiness is estimated as the average differences across block boundaries (where blocks are in size of 1 by 8). Afterwards the activity of the image signal is measured using two factors. The first factor is the average absolute differences between in-block image samples and the second factor is the zero-crossing rates. The same features are calculated for columns in the image and then overall blockiness, absolute difference between in-block image samples and zero-crossing rate are calculated as the average of horizontal and vertical correspondents. Then the three final features should be combined by entering some parameters. The parameters are estimated by subjective test data.
- Variance (VAR)[2]: It is the variance of the whole image.
- Spectrum [6]: It is the sum of the amplitudes of all Fourier transform coefficients.
- Laplacian (LAP), Gradient (GRA) and Auto-Correlation (AUTO)[1].
- Marichal [7]: This method is based on histogram computation of non-zero DCT transform.
- Kurtosis based metric by Zhang (ZHANG) [18]: Kurtosis is defined as a descriptor of the shape of a probability distribution of a random variable. A wider distribution has smaller kurtosis. In this method, spectral density function is considered as a probability density function.
- Marziliano Metric[8]: In this method first edge detection is done and then the width of any detected edge is estimated. The width of any detected edge is considered as the distance between two extrema in both sides of the edge pixel. Then the average of widths of all edge pixels is calculated as the sharpness metric.
- High-pass to band-pass frequency ratio (HP) [11]: The metric is based on the high-pass to band-pass frequency ratio applied to local features that are extracted by thresholding the bandpass filter output.
- Kurtosis of Wavelet Coefficients (Wavelet)[5]: In this method first the dyadic wavelet transform is calculated and then the Fourier transform of the wavelet coefficients across large scales is calculated. Finally the kurtosis of the Fourier transform is measured.
- Riemannian tensor based metric (Riemannian) [3]: In this method the Riemannian tensor is used by mapping the image into a non-Euclidean space and measuring the curve variation.
- Just Noticeable Blur (JNB) [4]: Ferzli et al. introduced the concept of just noticeable blur. Then a perceptual sharpness metric is derived based on measured just-noticeable blurs and probability summation over space, which

takes into account the response of HVS (human vision system) to sharpness at different contrast levels. This method gives the relative amount of blurriness in images with different content.

- Cumulative Probability Blur Detection (CPBD) [10]: In this method first edge detection is done and then for every detected edge, the probability of blur is estimated. Then a probability density function (Pdf) is derived from Pdfs of detected edges. Finally the cumulative probability of blur is calculated from derived Pdf.

5   Results

We have shown the results of applying mentioned methods to the stitched images of two experiments in tables 1 and 2. In these tables DC1 and DC2 rows are for values produced from LVDT which monitors online the change in dimension of the polymer specimen.

Table 1. Blur estimation of different methods for first experiment

Hour	0	2	4	6	8	10	12	14
DC1	-0.015	-0.016	-0.021	-0.010	-0.012	-0.009	-0.008	-0.012
NSS	49.270	43.302	44.305	44.083	45.376	45.907	45.727	45.535
NRJPEG	12.219	11.593	12.178	11.839	11.873	11.946	11.623	12.207
var	139.534	120.716	116.293	131.738	131.694	133.732	134.817	130.319
spectrum	2.95E8	2.81E8	2.65E8	2.86E8	2.90E8	2.98E8	2.94E8	2.92E8
lap	7.536	5.080	5.219	5.753	6.118	7.184	6.559	6.050
grad	1.863	1.770	1.605	1.733	1.780	1.914	1.861	1.773
auto	0.992	0.992	0.993	0.992	0.992	0.992	0.992	0.992
Marichal	0.904	0.904	0.904	0.904	0.904	0.904	0.904	0.904
Zhang	681.758	811.592	828.302	737.246	737.988	732.807	725.598	750.754
Marziliano	2.723	2.627	2.699	2.732	2.756	2.739	2.722	2.719
hp	0.053	0.019	0.028	0.049	0.013	0.012	0.024	0.041
wavelet	9.623	9.420	9.872	9.977	10.029	10.168	9.640	10.354
RIEM	5.101	5.032	3.99	5.270	5.451	5.712	6.072	5.137
JNB	8.652	9.688	8.493	9.748	8.196	7.770	10.358	8.973
CPBD	70.921	73.996	68.628	61.038	55.924	54.616	59.113	64.465

The absolute correlation between DC1 and DC2 with blur values of every method are presented in table 3. As can be seen from this table, variance, Zhang and CPBD methods have large correlations with both DC1 and DC2 (their values are bolded). Methods spectrum, grad, auto, Marziliano, hp and RIEM methods have a large correlation just in one of the experiments. Methods Marichal , wavelet and JNB have small correlations in both experiments. It should also be considered that stylus measurements may have some errors. These results confirm the possibility of using at least three of above blur estimation methods

Table 2. Blur estimation of different methods for second experiment

Hour	0	2	6	8	10	12	14
DC2	-0.018	-0.017	-0.015	-0.021	-0.017	-0.01	-0.010
NSS	43.443	45.856	44.749	45.413	42.880	44.775	42.832
NRJPEG	11.938	12.383	12.307	12.446	11.941	12.185	12.022
var	111.596	112.368	126.253	107.675	123.4	135.687	129.861
spectrum	2.61E+8	2.64E+8	2.63E+8	2.38E+8	2.48E+8	2.59E+8	2.57E+8
lap	4.972	7.815	5.924	4.532	4.062	5.173	4.090
grad	1.715	1.995	1.755	1.464	1.510	1.645	1.51
auto	0.992	0.992	0.992	0.993	0.993	0.993	0.993
Marichal	0.904	0.904	0.904	0.904	0.904	0.904	0.904
Zhang	865.445	872.251	782.756	907.222	785.533	752.471	756.690
Marziliano	2.587	2.603	2.601	2.595	2.599	2.587	2.611
hp	0.049	0.018	0.035	0.092	0.023	0.011	0.024
wavelet	10.178	9.874	10.166	9.418	9.474	10.422	9.608
RIEM	4.673	5.556	4.603	3.454	3.792	4.241	3.804
JNB	18.061	17.993	19.478	22.096	12,528	17.261	16.900
CPBD	84.821	80.763	85.901	93	82.037	83.059	76.308

Table 3. Correlation of blur values of different methods with values produced by the stylus instrument

Method	with DC1	with DC2
NSS	0.19	0.34
NRJPEG	0.36	0.33
var	**0.75**	**0.93**
spectrum	0.84	0.47
lap	0.52	0.15
grad	0.72	0.07
auto	0.77	0.24
Marichal	5E-017	67E-017
Zhang	**0.68**	**0.89**
Marziliano	0.56	0.19
hp	0.07	0.73
wavelet	0.33	0.41
RIEM	0.94	0.04
JNB	0.20	0.35
CPBD	**0.75**	**0.71**

for change detection of micro-graphs of this application. For more confidence we can combine results of several methods. In addition, these results show that a blur estimation method which works well for a kind of images, may fail for another kind.

6   Conclusion

We tested the ability of computer vision system to measure the amount of change in the dimension of a polymer composite specimen. We stitched frames of videos to produce one image of a big region of the surface. Then 15 blur estimation methods have been applied to stitched images and some of these methods have good correlation with the values provided by the stylus instrument. The results can be improved if a more powerful illumination can be provided.

References

1. Batten, C.F.: Autofocusing and Astigmatism Correction in the Scanning Electron Microscope. Master's thesis, Univ. Cambridge, Cambridge, U.K. (2000)
2. Erasmus, S., Smith, K.: An automatic focusing and astigmatism correction system for the sem and ctem. Microscopy 127, 185–199 (1982)
3. Ferzli, R., Karam, L.J.: A no reference objective sharpness metric using riemannian tensor. In: Third International Workshop on Video Processing and Quality Metrics for Consumer Electronics VPQM 2007, Scottsdale, Arizona (January 2007)
4. Ferzli, R., Karam, L.J.: A no-reference objective image sharpness metric based on the notion of just noticeable blur (jnb). IEEE Transactionscon Image Processing 18(4), 717–728 (2009)
5. Ferzli, R., Karam, L.J., Caviedes, J.: A robust image sharpness metric based on kurtosis measurement of wavelet coefficients. In: Proceedings of the 1st International Workshop on Video Processing and Quality Metrics for Consumer Electronics (2005)
6. Firestone, L., Cook, K., Talsania, N., Preston, K.: Comparison of autofocus methods for automated microscopy. Cytometry 12, 195–206 (1991)
7. Marichal, X., Ma, W., Zhang, H.J.: Blur determination in the compressed domain using dct information. In: IEEE Int. Conf. Image Processing, vol. 2, pp. 386–390 (1999)
8. Marziliano, P., Dufaux, F., Winkler, S., Ebrahimi, T.: Perceptual blur and ringing metrics: application to jpeg2000. Signal Processing: Image Communication 19(2), 163–172 (2004)
9. Murthy, A.V., Karam, L.J.: A matlab based framework for image and video quality evaluation. In: International Workshop on Quality of Multimedia Experience (QoMEX), pp. 242–247 (June 2010)
10. Narvekar, N., Karam, L.J.: A no-reference perceptual image sharpness metric based on the cumulative probability of blur detection. In: First International Workshop on Quality of Multimedia Experience (QoMEX) (July 2009)
11. Shaked, D., Tastl, I.: Sharpness measure: Towards automatic image enhancement. In: Proceedings of IEEE International Conference on Image Processing, vol. 1, pp. 937–940 (September 2005)
12. Sheikh, H.R., Bovik, A.C., Cormack, L.: No-reference quality assessment using natural scence statistics: Jpeg2000. IEEE Transactions on Image Processing 14(11), 1918–1927 (2005)
13. Sukumaran, J., Ando, M., Baets, P.D., Rodriguez, V., Szabadi, L., Kalacska, G., Paepegem, V.: Modelling gear contact with twin-disc setup. Tribology International 49(0), 1–7 (2012)

14. Sukumaran, J., Ando, M., Rodriguez, V., Baets, P.D.: Effect of velocity on roll/slip for low and high load conditions in polymer composite. Ugent Sustainable Construction and Design (2011)
15. Sukumaran, J.: Roll-slip phenomenon of polymer composites: online analysis assisted by computer vision. In: FEA PhD Symposium, 12th. Ghent University. Faculty of Engineering and Architecture (2011)
16. Thévenaz, P., Unser, M.: Optimization of mutual information for multiresolution image registration. IEEE Transactions on Image Processing 9, 2083–2099 (2000)
17. Wang, Z., Sheikh, H.R., Bovik, A.C.: No-reference perceptual quality assessment of jpeg compressed images. In: IEEE International Conference on Image Processing, vol. 1, pp. I-477– I-480 (September 2002)
18. Zhang, N., Vladar, A., Postek, M., Larrabee, B.: A kurtosis-based statititcal measure for two-dimensional processes and its application to image sharpness. In: Proceedings Section of Physical and Engineering Sciences of American Statistical Society, pp. 4730–4736 (2003)
19. Zitová, B., Flusser, J.: Image registration methods: a survey. Image and Vision Computing 21, 977–1000 (2003)

Hardware Implementation of a Configurable Motion Estimator for Adjusting the Video Coding Performances

Wajdi Elhamzi, Julien Dubois, Johel Miteran,
Mohamed Atri, and Rached Tourki

University of Burgundy, Laboratory Le2i, UMR CNRS 6306,
21000 Dijon - France
University of Monastir, Laboratory of EμE
Faculty of Sciences of Monastir, Tunisia
{wajdi.elhamzi,julien.dubois,johel.miteran}@u-bourgogne.fr,
{mohamed.atri,rached.tourki}@fsm.rnu.tn

Abstract. Despite the diversity of video compression standard, the motion estimation still remains a key process which is used in most of them. Moreover, the required coding performances (bit-rate, PSNR, image spatial resolution, etc.) depend obviously of the application, the environment and the network communication. The motion estimation can therefore be adapted to fit with these performances. Meanwhile, the real time encoding is required in many applications. In order to reach this goal, we propose in this paper a hardware implementation of the motion estimator which enables the integer motion search algorithms to be modified and the fractional search and variable block size to be selected and adjusted. Hence this novel architecture, especially designed for FPGA targets, proposes high-speed processing for a configuration which supports the variable size blocks and quaterpel refinement, as described in H.264.

Keywords: Configurable motion estimation, hardware implantation, H.264, search strategy, fractional search, video coding performances.

1   Introduction

Video coding has been the subject of many research works in last decades. A large number of coding solutions have been described to fit with the diversity of the compression standards and the required coding performances, which are correlated to the constraints defined by the user or fixed by the environment (i.e. networks used for data transmission and the target receiver setup). Consequently a large number of video codec has been developed. Despite this diversity, some particular processing stages, such as motion estimation [1], are implemented in most of the proposed solutions. The motion estimation is well known to be the most computation-intensive stage of video coding process. Any improvement on this stage can therefore impact on the whole video codec's performances. From another point of view, the motion estimation configuration can be adjusted to fit the application's constraints (image spatial resolution, frame-rate, bit-rate,

J. Blanc-Talon et al. (Eds.): ACIVS 2012, LNCS 7517, pp. 96–107, 2012.
© Springer-Verlag Berlin Heidelberg 2012

PSNR). For instance the motion estimation stage, described in the recent standards such as H.264 video or VP8, is highly efficient as well as highly sophisticated and complex. Meanwhile, different configurations can be defined to match with the required coding performances.

According to our analysis, the key features of motion estimation to be adjusted in current standard as H.264 are:

- The format of input data (i.e. the size of the blocks to match),
- The integer search method,
- The optional fractional search.

Software solutions can easily support any configuration nevertheless they may struggle to match the application's requirements. Indeed, for high-quality applications, the computational cost often exceeds the available resources of a standard computer. Meanwhile, to define an efficient hardware accelerator which supports such flexibility as well as high coding performances, it is still nowadays a challenge. Therefore, we propose in this paper, a motion estimation accelerator, fully compatible with H.264, which supports different configurations especially modifications on the three key features previously identified. The paper is structured as follow. In the section 2, we review the basic principles of the motion estimation. We recall and compare several integer search algorithms. Finally the impact fractional search on the coding performances (PSNR, processing-time) is presented. In section 3, we propose analysis on the integer motion estimation (IME). The common parts of these algorithms are then bringing out in order to prove that a generic structure can be proposed. The motion estimator's architecture has been designed and optimized to propose an efficient FPGA implementation in respect with the complexity and the regularity of the integer search and the fractional search. The hardware implementation results and discussion are finally presented in section 4.

2   Motion Estimation Technique

The Motion Estimation (ME) is an effective stage to detect temporal redundancies between successive frames in a video sequence. Therefore, it has become a crucial part of many video compression standards. The motion estimation aims to predict, as accurately as possible, the next frame from the current frame. The frame is split into fixed size macroblocks, currently 16x16 pixels. The prediction is processed for each macroblock of the current frame. As the motion estimation algorithm is not fixed by the video standard, many solutions have been proposed. The most popular is the Block-Matching Algorithm (BMA). In this method, the basic idea is to localize a reference block within the search area in the previous frame. A matching criterion is used to estimate similarities between any two given blocks. The applied BMA is performed using the Sum of Absolute Differences (SAD) matching criterion. This approach is known as the integer motion search as only integer displacements of the reference macroblock into the search window are performed. Some sub-pixel refinement can be processed. The Fractional Motion Estimation (FME) [2] is usually done for HalfPel and QuarterPel accuracy. The Variable Block Size Motion Estimation (VBSME) [3] is another major refinement which is included in recent standards. Indeed this approach is the use of BMA with the ability for the encoder to dynamically select the size of the blocks. The macro-block is split into smaller blocks and the estimation is performed on each sub-blocks. The VBS motion estimation can be processed at both integer and fractional levels. The motion estimation performances are therefore highly correlated not only to the selected integer search algorithm but also to the optional refinement stages VBSME and FME. Therefore the following sections discuss the impact of the integer search algorithms as well as the VBSME and the FME algorithms on the quality of image and other encoder's requirements.

2.1   Impact of the Search Strategy - Related Work

Many ME algorithms have been described in the literature. The most accurate strategy is the Full Search (FS) algorithm, which by exhaustively comparing all positions in the search window, gives the most accurate motion vector which causes SAD to be minimum. On the other hand, fast but sub-optimal algorithms compute the best matching candidate by guiding the search procedure using pre-defined search patterns. For instance, in Three-Step-Search (TSS) [4], the New Three Step Search (NTSS) [5] , Four Step Search (4SS) [6], the Hexagon-Based Search (HEXBS) [7] , the Diamond Search (DS) [8], the Cross-Diamond Search (CDS) [9], and the Block-Based Gradient Descent Search (BBGDS) [10] algorithms, square-shaped or hexagon-shaped or diamond-shaped search patterns with different sizes are employed. These algorithms performed well in relatively small search range and low-resolution video sequences. Improving the quality of image is achieved by finding the best possible motion vectors, which means motion vectors that will generate the smallest residual difference during the motion compensation. Reducing the total search time is achieved by selecting the proper fast motion estimation, which consists to reduce the Number of Search Points per block (NSP) to be checked. Nevertheless, the image quality can decrease compared with a FS approach. Hence, the mentioned fast search algorithms are also evaluated regarding the output PSNR. This fact is illustrated in [11]. It is noted that, for low and medium motion activity video sequences (Carphone, Foreman, and Mobile) the degradation of PSNR is slightly or negligible but the speedup is much improved. The situation is changed for the high-motion activity video sequences (Tennis Table, Football): the PSNR significantly decreases and the degradation of image quality is then visible. Otherwise, DS and BBGDS algorithms provide better PNSR performances than other fast algorithms while maintaining nearly the same search speed for the sequences Table tennis and Football. An enhanced efficient DS algorithm, named Modified Diamond Search (MDS), is proposed and compared with others fast approach and FS method in [12]. The proposed method as well as the others fast search methods DS, 4SS and N3SS achieves significant speed-up compared to FS. Hence the processing time respectively decreases of 99%, 94%, 73% and 65% for high motion video sequence (Football). A negligible degradation in both PSNR and bit-rate is observed. The low complexity of DS approach family induces that this kind of algorithms can be considered for hardware implementation. The FS algorithm is suitable to high-speed motion and/or high texture variation.

2.2 Impact of VBSME and FME - Related Work

H.264 introduces two new features to ME, the VBSME and the Sub-pixel accuracy motion estimation. The VBSME is carried out in two phases: integer motion estimation (IME) and fractional motion estimation (FME). In H.264, VP8 and others video codec, a 16x16 sized macroblock can be further partitioned into 16x8, 8x16, 8x8, 8x4, 4x8 and 4x4 sub-blocks. When all sub-blocks are in uniform motion, all sub-block motion vectors will be the same as the motion vector for the entire macroblock. However, if fine grain motion exists and sub-blocks are moving in different directions, sub-block motion vectors can differ significantly from each other and from the motion vector of the macroblock. Consequently the ME unit must be able to generate a separate motion vector for each of the sub-blocks. The advantages of a large block size are (i) simplicity and (ii) the limited number of vectors that must be encoded and transmitted. However, in areas of complex spatial structures and motion, better performance can be achieved with the smaller block size.

Usually, the motion of blocks does not match exactly in the integer positions. So, to find best matches, fractional position accuracy is used. If the best motion vector is a fractional position, an interpolation is needed to predict the current block. According to [2] and [13], fractional motion estimation (FME) upgrades rate distortion efficiency by + 4dB in peak signal-to-noise ratio (PSNR) and requests 45% of the inter-prediction processing time. In [14], four sequences with different characteristics are used for the experiment. Foreman stands for medium motions, Soccer sequence for high motions, Mobile and Optis have complex textures. Clearly using half or quarter-pel increases image quality. The accuracy of motion compensation is in quarter-pel resolution for H.264/AVC, which can provide significantly better compression performance, especially for images with complex texture. As shown in the state of the art analysis, the three key features which are the data block sizes (defined with VBSME), the IME strategy and the optional FME have high impact on the video codec's performances. Therefore, an efficient hardware implementation of a configurable motion estimator which supports modification on these three features can be considered as a significant contribution.

3   A Flexible Motion Estimation Architecture

3.1   Overview of the Proposed Architecture

Using a full search strategy, the motion detection process is regular. All possible positions of the pattern in the search window are scanned contrary to fast search approach. All the search strategies are intended to converge to the right motion vector with a regular process and can eventually be initialized by previous information (such as the vectors previously computed). Therefore using fast or reduced search strategies enables the number of matching to be reduced, decreasing the processing time. As mentioned previously, even if the number of matching is reduced, it is possible to achieve optimal coding results using appropriate (for the video application) reduced search algorithms. Our analysis of the IME approaches, lead us to propose a structure based on the highest possible common parts between fast motion algorithm and FS. Indeed, for all algorithms, a list of matching (positions) is processed during each Integer Motion Search Phase (IMEP). As shown in Fig.1, after the reception of the list and the number of matching, each matching is processed until all positions have been considered. Finally, the best vector and, optionally, all the resulting vectors are available. Depending on the search algorithms, all the vectors may be required and transmitted to the unit in charge of the address generation. All of the resulting vectors may be used during the generation of the next eventual list of matching. The iterative phase is depicted in figure 1.

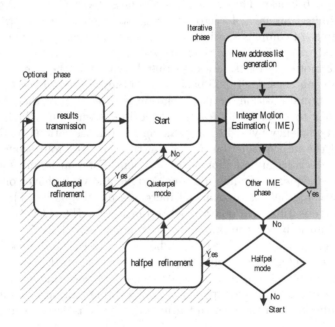

Fig. 1. Proposed algorithm

For all configurations, the address generation unit is described using a scheduler. This description could be very simple for a Full Search algorithm or more complex and irregular for more complex algorithms. The Diamond search has several phases of address generation. The full-search strategy is obviously supported in this scheme. Note that in this case, all possible addresses of the reference block in the search window are then transmitted to the operating part and therefore a unique phase is required to determine the best motion vector. In our implementation, a state machine has been used nevertheless a micro-processor (embedded in the FPGA) which represents a flexible solution as described in [15]. However, even if the state machine design may be more time consuming, higher system frequency can be achieved compared with the micro-processor based solution. Finally, depending of the user configuration, the optional fractional motion estimation (FME) can be performed with HalfPel or QuaterPel accuracy. The halfpel stage is processed systematically before the quaterpel refinement to reduce the search area and therefore memory requirement. Indeed, the subpel refinement and especially the interpolation phase are costly in terms of hardware resources [2,13,11]. Note that using a fast search for IME, induces that the FME represents the slower stage of the motion estimation. Therefore, an optimized and efficient architecture should be proposed for the FME unit. The architecture proposed is depicted Fig.2. The addresses of all matching are provided to the cache memory unit and the column extraction unit by the external address generation unit. A trade-off between the efficiency and the required resources, one matching is processed in several stages. A full parallel approach would request a large cache memory, to avoid important bottlenecks on the external memory, and extremely large processing resources for real-time implementation. We propose a trade-off between the complexity and performances with a matching done column by column.

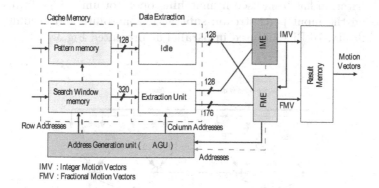

Fig. 2. The top-level view of the proposed motion estimation architecture

So as to guarantee the random access in any position of a search window the search window pixels have to be accessible to the matching engine and need to be stored in the FPGA to reduce the number of access to the external memory, so as not to exceed the available bandwidth. The cache memory permits access of two columns, one extracted from the block and the corresponding one in the search window. The architecture allows to access in one clock cycle any search window column and consecutive pattern matching evaluations do not need to be adjacent in terms of memory locations. The cache memory is obtained with dual-port memory blocks available into FPGA component. Our architecture enables an efficient random access, without any latency to be obtained. Moreover, any search-window width can be set according to the available processing. The Address Generator Unit (AGU) is charge of address generation for all configurations. The AGU allows selecting one column into the search window and one into the current block. The extraction unit enables the right amount of pixel to be selected into the search window column according to the selected matching and the motion estimation to be processed. Hence, for IME, 16 pixels (128 bits) are systematically extracted as the 16x16 macro-block and all possible sub-blocks can be processed in parallel. For FME, an interpolation phase is required. As 6 tap filters are used to interpolate the search window pixel, therefore the region to be extracted in slightly larger than the block width. The pixel number extracted also depends on the selected mode (16x16, 16x8, 8x8, 8x4, 4x4, etc.). For block's width equal to 16 pixels, 8 pixels and 4 pixels respectively, 22, 14 and 10 pixels should be extracted.

3.2   Proposed Integer Motion Estimator

The IME phase is highly regular. In our approach, each matching is operated column by column. A Processing Element (PE) is operating the comparison between a pattern pixel and the corresponding search window. The SAD matching evaluation criterion has been used in matching operator unit. It performs three operations on the input pixel stream: subtraction, absolute and accumulation. Due to regularity, 16 PEs are used in parallel as presented Fig.3.

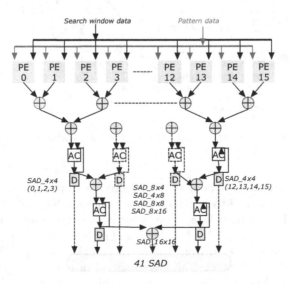

Fig. 3. IME processing Unit with VBSME supported

Moreover the architecture should support VBSME. Once again this estimation is regular as the different sub-blocks can be processed simultaneously with the 16x16 pixel macro-block. Accumulators (AC) are included inside the pipelined structure to enable the comparison to be done for all 40 sub-blocks. Such kind of efficient approach has been presented in [16]. Our version is adapted to the "two columns" process and represents therefore a low-cost approach in terms of hardware resources.

3.3 Proposed Fractional Motion Estimator

After the best integer motion vector is estimated, the fractional motion estimation accuracy can start. The HalfPel refinements of the surrounding eight half-search positions are computed, and then the QuarterPel refinements of eight quarter search positions surrounding the best half-search position are computed. In the MPEG-4/AVC H.264 standard, the QuarterPel accuracy luminance picture is interpolated with two successive filtering operations. The HalfPel refinement is more complex than the QuarterPel one and requires a 6-tap separable FIR filters with coefficients [1,-5, 20, 20, -5, 1] instead of bilinear filters. As shown in Fig.4a), each half pixel value is calculated from 6 adjacent pixels horizontally or vertically. The horizontal value h3,3 is computed from the six adjacent integer pixel samples located at horizontal direction according to the following equation:

$$h3, 3 = i1, 3 - 5i2, 3 + 20i3, 3 + 20i4, 3 - 5i5, 3 + i6, 3. \tag{1}$$

In a similar way, the vertical half-pel value v3,3 is performed using the six adjacent pixel values located in the vertical direction as:

$$v3, 3 = i3, 1 - 5i3, 2 + 20i3, 3 + 20i3, 4 - 5i3, 5 + i3, 6. \tag{2}$$

The diagonal half-pel value d3,3 is obtained from the six adjacent horizontal values hi or alternatively, verticals values vi,j according to:

$$d3, 3 = v1, 3 - 5v2, 3 + 20v3, 3 + 20v4, 3 - 5v5, 3 + v6, 3. \tag{3}$$

$$d3, 3 = h3, 1 - 5h3, 2 + 20h3, 3 + 20h3, 4 - 5h3, 5 + h3, 6. \tag{4}$$

Once half-pixel samples are available, the pixel values at QuarterPel locations are processed with basic bilinear weighting of the values at half-pel and integer-pel positions. Nevertheless, the quaterpel processing is less regular. As shown in Fig.4b), the orientation of the pixels is considered, and 12 different kinds of processing , which generate the QuaterPel positions, can be observed. Therefore we propose a novel architecture using four different memory banks for HalfPel processing and 12 banks for the QuaterPel refinement. For instance for HalfPel refinement, the original pixel named I and three kinds of interpolated pixel are stored respectively in I, H, V and D memory banks. This approach has been proposed by Ruiz [17] only for HalfPel refinement, we propose in this paper to apply it also to QuaterPel refinement. This architecture is highly efficient in term of

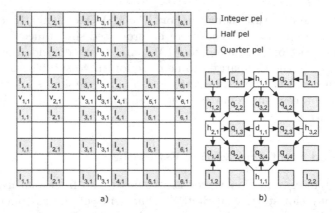

Fig. 4. a) Half-pel pixel values - (b) Quaterpel pixel values

data broadcasting therefore the processing decrease. Nevertheless the number of small cache memory is increased. Each bank is implemented with dual port memory embedded into the FPGA component. Only two memory blocks are required to store the reduced number of each class of interpolated pixels. Therefore, the used hardware resources are still low and suitable for FPGA implementation. For instance, the 32 memory blocks represent less than 8% of Virtex6 6vlx240 FPGA. The Fig.5 depicts the overall block diagram of the proposed architecture of FME. It consists of two processors used in pipeline: HalfPel and QuarterPel processors which are interpolation based units, processors units, memory unit and comparator unit. The architecture of processor and comparator unit is the same for both HalfPel and QuarterPel. In each refinement stage, eight candidates around the refinement center are evaluated simultaneously.

Our halfpel interpolation unit is based on the well-known Yang's solution [13] which processes a row 16-pixel interpolation unit. Indeed, a problem related to

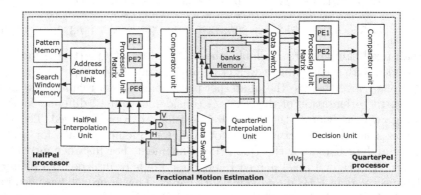

Fig. 5. Overall FME architecture

Chen's 4-pixel interpolation unit [2] is the redundant interpolating operations which appear in the overlapping area of the adjacent interpolation window. To overcome this problem, a new architecture based on 16-pixel interpolation unit with nine or eighteen 16x16 processing units is proposed by Yang's which removes all the redundancies. Our design, as Yang's, adopts a short-latency 16-pixel wide interpolator to increase throughput and eliminate redundant interpolation. Moreover, all sizes of blocks are processed by 16x16 processing units. Therefore, the hardware utilization is low when processing small size blocks (4x4 and 4x8). When 4x8 and 4x4 blocks are processed in parallel, a large memory bandwidth of search window memory is then required for reading the reference pixels in parallel. Yang's architecture enables higher processing performance to be obtained than with Chen's implementation. We used Half-pel interpolation unit proposed by Yang's. We proposed a pipeline architecture which enables Half-pel and Quarter-pel to be processed simultaneously. Consequently, the number of cycles is reduced. The processors request exactly the same scheduling in Half-pel and Quater-pel modes, therefore the performances are identical for both modes.

4   Implementation Results and Discussion

The proposed architecture can be considered as a low cost implementation of a motion estimator. The hardware ressources required for our implementation are presented in Table 1. The implementation have been done on a Virtex6 FPGA target (6vlx240tff784-3).

Table 1. Motion estimator's implementation results

Motion Estimator (Device :6vlx240tff784-3)				
Logic Utilization	Used (IME / FME)		Available	Utilization (IME / FME)	
Number of Slice Registers	1168	11944	301440	>1%	3%
Number of Slice LUTs	1281	17426	150720	>1%	11 %
Number of Block RAM/FIFO	1	32	416	>1%	8 %
Maximum Frequency	Frequency IME: 438 MHz -Frequency FME: 253 MHz				

The integer and fractional estimators are regrouped in this table. Note that only two search strategies are currently implemented: FS and DS. This flexible low-cost implementation for IME provides efficient results with a global frequency of 438 MHz. The architecture enables a matching to be processed in 16 cycles (36,5 ns) and without latency is required between two matching. With a 41x25 search window (1025 matching), 1080 HD (1920x1088) video streams can be processed at 3 fps in a FS mode. Meanwhile, using a DS method and considering a realistic average range of 15-30 matching per macro-blocks, a 1080 HD video stream can be processed between 223 and 111 fps. The same performances are obtained for HalfPel and QuaterPel mode. The Table 2, presents the number of cycle for each block size. The last row of Table 2 presents the full processing time of the 41 possible blocks in VSBME. As expected and detailed in section 3.3, the very low-cost architecture proposed by Chen is less performing than Yang's. Our architecture proposes very competitive performances and similar results to Yang's one. Comparing the two architectures, our solution reduces by two the memory size and decreases by 8 (instead of 18) the processor number for each sub-pel refinement. Our solution cannot process in parallel two 4x8 or 4x4 sub-blocks, nevertheless the pipeline structure enables Half and Quarter-Pel refinement to be processed simultaneously. Therefore, this architecture can save approximately 66% and 30% in processing time, compared with Chen's and Yang's respectively. The global time is reduced to 553 cycles .Yang's architecture has been implemented with a 0.18 μm technology. It can process 1080 HD video streams at frame rate of 30fps when running at 200 MHz. Our architecture, using the 40 nm technology available on Virtex 6 FPGA, can process this video stream at frame rate of 29 fps at 250 MHz (around 232K Macroblocks/s).

Table 2. Number of cycles required depending on sub-block size

sub-block types	block number	Chen's		Yang's		Our's	
		cycles/ block	total cycles	cycles/ block	total cycles	cycles/ block	total cycles
16x16	1	22x4	88	22	22	22	22
16x8	2	14x4	112	14	28	14	28
8x16	2	22x2	88	22	44	22	44
8x8	4	14x2	112	14	56	14	56
8x4	8	10x2	160	10	80	10	80
4x8	8	14x1	112	14÷2	56	14	112
4x4	16	10x1	160	10÷2	80	10	160
Latency		NA		29		29	
Total	41	1644		790		553	

5 Conclusion

We proposed in this paper, a flexible motion estimator which enables the integer search strategy to be adjusted and the optional VBSME and sub-pel refinements to be processed. This low-cost implementation, based on Virtex FPGA enables to reach high-speed performances. Hence for IME, 1080 HD video streams can be processed up to 200 fps. Moreover for FME mode, the same video streams can be processed at frame rate of 29 fps at 250 MHz (around 232K Macroblocks/s). Current developments aim to improve these performances, specially the sub-pel interpolation units. This solution can therefore represent an efficient adaptative solution more many video coding applications. Finally, the use of FPGA technology enables the dynamic reconfiguration to be considered. Therefore the ME accelerators could be even more scalable and can be dynamically adjusted according to the events happening in the video scene or some environment modifications (as a network bandwidth reduction).

References

1. Wiegand, T., Sullivan, G.J., Bjontegaard, G., Luthra, A.: Overview of the H.264/AVC video coding standard. IEEE Trans. on Circuits and Systems for Video Technology 13(7), 560–576 (2003)
2. Chen, T.C., Huang, Y.W., Chen, L.G.: Fully utilized and reusable architecture for fractional motion estimation of H.264/AVC. In: IEEE ICASSP, pp. 9–12 (2004)
3. Swee, Y.Y., McCanny, J.V.: A VLSI Architecture for Variable Block Size Video Motion Estimation. IEEE Trans. on Circuits and Systems for Video Technology 51(7), 384–389 (2004)
4. Koga, T., Ilinuma, K., Hirano, A., Iijima, Y., Ishiguro, T.: Motion Compensated Interframe Coding For Video Conferencing. In: Proc. Nat. Telecommun Conf., New Orleans, pp. G5.3.1–G5.3.5 (1981)
5. Li, R., Zeng, B., Liou, M.L.: A New Three-Step Search Algorithm for Fast Motion Estimation. IEEE Trans. on Circuits and Systems for Video Technology 4(4), 438–442 (1994)
6. Po, L.M., Ma, W.C.: A Novel Four-Step Search Algorithm for Fast Block Motion Estimation. IEEE Trans. on Circuits and Systems for Video Technology 6(3), 313–317 (1996)
7. Zhu, C., Lin, X., Chau, L.P.: Hexagon-Based Search Pattern for Fast Block Motion Estimation. IEEE Trans. on Circuits and Systems for Video Technology 12(5), 349–355 (2002)
8. Zhu, S., Ma, K.K.: A New Diamond Search Algorithm For Fast Block Matching Motion Estimation. IEEE Trans. on Image Process 9(2), 287–290 (2000)
9. Cheung, C., Po, L.M.: A Novel Cross-Diamond Search Algorithm for Fast Block Motion Estimation. IEEE Transactions on Circuits and Systems for Video Technology 12(12), 1168–1177 (2002)
10. Liu, L., Feig, E.: A Block-Based Gradient Descent Search Algorithm for Block Motion Estimation in Video Coding. IEEE Transactions on Circuits and Systems for Video Technology 6(4), 419–422 (1996)
11. Lee, Y.G., Ra, J.B.: Fast Motion Estimation Robust to Random Motions Based on a Distance Prediction. IEEE Transactions on Circuits and Systems for Video Technology 16(7), 869–875 (2006)
12. Ismail, Y., McNeely, J., Shaaban, M., Bayoumi, M.: Enhanced efficient diamond search algorithm for fast block motion estimation. In: IEEE ISCAS, Taipei, pp. 3198–3201 (2009)
13. Yang, C., Goto, S., Ikenaga, T.: High Performance VLSI Architecture of Fractional Motion Estimation in H.264 for HDTV. In: Proceedings of the IEEE ISCAS, Greece, pp. 2605–2608 (2006)
14. Chen, Y.H., Chen, T.C., Chien, S.Y., Huang, Y.W., Chen, L.G.: VLSI Architecture Design of Fractional Motion Estimation for H.264/AVC. Journal of Signal Processing Systems 53(3), 335–347 (2008)
15. Dubois, J., Mattavelli, M., Pierrefeu, L., Miteran, J.: Configurable Motion-Estimation Hardware Accelerator Module For The Mpeg-4 Reference hardware Description Platform. In: Proceedings of IEEE International Conference on Image Processing (ICIP 2005), Genova (2005)
16. Choudhury, A.R., Badawy, W.: A Quarter Pel Full Search Block Motion Estimation Architecture for H.264/AVC. In: IEEE ICME 2005 (2005)
17. Ruiz, G.A., Michell, J.A.: An Efficient VLSI Architecture of Fractional Motion Estimation in H.264 for HDTV. Journal of Signal Processing Systems 62(3), 443–457 (2010)

Quality Assurance for Document Image Collections in Digital Preservation*

Reinhold Huber-Mörk[1] and Alexander Schindler[1,2]

[1] Research Area Intelligent Vision Systems
Department Safety & Security Austrian Institute of Technology
reinhold.huber-moerk@ait.ac.at
[2] Department of Software Technology and Interactive Systems
Vienna University of Technology
schindler@ifs.tuwien.ac.at

Abstract. Maintenance of digital image libraries requires to frequently asses the quality of the images to engage preservation measures if necessary. We present an approach to image based quality assurance for digital image collections based on local descriptor matching. We use spatially distinctive local keypoints of contrast enhanced images and robust symmetric descriptor matching to calculate affine transformations for image registration. Structural similarity of aligned images is used for quality assessment. The results show, that our approach can efficiently asses the quality of digitized documents including images of blank paper.

1 Introduction

Large collections of image data include scanned or rendered document image data from historical archives or large-scale document preservation activities such as digital museum collections or the Google books initiative**. It is commonly observed that different versions of image collections with identical or near-identical content exist in such collections resulting from independent acquisitions or repeated downloads of Google books image collections with different post-processing, e.g. rectification, denoising, compression, rescaling, cropping etc.

We describe an approach for analysis and comparison of collections of digital document image data. Maintainers of image archives, such as libraries, as well as researchers in the field of digital preservation are typically confronted with inconsistencies in their collections. Due to independent acquisitions, digital file format migration or modification of image properties the task of content verification arises. Additionally, the long-term storage of data using deprecated hardware and data formats results in issues such as bit rot or limited or difficult access to the data.

From the point of document image content comparison a robust approach is required. Recently, stable image feature descriptors invariant to geometric and radiometric distortions became state of the art for various applications in computer vision. Although the

---

* This work was partially supported by the SCAPE Project. The SCAPE project is co-funded by the European Union under FP7 ICT-2009.4.1 (Grant Agreement number 270137).
** http://www.google.com/googlebooks/library.html

obtained quality and plausibility for human operators meets high expectations in various domains, image feature extraction and comparison based on advanced image analysis methods requires significant computational resources. Furthermore, image data in large collections of scanned documents is characterized by large volumes of data, therefore a compact representation of content information is aspired. Content-based representation and comparison of images requires image rectification and the use of expressive measures of structural similarity. Stable image correspondence is based on matching of local descriptors. From the point of storage consumption, the use of a condensed representation based on local descriptors enables a reduction of data volumes.

This paper is organized as follows. Section 2 provides an overview of document image comparison as well as the application of local features. In Sect. 3 we present our approach to document comparison. Section 4 shortly discusses image quality assessment as used in our work. Results are presented and Sect. 6 and Sect. 7 summarizes our work.

2 Related Work

Related work in the field of analysis of document image collections include tasks such as indexing, revision detection, duplicate and near-duplicate detection. Several authors mention that the use of optical character recognition, which is an obvious approach to extract relevant information from text documents, is quite limited with respect to accuracy and flexibility [2,8,18]. An approach combining page segmentation and Optical Character Recognition (OCR) for newspaper digitization, indexing and search was described recently [6], where a moderate overall OCR accuracy on the order of magnitude of 80 percent was reported. Page Segmentation is prerequisite for the document image retrieval approach suggested in [2] where document matching is based on the earth mover's distance measured between layout blocks. The PaperDiff system [18] finds text differences between document images by processing small image blocks which typically correspond to words. PaperDiff can deal with reformatting of documents but is restricted as it is not able to deal with documents with mixed content such as pages containing images, blank pages or graphical art. A method for duplicate detection in scanned documents based on shape descriptions for single characters also showed advantages with respect to robustness and speed when compared to OCR [8]. The most similar work, compared to our paper, is a revision detection approach for printed historical documents [3]. Contrarily to our approach, connected components are extracted from document images and Recognition using Adaptive Subdivisions of Transformation (RAST) [4] was applied to overlay images and highlight differences without providing details on the comparison strategy.

Apart from document image processing, several approaches to duplicate and near-duplicate image detection and image and sub-image retrieval were published in the related field of video and web image processing. Typically, approaches in this area make use of local image descriptors to match or index visual information. Near-duplicate detection of keyframes using one-to-one matching of local descriptors was described for video data [27]. A bag of visual keywords [7], derived from local descriptors, was described as an efficient approach to near-duplicate video keyframe retrieval[24]. For detection of near-duplicates in images and sub-images local descriptors were also employed [13].

In general, the application of local features ranges from texture recognition, robot localization to wide baseline stereo matching and object class recognition. In spite of their success and generality, these approaches are limited by the distinctiveness of the features and the difficulty of appropriate matching [9]. A survey and evaluation on the performance of local features in the context of their repeatability in the presence of rotation, scale, illumination, blur and viewpoint changes is provided in [15]. One of the most prominent local keypoint detection and description method, the Scale Invariant Feature Transform (SIFT) [14] descriptor is based on gradient distribution in salient regions. Faster keypoint detection and description method include Features from Accelerated Segment Test (FAST) [19], Speeded up Robust features (SURF) [1], and the recently developed Oriented Brief (ORB) based on Binary Robust Independent Elementary Features (BRIEF) [20].

3 Document Image Processing

Pixel-wise comparison of images is only possible as long as no geometric modifications were applied. Additionally, in cases of filtering, color or tone modifications the information at the pixel level might differ significantly, although the image content is well preserved. Therefore, we suggest to use interest point detection and derivation of local feature descriptors, which have proven highly invariant to geometrical and radiometrical distortions [14,23] and were successful applied to a variety of problems in computer vision.

To detect and describe interest regions in document images we used the SIFT keypoint extraction and description approach. SIFT selects an orientation by determining the peak of the histogram of local image gradient orientations at each keypoint location. Subpixel image location, scale and orientation are associated with each SIFT descriptor (4×4 location grid $\times 8$ gradient orientations). The keypoint locations itself are identified from a scale space image representation. All keypoints with low contrast or keypoints that are localized at edges are eliminated using a Laplacian function.

3.1 Contrast Enhancement

When investigating collections of historical artifacts it turned out that images of blank pages, e.g. images with no text or graphics are also important for historians. Therefore, images of blank pages need to be considered as well as images containing graphical art. In order to treat images with high textual or graphical information content as well as images showing blank pages we adopted a procedure for local contrast enhancement called Contrast-Limited Adaptive Histogram Equalization (CLAHE) [17]. Fig. 1 shows image pairs before and after local contrast enhancement. The number of tiles in CLAHE was chosen as 900. Clearly, the paper structure on blank images is enhanced while in region of rich information only small modifications are observed. Figure 1 shows two images before, one blank image and one image containing text, and after application of CLAHE. Especially in blank page the paper structure is enhanced, while in the text image lesser tone modifications are observed.

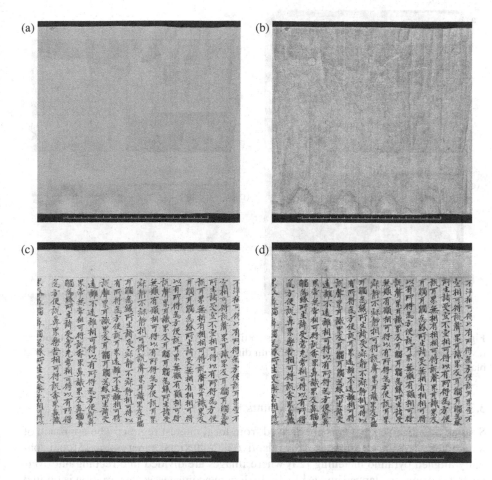

Fig. 1. Contrast enhancement of images: (a) blank image original, (b) blank image after CLAHE, (c) text image original, (d) text image after CLAHE

3.2   Robust Symmetric Matching

As suggested by Lowe [14], local descriptors are matched by identifying the first two nearest neighbors in Euclidean space. A descriptor is accepted only if the distance ratio to the second nearest neighbor is below a given threshold. An essential characteristic of this approach is that a descriptor can have several matches when different descriptors from the second image matched against the same descriptor from the first image. The overcome this problem, one can either ignore all ambiguous matches or keep the one with lowest distance. We also adopted this idea by enforcing one-to-one matching of descriptors. Figure 2 shows different typical cases of image pairs, e.g. text, rotated, noisy and blank images, with obtained correspondences of keypoints between the images overlaid as lines.

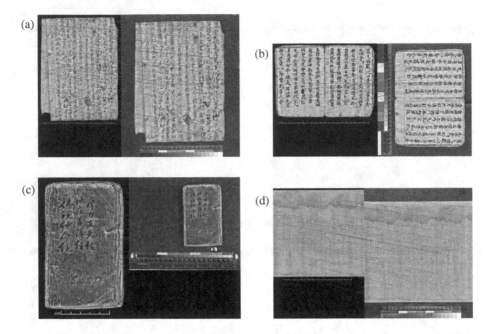

Fig. 2. Examples for matching of spatially distinctive local keypoints: (a) image pair containing text, (b) rotated image pair, (c) image pair with dirt and large scale and content difference, (d) blank image pair

3.3 Spatially Distinctive Local Keypoints

Spatially distinctive keypoints are derived from local interest regions. The approach of local interest regions was inspired by adaptive non-maximal suppression [5] and spatially aligned pyramid matching [25] where images are divided into rectangular overlapped and non-overlapped image blocks. In document images, scale variation is limited and it is not necessary to employ pyramid or scale-space schemes for the selection of interest regions. On the other hand, for the task of keypoint extraction a scale-space representation, as inherent to SIFT descriptors, is very valuable.

Centers of local interest regions are simply formed by a regular grid overlaid on the image with grid positions given by

$$(u_{i,j}, v_{i,j}), \quad 1 \le i \le m, 1 \le j \le n, \tag{1}$$

where m an n denote the number of grid points in horizontal and vertical dimensions. The overall number of interest regions is $k = m \cdot n$. The region of influence for each center local region of interest is described by a region of circular shape. The distance between given grid centers is given by $d = M/m = N/n$ and the influence area for each interest region becomes $r = \sqrt{2} \cdot d$. Image dimensions are $M \times N$, where M is the horizontal and N is the vertical resolution. As grid spacing d is commonly not an integer valued number, it has to be ensured to cover the full image domain. Figure 3 (a) shows all keypoints found in an image and Fig. 3 (b) the overlaid, partially overlapping interest regions.

Fig. 3. Selection of spatially distinctive local keypoints: (a) image with all keypoints, (b) local interest regions, (c) spatially distinctive keypoints

For each interest region centered at $(u_{i,j}, v_{i,j})$ we search for the keypoint with highest saliency in the circular neighborhood given by the search radius R. We employed the Harris corner detection approach [12] as simple measure of saliency in order to select keypoints inside interest regions. The 2D structure tensor A for pixel position (x, y) is given by

$$A(x,y) = \begin{bmatrix} I_x^2(x,y) & I_x(x,y)I_y(x,y) \\ I_x(x,y)I_y(x,y) & I_y^2(x,y) \end{bmatrix}, \tag{2}$$

where I_x and I_y are the partial derivatives of the image with respect to directions given by x and y. The eigenvalues of A provide information about the local image structure. Corner points are regarded as stable points for which both eigenvalues are large.

In order to avoid eigenvalue decomposition, the following measure of corner strength was suggested by Harris and Stephens [12]

$$R(x, y) = \det A(x, y) - k \operatorname{trace}^2 A(x, y), \tag{3}$$

where k is s constant, commonly chosen as $k = 0.04$. The set of spatially distinctive keypoints is derived from the strongest corner points from each local interest regions. Figure 3 (c) shows the selected keypoints with respect ro the interest regions.

3.4 Descriptor Matching

The matching of spatially distinctive keypoint descriptors is based on the established robust matching method called Random Sample Consensus (RANSAC) [10], where corresponding points are randomly drawn from the set of spatially distinctive keypoints and the concensus test is constrained on an affine fundamental matrix describing the transformation between image pairs. The obtained affine transformation parameters are used to overlay corresponding images by warping one image to the other.

4 Quality Assessment

Image quality assessment can roughly be dived into reference-based (non-blind) [21,23,26] and no reference-based (blind) [11,16] evaluation. Intermediate definitions exist, but they are of minor interest in the context of our paper. Blind image quality assessment considers single images and tries to quantify their information content either based on low level image features or using elaborate machine learning techniques. The

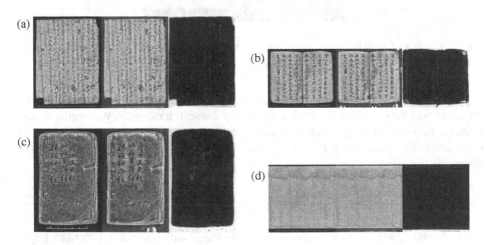

Fig. 4. Examples of image pairs after rectification and structural similarity at each pixel (black ... high structural similarity, white ... low structural similarity): (a) image pair containing text, (b) rotated image pair, (c) image pair with dirt and large scale and content difference, (d) blank image pair..

setup we are dealing with is to find out severe differences in content, which is addressed by non-blind image quality assessment. In such a setup, differences of visual appearance are quantified and the decision which image in a pair of images is visually more appealing is left to the human observer.

It is well known that image difference measures such as taking the mean squared pixel difference does not correspond to the human perception of image difference [22]. Therefore, we employed the structural similarity image (SSIM) non-blind quality assessment [23]. SSIM basically considers luminance, contrast and structure terms to provide a measure of similarity for overlaid images. The SSIM $s(I_1(x,y), I_2(x,y))$ between images I_1 and I_2 is calculated at each pixel location (x, y). In order to correct for small errors in image rectification we calculated the local minima $s_\mathcal{N}(x, y)$ of the SSIM between $I_1(x, y)$ and $I_2(\mathcal{N}(x, y))$, i.e. between the image I_1 and shifted versions of I_2. For the neighborhood $\mathcal{N}$ we used shifts of one pixel into all eight adjacent pixel directions

$$s_\mathcal{N}(x, y) = \min\{s(I_1(x, y), I_2(\mathcal{N}(x, y)))\}. \tag{4}$$

Figure 4 shows images pairs after registration and a derived image showing the SSIM at each pixel position. The examples are the same as shown in Fig. 2.

5 Evaluation

The goal of quality assurance in digital preservation is to reduce the manual interaction and assessment. Therefore, automatic assessment using the suggested procedure is used and a small subset of image pairs with low average SSIM are interactively checked. The best average SSIM and also the smallest set size for human assessment is obtained by using all keypoints in matching. The average number of keypoints per image was 32352 for the considered data set. Sampling of robust keypoints from all available keypoints offers the lowest possibility to obtain a small average SSIM due to mismatching followed by misregistration. On the other hand, matching of keypoints is the most time consuming part of the suggested algorithm and selection of a locally distinctive set of keypoints reduces the matching effort at the cost of increasing the subset of image pairs for manual assessment.

5.1 Dataset

The dataset is a sample of 1560 image-pairs of the International Dunhuang Project (IDP). The project focuses on preserving and cataloging forty thousand manuscripts, paintings and printed documents dating back to the end of the first millennium. The documents were discovered in 1900 in a sealed Buddhist cave near Dunhuang in western China and are now mostly dispersed to institutions worldwide. IDP started digitizing the manuscripts in 1998 to reassemble virtually the collections and make them accessible to all people.

The sample contains images of handwritten Chinese text and drawings as well as empty pages. Each image pair represents the same content, but has been digitized with different equipment and differs in size, color and alignment of the artifact.

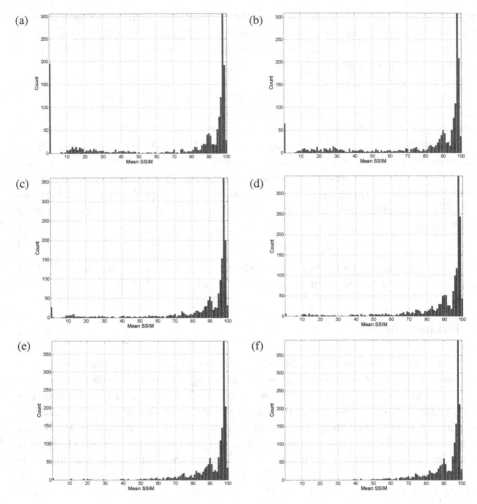

Fig. 5. Histograms of mean SSIM for different number of locally distinctive keypoints: (a) 64, (b) 256, (c) 512, (d) 1024, (e) 2048 and (f) all keypoints

6   Results

We will study the number of images with low values of mean SSIM depending on the number of keypoints. The distribution of the mean SSIM for different settings of the number of interest regions is shown in Fig. 5. Note that the number of keypoints is equal to the number of interest region provided that at least one keypoint is identified in each interest region.

For small numbers of 64 to 512 keypoints, see Figs. 5 (a)-(c), some entries for low mean SSIM are observed in the corresponding histograms. For larger numbers numbers of 1024 or 2048 keypoints, see Figs. 5 (d) and (e), the distributions already become close to the one observed for all keypoints used in Fig. 4 (f).

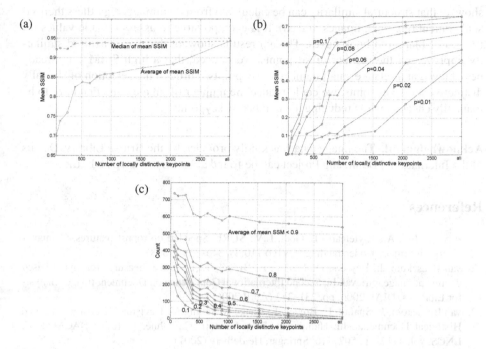

Fig. 6. Dependency of SSIM on the number of locally distinctive keypoints: (a) average and median values taken over the mean SSIM for all pairs of images, (b) quantiles on the average value of mean SSIM for all pairs of images, (c) Number of images below different thresholds on the average value of mean SSIM for all pairs of images

Figure 6 (a) shows the behavior of median and average values of mean SSIM depending on the number of keypoints. The median value of the mean SSIM is already quite high for small numbers of keypoints, e.g. for 384 keypoints. Figure 6 (b) presents the dependency of the mean SSIM with respect to p-quantiles, e.g. the $p = 0.1$ shows the best value of the mean SSIM for the lower ranking 10 percent of the image pairs. For p-quantiles larger than 5 a reasonable good mean SSIM value of 0.6 is obtained for keypoint sets larger than 1500. Figure 6 (c) presents observed numbers of keypoints which might be left to human inspection when thresholding on the mean SSIM value is applied. The numbers of images with low mean SSIM depending on the number of keypoints is observed from this plot, e.g. if one is interested in less than 100 images to check and a SSIM of 0.5 is assumed to be sufficiently good, at least 1024 keypoints per image were required.

7 Conclusion

We have presented an approach to image based quality assurance for digital collections. It enables automatic quality assessment of digitized documents using spatially distinctive local keypoints and robust symmetric descriptor matching. Experimental results showed, that structural similarity can be calculated from documents regardless their visual content (e.g. text, images, mixed). It is even possible to assess reliable values for images of blank old book pages. Though results showed, that the structured similarity improves on the number of keypoints, we noticed, that a high SSIM can already be achieved at a relative small number of keypoints. Through the selection of spatially distinctive local keypoints, we could reduce the number of image pairs that have to be manually checked while reducing the number of keypoints.

Acknowledgment. The image data was kindly provided by the British Library. Details of the International Dunhuang Project can be found at `http://idp.bl.uk/`

References

1. Bay, H., Ess, A., Tuytelaars, T., Gool, L.V.: SURF: Speeded up robust features. Computer Vision and Image Understanding (CVIU) 110(3), 346–359 (2008)
2. van Beusekom, J., Keysers, D., Shafait, F., Breuel, T.: Distance measures for layout-based document image retrieval. In: Second International Conference on Document Image Analysis for Libraries, DIAL 2006, pp. 231–242 (April 2006)
3. van Beusekom, J., Shafait, F., Breuel, T.: Image-Matching for Revision Detection in Printed Historical Documents. In: Hamprecht, F.A., Schnörr, C., Jähne, B. (eds.) DAGM 2007. LNCS, vol. 4713, pp. 507–516. Springer, Heidelberg (2007)
4. Breuel, T.: Fast recognition using adaptive subdivisions of transformation space. In: IEEE Computer Society Conference on Computer Vision and Pattern Recognition, Proceedings, CVPR 1992, pp. 445–451 (June 1992)
5. Brown, M., Szeliski, R., Winder, S.: Multi-image matching using multi-scale oriented patches. In: Proc. of Conf. on Comput. Vis. and Pat. Rec., San Diego, pp. 510–517 (June 2005)
6. Chaudhury, K., Jain, A., Thirthala, S., Sahasranaman, V., Saxena, S., Mahalingam, S.: Google newspaper search - image processing and analysis pipeline. In: 10th International Conference on Document Analysis and Recognition, ICDAR 2009, pp. 621–625 (July 2009)
7. Csurka, G., Dance, C.R., Fan, L., Willamowski, J., Bray, C.: Visual categorization with bags of keypoints. In: Workshop on Statistical Learning in Computer Vision, ECCV 2004, pp. 1–22 (2004)
8. Doermann, D., Li, H., Kia, O.: The detection of duplicates in document image databases. Image and Vision Computing 16(12-13), 907–920 (1998)
9. Ferrari, V., Tuytelaars, T., Gool, L.V.: Simultaneous object recognition and segmentation from single or multiple model views. Intl. J. of Comp. Vis. 67(2), 159–188 (2006)
10. Fischler, M.A., Bolles, R.C.: Random sample consensus: a paradigm for model fitting with applications to image analysis and automated cartography. Commun. ACM 24, 381–395 (1981)
11. Gabarda, S., Cristóbal, G.: Blind image quality assessment through anisotropy. J. Opt. Soc. Am. A 24(12), B42–B51 (2007)
12. Harris, C., Stephens, M.: A combined corner and edge detector. In: Proc. of ALVEY Vision Conf., pp. 147–152 (1988)
13. Ke, Y., Sukthankar, R., Huston, L.: An efficient parts-based near-duplicate and sub-image retrieval system. In: Proceedings of the 12th Annual ACM International Conference on Multimedia, MULTIMEDIA 2004, pp. 869–876. ACM, New York (2004)

14. Lowe, D.G.: Distinctive image features from scale-invariant keypoints. Int. J. of Comput. Vision 60(2), 91–110 (2004)
15. Mikolajczyk, K., Schmid, C.: A performance evaluation of local descriptors. IEEE Trans. on Pat. Anal. and Mach. Intel. 27(10), 1615–1630 (2005)
16. Moorthy, A., Bovik, A.: Blind image quality assessment: From natural scene statistics to perceptual quality. IEEE Transactions on Image Processing 20(12), 3350–3364 (2011)
17. Pizer, S.M., Amburn, E.P., Austin, J.D., Cromartie, R., Geselowitz, A., Greer, T., Romeny, B.T.H., Zimmerman, J.B., Zuiderveld, K.: Adaptive histogram equalization and its variations. Computer Vision, Graphics, and Image Processing 39 (1987)
18. Ramachandrula, S., Joshi, G., Noushath, S., Parikh, P., Gupta, V.: Paperdiff: A script independent automatic method for finding the text differences between two document images. In: The Eighth IAPR International Workshop on Document Analysis Systems, DAS 2008, pp. 585–590 (September 2008)
19. Rosten, E., Drummond, T.W.: Machine Learning for High-Speed Corner Detection. In: Leonardis, A., Bischof, H., Pinz, A. (eds.) ECCV 2006. LNCS, vol. 3951, pp. 430–443. Springer, Heidelberg (2006)
20. Rublee, E., Rabaud, V., Konolige, K., Bradski, G.: ORB: An efficient alternative to SIFT or SURF. In: International Conference on Computer Vision, Barcelona (November 2011)
21. Wang, Z., Bovik, A,.: A universal image quality index. IEEE Signal Processing Letters 9(3), 81–84 (2002)
22. Wang, Z., Bovik, A.: Mean squared error: Love it or leave it? A new look at signal fidelity measures. IEEE Signal Processing Magazine 26(1), 98–117 (2009)
23. Wang, Z., Bovik, A., Sheikh, H., Simoncelli, E.: Image quality assessment: from error visibility to structural similarity. IEEE Transactions on Image Processing 13(4), 600–612 (2004)
24. Wu, X., Zhao, W.L., Ngo, C.W.: Near-duplicate keyframe retrieval with visual keywords and semantic context. In: Proceedings of the 6th ACM International Conference on Image and Video Retrieval, CIVR 2007, pp. 162–169. ACM, New York (2007), http://doi.acm.org/10.1145/1282280.1282309
25. Xu, D., Cham, T.J., Yan, S., Duan, L., Chang, S.F.: Near duplicate identification with spatially aligned pyramid matching. IEEE Transactions on Circuits and Systems for Video Technology 20(8), 1068–1079 (2010)
26. Zhang, L., Zhang, L., Mou, X., Zhang, D.: FSIM: A feature similarity index for image quality assessment. IEEE Transactions on Image Processing 20(8), 2378–2386 (2011)
27. Zhao, W.L., Ngo, C.W., Tan, H.K., Wu, X.: Near-duplicate keyframe identification with interest point matching and pattern learning. IEEE Transactions on Multimedia 9(5), 1037–1048 (2007)

The Sampling Pattern Cube – A Representation and Evaluation Tool for Optical Capturing Systems

Mitra Damghanian, Roger Olsson, and Mårten Sjöström

Mid Sweden University, Holmgatan 10, 85170, Sundsvall, Sweden
mitra.damghanian@miun.se

Abstract. Knowledge about how the light field is sampled through a camera system gives the required information to investigate interesting camera parameters. We introduce a simple and handy model to look into the sampling behavior of a camera system. We have applied this model to single lens system as well as plenoptic cameras. We have investigated how camera parameters of interest are interpreted in our proposed model-based representation. This model also enables us to make comparisons between capturing systems or to investigate how variations in an optical capturing system affect its sampling behavior.

Keywords: camera modeling, light field sampling, camera system representation.

1 Introduction

Properties such as focal plane, angle of view, and depth-of-field are important features when describing a camera. These high-level properties can be inferred from in-depth knowledge about how the image capturing system samples the 5D plenoptic function, which describes the radiance through any point in three-dimensional space incoming light field. A model that describes this sampling behavior is therefore a valuable tool in understanding the system and its potential and limitations, facilitating the development of more efficient post-processing algorithms and insightful system manipulations in order to get desired system features.

In previous works, models have been proposed that describe the light field and how it is sampled by different image capturing systems [1,2,3]. The plenoptic function is a ray-based model for light that includes the chromacity as well as spatial, temporal, and directional variation. The plenoptic function of a given scene contains a large degree of redundancy. Sampling and storing the full plenoptic dimensional function for any useful region of space is impractical. Since the radiance of a given ray does not change in free space, the plenoptic function can be expressed with one less dimension as a light field in a region free of occluders. The light field or radiance can be considered as a density function in the ray space. The light field representation has been utilized to investigate camera

J. Blanc-Talon et al. (Eds.): ACIVS 2012, LNCS 7517, pp. 120–131, 2012.

trade-offs [4] and has proven useful for applications spanning computer graphics, digital photography, and 3D reconstruction. The scope of the light field has also been broaden by employing wave optics to model diffraction and interference [5].

In this work we introduce a simple and practical model for exploring the sampling behavior of an image capturing systems. This model is simplified compared to previously proposed models but includes focus information, which is vital for inferring high-level properties such as depth-of-field. Being able to easily quantify such properties is of practical use for conventional image capturing systems in general but of specific interest when working with more complex systems such as camera arrays [6] and light field or plenoptic cameras [7].

The practical usage of the proposed model is presented by applying it on a set of plenoptic cameras. There are high-level properties of a plenoptic camera that are of interest to describe in a unique and compact way but have a complex relationship to the sampling behavior of this capturing system. A plenoptic camera captures the angular and spatial information of the 4D light field collected by the camera's main lens. This is done by adding an array of lenslets to the camera system close to the image sensor [7]. From two configurations proposed for a plenoptic camera, the first configuration or as we call it PC-i, places the lenslet array at the main lens image plane. In the second configuration, called here as PC-f, the lenslet array is focused at the image plane of the main lens (focused plenoptic camera)[8]. Different optical arrangements in these two camera configurations cause significant difference in their light field sampling properties. Taking a broad view on the case, a representation and evaluation tool for investigating the sampling behavior of various capturing systems is the aim of this work.

In the following sections we first introduce the proposed model. We then apply it to a single lens system in order to explain how the model relates to this well-known optical system and how the system variations are reflected in the model. Then we present the records about the investigated sampling behavior of plenoptic cameras using provided model. We observe the effect of system variations on the light field sampling behavior of the camera system and explore how system variations are revealed in the model based interpretation of the optical system.

2   Problem Description

The aim of this work is to investigate light field sampling behavior of complex capturing systems using a proposed model and infer and visualize properties that allow for comparison of how different capturing configurations are affected by various optical arrangements. Properties of interest include, but are not limited to spatial and/or angular resolution, depth of field, refocusing possibilities (all in focus depth, minimum distance for the in-focus plane). Properties excluded from the model are those caused by the wave nature of light like diffraction and polarization.

3 Proposed Model

3.1 Data Structure

We consider the light intensity captured in each image sensor pixel as the fundamental data from which our model is derived. From where within the scene this data set originates is described in terms of both spatial position and angular span. The explicit knowledge about the exact origin of each light field sample makes the model a tool capable of observing and investigating the light field sampling behavior of a camera system.

Contrary to previously proposed single light ray based models, that are parameterized using a position and direction in 3D space or a two plane representation, our proposed model uses a light cone with an infinitesimal tip and finite base.

Light Cone. is here defined as the bundle of light rays passing through the tip of the cone represented by a 3D point (x_c, y_c, z_c), within a certain span of angles $[\theta_s, \theta_f]$ which are defined relative to the normal of the plane $< z_c >$ where $< z_c >= \{x, y, z = z_c\}$. θ_s and θ_f are angle pairs showing the start and finish of the cone's angular span in $< x_c >$ and $< y_c >$ planes (see Fig. 1). Using the notation of $r(x, y, z, \theta)$ as a single light ray passing through (x, y, z) with the angle of θ relative to the normal of plane $< z >$, the following notation is utilized for a light cone:

$$C(x_c, y_c, z_c, \theta_s, \theta_f) = \{\forall r(x_c, y_c, z_c, \theta) : \theta \in [\theta_s, \theta_f])\}. \tag{1}$$

A light cone is hence uniquely defined by its tip location and the angular span. The radiance contained in a light cone is obtained by integrating all light rays within that light cone:

$$I(x_c, y_c, z_c) = \int C(x_c, y_c, z_c, \theta_s, \theta_f)d\theta = \int_{\theta_s}^{\theta_f} r((x_c, y_c, z_c), \theta)d\theta \tag{2}$$

If we consider the image pixel size being as the maximum precision of a point, we come to a sampled space of the proposed model. To parameterize the model, we first consider the fundamental data captured by an image sensor to be a set of light cones and second, this data set being back-traceable into the captured scene as a new set of light cones. The first set of light cones have their tip locations positioned at the image sensor pixel locations and their angular span defined by the light acceptance angle of the sensor and the combined aperture of the optical system. When back-tracing this set of light cones into the scene a new set of light cones is finally produced. A combination of transformations acts on the light cones as a consequence of back-tracing through the optical system. For example a translation through free space neither affects the tip position nor the angular span of a light cone, while a lens effect transforms a light cone into one with a tip location and angular span obtained by the lens equation (see Fig. 1). Regardless of the number of transformations, all light rays

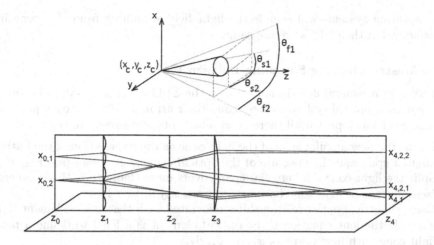

Fig. 1. Illustrating an example of light cones and how they are back-traced from the plane of sensor pixels at z_0, to a space in front of the light capturing system, z_4 in this case

within a light cone are preserved. However a single light cone might split into a number of light cones when straddling two or more optical elements, e.g. in the case of passing through a lens array. The final set of light cones, located outside the image capturing system but within the captured scene forms the sampling pattern cube (SPC).

Sampling Pattern Cube. describes the qualitative as well as quantitative behavior of the optical system. The SPC is thus a mapping between the pixel content captured by the image sensor and the 3D space outside the image capturing system. To simplify further descriptions of the model, as well as illustrations of the same, we henceforth reduce the dimensionality by ignoring the parameters relating to the y-plane. Expanding the model to its full dimensionality is straightforward. Given this simplification the first dimension of the SPC is the location of the light cone tip x, relative to the optical axis of the capturing system. The second dimension being the angular span of the light cone θ and the third dimension being the light cone tip's depth z along the optical axis, relative to the reference plane $< z_0 >$. This reference plane can be arbitrarily chosen to be located at the image sensor plane, the main lens plane, or any other parallel plane as long as it is explicitly defined. Although an axial symmetry of the optical system is assumed in this description, the approach can be easily extended to a nonsymmetrical system.

The choice of using light cones renders a more straightforward handling of in-focus light ray information compared to previously proposed two-plane and point-angle representations [1,2,3] and is unique for a determined optical system. In addition, by letting the SPC only contain the final set of light cones, we decouple the sampling behavior of the capturing system from the scene properties.

Two capturing systems will sample the light field stemming from the scene in the same way if their SPCs are the same.

3.2 Constructing the Sampling Pattern Cube

Here we give a general description on how the SPC is constructed based on a set of common optical system elements and their arrangement. For each pixel in the image sensor, repeat until there is no more optical elements to consider:

1. Define the new angular span of the light cone as the intersection of the initial angular span and the aperture of the optical element it passes (see Fig. 1).
2. Split the light cone if its angular span covers more than one optical element (see the case of light cone back-traced from x_{02} in Fig. 1).
3. Use geometrical optics relationships associated with the optical element (for example the lens equation if the optical element is a lens) to define a new light cone with new values of x_c, z_c, θ_s, θ_f.

A section of the three dimensional space is illustrated in Fig 1. This figure shows how the above algorithm is applied to two initial light cones, corresponding to two image sensor pixels located at x_{01} and x_{02}. In the back-tracing process, the first lens effect associated with the lens array located on plane $< z_1 >$ results in a new set of light cone with tips located on plane $< z_2 >$ with their respective angular spans. The final lens effect associated with the lens located on plane $< z_3 >$ gives the final light cones with tips located on plane $< z_4 >$ which are $x_{4,1}, x_{4,2,1}, x_{4,2,2}$. The first subscript indicates on which z plane in depth the tip is located, the second indicates from which initial light cone it is traced and the third indicates if the light cone has been split.

Properties of the Sampling Pattern Cube. The obtained SPC carries information specifying angular and spatial positions from which the captured information by each pixel originates. This knowledge is scene independent and provides the necessary information about the sampling behavior of the image capturing system. The number of non-overlapping light cone tips in the SPC gives an upper limit for the extractable spatial resolution focused on the plane where they are located. In the final set of light cones the depth for each light cone is defined as z_c with tip position (x_c, z_c). Parallel light rays are treated as a cone with their origin at depth plane of infinity and an infinitively small angular span. Here we apply the SPC model to a number of imaging capturing systems. We continue to reduce the dimensions of the model in the given examples to simplify the discussion as well as the illustrations.

4   Applying the SPC Model to Specific Optical Capturing Systems

4.1   Sampling Pattern Cube for a Single Lens Relay System

Figure 2 represents a single lens relay system as described by the SPC. The system follows the lens equation $\frac{1}{a} + \frac{1}{b} = \frac{1}{f}$, where a is the object distance and b is the image sensor distance from the optical center of the main lens with focal length f. Within this context the focal plane and depth of field are the parameters of interest in this system. Here, the focal plane is defined as the plane upon which the lens is actually focused. The depth of field is defined as the maximum possible depth variations around the focal plane while the image remains in focus (according to the resolution of the image sensor). The depth of field is known to be proportional to the image sensor pixel size and lens focal length, and inversely proportional to the lens aperture size.

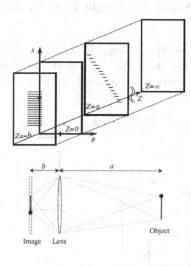

Fig. 2. A single lens relay system represented in a SPC

Focal Plane. The knowledge about the single lens relay system tells us that it is focused at the plane with distance a from the main lens, which is located outside the camera. The SPC representation of the system also shows that light information collected by the image sensor pixels is originating from the single plane of $z = a$.

Depth of Field. To infer depth of field from the SPC we look for the maximum possible depth variations around the focal plane, without any interference between the adjacent light cones. This variation is a function of the angular span of adjacent light cones and the distance between their tip positions. Considering how the SPC is constructed, the smaller aperture size will cause smaller angular span of the final set of light cones. Moreover, bigger distances between final positions of the cone tips is achieved by a bigger pixel size on the image sensor and a bigger focal length of the main lens. Thus, the SPC model shows that the smaller angular span of the light cones, and the bigger the distance between adjacent light cone tips, the larger depth of field.

Variation of System Parameters. In the SPC representation of a single lens relay system we observe a continuous shift in the angular span, and the light cone tip positions moving from one light cone to the next (Fig. 2). A change in the focal length of the lens will result in a shift in depth of the $z = a$ plane, a variation in the tip location and angular span of the light cones while preserving their number. A change in the aperture size will not affect the depth position of the plane $z = a$ nor the tip position of the final set of light cones on this plane, but will proportionally affect the angular span of the cones.

4.2   Sampling Pattern Cube for Single Lens System Focused at Optical Infinity

This second example is representing a single lens system that is focused at optical infinity (see Fig. 3). Light cone tips are located at the plane of optical infinity. They are distributed more sparsely compared to the case shown in Fig. 2 and have a narrower angular span.

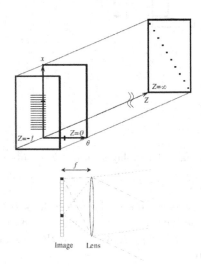

Fig. 3. An infinity focused single lens system represented in a SPC

Focal Plane. The plane at optical infinity is known as the focal plane of this system. The SPC also shows that light information collected on the image sensor is originating from the plane at optical infinity.

Depth of Field. The depth of field in an infinitely focused single lens system does not have a clear starting point, but extends into infinity. In the SPC we also cannot determine any minimum distance where light cones start to overlap since the angular span of the cones are infinitively small.

Variation of System Parameters. If we apply a slight increase in the distance between image sensor and the lens the focal plane is shifted from infinity to the hyper focal distance. In this case, the depth of field is starting from a point halfway between the lens and hyper focal distance and extends to optical infinity. By examining the SPC, and considering how its generated, we again find the hyper focal plane as the plane where cone tips are located. For the depth of field parameter, we are back to the case of a relay system where maximum possible depth variations around the focal plane, without any interference between the adjacent light cones, determine the depth of field.

4.3   Sampling Pattern Cube for Plenoptic Cameras

To explain the sampling behavior of plenoptic cameras using the introduced model, we first generated the SPC for two configurations of a plenoptic camera, PC-i and PC-f. Parameters of the main lens and the lenslets array were considered to be the same in both configurations and the main lens was focused at the optical infinity. The utilized camera parameters taken from [9] are summarized in Table 1. We considered spatial and angular resolution as the parameters of interest for plenoptic cameras. We define spatial and angular resolution as the resolvable positional and angular data respectively. The SPCs for the plenoptic camera configurations are generated and shown in Figs. 4, 5, 6. The plenoptic cameras have a 4D sampling behavior, in contrast to conventional 2D camera systems. Again, for clarity we only present a subset of the resulting 4D SPC, corresponding to a single row of pixels behind a single row of lenslets. Also multiple insets in one figure have the same scale for easier comparison and values are excluded to keep the cases general.

Table 1. Utilized camera parameters

Parameter	PC-i	PC-f
Main lens focal length, F	$80mm$	
Spacing between main lens and lenslet array	$80mm$	$97mm$
Lenslet focal length, f	$1.5mm$	
Lenslet pitch	$0.5mm$	
Lenslet array size	100×100	
Spacing between lenslet array and image sensor	$1.5mm$	$1.7mm$
Image sensor pixel size	$6.8\mu m \times 6.8\mu m$	

Spatial Resolution. Examining the SPC of the PC-i, light cones from the pixels behind a single lenslet differ in their position, hence appear in columns as Fig. 5 shows. Light cones from pixels behind adjacent lenslets share position and add to the angular span. Considering the spatial resolution as the resolvable positional data, sharing the tip location among the cone tips does not increase the spatial resolution. Observing the SPC associated with the PC-f, light cones

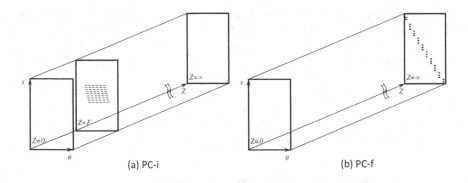

(a) PC-i   (b) PC-f

Fig. 4. Schematic SPCs for two configurations of a plenoptic camera (a)PC-i (b)PC-f

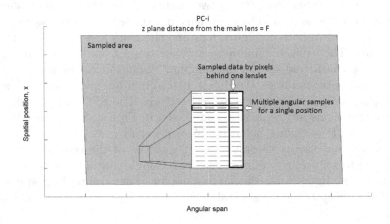

Fig. 5. The plane containing light cone tips in the SPC representation of PC-i

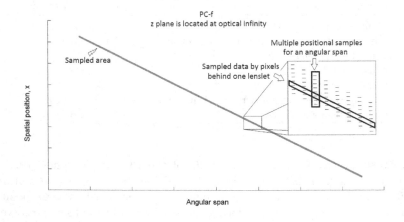

Fig. 6. The plane containing light cone tips in the SPC representation of PC-f

from adjacent lenslets do not share their tip location. In this case each light cone instead adds the number of individual light cone tips in the SPC that will give a bigger number of resolvable positional data. The knowledge about higher number of resolvable spatial samples in the PC-f structure compared to PC-i is in line with prior knowledge about these two configurations of plenoptic camera.

Angular Resolution. Examining the SPC of the PC-i (see Fig. 5), light cones from the pixels behind a single lenslet have similar angular span and light cones from pixels behind adjacent lenslets add to that angular span. This sampling behavior gives multiple angular samples for one single spatial position. Observing the SPC associated with the PC-f, the number of angular sample associated with one spatial position is limited due to the constant shift of the light cones from the pixels behind one lenslet. The knowledge about higher number of resolvable angular samples for one positional data in the PC-i structure compared to PC-f is in line with our prior knowledge about the two configurations of plenoptic camera.

The following section investigates the effect of certain optical system variations on the sampling behavior of the plenoptic cameras by observing the generated SPCs in each case.

Varying Pitch of the Lenslets. Figure 7 shows how changes in the pitch size of the lenslets, l_p, will affect the sampling pattern of the PC-i. When examining the SPC of the PC-i, we see that the information captured by each pixel originates from a plane $z = F$ in front of the main lens. In this case the main lens plane is selected as the zero depth plane. Keeping the total area in camera covered by the lenslets constant, variation of the pitch size does not affect the total sampled angular span (constant width of the sampled area in the SPC). A decreased lenslet pitch size gives fewer samples in the fixed total angular span, but a denser spatial sampling. In the PC-f, a decreased lenslet pitch size reduces the angular span (for each light cone), which results in a narrower total angular span at each spatial position (see Fig. 8). In the PC-f, the lenslet pitch size does not change the number of spatial samples associated with one angular span.

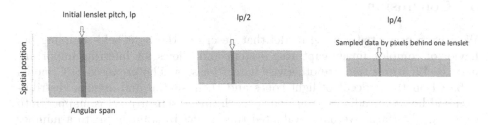

Fig. 7. Illustrating of how the SPC changes with variations of the lenslet pitch size in PC-i

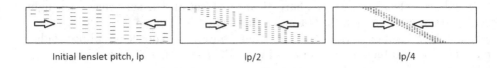

Initial lenslet pitch, lp   lp/2   lp/4

Fig. 8. Illustration of how the SPC changes with variations of the lenslet pitch size in PC-f

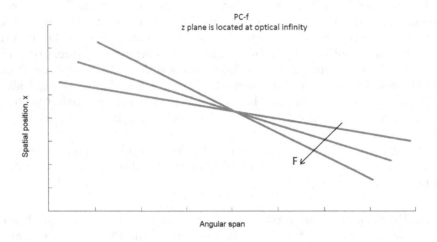

Fig. 9. Illustration of how SPC changes in PC-f with variations of the main lens focal length, F

Varying Focal Length of the Main Lens in PC-f. Smaller F moves $< z_c >$ in the SPC towards the camera, extends the angular span of the cones and brings their tip location closer to each other (Fig. 9). These changes causes interference of the light rays in the cones happen in a shorter translation in depth and hence reducing the depth of field.

5   Conclusion

We have represented a novel model that describes the light field sampling behavior of complex image capturing system and allows for inferring important high level features that are otherwise hard to assess. The proposed SPC model is based on the concept of light cones and their spatial and angular distribution and how the radiance captured by each image sensor pixel is mapped into captured 3D space. We have evaluated this model by applying it to a number of image capturing systems, starting from simple single lens systems and then continuing with more complex systems in the form of two types of plenoptic camera. We investigated the high level parameters focal plane, depth of field, and spatial and angular resolution and showed how these could be derived from the SPC model properties. Our proposed model enables comparisons between various imaging capturing systems and investigations on how variations in the optical sub-system affect the capturing system's sampling behavior. In future work, we will extend the concept of SPC to include more optical elements and operations with which SPCs can be processed, compared and evaluated. We will also apply our model to more systems such as multi-camera arrays and more complex plenoptic cameras.

Acknowledgment. This work has been supported by grant 00156702 of the EU European Regional Development Fund, Mellersta Norrland, Sweden, and by grant 00155148 of Länsstyrelsen i Västernorrland, Sweden.

References

1. Fujii, T.: Ray Space Coding for 3D Visual Communication. In: Picture Coding Symposium, vol. 2, pp. 447–451 (1996)
2. Gortler, S.J., Grzeszczuk, R., Szeliski, R., Cohen, M.F.: The lumigraph. In: Proc. Computer Graphics and Interactive Techniques, pp. 43–54 (1996)
3. Levoy, M., Hanrahan, P.: Light field rendering. In: Proc. Computer Graphics and Interactive Techniques, pp. 31–42 (1996)
4. Levin, A., Freeman, W., Durand, F.: Understanding camera trade-offs through a Bayesian analysis of light field projections. MIT CSAIL TR 2008-049
5. Oh, S.B., Kashyap, S., Garg, R., Chandran, S., Raskar, R.: Rendering Wave Effects with Augmented Light Field. Computer Graphics Forum 29(2), 507–516 (2010)
6. Wilburn, B., Joshi, N., Vaish, V., Talvala, E.V., Antunez, E., Barth, A., Adams, A., Horowitz, M., Levoy, M.: High performance imaging using large camera arrays. ACM Trans. Graph. 24(3), 765–776 (2005)
7. Adelson, E.H., Wang, J.Y.A.: Single lens stereo with a plenoptic camera. IEEE Trans. Pattern Analysis and Machine Intelligence 14(2), 92–106 (1992)
8. Lumsdaine, A., Georgiev, T.: The focused plenoptic camera. In: 2009 IEEE International Conference on Computational Photography (ICCP), pp. 1–8 (2009)
9. Georgiev, T., Chunev, G., Lumsdaine, A.: Superresolution with the focused plenoptic camera. In: Proc. SPIE-IS&T Electronic Imaging, vol. 7873 (2011)

Improving Image Acquisition:
A Fish-Inspired Solution

Julien Couillaud, Alain Horé, and Djemel Ziou

MOIVRE, Département d'informatique, Université de Sherbrooke
2500, Boulevard de l'Université, Sherbrooke (Québec), J1K2R1, Canada
{julien.couillaud,alain.hore,djemel.ziou}@usherbrooke.ca

Abstract. In this paper, we study the rendering of images with a new mosaic/color filter array (CFA) called the Burtoni mosaic. This mosaic is derived from the retina of the African cichlid fish *Astatotilapia burtoni*. To evaluate the effect of the Burtoni mosaic on the quality of the rendered images, we use two quality measures in the Fourier domain which are the resolution error and the aliasing error. In our model, no demosaicing algorithm is used, which makes it independent of such algorithms. We also use 11 semantic sets of color images in order to highlight the images classes that are well fitted for the Burtoni mosaic in the process of image acquisition. We have compared the Burtoni mosaic with the Bayer CFA and with an optimal CFA proposed by Hao *et al*. Experiments have shown that the Burtoni mosaic gives the best performances for images of 9 semantic sets which are the high frequency, aerial, indoor, face, aquatic, bright, dark, step and line classes.

Keywords: Image formation, color measurement, sensors, color filter arrays, Burtoni mosaic, image quality.

1 Introduction

Image quality is an essential concept in image processing and perception. The concept of image quality is complex since it depends on several factors such as the human perception characteristics, the various physical components (lenses, sensors, etc.) and the algorithms (sampling, quantization, denoising, compression, radiometric corrections, etc.) implied in the image formation process. At the sensor level, the arrangement of the photosensitive cells (called photosites) greatly influences the image quality. This arrangement is sometimes called mosaic or color filter array (CFA). Many mosaic implementations have been used in digital image sensors. In 1976, Bayer proposed a mosaic configuration which is now widely used in digital cameras [1]. The Bayer pattern, shown in Fig. 1a, provides an RGB mosaic in which only one primary color element is available in a given photosite, whereas the two missing primary colors must be estimated from the adjacent photosites via a demosaicing algorithm. Over the years, new cameras have incorporated many other mosaic implementations [3, 4, 13, 15]. Getting inspiration from the natural world, Kröger has proposed a new mosaic

J. Blanc-Talon et al. (Eds.): ACIVS 2012, LNCS 7517, pp. 132–141, 2012.

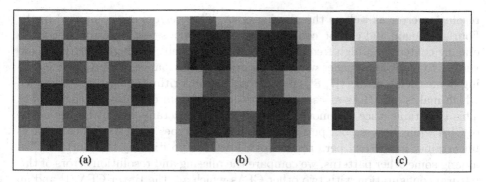

Fig. 1. Examples of mosaics: (a) Bayer mosaic (b) Burtoni mosaic (c) Optimal mosaic Cfa4b [7]

which corresponds to the retina of the African cichlid fish Astatotilapia burtoni shown in Fig. 2 [12].

The Burtoni mosaic has been shown to use trichromatic representation of colors [5], as displayed in Fig. 1b. In addition, as can be seen in Fig. 2b, the photoreceptors in the retina of the Burtoni eye are arranged in a quasi-regular mosaic similar to the mosaics of manufactured devices, making them electronically realizable. CFAs can also be designed as the solution of a constrained optimization problem that aims at minimizing a demosaicing error [7]. An example of such CFAs is the optimal CFA pattern shown in Fig. 1c.

The mosaics described in the preceding paragraphs all aim at improving image acquisition and color perception. However, the arrangement of pattern in these mosaics can lead to aliasing and resolution errors [9]. Both spatial and chromatic information can be affected. Pursuing the work of Kröger [12], the present study intends to investigate the possibility of transferring nature's solutions to electronic devices in order to minimize the reconstruction errors of images. For this purpose, we study the mosaic of the fish Astatotilapia burtoni and we assess the quality of the rendered images at the output of that mosaic by using the

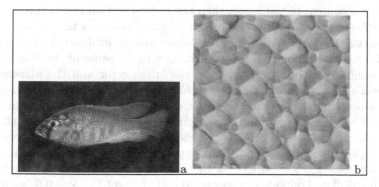

Fig. 2. (a) Astatotilapia burtoni and (b) a section of its retina [12]

resolution error as well as the aliasing error. These errors are computed in the Fourier domain and can be coarsely seen as the reconstruction error of low frequency content and high frequeny content respectively. We highlight that, conversely to many approaches which evaluate the performance of CFAs by measuring demosaicing errors ([7, 8]), no demosaicing algorithm is used in our model, which makes our CFAs-assessment approach free from demosaicing algorithms. This is suitable since a demosaicing algorithm is generally well fitted for a type of CFA while it gives poor performances for other types of CFAs, which involves uncertainty in the real performance of CFAs. For positioning the Burtoni CFA among some other patterns, we compare the aliasing and resolution errors of this natural configuration with two other CFAs which are the Bayer CFA [1] and an optimal CFA designed by Hao *et al.* [7].

The outline of the paper is as follows: in section 2, we describe our methodology. Experimental results and discussions are presented in section 3, and we end the paper with concluding remarks.

2   Methodology

For the assessment of the fidelity of images at the sensor level, we consider real scenes represented by continuous images as input of the sensor while their corresponding discrete images are the output. The scenes are built from discrete images by using the generalized sampling theorem proposed by Papoulis [14] and used for image resolution enhancement and depth from defocus [2, 11]. Although this reconstruction model leads to more accurate estimations when compared to certain other existing models [11], it may cause deformations of the reconstructed images. However, these deformations can be seen as inherent to the image structure and therefore to the scene. In other words, the continuous images, as 2D representation of the 3D scene, are enough for the quality assessment because they encode the projection of physical phenomena inherent to the realistic scene. Having a continuous image and its discrete version, the fidelity measures can be defined. Their goal is to capture how the informational content of the scene is reproduced in the discrete image. If the CFA preserves the informational content of the scene, then the reconstruction errors corresponding to the fidelity measures will be small. The fidelity measures that we use are the aliasing error and the resolution error, which aim to evaluate loss of information in the reconstruction of continuous images in the sense of the Shannon and Nyquist sampling theorem. In fact, the resolution error and the aliasing error can be seen as the reconstruction error of the low frequency and high frequency content respectively. The resolution error, denoted by E_r, gives a measure of the accuracy of the reconstruction of an original signal in the baseband defined by $[-0.5fs_x, 0.5fs_x] \times [-0.5fs_y, 0.5fs_y]$, where fs_x and fs_y are respectively the horizontal and vertical sampling frequency associated to the CFA. The aliasing error, denoted by E_a, measures how the high frequencies interfere with the signal, and is calculated outside the baseband $[-0.5fs_x, 0.5fs_x] \times [-0.5fs_y, 0.5fs_y]$. The analytical formulas for E_r and E_a are given by:

$$\begin{cases} E_r = \int_{-fs_x/2}^{fs_x/2} \int_{-fs_y/2}^{fs_y/2} \|I_c(f_x, f_y) - I_d(f_x, f_y)\|^2 \mathrm{d}f_x \mathrm{d}f_y \\ E_a = \int_{F_a} \int_{F_a} \|I_c(f_x, f_y) - I_d(f_x, f_y)\|^2 \mathrm{d}f_x \mathrm{d}f_y \end{cases} \tag{1}$$

If we denote by I_p the continous image obtained by the Papoulis theorem [11], then I_c is the Fourier transform of the discrete image obtained from I_p. I_d is the Fourier transform of the mosaiced image formed by the CFA from the continuous image I_p. The computation of the mosaiced image is described in Appendix 4. In Eq. (1), F_a represents the frequencies outside the baseband $[-0.5fs_x, 0.5fs_x] \times [-0.5fs_y, 0.5fs_y]$. fs_x and fs_y are computed as follows:

$$fs_x = \frac{1}{n_x} \quad \text{and} \quad fs_y = \frac{1}{n_y} \tag{2}$$

where n_x and n_y are respectively the number of horizontal pixels and the number of vertical pixels used in the repeating pattern that characterizes the CFA. For example, in the case of the Bayer CFA shown in Fig. 1a, $n_x = n_y = 2$. In the case of the Burtoni CFA shown in Fig. 1b, $n_x = n_y = 10$. Ideally, the image is well reconstructed when E_r and E_a tend toward 0. In order to be able to measure the perceptual impact of a CFA to the quality of images, we will compute the aliasing and the resolution errors in the non-correlated color space YCbCr instead of the correlated color space RGB. The YCbCr enables to separate the luminance from the chrominance (as the human visual system does indeed), which gives more accuracy in the detection of color errors. Consequently, the aliasing and resolution errors are computed for each of the bands Y, Cb and Cr. In Fig. 3, we show the spectrum of a mosaiced image corresponding to three different CFAs, and we indicate the parts corresponding to the resolution and aliasing errors. We note that in our model, we focus in fact on the sum of squared errors that are generated in the acquisition of images by the CFA. No demosaicing algorithm is used in our model, which makes our CFAs-assessment approach free from demosaicing algorithms. This enables to focus on the CFA pattern and not on any algorithm that may be used to form a color image from the CFA. In fact, a bias is created when any demosaicing algorithm is used in the evaluation of a CFA (as commonly found in the literature [7, 10]) since we are no longer assessing only the CFA but the combination of the CFA with the demosaicing algorithm. As a demosaicing algorithm may be better fitted for a

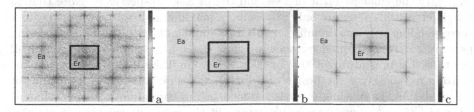

Fig. 3. Spectrum of a mosaiced image in the Y band (a) Burtoni mosaic (b) Bayer mosaic (c) Optimal mosaic Cfa4b [7]

type of CFA than for another, it is not really fair to measure the performance of a CFA based on the quality of the images that it renders through a (possibly non-adapted) demosaicing algorithm. Thus, in simple terms, we focus in our model on the acquisition errors introduced by the CFA, while approaches that use demosaicing algorithms focus in fact on the reconstruction errors introduced by the combination of the CFA combined to these demosaicing algorithms.

3   Experimental Results

The performances of the Burtoni mosaic are compared with those obtained with the Bayer pattern [1] and the optimal pattern Cfa4b proposed in [7] (see Fig. 1). As it is generally observed and known that the quality of images greatly depends on the CFA used in the image formation process ([6, 10, 13]), we use a set of 132 color images of 11 semantic classes : high frequency images (HF), aerial images (Aer), face images (Face), indoor images (Ind), aquatic images (Aqu), bright images (Bri), dark images (Dark), step images (Step), homogenous images (Hom), line images (Line) and texture images (Tex). A sample of this set of images is displayed in Fig. 4. To the best of our knowledge, no previous study on CFAs has focused on semantic classes of images in order to better highlight the images classes or the types of 3D scenes that are well adapted for a given CFA. We also note that we have used a scale ratio of 1×1 for the reconstruction of a continuous image using the Papoulis theorem [11] in order to be as close as possible to the original discrete image. As indicated previously, all images are transformed into the YCbCr color space in order to study luminance and chrominance separately. The aliasing and resolution errors are then estimated for each band separately. In Tables 1-4, we show the scores obtained for the different CFAs. Note that the Burtoni, Bayer and optimal CFA are represented by the capital letters F, B and C respectively. The values in Table 1 (resp. Table 2) represent the percentage of the number of images for which a given CFA gives the smallest (resp. highest) aliasing error compared to the two others. In the same way, the values in Table 3 (resp. Table 4) represent the percentage of the number of images for which a given CFA gives the smallest (resp. highest) resolution error compared to the two others. As an example in Table 1, for the texture class and regarding the resolution error at the Y band, the Burtoni CFA gives the smallest error in 82% of cases while the optimal CFA and the Bayer CFA give the smallest error in 18% and 0% of cases respectively. Note that in the different tables, we are only displaying a maximum of two percentage values corresponding to a maximum of two CFAs among three possible; the missing percentages are computed by knowing that the sum of the percentages for all the three CFAs is always 100% for each band. In Table 1, it appears that the Burtoni mosaic gives the best scores for all the semantic classes used and for all bands. As the aliasing error is reduced in the chrominance bands (that is, Cb and Cr) and since these bands represent the color information, it appears that the Burtoni mosaic is prone to little color errors compared to the Bayer mosaic and the optimal mosaic CFA4b. This simply means that the Burtoni

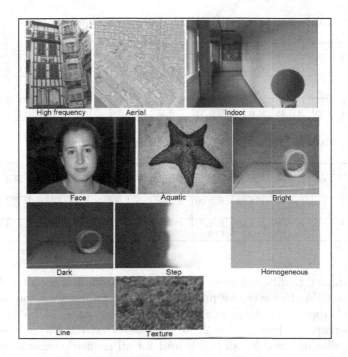

Fig. 4. Sample of each semantic set of images used in the experiments

mosaic is less subject to interferences (such as areas of high-contrast and fine details) that may cause color aliasing. In fact, by using knowledge about the human visual system, high frequency errors or differences are more noticeable than low frequency errors, and thus aliasing errors in the Cb and Cr bands translate into noticeable color errors or defects in images. These errors may appear for example, for the human visual system, in the form of desaturated

Table 1. Aliasing error : percentage of minimal values. Note that B denotes the Bayer mosaic, F the Burtoni mosaic, and C the optimal mosaic Cfa4b.

	HF.	Aer.	Ind.	Face	Aqu.	Bri.	Dark	Step.	Hom.	Line	Text.
Y	F 1.00	F 1.00	F 1.00	F 1.00	F 1.00	F 1.00	F 1.00	F 1.00	F 0.82 B 0.18	F 1.00	F 0.82 C 0.18
Cb	F 1.00	F 1.00	F 1.00	F 1.00	F 1.00	F 1.00	F 1.00	F 1.00	F 0.82 B 0.18	F 1.00	F 0.91 B 0.09
Cr	F 1.00	F 1.00	F 1.00	F 1.00	F 1.00	F 1.00	F 1.00	F 1.00	F 1.00	F 1.00	F 1.00

Table 2. Aliasing error : percentage of maximal values

	HF.	Aer.	Ind.	Face	Aqu.	Bri.	Dark	Step.	Hom.	Line	Text.
Y	B 0.93 C 0.07	B 1.00	B 1.00	B 1.00	B 0.94 C 0.06	B 1.00	B 1.00	B 1.00	B 0.55 C 0.45	B 0.82 C 0.18	B 0.82 F 0.09
Cb	B 1.00	B 1.00	B 1.00	B 0.94 C 0.06	B 1.00	B 1.00	B 1.00	B 1.00	C 0.73 B 0.27	B 0.64 C 0.36	B 0.64 C 0.27
Cr	B 1.00	B 1.00	B 1.00	B 1.00	B 0.94 C 0.06	B 1.00	B 1.00	B 1.00	C 0.64 B 0.36	B 1.00	B 1.00

Table 3. Resolution error : percentage of minimal values

	HF.	Aer.	Ind.	Face	Aqu.	Bri.	Dark	Step.	Hom.	Line	Text.
Y	B 0.93	B 1.00	B 0.82	B 0.88	F 0.83	B 0.83	B 0.83	B 0.91	B 0.91	B 0.73	B 0.55
	C 0.07		C 0.18	C 0.12	C 0.17	C 0.17	C 0.17	C 0.09	C 0.09	C 0.27	C 0.45
Cb	C 0.67	C 1.00	B 0.55	C 0.81	C 0.72	B 0.67	B 0.83	B 0.55	B 0.82	B 0.73	C 0.73
	F 0.20		C 0.36	B 0.19	B 0.28	C 0.33	C 0.17	C 0.45	C 0.18	C 0.27	B 0.27
Cr	C 0.67	C 0.71	C 0.55	C 0.75	C 0.61	B 0.50	C 0.67	B 0.55	B 0.82	C 0.55	C 0.73
	B 0.27	B 0.29	B 0.45	B 0.25	B 0.33	C 0.50	B 0.33	C 0.45	C 0.18	B 0.36	B 0.27

Table 4. Resolution error : percentage of maximal values

	HF.	Aer.	Ind.	Face	Aqu.	Bri.	Dark	Step.	Hom.	Line	Text.
Y	F 1.00	F 1.00	F 1.00	F 0.94	F 1.00	F 1.00	F 1.00	F 1.00	F 0.91	F 1.00	F 1.00
				C 0.06					C 0.09		
Cb	F 0.93	F 1.00	F 0.91	F 1.00	F 1.00	F 1.00	F 1.00	F 1.00	F 1.00	F 1.00	F 1.00
	C 0.07		C 0.09								
Cr	F 1.00	F 1.00	F 1.00	F 1.00	F 0.94	F 1.00	F 1.00	F 1.00	F 1.00	F 1.00	F 1.00
					C 0.06						

colors or completely different colors between the original scene and the image given by the CFA. However, we precise here that we do not know how these errors would appear for Astatotilapia Burtoni since we have no information about its perception. From Table 2, we conclude that the Bayer mosaic gives the highest aliasing error for all bands and for all semantic classes, except the homogenous class. Thus, the Bayer mosaic may be more sensitive in most cases to color aliasing than the Burtoni mosaic and the optimal CFA. Regarding the resolution errors in Table 3, it appears that the Bayer and CFA4b mosaics share/permute the best scores in almost all the semantic classes and for all bands, the Bayer mosaic performing particularly well in the Y band. The Bayer mosaic has the smallest resolution error for all bands in the case of the bright, step and homogenous classes of images. For all the other classes, no CFA pattern has the best performances for simultaneously all the bands, and thus none can be said to be better than the two others. However, each of the Bayer and CFA4b mosaics performs better than the Burtoni mosaic regarding the resolution error. In fact, we can observe in Table 4 that the Burtoni mosaic gives the highest resolution error for all the semantic sets and for all bands. As the resolution error is generally mostly apparent in the Y band compared to the Cb and Cr bands, the scores in Tables 3-4 suggest for example that the Burtoni mosaic is inferior to the Bayer and CFA4b mosaics in representing smooth regions or smooth details in an image. The scores in Tables 1-4, regarding the aliasing and resolution errors, confirm the choice of semantic classes for assessing the performance of CFAs since we can observe that some CFAs respond well to some types of scenes than others. Consequently, we can imagine the design of specialized cameras that are particularly efficient for the acquisition of some specific types of scenes. In general, the aliasing error increases when the resolution error decreases. In order to give a unique value to the errors generated by the different CFAs, we propose to compute the product of the aliasing and resolution errors. We note that the multiplication is not motivated by any human perception aspect, but is simply used as a numerical criteria for optimality in order to make a compromise

Table 5. Product of the resolution and aliasing errors : percentage of minimal values

	HF.	Aer.	Ind.	Face	Aqu.	Bri.	Dark	Step.	Hom.	Line	Text.
Y	F 0.87	F 1.00	F 0.91	F 1.00	F 0.94	F 1.00	F 1.00	F 0.73	B 0.55	F 0.64	B 0.45
	B 0.07		C 0.09		B 0.06			C 0.18	F 0.45	B 0.27	C 0.45
Cb	F 0.93	F 0.71	F 1.00	F 0.88	F 0.89	F 1.00	F 1.00	F 0.73	B 0.82	F 0.55	F 0.36
	C 0.07	C 0.29		C 0.13	C 0.11			C 0.27	F 0.09	B 0.45	C 0.36
Cr	F 1.00	F 1.00	F 1.00	F 1.00	F 0.89	F 1.00	F 1.00	F 0.91	B 0.64	F 0.82	F 0.36
					B 0.06			B 0.09	C 0.27	B 0.09	C 0.36

Table 6. Product of the resolution and aliasing errors : percentage of maximal values

	HF.	Aer.	Ind.	Face	Aqu.	Bri.	Dark	Step.	Hom.	Line	Text.
Y	C 0.60	B 0.43	B 0.82	B 0.50	C 0.61	B 0.83	B 0.50	C 0.45	C 0.73	B 0.45	F 0.73
	B 0.27	C 0.43	F 0.09	C 0.50	B 0.33	C 0.17	C 0.50	F 0.27	F 0.27	C 0.45	B 0.18
Cb	B 0.93	B 1.00	B 0.91	B 0.88	B 0.89	B 0.67	B 0.67	B 0.82	F 0.55	C 0.45	F 0.55
	C 0.07		C 0.09	C 0.13	C 0.11	C 0.33	C 0.33	F 0.09	C 0.45	B 0.36	C 0.27
Cr	B 0.73	B 0.43	B 0.64	B 0.75	B 0.61	B 0.50	B 0.67	C 0.55	F 0.91	B 0.55	B 0.55
	C 0.27	C 0.43	C 0.36	C 0.25	C 0.33	C 0.50	C 0.33	B 0.36	C 0.09	F 0.27	F 0.27

between the resolution error and the aliasing error. The results of this product for the different CFAs, in percentage as in the case of the aliasing and resolution errors, are shown in Tables 5-6. The analysis which is made is that the CFA with the smallest value of the product has better performances in overall than the other CFAs. As can be seen in Table 5, the Burtoni mosaic gives the best results for the high frequency, aerial, indoor, face, aquatic, bright, dark, step and line semantic classes and for all bands. Thus, for scenes corresponding to those semantic classes, the Burtoni mosaic should be used preferably, compared to the Bayer and the CFA4b mosaics, for capturing images. The Burtoni mosaic is not the best for the homogenous and texture classes. In Table 6, we observe that the Bayer CFA gives the poorest results for the aerial, indoor, face, bright and dark classes and for all bands.

4 Conclusion

In this paper, we have proposed a simple methodology for comparing the performances of color filter arrays in capturing images. Our methodology does not involve demosaicing algorithms. It is based on the computation in the Fourier domain of the resolution and aliasing errors, which are two types of errors that can be coarsely seen as the reconstruction errors of the low frequency and high frequeny content respectively. We have applied our methodology to evaluate a new CFA inspired from the retina of the fish Astatotilapia Burtoni, and we have compared that CFA to the Bayer mosaic and to an optimal CFA that includes non-RGB colors. The experimental results have shown that the Burtoni mosaic gives in overall the best performances for images belonging to the high frequency, aerial, indoor, face, aquatic, bright, dark, step and line classes, while it is not the best for the texture and homogenous classes. In a more general sense, the experimental tests undertaken in this paper have revealed that some CFAs are better fitted for some types of 3D scenes or semantic classes of images. This gives rise to what we call the specialization of cameras, which is the process that should lead to the design of cameras that are specialized and more efficient in the acquisition of some particular 3D scenes or types of images.

Appendix A. Computation of the Mosaiced Image

Let us define by I a color image with color pixels $I(p,q) = \{I(p,q)_k\}_{k \in \{1,2,3\}}$ in the RGB vectorial color space. $I(p,q)_1$ represents the red (R) component, $I(p,q)_2$ the green (G) component, and $I(p,q)_3$ the blue (B) component. Since information about the arrangement of color filters in the actual CFA is readily available either from the camera manufacturer (when demosaicing is implemented in the camera), or obtained from the raw CFA image, a $M \times N$ vectorial field $d : \mathbb{N}^2 \to \{0,1\}^3$ of the corresponding location flags $d(p,q)_k$, $k \in \{1,2,3\}$, is initialized using the default value $d(p,q)_k = 1$ to indicate that the primary color indexed by k is found in the CFA at position (p,q). In the CFA pattern shown in Fig. 5a for example, we have $d(p,q)_1 = 0$, $d(p,q)_2 = 1$, $d(p,q)_3 = 0$, $d(p,q-2)_3 = 1$, $d(p,q-1)_1 = 1$, $d(p,q+1)_3 = 1$, and $d(p,q+2)_1 = 1$.

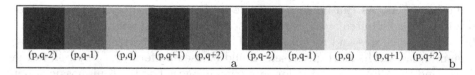

Fig. 5. Parts of a CFA pattern (a) with only RGB primary colors (b) with non-primary colors

The mosaiced image M, associated to the image I and to the CFA characterized by the vectorial field d, is given by:

$$M(p,q) = I(p,q) \otimes d(p,q) \tag{3}$$

where $\otimes$ denotes the element-wise product. In the case of CFAs that include non-primary color pixels, $d(p,q)_k = 1$ if the primary color indexed by k is used in the additive color synthesis that produces the color found in the CFA at position (p,q). In the CFA pattern shown in Fig. 5b (made up of blue, green, yellow, cyan and red colors), we have $d(p,q)_1 = 1$, $d(p,q)_2 = 1$, $d(p,q)_3 = 0$, $d(p,q+1)_1 = 0$, $d(p,q+1)_2 = 1$, $d(p,q+1)_3 = 1$, $d(p,q-2)_3 = 1$, $d(p,q-1)_2 = 1$, and $d(p,q+2)_1 = 1$. For this type of CFA, the mosaiced image M is given by:

$$M(p,q)_k = \frac{I(p,q)_k \times d(p,q)_k}{\sum_{k=1}^{3} d(p,q)_k} \tag{4}$$

References

[1] Bayer, B.E.: Color imaging array (1976)

[2] Deschênes, F., Ziou, D., Fuchs, P.: An unified approach for a simultaneous and cooperative estimation of defocus blur and spatial shifts. Image and Vision Computing 22(1), 35–57 (2004)

[3] Elliot, C.: Reducing pixel count without reducing image quality. Information Display 15(12), 22–25 (1999)

[4] Elliot, C., Credelle, T., Han, S., Im, M., Higgins, M., Higgins, P.: Development of the pentile matrix color amlcd subpixel architecture and rendering algorithms. Journal of the Society for Information Display 11(1), 89–98 (2003)

[5] Fernald, R.D., Liebman, P.A.: Visual receptor pigments in the african cichlid fish haplochromis burtoni. Vision Research 20(10), 857–864 (1980)

[6] Hain, R., Kahler, C.J., Tropea, C.: Comparison of ccd, cmos and intensified cameras. Experiments in Fluids 42(3), 403–411 (2007)

[7] Hao, P., Li, Y., Lin, Z., Dubois, E.: A geometric method for optimal design of color filter arrays. IEEE Transactions on Image Processing 20(3), 709–722 (2011)

[8] Hirakawa, H., Wolfe, P.J.: Spatio-spectral color filter array design for optimal image recovery. IEEE Transactions on Image Processing 17(2), 1876–1890 (2008)

[9] Holst, G.C.: Holst, G.C.: Sampling, aliasing and data fidelity. JCD Publishing, Bellingham, Winter Park (1998)

[10] Horé, A., Ziou, D.: An edge-sensing generic demosaicing algorithm with application to image resampling. IEEE Transactions on Image Processing 20(11), 3136–3150 (2011)

[11] Horé, A., Ziou, D., Deschênes, F.: A new image scaling algorithm based on the sampling theorem of papoulis and application to color. In: International Conference on Image and Graphics, pp. 39–44 (2007)

[12] Kröger, R.: Anti-aliasing in image recording and display hardware: lessons from nature. Journal of Optics: Pure and Applied Optics 6(8), 743–748 (2004)

[13] Lukac, R., Plataniotis, K.N.: Color filter arrays: design and performance analysis. IEEE Transactions on Consumer Electronics 51(4), 1260–1267 (2005)

[14] Papoulis, A.: Generalized sampling theorem. IEEE Transactions on Circuits and Systems 24, 652–654 (1977)

[15] Ramanath, R., Snyder, W.E., Bilbro, G.L., Sander III, W.A.: Demosaicking methods for bayer color arrays. Journal of Electronic Imaging 11(3), 306–315 (2002)

Evaluating the Effects of MJPEG Compression on Motion Tracking in Metro Railway Surveillance

Angelo Cozzolino[2], Francesco Flammini[1], Valentina Galli[1], Mariangela Lamberti[1], Giovanni Poggi[3], and Concetta Pragliola[1]

[1] Ansaldo STS, Via Argine 425, Naples, Italy
{francesco.flammini,valentina.galli,
mariangela.lamberti}@ansaldo-sts.com
[2] Nexera Scpa, Centro Direzionale Isola A/3, Naples, Itlay
acozzolino@nexera.it
[3] University of Naples Federico II, Via Claudio 21, Naples, Italy
giovanni.poggi@unina.it

Abstract. Video content analytics is being increasingly employed for the security surveillance of mass-transit systems. The growing number of cameras, the presence of legacy networks, the limited bandwidth of wireless links, are some of the issues which highlight the importance of evaluating the performance of motion tracking against different levels of video compression. In this paper, we report the results of such an evaluation considering false-negative and false-positive metrics applied to videos captured from cameras installed in a real metro-railway environment. The evaluation methodology is based on the manual generation of the Ground Truth on selected videos at growing levels of MJPEG compression, and on its comparison with the Algorithm Result automatically generated by the Motion Tracker. The computation of reference performance metrics is automated by a tool developed in Matlab. Results are discussed with respect to the main causes of false detections, and hints are provided for further industrial applications.

Keywords: performance evaluation, motion tracking, MJPEG codec, intelligent video surveillance, mass-transit systems.

1 Introduction

Many transit systems can be spread through hundreds of kilometers and require thousands of employees for daily operations. A complete deployment of visual surveillance to cover a system of this magnitude requires thousands of cameras, which makes human-based surveillance unfeasible. Detecting specific activities almost completely relies on costly and scarce human resources. Manual analysis of video is labor intensive, fatiguing, and prone to errors. Additionally, psychophysical research indicates that there are severe limitations in the ability of humans to monitor simultaneous signals. Thus, it is clear that there is a fundamental contradiction between the current surveillance model and human surveillance capabilities. The ability to monitor real-time footage provides dramatic capabilities to transit agencies. Software-aided real-time video content analytics (VCA) considerably alleviates the

J. Blanc-Talon et al. (Eds.): ACIVS 2012, LNCS 7517, pp. 142–154, 2012.

human constraints, which currently are the main handicap for analyzing continuous surveillance data [4].

Past experiences (see e.g. [11] for Madrid Metro) using state-of-the-art systems reported poor performance, with up to 1700 false alarms per camera per day, literally overwhelming central operators. Those results lead to the conclusion that the video-analytics technology was not yet mature to be adopted in real mass-transit environments. Our experience proved instead that, though very initial results can be disappointing, after careful testing and optimization a huge improvement could be achieved, making the technology usable in practice. In fact, we developed and succesfully adopted in real installations (e.g. Metrocampania Nord-Est [3]; see Fig. 1) a methodology based on rigorous testing procedures for 'black-box' performance evaluation of VCA in the specific contexts (camera type and position, scene, external noise, weather, indoor/outdoor surrounding environment, etc.). Hence, key parameters of the algorithms are modified according to the results of performance assessment, and the evaluation is repeated until satisfactory results are achieved. In order to speed-up the process, those parameters (including area of interest, size/speed of the objects, alarm latencies, inhibition times, etc.) are grouped considering camera categories which are homogenous in terms of installation and lighting conditions (e.g. platform cameras, tunnel cameras, etc.). In a few iterations, the fine-tuning methodology converges to the optimal trade-off between false/nuisance alarm rate and detection probability.

In this paper we present a method to go a step forward with respect to our previous experience: the aim here is to evaluate the performance of the motion tracker without using filters on the speed and size of the objects, like we did when performing black-box testing. In such a way, the tracking of any object of any size is taken into account and therefore it is possible to investigate more precisely on the causes of false detections (positive or negative). However, that obliges to employ lower level metrics, that we borrowed from the past research in this field. Furthermore, we wanted to evaluate the performance of motion tracking with respect to the MJPEG video compression, which is notoriously much less efficient than more recent codecs like H264 [9], but still widespread especially in legacy installations. The results we achieved allow to fine tune the compression level to obtain the optimal trade-off between bandwidth occupation and VCA performance, when video quality is not required to be 100% (e.g. because of redundant coverage with other standard, megapixel or PTZ cameras).

Fig. 1. Control room for the security management system

2   Reference Metrics

Several metrics have been proposed in literature to evaluate VCA performance. Those metrics usually require a comparison of the Algorithm Result (AR) with optimal results stored in the so called Ground Truth (GT) [1]. Therefore the first step towards performance evaluation is to build a valid Ground Truth [8].

In this paper, the method used for ground truthing is one in which objects are manually bounded by geometric shapes, typically rectangles; unique IDs are assigned to individual objects and are consistently maintained over subsequent frames.

A variety of annotation tools exist to generate GT data manually, such as Anvil, VideoAnnex, ViPER-GT. Though more time-consuming with respect to possible automatic or semi-automatic methods, manually generated GT are obviously more reliable; this is the reason why this is still the most widespread method for GT generation. Hence, a typical GT consists of a text file including information about the labels and the coordinates of the bounding boxes for each object present in the scene. In order to automate the evaluation of metrics, GT and AR files should include coherent information.

The tracking method has been used for the definition of reference metrics. Tracking is defined as the problem of estimating the spatial extent of the non-background objects for each frame of a video sequence. The result of tracking is a set of tracks for all non-background objects [14]. Tracking is based on the fact that objects are present in the scene for a certain time frame; hence, objects can be characterized spatially by their positioning information (i.e. the up-left and down-right coordinates of their bounding box) and temporally by the number of frames in which they are present, that is their track.

To quantify the level of matching between GT and AR tracks, both in space and time, it is necessary to define the concepts of spatial and temporal overlap between tracks. The spatial overlap is the bounding box overlapping $A(Gi, ARj)$ between Gi and ARj tracks in a specific frame k:

$$A(G_{ik}, AR_{jk}) = \frac{Area(G_{ik} \cap AR_{jk})}{Area(G_{ik} \cup AR_{jk})} \tag{1}$$

The temporal overlap associates AR tracks to GT tracks according to the following condition in order to find candidates for GT and AR tracks association:

$$\frac{L(G_i \cap AR_j)}{L(G_i)} \geq T_{ot} \tag{2}$$

where $L(Gi \cap Ai)$ is the number of frames of the intersection between GT track i and AR track j, $L(Gi)$ is the number of frames of GT track i and Tot is an appropriate threshold.

In the following we introduce the basic metrics used in this paper to evaluate the performance of the motion tracker.

- *False Negative (FN) o Track Detection Failure (TDF)*: a GT track will not be considered detected (i.e. track detection failure), if it satisfies any of the following conditions.
  1) a GT track i has temporal overlap smaller than Tot with any AR track j:

$$\frac{L(G_i \cap AR_j)}{L(G_i)} < T_{ot} \qquad\qquad \forall j \qquad\qquad (3)$$

  2) although a GT track i has enough temporal overlap with AR track j, it has insufficient spatial overlap with any AR tracks (smaller than Tos):

$$\frac{\sum_{k=1}^{N} A(G_{ik}, AR_{jk})}{N} < T_{OS} \qquad\qquad \forall j \qquad\qquad (4)$$

- *False Positive (FP) o False Alarm Track (FAT)*: an AR track will be not associated with any GT tracks (i.e. false alarm), if the AR track meets any of the following conditions:
  1) a AR track j has temporal overlap smaller than Tot with any GT track i:

$$\frac{L(G_i \cap AR_j)}{L(AR_i)} < T_{ot} \qquad\qquad \forall i \qquad\qquad (5)$$

  2) a AR track j does not have sufficient spatial overlap with any GT track i although it has enough temporal overlap with GT track i:

$$\frac{\sum_{k=1}^{N} A(G_{ik}, AR_{jk})}{N} < T_{OS} \qquad\qquad \forall i \qquad\qquad (6)$$

The above listed metrics have been validated in previous studies on performace evaluation of artificial vision using publicly available datasets (like PETS, i-LIDS, ETISEO, etc.).

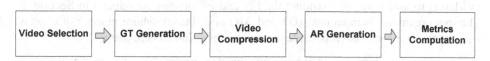

Fig. 2. Steps of the evaluation method

3   Evaluation Method

The main steps of the method used for performance evaluation are shown in Fig. 2.

In the first step (i.e. 'Video Selection') we had to collect a set of uncompressed video recordings from cameras representing a comprehensive picture of the main metro railway scenarios, that is:

- Concourse
- Platform
- Turnstiles
- Tunnel portal

Those scenarios are very diverse, going from possibly crowded areas featuring quick movements (especially near turnstiles) or almost stationary conditions (mainly in platform), to situations (i.e. tunnel portals) in which human presence is rare but false alarms can be generated by the light change of passing trains. More specifically, real footage has been selected for the duration of 1 minute, featuring:

- Concourse, 7 objects in the scene;
- Platform, simulation of object left behind;
- Turnstile, 7 objects in the scene;
- Tunnel portal, train passing.

All cameras are analogue featuring 4CIF resolution and 25FPS. The camera watching tunnel portal features an IR lamp to be able to see in very low light conditions.

In the second step (i.e. 'GT Generation') the GT has been generated using an appropriate criterion for the organisation of the information (ID and box coordinates) in the text file including for each frame the list of manually detected objects.

In the third step (i.e. 'Video Compression') the 1500 frames of the selected videos have been MJPEG compressed using the following quality levels (in percentage) and subsequent compression factors ('C'): 100% (C = 1); 50% (C ≈ 5); 20% (C ≈ 10); 10% (C ≈ 15); 5% (C ≈ 20); 1% (C ≈ 25) (see Fig. 3).

In the fourth step ('AR Generation'), videos have been analyzed by a Motion Tracker [10] identical to the one installed in the metro-railway but without using filters for alarm generation. The Motion Tracker has generated for each compression level an AR text file with detected objects, whose information was structured coherently with the ones included in the GT.

In the fifth step ('Metrics Computation'), we have applied the SW tool developed in Matlab to automatically compute the FN and FP metrics introduced in Section 2. The tool organizes its input data (GT and AR) in cell array whose number of rows is equal to the number of objects while the number of columns is 5, that is:

- The list of frames in which the object is present (i.e. the track), that is a vector whose length is equal to the number of frames of the track;
- Top-left and bottom-right coordinates of the bounding-boxes (2 vectors of length 2)

By comparing GT and AR cells, the algorithm computes the FN and FP metrics verifying conditions on temporal and spatial overlaps (*Tot* and *Tos* thresholds), as discussed in Section 2.

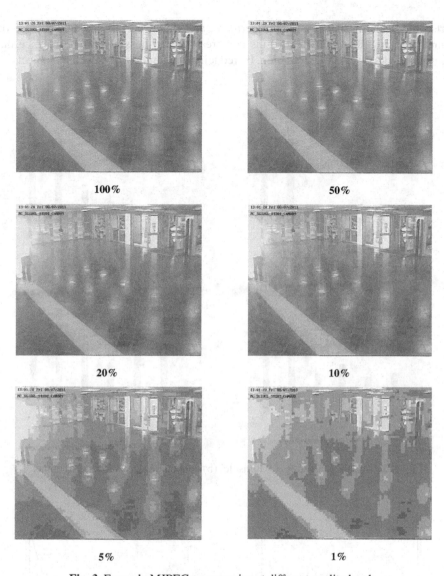

Fig. 3. Example MJPEG compression at different quality levels

4   Discussion of Results

In Fig. 4 we report the numerical results (represented by bar diagrams) of FN and FP evaluation against video compression quality, in the different scenarios, while in Fig. 5 the same results are shown by means of smoothing functions in order to highlight the trends; in fact, since algorithm adaptive thresholds are variable depending on scene characteristics (e.g. objects size, ambient light, etc.), slight unpredictable fluctuations of results around an average are possible, until the effect of compression starts predominating the results. Furthermore, and this especially evident in case of Tunnel FP, the 'filtering' effect of the compression can possibly counterbalance the negative effect of quality degradation, by reducing the number of detectable objects.

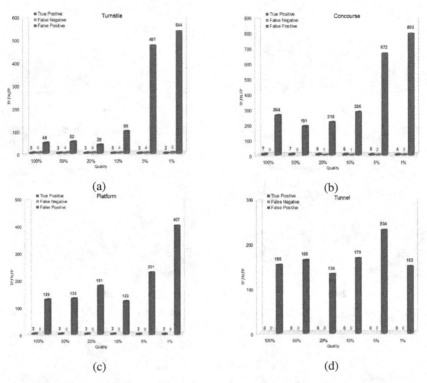

Fig. 4. TP and FP evaluation: (a) turnstile; (b) concourse; (c) platform; (d) tunnel

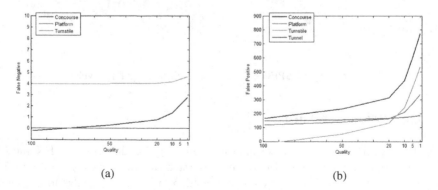

Fig. 5. False Negative (a) and False Positive (b) trends w.r.t. quality levels

As expected, tracking performance degrades generally with quality, and this has a much relevant impact at higher levels of compression, in particular when the image quality threshold is lower than 20%, that is at compression ratios higher than 10 (corresponding approximately to 4 Mbps bandwidth occupation).

Starting from those results, a more detailed analysis allowed us to discover the causes of FN and FP and their relevance at higher compression levels.

For FN, the main causes appear to be *tiling* (see Fig. 6) and *occlusions* (see Fig. 7), preventing the tracker to 'hook' the objects in the scene, and thus to track their trajectory, since their IDs change frequently as they were different objects.

For FP, there can be several possible causes (see Fig. 8), including:

- *Glare*: a strong light source saturates a certain area of the camera sensor causing charge leaks in adjacent pixels; when an object moves, the light reaching the sensor decreases suddenly and so do charge leaks, modifying the appearance of the light source even when it is not covered by any objects.
- *Light Change*: the movement of an object in an area which has a light level that is different from the rest of the scene (e.g. natural light) causes a light variation in the same area, and hence a variation in chromatic components that the Motion Tracker can associate to a new object.
- *Reflection*: such a phenomenon happens when the image of an object is reflected on the floor, generating a variation on chromatic components in that area; the consequent effect is the detection of a 'phantom' object.
- *Camouflage*: it happens when the chromatic components of object parts melt into the background so that the object is no more identified with a single box but it is partitioned into blocks featuring different identifiers.
- *Large Artefacts*: it happens when a group of adjacent pixels undergo a relevant variation of chromatic components in areas in which there is no object movement, caused by reflections or light variations generating tiling artefacts detected by the algorithm as objects.

More specifically, as shown in Fig. 9, in the Concourse all FP causes (especially glare) increase considerably with compression, while in Platform and Turnstiles the effects of artefacts is largely predominant with respect to other causes, which, however, continue to be relevant.

Tunnel FP are not reported since they feature a singular unpredictable behavior, as already shown in Fig. 4d: since there is no real object moving in the scene, they show up only at train passage due to the light change in the scene; furthemore, the absence of most chromatic components with respect to other standard cameras (IR cameras only provide greyscale images) reduces the numerosity of FP causes varying with compression levels.

Using deblocking as a pre-processing tool prior to VCA may improve the results, therefore we are going to experiment this filter on the test-set in the future. We will also add more granularity in the 20%-50% range to highlight possible non-linear behaviors.

Finally, it is important to state that the results reported above are largely conservative, since the areas of interest configured in the real installation are usually smaller; moreover, most FP are filtered at a higher level by scene calibration and by setting object size/speed thresholds to configure the VCA alarms actually active, like: person in restricted area, object left behind, platform line crossing, etc.

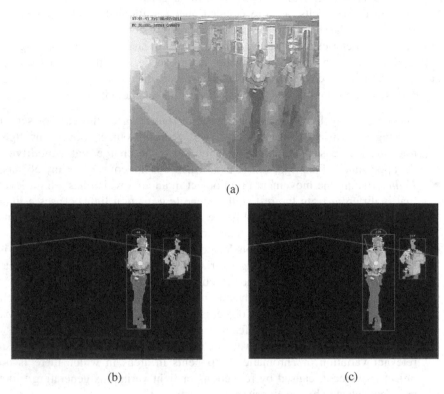

(a)

(b)   (c)

Fig. 6. Example of tiling

(a)   (b)

Fig. 7. Example of occlusion

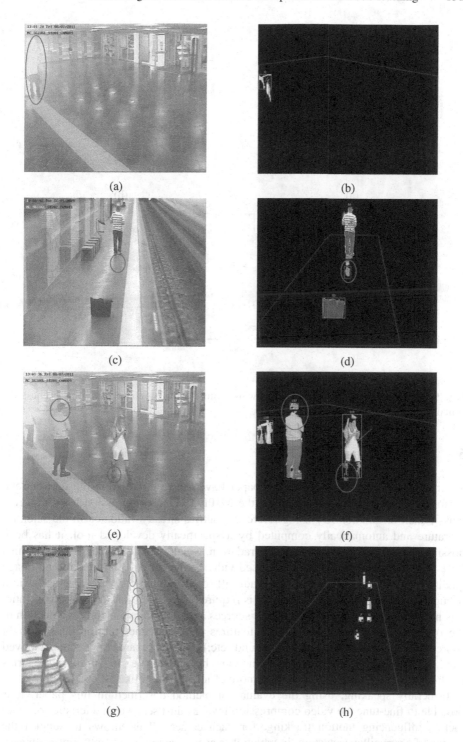

Fig. 8. FP sources: (a)(b) glare; (c)(d) reflection; (e)(f) camouflage; (g)(h) large artefacts

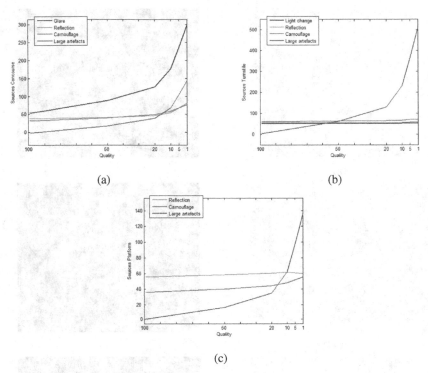

(a)   (b)

(c)

Fig. 9. Relevance of FP sources at growing compression levels in different scenes: (a) concourse; (b) turnstiles; (c) platform

5   Conclusions

The research results presented in this paper have shown the relationship between the performance of a Motion Tracker and the MJPEG video compression level in a real mass-transit installation. By using reference metrics already validated in the scientifc literature and automatically computed by a specifically developed tool, it has been possibile to evaluate a performance degradation, which is critical when passing from a 20% till a 1% quality level of compressed videos, whereas a 50% reduction on image quality representes a very acceptable trade-off (corresponding to ≈ 7 Mbps bandwidth occupation). In all the cases in which it is required to go over that 'conservative' ratio, it is necessary to evaluate how the error sources are affected in the correct detection of the objects, according to the specific features of each scene (motion density, light sources, camera shots, type of background, etc.). On this regard, the results achieved can provide some guidelines which can be applicable in similar scenarios (technologies and contexts), e.g. using more efficient codecs like HEVC.

Generally speaking, using the evaluation method described in this paper, it is possible to fine-tune the video compression level against scene characteristics or other factors influencing motion tracking, for each camera. This allows to support the design of a surveillance system, in which it is necessary to concurrently optimize a set of parameters, including the bandwidth of transmitted videos, that are the most relevant contribution in practical applications, since:

- the number of security cameras is ever growing, especially in transit applications
- VCA requirements are increasingly demanding in terms of events to be detected and expected performance

The method and tool used for the analysis provided in this paper are suitable to other evaluations, e.g. considering other quality factors (sensitivity, resolution, frame rate, etc.) or noise factors (vibrations, electro-magnetic interference, chromatic distortions, etc.). Therefore, it is possible to envisage several useful applications in industrial settings considering any other domains, like distributed urban surveillance which can be based on low-band wireless networks [6].

References

[1] Baumann, A., Boltz, M., Ebling, J., Koeing, M., Loors, H.S., Merkel, M., Niem, W., Warzelhan, J.K., Yu, J.: A Review and Comparison of Measures for Automatic Video Surveillance Systems. EURASIP Journal on Image Video Processing (June 2008)

[2] Black, J., Velastin, S.A., Boghossian, B.: A real time surveillance system for metropolitan railways. In: IEEE Conference on Advanced Video and Signal Based Surveillance, pp. 189–194 (2005)

[3] Bocchetti, G., Flammini, F., Pappalardo, A., Pragliola, C.: Dependable integrated surveillance systems for the physical security of metro railways. In: Proc. 3rd ACM/IEEE International Conference on Distributed Smart Cameras (ICDSC 2009), Como (Italy), August 30-September 2, pp. 1–7 (2009)

[4] Candamo, J., Shreve, M., Glodgof, D.B., Sapper, D.B., Kasturi, R.: Understanding Transit Scenes: A Survey on Human Behavior-Recognition Algorithms. IEEE Transactions on Intelligent Transportations Systems 11(1) (March 2010)

[5] Chang, J.-Y., Liao, H.-H., Che, L.-G.: Localized Detection of Abandoned Luggage. EURASIP Journal on Advances in Signal Processing, Article ID 675784 (2010)

[6] Flammini, F.: Critical Infrastructure Security: Assessment, Prevention, Detection, Response. WIT Press (2011)

[7] Grabner, H., Roth, P., Grabner, M., Bischof, H.: Autonomous Learning of a Robust Background Model for Change Detection. In: Proc. 9th IEEE International Workshop on Performance Evaluation of Tracking and Surveillance, pp. 39–46 (2006)

[8] Manohar, V., Soundararajan, P., Raju, H., Goldgof, D.B., Kasturi, R., Garofolo, J.S.: Performance Evaluation of Object Detection and Tracking in Video. In: Narayanan, P.J., Nayar, S.K., Shum, H.-Y. (eds.) ACCV 2006. LNCS, vol. 3852, pp. 151–161. Springer, Heidelberg (2006)

[9] Marpe, D., Wiegand, T., Sullivan, G.J.: The H.264/MPEG4 Advanced Video Coding Standard and its Applications. IEEE Communication Magazine (August 2006)

[10] Nexera Motion Tracker, http://www.nexera.it/files/VMT_110426.pdf

[11] Piñero, J.C.: Intelligent Video Results of testing 4 technologies on Madrid Metro. In: Procs. Joint UITP-CUTA International Security Conference, Montreal, Canada, November 11-12 (2009)

[12] Räty, T.: Survey on Contemporary Remote Surveillance Systems for Public Safety. IEEE Transactions on Systems, Man and Cybernetics-Part C 40(5) (September 2010)
[13] Spirito, M., Regazzoni, C.S., Marcenaro, L.: Automatic detection of dangerous events for underground surveillance. In: IEEE Conference on Advanced Video and Signal Based Surveillance, pp. 195–200 (2005)
[14] Yin, F., Makris, D., Velastin, S.A., Orwell, J.: Quantitative evaluation of different aspects of motion trackers under various challenges. In: Quantitative Evaluation of Trackers, Annual of the BMVA, vol. 2010(5) (2010)

Annotating Images with Suggestions — User Study of a Tagging System

Michal Hradiš, Martin Kolář, Aleš Láník, Jiří Král,
Pavel Zemčík, and Pavel Smrž

Faculty of Information Technology
VUT — Brno University of Technology
Brno Czech Republic

Abstract. This paper explores the concept of image-wise tagging. It introduces a web-based user interface for image annotation, and a novel method for modeling dependencies of tags using Restricted Boltzmann Machines which is able to suggest probable tags for an image based on previously assigned tags. According to our user study, our tag suggestion methods improve both user experience and annotation speed. Our results demonstrate that large datasets with semantic labels (such as in TRECVID Semantic Indexing) can be annotated much more efficiently with the proposed approach than with current class-domain-wise methods, and produce higher quality data.

Keywords: Restricted Boltzmann Machine, human-assisted learning, user interface, image tagging, crowdsourcing, image classification.

1 Introduction

Automatic or semi-automatic image tagging, classification, and semantic analysis is one of the important and open problems of the contemporary image data management.

Obtaining high-quality annotations for large image and video datasets is paramount in the area of all types of classification and especially semantic classification[1]. The annotated datasets are being used not only to learn the semantic classifiers, but they are needed also for evaluation of different approaches, and for comparisons of the results in order to reliably identify and evaluate the promising methods. We propose the idea that such datasets including large number of semantic categories could be efficiently obtained through annotation of one image or video shot at a time (*image-wise* tagging) provided the system suggests the likely tags based on the content, tags assigned to near-by images, and also based on tags already assigned to the currently annotated image or video.

---

[1] Semantic classification of images is understood as an assignment of semantic tags to images or parts of images. The tags can represent objects (e.g. car, person, building), conditions (e.g. sunny, winter, outdoor, fog), activities (e.g. singing, dancing, running), or possibly other relevant semantic categories.

J. Blanc-Talon et al. (Eds.): ACIVS 2012, LNCS 7517, pp. 155–166, 2012.

ITS (*Intelligent Tagging System*), the web-based image tagging system we implemented for this purpose, suggests tags for an image or video by modeling dependencies between tags assigned to an image using Restricted Boltzmann Machines [3] (RBM), and through utilizing tags of temporally collocated images from the same gallery. The objective of the tag suggestion methods is to allow *image-wise* tagging (assign tags to an image) rather than *class-domain-wise* tagging (assign images to a tag). According to the user testing we performed, this approach makes tagging faster, easier to use, more intuitive, and more precise. The produced dataset contains significantly more annotations of infrequent tags, since it makes tagging of rare classes more probable compared to the class-domain-wise tagging.

Several existing datasets contain enough tagged images to make learning and comparison of semantic image classifiers possible [11,4,12,6,5]. These datasets were annotated using various tagging methods, typically by creating a taxonomy and adding positive and negative examples in each class manually, or by searching on Internet and checking the search results by hand [4,12]. Each image in such datasets is assigned only to a single class, which inhibits class correlation analysis. When attempting to find tag correlations, for example for the suggestion of co-occurring tags, data generated this way cannot be used.

Alternatively, TRECVID semantic indexing dataset [9] is annotated by *Active Learning* [1] and contains annotations of possibly 500 tags for each video-shot; however, positive examples are rather sparse in this dataset. The Active Learning is a class-domain-wise annotation approach. It utilizes a network of classifiers, which are organized in such a way as to take into account a variety of low level features and descriptors. These include text, local and global visual information, as well as conceptual context. The classifiers are iteratively trained on currently available annotations and provide users with examples which would be most informative when annotated for a given tag.

Outside computer vision research, usage of visual media databases becomes more common and the amount of available content grows rapidly. Semantic information in the form of tags greatly improves the ability to search and browse such databases. As opposed to visual information, semantic information is more useful for navigation in the databases; however, it is also much harder to extract from the contents. At the present, reliable extraction of general tag-level semantic information from images is not possible, and state-of-the-art methods provide only mediocre results [9]. Reliable and broad semantic information has to be currently provided by users.

Existing media databases (e.g. Flickr and YouTube) allow users to tag the content they upload by typing words or by selecting from a list of tags automatically suggested based on previously added tags. Methods used in our image tagging system are directly applicable in such databases, and the obtained experimental results are relevant, to an extent, for such applications as well. Among others, the experiments show that tagging using the tag suggestion provides richer information, and that the users find it more pleasant and straightforward, indicating that users would be more inclined to tag content with good suggestions.

The paper first presents the description of the proposed semi-supervised prediction method and the technical description of the web user interface. The experiments and results are presented in Section 3 together with discussion of the results. Finaly, the paper is concluded in Section 4.

2   Suggestion Engine

A key part of ITS is the suggestion engine[2], which makes a prediction of likely tags, given current positive and negative tags on an image. We have combined a method with a global prior on tag co-occurrence (Restricted Boltzmann Machine), with a method for using information from tags in concurrent images (local tag suggestion). We have chosen these methods to make it possible to use the annotation system for various types of data (independent images, related images, video sequences), and in various ways to allow flexibility.

2.1   Restricted Boltzmann Machine

RBM is an undirected bipartite graphical model [3]. It defines a probability distribution over a vector of visible variables $\mathbf{v}$ and a vector of hidden variables $\mathbf{h}$. In the RBM model, the visible variables are independent of each other when the hidden variables are observed and vice versa.

For the purpose of modeling dependencies among semantic tags, the visible variables $\mathbf{v}$, each corresponding to presence of a tag, are binary. In our work, the hidden variables $\mathbf{h}$ are binary as well.

The joint probability over $\mathbf{v}$ and $\mathbf{h}$ is defined as

$$p(\mathbf{v}, \mathbf{h}) = \frac{exp(-E(\mathbf{v}, \mathbf{h}))}{Z}, \tag{1}$$

where Z is a normalization constant and E is energy function given by

$$E(\mathbf{v}, \mathbf{h}) = -\mathbf{v}^\top \mathbf{W} \mathbf{h} - \mathbf{v}^\top \mathbf{b}^v - \mathbf{h}^\top \mathbf{b}^h, \tag{2}$$

where (W) is a matrix of weights between elements of $\mathbf{v}$ and $\mathbf{h}$, and $\mathbf{b}^v$ and $\mathbf{b}^h$ are biases of visible respective hidden variables. Conditional dependencies between the visible and hidden variables are expressed as

$$p(\mathbf{h}|\mathbf{v}) = \sigma\left(\mathbf{W}\mathbf{v} - \mathbf{b}^v\right) \text{ and } p(\mathbf{v}|\mathbf{h}) = \sigma\left(\mathbf{W}^\top \mathbf{h} - \mathbf{b}^h\right), \tag{3}$$

where $\sigma()$ is a sigmoid function.

As a generative model, RBM could be trained using maximum likelihood. However, derivatives of the likelihood are intractable. To overcome this problem, Hinton [7] introduced a practical approximation called *Contrastive Divergence* (CD). The CD algorithm computes gradients for optimization as

$$\nabla \mathbf{W} = \langle \mathbf{vh} \rangle_{data} - \langle \mathbf{vh} \rangle_{recon} \tag{4}$$

$$\nabla \mathbf{b}^v = \langle \mathbf{v} \rangle_{data} - \langle \mathbf{v} \rangle_{recon} \tag{5}$$

$$\nabla \mathbf{b}^h = \langle \mathbf{h} \rangle_{data} - \langle \mathbf{h} \rangle_{recon}, \tag{6}$$

---

[2] The ITS system is available at http://medusa.fit.vutbr.cz:15161.

where $\langle.\rangle_{data}$ are expectations with respect to the distribution of data and $\langle.\rangle_{recon}$ are expectations with respect to the distribution of reconstructed data. The reconstructed data is obtained by starting with a data vector on visible variables, and sampling first from distribution $p(\mathbf{h}|\mathbf{v})$ and then $p(\mathbf{v}|\mathbf{h})$ (Equation 3).

In the context of tag suggestion, the task of RBM is to provide marginal probabilities of unobserved tags which constitute the visible variables $\mathbf{v}$ as more and more tags become observed (by actions of a user). Several algorithms could solve inference in in the RBM model. We chose *Gibbs sampling* which draws several samples from the RBM distribution. The means of marginal distributions $E(p(v_i))$ can then be computed from the the samples. Gibbs sampling starts by assigning random values to unobserved variables, and a sample is obtained by iterating between computing $p(\mathbf{h}|\mathbf{v})$ (Equation 3) and sampling from it, followed by computing $p(\mathbf{v}|\mathbf{h})$.

As it is not practical and/or desirable to obtain a large training dataset where presence or absence of all tags for all images would be known due to a large number of possible tags (hundreds or thousands), inevitably, such dataset has to have sparse annotations, and the learning algorithm has to handle situations where potentially large portion of the tags is unobserved. Several methods for handling missing training data in the context of RBM were proposed. Single missing value can be easily filled by sampling from its exact conditional distribution (it is known for single unobserved variable). More missing values can be treated in the same way as the other parameters [8] if they are updated often during learning. This approach is efficient only on training sets of limited size. Salakhundinov et al. [10] introduced a radical way of dealing with missing values by using RBMs with different numbers of visible units for different training cases. This approach is able to handle very sparse data; however, it no longer produces a single RBM model.

In our work, we decided to use Gibbs sampling to fill the unobserved values in the training data. For the CD gradients (Equation 4), the data means $\langle.\rangle_{data}$ have to be computed. This can be done by drawing samples from the distribution of the unobserved visible variables conditioned on the observed visible variables. This distribution is not known during learning of the RBM model. However, current imperfect RBM model can be used instead as an approximation. When a sample from the distribution of the visible data is obtained, the CD algorithm proceeds exactly as described in Section 2.1.

2.2   Local Tag Suggestion

Aside from the RBM suggestion method, tags are also suggested if they are positively annotated in nearby images in the gallery. A gallery is viewed as a chronological sequence, with images $\{I_i\}_{i=1}^{N}$. When generating suggestions for a given image I_i, each tag is given a weight ω, given by

$$\omega = \sum_{i=1}^{N} \frac{1}{log(|p - i| + 1)} * has\_tag(I_i), \tag{7}$$

where

$$has\_tag(I_i) = \begin{cases} 1 & \text{if the tag is positively annotated on } I_i \\ -1 & \text{if the tag is negatively annotated on } I_i \\ 0 & \text{if the tag is not annotated on } I_i \end{cases}$$

The $\frac{1}{log(|p-i|+1)}$ term ensures that closer annotations have more weight on ω, and the $has\_tag(I_i)$ term ensures that positive annotations have positive weight, negative annotations negative weight, and all others are ignored. Tags are then ordered by their ω from highest to lowest. Any tags with $\omega > 0$ are then suggested, in this order.

2.3   Integration of Suggestion and User Interface

When suggesting n tags, $\lfloor n/2 \rfloor$ are from the RBM model, $\lfloor n/2 \rfloor$ from local tag suggestion, and if n is odd the remaining one is chosen with either method with equal probability. That ensures that when only one tag is being added, neither method is favoured.

When an image is loaded, 15 tags are chosen and three annotating options are available to the user. As seen in Figure (picture of the web), they are as follows:

1. Each of the 15 suggested tags is presented with a "check" and a "cross". When clicking check, the tag is added as positive annotation, the cross adds negative annotation. When clicking either, the tag dissapears from the suggestion list, and a new one is added at the end of the list.
2. The user can use an autocompleting text field, where any typed word or part of a word is matched with all occurrences in existing tags as a substring. For example, when typing person, the user is presented with "person", "male person", "female person", and others. This ensures that when no information is given yet, the user can easily add information that's compatible with the current collection of tags in the database. When any of these is clicked, it gets added to the current suggestion, and the suggested tags are refreshed accordingly. Users are allowed to enter new tags which are not yet in the database; however, such tags are not immediately considered by the RBM model. It is more appropriate to add new tags to the RBM model when the number of positive annotations of such tags increases over certain threshold in order to prevent saturating the model by rare or otherwise irrelevant tags.
3. Given the chronological sequence of images, three preceding and three succeeding images are shown on the right. When any of these is clicked, the positive tags that have been annotated on that image are copied over to the current image, and the suggested tags are refreshed accordingly.

The suggestion operation takes on average 0.1 seconds, making the system responsive and allowing quick interaction with the user. In case of sequential video frames, this interface allows users to seamlessly copy tags from previous images to the current one, either by copying tags from the three preceding and three succeeding images, or by selecting the suggested local tags. Another use scenario

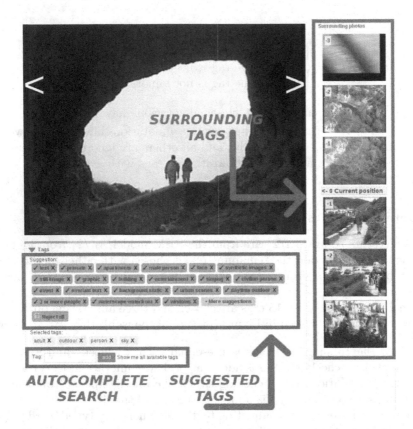

Fig. 1. Typical view of the ITS web interface. Annotation option parts are outlined in red.

is the annotation of holiday photos with recurring themes, people, and elements. In the case of unusual images and tags that are not a priory likely, the RBM suggestions may not be accurate very useful at first; however, by providing one or several tags relevant to the image (e.g. by using the autocompleting text field) will make co-occuring tags likely to be suggested.

3   Experiments and Results

In order to identify the usability and usefulness of our system, we performed two experiments with users: testing with untrained individuals with minimal support, and testing with expert annotators for an extended period of time. In order to make the test replicable, we used only images and tags[3] from the

---

[3] Examples of the classes are Actor, Airplane Flying, Bicycling, Canoe, Doorway, Ground Vehicles, Stadium, Tennis, Armed Person, Door Opening, George Bush, Military Buildings, Researcher, Synthetic Images, Underwater and Violent Action.

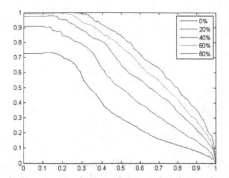

Fig. 2. Precision-Recall Curves of tag suggestion for different numbers of known tags per image. The curves are for different probabilities that the tags in the TRECVID 2011 semantic indexing dataset are known.

TRECVID 2011 Semantic Indexing task[4], and disabled the feature to add new tags.

Besides the reproducibility of the experiments by others, there are several other advantages of using the TRECVID data. A part of the data is already annotated and can be used to learn the RBM tag-dependency model. Further, the dataset was annotated by Active Learning [2] which provides a baseline for comparison.

In addition to the user study, the ability of RBM to model dependencies among tags and the ability to estimate marginal tag probabilities by Gibbs sampling was tested on the TRECVID data. This experiment gives an objective information of the RBM suggestion system alone.

3.1   RBM Suggestion

The RBM tag suggestion was tested on a training dataset for semantic indexing task from TRECVID 2011 evaluations. The dataset consists of 400 hours of video from which over 260 thousand images (key-frames) were extracted. For the dataset, 345 semantic classes were annotated by Active Learning[5] [2]. Total 14M shots-level annotations were collected (approximately 16 %). Note, that only 400 thousand of the annotations are positive. On average, there is over 1100 positive and 42 thousand negative annotations for each class. Distribution of annotations is shown in Figure 3.

The TRECVID dataset was divided into two parts. First[6] 200 thousand key-frames were used for training. From the remaining 60 thousand key-frames 20 thousand were randomly selected for testing. Key-frames from a single video were assigned exlusively to only one of the sets.

---

[4] http://www-nlpir.nist.gov/projects/tv2011/tv2011.html
[5] http://mrim.imag.fr/tvca/
[6] Videos were sorted according to their titles.

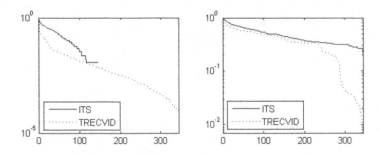

Fig. 3. Normalized numbers of positive (left), respective negative (right) annotations for classes in TRECVID 2011 semantic indexing dataset as annotated by Active Learning [1] and ITS expert users. Scales of y-axes are logarithmic

Precision-recall curves (PRC) were computed on the testing part of the dataset for for probabilities 0 %, 20 %, 40 %, 60 % and 80 % that the annotated tags are known - known tags were sampled randomly and independently for each key-frame. Note that even for the high probabilities, only a small number of tags per a key-frame are actually known due to the fact that only 53 tag annotations are available for a key-frame on average.

The optimal strength of L2 regularization (*weight decay*) and size of the hidden layer was selected by grid search using cross-validation. The CD training process iterated 20 times over the training set before terminating, and the marginal probabilities of tags on the testing set were estimated using fifty samples. The actual size of the optimal hidden layer was 64. Adding more hidden variables did not improve modeling tag dependencies, and it reduced the ability of RBM to model a priori probabilities (when no tags are known for an image).

Results in Figure 2 clearly show that the RBM combined with Gibbs sampling can utilize the information provided by the known tags, and that precision

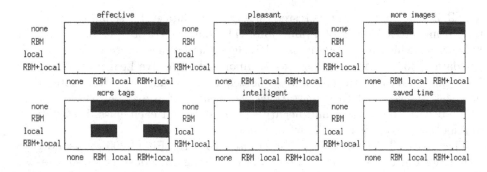

Fig. 4. Black squares represent a significantly better outcome in the user evaluation, according to the questionnaire. The questions allowed a 1 − 5 rating on effectiveness, pleasantness, amount of images, amount of tags per image, perceived method intelligence, and whether the method saved time.

significantly improves with the number of known tags. The PRC for 0 % of known tags corresponds to a priori probabilities of tags, and it exhibits the relatively good results due to unbalanced counts of positive annotations of the individual classes.

3.2 Testing by Untrained Users

10 randomly selected technical university students were asked to use 4 different tag suggestion methods using our system, with as little training as possible. The 4 methods are:

1. **none** — no suggestion method
2. **RBM** — only Restricted Boltzmann Machine suggestion (Section 2.1)
3. **local** — only local tag suggestion (Section 2.2)
4. **RBM+local** — the combination of Restricted Bolzmann Machine and local tag suggestion, as presented in section 2.3

The methods were ordered randomly and the user was not told which is which. After using each method, the user was asked to answer a questionnaire with questions regarding the rating and usability of the method, and data regarding the amount of annotations created was stored.

According to the results (Figure 5), **RBM** and **RBM+local** suggestion methods allow significantly[7] faster annotation. There were no significant differences between **RBM** and **RBM+local**, nor between **none** and **local**. According to the questionnaire, method **none** is found by the users to be significantly[8] inferior to all the other methods in almost all aspects. No other significant differences were found, except that **RBM** and **RBM+local** received better marks in the ability to facilitate annotating more tags per image compared to **local**.

3.3 Testing by Expert Users

Three expert users were asked to use the combined tag suggestion method (Section 2.3). The users previously took part in TRECVID 2011 collaborative annotations [1], and had at least two hours experience with ITS. The users spent a total of three hours annotating randomly selected videos from the TRECVID dataset.

In this setting, the number of positive and negative annotations assigned per hour was 448 and 3085 respectively, averaging 13.1 positive annotations per image. The annotating speed compares very favorably to class-domain-wise annotation for which the authors of [1] expect 2 seconds per annotation; moreover, only 2.5% of the annotations in the TRECVID 2011 SIN [9] dataset are positive. Distribution of the annotated tags is shown in Figure 3. When compared to the original distribution of tags obtained by the Active Learning method [1], the ITS tags have a heavier tail distribution for both positive (kurtosis 8.35 in TRECVID and 4.18 by ITS), and negative annotations (kurtosis 2.18 in TRECVID and 1.98 by ITS).

---

[7] Using the paired t-test at the 10% significance level.
[8] Using the Mann-Whitney U test at the 10% significance level.

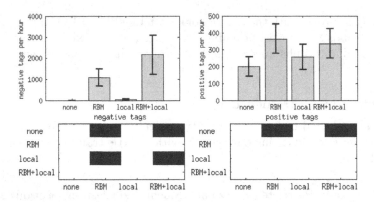

Fig. 5. The top graphs show the mean number of tags assigned per hour with confidence intervals at 90% significance level. The bottom graphs show black squares where the column methods annotate significantly more tags per hour than the row methods.

3.4   Discussion

According to the distribution of tags obtained by ITS (Figure 3), infrequent classes are more likely to get tagged with this method than with class-domain-wise Active Learning [1]. One of the probable causes is that users are able to assign the most relevant tags to images using the autocompleting text field even though the tags are not suggested. This is a clear advantage, as positive examples of less frequent classes are hard to obtain by Active Learning, which forces users to asses a huge number of almost random images for each of the infrequent classes. This effect would be even more pronounced if the set of annotated tags was larger.

Another problem of the class-domain-wise Active Learning is that the underlying classifiers may drift according to early examples to a specific type of images which are not representative of a whole class. For example, consider the first annotated images for a dog class happen to be grayscale. The classifier could focus on the color in such case, and it may never recover. The **local** suggestion method does not exhibit this type of issues. The RBM model could learn inaccurate a priori probabilities on early examples. However, these inaccurate a priori probabilities will get corrected: as tags become more likely, they are more likely to be suggested, and consequently they will become more likely annotated as negative.

In our experiments, previously annotated data is used to overcome the cold start problem. If such data was not available, the RBM model could be initialized according to a text corpus. However, it would be feasible to start without any tag dependency knowledge at all, as the **local** suggestion method already allows good suggestions in many situations. Only the speed of annotation would be negatively affected in such case. We suspect that the TRECVID Semantic Indexing (SIN) 2011 dataset does not allow the RBM model to provide as good suggestions as could be reached due to very sparse positive annotations, and we expect that speed of annotation would increase if more densely annotated dataset was used.

In TRECVID SIN, the annotated objects are short video shots. In the class-domain-wise Active Learning [1], a single shot is assessed multiple times by different users for different tags. To make the annotations highly reliable, the assessors would have to view a video-shot again for each annotated tag. Viewing each shot would be very time-consuming. On the other hand, extending ITS to video-shots would introduce only minor overhead, as a shot has to be viewed only once to annotate all tags.

4   Conclusion

We created a system for human-assisted image-wise annotation with tag suggestions which could be used to obtain large semantically labeled datasets. The suggestion methods, as well as the annotating system itself, could be applied in the context of public media databases.

According to the experiments, the proposed method for modeling dependencies of tags using RBM is able to utilize previously assigned tags and estimate marginal probabilities of other tags. Both suggestion methods improve user experience when annotating images, and the RBM model and its combination with local tag suggestion improve annotation speed as well. Experienced users are able to produce positive annotations at a much faster rate using ITS compared to class-domain-wise Active Learning [1]. In addition, the obtained annotations contain a higher percentage of positive examples of infrequent classes.

As a future work we intend to combine ITS with research in image feature extraction and semantic image classification [9]. The RBM suggestion method can be extended to integrate information from the assigned tags with visual information, so that suggestions are made more reliable, especially when no tags are yet assigned. A natural way to combine the information is, for instance, provided by Conditional-RBM models [8]. Further, the current local tag suggestion method could be given a stronger foundation by being integrated in the probabilistic suggestion model as well.

Acknowledgements. This work has been supported by EU-7FP-IST - GLO-CAL - EEU - 248984, and BUT FIT grant No. FIT-11-S-2, and Research and Development Council of the Czech Republic - CEZ MMT, MSM0021630528.

References

1. Ayache, S.: Video corpus annotation using active learning. In: 30th European Proceedings of the IR research (2008)
2. Ayache, S., Quénot, G.: Evaluation of active learning strategies for video indexing. Signal Processing: Image Communication 22(7-8), 692–704 (2007)
3. Carreira-Perpinan, M.A., Hinton, G.E.: On Contrastive Divergence Learning. In: Cowell, R.G., Ghahramani, Z. (eds.) Artificial Intelligence and Statistics, Society for Artificial Intelligence and Statistics, p. 17. Citeseer (2005)

4. Deng, J., Dong, W., Socher, R., Li, L.-j., Li, K., Li, F-f.: ImageNet: A Large-Scale Hierarchical Image Database, pp. 2–9
5. Everingham, M., Gool, L., Williams, C.K.I., Winn, J., Zisserman, A.: The Pascal Visual Object Classes (VOC) Challenge. International Journal of Computer Vision 88(2), 303–338 (2009)
6. Griffin, G., Holub, A.: Caltech-256 object category dataset (2007)
7. Hinton, G.E.: Training products of experts by minimizing contrastive divergence. Neural Computation 14(8), 1771–1800 (2002)
8. Hinton, G.E., Osindero, S., Teh, Y.-W.: A fast learning algorithm for deep belief nets. Neural Computation 18(7), 1527–1554 (2006)
9. Over, P., Awad, G., Michel, M., Fiscus, J., Kraaij, W., Smeaton, A.F., Quéenot, G.: TRECVID 2011 – An Overview of the Goals, Tasks, Data, Evaluation Mechanisms and Metrics. In: Proceedings of TRECVID 2011. NIST, USA (2011)
10. Salakhutdinov, R., Mnih, A., Hinton, G.: Restricted Boltzmann machines for collaborative filtering. In: Proceedings of the 24th International Conference on Machine Learning, pp. 791–798 (2007)
11. Smith, J.R., Naphade, M., Tesic, J., Chang, S.-f., Hsu, W.: Standards Large-Scale Concept Ontology for Multimedia. Evaluation, 86–91 (2006)
12. Torralba, A., Fergus, R., Freeman, W.T.: 80 Million Tiny Images: a Large Data Set for Nonparametric Object and Scene Recognition. IEEE Transactions on Pattern Analysis and Machine Intelligence 30(11), 1958–1970 (2008)

Cross-Channel Co-occurrence Matrices for Robust Characterization of Surface Disruptions in $2^1/_2$D Rail Image Analysis*

Daniel Soukup and Reinhold Huber-Mörk

Safety & Security Department
Research Area Intelligent Vision Systems
Austrian Institute of Technology
{daniel.soukup,reinhold.huber}@ait.ac.at

Abstract. We present a new robust approach to the detection of rail surface disruptions in high-resolution images by means of $2^1/_2$D image analysis. The detection results are used to determine the condition of rails as a precaution to avoid breaks and further damage. Images of rails are taken with color line scan cameras at high resolution of about 0.2 millimeters under specific illumination to enable $2^1/_2$D image analysis. Pixel locations fulfilling the anti-correlation property between two color channels are detected and integrated over regions of general background deviations using so called cross-channel co-occurrence matrices, a novel variant of co-occurrence matrices introduced as part of this work. Consequently, the detection of rail surface disruptions is achieved with high precision, whereas the unintentional elimination of valid detections in the course of false and irrelevant detection removal is reduced. In this regard, the new approach is more robust than previous methods.

1   Introduction

Rails need to be inspected regularly to determine the condition of the material. This is an indispensable precaution in order to be able to take action timely to avoid severe rail damage and therefore possible train accidents. Originally, this inspection was conducted by humans by visual and acoustical means (hammer sounding). Later automated inspection was based on ultrasonic or magnetic sensors, X-ray, etc., e.g. [5]. These first automated methods offered the possibility to detect material defects in the inner of the rail body.

Recently, automated vision inspection systems have been deployed. A vision based system for image based inspection of clips holding the rail track was presented in [9] and image based detection of general rail defects is described in [6]. Even though automated visual inspection systems are restricted to the view onto

* This work is supported by the Austrian Federal Ministry for Transport, Innovation and Technology BMVIT, program line I2V "Intermodalität und Interoperabilität von Verkehrssystemen", project fractINSPECT.

J. Blanc-Talon et al. (Eds.): ACIVS 2012, LNCS 7517, pp. 167–177, 2012.

surfaces, they facilitate a higher resolution inspection and thus even the detection of small (surface) defects. Especially, in the analysis of rail wear resulting from rolling contact fatigue (RCF) [1], automated visual inspection seems to be an appropriate approach. RCF evokes so called spallings and headchecks, which emerge from small break outs on the rail surface[12]. Spallings and headchecks are commonly regarded to be preliminary stages of cracks and even rail breaks. Precisely, the robust detection of such rail surface disruptions is the goal of the actual work.

Our ideas are based on a previous paper [4] dealing with a wider range of visual rail surface analysis techniques. We focus on one special aspect of this earlier work, which comprises the $2^1/_2$D analysis of rail images taken under special illumination conditions in order to detect rail surface disruptions, i.e. spallings and headchecks (Section 2 gives a detailed introduction to $2^1/_2$D image analysis). Our goal was to find a more robust detection algorithm, namely robust in the sense of detection accuracy. In order that, we extended the mathematical treatment in a certain way to achieve this goal. The principle of the analysis of reflection properties in the presented $2^1/_2$D analysis is related to the shape from shading (SFS) and photometric stereo (PS) methods. SFS deals with the determination of three-dimensional shape from a single image irradiance, whereas in PS the shading based reconstruction is based on two or more images [7]. Recently, a method similar to our approach of $2^1/_2$D analysis was used for solder paste inspection [8]. An experimental study on specular reflection from metallic surfaces and application to coin classification is discussed in [3].

This paper is organized as follows: Section 2 gives an overview on the image acquisition setup and introduces the central term of anti-correlation. In Sect. 3, we derive the new criterion for rail disruption detection, including the image preprocessing and the definition of the novel cross-channel co-occurrence matrices. We present results on detection results and the analysis of structures in cross-channel co-occurrence matrices in Sect. 4 and conclude in Sect. 5.

2 $2^1/_2$D Image Analysis and Anti-correlation

$2^1/_2$D means that information about distortions on a rail surface are to be detected, whereas these distortions (e.g. spallings and headchecks) are not measured in a complete 3D sense. That is, we are not interested in the actual depth measures of such distortions, but simply want to assess their existence. We do this by means of a special configuration of differently colored light sources and a color line scan camera.

Illuminating line light sources are placed parallel to the line scan camera. The lights and the camera itself are mounted on a railway vehicle and oriented orthogonal to the rail direction. The setup is shown in Fig.1(a). It is based on a dark-field illumination principle, i.e. for undistorted surface patches only a small amount of light is reflected towards the sensor, whereas surface disruptions typically cause reflections. The image resolution is approximately 0.2 millimeters.

One light source, e.g. a red one, is placed in front and another light source, e.g. the blue one, is placed behind the line scan camera with respect to the

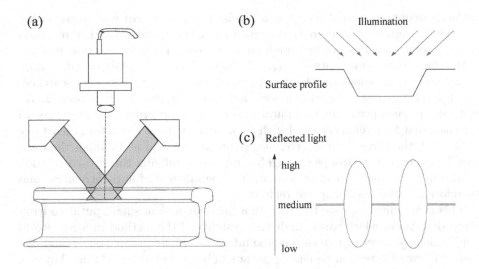

Fig. 1. Acquisition setup and model of reflection properties: (a) top-down view of the head surface using a line camera and illumination by different line light sources under oblique angles, (b) distorted surface profile into driving direction and direction of sources of illumination, (c) model of reflectance for a distorted surface profile

driving direction. The angle of specular reflection from undistorted rail surfaces into the camera is avoided [3] and strong reflections and shadows are observed in cases of surface disruptions only. The expected reflection properties due to a surface distortion, i.e. a spalling, is shown in Fig.1 (b). Light from two spectral channels, e.g. from a blue light source at the left and a red light source on the right, approach the object surface at oblique angles. The shown surface profile is taken along the rail direction. Due to the dominating specular reflection on metal surfaces light in the red channel is typically strongly reflected back to the camera when hitting the left edge of the surface disruption, see Fig.1 (c). On the other hand, no specular reflection happens in the red channel on the edge on the right. The blue channel shows an opposite behavior when compared to the red channel, this property is termed *anti-correlation*.

Note that the color line scan camera is mounted orthogonally to the rail direction. Correspondingly, in the acquired images, disruptions appear (according to the anti-correlation model) as pixel configurations with a bright bluish image region in the upper part (with respect to the image coordinates) and a bright reddish area in the lower part of the disruption's image region.

3   Robust Characterization of Rail Surface Disruptions by Means of Anti-correlation

A primary method to characterize the occurrence of pixel configurations exhibiting the anti-correlation property was presented in [4]. In that approach, the rail surface disruptions were detected in a pixel-wise manner. For each pixel with a sufficiently high $b - r$ (blue-red) difference (high blue pixel value, low red pixel value), a corresponding pixel with a high $r - b$ (red-blue) difference was searched in the same pixel column, just $d = 1, ..., 6$ pixels adjacent in rail driving direction, i.e. adjacent lines below. In other words, pixel pair configurations were searched, which fulfill the anti-correlation model that has been introduced in Sect. 2. We will refer to such pixel pair configurations as *anti-correlation configurations*. In the case, that for a reference pixel such a configuration was found for at least one value of d, the corresponding reference pixel was marked as fulfilling the anti-correlation property. Groups of neighboring pixels fulfilling the anti-correlation condition were combined to regions with a high degree of anti-correlation and therefore classified as disruption regions.

This proceeding is prone to generate a huge amount of small, putative irrelevant detections, which would limit the usability of the method in a real world application. In order to reduce the amount of these false alarms, one would discard very small detection regions by means of some area thresholding. Anyway, in doing so one would possibly oversee disruptions comprised of a set of small, separated, single anti-correlation regions, which – standing singularly – would be ignored due to the area thresholding.

A more robust approach would integrate detection results over meaningful regions, so that anti-correlation regions with a mutual relation to each other are treated together. Such a relation must be some additional information, which complements the information of local presence of anti-correlation. In this way, accidental discarding of putative irrelevant detections can be attenuated. Additionally, these integration regions would represent a prior estimate about the expectable extent of a disruption region, which allows for flexible variations of distance values d.

In the actual work, we introduce such additional information of mutual relation in form of deviations from the local background. A surface disruption primarily shows up as a deviation from the local background in the image. According to the model, at least some parts of a deviation due to a surface disruption exhibit anti-correlation configurations. These could be a set of distributed small spots, which are prone to be eliminated as irrelevant when considered as single detections. Using the information of background deviation clings all occurrences of anti-correlation configurations regarding the same disruption together, no matter if these configuration regions are adjacent. This proceeding increases the probability for small relevant detections to come through the elimination process. In this manner, a background deviation object is considered a rail surface disruption, if a significant amount of member pixels of that deviation region displays the anti-correlation model.

We arrange the presentation of the entire process into the following three steps, each of which being treated in a particular section.

1. Determine background deviations (Sect. 3.1),
2. measure the amount of anti-correlation configurations for each of the background deviation regions (Sect. 3.2),

3. draw final decision, if deviation is a disruption, on basis of frequencies of anti-correlation configurations in each background deviation region (Sect. 3.3).

3.1 Determining Background Deviations

The local image background is computed as the convolution of the original image I with a large averaging filter h, i.e. $I_B = I * h$. In the used data, a 21×21 box filter showed satisfying results. The background image I_B is then subtracted from the original image I giving the deviation image $(I_D = I - I_B)$. Actually, $I_D = I - I_B - 5$ to be sure to separate the deviation regions distinctly from each other with zero areas. The resulting difference image I_D is comprised of the background deviations. By means of a connected-component extraction algorithm, applied to the luminance image of I_D, we extracted the deviation regions, and evaluated the amount of anti-correlation configurations within their region boundaries in I_D.

3.2 Measuring the Amount of Anti-correlation Configurations

As a measure of the score of anti-correlation configurations in a region of interest, we determine the relative frequencies of pixel pairs within the region, which fulfill the anti-correlation condition, i.e.

1. both pixels are within the region of interest,
2. both pixels are in the same column but in different lines,
3. the upper pixel is significantly more blue than red,
4. the lower pixel, at the same time, is significantly more red than blue.

That means, we are interested in counting vertical pixel pair configurations showing the co-occurrence of an upper blue and a lower red pixel partner. Recall that the anti-correlation property appears along rail driving direction, which means vertically in the image columns in consequence of the setup of the light sources and the line scan camera.

A classical method for representing the co-occurrence of special brightness configurations of pixel pairs in image patches is the *co-occurrence matrix* [2]. Usually, it is used for texture description in gray-scale images. For a special gray-scale image patch G and a fixed pixel distance d, a gray-scale co-occurrence matrix[1] may be expressed in a non-normalized form as[2]

$$P_d(v_1, v_2) = |\{((k, l), (m, n)) \in G \times G :$$
$$m - k = d, l = n, \tag{1}$$
$$I(k, l) \in I(v_1), I(m, n) \in I(v_2)\}| \; ,$$

where $|\{...\}|$ refers to set cardinality and $I(v_1)$, $I(v_2)$ are brightness value intervals. Using intervals of brightness values rather than individual brightness values

---

[1] The notation corresponds to [10].

[2] In the original formulation, co-occurrence matrices also depend on an angle ϕ, which indicates in which direction d is meant. In our application, only the vertical direction is of interest, why we omit the use of ϕ in our descriptions.

is reasonable, because co-occurrence matrices dealing with individual brightness values are very large (e.g. 255×255). Moreover, the handling of configurations in such a brightness resolution is unnecessary. Hence, a disjoint partition $\mathcal{P}$ of intervals is defined on the set of brightness values, which corresponds to a quantization of the range of brightness values. In this way, the co-occurrence matrices become smaller ($|\mathcal{P}| \times |\mathcal{P}|$), thus easier manageable and evaluable. According to this notation, $I(v)$ corresponds to an interval, for which $I(v) \in \mathcal{P} \wedge v \in I(v)$.

However, $P_d(v_1, v_2)$ describes how frequently two pixels with gray-levels in $I(v_1)$, $I(v_2)$ appear in the region G. In order to fit our problem at hand, we propose to use the concept of co-occurrence matrices to describe the frequencies of anti-correlation configurations of the extracted regions of interest (G) for characterization of rail surface disruptions. Thus we introduce *cross-channel co-occurrence matrices* for color images (see (2)), in which co-occurrences in two different color channels, particularly differences of color channels ($b-r$ and $r-b$), are considered, rather than only in one gray-scale image.

$$C_d(v_1, v_2) = |\{((k,l),(m,n)) \in G \times G :$$
$$m - k = d, l = n, \tag{2}$$
$$I_D^{b-r}(k,l) \in I_D^{b-r}(v_1), I_D^{r-b}(m,n) \in I_D^{r-b}(v_2)\}| \quad ,$$

where I_D^{b-r} is the difference of the blue color channel of I_D minus its red color channel, and I_D^{r-b} is the $r - b$ color channel difference of I_D. $I_D^{b-r}(v_1)$, $I_D^{r-b}(v_2)$ are intervals of a corresponding disjoint partition $\mathcal{C}$ of the set of difference values between two color channels. As we are interested in analyzing high difference values, we only treat positive difference values, i.e. $[0, 255]$, and crop negative differences to zero.

The presented definitions of co-occurrence matrices so far describe absolute frequencies of pixel configurations. Yet, deviation regions are of different sizes. To be able to compare co-occurrence matrices for regions of different sizes, we need to normalize $C_d(v_1, v_2)$ by its matrix sum (i.e. the total amount of pixel configuration pairs considered), giving a cross-channel co-occurrence matrix of relative frequencies:

$$\bar{C}_d(v_1, v_2) = \frac{C_d(v_1, v_2)}{\sum_{i,j} C_d(i,j)} \quad . \tag{3}$$

$\bar{C}_d(v_1, v_2)$ reflects the relative frequencies of pixel configurations in G for one fixed pixel distance d. Rail surface disruptions can comprise anti-correlation configurations for a variety of distances d. Therefore, for each region of interest, we compute a set of matrices $\bar{C}_d(v_1, v_2)$, where $d = 1, ..., d_{max}$ and d_{max} is the maximal vertical distance of pixel configurations in that region of interest. Then we compute the average over all these matrices, in which way we take account for any possible anti-correlation configuration distance d:

$$\bar{C}(v_1, v_2) = \frac{1}{d_{max}} \sum_{d=1}^{d_{max}} \bar{C}_d(v_1, v_2) \quad . \tag{4}$$

3.3   Rail Disruption Criterion

With the cross-channel co-occurrence matrix $\bar{C}$ (see (4)), we have generated a tool for determining the relative frequencies of anti-correlation configurations that are present in a region G of I_D. As anti-correlation is the co-occurrence of high $b - r$ values and high $r - b$ values in distance d, one would expect to measure a significant amount of entries apart from the first few lines and first few columns only for disruption regions. Consequently, the criterion to characterize disruptions is based on the sum of entries in a right, lower sub-matrix of $\bar{C}$:

$$G \text{ is surface disruption if } \left(\sum_{i=i_0}^{n} \sum_{j=j_0}^{n} \bar{C}(i,j) \right) > t \, , \qquad (5)$$

where $i_0 > 1$, $j_0 > 1$ (usually $i_0 = j_0$), and $i = 1$, $j = 1$ indicate the first line and column of $\bar{C}$, respectively. t is a threshold value, that has been determined in experiments (see Sect. 4).

Originally, we expected to observe more distinct structures in $\bar{C}$ in the case of disruptions. E.g., a concentration of high frequencies on the right lower diagonal, because our idea of the anti-correlation model was more symmetrical. However, we could not detect any other structures except the significant amount of relative frequencies in the right, lower sub-matrix. A statistical analysis on the structure of cross-channel co-occurrence matrices of rail surface disruptions will be presented in Sect. 4.

4   Results

4.1   Detection of Rail Surface Disruptions

We demonstrate the results of the proposed method by means of an example image of a piece of rail that comprises a lot of surface disruptions. Experiments have been performed in order to determine a reasonable parameter setting for the threshold parameter t in (5), which is our criterion for characterizing rail surface disruptions. No ground truth information was given, hence, no objective target results were available, on the basis of which an optimization algorithm could have been applied. Consequently, the results have been evaluated by human visual judgment in a way that the detection results are acceptable. The partition of the set of brightness difference values was set to 8 equidistant, disjoint intervals yielding 8×8 cross-channel co-occurrence matrices $\bar{C}$. The parameters i_0, j_0 defining the size of the right, lower sub matrix of $\bar{C}$ were determined by analyzing samples of $\bar{C}$. For the given partition of 8 equidistant brightness intervals it became apparent that $i_0 = j_0 = 2$. The best result has been found for $t = 0.015$. t corresponds with the proportion of entries in the sub-matrix relatively to the overall entries in $\bar{C}$. From $t = 0.015$, one can see that this amount is very small even in the cases of actual disruptions. Anyway, the criterion correctly discriminates disruptions and non-disruptions on the basis of these parameters. Once more, we want to emphasize that, due to the absence of ground truth information, the determination of t has been accomplished only by human visual judgement. For $t = 0.015$ all relevant disruptions in the data have been detected, while the rate of erroneously as disruptions misclassified non-disruptions was negligible.

Figure 2 shows an example result image, which displays approximately a $3cm \times 3cm$ detail of a rail head. The blue lines to the right stem from grinding, which is a maintenance activity for rails, whereas the large purple area on the left is the rail/train contact area. The surface disruptions that have to be detected appear in the contact area due to RCF. Bounding boxes of detected deviations have been overlaid over the original rail image I. For those deviations in the green rectangles, criterion (5) is fulfilled. Hence, they are considered disruptions. It is distinctly perceivable that the disruptions show a lot of vertical blue-red pixel configurations corresponding to our model of anti-correlation. There are small, single anti-correlation regions in Fig. 2 that are not indicated as deviations at all. These have fallen victim to the false alarm elimination procedure, because they where not part of a significant large background deviation region.

Figure 3 shows three examples of disruptions consisting of several separated anti-correlation configuration areas. These examples demonstrate that the goal of generating connecting relations between separated anti-correlation regions has been achieved. Thus making the detection procedure more robust against over-seeing disruptions comprised of a set of small, separated, single anti-correlation regions, which could unintentionally be deleted in the course of elimination of non relevant, small detection areas.

4.2   Structures in Cross-Channel Co-occurrence Matrices

We have already mentioned that we also expected to observe more distinct, spatial structures in cross-channel co-occurrence matrices reflecting the structure of disruptions in some way. Thus we analyzed the co-occurrence matrices, that have correctly been classified as surface disruptions on the basis of criterion (5), by applying a principle components analysis (PCA) to them, corresponding the approach of eigen faces [11]. In Fig. 4, the first 6 "eigen(-cross-channel)-co-occurrence" matrices (regarding the 6 highest eigen values) are given. Except the fact, that there are distinctly perceivable entries in the right, lower sub matrices of these eigen matrices, we could not find any higher structures. This is an interesting observation, anyway, the relatively simple criterion (5) works quite satisfactorily. For the sake of completeness, we mention that the corresponding eigen matrices for the non-disruptions exhibit almost no significant entries in the right, lower sub matrices. However, this is not a surprise as the classification was based on this very criterion.

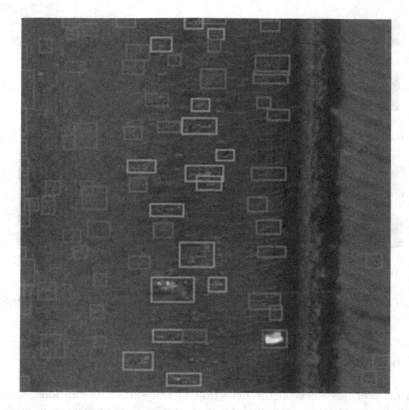

Fig. 2. Detection results for rail surface disruptions. Green rectangles indicate background deviations comprising a significant amount of anti-correlation configurations (i.e. surface disruptions), whereas red rectangles indicate general background deviations (often a result of texture resulting from uneven textured surface structure). Small unmarked anti-correlation configuration regions were ignored as part of the false alarm elimination procedure, because they were too small and not part of any bigger background deviation.

Fig. 3. Examples of deviations that have been classified as rail surface disruptions and consist of several separated anti-correlation regions

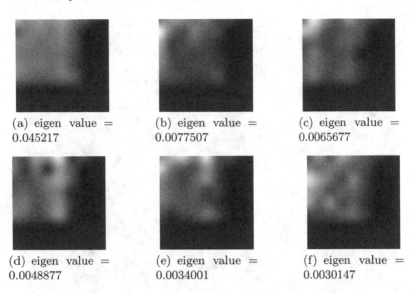

(a) eigen value = 0.045217

(b) eigen value = 0.0077507

(c) eigen value = 0.0065677

(d) eigen value = 0.0048877

(e) eigen value = 0.0034001

(f) eigen value = 0.0030147

Fig. 4. (a)-(f) The first 6 "eigen cross-channel co-occurrence" matrices determined from the set of all disruptions by PCA

5   Conclusion

Based on previous work on the detection of rail surface disruptions, we have presented a more robust approach to characterize the appearance of such disruptions. The images are taken in a specific setup of a color line scan camera and two light sources of different colors, which are mounted in different angles with respect to the rail surface. In the resulting dark-field images, rail surface disruptions have a specific appearance, a combination of bluish and reddish pixel configurations, according to the two light sources. We have illustrated a new, more robust method to exploit these pixel constellations. The originally more pixel-based method has been extended to integrate detections over meaningful regions of background deviations, which makes the algorithm more robust against the unintentional elimination of valid detection results in the course of putative irrelevant detection removal. This region integration process has been realized by the application of cross-channel co-occurrence matrices, a multi-spectral extension of classical gray-scale co-occurrence matrices we have introduced. The experimental results show, that the detection as well the integration work satisfactorily. Hence, the co-occurrence based approach to rail surface detection is more suitable in a real world application. Nonetheless, the new algorithm represents a specific adaption of the surface detection method, which has not yet been compared to other possible approaches. Thus future work will focus on finding alternative solutions and on comparing them with the cross-channel co-occurrence matrix method.

References

1. Doherty, A., Clark, S., Care, R., Dembowsky, M.: Why rails crack. Ingenia (23), 23–28 (June 2005)
2. Haralick, R.M., Shanmugam, K., Dinstein, I.: Textural features for image classification. IEEE Transactions on Systems, Man, and Cybernetics 3(6), 610–621 (1973)
3. Hoßfeld, M., Chu, W., Adameck, M., Eich, M.: Fast 3D-vision system to classify metallic coins by their embossed topography. Electronic Letters on Computer Vision and Image Analysis 5(4), 47–63 (2006)
4. Huber-Mörk, R., Nölle, M., Oberhauser, A., Fischmeister, E.: Statistical Rail Surface Classification Based on 2D and 2.5D Image Analysis. In: Blanc-Talon, J., Bone, D., Philips, W., Popescu, D., Scheunders, P. (eds.) ACIVS 2010, Part I. LNCS, vol. 6474, pp. 50–61. Springer, Heidelberg (2010)
5. Jarmulak, J., Kerckhoff, E.J.H., van't Veen, P.P.: Case-based reasoning for interpretation of data from non-destructive testing. Engineering Applications of Artificial Intelligence (4), 401–417 (2001)
6. Khandogin, I., Kummert, A., Maiwald, D.: Nonlinear image processing for automatic inspection of railroad lines. In: Proceedings of IEEE Workshop on Nonlinear Signal and Image Processing, vol. 1 (1997)
7. Klette, R., Schlüns, K., Koschan, A.: Shape from Shading. In: Computer Vision: Three-Dimensional Data from Images, ch. 7, pp. 263–300. Springer (1998)
8. Pang, G.K., Chu, M.H.: Automated optical inspection of solder paste based on 2.5D visual images. In: Proceedings of International Conference on Mechatronics and Automation, pp. 982–987 (2009)
9. Singh, M., Singh, S., Jaiswal, J., Hempshall, J.: Autonomous rail track inspection using vision based system. In: Proceedings of International Conference on Computational Intelligence for Homeland Security and Personal Safety, pp. 56–59 (2006)
10. Sonka, M., Hlavac, V., Boyle, R.: Co-occurrence Matrices. In: Image Processing, Analysis, and Machine Vision, 3rd edn., ch. 15.1.2, pp. 723–725. Thomson (2008)
11. Turk, M.A., Pentland, A.P.: Eigenfaces for recognition. Journal of Cognitive Neuroscience 3(1), 71–86 (1991)
12. Zacher, M., Baumann, G., Le, R.: Modelle zur Prognose von Rollkontaktermüdungsschäden an Schienen. EI - Der Eisenbahningenieur 60(7), 44–52 (2009)

Improving HOG with Image Segmentation: Application to Human Detection

Yainuvis Socarrás Salas[1,2], David Vázquez Bermudez[1,2],
Antonio M. López Peña[1,2], David Gerónimo Gomez[1,2], and Theo Gevers[1,3]

[1] Computer Vision Center, Universitat Autónoma de Barcelona, Spain
[2] Department of Computer Science, Universitat Autónoma de Barcelona, Spain
[3] Informatics Institute, Faculty of Science, University of Amsterdam, The Netherlands
{ysocarras,dvazquez,antonio,dgeronimo}@cvc.uab.es,
th.gevers@uva.nl

Abstract. In this paper we improve the *histogram of oriented gradients* (HOG), a core descriptor of state-of-the-art object detection, by the use of higher-level information coming from image segmentation. The idea is to re-weight the descriptor while computing it without increasing its size. The benefits of the proposal are two-fold: (i) to improve the performance of the detector by enriching the descriptor information and (ii) take advantage of the information of image segmentation, which in fact is likely to be used in other stages of the detection system such as candidate generation or refinement.

We test our technique in the INRIA person dataset, which was originally developed to test HOG, embedding it in a human detection system. The well-known segmentation method, mean-shift (from smaller to larger super-pixels), and different methods to re-weight the original descriptor (constant, region-luminance, color or texture-dependent) has been evaluated. We achieve performance improvements of 4.47% in detection rate through the use of differences of color between contour pixel neighborhoods as re-weighting function.

1 Introduction

Vision-based human detection is a key component in fields such as advanced driving assistance [14,8,12] and video surveillance [21,17,27]. Detecting people in images represents a challenging task given their intra-class variability, the diversity of backgrounds and the different image acquisition conditions. Nowadays, even detecting non-occluded standing persons is still a hot topic of research. As can be seen in [14], building a vision-based human detector requires to develop different modules. In this work we want to improve human detection by focusing on *classification*, i.e., on building a classifier that given an image window decides if it contains a person or not.

Nowadays, most successful classification processes for human detection follow the learning-from-examples paradigm [14,8], where core ingredients are the set of *descriptors* used to represent the humans as well as the learning algorithm itself. Indeed, finding good sets of descriptors for developing a human classifier is a major key for its success. Different sets try to exploit (combinations of) cues as shape and texture [28,7], even adding motion and depth [9,27]. Among all possible sets of descriptors, one that is being specially useful for building human detectors (and object detectors in general) is

J. Blanc-Talon et al. (Eds.): ACIVS 2012, LNCS 7517, pp. 178–189, 2012.
© Springer-Verlag Berlin Heidelberg 2012

the so-called HOG, i.e., the histograms of oriented gradients. This descriptor was proposed in [6] for building a holistic classifier, using linear support vector machines (linear SVM) as learning algorithm. HOG still remains as a competitive baseline method for comparison with new human classifiers [8,7]. Although HOG descriptors capture the shape of the humans in a dense way, i.e., the positive weights learnt when using a linear classifier resemble the human silhouette, they are also affected by local noise and texture given that gradient is a local measure. On the other hand, there are works that explicitly exploit the human's shape either holistically [13] or in part-based approaches [22]. In this cases, however, the image pixels out of the silhouette are not taken into account, i.e., there is not such a non-human class.

In this work, we aim to enhance human silhouette orientations, without explicitly computing such silhouettes, but using information not as local as the own gradient magnitude. Thus, we propose to use image segmentation to obtain image segments (or regions) with their corresponding frontiers, in order to later re-weight the HOG descriptor according to this frontier information as well as appearance differences between the segments.

The inspiration for this proposal comes from two sources. The first is the idea of using appearance information, whose importance in object detection has been widely demonstrated [26,28], and specially the idea of combining cues with the HOG descriptor, e.g., co-occurrence HOG [29], color HOG [24], etc. It has been largely demonstrated by the proposal of different descriptors that appearance is an important cue for object detection. The second source is the increasing trend of using segmentation for both detection and segmentation, which in our case has the potential of highlighting the shape of the human. Segmentation has been used for pixel-based object detection [2,19], for providing shape-based outputs [15] and even also to generate candidate windows [25], so exploiting global image segmentation is likely to be useful also in other stages of the detection system. In fact, there exists a very related work by Ott et al. [23] which also combines the concepts of HOG descriptor and image segmentation. In such a work, given a window to be classified as human or not, a *soft segmentation* is carried out aimed at separating between foreground (human) and background pixels in order to compute an additional color-based HOG (CHOG) descriptor to be combined with the usual HOG in an augmented descriptor space. In our proposal we do not require to distinguish between foreground and background but rely on a global image segmentation. Besides, in our case we do not augment the original descriptor, thus not increasing the complexity of the classifier.

The outline of the paper is as follows. Sect. 2 describes the proposed algorithm and its parameters (segmentation method, and descriptor re-weighting approaches). The experimental results, including the details of the dataset and detection system, together with discussion, is presented in Sect. 3. Finally, the main conclusions and future work are summarized in Sect. 4.

2   HOG Re-weighting Using Global Image Segmentation

The proposed approach consists in re-weighting the HOG descriptor for each one of the cells while it is computed. Basically, HOG consists in an intelligent grouping of gradient information (cells and blocks), as well as well-engineered histograms of gradient orientations (weighting by gradient magnitude, bin interpolation, histogram normalization and outliers clipping are the major steps[1]). The window of interest is covered by overlapping blocks, therefore, the HOG descriptor of the whole window usually ends up being thousand-dimensional. A linear SVM is used for learning the human classifier works in such high dimensional space. Accordingly, the obtained classifier is just a weighted summation running on such number of dimensions.

When computing HOG, the gradient orientation θ_P at a given pixel P is *weighted* by the corresponding magnitude μ_P, i.e., μ_P is accumulated in the histogram bin corresponding to θ_P(of course, taking into account the discretization, Gaussian weighting and interpolation proposed in [6]). Notice that the gradient at P, only encodes local differences in intensity or color, i.e., differences between adjacent pixels. In this paper, we want to incorporate differences based on a wider spatial support into the process in order to assess if they allow to obtain a human detector with higher performance. In particular, we want to weight μ_P by a given ω_P coming up from an image segmentation process, i.e., the vote of θ_P in the histogram will be the re-weighted magnitude λ_P instead of μ_P. Fig. 1 illustrates the idea.

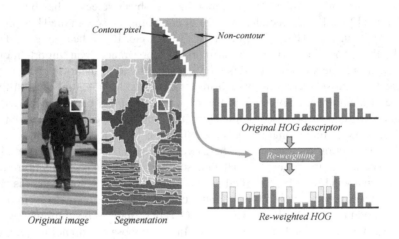

Fig. 1. Re-weighting of the HOG descriptor according to the image segmentation cues

2.1 Proposed Algorithm

Given an input image I and HOG parameters ϕ, our proposal can be summarized as follows:

1. Compute the image gradient of I, i.e., δ_I, using the corresponding parameters in ϕ.
2. Compute a global image segmentation of I using method $\mathcal{S}$, i.e., $\mathcal{S}(I) = \mathcal{S}_I$. Let $\mathcal{S}_I$ be the segmented image in which it is easy to distinguish the resulting segments and segment frontiers/contours.

---

[1] The computation of the HOG has many details and we refer the reader to [6] for a comprehensive explanation.

3. Use δ_I, $\mathcal{S}_I$ and ϕ to compute the modified HOG of all desired windows of I. This means to proceed like for standard HOG but rather than weighting each orientation θ_P by its corresponding magnitude μ_P (in the histogram voting), we weight it by λ_P, where $\lambda_P = \omega_P * \mu_P$ and $\omega_P = \mathcal{W}(\mathcal{S}_I(P))$.

$\mathcal{W}$ is the weighting function of each pixel, which will be detailed in the next subsections. As an example, setting $\mathcal{W} = 1$ means that each pixel is not altered, thus getting the original HOG descriptor. Note that δ_I and $\mathcal{S}_I$ are computed at once over the whole I, i.e., they are not computed in a per window basis (except if I is a window).

2.2 Image Segmentation

Providing a spatial partition of an image, i.e., a segmentation, remains as an active topic in Computer Vision. Some of the open issues are the type of descriptors to use, the similarity criteria to merge and split regions or joint pixels, the combination of top-down and bottom-up approaches, etc. Indeed, there is a plethora of proposals in the literature for image segmentation task. Not surprisingly, it is one of the most difficult tasks of the popular PASCAL challenge [10].

In the context of human detection a relevant issue is real-time. Thus, after some initial tests, we discarded some possibilities as using [1] method for gradient computation, as well as other more sophisticated image segmentation techniques (graph-cuts, top-down/bottom-up fusion, etc.) [3,18,2,1]. We did not consider basic methods as K-Means and watershed because parametrization can become a hard task, e.g., provide a good K for K-Means or appropriate markers for watershed was difficult. Instead, we relied on mean-shift algorithm applied to the CIE Luv color space because its computation

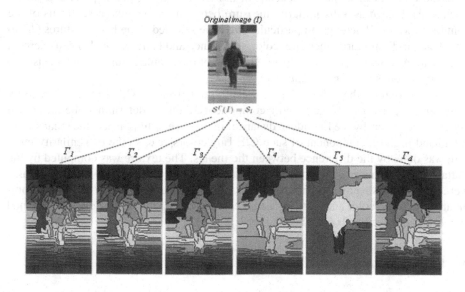

Fig. 2. Mean-shift image segmentation with different parameters (Γ)

is fairly fast and the parametrization is done in a relatively simple way. Moreover, we have chosen CIE Luv because the Euclidean distance between two colors in this space is strongly correlated with the human visual perception [30]. For instance, Fig. 2 shows the result of segmenting an image using mean-shift algorithm [4] with different parameters (Γ), computed in CIE Luv color space. Here we do not claim CIE Luv to be the most suited colorspace, therefore, in the future we want to consider other color spaces as well.

We compute the segmentation of image I with mean-shift algorithm $\mathcal{S}$ according to a set of different parameters that can be defined as Γ, so that $\mathcal{S}^\Gamma(I) = \mathcal{S}_I$. Such Γ represents the bandwidth parameter of the mean-shift algorithm, such parameter takes into account the segmentation spatial radius, segmentation feature space radius and minimum segment area [4]. We tuned Γ values according to the proposed in [4] in order to obtain different number of segments and, therefore, homogeneous regions of dissimilar sizes, i.e., segmentation results that varies from smaller super-pixels to larger super-pixels. In Fig. 2 is illustrated the idea, different segmentations of an image where the number and size of segments varies according to the Γ used, the case of Γ_d shows the resulting image segmented with the default mean-shift parameters.

2.3 Pixel Weighting Functions

As previously mentioned, the simplest case of $\mathcal{W}$ can be defined as $\mathcal{W}(P) = 1$ without considering the pixel position (contour or non-contour), which would make the image segmentation useless since we would be computing the standard HOG. In fact, we are interested in rules of the form $\mathcal{W}(P) = \omega_c$ if P is a contour pixel in $\mathcal{S}_I$ and $\mathcal{W}(P) = 1$ otherwise.

In our case, ω_c of a pixel P depends of the location of P, i.e., is pixel-dependent. Such ω_c is defined as a dissimilarity measure between the neighbour segments of the contour to which P belongs. In particular, we have selected some basic features (F) to establish our dissimilarity measure: color, luminance and texture, we also considered a combination between color and texture. Because of the simple nature of such measures, its computation is done in a simple way.

For each region, the color measure was computed in the CIE Luv colorspace by computing the average of the u and v components, then we determined the difference between the means by the Euclidean distance. In the case of luminance, the means were calculated in the L component of such CIE Luv colorspace, so the dissimilarity measure was done by the difference between the means. The texture was computed by the Battacharyya distance between the histograms of the adjacent regions, such histograms were calculated using local binary patterns, i.e., LBP values [16]. In the case of the combination between color and texture, each measure is computed separately, as explained above, and the average is calculated.

3   Experimental Results

In this section we evaluate the proposed algorithm in a publicly available dataset.

3.1   Dataset

In order to conduct the mentioned experiments, we make use of the INRIA person dataset [6], which contains color images. This dataset shows a wide range of human variations in pose, clothing, occlusions as well as complex backgrounds. Moreover, the dataset is divided in separated sets of null intersection for training and testing.

The training set contains 2,416 *positive* samples consisting in image windows (original and vertical mirror), each one containing a person framed by certain amount of background. All the positives are of the same size (*canonical detection window, 64x128*), although many of them come from an isotropic down scaling. We term this set of windows as $\mathcal{V}_+^{train}$. For collecting *negative* samples, i.e., image windows that do not contain persons, there are 1,218 person-free images available. We term this set of images as $\mathcal{I}_-^{train}$. The testing set consists of: (1) $\mathcal{I}_-^{test}$: 453 person-free images; (2) $\mathcal{I}_+^{test}$: 288 images containing labeled persons (ground truth); (3) $\mathcal{V}_+^{test}$: 1,126 positives analogous to the ones in $\mathcal{V}_+^{train}$ after cropping and mirroring the ground truth of $\mathcal{I}_+^{test}$.

3.2   Training

We use the standard training procedure for the INRIA dataset [6,5]. First, we collect random negative windows from the images in $\mathcal{I}_-^{train}$ (10 windows per image to have 12,180 negatives) and down scale them to the size of the canonical detection window; let us call this set of windows $\mathcal{V}_-^{train}$. Then, given the sets $\mathcal{V}_+^{train}$ and $\mathcal{V}_-^{train}$, we compute the HOG of such labeled windows on top of the desired color space, and train a human classifier using the linear SVM. Finally, we run the corresponding human detector on $\mathcal{I}_-^{train}$ in order to follow the recommended *bootstrapping* technique, i.e., to append the set $\mathcal{V}_-^{train}$ with *hard negative windows* and re-train the human classifier. We apply two bootstrapping iterations.

3.3   Testing

In order to perform multi-scale human detection we use the *pyramidal sliding window* strategy as proposed in Dalal's PhD [5]. The original image is resized by a scaling factor s^i to obtain the image corresponding to the pyramid level i. Then, given a pyramid level, we shift the search window along the horizontal and vertical directions with a given stride. The smaller the scaling factor and window stride, the finer the sliding window search, so a better detection performance is expected. However, this is to the expense of a higher processing time. In our framework we have reproduced Dalal's approach [5] in order to perform experiments. While Dalal sets scaling to 1.2 and window stride to (8,8) pixels, in our experiments we found that a 1.05 scaling factor and (4,4) pixels stride provides a better tradeoff between processing time and performance. Additionally, we have added anti-aliasing operations [11] in our implementation of Dalal's approachwhich improve performance around a 9% in the INRIA dataset with respect to the original proposal in [5], which, in fact, makes more challenging to improve the standard HOG results. Therefore, all our experiments are done with these operations.

Here, in order to compute the weighted HOG, we apply the selected image segmentation algorithm (i.e., $\mathcal{S}$) to each level of the pyramid. Thus, we obtain a sort of multi-scale segmentation of the original image (Fig. 3).

Fig. 3. Pyramid-segmentation. The scale of the slice in the pyramid affects the segmentation, similarly as it affects the HOG descriptor.

Since in multi-scale human detection a single person can be detected several times at slightly different positions and scales but a unique detection per human is desired, multiple overlapped detections shall be grouped by a clustering (*non-maximum-suppression*) procedure. In this case, we rely on the iterative confidence clustering approach of Laptev [20], which is a simpler and faster technique than Dalal's proposal and yields similar results.

3.4 Evaluation

In our experiments we use the widely extended *per image* evaluation procedure[2], which consists in running the detection system in a set of images containing persons and then comparing with the groundtruth for counting how many of such detections are true positives (T^{TP}) and how many are false positives (T^{FP}). If $I^{\#}$ is the cardinality of $\mathcal{I}^{test}$ and $H^{\#}$ the number of labeled persons in $\mathcal{I}^{test}_{+}$, then we can define the per image detection rate as $DR = T^{TP}/H^{\#}$ ($DR \in [0,1]$; per image miss rate $MR = 1 - DR$) and the false positives per image as $FPPI = T^{FP}/I^{\#}$. In order to determine if a detection overlaps sufficiently with a labeled human of $\mathcal{I}^{test}_{+}$ we follow the so-called PASCAL criterion [7] (also for bootstrapping during training). Now, we can define a curve to compare the algorithms. Note that FPPI can be greater than one, which would mean to have more than one false positive per image).

---

[2] Through the literature it has been demonstrated [7] that *per image* evaluation is more realistic than *per window* evaluation for assessing object detectors, which consists in classifying cropped examples and counterexamples, so in this paper we only use the former.

Taking into account $\mathcal{S}$ and $\mathcal{W}$, we have performed experiments in which the weight in the contour pixels is given by different criteria, $\omega_c = \Delta$. Such difference (Δ) is computed considering the variation in color, luminance (gray), texture (LBP) and combination of color and texture means between adjacent regions.

Fig. 4 illustrates the performance of the different algorithms. In all cases the result of the standard HOG is included for comparison. Within the legend parentheses, for the different plotted curves, we will indicate missrate at FPPI=10^0 and average area under the curve (A-AUC) between FPPI=10^{-1} and FPPI=10^0. Such FPPI points are relevant to detectors for driver assistance, the application field in which we will focus, taking into account that temporal coherence can help in reducing false positives if they are few per image.

3.5 Discussion

According to the experiments, it is clear that our proposal outperforms the standard HOG, i.e., the contribution of the segmentation cues in the computation of the HOG features seems to be significant for detecting pedestrians in the INRIA dataset. However, we can see how our proposal is sensitive to the segmentation output. A plausible explanation is the following, mean-shift with Γ_1 (Fig. 4a) outputs many small regions, also called super-pixels. Thus, such super-pixels are still too local, i.e., too close to pixels size. In the case of mean-shift with Γ_2 (Fig. 4b), the performance of the algorithm is slightly better due to the increased sizes of the segmented regions. On the contrary, Γ_4 (Fig. 4d) and Γ_5 (Fig. 4e) provides larger super-pixels so the information provided to the classifier is too general, i.e., such contribution is not enough detailed. In the case of mean-shift with Γ_3 (Fig. 4c) the resulting super-pixels are larger than mean-shift obtained with Γ_1 (Fig. 4a) and Γ_2 (Fig. 4b) but smaller than the obtained with Γ_4 (Fig. 4d) and Γ_5 (Fig. 4e) providing detailed information to the classifier but not too local. In the case of Γ_d (Fig. 4f) our proposal is computed with the default parameters provided by mean-shift method. The obtained results are quite good but not as good as those obtained with Γ_3, therefore, it is necessary a validation set to adjust the segmentation parameters. However, in all the cases our proposal outperforms standard HOG descriptor, although mean-shift with Γ_3 (Fig. 4c) achieves the best results.

Regarding the tested $\mathcal{W}$, the best option consists in weighting HOG at contour pixels (ω_c) according to the difference in color between the segments separated by the contour. Overall, using mean-shift (Γ_3), differences of color between segments for setting ω_c, we have down shifted missrate an average of 4.47% in our area of interest (from FPPI=10^{-1} to FPPI=10^0) compared to our HOG implementation explained in section 3.3.

An interesting further question is whether this improvement is maintained when combining HOG with other descriptors as it is normally done. In order to test this we have reproduced the recent HOG-LBP approach (combining HOG with local binary patterns), presented in [28,31] with satisfactory results. In addition to the original LBP implementation, we have introduced three improvements with respect to [28] which increase its performance: (i) we use a threshold in the pixel comparisons, which increases the descriptor tolerance to noise; (ii) we do not interpolate the pixels around the compared central one; and (iii) we perform the computation directly in the luminance channel instead of separately computing the histograms in the three color channels.

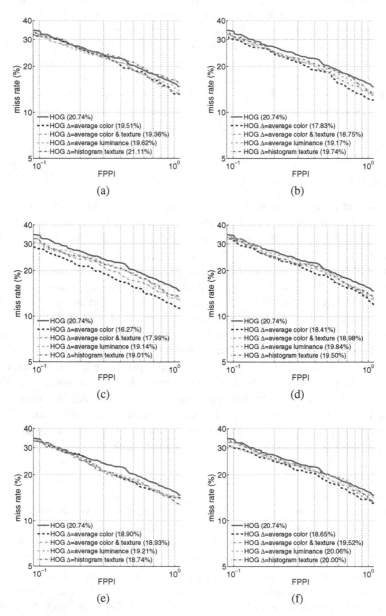

Fig. 4. Performance curves of the different parameters (Γ) for the segmentation algorithm mean-shift. The curves (a)-(e) shows the results of our proposal with different segmentation parameters, obtaining from smaller to larger super-pixels. The diagrams (a)-(e) shows the results of the contribution coming from the segmentation with parameters Γ_1-Γ_5, in the case of (f) corresponds to the default parameters (Γ_d) of the mean-shift algorithm.

Fig. 5 illustrates the comparison among [28] (Wang's approach), our implementation of HOG-LBP and our proposal. As can be seen, our implementation already outperforms Wang's in 6.02% MR, and including the proposed segmentation-based weighting we further decrease MR to 7.31%, which demonstrates that our proposal is complementary to combining HOG with other cues.

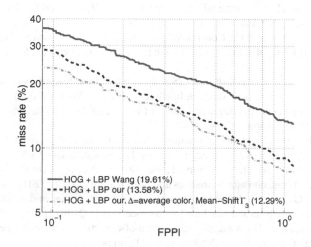

Fig. 5. Comparison between HOG-LBP with and without our proposed algorithm

4   Conclusions

In this work we have investigated the possibility of improving HOG descriptors in the context of human detection. In particular by weighting HOG with information coming from image segmentation. We have conducted different experiments to clarify what type of segmentation is preferred (from smaller to larger super-pixels) and how such HOG re-weighting must be performed. Overall, we have seen that using mean-shift with Γ_3 and differences of color between segments for setting HOG weights at contours, we have down shifted missrate an average of 4.47% in our area of interest (from FPPI=10^{-1} to FPPI=10^0). Furthermore, our proposal is complementary to combining HOG with other descriptors such as LBP, achieving a decrease of 1.29% in MR.

As future work we plan both to analyze the cases in which segmentation-based HOG weight is helping most in order to exploit this a prior information in the design of further detectors. Furthermore, we want to take advantage of the image segmentation for other tasks different than classification, e.g., candidate generation or refinement.

Acknowledgements. This work is supported by Spanish MICINN projects TRA2011-29454-C03-01, TIN2011-29494-C03-02, and Consolider Ingenio 2010: MIPRCV (CSD200700018. Y. Socarrás and D. Vázquez are supported by Universitat Autónoma de Barcelona, Spain.

References

1. Arbeláez, P., Maire, M., Fowlkes, C., Malik, J.: Contour detection and hierarchical image segmentation. IEEE Trans. on Pattern Analysis and Machine Intelligence 99(1), 898–916 (2010)
2. Boix, X., Gonfaus, J., van de Weijer, J., Bagdanov, A., Serrat, J., Gonzàlez, J.: Harmony potentials for joint classification and segmentation. In: IEEE Conf. on Computer Vision and Pattern Recognition, San Francisco, CA, USA (2010)
3. Carreira, J., Sminchisescu, C.: Constrained parametric min-cuts for automatic object segmentation. In: IEEE Conf. on Computer Vision and Pattern Recognition, San Francisco, CA, USA (2010)
4. Comaniciu, D., Meer, P.: Mean shift: a robust approach toward feature space analysis. IEEE Trans. on Pattern Analysis and Machine Intelligence 24(5), 603–619 (2002)
5. Dalal, N.: Finding people in images and videos. PhD Thesis, Institut National Polytechnique de Grenoble / INRIA Rhône-Alpes (2006)
6. Dalal, N., Triggs, B.: Histograms of oriented gradients for human detection. In: IEEE Conf. on Computer Vision and Pattern Recognition, San Diego, CA, USA (2005)
7. Dollár, P., Wojek, C., Schiele, B., Perona, P.: Pedestrian detection: an evaluation of the state of the art. IEEE Trans. on Pattern Analysis and Machine Intelligence (2011) (in press)
8. Enzweiler, M., Gavrila, D.: Monocular pedestrian detection: survey and experiments. IEEE Trans. on Pattern Analysis and Machine Intelligence 31(12), 2179–2195 (2009)
9. Enzweiler, M., Gavrila, D.: A multi-level mixture-of-experts framework for pedestrian classification. IEEE Trans. on Image Processing (2011) (in press)
10. Everingham, M., van Gool, L., Williams, C., Winn, J., Zisserman, A.: The PASCAL visual object classes (VOC) challenge. Int. Journal on Computer Vision 88(2), 303–338 (2010)
11. Felzenszwalb, P., McAllester, D., Ramanan, D.: A discriminatively trained, multiscale, deformable part model. In: IEEE Conf. on Computer Vision and Pattern Recognition, Anchorage, AK, USA (2008)
12. Gandhi, T., Trivedi, M.: Pedestrian protection systems: issues, survey, and challenges. IEEE Trans. on Intelligent Transportation Systems 8(3), 413–430 (2007)
13. Gavrila, D.: A bayesian, exemplar-based approach to hierarchical shape matching. IEEE Trans. on Pattern Analysis and Machine Intelligence 29(8), 1408–1421 (2007)
14. Gerónimo, D., López, A., Sappa, A., Graf, T.: Survey of pedestrian detection for advanced driver assistance systems. IEEE Trans. on Pattern Analysis and Machine Intelligence 32(7), 1239–1258 (2010)
15. Gould, S., Gao, T., Koller, D.: Region-based segmentation and object detection. In: Advances in Neural Information Processing Systems, Vancouver, BC, Canada (2009)
16. Guo, Z., Zhang, L., Zhang, D.: A completed modeling of local binary pattern operator for texture classification. IEEE Trans. on Pattern Analysis and Machine Intelligence 19(6), 1657–1663 (2010)
17. Jones, M., Snow, D.: Pedestrian detection using boosted features over many frames. In: IEEE Conf. on Computer Vision and Pattern Recognition, Anchorage, AK, USA (2008)
18. Kumar, M., Torr, P., Zisserman, A.: Objcut: Efficient segmentation using top-down and bottom-up cues. IEEE Trans. on Pattern Analysis and Machine Intelligence 32(3), 530–545 (2010)
19. Ladický, Ľ., Sturgess, P., Alahari, K., Russell, C., Torr, P.H.S.: What, Where and How Many? Combining Object Detectors and CRFs. In: Daniilidis, K., Maragos, P., Paragios, N. (eds.) ECCV 2010. LNCS, vol. 6314, pp. 424–437. Springer, Heidelberg (2010)
20. Laptev, I.: Improving object detection with boosted histograms. Image and Vision Computing 27(5), 535–544 (2009)

21. Liao, C.T., Lai, S.H., Wang, W.H.: A hierarchical image kernel with application to pedestrian identification for video surveillance. In: IEEE Int. Conf. on Image Processing, Cairo, Egypt (2009)
22. Lin, Z., Davis, L.: Shape-based human detection and segmentation via hierarchical part-template matching. IEEE Trans. on Pattern Analysis and Machine Intelligence 32(4), 604–618 (2010)
23. Ott, P., Everingham, M.: Implicit color segmentation features for pedestrain and object detection. In: Int. Conf. on Computer Vision, Kyoto, Japan (2009)
24. Rao, M., Vázquez, D., López, A.: Color contribution to part-based person detection in different types of scenarios. In: International Conference on Computer Analysis of Images and Patterns, Seville, Spain (2011)
25. van de Sande, K., Uijlings, J., Gevers, T., Smeulders, A.: Segmentation as selective search for object recognition. In: Int. Conf. on Computer Vision, Barcelona, Spain (2011)
26. Viola, P., Jones, M.: Rapid object detection using a boosted cascade of simple features. In: IEEE Conf. on Computer Vision and Pattern Recognition, Kauai, HI, USA (2001)
27. Viola, P., Jones, M., Snow, D.: Detecting pedestrians using patterns of motion and appearance. Int. Journal on Computer Vision 63(2), 153–161 (2005)
28. Wang, X., Han, T., Yan, S.: An HOG-LBP human detector with partial occlusion handling. In: Int. Conf. on Computer Vision, Kyoto, Japan (2009)
29. Watanabe, T., Ito, S., Yokoi, K.: Co-Occurrence Histograms of Oriented Gradients for Pedestrian Detection. In: Wada, T., Huang, F., Lin, S. (eds.) PSIVT 2009. LNCS, vol. 5414, pp. 37–47. Springer, Heidelberg (2009)
30. Wyszecki, G., Stiles, W.: Color science: concepts and methods, quantitative data and formulae. Wiley Series in Pure and Applied Optics (1982)
31. Zhang, J., Huang, K., Yu, Y., Tan, T.: Boosted local structured hog-lbp for object localization. In: IEEE Conf. on Computer Vision and Pattern Recognition, Providence, RI, USA (2011)

A Supervised Learning Framework for Automatic Prostate Segmentation in Trans Rectal Ultrasound Images

Soumya Ghose[1,2], Jhimli Mitra[1,2], Arnau Oliver[1], Robert Martí[1],
Xavier Lladó[1], Jordi Freixenet[1], Joan C. Vilanova[3], Josep Comet[4],
Désiré Sidibé[2], and Fabrice Meriaudeau[2]

[1] Computer Vision and Robotics Group, University of Girona, Campus Montilivi,
Edifici P-IV, Av. Lluís Santaló , s/n, 17071 Girona, Spain
[2] Laboratoire Le2I - UMR CNRS 5158, Université de Bourgogne,
12 Rue de la Fonderie, 71200 Le Creusot, France
[3] Girona Magnetic Resonance Imaging Center, Girona, Spain
[4] University Hospital Dr. Josep Trueta, Girona, Spain

Abstract. Heterogeneous intensity distribution inside the prostate gland, significant variations in prostate shape, size, inter dataset contrast variations, and imaging artifacts like shadow regions and speckle in Trans Rectal Ultrasound (TRUS) images challenge computer aided automatic or semi-automatic segmentation of the prostate. In this paper, we propose a supervised learning schema based on random forest for automatic initialization and propagation of statistical shape and appearance model. Parametric representation of the statistical model of shape and appearance is derived from principal component analysis (PCA) of the probability distribution inside the prostate and PCA of the contour landmarks obtained from the training images. Unlike traditional statistical models of shape and intensity priors, the appearance model in this paper is derived from the posterior probabilities obtained from random forest classification. This probabilistic information is then used for the initialization and propagation of the statistical model. The proposed method achieves mean Dice Similarity Coefficient (DSC) value of 0.96 ± 0.01, with a mean segmentation time of 0.67 ± 0.02 seconds when validated with 24 images from 6 datasets with considerable shape, size, and intensity variations, in a leave-one-patient-out validation framework. The model achieves statistically significant t-test p-value<0.0001 in mean DSC and mean mean absolute distance (MAD) values compared to traditional statistical models of shape and intensity priors.

Keywords: Prostate Segmentation, Random Forest, Statistical Shape and Posterior Probability Models, Ultrasound.

1 Introduction

Prostate cancer is the most commonly diagnosed cancer in North America and accounted for 33,000 estimated deaths in 2011 [1]. Accurate prostate

J. Blanc-Talon et al. (Eds.): ACIVS 2012, LNCS 7517, pp. 190–200, 2012.

segmentation in TRUS may aid in radiation therapy planning, motion monitoring, biopsy needle placement and multimodal image fusion between TRUS and magnetic resonance imaging (MRI) to improve malignant tissue extraction during biopsy [19]. However, accurate computer aided prostate segmentation from TRUS images is a challenging task due to low contrast of TRUS images, speckle, and shadow artifacts. Moreover, inter-patient prostate shape, size and deformation may vary significantly and heterogeneous intensity distribution inside the prostate gland may introduce further challenges in automatic prostate segmentation.

Deformable models and statistical shape models are commonly used for prostate segmentation in TRUS images. For example Badiei et al. [2] used a deformable model of warping ellipse and Ladak et al. [14] used discrete dynamic contour to achieve semi-automatic prostate segmentation. However, prostate segmentation during TRUS guided biopsy procedures should necessarily be automatic. Shen et al. [18] and Zhan et al. [20] presented an automatic method that incorporated a priori shape and texture information from Gabor filters to produce accurate prostate segmentation. However, the method is computationally expensive and probably unsuitable for TRUS guided prostate intervention [19]. In recent years, Cosio et al. [6] reported an automatic method for prostate segmentation with active shape models [4]. However, the computationally intensive optimization framework of genetic algorithm is unsuitable for TRUS guided intervention.

In recent years, supervised machine learning methods have been adopted for solving prostate segmentation problems in medical images [15,10]. Motivated by these approaches we propose a novel prostate segmentation method in which appearance and spatial context based information from the training images are used to classify a new test image to achieve probabilistic classification of the prostate. Further, statistical shape and appearance model derived from PCA of prostate shape and posterior probabilistic values of the prostate region of the training TRUS images are propagated in a multi-resolution framework to segment a test image. The key contributions of this work are:

- The use of random forest classification framework to obtain a soft classification of the prostate.
- Using such information in training, automatic initialization and propagation of our model.

The performance of our method is compared with the traditional active appearance model (AAM) [5] and also with our previous work [11]. Compared to the use of intensity as in [5] and to the use of texture obtained from quadrature filter in [11], the posterior probabilistic information is used to train, initialize and propagate our model. Statistically significant improvement is achieved when validated with 24 images that have significant shape, size, and contrast variations of the prostate in a leave-one-patient-out validation framework.

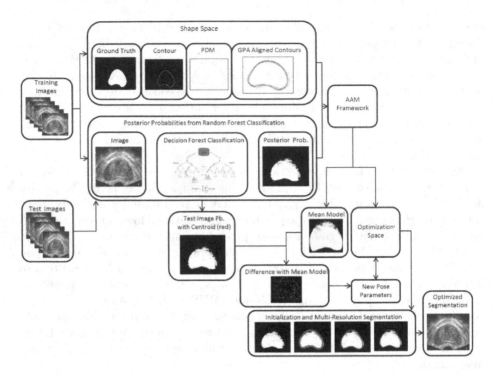

Fig. 1. Schematic representation of our approach. Abbreviations used PDM = Point Distribution Model, GPA = Generalized Procustes Analysis, Pb. = Probability.

2   Proposed Segmentation Framework

The proposed method is developed on two major components: 1) Supervised learning framework of decision trees (random forest) to determine the posterior probability of a pixel being prostate, and 2) adapting statistical models of shape and intensity priors to incorporate the posterior probabilities of the prostate region for training, initialization and propagation of the parametric model. We present the random forest framework for determining posterior probability of the prostate region, followed by our statistical shape and probability prior model of the prostate region in the following subsections. The schema of our proposed method is illustrated in Fig. 1.

2.1   Random Forest Based Probabilistic Classification

In traditional AAM [5], the point distribution model (PDM) [4] of the contour is aligned to a common reference frame by generalized Procrustes analysis [13]. Intensities are warped into correspondence using a piece-wise affine warp and sampled from a shape-free reference. Intensity distribution inside the prostate region may vary significantly from one dataset to another depending on the ultrasound image acquisition parameters and nature of the prostate tissue of a patient. Hence, the use of intensity distribution of the prostate region to build the texture model as in traditional AAM introduces larger variations producing an inaccurate texture model that adversely affects segmentation results. To reduce the inter-dataset intensity variations and intensity variations inside the prostate region, we propose to determine the posterior probability of the image pixels being prostate in a supervised learning framework and use PCA of the posterior probabilities of the prostate region to build our appearance model.

Our approach of using pixel location to determine the prior position information of the prostate is based on the works of Cosio et al. [6] and Shen et al. [18]. Both used prior prostate location information in TRUS images to automatically initialize their model. Cosio et al. [6] used a 3D feature vector of pixel location and intensity value to classify and localize prostate in TRUS images for initialization of their model. Similarly, Shen et al. [18] proposed to use the relative position of the prostate with respect to the TRUS probe (located at the center of the base line of the TRUS image) for initialization. More recently Li et al. [15] used a spatial context based machine learning approach to achieve a probabilistic segmentation of the prostate. Motivated by these approaches we propose a supervised learning framework that exploits the location and image feature information of the prostate in TRUS images to determine the posterior probability of the prostate region.

In this paper, the probabilistic classification addressed by supervised random decision forest may be formalized as a soft classification of pixels into either background or prostate. Decision trees are discriminative classifiers which are known to suffer from over-fitting. However, a random decision forest achieves better generalization by growing an ensemble of many independent decision trees on a random subset of the training data and by randomizing the features made available at each node during training [10].

During **training**, to minimize the pose and intensity variations, our datasets are rigidly aligned based on intensities. We have used Evangelidis et al. [9] for rigid alignment. The inter-patient intensity variations are linearly normalized between 0 and 1. The data consists of a collection of features obtained from 3×3 neighborhood of pixels, each centered at $V = (X, F)$. Where, $X = (x, y)$ denotes the position of the pixel associated with a feature vector F. The mean and standard deviation of the 3×3 pixel neighborhood are used as the feature vector F. Each tree $\tau_i, i = 1, \ldots, T$ in the decision forest receives the full set V, along with the label and the root node and selects a test to split V into two subsets to maximize information gain. A test consists of a feature (like the mean of a pixel neighborhood) and a feature response threshold. The left and the right child nodes receive their respective subsets of V and the process is repeated at each child node to grow the next level of the tree. Growth is terminated when either information gain is minimum or the tree has grown to maximum depth. Each decision tree in the forest is unique as each tree node selects a random subset of features and threshold.

During **testing**, the test image is rigidly aligned to the same frame of the training datasets and its intensities are normalized. The pixels are routed to one

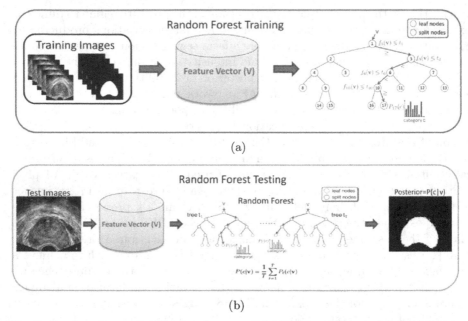

Fig. 2. Random forest classification framework (a) Random forest training (b) Random forest classification with a test image

leaf in each tree by applying the test (selected during training). Each pixel of the test dataset is propagated through all the trees by successive application of the relevant binary test to determine probability of belonging to a class c. When reaching a leaf node l_τ in all trees where $\tau \in [1, \ldots, T]$, posterior probabilities $P_\tau(c|V)$ are gathered in order to compute the final posterior probability of the pixel defined by $P(c|V) = \frac{1}{T} \sum_{\tau=1}^{T} P_\tau(c|V)$. Computation of class posterior probabilities in decision forest is illustrated in Fig. 2.

2.2   Statistical Shape and Appearance Model

The process of building the parametric statistical model of shape and appearance variations involves the task of building a shape model, an appearance model, and consecutively a combined model of shape and appearance priors. To build the shape model, a PDM [5] is built by equal angle sampling of the prostate contours to determine the landmarks automatically. The PDM of the contours are aligned to a common reference frame by generalized Procrustes analysis [13]. PCA of the aligned PDMs identifies the principal modes of shape variations. Posteriori probabilistic information (of pixels being prostate) of the segmented region are warped into correspondence using a piece-wise affine warp and are sampled from a shape-free reference similar to that of AAM [5]. PCA of the posterior probabilities from Section 2.1 is used to identify their principal modes of variation. The model may be formalized in the following manner. Let s and t represent the shape and posterior probability models, then

$$s = \bar{s} + \Phi_s \theta_s, \quad t = \bar{t} + \Phi_t \theta_t \tag{1}$$

where $\bar{s}$ and $\bar{t}$ denote the mean shape and posterior probability information respectively, then Φ_s and Φ_t contain the first p eigenvectors (obtained from 98% of total variations) of the estimated joint dispersion matrix of shape and posterior probability information and θ represent the corresponding eigenvalues. The model of shape and posterior probability variations are combined in a linear framework as,

$$b = \begin{bmatrix} W\theta_s \\ \theta_t \end{bmatrix} = \begin{bmatrix} W\Phi_s^T(s - \bar{s}) \\ \Phi_t^T(t - \bar{t}) \end{bmatrix} \tag{2}$$

where W denotes a weight factor (determined as in AAM [5]) coupling the shape and the probability space. A third PCA of the combined model ensures the reduction in redundancy of the combined model, and is given as,

$$b = E\alpha \tag{3}$$

where E is the matrix of eigenvectors and α the appearance parameters.

2.3 Optimization and Segmentation of a New Instance

In our model, we use the optimization framework similar to that proposed by Cootes et al. [5]. The objective function of our model is similar to AAM. However, instead of minimizing the sum-of-squared differences of intensities between the mean model and target image, we minimize the sum-of-squared differences of the posterior probabilities of the mean model and the target image. The prior knowledge of the optimization space is acquired by perturbing the combined model with known model parameters and perturbing the pose (translation, scale and rotation) parameters. Linear relationships between the perturbation of the combined model (δc) and the residual posterior probability values (δt) (obtained from the sum-of-squared differences between the posterior probabilities of the mean model and the target image), and between the perturbation of the pose parameters (δp) and the residual posterior probability values are acquired in multivariate regression frameworks as,

$$\delta c = R_c \delta t, \quad \delta p = R_p \delta t \tag{4}$$

R_c and R_p refer to the correlation coefficients. Given a test image, the posterior probability values of the pixels being prostate is determined with random forest soft classification. The sum-of-squared differences of the posterior probability values with the mean model is used to determine the residual value δt. The combined model (δc) and the pose parameters (δp) are then updated using Eq. (4) to generate a new shape, and combined model and consequently the new posterior probabilities. The process continues in an iterative manner until the difference of the mean model with the target image remains unchanged. The model is initialized at a resolution one fourth the size of the original image and the model propagates in a multi-resolution schema from lower to higher resolution to achieve segmentation.

Table 1. Prostate segmentation quantitative comparison (HD, MAD and MaxD in mm, Spec., Sens., and Acc., are for Specificity, Sensitivity and Accuracy respectively.) Statistically significant values are italicized

Method	DSC	HD	MAD	MaxD	Spec.	Sens.	Acc.
AAM [5]	0.94±0.03	4.92±0.96	2.15±0.94	5.3±0.48	0.89±0.03	0.993±0.006	0.97±0.009
Ghose et al. [11]	0.95±0.02	3.82±0.88	1.26±0.51	3.92±0.93	0.94±0.03	0.97±0.02	0.97±0.01
Our Method	*0.96±0.01*	*2.99±0.73*	*0.96±0.31*	3.01±0.73	0.94±0.02	0.991±0.005	0.98±0.007

3   Experimental Results and Discussions

We have validated the accuracy and robustness of our method with 24 axial mid-gland TRUS images of the prostate with a resolution of 354×304 pixels from 6 prostate datasets in a leave-one-patient-out evaluation strategy. The ground truth for the experiments are prepared in a schema similar to MICCAI prostate challenge 2009 [17], where manual segmentations performed by an expert radiologist were validated by an experienced urologist. Both doctors have over 15 years of experience in dealing with prostate anatomy, prostate segmentation, and ultrasound guided biopsies. We have fixed the number of trees to 100, tree depth to 30 and the lower bound of information gain to 10^{-7} in decision forest. These parameters were chosen empirically as they produced promising results with test images.

We have used most of the popular prostate segmentation evaluation metrics like DSC, 95% Hausdorff Distance (HD) [17], MAD [19], Maximum Distance (MaxD) [16], specificity [8], sensitivity, and accuracy [2] to evaluate our method. Furthermore, the results are compared with the traditional AAM [5], and to our previous work in which we used texture features extracted with quadrature filters in the statistical shape and appearance model [11]. It is observed from Table 1 that a probabilistic representation of the prostate regions in TRUS images significantly improves segmentation accuracy when compared to traditional AAM and to [11]. As opposed to the manual initialization of traditional AAM and as in [11], we use the posterior probability information for automatic initialization and training of our statistical shape and appearance model. We achieved a statistically significant improvement in t-test p-value for DSC, HD and MAD compared to traditional AAM [5] and to [11]. A high DSC value and low values of contour error metrics of HD and MAD are all equally important in determining the segmentation accuracy of an algorithm. In this context, we obtained better segmentation accuracies compared to [5] and [11]. To provide qualitative results of our method we present a subset of results in Fig. 3.

Our method is implemented in Matlab 7 on an Intel Core i5, 2.8 GHz processor and 8 GB RAM. The mean segmentation time of the method is 0.67±0.02 seconds with an unoptimized Matlab code. Even with an unoptimized Matlab

Table 2. Qualitative comparison of prostate segmentation

Reference	Area Accuracy	Contour Accuracy	Datasets	Time
Betrouni [3]	Overlap 93±0.9%	Distance 3.77±1.3 pixels	10 images	5 seconds
Shen [18]	Error 3.98±0.97%	Distance 3.2±0.87 pixels	8 images	64 seconds
Ladak [14]	Accuracy 90.1±3.2%	MAD 4.4±1.8 pixels	117 images	-
Cosio [6]	-	MAD 1.65±0.67 mm	22 images	11 minutes
Yan [19]	-	MAD 2.10±1.02 mm	19 datasets /301 images	0.3 seconds
Ghose [12]	DSC 0.96±0.01	MAD 0.80±0.24 mm	6 datasets/ 24 images	5.95 seconds
Our Method	DSC 0.96±0.01	MAD 3.44±1.11 pixels/ 0.96±0.31 mm	6 datasets/ 24 images	0.67 seconds

code in Table 2 we observe that our mean segmentation time is better when compared to [3], [18] and [6], although inferior to [19]. However, [19] used an optimized C++ code to achieve their results. We believe that a speed-up of computational time is possible with a parallelized and optimized code in GPU environment.

A quantitative comparison of different prostate segmentation methodologies is difficult in the absence of a public dataset and standardized evaluation metrics. Nevertheless, to have an overall qualitative estimate of the functioning of our method, we have compared with some of the existing 2D segmentation methods as shown Table 2. In Table 2, we may consider the area overlap and the area accuracy as equivalent of DSC measure and the average distance as equivalent of the average MAD. Analyzing the results, we observe that our mean DSC value is better than the area overlap accuracy values of Betrouni et al. [3] and Ladak et al. [14] and very similar to the area overlap error of Shen et al. [18]. However, it is to be noted that we have used more images compared to Shen et al. Our MAD value also shows improvement when compared to [3], [18], [14], [6] and [19]. From these observations we may infer our method performs well in overlap and contour accuracy measures when assessed qualitatively.

Furthermore, the obtained contour and area overlap accuracies are similar to the results obtained in [12]. In our previous work [12] we fused probabilities obtained from expectation maximization (EM) [7] based clustering and spatial probabilities to achieve a soft clustering of the prostate. In a schema similar to our proposed model in this article, automatic initialization and propagation of the deformable model was achieved with posterior probabilities. However, our previous work [12] computationally more expensive due to the EM framework adopted for the model. Transforming the EM framework with a supervised learning framework, our proposed method achieves prostate segmentation in significantly less time than that required for [12]. The mean segmentation time of [12] with current machine configuration is 4.33±0.21 seconds while the proposed method using supervised learning with random forest takes 0.67±0.02 seconds without compromising the segmentation accuracies. Mean segmentation time is often a critical element in selecting one segmentation method over the other for

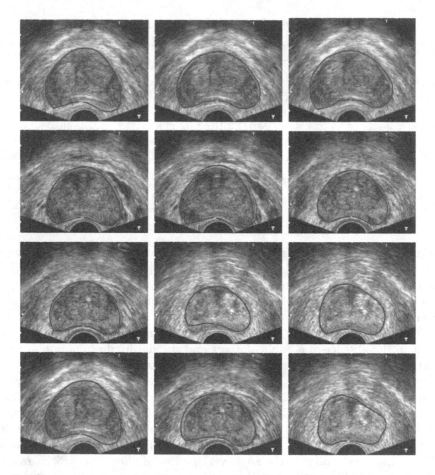

Fig. 3. The green contour gives the ground truth and the red contour gives the obtained result

near real-time multimodal image fusion between TRUS and MRI to improve malignant tissue sampling during biopsy. In this context, we may claim that our present method shows improvement over our previous work in [12].

4   Conclusion and Future Works

A novel approach of multiple statistical models of shape and posterior probability information of prostate region with the goal of segmenting the prostate in 2D TRUS images has been proposed. Our approach is accurate, and robust to significant shape, size and contrast variations in TRUS images compared to traditional AAM. While the proposed method is validated with prostate mid-gland images, effectiveness of the method for the base and the apical slices is yet to be validated.

Acknowledgements. This research has been funded by VALTEC 08-1-0039 of Generalitat de Catalunya, Spanish Science and Innovation grant nb. TIN2011-23704, Spain and Conseil Régional de Bourgogne, France.

References

1. Cancer Society Atlanta, A. Prostate Cancer (2011), http://www.cancer.org (accessed on January 28, 2012)
2. Badiei, S., Salcudean, S.E., Varah, J., Morris, W.J.: Prostate Segmentation in 2D Ultrasound Images Using Image Warping and Ellipse Fitting. In: Larsen, R., Nielsen, M., Sporring, J. (eds.) MICCAI 2006. LNCS, vol. 4191, pp. 17–24. Springer, Heidelberg (2006)
3. Betrouni, N., Vermandel, M., Pasquier, D., Maouche, S., Rousseau, J.: Segmentation of Abdominal Ultrasound Images of the Prostate Using A priori Information and an Adapted Noise Filter. Computerized Medical Imaging and Graphics 29, 43–51 (2005)
4. Cootes, T.F., Hill, A., Taylor, C.J., Haslam, J.: The Use of Active Shape Model for Locating Structures in Medical Images. Image and Vision Computing 12, 355–366 (1994)
5. Cootes, T.F., Edwards, G.J., Taylor, C.J.: Active Appearance Models. In: Burkhardt, H., Neumann, B. (eds.) ECCV 1998. LNCS, vol. 1407, pp. 484–498. Springer, Heidelberg (1998)
6. Cosío, F.A.: Automatic Initialization of an Active Shape Model of the Prostate. Medical Image Analysis 12, 469–483 (2008)
7. Dempster, A.P., Laird, N.M., Rubin, D.B.: Maximum Likelihood from Incomplete Data via the EM Algorithm. Journal of the Royal Statistical Society 39, 1–38 (1977)
8. Diaz, K., Castaneda, B.: Semi-automated Segmentation of the Prostate Gland Boundary in Ultrasound Images Using a Machine Learning Approach. In: Reinhardt, J.M., Pluim, J.P.W. (eds.) Procedings of SPIE Medical Imaging: Image Processing, pp. 1–8, SPIE, USA (2008)
9. Evangelidis, G.D., Emmanouil, Z.P.: Parametric Image Alignment Using Enhanced Correlation Coefficient Maximization. IEEE Trans. Pattern Anal. Mach. Intell. 30, 1858–1865 (2008)
10. Geremia, E., Menze, B.H., Clatz, O., Konukoglu, E., Criminisi, A., Ayache, N.: Spatial Decision Forests for MS Lesion Segmentation in Multi-Channel MR Images. In: Jiang, T., Navab, N., Pluim, J.P.W., Viergever, M.A. (eds.) MICCAI 2010. LNCS, vol. 6361, pp. 111–118. Springer, Heidelberg (2010)
11. Ghose, S., Oliver, A., Martí, R., Lladó, X., Freixenet, J., Mitra, J., Vilanova, J.C., Comet, J., Meriaudeau, F.: Statistical shape and texture model of quadrature phase information for prostate segmentation. International Journal of Computer Assisted Radiology and Surgery 7, 43–55 (2012)
12. Ghose, S., Oliver, A., Martí, R., Lladó, X., Freixenet, J., Vilanova, J.C., Meriaudeau, F.: A probabilistic framework for automatic prostate segmentation with a statistical model of shape and appearance. In: IEEE ICIP, pp. 713–716 (2011)
13. Gower, J.C.: Generalized Procrustes Analysis. Psychometrika 40, 33–51 (1975)
14. Ladak, H.M., Mao, F., Wang, Y., Downey, D.B., Steinman, D.A., Fenster, A.: Prostate Segmentation from 2D Ultrasound Images. In: Proceedings of the 22nd Annual International Conference of the IEEE Engineering in Medicine and Biology Society, pp. 3188–3191. IEEE Computer Society Press, Chcago (2000)

15. Li, W., Liao, S., Feng, Q., Chen, W., Shen, D.: Learning Image Context for Segmentation of Prostate in CT-Guided Radiotherapy. In: Fichtinger, G., Martel, A., Peters, T. (eds.) MICCAI 2011, Part III. LNCS, vol. 6893, pp. 570–578. Springer, Heidelberg (2011)
16. Liu, H., Cheng, G., Rubens, D., Strang, J.G., Liao, L., Brasacchio, R., Messing, E., Yu', Y.: Automatic Segmentation of Prostate Boundaries in Transrectal Ultrasound (TRUS) Imaging. In: Sonka, M., Fitzpatrick, J.M. (eds.) Proceedings of the SPIE Medical Imaging: Image Processings, pp. 412–423, SPIE, USA (2002)
17. MICCAI: 2009 prostate segmentation challenge MICCAI (2009), http://wiki.na-mic.org/Wiki/index.php (accessed on April 1, 2011)
18. Shen, D., Zhan, Y., Davatzikos, C.: Segmentation of Prostate Boundaries from Ultrasound Images Using Statistical Shape Model. IEEE Transactions on Medical Imaging 22, 539–551 (2003)
19. Yan, P., Xu, S., Turkbey, B., Kruecker, J.: Discrete Deformable Model Guided by Partial Active Shape Model for TRUS Image Segmentation. IEEE Transactions on Biomedical Engineering 57, 1158–1166 (2010)
20. Zhan, Y., Shen, D.: Deformable Segmentation of 3D Ultrasound Prostate Images Using Statistical Texture Matching Method. IEEE Transactions on Medical Imaging 25, 256–272 (2006)

Simultaneous Segmentation and Filtering via Reduced Graph Cuts

Nicolas Lermé[1] and François Malgouyres[2]

[1] LAGA UMR CNRS 7539,
LIPN UMR CNRS 7030, Université Paris 13
nicolas.lerme@lipn.fr
[2] IMT UMR CNRS 5219, Université Paul Sabatier
fmalgouy@math.univ-toulouse.fr

Abstract. Recently, optimization with graph cuts became very attractive but generally remains limited to small-scale problems due to the large memory requirement of graphs, even when restricted to binary variables. Unlike previous heuristics which generally fail to fully capture details, [8] proposes another band-based method for reducing these graphs in image segmentation. This method provides small graphs while preserving thin structures but do not offer low memory usage when the amount of regularization is large. This is typically the case when images are corrupted by an impulsive noise. In this paper, we overcome this situation by embedding a new parameter in this method to both further reducing graphs and filtering the segmentation. This parameter avoids any post-processing steps, appears to be generally less sensitive to noise variations and offers a good robustness against noise. We also provide an empirical way to automatically tune this parameter and illustrate its behavior for segmenting grayscale and color images.

Keywords: graph cuts, reduction, image segmentation, filtering.

1 Motivation and Scope

Graph cuts have become increasingly popular due to their ability to efficiently compute the Maximum A Posteriori of Markov Random Fields (MRF). This popularity is notably driven by the introduction of a fast maximum-flow (max-flow) algorithm [3] making near real-time performance possible for solving numerous labeling problems such as denoising, image segmentation, stereovision, etc.

In parallel, technological advances in image acquisition have both increased the amount and the diversity of data to process. As an illustration, in the satellite SPOT-5 launched by Arianespace in 2002, the embedded high resolution sensors can capture multispectral and panchromatic images of about 1GB.

Processing this type of data amounts to solve large scale optimization problems. In the image segmentation context, almost all graph cuts-based methods are impractical to solve such problems due to the memory requirements for storing the underlying graphs. To overcome this situation, some amount of work

J. Blanc-Talon et al. (Eds.): ACIVS 2012, LNCS 7517, pp. 201–212, 2012.

has been done in this direction and a number of heuristics [9,10,12,5] and exact methods [7,4,13] have been proposed in recent years.

To our best knowledge, this problem seems to be first addressed in [9] where the underlying graph is built upon a pre-segmentation. Although this approach greatly reduce the computational burden of graph cuts, the results strongly depend on the algorithm used for computing the pre-segmentation. Also, better results are obtained when over-segmentation occurs, losing in this way the main benefit of such a reduction.

Others have also reported band-based methods [10,12,5]. A low-resolution of the image is first segmented and the solution is propagated to the finer level by only building the graph in a narrow band surrounding the interpolated foreground/background interface at that resolution. While such an approach drastically reduce time and memory consumption, it is limited to segment roundish objects. This problem is notably reduced in [12] but still present for low-contrasted details. In [5], finer bands are obtained using an uncertainty measure associated to each pixel.

Exact methods have been also investigated [7,4,13]. In [7], binary energy functions are minimized for the shape fitting problem with graph cuts in a narrow band while ensuring the optimality on the solution. One makes a band evolve around the object to delineate by expanding it when the minimum-cut (min-cut) touches its boundary. This process is iterated until the band no longer evolves. Although the algorithm generally converges in few iterations toward the optimal solution, an initialization is required and no bound on the band size is given.

A parallel max-flow algorithm yielding a near-linear speedup with the number of processors is described in [4]. Nevertheless, the algorithm is relatively sensitive to the available amount of physical memory and remains less efficient on small graphs.

The approach used in [13] is different: instead of reducing the graphs, the problem is decomposed into optimizable sub-problems, solved independently and updated according to the results of the adjacent problems. This process is iterated until convergence and optimality is guaranteed by Lagrangian decomposition.

Finally, another band-based method called Reduced Graph Cuts (RGC) was proposed for reducing graphs in binary image segmentation [8]. The graph is progressively built by only adding nodes which locally satisfy a condition. In the manner of [12,5], the graph nodes are typically located in a narrow band surrounding the object edges to segment. Empirically, the authors show in [8] that the solutions obtained with and without reduction are identical and the time for reducing the graph is even compensated by the time for computing the min-cut in the reduced graph when the regularization is of moderate level.

The rest of this paper is organized as follows. We first briefly review the graph cuts framework in Section 2 as well as the band-based strategy of [8] in Section 3 for reducing graphs. Afterwards, a new parameter is introduced in Section 4 for further reducing the graphs and removing small undesired segments in the segmentation due to noise. The sensitivity of this parameter as well as its robustness against noise are also evaluated through experiments for segmenting grayscale and color images.

2 Preliminaries

Consider a multi-channels image $I : \mathcal{P} \subset \mathbb{Z}^d \rightarrow [0,1]^c$ $(c > 0)$ as a function, mapping each pixel $p \in \mathcal{P}$ to a vector $I_p \in [0,1]^c$ [1]. We define a binary segmentation as an application u affecting to each pixel $p \in \mathcal{P}$ either 0 (background) or 1 (object) and we write $u \in \{0,1\}^{\mathcal{P}}$. A popular strategy to segment I is to minimize a MRF of the form [2]:

$$E(u) = \beta \sum_{p \in \mathcal{P}} E_p(u_p) + \sum_{(p,q) \in \mathcal{N}} E_{p,q}(u_p, u_q), \qquad (1)$$

among $u \in \{0,1\}^{\mathcal{P}}$ and for a fixed parameter $\beta \in \mathbb{R}^+$. The neighborhood system $\mathcal{N} \subset (\mathcal{P} \times \mathcal{P})$ is a subset of all pixel pairs. In the sequel, "connectivity 0" will denote 4 and 6 neighbors in 2D and 3D images while "connectivity 1" will denote 8 and 26 neighbors for the same images. In (1), the data term $E_p(.)$ is defined as the negative log-likelihood of a label being assigned to pixel p and is computed from its color and the appearance models of the object and background seeds [2]:

$$\begin{cases} E_p(1) = -log\, \mathbb{P}(I_p | p \in \mathcal{O}) \\ E_p(0) = -log\, \mathbb{P}(I_p | p \in \mathcal{B}) \end{cases} \qquad (2)$$

For any pixels pair $(p,q) \in \mathcal{N}$, the corresponding smoothness term in (1) is defined as a contrast-sensitive Ising model:

$$E_{p,q}(u_p, u_q) = \begin{cases} 0 & \text{if } u_p = u_q, \\ \frac{1}{\|p-q\|_2} exp\Big(-\frac{\|I_p - I_q\|_2^2}{2\sigma^2} \Big) & \text{otherwise,} \end{cases} \qquad (3)$$

where $\|.\|_2$ is the Euclidean norm (either in $\mathbb{R}^d$ or $\mathbb{R}^c$) and σ is a free parameter generally related to noise acquisition. As an illustration, when pixels p and q belong to a uniform area, we have $\|I_p - I_q\|_2 < \sigma$. This implies a large cost in the exponential and discourages any cut between pixels p and q. Conversely, when these pixels are on both sides of a contour, we have $\|I_p - I_q\|_2 > \sigma$. This encourages any cut between pixels p and q due to low value of the exponential.

When the smoothness terms are submodular [6], the minimizer of (1) can be efficiently obtained by computing a min-cut in a weighted digraph $\mathcal{G} = (\mathcal{V}, \mathcal{E})$ with a set of nodes $\mathcal{V} = \mathcal{P} \cup \{s,t\}$, a set of edges $\mathcal{E} \subset (\mathcal{V} \times \mathcal{V})$ and edge capacities $c : (\mathcal{V} \times \mathcal{V}) \rightarrow \mathbb{R}^+$. The terminal nodes s and t are called the source and the sink, respectively. The set of edges $\mathcal{E}$ is split into two disjoint sets $\mathcal{E}_n$ and $\mathcal{E}_t$ denoting respectively n-links (edges linking two nodes of $\mathcal{P}$) and t-links (edges linking a node of $\mathcal{P}$ to the terminal s or t). Once the min-cut is computed in $\mathcal{G}$, we set $u_p = 1$ if a node p is connected to the source s and $u_p = 0$ if p is connected to the sink t.

---

[1] Usually, $\mathcal{P}$ corresponds to a rectangle.

[2] In this setting, the distributions are estimated using a Gaussian Mixtures Model. The number of Gaussians is automatically computed using a statistical criterion [1].

3 Reduction

As explained before, the memory consumption of graph cuts for segmenting high-resolution data can be very large. As an illustration, the max-flow algorithm of [3] v3.01 used in the experiments of Section 4, allocates $25 \sharp \mathcal{P} + 16 \sharp \mathcal{E}_n$ bytes [3]. For a fixed amount of RAM, one clearly see that the maximum image size quickly decreases as the dimensionality d of $\mathcal{P}$ increases. As shown in [8], most of the nodes in the graph are however useless during the max-flow computation since they are not traversed by any flow. Ideally, one would like to extract the smallest possible graph $\mathcal{G}' = (\mathcal{V}', \mathcal{E}')$ from $\mathcal{G} = (\mathcal{V}, \mathcal{E})$ while keeping the max-flow value f'^* in $\mathcal{G}'$ identical or very close to the max-flow value f^* in $\mathcal{G}$. This corresponds to an ideal optimization problem which we will not try to solve since the method for determining $\mathcal{G}$ also needs to be (very) fast.

Let us first introduce some terminology before reviewing the method of [8] for building $\mathcal{G}'$. For the sake of clarity, the same notations are used as in [8]. In accordance with the construction given in [6], we consider (without loss of generality) that a node is connected to at most one terminal

$$(s, p) \in \mathcal{E}_t \Rightarrow (p, t) \notin \mathcal{E}_t, \qquad \forall p \in \mathcal{P}. \tag{4}$$

We also summarize t-links capacities by

$$c(p) = c(s, p) - c(p, t), \qquad \forall p \in \mathcal{P}. \tag{5}$$

For any $B \subset \mathbb{Z}^d$ [4] and a node $p \in \mathcal{P}$, we denote by B_p the set translation of B at p

$$B_p = \{q + p \mid q \in (B \cap \mathcal{P})\}. \tag{6}$$

For $Z \subset \mathcal{P}$ and $B \subset \mathbb{Z}^d$, we denote by Z_B the dilation of Z by B as

$$Z_B = \{p + q \mid q \in (B \cap \mathcal{P}), p \in Z\} = \bigcup_{p \in Z} B_p. \tag{7}$$

From here, the idea developed in [8] for building $\mathcal{G}'$ is to remove from the nodes of $\mathcal{G}$ any $Z \subset \mathcal{P}$ where all nodes are linked to s (resp. to t) and such that all the flow that might get in (resp. out of) the region Z_B does so by traversing its boundary and can be absorbed (resp. provided) by the band $Z_B \setminus Z$. Building such Z is done by testing each individual pixel $p \in \mathcal{P}$. In the manner of [12,5], the remaining nodes are therefore located in a narrow band surrounding the object edges to segment. In practice, the authors of [8] use a more conservative test by testing each node $p \in Z$ in a square window B of size $(2r + 1)^d$ centered in p:

$$\begin{cases} \text{either} & \left(\forall q \in B_p, \ c(q) \geq +\delta_r\right), \\ \text{or} & \left(\forall q \in B_p, \ c(q) \leq -\delta_r\right). \end{cases} \tag{8}$$

---

[3] The operator '$\sharp$' stands for the cardinality of a set.
[4] In practice, B is a square centered at the origin.

where $\delta_r = \frac{P(B)}{(2r+1)^d - 1}$ and $P(B)$ is defined as

$$P(B) = \max(\sharp\{(p,q) \; : \; p \in B, q \notin B \text{ and } (p,q) \in \mathcal{N}\},$$
$$\sharp\{(q,p) \; : \; p \in B, q \notin B \text{ and } (q,p) \in \mathcal{N}\}). \tag{9}$$

In words, for any node $p \in Z$ satisfying the first (resp. second) condition of (8), all its neighbors $q \in B_q$ are only linked to s (resp. t) and the flow that might get in (resp. out) through t-links in $B_p \setminus \{p\}$ suffices to saturate the n-links going out (resp. in) B_p. Thus, p becomes useless and need not to be added to $\mathcal{G}'$. An algorithm of complexity $O(1)$ (i.e. independent of r) is also mentioned in [8] for computing (8). Additionally, the extra memory storage required by this algorithm is a table of dimensionality $(d - 1)$ and is therefore negligible over the image and the graph size. A key point of [8] is that the pixel error between segmentations obtained with and without reduction remains extremely low, hence preserving thin structures which are ubiquitous in some applications.

The experiments presented in [8] confirm the intuitive dependence between the size of the reduced graph $\mathcal{G}'$ and the model parameters. Indeed, when minimizing (1) by graph cuts, the t-links capacities are all multiplied by β. It is therefore straightforward to observe that the test (8) is harder to satisfy as β decreases. In such a situation, we need a larger window radius for decreasing δ_r in order to reduce the size of the reduced graph $\mathcal{G}'$. This results in wider bands around the object contours. Conversely, when β is large, we can afford a large δ_r and therefore a small window radius to decrease the size of the reduced graph $\mathcal{G}'$. An ideal situation therefore consists of large area of nodes connected to the same terminals separated by rough borders. As opposite, a less favorable situation occurs when these area consist of nodes connected to different terminals. This is typically the case when dealing with noisy images. In the next section, we embed a new parameter in (8) to both further reducing $\mathcal{G}'$ and filtering the segmentation while keeping β large.

4 Simultaneous Segmentation and Filtering

A naive approach to filter the segmentation is to apply morphological operators (e.g. opening or closing). Nonetheless, when the amount of noise is large, such an approach fail during the reduction since a lot of nodes would be added to the reduced graph. Another approach would consist in denoising the image first and then applying [8]. This would lead to unsatisfactory results in the case for instance of echographic images since contours of objects would be over-smoothed.

Another way to filter the segmentation is to relax (8) is to allow some nodes in B_p to fail complying the test. The proportion of nodes satisfying (8) can be controlled by a parameter $\eta \in [0,1]$. As η decreases, the test (8) becomes easier to satisfy since a larger proportion of nodes can be connected to opposite terminals. Embedding η in (8) leads to

$$\begin{cases} \text{either} & \left(\sharp\{q \in B_p \mid c(q) \geq +\delta_r\} \geq \eta \sharp B_p\right), \\ \text{or} & \left(\sharp\{q \in B_p \mid c(q) \leq -\delta_r\} \geq \eta \sharp B_p\right). \end{cases} \tag{10}$$

4.1   Further Reducing Graphs

The parameter η can be used for decreasing the memory consumption of graph cuts. The Figure 3 illustrates how far the test (8) can be relaxed for further reducing graphs while getting nearly the same segmentation. In this experiment, the segmentation as well as the reduced graph are shown for segmenting a 2D noisy image. Since the test (10) is easier to satisfy as η decreases, the reduced graph $\mathcal{G}'$ becomes thicker around the object contours.

4.2   Automatic Tuning of η

Lower Bound. For a fixed window radius, notice first that the value of η must be large enough to not increase the number of components in the reduced graph $\mathcal{G}'$ (see Figure 2). Indeed, below some value (denoted by η_{min}), the reduced graph $\mathcal{G}'$ is split into multiple pieces in areas with high-curvature and the min-cut is no longer ensured of being fully embedded into $\mathcal{G}'$. This implies that some voxels could be wrongly labeled in the segmentation.

The Figure 1 illustrates a situation where η_{min} can be easily computed with an image consisting of two highly-contrasted areas. Using (10) with a square window of radius r and $\eta = 1$, the reduced graph $\mathcal{G}'$ corresponds to a thin band of size $2r$. An easy under-estimation of η_{min} is obtained by imposing that η_{min} permits to segment these two contrasted areas. In order to do so, we want the test (10) to be false for any pixel p at the boundary between these areas. For such a pixel, we have (assuming e.g. that $c(p) \geq +\delta_r$)

$$\sharp\{q \in B_p \mid c(q) \geq +\delta_r\} = (r+1)(2r+1)^{d-1}. \tag{11}$$

As a consequence, if

$$\eta \leq \frac{(r+1)(2r+1)^{d-1}}{(2r+1)^d}, \tag{12}$$

the node p does not belong to the reduced graph $\mathcal{G}'$. Since we want to avoid the situation, we must therefore have

$$\eta > \frac{(r+1)(2r+1)^{d-1}}{(2r+1)^d}$$
$$= 1 - \frac{r}{2r+1} = \eta_{min}. \tag{13}$$

Remark that (13) does not depend on the dimensionality d of $\mathcal{P}$. By observing (13), it is straightforward to see that, as the window radius r tends to infinity, the proportion of nodes allowed to be connected to opposite terminals tends to $\frac{1}{2}$. In practice, we also observed that (13) is less accurate in connectivity 0 than in connectivity 1 (see Figure 2).

Upper Bound. For a fixed window radius r and a positive amount of noise ξ, one can observe in Figure 3 that there exists a value of the parameter η for which most of the nodes in noisy regions are removed from the graph $\mathcal{G}$, leading to a diminution of the size of the reduced graph $\mathcal{G}'$.

The purpose of this paragraph is to identify, from a statistical point of view, a reliable value of the parameter η for which all nodes of $\mathcal{P}$ are very likely to be removed from $\mathcal{G}$. For a fixed amount of noise ξ in the image I, we therefore want to find an upper bound on η by finding the maximum value of η in such a way that we control the proportion of nodes corresponding to noisy pixels in homogeneous areas.

Consider a noisy constant image I with a noise generated by a Bernoulli distribution of parameter $\xi \in]0,1[$, corresponding to the amount of noise in I [5]. The two cases where $\xi = 0$ and $\xi = 1$ are trivial and are not considered in our analysis. Assume now that the graph $\mathcal{G}$ is defined as in Section 3 where the nodes corresponding to noise-free pixels are connected to the sink t with a capacity $c(q) \leq -\delta_r$ and the nodes corresponding to noisy pixels have a capacity $c(q) > -\delta_r$.

First, let X be a discrete random variable counting degraded pixels in a square window B of size $n = (2r + 1)^d$ in the image I. Then, the probability that at least k pixels are corrupted in B is given by

$$\mathbb{P}(X > k) = \sum_{i=k+1}^{n} \binom{n}{i} \xi^i (1 - \xi)^{n-i}, \tag{14}$$

where $\binom{n}{i} = \frac{n!}{i!(n-i)!}$. For a fixed window radius r, it is straightforward to see that (14) is decreasing in k and tends to ξ^n if we impose that $\xi \in]0,1[$. According to the test (10) and the hypothesis on $\mathcal{G}$: a node $p \in \mathcal{P}$ can be removed from $\mathcal{G}$ if and only if

$$\sharp\{q \in B_p \mid c(q) \leq -\delta_r\} = \sharp\{q \in B_p \mid q \text{ is noise-free}\} \geq \eta n \tag{15}$$

Moreover, we assumed

$$\sharp\{q \in B_p \mid q \text{ is noise-free}\} \sim (n - X). \tag{16}$$

Therefore, we have

$$\mathbb{P}(p \text{ is not removed}) = \mathbb{P}((n - X) < \eta n) = \mathbb{P}(X > (1 - \eta)n). \tag{17}$$

Fixing a proportion $\varepsilon \simeq 0$ of wrongly constructed nodes, we choose

$$\eta^+ = \max \{\eta \in [0, 1] \mid \mathbb{P}(X > (1 - \eta)n) \geq \varepsilon\}, \tag{18}$$

Considering the lower bound η_{min} defined in (13), we set

$$\eta_{max} = \max \{\eta_{min}, \eta^+\}. \tag{19}$$

Combining the definitions of the lower and upper bounds (see (13) and (19)), it now becomes easy to get an estimation of the parameter η^* for a fixed window radius by setting

$$\eta^* = \left(\frac{\eta_{min} + \eta_{max}}{2}\right). \tag{20}$$

---

[5] Histogram-based techniques can be for instance used to estimate ξ.

Let us now analyze the joint behavior of the lower and the upper bounds. When the amount of noise ξ is fixed, one can easily observe that the gap

$$\Delta\eta = (\eta_{max} - \eta_{min}), \tag{21}$$

grows as the window radius r increases. Indeed, we have previously seen that the lower bound η_{min} tends to $\frac{1}{2}$ as the window radius r increases (see (13)). The previous observation is also due to the fact that the upper bound η_{max} grows as the window radius r increases.

Similarly, when the window radius r is fixed, remark that (21) decreases when the amount of noise ξ increases. This situation is consistent because η_{min} remains the same but η_{max} tends to $\frac{1}{2}$ since it is more likely that the number of degraded pixels increase in the window B. Increasing the window radius r can compensate the augmentation of the amount of noise only up to $\xi = 0.5$. Finally, we empirically found that setting $\varepsilon = 0.05$ gives best estimate of η_{max} in (18).

4.3   Filtering

The parameter η can also serves to filter the segmentation. This behavior is illustrated in Figure 4 for segmenting a 3D noisy image acquired from a confocal microscope. White spots correspond to cell nuclei in a mouse cerebellum. Observe how far the filtering acts for small values of η: small regions in the reduced graph $\mathcal{G}'$ as well as in the segmentation are progressively removed as η decreases.

The robustness (see Figure 6 and 5) and sensitivity to noise of the parameter η are now (see Figure 7) are now analyzed. Let us describe the experimental setup. The experiment consists in segmenting four grayscale and five 2D color images in connectivity 1 with an increasing noise level ranging from 4 to 48%. For each image, we compute a reference segmentation on the noise-free image by placing the seeds by hand. We set $\beta = +\infty$ and automatically estimate the σ parameter as explained in [11]. Then, for each impulsive noise level, we select the segmentation maximizing the Dice Similarity Coefficient (DSC) between the reference image and all segmentations obtained through a fixed range of window radii and η values. We choose window radii r from 1 to 12 and eight linearly spaced values of η from η_{min} (w.r.t. r) to 1. Then, each segmentation is computed using the same seeds as those used for the computing the reference segmentation. Again, the σ parameter is automatically estimated as in [11].

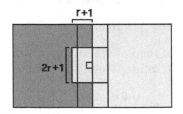

Fig. 1. Toy example for computing the lower bound η_{min}

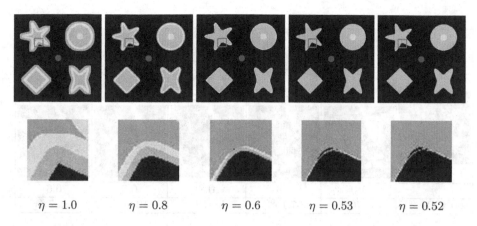

$\eta = 1.0 \qquad \eta = 0.8 \qquad \eta = 0.6 \qquad \eta = 0.53 \qquad \eta = 0.52$

Fig. 2. Illustration of the lower bound η_{min} for segmenting a 2D synthetic image. In this experiment, $\eta_{min} \simeq 0.523$ and we set $r = 10$ using connectivity 1. On all images, the nodes of $\mathcal{G}'$ are superimposed in yellow to the image by transparency. The bottom row correspond to a close-up of the box in purple color. Observe how the reduced graph $\mathcal{G}'$ splits into multiple pieces as soon as $\eta \leq \eta_{min}$.

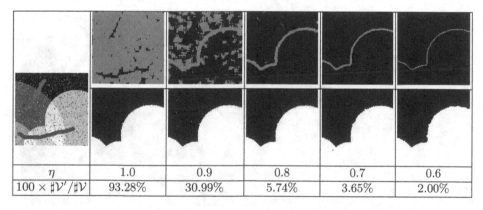

η	1.0	0.9	0.8	0.7	0.6
$100 \times \sharp\mathcal{V}'/\sharp\mathcal{V}$	93.28%	30.99%	5.74%	3.65%	2.00%

Fig. 3. Memory gain when segmenting a 2D synthetic image corrupted by 10% of impulsive noise (left). Top row shows the nodes of the reduced graph in light gray while bottom row shows the corresponding segmentation. In this experiment, we set $r = 3$ and use connectivity 1.

As shown in Figure 6, for an impulsive noise level up to 45%, the parameter η appears to be reasonably robust with a DSC always greater than 94% for all images, except for the image "rice". However, such high and stable noise robustness can only be reached by increasing the amount of seeds (see Figure 6). The reason why the algorithm behaves poorly on the "rice" image is the following. As said earlier, r must be large enough when ξ increases for removing a maximum number of segments due to noise. This implies wider bands in $\mathcal{G}'$ around the object contours. However, the object contours further oscillate as ξ increases.

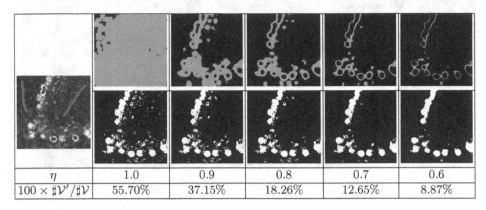

η	1.0	0.9	0.8	0.7	0.6
$100 \times \#\mathcal{V}'/\#\mathcal{V}$	55.70%	37.15%	18.26%	12.65%	8.87%

Fig. 4. Simultaneous segmentation and filtering of a 3D noisy image (left). In this picture, the white spots correspond to cell nuclei in a mouse cerebellum. Top row shows the nodes of the reduced graph in light gray while bottom row shows the corresponding segmentation. In this experiment, we set $r = 5$ and use connectivity 1.

Fig. 5. Qualitative analysis of the robustness to noise for segmenting the images "f117" (left-most column), "pyramid" (left column), "sunflower" (right column) and "flamingo" (right-most column) in with a fixed impulsive noise level of 36%. Seeds and model parameters are the same than those used in Figure 6 (top row).

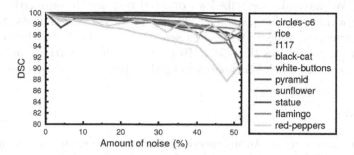

Fig. 6. Quantitative analysis of the robustness to noise for segmenting in connectivity 1 four 2D grayscale images (top-most curves in the list) and five 2D color images with an impulsive noise level ranging from 4 to 48%.

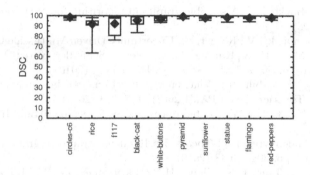

Fig. 7. Sensitivity of η for segmenting the images in Figure 6 with an impulsive noise level of 36%. The seeds and model parameters are the same than those used in Figure 6.

Another reason is due to the proximity of the objects to segment. As an illustration, consider two circles over a uniform background, separated by a distance $d_0 > 0$. We clearly see that the test (10) becomes more and more difficult to satisfy when the window radius r increases. When $(2r + 1) \geq d_0$, the reduced graphs of both circles fuse into one component. This is typically the case for the image "rice" because it consists of small assembled rice grains near from each other. Finally, the Figure 7 also illustrates that the parameter η is not very sensitive to the variations of r and η. The DSC does not vary much with respect to noise, except for the image "rice". This exception can be explained for the same reasons as before.

5   Conclusion

In this paper, we have presented a new parameter to embed in [8] for simultaneously reduce graphs and filter segmentations with the same computational complexity. We have also described an original manner to automatically tune it with the window radius parameter. In the proposed experiments, this new parameter generally appears to be less sensitive to noise but only for a limited amount, typically less than 50%. To overcome this situation, we could for instance inspect larger neighborhoords to further discriminate signal from noise.

References

1. Bouman, C.A.: Cluster: An unsupervised algorithm for modeling Gaussian mixtures (April 1997), http://www.ece.purdue.edu/string~bouman
2. Boykov, Y., Jolly, M.-P.: Interactive graph cuts for optimal boundary and region segmentation of objects in N-D images. In: ICCV, vol. 1, pp. 105–112 (2001)
3. Boykov, Y., Kolmogorov, V.: An experimental comparison of min-cut/max-flow algorithms for energy minimization in vision. IEEE Transactions on PAMI 26(9), 1124–1137 (2004)
4. Delong, A., Boykov, Y.: A scalable graph-cut algorithm for N-D grids. In: CVPR, pp. 1–8 (2008)
5. Kohli, P., Lempitsky, V., Rother, C.: Uncertainty Driven Multi-scale Optimization. In: Goesele, M., Roth, S., Kuijper, A., Schiele, B., Schindler, K. (eds.) DAGM 2010. LNCS, vol. 6376, pp. 242–251. Springer, Heidelberg (2010)
6. Kolmogorov, V., Zabih, R.: What energy functions can be minimized via graph cuts? IEEE Transactions on PAMI 26(2), 147–159 (2004)
7. Lempitsky, V., Boykov, Y.: Global optimization for shape fitting. In: CVPR, pp. 1–8 (2007)
8. Lermé, N., Malgouyres, F., Létocart, L.: Reducing graphs in graph cut segmentation. In: ICIP, pp. 3045–3048 (2010)
9. Li, Y., Sun, J., Tang, C.K., Shum, H.Y.: Lazy Snapping. ACM Transactions on Graphics 23(3), 303–308 (2004)
10. Lombaert, H., Sun, Y.Y., Grady, L., Xu, C.Y.: A multilevel banded graph cuts method for fast image segmentation. In: ICCV, vol. 1, pp. 259–265 (2005)
11. Rother, C., Kolmogorov, V., Blake, A.: "GrabCut": Interactive foreground extraction using iterated graph cuts. In: SIGGRAPH, pp. 309–314 (2004)
12. Sinop, A.K., Grady, L.: Accurate Banded Graph Cut Segmentation of Thin Structures Using Laplacian Pyramids. In: Larsen, R., Nielsen, M., Sporring, J. (eds.) MICCAI 2006. LNCS, vol. 4191, pp. 896–903. Springer, Heidelberg (2006)
13. Strandmark, P., Kahl, F.: Parallel and distributed graph cuts by dual decomposition. In: CVPR, pp. 2085–2092 (2010)

Rectangular Decomposition of Binary Images[*]

Tomáš Suk, Cyril Höschl IV, and Jan Flusser

Institute of Information Theory and Automation of the ASCR,
Pod vodárenskou věží 4, 182 08 Praha 8, Czech Republic
{suk,hoschl,flusser}@utia.cas.cz
http://zoi.utia.cas.cz/

Abstract. The contribution deals with the most important methods for decomposition of binary images into union of rectangles. The overview includes run-length encoding and its generalization, decompositions based on quadtrees, on the distance transformation, and a theoretically optimal decomposition based on maximal matching in bipartite graphs. We experimentally test their performance In binary image compression and in convolution calculation and compare their computation times and success rates.

Keywords: Binary image decomposition, generalized delta-method, distance transformation, quadtree, bipartite graph, image compression, fast convolution.

1 Introduction

Binary images can be represented in a more efficient way, than just as a full-sized matrix consisting of zeros and ones. The terms "good representation" and "optimal representation" cannot be generally defined and are always dependent on what we are going to do with the image. The methods of binary image representation can be divided into two groups referred as *decomposition methods* and *boundary-based methods* (which we do not discuss in this paper).

Decomposition methods try to express the object as a union of simple disjoint subsets called *blocks* or *partitions* which can be effectively stored and consequently used for required processing. Having a binary object B (by a binary object we understand a set of all pixels of a binary image whose values equal one), we decompose it into $K \geq 1$ blocks $B_1, B_2, \ldots, B_K$ such that $B_i \cap B_j = \emptyset$ for any $i \neq j$ and $B = \bigcup_{k=1}^{K} B_k$. Although in a continuous domain we may consider various shapes of the blocks (convex, star-shaped, hexagonal, rectangular, etc., see [10]), all decomposition methods which perform in a discrete domain use only rectilinear rectangular or square blocks because of a native rectangular structure of the discrete image domain.

---

[*] This work has been supported by the grant No. P103/11/1552 of the Czech Science Foundation.

J. Blanc-Talon et al. (Eds.): ACIVS 2012, LNCS 7517, pp. 213–224, 2012.

The power of any decomposition method depends on its ability to decompose the object into a small number of blocks in a reasonable time. Most authors have measured the decomposition quality just by the number of blocks K, while ignoring the complexity of the algorithms, claiming that such decomposition that minimizes K is the optimal one. This criterion is justified by the fact that the complexity of subsequent calculations uses to be $\mathcal{O}(K)$ and compression ratio (if the decomposition is used for compression purposes) also increases as the number of blocks decreases. However, this viewpoint may be misleading. Simple algorithms produce relatively high number of blocks but perform fast, while more sophisticated decomposition methods end up with the small number of blocks but require more time. Even if the decomposition is in most tasks performed only once per object and can be done off-line, the time needed for decomposing the image is often so long that it substantially influences the efficiency of the whole method.

Image rectangular decomposition has found numerous straightforward applications in image compression methods and formats (RLE, TIFF, BMP and others), in calculation of image features (mainly moments and moment invariants) [7] in fast convolution algorithms with binary kernels, and in VLSI design.

The aim of this paper is to review existing decomposition methods, to present one which is new in this context and which is theoretically optimal in terms of the number of blocks, and to compare their performance in loss-less image compression and in fast convolution calculation.

2   Decomposition into Row Segments

Decomposition of an object into rows or columns is the most straightforward and the oldest method. The blocks are continuous row segments for which only the coordinate of the beginning and the length are stored. In image compression this has been known as run-length encoding (RLE). This principle and its modifications (CCITT, PackBits) are used in several image formats such as TIFF and BMP. In feature calculation, Zakaria [18] used the same representation for fast computation of image moments of convex shapes and called it "Delta-method" (DM). It is very fast but leads to the number of blocks which uses to be (much) higher than the minimal decomposition.

A simple but powerful improvement of the delta method was proposed by Spiliotis and Mertzios [17]. This "Generalized Delta-method" (GDM) employs a rectangular-wise object representation instead of the row-wise one. The adjacent rows are compared and if there are some segments with the same beginning and end, they are unified into a rectangle (see Fig. 1a). For each rectangle, the coordinates of its upper-left corner, the length and the width are stored. The GDM is only slightly slower than DM while producing (sometimes significantly) less number of blocks. Surprisingly, under our knowledge this method has not been implemented in any commercial image format.

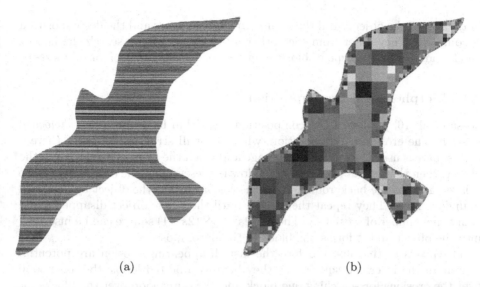

Fig. 1. Decomposition of the bird image. (a) Generalized Delta-method (GDM – 983 blocks in total), (b) Quadtree decomposition (QTD – 4489 blocks in total).

3 Quadtree Decomposition

Quadtree decomposition (QTD) is a popular hierarchical decomposition scheme used in (but not limited to) image representation and compression [9]. The QTD works with square images of a size of a power of two; if it is not the case, the image can easily be zero-padded to the nearest such size. The image is iteratively divided into four quadrants. Homogeneity of each quadrant is checked and if the whole quadrant lies either in the object or in the background, it is not further divided. If it contains both object and background pixels, it is divided into quadrants, and the process is repeated until all blocks are homogeneous. The decomposition can be efficiently encoded into three-symbol string, where 2 means division, 1 means a part of the object and 0 stands for the background. An example of the quadtree decomposition is in Fig. 1b.

The algorithm always yields square blocks that may be advantageous for some purpose but usually leads to a higher number of blocks than necessary. A drawback of this decomposition algorithm is that the division scheme is not adapted with respect to the content of the image, but it is defined by absolute spatial coordinates. Hence, the decomposition is not translation-invariant and may lead to absurd results when for instance a large single square is uselessly decomposed up to individual pixels.

4 Decomposition to the Largest Inscribed Blocks

This group of methods can be described as "the largest first". They search the largest block that can be inscribed into the object, remove it and repeat searching in the rest of the object until the entire object disappears and the decomposition is complete. They differ from each other by the way, how to search the largest block and also by the type of blocks (squares or rectangles, even or odd sizes).

4.1 Morphological Decomposition

Sossa et al [16] published a decomposition algorithm based on a *morphological erosion*. The erosion is an operation, where a small structural element (here a 3×3 square is used) moves over the image and when the whole element lies in the object, then the central pixel of the window is preserved in the object, otherwise it is assigned to the background. So, each erosion shrinks the object by one-pixel boundary layer. They repeat the erosion until the whole object disappears and count the number of erosions s. Then a $(2s-1) \times (2s-1)$ square can be inscribed into the object and it forms one block of the decomposition.

The pixels of the object before the last disappearing erosion are potential centers of the inscribed square. So, they have two nested loops: the inner loop over the erosions for searching one block and the outer loop over the blocks for whole decomposition. If we consider that erosion is a relatively time consuming operation, it suggests this method performs much slower comparing to the previous decomposition algorithms. Although the original method [16] considers decomposition into squares only, it can be generalized also to rectangles which decreases the number of the resulting blocks.

4.2 Distance Transformation Decomposition

We proposed to speed up the previous algorithm by means of the *distance transformation* (DT), which we use for finding of the centers of the inscribed rectangles. In morphological decomposition, we must repeat the erosions s-times for finding $(2s - 1) \times (2s - 1)$ inscribed square, while the distance transformation with a suitable metric can be calculated only once. The DT of a binary image is an image, where each object pixel shows the distance to the nearest boundary pixel and the background pixels are zero [1].

DT strongly depends on the metric used for the distance measurement. Seaidoun [15] proposed an algorithm for the Euclidean metric, we used a simplified version for the chessboard metric

$$d(a,b) = \max\{|a_x - b_x|, |a_y - b_y|\}. \tag{1}$$

The metric is closely related to the form of the blocks, the chessboard metric leads to the decomposition to rectilinear squares, the Euclidean metric to circular blocks and a city block metric to the squares rotated by $45°$.

We successively search the image from the left, right, top and bottom, count distances from the last boundary pixel and calculate the minimum from the four directions. The result is DT, the maximum of the result equals s for the inscribed square $(2s - 1) \times (2s - 1)$ and the pixels with this maximum value are potential centers of the inscribed squares.

We use an improved version of DT inspired by [14]. If we change only a small part of the original image, then upgrading its close neighborhood is sufficient. In our case, if we remove a rectangle from the image, then the rectangle is zeroed and DT is recomputed in a small frame around it. If the frame in some distance d from the rectangle is not changed, then the rest of DT is left unchanged.

The potential center(s) of the largest inscribed blocks are the pixels with the maximum values of DT. If the maximum s is unique, then a square $(2s - 1) \times (2s - 1)$ is inscribed. However, often the maximum is not unique and the choice of the block center is ambiguous. We try to keep the blocks as large as possible. Hence, if there is a 2×2 square of the maxima, an even-sized square $2s \times 2s$ can be inscribed into the object. If the potential square centers create a line segment (with a single or double-pixel width), then the corresponding squares are unified into one rectangle. At the end of the loop, the inscribed rectangle is removed from the object and the procedure starts the next loop, which is applied to the rest of the image. The decomposed bird image is shown in Fig. 2a.

Both morphological and DT decompositions end up with the same set of blocks. However, they are still only sub-optimal even on many simple shapes. This is because a sequence of locally optimal steps which these "greedy" algorithms apply to an image (placing always the largest inscribed rectangle) may not yield an optimal solution. As soon as a block is created, it cannot be removed any more because the methods do not include any backtracking. These two algorithms differ from each other by computing complexity. Erosion is a relatively complex operation while the DT can be calculated faster thanks to its simple upgrading. Anyway, both methods perform slower comparing to the previous decomposition algorithms, see the experiments.

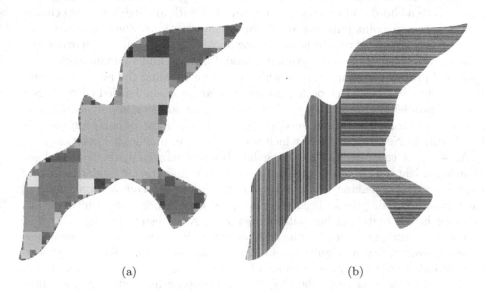

(a)   (b)

Fig. 2. (a) Distance transformation decomposition (DTD) of the bird image (1306 blocks in total), (b) GBD decomposition (923 blocks in total)

5   Graph-Based Decomposition

A large group of decomposition algorithms appeared in 80's in computational geometry [10]. Surprisingly, they have not received almost any attention from image analysis community. Their formulation was usually much more general than ours. They tried to decompose general polygons into specific polygonal components (convex polygons, star-shape polygons, triangles, generally oriented rectangles, etc.). A common feature of these methods was that they transformed the decomposition problem to a graph partitioning problem and employed known tools from graph theory. The only subgroup relevant to our purposes is a decomposition of a digital polygon into rectilinear rectangles. An algorithm that was proved to be optimal in terms of the number of blocks was independently proposed in the same form by three different authors [12], [13], [6] (in this order) and later discussed by [8], [4] and others. The method (denoted here as graph-based decomposition – GBD) works for any object even if it contains holes.

The vertices of a binary object can be divided into two groups, those having the inner angle 90° (we can call them "convex") and those having the inner angle 270° (we can call them "concave"). The method performs hierarchically on two levels. On the first level, we detect all concave vertices of the input object and identify pairs of "cogrid" concave vertices (i.e. those having the same horizontal or vertical coordinates). Then we divide the object into subpolygons by constructing chords which connect certain cogrid concave vertices. It is proved in [6] that the optimal choice of the chord set is such that the chords do not intersect each other and their number is maximum possible.

The problem of optimal selection of the chords is equivalent to the problem of finding the maximal set of independent nodes in a graph, where each node corresponds to a chord and two nodes are connected with an edge if the two chords have a common point (either a vertex or an intersection). Since any two horizontal (vertical) edges cannot intersect one another, our graph is a bipartite one which implies a solution in a polynomial time. First, we find a maximal matching (classical problem in graph theory which looks for labeling the maximum number of edges such that each node is incident to at most one labeled edge). It is a classical problem in graph theory, whose algorithmic solution in polynomial time has been published in various versions (probably the most popular approach is by Maximum Network Flow [3] which we also used in our implementation).

As soon as the maximal matching has been constructed, the maximal set of independent nodes can be found much faster than the maximal matching itself – roughly speaking, the maximal independent set contains one node of each matching pair plus all isolated nodes plus some other nodes which are not included in the matching but still independent. As a result we obtain a set of nodes that is unique in terms of the number but ambiguous in terms of particular nodes. However, this ambiguity does not play any role – although each set lead to different partitioning, the number of partitions is always the same. Hence, at the end of the first level, the object is decomposed into subpolygons, which (when considered individually) do not contain any cogrid concave vertices (see Fig. 3d).

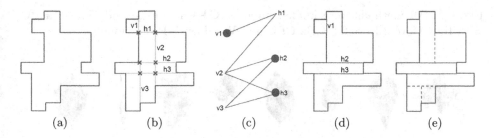

Fig. 3. (a) The object to be decomposed. (b) All possible chords connecting the cogrid concave vertices. The crosses indicate the chord intersections. (c) The corresponding bipartite graph with a maximum independent set of three nodes. (d) The first-level decomposition of the object. (e) The second-level decomposition which adds the decomposition of subpolygons. From each concave vertex a single chord of arbitrary direction is constructed.

The second level is very simple. Each subpolygon coming from the first level is further divided. From each its concave vertex a single chord is constructed such that this chord terminates either on the boundary of the subpolygon or on the chord constructed earlier. This is a sequential process in which each concave vertex is visited only once. Between two possible chords offered in each concave vertex we may choose randomly. After that, the subpolygon is divided into rectangles because rectangle is the only polygon having no concave vertices (see Fig. 3e).

The strength of this algorithm is in the fact that it guarantees minimizing the number of decomposing rectangles regardless of the particular choices on the both levels. On the other hand, one may expect slower performance than in the previous algorithms namely because of expensive finding the maximum set of independent graph nodes.

If the object does not have any cogrid concave vertices or if one of the maximum independent sets of nodes contains only the nodes corresponding to the horizontal (or vertical) chords, then also all chords in the second level may be constructed in the same direction and, consequently, the GBD decomposition leads exactly to the same partitioning as the GDM applied in that direction. It corresponds with the surprisingly good results of the GDM. An example of the GBD decomposition is in Fig. 2b.

6   Experimental Comparison of Image Compression

In this section, we compare the performance of the above decomposition methods in binary image compression. The experiments were performed on the publicly available LEAF database [2] which is a database of 795 scanned and binarized leaves of trees and shrubs of vegetation growing in the Czech Republic (see

Fig. 4)[1]. All methods were implemented in C++ language and run on a PC with Intel Core 2 Duo, 2.8 GHz CPU and Windows 7 Professional.

Fig. 4. Examples of the LEAF database (acer platanoides, aesculus hippocastanum, betula pendula, fagus sylvatica, hedera helix, quercus robur, salix alba, ulmus glabra)

First, we monitor and compare two parameters: the number of blocks and the corresponding decomposition time for the GDM, QTD, DTD and GBD methods, respectively. The data presented in Table 1 are cumulative for all objects in the database. The time was always measured just of the decomposition itself, no input/output operations were included. The minimum number of blocks was achieved by GBD, as was expected. This is of course on the expense of the time but surprisingly the time is lower than that of DTD and only five times higher than the time of QTD. The winner of this test is the GDM method yielding only a slightly worse number of blocks than GBD but in the by far shortest time. On the other hand, QTD produce the highest block number and the DTD is the slowest.

Table 1. The number of blocks and decomposition time achieved on the LEAF database

Method	Number of blocks	Number of blocks [%]	Time [s]
GDM	419489	112	1.3
QTD	1913275	511	7.2
DTD	545528	146	50.3
GBD	374149	100	37.5

Although the decomposition itself makes a substantial compression, we further increase the compression ratios of all methods by a proper block ordering. We propose a new file format denoted as BLK. It uses three types of compression: the blocks from DTD are grouped according their size, this allows to store the size only once per each group and then to store just upper left corner of each block. The long narrow blocks from GDM and GBD are sorted by the coordinates in the "narrow" direction and sizes and coordinate differences in this direction are encoded in the decreased number of bits. QTD uses its traditional three-symbol

---

[1] The database exists in two versions – original (the leaves with petioles, high resolution) and simplified (the leaves without petioles, twice downsampled). Tab. 1 refers to the simplified version, Tab. 2 to the original one.

encoding. The label of the actual decomposition method is stored in the file header along with other auxiliary parameters.

We compared compression ratios of BLK format (with all these four decomposition methods) to commercial formats. As we already explained it does not reflect only the number of blocks since other factors playing role there. We calculated average compression ratios (ACR) over the LEAF database. ACR is a ratio of the size of all files in the database in the specific format and the size without any compression. The results are in Table 2. In this experiment, it is not meaningful to measure the time because it inherently includes I/O operations. Since we do not have an access to source codes of commercial compressions, it would be impossible to ensure an objective time comparison.

Table 2. Compression ratios on the LEAF database

Format	Method	size [byte]	ACR [%]
TIFF	no compression	172886448	100.00
TIFF	PackBits	13282998	7.68
TIFF	RLE	8297340	4.80
GIF	LZW	6914637	4.00
BLK	DTD	5173371	2.99
PNG	deflate	5066019	2.93
BLK	GDM	4723166	2.73
BLK	GBD	4603942	2.66
BLK	QTD	3012532	1.74

Surprisingly the best performance of QTD (comparing to the previous experiment) was achieved namely because the three-symbol encoding in the BLK format is very efficient. The ACR of GBD and GDM is slightly worse, but still very good; the GBD method is better because it guarantees the minimum number of blocks. The good result of DTD was achieved by efficient encoding of one-pixel blocks, but in the longest time. The only commercial format with comparable ACR is PNG with a deflate method, others provide worse compression ratios than all BLK methods.

Based on these two measurements a general recommendation can be as follows: the QTD method yields good compression ratio because of efficient implementation in BLK format, but we should keep in mind that the number of blocks was four times higher and the decomposition time even six times higher than GDM offering a very good compromise between compression ratio and decomposition speed. The GBD and DTD methods are suitable mainly for applications, where the compression is performed only once (usually off-line) and thus the time of the compression is not critical. GBD provides minimum number of blocks and slightly better ACR and time of compression.

7   Experimental Comparison of Computing Convolution

In this experiment we show that the decomposition can be a powerful tool for speeding-up convolution filtering of an image with a binary kernel. While traditional "by definition" discrete convolution of an $M \times N$ image with an arbitrary $m \times n$ mask requires $\mathcal{O}(mnMN)$ operations and convolution via fast Fourier transformation (FFT) $\mathcal{O}(MN \log MN)$ operations, convolution with a constant-valued rectangle takes only $\mathcal{O}(MN)$ operations regardless of the mask size. There are several ways how to implement such algorithm. The best one is probably to employ precalculations of row-wise and consequently column-wise sums of the image. Let us denote $S(X)$ the row-wise and column-wise sum of the original image from (0,0) to pixel X, then the convolution with a rectangular mask $ABCD$ is given as $S(D) - S(C) - S(B) + S(A)$.

Now let us imagine a binary kernel where the non-zero values form a more complex set than a single rectangle. Such a situation typically appears for instance in *coded aperture* (CA) imaging. CA is a method of recovering the depth map of the scene from a single image [11]. The trick is to insert a special occluder within the aperture of the camera lens to create a coded aperture. The CA output must be deconvolved, which incorporates (if an iterative deconvolution method such as Richardson-Lucy or similar is applied) repeating calculations of convolution of an estimated image with the aperture mask.

If the mask has a full or close-to-full rank, we cannot effectively use any factorization that seemingly takes us back to the calculation from the definition or via FFT. However, if we decompose the mask into rectangles $B_1, \cdots, B_K$, we can, thanks to the linearity of convolution, calculate the convolutions with each B_j separately by the method described above and then just sum up the results. (This method can be used even if the kernel is not binary and thus the blocks have different values but that is a rare case in practice.) In that way we achieve the overall complexity of $\mathcal{O}(KMN)$. In this experiment we demonstrate that for $K << mn$ the speed up is really huge comparing to the direct calculation from the definition and still significant comparing to the FFT.

We filtered a 3456×2592 image with two binary kernels of the same shape but different size – the small one of (35×38) and the large one of (141×152) pixels. The small kernel is a downsampled version of the large one (see Fig. 5a). The kernels were decomposed by the GBD method into 10 rectangles (see Fig. 5b).

We tested three methods – direct convolution in the image domain from the definition, convolution via FFT in the frequency domain (we used popular public-domain FFTPack software [5]), and fast convolution using kernel decomposition as described above. In the last case, the matrix of the partial sums of the image was precomputed and then the (cyclic) convolution was calculated.

We wanted to measure the time of each individual step separately because in practice either the mask decomposition or the precomputing of partial sums uses to be done only once and hence its complexity is negligible (in batch processing either the mask or the image stays the same while the other factor varies).

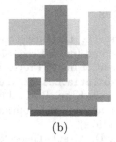

(a)   (b)

Fig. 5. (a) The binary convolution kernel used in the experiment. (b) Its 10 blocks of GBD decomposition.

However, the mask decomposition was so fast that the corresponding time was not measurable.

As expected, the slowest calculation is from the definition in the image domain – 26 seconds for the small and 411 seconds for the large kernel, respectively. The speed of the calculation via FFT is independent of the kernel size – 4.3 seconds in both cases. Also the time of the decomposition method actually does not depend on the mask size. It took only 0.96 seconds including precomputing of the partial sums (0.1 s) and the mask decomposition (negligible time).

This experiment illustrates that the convolution with a binary mask can be implemented by means of mask decomposition in a very efficient way. Two main factors influence whether or not the convolution via decomposition is faster than via FFT – the image size (not the mask size – we expect masks much smaller than the images) and the number of blocks of the mask. In our implementation and hardware and for 8 – 10 Mpix images the threshold value is about 40 blocks. If the number of blocks is lower, the decomposition-based convolution is the best choice.

8   Conclusion

We presented an overview of methods which decompose an arbitrary binary object into rectilinear rectangles, starting from very simple one up to the optimal graph-based decomposition. We tested their performance in two frequent tasks – image compression and linear filtering. We showed that there is no "generally best" method; the choice must reflect our requirements and is always a compromise between complexity on one hand and time and memory consumption on the other hand. The weights given to these two factors are user-defined parameters.

This paper should help the users to select proper decomposition method according to their preferences. In our opinion, GDM is the most appropriate in common situations, while GBD is recommended if we want to achieve as few blocks as possible on the expense of higher complexity. The other two tested methods either produce too many blocks (QTD) or perform slowly (DTD). They may find applications in specific tasks only. The decomposition methods can be used for speed-up of various other computations, e.g. computing features for pattern recognition as moments etc.

References

1. Borgefors, G.: Distance transformations in digital images. Computer Vision, Graphics, and Image Processing 34(3), 344–371 (1986)
2. Department of Image Processing: Tree leaf database,
   http://zoi.utia.cas.cz/tree_leaves
3. Edmonds, J., Karp, R.M.: Theoretical improvements in algorithmic efficiency for network flow problems. Journal of the Association for Computing Machinery 19(2), 248–264 (1972)
4. Eppstein, D.: Graph-Theoretic Solutions to Computational Geometry Problems. In: Paul, C., Habib, M. (eds.) WG 2009. LNCS, vol. 5911, pp. 1–16. Springer, Heidelberg (2010)
5. Fernandes, A.: FFTPACK translated to pure iso c/c++,
   http://www.fernandes.org/txp/article/
   4fftpack-translated-to-pure-iso-cc
6. Ferrari, L., Sankar, P.V., Sklansky, J.: Minimal rectangular partitions of digitized blobs. Computer Vision, Graphics, and Image Processing 28(1), 58–71 (1984)
7. Flusser, J., Suk, T., Zitová, B.: Moments and Moment Invariants in Pattern Recognition. Wiley, Chichester (2009)
8. Imai, H., Asano, T.: Efficient algorithms for geometric graph search problems. SIAM Journal on Computing 15(2), 478–494 (1986)
9. Kawaguchi, E., Endo, T.: On a method of binary-picture representation and its application to data compression. IEEE Transactions on Pattern Analysis and Machine Intelligence 2(1), 27–35 (1980)
10. Keil, J.M.: Polygon decomposition. In: Handbook of Computational Geometry, pp. 491–518. Elsevier (2000)
11. Levin, A., Fergus, R., Durand, F., Freeman, W.T.: Image and depth from a conventional camera with a coded aperture. In: Special Interest Group on Computer Graphics and Interactive Techniques Conference, SIGGRAPH 2007. ACM, New York (2007)
12. Lipski Jr., W., Lodi, E., Luccio, F., Mugnai, C., Pagli, L.: On two-dimensional data organization II. In: Fundamenta Informaticae. Series IV, vol. II, pp. 245–260 (1979)
13. Ohtsuki, T.: Minimum dissection of rectilinear regions. In: Proceedings of the IEEE International Conference on Circuits and Systems, ISCAS 1982, pp. 1210–1213. IEEE (1982)
14. Schouten, T.E., van den Broek, E.L.: Incremental distance transforms (IDT). In: 20th International Conference on Pattern Recognition, ICPR 2010, pp. 237–240. IEEE Computer Society (August 2010)
15. Seaidoun, M.: A Fast Exact Euclidean Distance Transform with Application to Computer Vision and Digital Image Processing. Ph.D. thesis, Northeastern University, Boston, USA (September 1993) advisor John Gauch
16. Sossa-Azuela, J.H., Yáñez-Márquez, C., Díaz de León Santiago, J.L.: Computing geometric moments using morphological erosions. Pattern Recognition 34(2), 271–276 (2001)
17. Spiliotis, I.M., Mertzios, B.G.: Real-time computation of two-dimensional moments on binary images using image block representation. IEEE Transactions on Image Processing 7(11), 1609–1615 (1998)
18. Zakaria, M.F., Vroomen, L.J., Zsombor-Murray, P., van Kessel, J.M.: Fast algorithm for the computation of moment invariants. Pattern Recognition 20(6), 639–643 (1987)

A New Level-Set Based Algorithm for Bimodal Depth Segmentation

Michal Krumnikl, Eduard Sojka, and Jan Gaura

VŠB - Technical University of Ostrava,
Faculty of Electrical Engineering and Computer Science,
17. listopadu 15, 708 33 Ostrava-Poruba, Czech Republic
{michal.krumnikl,eduard.sojka,jan.gaura}@vsb.cz

Abstract. In this paper, a new algorithm for bimodal depth segmentation is presented. The method separates the background and the planar objects of arbitrary shapes lying in a certain height above the background using the information from the stereo image pair (more exactly, the background and the objects may lie on two distinct general planes). The problem is solved as a problem of minimising a functional. A new functional is proposed for this purpose that is based on evaluating the mismatches between the images, which contrasts with the usual approaches that evaluate the matches. We explain the motivation for such an approach. The minimisation is carried out by making use of the Euler-Lagrange equation and the level-set function. The experiments show the promising results on noisy synthetic images as well as on real-life images. An example of the practical application of the method is also presented.

Keywords: image segmentation, stereo correspondence, level set.

1 Introduction

The level sets are generally known to the computer vision community mainly as the image segmentation methods. The basic approach was originally introduced by Osher and Sethian [19], and since then is being extensively developed and improved in many ways [6,16,12]. The main advantage of the level sets is the ability to extract objects of various shapes and surfaces without the need to parametrise them. Most of the algorithms rely on the pixel intensities and functional models [20,15,21].

However, the image segmentation is not the only application, the level sets can also be used for solving the stereo correspondence problem. Many stereo matching algorithms determine the disparity using the energy minimisation techniques, such as dynamic programming [18,7], graph cuts [3,14], or belief propagation [13]. In addition to these classical approaches, new ones are being developed. Energy minimisation approaches using the partial differential equations have been proposed recently [1,2]. In former studies, level sets already showed the ability to solve the spatial problems such as the 3D shape extraction. A method for recovering the projections of 3D planar curves using the level sets was proposed in

J. Blanc-Talon et al. (Eds.): ACIVS 2012, LNCS 7517, pp. 225–236, 2012.
© Springer-Verlag Berlin Heidelberg 2012

[8,9]. Later, this approach was extended to solve the stereo matching problem for an arbitrary number of images [11], where a proposed functional is based on evaluating the brightness correlation between the corresponding points. Latest methods use regularization terms based on the Mumford-Shah functional for discontinuity preserving, combined with a functional for occlusion handling [2].

In this paper, we present a new algorithm for bimodal depth segmentation. The method separates the planar objects of arbitrary shapes lying in a certain height above a background (base plane) using the information from the stereo image pair. (More exactly, the objects and the background can lie on two distinct planes in a general mutual position.) We work with the gray-scale images. The brightness of particular objects in one image may be different and may vary along each object. The brightness of the base plane may vary too. The problem is solved as a problem of minimisation. A new functional is proposed for this purpose that is based on evaluating the mismatches between the images, which contrasts with the usual approaches that evaluate matches (i.e., small brightness difference or big correlation between the corresponding points). We explain why the approach based on the mismatches may be advantageous. The minimisation is carried out by making use of the Euler-Lagrange equation and the level-set function. In its essence, the algorithm was inspired by the algorithm proposed by Chan and Vese [4,5]. The experiments show the promising results on noisy synthetic images as well as on real-life images. We also present an example of application of the method.

The paper is organised as follows. In the following section, the Chan and Vese method is briefly summarised. Section 3 contains the description of the proposed method. The results of testing are presented in Section 4.

2 Review of Chan and Vese's Method

This section introduces the reader to the original Chan and Vese method that was an inspiration for the method we propose. Rather than presenting all the details [4,5], we describe only the basic ideas.

Let $u(x)$ be the brightness function of the input image that is defined over a two-dimensional area, denoted by Ω. It is being assumed that the image consists of objects and a background. All the objects as well as the background have nearly constant brightness; the quantities c_o and c_b denote the average brightness of the objects and the background, respectively. Let C stand for the collection of closed curves that separate the objects from the background. The original Chan and Vese algorithm is based on minimizing the fitting energy functional that is defined by the equation

$$F(c_o, c_b, C) = \mu \cdot Length(C) + \nu \cdot Area(inside(C)) +$$
$$+\lambda_o \int_{inside(C)} (u(x) - c_o)^2 \, dx + \lambda_b \int_{outside(C)} (u(x) - c_b)^2 \, dx, \qquad (1)$$

where $\mu \geq 0$, $\nu \geq 0$, and $\lambda_o, \lambda_b \geq 0$ are suitably chosen parameters adapting the functional to a particular class of images.

In order to minimise the functional from Eq. (1), a function $\phi(x), x \in \Omega$, referred to as a *level set function*, is introduced. By the level set function, the image is partitioned into a set of regions. Inside the objects, the value of the level set function is $\phi(x) > 0$; $\phi(x) < 0$ holds outside the objects. The object contours are found at points where $\phi(x) = 0$. Using the Heaviside function

$$H(z) = \begin{cases} 1 & \text{if } z \geq 0 \\ 0 & \text{if } z < 0 \end{cases}, \tag{2}$$

the functional from Eq. (1) can be rewritten in the following way (we omit the parameter x of u and ϕ)

$$F(c_o, c_b, \phi) = \mu \int_\Omega |\nabla H(\phi)| dx + \nu \int_\Omega H(\phi) dx +$$

$$+ \lambda_o \int_\Omega (u - c_o)^2 H(\phi)\, dx + \lambda_b \int_\Omega (u - c_b)^2 (1 - H(\phi))\, dx. \tag{3}$$

Keeping the level set function ϕ fixed and minimising $F(c_o, c_b, \phi)$ with respect to c_o, c_b, we can find the following expressions

$$c_o(\phi) = \frac{\int_\Omega u H(\phi) dx}{\int_\Omega H(\phi) dx},$$

$$c_b(\phi) = \frac{\int_\Omega u(1 - H(\phi)) dx}{\int_\Omega (1 - H(\phi)) dx}, \tag{4}$$

where $c_o(\phi)$ and $c_b(\phi)$ stand for the brightness of the objects and the brightness of the background, respectively. Keeping c_o, c_b fixed and minimizing $F(c_o, c_b, \phi)$ with respect to ϕ, we obtain the Euler-Lagrange equation in the form of

$$\delta(\phi) \left[\mu \operatorname{div} \left(\frac{\nabla \phi}{|\nabla \phi|} \right) - \nu - \lambda_o (u - c_o)^2 + \lambda_b (u - c_b)^2 \right] = 0. \tag{5}$$

For practical computation, a regularized version of H (denoted by H_ε) and its derivative are introduced as follows

$$H_\varepsilon(z) = \frac{1}{2} \left(1 + \frac{2}{\pi} \arctan \left(\frac{z}{\varepsilon} \right) \right),$$

$$\delta_\varepsilon(z) = H'_\varepsilon(z) = \frac{1}{\pi} \cdot \frac{\varepsilon}{\varepsilon^2 + z^2}, \tag{6}$$

where ε is a suitably chosen constant.

The Euler-Lagrange equation can be solved iteratively by introducing the parametrisation $\phi(t, x)$ in time, by considering the boundary conditions, and by iteratively updating the values of $\phi(t, x)$. The following is computed

$$\begin{cases} \dfrac{\partial \phi}{\partial t} = \delta_\varepsilon(\phi) \left[\mu \operatorname{div} \left(\frac{\nabla \phi}{|\nabla \phi|} \right) - \nu - \lambda_o (u - c_o)^2 + \lambda_b (u - c_b)^2 \right] \text{ in } \Omega, \\ \phi(0, x) = \phi_0(x) \text{ in } \Omega, \\ \dfrac{\delta_\varepsilon(\phi)}{\nabla \phi} \dfrac{\partial \phi}{\partial \mathbf{n}} \text{ in } \partial \Omega, \end{cases} \tag{7}$$

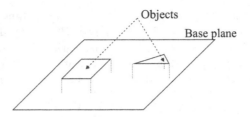

Fig. 1. A scene with two height levels containing a base plane (bottom points) and the objects that lie on another plane (top points)

where $\mathbf{n}$ denotes the exterior normal to the boundary $\partial\Omega$ of Ω, and $\frac{\partial\phi}{\partial\mathbf{n}}$ is the normal derivative of ϕ at the object boundaries. The initial value $\phi_0(x)$ of the level set function is often determined from an initial estimation of the object boundaries. The values of ϕ_0 are computed as the distance from the initial boundary curves.

We point out that an alternative method was presented in [17] converting the problem of minimising the functional from Eq. (3) into the problem of convex minimisation. General acquaintance of the original method and original paper, however, was a motivation for us to use the original method as a basis also in this paper since we believe that the essential thing that is always important is to formulate the basic functional first. The techniques how the minimisation can be carried out effectively are certainly important too, but to a lesser degree.

3   Description of the New Method

We suppose that we deal with the following scenes (Fig. 1). A base plane is present in the scene. The objects have the form of pieces of another plane lying in a certain height above the base plane; this second plane is not necessarily parallel to the base plane. The shape of objects is arbitrary. For the points of the base plane and the objects, respectively, we will also use the terms *bottom points* and *top points*. We consider the grey-scale images and scenes. The brightness of particular objects may be different and need not be constant. The restriction is that all the objects should be either darker or brighter than is the background.

We suppose that we have two images of a scene that are obtained by two pinhole cameras at different positions. To distinguish between the cameras and images, we will use the term the *left* and the *right* camera or image. Due to the pinhole model, both the images are connected by a projective transformation. We suppose that this transformation is known. The goal is to segment the images, i.e., to find the whole areas of particular objects, i.e., to classify all pixels as the pixels containing the projections of either the top points or bottom points.

Firstly, we focus only on the geometric transformations without considering any occlusions. Say that we see a certain point whose position is described by x_L in the left image (Fig. 2). It can either be the image of a bottom point or the image of a top point. In the case of the top point, the position of the corresponding point in the right image is $\pi_\mathrm{LTR}(x_\mathrm{L})$, where $\pi_\mathrm{LTR}(\cdot)$ is the projective

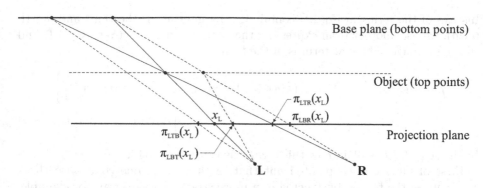

Fig. 2. Projective transforms between images (without occlusions): If a top point is seen at x_L in the left image, then it should also be seen at $\pi_{LTR}(x_L)$ in the right image; otherwise, if a bottom point is seen at x_L, it should be seen at $\pi_{LBR}(x_L)$. The point that can be seen at the position of $\pi_{LTR}(x_L)$ in the right image need not necessarily be only the top point that is seen at x_L; at the same place a bottom point can also be seen whose projection in the left image is at $\pi_{LTB}(x_L)$ (see the text). Similarly, the point that can be seen at $\pi_{LBR}(x_L)$ in the right image need not be the bottom point only that is seen at x_L; it can also be a top point that, in the left image, is seen at $\pi_{LBT}(x_L)$.

transformation; the subscript LTR stands for the transformation for the top points from the left to the right image (the other subscripts introduced in this paragraph are created according to the similar rule). In the case that x_L is a projection of a bottom point, its corresponding projection in the right image should be at $\pi_{LBR}(x_L)$. We can also think about a point x_R in the right image and introduce two possible positions of the corresponding points in the left image, namely $\pi_{RTL}(x_R)$ and $\pi_{RBL}(x_R)$ for the top and bottom points, respectively. From the geometrical point of view, the point that can be seen at the position of $\pi_{LTR}(x_L)$ in the right image need not necessarily be only the top point that is seen at x_L; at the same place a bottom point can also be seen whose position in the left image is $\pi_{RBL}(\pi_{LTR}(x_L)) \equiv \pi_{LTB}(x_L)$. Similarly, the point that can be seen at $\pi_{LBR}(x_L)$ in the right image need not be only the bottom point that is seen at x_L; it can also be a top point that, in the left image, is seen at $\pi_{RTL}(\pi_{LBR}(x_L)) \equiv \pi_{LBT}(x_L)$.

In the method we propose, the level-set function ϕ distinguishes between the objects and the base plane, i.e., between the areas containing the projections of either the top or the bottom points. We evaluate the level-set function over the left image, i.e., we will often write $\phi(x_L)$. In accordance with the original Chan and Vese functional in Eq. (3), we use the term requiring the boundary between the objects and the background to be short (the first term in the following expression) and the term requiring the area of objects to be small (the second term), i.e., we use

$$\mu \int_\Omega |\nabla H(\phi(x_L))|dx + \nu \int_\Omega H(\phi(x_L))\, dx\,. \tag{8}$$

Instead of the terms in Eq. (3) containing the intensities (the third and fourth term), we use another term expressing the correspondence between the left and the right image. The new term is of the form

$$\int_{\Omega} \left\{ \left[u_R\big(\pi_{LBR}(x_L)\big) - u_R\big(\pi_{LTR}(x_L)\big) \right] - \left[u_L(x_L) - u_L\big(\pi_{LTB}(x_L)\big) \right] \right\}$$
$$\left[H\big(\phi(x_L)\big) - 0.5 \right] dx. \quad (9)$$

In the sequel, we explain how this term was constructed (Fig. 3).

First of all, let it be pointed out that, alternatively, one could also think about using the terms constructed in a more straightforward way, for example, according to the following formula

$$\int_{\Omega} \left[u_R\big(\pi_{LTR}(x_L)\big) - u_L(x_L) \right]^2 H\big(\phi(x_L)\big) dx$$
$$+ \int_{\Omega} \left[u_R\big(\pi_{LBR}(x_L)\big) - u_L(x_L) \right]^2 \left[1 - H\big(\phi(x_L)\big) \right]$$
$$\left[1 - H\Big(\phi\big(\pi_{LBT}(x_L)\big)\Big) \right] dx \quad (10)$$

expressing the fact that the left and right image should correspond at the points where both the cameras see the objects or both the cameras see the base plane. (Later, however, we will show that such terms are not too useful.) For the objects, no occlusion occurs. Therefore, the objects are always seen by both cameras, i.e., the correspondence for the objects can be expected whenever $\phi(x_L) > 0$, which explains the term $H(\phi(x_L))$. The value $\phi(x_L) < 0$ indicates that the left camera sees the base plane. Due to the occlusions by objects, however, not every point of the base plane that can be seen by the left camera can also be seen by the right camera. Matching the base plane can only be done on the area that is seen by both cameras, which is expressed by the terms $1 - H(\phi(x_L))$ (which is the part of the bottom plane that is seen by the left camera) and $1 - H(\phi(\pi_{LBT}(x_L)))$ (the part that is seen by the right camera). Clearly, if $\phi(x_L)$ correctly separates between the objects and the base plane, the value of the expression stated above is minimal and, for theoretical images, it can even take the value of zero. Unfortunately, the expression is not suitable for the use in the functional that should be minimised, which is due to the fact that the minimum can also be achieved for incorrect object detections. Consider, for example, a scene that contains only the base plane with a constant brightness and no object. The zero, i.e., the minimal value of the expression from Eq. (10) is achieved even though ϕ incorrectly indicates an object in such a scene, which is simply because $u_R(\pi_{LTR}(x_L)) = u_L(x_L)$ and $u_R(\pi_{LBR}(x_L)) = u_L(x_L)$ since both the cameras see only the base plane everywhere. In other words, the term itself from Eq. (10) does not prevent from the detection of false objects, which is threatening in the situation that cannot be regarded as rare (objects on a base plane with a constant brightness). The terms of this type are used in more approaches [1,2,9]; similar problems can also be seen in the methods based on correlation [11]. Generally speaking, the methods based on concordance of brightness between the image points (small brightness difference or big correlation) are suspected to have problems since the brightness concordance between two points is ambiguous. In the case of concordance, we can only say that they can, but need not, correspond. In the case of a brightness mismatch, on the other hand, we are sure that the points do not correspond.

For evaluating the degree of correspondence, therefore, we introduce the term from Eq. (9) that takes into account the mismatch of brightness. (The whole functional is presented in Eq. (11).) The way in which the new term works is illustrated in Fig. 3. The value of the difference $[u_R(\pi_{LBR}(x_L)) - u_R(\pi_{LTR}(x_L))] - [u_L(x_L) - u_L(\pi_{LTB}(x_L))]$ is depicted for the case that the object is brighter than the base plane and providing that the object and the base plane have a constant brightness. The value of the term $H(\phi(x_L)) - 0.5$ from Eq. (9) is either 0.5 for $\phi(x_L) > 0$ indicating the hypothesis that the object is present in that area or -0.5 otherwise (Fig. 3). It can be easily seen that the correspondence term from Eq. (9) takes its lowest possible value if $\phi(x_L)$ fits to the object boundary and in no other cases; the lowest possible value is negative. The correspondence term can also be viewed as a dot product between the difference term and $H(\phi(x_L)) - 0.5$. The value of the dot product is the lowest (highest in absolute value) if $\phi(x_L)$ fits to the object. The restriction of the term is that all the objects should be either darker or brighter than is the background.

We can conclude that the functional we use is the following one

$$F(\phi) = \mu \int_\Omega \Big|\nabla H\big(\phi(x_L)\big)\Big| dx + \nu \int_\Omega H\big(\phi(x_L)\big) dx$$

$$+ \lambda \int_\Omega \Big\{ \Big[u_R\big(\pi_{LBR}(x_L)\big) - u_R\big(\pi_{LTR}(x_L)\big)\Big] - \Big[u_L(x_L) - u_L\big(\pi_{LTB}(x_L)\big)\Big] \Big\}$$

$$\Big[H\big(\phi(x_L)\big) - 0.5\Big] dx$$

$$+ \kappa \int_\Omega \Big|\nabla u_L(x_L)\Big|^2 H\big(\phi(x_L)\big) dx + \kappa \int_\Omega \Big|\nabla u_R\big(\pi_{LTR}(x_L)\big)\Big|^2 H\big(\phi(x_L)\big) dx . \quad (11)$$

The last two terms in the last row are optional. They were added to express the fact that the edges (big gradients) are not usually expected in the area of objects. The terms are not needed in the theoretical images according to the model that was introduced before, but may be useful in real-life images.

The rationale behind the construction of the functional in this way can be easily seen. The new term (with the λ coefficient) detects the places of mismatch between the images (Fig. 3) and should be minimised as was explained before. The term with the μ coefficient contributes to connecting such places into the whole objects, i.e., it does not allow that ϕ only indicates the places with the differences that occur near the object boundary (Fig. 3).

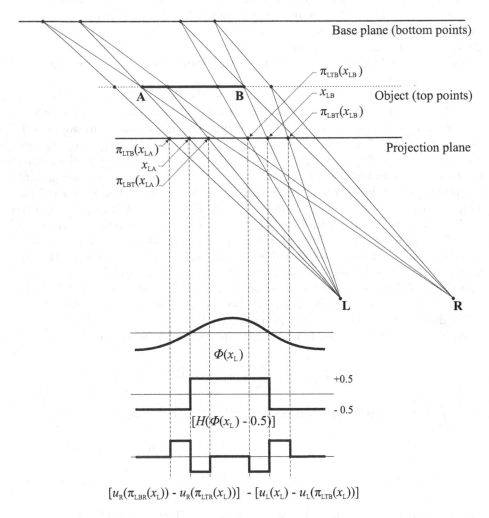

Fig. 3. The values of the terms from Eq. (9) for the image in which the base plane has a constant brightness of b_B and the object has the brightness of b_T. We suppose that $b_T > b_B$ and we introduce $b_T - b_B \equiv \delta b$. Independently on $\phi(\cdot)$, the difference term $[u_R(\pi_{LBR}(x_L)) - u_R(\pi_{LTR}(x_L))] - [u_L(x_L) - u_L(\pi_{LTB}(x_L))]$ takes the value of $+\delta b$ in the neighbourhood of object, the value of $-\delta b$ inside the object but in the neighbourhood of its boundary, and the value of zero otherwise. The term $H(\phi(x_L)) - 0.5$ takes the value of either -0.5 or $+0.5$. The value of Eq. (9) is minimised if $\phi(x_L)$ fits to the object.

The Euler-Lagrange equation corresponding to the functional from Eq. (11) (including the last two optional terms) is of the form

$$\delta\big(\phi\left(x_{\mathrm{L}}\right)\big)\left[\mu\operatorname{div}\left(\frac{\nabla\phi(x_{\mathrm{L}})}{|\nabla\phi(x_{\mathrm{L}})|}\right)-\nu\right]$$

$$+\lambda\delta\big(\phi\left(x_{\mathrm{L}}\right)\big)\left[\Big(u_{\mathrm{R}}\big(\pi_{\mathrm{LBR}}\left(x_{\mathrm{L}}\right)\big)-u_{\mathrm{R}}\big(\pi_{\mathrm{LTR}}\left(x_{\mathrm{L}}\right)\big)\Big)-\Big(u_{\mathrm{L}}\left(x_{\mathrm{L}}\right)-u_{\mathrm{L}}\big(\pi_{\mathrm{LTB}}\left(x_{\mathrm{L}}\right)\big)\Big)\right]$$

$$-\kappa\delta\big(\phi\left(x_{\mathrm{L}}\right)\big)\left[\big|\nabla u_{\mathrm{L}}\left(x_{\mathrm{L}}\right)\big|^{2}+\big|\nabla u_{\mathrm{R}}\big(\pi_{\mathrm{LTR}}\left(x_{\mathrm{L}}\right)\big)\big|^{2}\right]=0.$$

$$(12)$$

The equation can be solved in the usual way by making use of $H_{\varepsilon}(\cdot)$, $\delta_{\varepsilon}(\cdot)$, and the time parametrisation [4,5]. The projective transformations $\pi_{\mathrm{LBR}}(\cdot)$ etc. can be determined from the positions of the planes containing the bottom and top points and from the positions of both cameras. Practically, they can also be determined from the point correspondences in a pair of calibrating images containing both bottom and top points.

4   Tests and Results

The algorithm has been tested on artificial and real-life images complying with the model introduced before. We believe that the results can be regarded as good and promising. The general explanation is that by exploiting strong a priori known properties of scene, it is possible to achieve better results, which especially holds for the real-life images that are often difficult for the general-purpose algorithms. In the sequel, we describe the tests in more details.

4.1   Testing with Artificial Images

Firstly, synthetic images with objects of different shapes and added noise were generated. Fig. 4 depicts several examples. The brightness of images was normalised into the range $[0, 1]$. The parameters from Eq. (12) were chosen to be $\mu = 1$, $\nu = 0.01$, $\lambda = 1$, $\kappa = 0$, and $\Delta t = 10$. As can be seen (Fig. 4), the objects were successfully detected even in relatively noisy images.

4.2   Testing with Real-Life Images and Practical Usage of the Method

In this section, we describe the experiments with real-life images. The method benefits from a strong a priori knowledge of the scene. The model of the scene, on the other hand, is also a strong limitation of the method; the method can be used only in specific cases. We use the method for detecting the cars on parking lots for the purpose of detecting the occupancy of particular places. The motivation for using the stereo pair for solving the mentioned problem is to overcome some difficulties that are reported by the authors using only one image (e.g., [10]).

Fig. 4. Artificial test images: height levels, left input images with the results depicting the found objects (*right images*)

Moreover, the detection of an object with a certain height is a reliable marker that the place is occupied, which is not offered by one-image approaches that may be deceived more easily.

The usual situation in the parking lots nearly corresponds to the model we introduced before (Fig. 5). The base plane is present and the roofs of cars may be regarded as objects. Some differences from the model, however, exist. Namely: (1) the cars do not have only the roof, but they also have the whole body containing the parts at different heights; (2) the cars may be of different heights. Nevertheless, the following can be assumed: (1) the roof is usually the most prominent part of car in the images (Fig. 5), (2) for cars of a certain category, e.g., the passenger cars, more or less the same height of them can be expected.

The images are provided by a pair of uncalibrated cameras; the lens distortion is not compensated. The transformations $\pi_{\mathrm{LTR}}(x_\mathrm{L})$, $\pi_{\mathrm{LBR}}(x_\mathrm{L})$, $\pi_{\mathrm{LTB}}(x_\mathrm{L})$, and $\pi_{\mathrm{LBT}}(x_\mathrm{L})$ have chosen to be two-value functions that have the form of bicubic polynomials whose coefficients were found by the least squares method from two sets of calibrating points that were determined manually (only the mentioned transformations are needed for each x_L; the exact type of projection and distortion need not be known). The first set of calibrating points contained selected corresponding points lying on the ground of parking lot; the second set contained selected corresponding points on the car roofs (each pair of images offers a lot of suitable calibrating points of both types). The bicubic polynomials proved to be fully capable to model the values of the transformations in our rather heavily distorted images. The size of images was 1920×1080 pixels. The initial value of $\phi(x)$ was set on the basis of the difference $[u_\mathrm{R}(\pi_{\mathrm{LBR}}(x_\mathrm{L})) - u_\mathrm{R}(\pi_{\mathrm{LTR}}(x_\mathrm{L}))] - [u_\mathrm{L}(x_\mathrm{L}) - u_\mathrm{L}(\pi_{\mathrm{LTB}}(x_\mathrm{L}))]$. At the places, where the value of difference was less than a small negative threshold, the value of $\phi_0(x)$ was set to 1 (object); otherwise, it was set to -1 (background). Objects brighter than is the background were expected. The results of detection can be seen in Fig. 5.

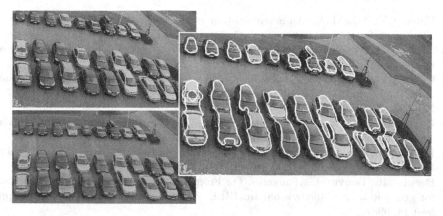

Fig. 5. The result of the "car roofs" detection from a given stereo pair. As can be seen, higher parts of car bodies are detected too.

5   Conclusions

We have presented a new algorithm for bimodal depth segmentation. The method separates the planar objects of arbitrary shapes lying in a certain height above a background (base plane) using the information from the stereo image pair. The problem has been solved as a problem of minimisation. A new functional has been proposed for this purpose that is based on evaluating the mismatches between the images, which contrasts with the usual approaches that evaluate the matches. We have explained that this difference is important. The minimisation has been carried out by making use of the Euler-Lagrange equation and the level-set function. We have also presented some results of testing and an example of practical application of the method, which was detecting the occupancy of parking slots.

Acknowledgements. This work was partially supported by the SGS grant No. SP2012/58 of VŠB - Technical University of Ostrava, Faculty of Electrical Engineering and Computer Science.

References

1. Alvarez, L., Deriche, R., Weickert, J., Sanchez, J.: Dense disparity map estimation respecting image discontinuities: A PDE and scale-space based approach. Journal of Visual Communication and Image Representation, Special Issue on Partial Differential Equations in Image Processing, Computer Vision and Computer Graphics 13(1/2), 3–21 (2002)
2. Ben-Ari, R., Sochen, N.: Stereo matching with mumford-shah regularization and occlusion handling. IEEE Trans. Pattern Analysis and Machine Intelligence 32(11), 2071–2084 (2010)
3. Boykov, Y., Veksler, O., Zabih, R.: Fast approximate energy minimization via graph cuts. IEEE Trans. Pattern Analysis and Machine Intelligence 23, 1222–1239 (2001)

4. Chan, T.F., Vese, L.A.: An active contour model without edges. In: International Conference Scale-Space Theories in Computer Vision, pp. 141–151 (1999)
5. Chan, T.F., Vese, L.A.: Active contours without edges. IEEE Trans. on Image Processing 10(2), 266–277 (2001)
6. Chan, T.F., Vese, L.A.: A multiphase level set framework for image segmentation using the Mumford and Shah model. International Journal of Computer Vision 50, 271–293 (2002)
7. Cox, I.J., Hingorani, S.L., Rao, S.B., Maggs, B.M.: A maximum likelihood stereo algorithm. Computer Vision and Image Understanding 63, 542–567 (1996)
8. Deriche, R., Bouvin, C., Faugeras, O.: Level-set approach for stereo. Investigative Image Processing 2942(1), 150–161 (1997)
9. Deriche, R., Bouvin, C., Faugeras, O.: Front propagation and level-set approach for geodesic active stereovision. In: IEEE Workshop on Visual Surveillance, pp. 56–63 (1998)
10. Fabián, T.: An algorithm for parking lot occupation detection. In: Proceedings of the 7th Computer Information Systems and Industrial Management Applications, pp. 165–170 (2008)
11. Faugeras, O., Keriven, R.: Variational principles, surface evolution, pde's, level set methods and the stereo problem. IEEE Trans. on Image Processing 7, 336–344 (1999)
12. Hsu, C.Y., Yang, C.H., Wang, H.C.: Topological control of level set method depending on topology constraints. Pattern Recognition Letters 66, 537–546 (2008)
13. Klaus, A., Sormann, M., Karner, K.F.: Segment-based stereo matching using belief propagation and a self-adapting dissimilarity measure. In: Proceedings of the 17th International Conference on Pattern Recognition, vol. 3, pp. 15–18 (2006)
14. Kolmogorov, V., Zabih, R.: Computing visual correspondence with occlusions using graph cuts. In: Proceedings of the IEEE International Conference on Computer Vision, vol. 2, pp. 508–515 (2001)
15. Leventon, M.E., Grimson, W.E.L., Faugeras, O., Wells, W.: Level set based segmentation with intensity and curvature priors. In: Proceedings of the IEEE Workshop on Mathematical Methods in Biomedical Image Analysis, pp. 4–11 (2000)
16. Malladi, R., Sethian, J.A., Vemuri, B.C.: Shape modeling with front propagation: A level set approach. IEEE Trans. Pattern Analysis and Machine Intelligence 17, 158–175 (1995)
17. Nikolova, M., Esedoglu, S., Chan, T.F.: Algorithms for finding global minimizers of image segmentation and denoising models. SIAM Journal of Applied Mathematics 66(5), 1632–1648 (2006)
18. Ohta, Y., Kanade, T.: Stereo by intra- and inter-scanline search using dynamic programming. IEEE Trans. Pattern Analysis and Machine Intelligence 7(1), 139–154 (1985)
19. Osher, S., Sethian, J.: Fronts propagating with curvature-dependent speed: algorithms based on the Hamilton-Jacobi formulation. Journal of Computational Physics 79, 12–49 (1988)
20. Rousson, M., Paragios, N.: Prior Knowledge, Level Set Representations & Visual Grouping. International Journal of Computer Vision 76(3), 231–243 (2008)
21. Sojka, E., Gaura, J., Krumnikl, M.: Active Contours without Edges and with Simple Shape Priors. In: Blanc-Talon, J., Bourennane, S., Philips, W., Popescu, D., Scheunders, P. (eds.) ACIVS 2008. LNCS, vol. 5259, pp. 730–741. Springer, Heidelberg (2008), http://dx.doi.org/10.1007/978-3-540-88458-3_66

3D Shape from Focus Using LULU Operators

Roushanak Rahmat[1], Aamir Saeed Mallik[2], Nidla Kamel[2],
Tae-Sun Choi[3], and Monson H. Hayes[1]

[1] Graduate School of Advanced Imaging Science, Multimedia, and Film
Chung-Ang University, Seoul, Korea
[2] Center for Intelligent Signal & Imaging Research (CISIR)
Department of Electrical and Electronic Engineering
Universiti Teknologi Petronas, Perak, Malaysia
[3] Department of Mechatronics
Gwangju Institute of Science and Technology, Gwangju, Korea
{roushanakrahmat@gmail.com}

Abstract. Extracting the shape of an object is one of the important
tasks to be performed in many vision applications. One of the difficult
challenges in 3D shape extraction is the roughness of the surfaces of
objects. Shape from focus (SFF) is a shape recovery method that reconstructs the shape of an object from a sequence of images taken from the
same viewpoint but with different focal lengths. This paper proposes the
use of LULU operators as a preprocessing step to improve the signal-to-
noise ratio in the estimation of 3D shape from focus. LULU operators are
morphological filters that are used for their structure preserving properties. The proposed technique is tested on simulated and real images
separately, as well as in combination with traditional SFF methods such
as sum modified Laplacian (SML), and gray level variance (GLV). The
proposed technique is tested in the presence of impulse noise with different noise levels. Based on the quantitative and qualitative experimental
results it is shown that the proposed techniques is more accurate in focus
value extraction and shape recovery in the presence of noise.

Keywords: Shape from Focus, LULU operators, Discrete Pulse
Transform.

1 Introduction

One of the basic problems in capturing images with digital cameras is the loss of
information about the objects in a scene, such as the distance of the objects from
the camera, and the shape of each object. For applications in computer vision,
it is often necessary to estimate the distance of an object from the camera and
possibly its three-dimensional shape. In general, it is possible to estimate the
distance of an object from a camera when the object is within the plane of focus,
and knowing the focus points of an object in multiple focus planes allows for the
recovery of shape information. Thus, focusing is an important area of research
in 3D shape extraction. There are many different techniques for estimating the

J. Blanc-Talon et al. (Eds.): ACIVS 2012, LNCS 7517, pp. 237–245, 2012.
© Springer-Verlag Berlin Heidelberg 2012

focus of an image, such as the Fourier transform [1], aperture-plane distortion [2], Gaussian interpolation [3], second and fourth order moments [5], and Chebyshev moments [6]. In addition to focussing methods, there are 3D shape recovery techniques that are based on shape extraction from stereo, texture, defocus, or motion and shading, which are sometimes combined with shape from focus to improve the shape recovery result. In this paper, we discuss and analyze the proposed techniques based on shape from focus (SFF).

SFF is less complicated compared to other shape recovery techniques since all that is required is a sequence of images with different focal lengths that are captured from the same position. There are many different Focus Measures (FMs) to determine the focus value for a given region of an image from a sequence of images with different focus values. These include Laplacian, modified Laplacian (ML), sum of the modified Laplacian (SML) [3], Tenenbaum [4] gray level variance (GLV), mean, curvature and M2 [7,8]. In this paper, we consider the use of LULU operators to improve the signal-to-noise ratio when estimating shape from focus. LULU operators are morphological filters that are popular because of their structure preserving properties. We cascaded and compared our results with two of the best focus measurement techniques, which are SML and GLV. Applying LULU operators on noisy SFF data to detect focus values shows great improvement in performance compared to standard methods. This improvement is due the ability of LULU operators to reduce reduce noise, in general, and impulse noise in particular while preserving shape information (structure). The results of depth estimation is compared qualitatively and quantitatively using simulated and real objects.

1.1 Shape from Focus

The fundamental principle behind the estimation of the shape of an object from focus is that different parts of an object that lie at different distances from the camera will have different focus values. Therefore, generating a sequence of images that are captured using a different focus may be used to estimate the depth and, therefore, shape from focus. Six frames with different focus values of a simulated cone are shown in Figure 1(a) and six different frames with different focus values of a real cone are shown in Figure 1(b).

Once a sequence of images has been captured using different camera focal lengths, the next step is to detect the best focus value for each pixel or pixel region. The standard shape-from-focus sharpness methods compute a sharpness value within a small neighborhood of a pixel in each frame, and replace the pixel value with its sharpness value. The shape of an object can be estimated by finding the sharpest focus value for each pixel from the set of focus values obtained for each pixel within the sequence of images captured with different focal lengths.

The success of any SFF method for estimating the best focus of an object is dependent upon the accuracy of the digital camera in capturing the focus values and the focus measurement metric in detecting the focus value in each image frame. Two of the most popular SFF methods, sum of modified Laplacians

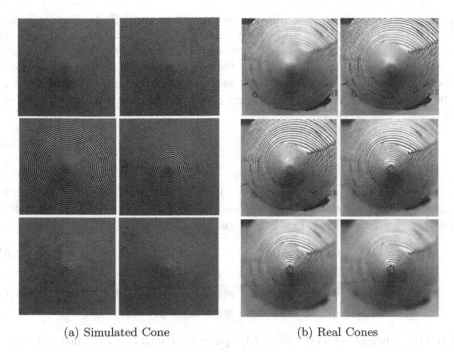

(a) Simulated Cone   (b) Real Cones

Fig. 1. (a) Test images of the simulated cone with different focus values, and (b) Test images of the real cone with different focus values

(SML) and Gray Level Variance (GLV), are used in this work and compared with LULU.

The Sum of Modified Laplacians is a symmetric differential operator that is used to measure the sharpness of each pixel and is given by [9],

$$\text{SML}(x_0, y_0) = \sum_{(x,y) \in U(x_0, y_0)} \left(\frac{\partial^2 f(x,y)}{\partial x^2} \right) + \left(\frac{\partial^2 f(x,y)}{\partial y^2} \right) \tag{1}$$

where (x, y) is the location of a pixel and $U(x_0, y_0)$ is a neighborhood of a given pixel (x_0, y_0).

Another commonly measure to estimate the sharpness or focus of an object is the Gray Level Variance (GLV). Specifically, the GLV is defined as follows

$$\text{GLV}(x_0, y_0) = \frac{1}{N-1} \sum_{(x,y) \in U(x_0, y_0)} [f(x,y) - \mu_U(x_0, y_0)]^2 \tag{2}$$

where again (x, y) denotes the location of a pixel and $m_U(x_0, y_0)$ is the mean gray level value within a neighborhood $U(x_0, y_0)$ of a pixel at (x_0, y_0) [7,10].

2   LULU Operators

In the late 1980s, Rohwer introduced LULU smoothers that are based on extreme order statistics within moving windows [11]. Initially, these local non-linear operators were used for noise removal applications, especially for impulse noise, and they have been widely compared to median filters [12,13]. LULU operators are a combination of the two basic operators L (low) and U (upper) with individual arrangements in different filters. One-dimensional LULU filters have been used in applications such as statistics and filtering to remove local peaks and valleys. For a one-dimensional sequence x_i, the one dimensional LULU operators are defined as follows [14]:

$$L_n(x_i) = \max\{\min\{x_{i-n}, \ldots, x_i\}, \min\{x_i, \ldots, x_{i+n}\}\} \tag{3}$$
$$U_n(x_i) = \min\{\max\{x_{i-n}, \ldots, x_i\}, \max\{x_i, \ldots, x_{i+n}\}\} \tag{4}$$

For 2D data, LULU operators have been used in image denoising [12] and, more recently, in object extraction application [14]. For 2D data, the neighbors of a pixel $p(i, j)$ may be divided into four different parts as follows (See Figure 2):

$$I_1 = [p(i-1, j-1), \ p(i-1, j), \ p(i, j), \ p(i, j-1)] \tag{5}$$
$$I_2 = [p(i-1, j+1), \ p(i-1, j), \ p(i, j), \ p(i, j+1)] \tag{6}$$
$$I_3 = [p(i, j-1), \ p(i, j), \ p(i+1, j-1), \ p(i+1, j)] \tag{7}$$
$$I_4 = [p(i, j+1), \ p(i, j), \ p(i+1, j), \ p(i+1, j+1)] \tag{8}$$

Given these neighborhoods, the LULU operators L and U are defined as follows,

$$L(i, j) = \max\{\min(I_1), \min(I_2), \min(I_3), \min(I_4)\} \tag{9}$$
$$U(i, j) = \min\{\max(I_1), \max(I_2), \max(I_3), \max(I_4)\} \tag{10}$$

By knowing the strength of LULU operators in object detection, we can expand these methods to 3D shape recovery. Since LULU can recover the images in the presence of noise and it has recently applied as a object detection technique, they can perform well in focus detection in SFF by reducing the noise in SFF data. See [15] for a detailed discussion of LULU operators.

3   Simulation Results

The test objects that are studied for this work include simulated and real objects with different textures. These objects include:

- *A Plane*: This is an image with uniform texture. The images are of size 200×200 and eighty-seven images with different focus values were created.
- *Simulated Cone and a Real Cone*: These are 300×360 images that are densely textured. Ninety-seven different images with different focus were generated.
- *Real LCD*: These are Thin Film Transistor-Liquid Crystal Display (TFT-LCD) images of a microscopic object. Sixty real data frames were obtained, and each frame is 300×300 pixels.
- *Real Coin*: This object is the head of Lincoln on a one penny coin. This highly-textured object has a resolution of 300×300 and 68 frames were created.

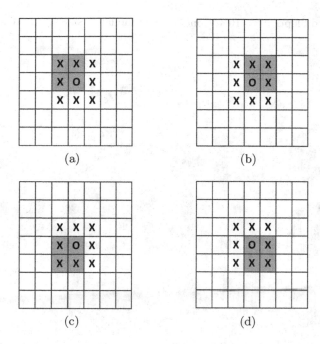

Fig. 2. Illustration of the four different neighborhood of a pixel $p(i,j)$ as defined in Eq. (5)-(8), (a) I_1, (b) I_2, (c) I_3, and (d) I_4

- *Simulated Cosine*: This is sequence of 60 frames of a simulated cosine with a resolution of 300 × 300.

The ground truth of these objects is shown in Figures 3(a) and 4(a).

In this work, we applied LULU on SFF separately using different window sizes. The windows were moved along each frame and in some other cases were extended into 3D window by evaluating a pixel not only with the neighbor pixels of the same frame but also with neighbor pixels of frames before and after. After considering LULU alone on SFF, we cascaded it with SML and GLV separately with applying LULU operators first followed by SML or GLV. The results are compared with the original depth map of each object through root mean square error (RMSE), correlation and peak signal to noise ratio (PSNR). Each experiment is repeated ten times in the presence of impulse noise. Three different levels of impulse noise is considered, high (noise density=0.5), medium (noise density=0.05) and low (noise density=0.005). The selected results for all the objects for low and medium levels of noise is illustrated in Figures 3 and 4. Figure 3 shows that the performance of proposed method is good in a low level of impulse noise on SFF data. Applying LULU, GLV or SML alone fails to recover 3D shape even though LULU is slightly performing better than others. But as SML or GLV are cascaded with LULU, their performance improves and provides good result for 3D shape recovery.

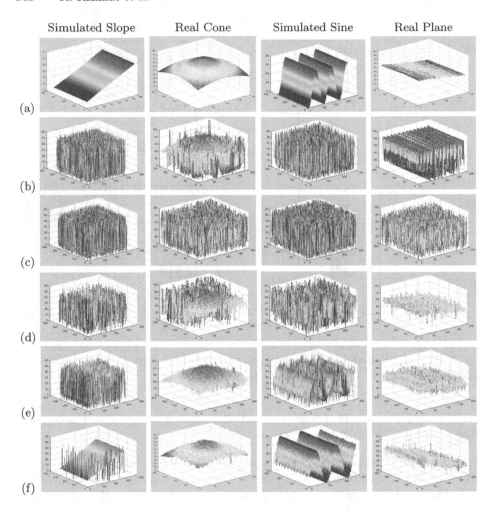

Fig. 3. 3D Shape recovery of SFF objects in the presence of impulse noise with noise density of 0.05. (a) Ground truth, (b) LULU, (c) SML, (d) GLV, (e) LULU+SML, (f) LULU+GLV.

Figure 4 shows the 3D shape recovered with proposed and other mentioned techniques in the presence of medium level of impulse noise for four other objects that are used for testing proposed method. The better performance of LULU compared to GLV and SML alone in the presence of impulse noise is clear based on simulated cone object results. Also, the better 3D shape based on LULU+GLV is obvious for all four objects in f) row. The quantitative analysis for simulated cone, real cone and simulated cosine objects are tabulated in Table 1, for all three level of impulse noise. Table 1 shows that applying LULU alone is a very good 3D shape recovery method at higher noise level as it is performing better than both GLV and SML in higher amount of impulse noise.

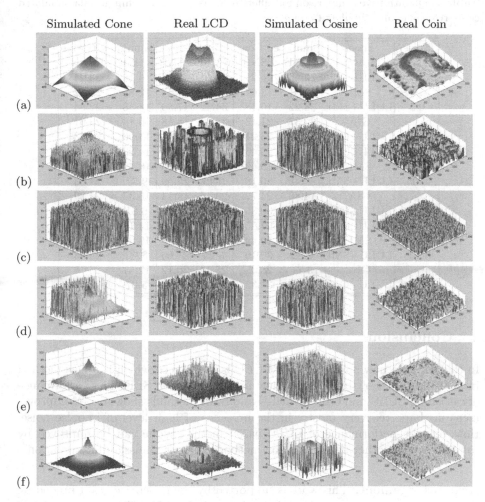

Fig. 4. 3D Shape recovery of SFF objects in the presence of impulse noise with noise density of 0.005. (a) Ground truth, (b) LULU, (c) SML, (d) GLV, (e) LULU+SML, (f) LULU+GLV.

If we cascade proposed method with other traditional methods, their performance improves. For example, applying LULU and SML shows a better result rather than applying LULU itself or SML alone generally. This can be explained due to filtering property of LULU filters. In LULU+SML/GLV focus measure, firstly, LULU removes the noise from SFF data and extracts new best focused points. Next, GLV/SML can perform well by refining the focused points and build a more accurate 3D shape. In general, the cascading methods improve the accuracy of focus detection.

Table 1. Quantitative comparison for different focus measure techniques for simulated cone, real cone, and simulated cosine

Noise Density	Focus Measure	Simulated Cone RMSE	Simulated Cone PSNR	Real Cone RMSE	Real Cone PSNR	Simulated Cosine RMSE	Simulated Cosine PSNR
	LULU	15.69	24.21	31.11	12.00	16.18	23.94
	SML	32.01	18.02	34.13	17.47	18.85	22.62
0.5	LULU+SML	38.22	16.48	34.42	17.40	18.38	22.84
	GLV	22.37	21.13	31.43	18.18	16.83	23.61
	LULU+GLV	17.62	23.21	28.91	20.01	14.96	24.63
	LULU	12.12	26.46	35.92	17.60	14.23	25.06
	SML	29.34	19.49	33.03	17.75	18.79	22.65
0.05	LULU+SML	7.89	30.18	9.46	28.50	9.77	28.33
	GLV	14.80	24.72	28.14	19.14	15.37	24.39
	LULU+GLV	7.75	30.35	6.65	31.73	6.81	31.47
	LULU	15.01	24.55	31.97	18.03	14.17	25.10
	SML	27.04	19.49	31.71	18.11	19.09	22.51
0.005	LULU+SML	7.89	30.19	5.29	33.66	8.22	29.83
	GLV	9.71	28.38	25.13	20.12	12.51	26.18
	LULU+GLV	7.75	30.33	3.62	36.95	5.67	32.64

4   Conclusion

In this paper, a new application for LULU is introduced which is a new method in 3D shape recovery from single view images based on SFF. The performance of cascading LULU and GLV or LULU and SML methods show a good improvement in shape recovery mostly in the presence of high level of impulse noise. However, the performance of LULU-based method alone can be improved by combing it with other approximation methods such as Gaussian interpolation.

Acknowledgement. This work is supported by the E-Science grant funded by the Ministry of Science, Technology and Innovation (MOSTI), Government of Malaysia (No: 01-02-02-SF0064).

References

1. Horn, B.K.P.: Focussing. M.I.T. Project MAC, AI Memo (1968)
2. Muller, R.A., Buffington, A.: Real-Time Correlation of Atmospherically Degraded Telescope Images Through Sharpening. Journal of the Opical Society of America 64(9), 1200–1210 (1974)
3. Nayar, S.K.: Shape from Focus. IEEE Transactions on Pattern Analysis and Machine Intelligence 16(8), 824–883 (1994)
4. Tenenbaum, J.M.: Accomodation in Computer Vision, Ph.D. Thesis, Stanford University (1970)
5. Zhang, Y., Zhang, Y., Wen, C.: A New focus Measure Method Using Moments. Image and Vision computing 18(12), 949–965 (2000)

6. Yap, P.T., Raveendran, P.: Image Focus Measure Based on Chebyshev Moments. IEE Proceedings - Vision, Image, and Signal Processing 151(2), 128–136 (2004)
7. Helmli, F.S., Scherer, S.: Adaptive Shape from Focus with an Error Estimation in Light Microscopy. In: Proceedings of the 2nd International Symposium on Image and Signal Processing and Analysis, pp. 188–193 (2001)
8. Xiong, Y., Shafer, S.A.: Depth from Focusing and Defocusing. In: Proceedings of the IEEE Computer Society Conference on Computer Vision and Pattern Recognition, CVPR 1993, pp. 68–73 (1993)
9. de Wet, T., Conradie, W.: In: Proceedings of ICOTS7 2006: The 7th International Conference on Teaching Statistics, alvador, Bahia, Brazil (2006)
10. Malik, A.S., Choi, T.-S.: Consideration of illumination effects and optimizatino of window size for accurate calculations of depth map for 3D shape recovery. Pattern Recognition 40, 154–170 (2007)
11. Rohwer, C.H.: Idempotent one-sided approximation of median smoothers. Journal of Approximation Theory 58, 151–163 (1989)
12. Rahmat, R., Malik, A.S., Kamel, N.: Comparative analysis of LULU Filters and other Image Denoising Filters. In: 3rd International Conference on Signal Acquisition and Processing, ICSAP (2011)
13. Pierre du Toit, J.: The Discrete Pulse Transform and Applications. Masters Thesis, University of Stellenbosch (2007)
14. Anguelov, R., Fabris-rotelli, I.: LULU Operators and Discrete Pulse Transform for Multidimensional Arrays. IEEE Transaction on Image Processing 19(11), 3012–3023 (2010)
15. Conradie, W.J., Wet, T.D., Jankowitz, M.: Exact and asymptotic distributions of LULU smoothers. Journal of Computational and Applied Mathematics 186(1), 253–267 (2006)

Overlapping Local Phase Feature (OLPF) for Robust Face Recognition in Surveillance

Qiang Liu and King Ngi Ngan

Dept. of Electronic Engineering, The Chinese University of Hong Kong, Hong Kong
{qliu,knngan}@ee.cuhk.edu.hk

Abstract. As a non-invasive biometric method, face recognition in surveillance is a very challenging problem because of the concurrence of conditions, such as under the variable illumination with uncontrolled pose and movement in low-resolution of subject. In this paper, we present a robust human face recognition system for surveillance. Unlike traditional recognition system which detect face region directly, we use a Cascade Head-Shoulder Detector (CHSD) and a trained human body model to find the face region in an image. To recognize human face, an efficient feature, Overlapping Local Phase Feature (OLPF), is proposed, which is robust to pose and blurring without adversely affecting discrimination performance. To describe the variations of faces, Adaptive Gaussian Mixture Model (AGMM) is proposed which can describe the distributions of the face images. Since AGMM does not need the topology of face, the proposed method is resistant to the face detection errors caused by wrong or no alignment. Experimental results demonstrate the robustness of our method on public dataset as well as real data from surveillance camera.

Keywords: Face Detection, Face Recognition, Local Binary Pattern (LBP), Local Phase Feature (LPF), Gaussian Mixture Model (GMM), Adaptive Gaussian Mixture Model (AGMM).

1   Introduction

In surveillance, human recognition through face is a popular way to prevent crime and terrorism. However, in many real-world applications, face recognition is still a challenging and unsolvable problem, although it performs well to deal with the cooperative subjects in some controlled applications, such as passport verification system. While for general surveillance cases, the captured faces may have different illuminations, expressions or poses. Besides, the surveillance video may have low quality issues such as low resolution, motion blur, out-of-focus blur or even the concurrence of them. Additionally, camera noise and compression distortion occurring during network transmission also affect the accuracy of the face recognition.

There existed a large number of face recognition algorithms in the past few decades, from utilizing the facial properties and relations, such as areas, distances, and angles [1] to projecting face image to feature spaces, such as Eigenface [2], Fisherface[3], Laplacianface [4][5] and derivative domain [6][7]. However, those methods

J. Blanc-Talon et al. (Eds.): ACIVS 2012, LNCS 7517, pp. 246–257, 2012.
© Springer-Verlag Berlin Heidelberg 2012

were designed for well aligned, uniformly illuminated, and frontal face images. While, in practice, it is almost impossible to satisfy these requirements, especially in security surveillance system. Consequently, many efforts have been made to develop algorithms for unconstrained face images [8][9][10][11]. Instead of using global features, they advocated using local appearance descriptors such as Gabor jets [12][13], SURF [14], SIFT [15][16], HOG [17] and Local Binary Patterns [19]. Because local appearance descriptors are more robust to occlusion, expression and small sample sizes than global features.

To be robust to low-resolution and blurring arising in the surveillance image, Gupta et al. [20] alternated between recognition and restoration with the assumption of a known blurring kernel. Hennings-Yeomans et al. [21] proposed a method to extract features from both the low-resolution faces and their super-resolved ones within a single energy minimization framework. Nishiyama et al. [22] proposed to improve the recognition of blurry faces with a pre-defined finite set of blurring kernels. Using the theory of sparse representation and compressed sensing, Wright et al. [23] yields new insights into two crucial issues in face recognition: the role of feature extraction and the difficulty due to occlusion.

For above methods, alignment is an indispensable preprocessing step, i.e., fix the coordinates of corners (e.g., eyes, nose) and then normalize to the same scale. However, it is known that automatic alignment is still a challenging problem for real-time system. Especially, the face detected automatically is often unsatisfactory and may be at different scales or coordinates. In surveillance, face detection is more difficult because of the highly uncontrolled pose, high noise and compression distortion in transmission.

In this paper, instead of finding the face directly, we propose to find the head-shoulder (HS) region first, and then employ the trained body model to get the face region. Also, to represent face region discriminatively, we propose an Overlapping Local Phase Feature (OLPF) which is not only robust to pose variation but also to image blurring. To robustly model faces, an Adaptive Gaussian Mixture Model (AGMM) is developed to describe the distributions of the training data. Since AGMM does not require the topology of face, the model is resistant to the initial errors induced by automatic face detector. Combining AGMM with OLPF, our method can handle faces with multiple uncontrolled issues in surveillance, such as pose, illumination, blurring, as well as resolution and scaling problems.

The structure of the paper: in the section 2, we briefly discuss on how to detect face by CHSD in surveillance image and detail the proposed face recognition algorithm in the section 3. In the section 4, we give extensive experiments to demonstrate the robustness of our method and conclusions are summarized in the section 5.

Fig. 1. Examples of images from surveillance videos

2   Face Detection Using CHSD

As aforementioned, in general surveillance condition, people and the target scene cannot be controlled strictly. So the captured faces may differ much in pose, illumination and expression. Some examples are given in Fig. 1. For these cases, traditional face detector [24] cannot locate the face region correctly. To account for those issues in uncontrained conditions, we propose a Cascade Header and Shoulder Detector (CHSD) to detect Head and Shoulder (HS) region firstly, and then use the HS model to obtain the face region.

The proposed is inspired by Dalal and Triggs [26] who use a dense grid of Histograms of Oriented Gradients (HoG) and linear Support Vector Machine (SVM) [27] to detect human. This method works slowly, and can only process QVGA images at 1FPS in a sparse scanning manner that needs to evaluate about 800 detection windows per image. In this paper, we intend to speed it up to real-time by combining the cascade rejecters [28][29].

The idea of CHSD is to use a cascade of rejecters to filter out a large number of non-HS samples while preserving almost 100% of HS regions in the early steps. Thus the computation time can be reduced significantly before more complex classifiers are called upon to achieve low false positive rates. As shown in Fig. 2, CHSD includes three parts: simple rejecter, Harr-like rejecter [24], and HoG classifier. The first layer is a simple feature rejecter where common features like variance and difference are efficiently calculated from integral images[1]. The second layer is the AdaBoosting HS classifiers constructed by a cascade of Harr-like features. The last layer is the HoG feature classifier which only needs to deal with tens of HS candidates. So the classification can be finished quickly even for high dimensional data. Once the HS region is obtained, the face region will be extracted by the structure model learnt from the training dataset, as illustrated in Fig. 2 (b) and (c). Multiple layers of classifiers is employed to reject as many non-HS samples as possible at the earliest stage with limited computation, which decrease the detection time significantly (20-40 FPS).

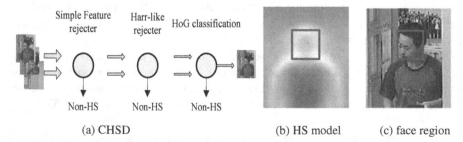

(a) CHSD   (b) HS model   (c) face region

Fig. 2. Face detection use CHSD and HS model. (a) Structure of CHSD. (b) HS mode and learnt face region with the red rectangle. (c) Detected face region uses HS region.

---

[1] In the first two rejecters, any two-rectangle feature can be computed in six array references, any three-rectangle feature in eight, and any four-rectangle feature in just nine.

3   Face Recognition

Local Binary Pattern (LBP) [18] as a local feature has proven to be highly discriminative for various applications, including image retrieval, surface inspection, texture
classification and segmentation. However, most LBP-based algorithms [19][31] use a
rigid descriptor matching strategy that is sensitive to pose variation and misalignment
of face, and thus cannot work well in surveillance. In this section, we propose an improved LBP-like algorithm by using OLPF to account for the low quality face recognition in surveillance, such as the pose variation with image blurring.

3.1   Overlapping Local Phase Feature (OLPF)

The proposed OLPF is mainly based on the phase feature [33], which is extracted
from the frequency domain by Fourier Transform. The image blurring process in the
Fourier domain can be represented as:

$$B(\mathbf{u}) = (I \cdot H)(\mathbf{u}) \tag{1}$$

where $B(\mathbf{u})$, $I(\mathbf{u})$ and $H(\mathbf{u})$ are the Discrete Fourier Transforms (DFT) of the blurred
image $b(\mathbf{m})$, the original image $i(\mathbf{m})$, and the blurring kernel $h(\mathbf{m})$, respectively. $\mathbf{m}$
and $\mathbf{u}$ are vectors of coordinates $[m, n]^T$ and $[u, v]^T$. We may separate the magnitude
and phase parts of (1) into

$$|B(\mathbf{u})| = |I(\mathbf{u})| \cdot |H(\mathbf{u})| \quad \text{and} \quad \angle B(\mathbf{u}) = \angle I(\mathbf{u}) + \angle H(\mathbf{u}) \tag{2}$$

If the blurring kernel $h(\mathbf{m})$ is assumed to be centrally symmetric, namely $h(\mathbf{m}) = h(-\mathbf{m})$, its Fourier transform is always real-valued $H(\mathbf{u})=Re\{H(\mathbf{u})\}$, and as a consequence
its phase part is only two-valued function, given by

$$\angle H(u) = \begin{cases} 0 & \text{if } H(u) \geq 0 \\ \pi & \text{if } H(u) < 0 \end{cases} \tag{3}$$

The transform can be efficiently evaluated for all image position using 1-D convolutions for the rows and columns successively. The local Fourier coefficients are com-
puted at four frequency points $\mathbf{u}_1=[a, 0]^T$, $\mathbf{u}_2=[0, a]^T$, $\mathbf{u}_3=[a, a]^T$, and $\mathbf{u}_4=[a, -a]^T$,
where a is a sufficiently small scalar to satisfy $H(\mathbf{u}_i)>0$. $I_\mathbf{m} = [I(\mathbf{u}_1, \mathbf{m}), I(\mathbf{u}_2, \mathbf{m}), I(\mathbf{u}_3, \mathbf{m}), I(\mathbf{u}_4, \mathbf{m})]$ as an invariant feature to blur is extracted for recognition by observing
the signs of the real and imaginary parts of each component in $I(\mathbf{m})$. A LBP-like me-
thod quantizes the phase information:

$$q_j = \begin{cases} 1, & \text{if } b_j(m) \geq \xi \\ 0, & otherwise \end{cases} \tag{4}$$

where $b_j(\mathbf{m})$ is the jth component the vector $B_m= [Re\{I_m\}, Im\{I_m\}]$. ξ is a small
enough valued to tolerate the image noise. The resulting eight binary coefficients $q_j(\mathbf{x})$
(8-neigborhood) are represented as integer values between 0-255 using binary coding.

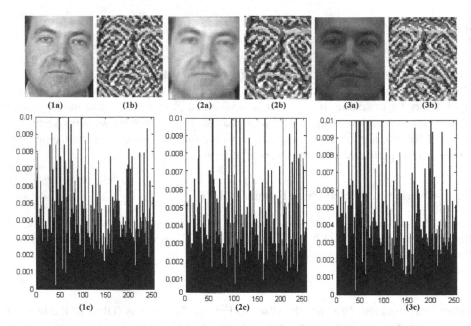

Fig. 3. Invariant property of LPF to blur and illumination. 1, 2, and 3 show the original image, blurred image ($\sigma=2$), and the image with different illumination, respectively. a, b, and c denote original image, the LPF image, and the LPF histogram. Bhattacharyya distances between two histograms are 0.0846 (1c and 2c) and 0.1035(1c and 3c).

$$f_{LPF} = \sum_{j=1}^{8} q_j(x)2^{j-1} \qquad (5)$$

An example of LPF features to represent the original image, the blurred image, and different illumination image by histograms are given in Fig. 3.

Head pose is believed to be one of the hardest issues for face recognition [34]. Although LPF feature can tolerate with blurred image, it is sensitive to the pose variation and misalignment common in surveillance image. Inspired by bag-of-feature, we develop an Overlapping LPF (OLPF), which describes a face as a set of feature vectors. For each face, we first divide it into small, uniformly sized, overlapped blocks. Then descriptive features are extracted from each block to form a vector. The robustness to pose variations is attributed to the explicit allowance for movement of face areas, when comparing face images of a particular person at various poses. Changes occurring at one facial component (e.g. the mouth) only affect the subset of face areas that cover this particular component. Therefore, OLPF-based face descriptor is not only robust to blurring but also robust to pose, expression, and misalignment.

3.2 Fixed Gaussian Mixture Model (FGMM)

In surveillance system, it is difficult to get an ideally frontal face image, because cameras are normally mounted under the ceiling where subjects rarely pose for. Although the face synthesis algorithm like [36] can convert the lateral faces to frontal ones, the synthesized faces often have residual artifacts which may degrade the performance of recognition significantly. In [35][37], a "bag-of-feature" approach was shown to perform well in the presence of pose variations. It is based on dividing the face into overlapping uniform-sized blocks, analyzing each block with the Discrete Cosine Transform (DCT) and modeling the resultant set of features via a Gaussian Mixture Model (GMM).

In our method, LPF is employed to replace the DCT feature used in [35]. Thus, we use a 1073x64 feature matrix to represent a face (64×80) divided by 8×8 block with 4-pixel overlapping. By assuming the feature vectors $\mathbf{X}$ are independent and identically distributed (i.i.d.), the likelihood of it belonging to the person i is

$$P\left(X \mid \lambda^{[i]}\right)=\prod_{n=1}^{N} P\left(x_{n} \mid \lambda^{[i]}\right)=\prod_{n=1}^{N} \sum_{g=1}^{G} \omega_{g}^{[i]} N\left(x_{n} \mid \mu_{g}^{[i]}, \Sigma_{g}^{[i]}\right) \tag{6}$$

where $N\left(x \mid \mu, \Sigma\right)=\left((2\pi)^{d} \cdot |\Sigma|\right)^{-\frac{1}{2}} e^{-\frac{1}{2}(x-\mu)^{T} \Sigma^{-1}(x-\mu)}$ is a multi-variant Gaussian function, while $\lambda^{[i]}=\{\omega_{g}^{[i]}, \mu_{g}^{[i]}, \Sigma_{g}^{[i]}\}_{1}^{G}$ is the set of parameters for person i. Its parameters are optimized by the Expectation Maximization (EM) algorithm. To initialize the EM, a fixed number of Gaussians should be set to describe those faces. Generally, the number of Gaussians affects the accuracy of the face model. More Gaussians can give more precise face model, but it may not convergent due to the limited data. In order to ensure the convergence of each face model, the smallest Gaussian number of the training faces is selected to initialize EM, which can be referred as Fixed Gaussian Mixture Model (FGMM). We propose face recognition which combines OLPF with FGMM can handle the concurrence of blur, pose, expression and illumination robustly.

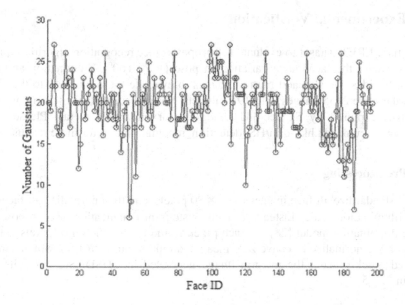

Fig. 4. The adaptive number of GMMs for each subject in FERET

3.3   Adaptive Gaussian Mixture Model (AGMM)

Fig. 4 shows the optimal number of Gaussians needed for the faces (64×80) in FERET dataset divided by 8×8 block with 4-pixel overlapping. We found that the minimum and maximum numbers of Gaussians are six for the 50th face and twenty-eight for the 4th, respectively, for a face. For FGMM, if setting G=6 as the number of Gaussians for each face, the faces such as the 4th one which have large variations cannot be modeled well. Similarly, if using too many Gaussians like G=28, EM may not be able to converge in the 50th face, because the samples with the high dimensions is too sparse to be used to build the face model with 28 Gaussians.

Unlike FGMM using fixed number of Gaussians to model the distributions of each face, we propose to use adaptive number of Gaussian Mixture Model to represent each face. As shown in (7), the number of Gaussian and the other parameters ($\lambda^{[i]} = \{\omega_g^{[i]}, \mu_g^{[i]}, \Sigma_g^{[i]}\}_1^{G_i}$) are estimated from the training dataset by maximizing the Log likelihood with iterative EM [40]. Apparently, this issue can be solved when using AGMM as appropriate number of Gaussians can be obtained adaptive to each face, which can give 5% improvement approximately.

$$\arg\max_{\lambda} \ln p\left(X|\lambda^{[i]}\right) = \arg\max_{\lambda} \sum_{n=1}^{N} \ln\left\{p\left(\bar{x}_n|\lambda^{[i]}\right)\right\}$$

$$= \arg\max_{\lambda} \sum_{n=1}^{N} \ln\left\{\sum_{g=1}^{G} \omega_g^{[i]} N\left(\bar{x}_n|\mu_g^{[i]}, \Sigma_g^{[i]}\right)\right\} \qquad (7)$$

4   Experimental Verification

We use the FERET dataset to evaluate the proposed face recognition algorithm quantitatively, where the faces have variation in pose [-60°, +60°], illumination and expression. Besides, we also add blurred images to evaluate the robustness to the blur. Totally, there are 2955 images with 197 subjects. For real surveillance testing, we use the images captured by SCface [41] and our surveillance cameras. Please visit http://www.ee.cuhk.edu.hk/~qliu/HS_detection_recognition.htm for more results

4.1   Pre-processing

First, we standardize all face images to 64×80 pixels, and then normalize all faces to similar illumination scale. Instead of using histogram equalization, we proposed a new the illumination model [28] for each pixel. In the model, the set of pixels within each block are normalized to have zero mean and unit variance $N(0, 1)$, which can be calculated quickly using the integral image generated in CHSD. Some results are shown in Fig. 5.

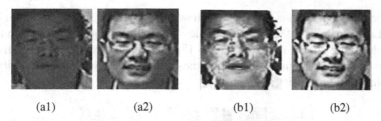

(a1)   (a2)   (b1)   (b2)

Fig. 5. Illumination normalization: (a) are the original images; (b) are the normalized ones

4.2   Face Recognition Results

For AGMM, the blocks size is set to 8×8 and with 4-pixel overlapping. This results in 1073 feature vectors per face. Each feature vector contains 64 phase histogram bins (down-sample the phase histogram bins to 64).

For the FERET dataset, we use the frontal image (0^0) as the gallery and the others as probe images. Table 1 and Table 2 show the comparisons with existing methods on pose, illumination, expression and blur variations. Apparently, our method has high recognition rate and outperforms the other algorithms significantly. Please note that [36] and [39] are excluded in Table 2, because they cannot handle the variations on illumination, expression and blur.

Table 1. Comparison with existing algorithms on FERET with pose variation

method	Pose							
	-60^0	-40^0	-25^0	-15^0	15^0	25^0	40^0	60^0
[3]	3.2	8.5	23.7	54.3	49.7	36.1	11.5	5.2
[36]	NO^2	NO	85.6	88.2	88.1	66.8	NO	NO
[39]	NO	NO	83.6	93.4	100	72.1	NO	NO
FGMM (G=25)	40.8	73.4	87.3	95.9	96.6	78.1	65.3	43.1
AGMM	56.4	80.6	91.3	100	100	88.4	76.8	58.4

Table 2. Comparison with existing algorithms on FERET with illumination, expression and blur variation

	illumination	expression	Blur (σ=1.0)	Blur (σ=2.0)	Blur (σ=3.0)
[3]	58.0	36.8	78.9	64.7	53.4
[42]	NO	NO	89.6	85.0	73.7
FGMM	81.3	75.8	96.6	93.5	81.6
AGMM	89.5	78.1	100	95.7	83.9

It is noted that apart from pose variations, imperfect face localization [25] is also an annoying issue in a real life surveillance system. Imperfect localization results in

---

^{2} Not given in the papers.

translations as well as scale change, which adversely affects face recognition performance. To evaluate AGMM, some examples with misalignment on scales and detection windows are shown in the 1st row o Fig. 6. Apparently, face images from the same person have misalignment problem, they are more similar (high similarity probability) than those from different person.

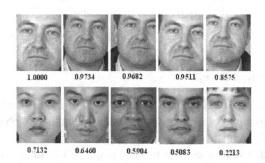

Fig. 6. Evaluation of the robustness of AGMM to misalignment. The normalized similarity probability with original face image (the first one) is given below the image.

Besides, we also build a dataset with totally 9164 color images collected from an indoor surveillance camera. Some samples are given in Fig. 1. For this dataset, the recognition rate of our method can reach 73% by using OLPF+FGMM and 81.4% by using OLPF+AGMM with 6 training sample and 4-pixel overlapping, respectively. Table 3. Comparison with existing algorithms on our dataset shows the recognition results for different descriptors on our data. Both FGMM and AGMM with OLPF feature outperform the state-of-art methods.

Table 3. Comparison with existing algorithms on our dataset

Methods	PCA[3]	LBP[18]	LPQ[33]	LFD[42]	OLPF+FGMM	OLPF+AGMM
Rec. Rate	46.3%	49.1%	57.9%	69%	73%	81.4%

Compared to PCA, we use the same size of training samples (six images) of each subject and the others for testing. With the same training data, PCA is worse than our method, because it needs accurate alignment and thus sensitive to the size of training dataset, pose, illumination, and blurring. While as illustrated in Fig. 7, the size of training set rarely affect the performance of the recognition rate of proposed method. But the number of overlapping pixels significantly impact on the recognition rate. Because, in the high dimensions space, overlapped samples can provide more crowding clusters, which can be easily modeled by AGMM. Although LPQ and LFD have used the phase feature, they cannot handle the pose variation and misalignment without a robust face model, such as FGMM and AGMM.

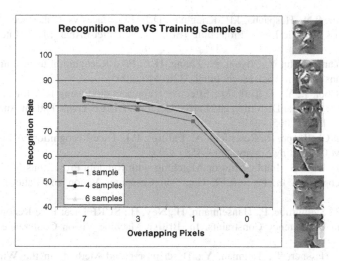

Fig. 7. The relationship between the size of training sample and recognition rate (AGMM); 1sample and 4 samples corresponds to the first one and four image in the right side image; and 6 samples use the entire samples listed in the right side

5   Conclusions

A robust human face recognition system for surveillance is presented in this paper. The contributions can be summarized as follows: first, we used CHSD to solve the unconstrained face detection problem in surveillance. Second, we proposed a new face feature OLPF to represent face distinctively which is not only robust to illumination but also invariant to blurring. At last, we proposed an AGMM model to describe the distribution of the faces which is robust to both pose variation and imperfect detection which are very important properties in surveillance detection. The experimental results on FERET and our surveillance dataset show that our method outperforms the existing algorithms in surveillance.

Acknowledgement. We are thankful to Dr. ZHANG Wei, Dr. OUYANG Wanli, who provided useful suggestions and help on revising this paper.

References

1. Cox, J., Ghosn, J., Yianilos, P.N.: Feature-Based Face Recognition Using Mixture-Distance. In: Proc. IEEE Conf. on Computer Vision and Pattern Recognition, pp. 209–216 (1996)
2. Turk, M., Pentland, A.: Eigenfaces for Recognition. Journal of Cognitive Neuroscience, 71–86 (1991)
3. Turk, M., Pentland, A.: Face Recognition Using Eigenfaces. In: Proc. IEEE Conf. on Computer Vision and Pattern Recognition, pp. 586–591 (1991)

 4. Belhumeur, P.N., Hespanha, J.P., Kriegman, D.J.: Eigenfaces vs. Fisherfaces: Recognition using Class Specific Linear Projection. IEEE Trans. Pattern Anal. Mach. Intell., 711–721 (1997)
 5. He, X., Yan, S., Hu, Y., Niyogi, P., Zhang, H.J.: Face Recognition using Laplacianfaces. IEEE Trans. Pattern Anal. Mach. Intell., 328–340 (2005)
 6. Kim, J., Choi, J., Yi, J., Turk, M.: Effective Representation using ICA for Face Recognition Robust to Local Distortion and Partial Occlusion. IEEE Trans. Pattern Anal. Mach. Intell., 1977–1981 (2005)
 7. Zhao, W., Chellappa, R., Rosenfeld, A., Phillips, P.J.: Face Recognition: A Literature Survey. ACM Computing Surveys, 399–458 (2003)
 8. Wright, J., Hua, G.: Implicit Elastic Matching with Random Projections for Pose-Variant Face Recognition. In: Proc. IEEE Conf. on Computer Vision and Pattern Recognition (2009)
 9. Dreuw, P., Steingrube, P., Hanselmann, H., Ney, H.: SURF Face: Face Recognition under Viewpoint Consistency Constraints. In: British Machine Vision Conference (September 2009)
10. Wolf, L., Hassner, T., Taigman, Y.: Descriptor based Methods in the Wild. In: Proc. ECCV (2008)
11. Ruiz-del-Solar, J., Verschae, R., Correa, M.: Recognition of Faces in Unconstrained Environments: A Comparative Study. EURASIP Journal on Advances in Signal Processing, 1–20 (2009)
12. Zou, J., Ji, Q., Nagy, G.: A Comparative Study of Local Matching Approach for Face Recognition. IEEE Transactions on Image Processing, 2617–2628 (2007)
13. Tan, X., Triggs, B.: Fusing Gabor and LBP Feature Sets for Kernel-Based Face Recognition. Analysis and Modeling of Faces and Gestures, 235–249 (2007)
14. Bay, H., Tuytelaars, T., Gool, L.V.: Surf: Speeded up Robust Features. LNCS, p. 404 (2006)
15. Lowe, D.G.: Distinctive Image Features from Scale-Invariant Keypoints. Int. J. Comput. Vision, 91–110 (2004)
16. Bicego, M., Lagorio, A., Grosso, E., Tistarelli, M.: On the Use of SIFT Features for Face Authentication. In: Proc. IEEE Conf. on Computer Vision and Pattern Recognition Workshop (2006)
17. Albiol, A., Monzo, D., Martin, A., Sastre, J., Albiol, A.: Face Recognition using HOG-EBGM. Pattern Recogn. Lett., 1537–1543 (2008)
18. Ahonen, T., Hadid, A., Peitikaimen, M.: Face Description with Local Binary Patterns: Application to Face Recognition. IEEE Trans. Pattern Anal. Mach. Intell., 2037–2041 (2006)
19. Ojala, T., Pietikainen, M., Maenpaa, T.: Gray Scale and Rotation Invariant Texture Classification with Local Binary Patterns. LNCS, pp. 404–420 (2000)
20. Gupta, M.D., Rajaram, S., Petrovic, N., Huang, T.S.: Restoration and Recognition in A Loop. In: Proc. IEEE Conf. on Computer Vision and Pattern Recognition, pp. 638–644 (2005)
21. Hennings-Yeomans, P.H., Baker, S., Kumar, B.V.K.V.: Simultaneous Super-resolution and Feature Extraction for Recognition of Low-resolution Faces. In: Proc. IEEE Conf. on Computer Vision and Pattern Recognition, pp. 1–8 (2008)
22. Nishiyama, M., Takeshima, H., Shotton, J., Kozakaya, T., Yamaguchi, O.: Facial Deblur Inference to Improve Recognition of Blurred Faces. In: Proc. IEEE Conf. on Computer Vision and Pattern Recognition, pp. 1115–1122 (2009)
23. Wright, J., Yang, A.Y., Ganesh, A., Sastry, S.S., Ma, Y.: Robust Face Recognition via Sparse Representation. IEEE Trans. Pattern Anal. Mach. Intell., 210–227 (2008)

24. Viola, P., Jones, M.: Robust Real-time Face Detection. In: International Conference on Computer Vision (2001)
25. Rodriguez, Y., Cardinaux, F., Bengio, S., Mariéthoz, J.: Measuring the Performance of Face Localization Systems. Image and Vision Computing, 882–893 (2006)
26. Dala, N., Triggs, B.: Histograms of Oriented Gradients for Human Detection. In: Proc. IEEE Conf. on Computer Vision and Pattern Recognition (2005)
27. Dollar, P., Wojek, C., Schiele, B., Perona, P.: Pedestrian Detection: An Evaluation of the State of art. In: Proc. IEEE Conf. on Computer Vision and Pattern Recognition, pp. 743–761 (2011)
28. Li, H., Ngan, K.N., Liu, Q.: FaceSeg: Automatic Face Segmentation for Real-time Video. IEEE Transactions on Multimedia, 77–88 (2009)
29. Zhu, Q., Yeh, M., Cheng, K., Avidan, S.: Fast Human Detection Using a Cascading of Histograms of Oriented Gradients. In: Proc. IEEE Conf. on Computer Vision and Pattern Recognition, pp. 1491–1498 (2006)
30. Zhang, C., Zhang, Z.: A Survey of Recent Advances in Face Detection. Microsoft Research Technical Report, MSR-TR-2010-66 (2010)
31. Fang, Y., Luo, J., Lou, C.: Fusion of Multi-directional Rotation Invariant Uniform LBP Features for Face Recognition. In: Third International Symposium on Intelligent Information Technology Application, pp. 332–335 (2009)
32. Ojala, T., Pietikainen, M., Maenpaa, T.: Multi-resolution Gray-scale and Rotation Invariant Texture Classification with Local Binary Patterns. IEEE Transactions on Pattern Analysis and Machine Intelligence, 971–987 (2002)
33. Ojansivu, V., Heikkilä, J.: Blur Insensitive Texture Classification Using Local Phase Quantization. In: Proc. Image and Signal Processing, pp. 236–243 (2008)
34. Phillips, P.J., Grother, P., Micheals, R., Blackburn, D.M., Tabassi, E., Bone, M.: Face Recognition Vendor Test 2002. In: IEEE International Workshop on Analysis and Modeling of Faces and Gestures (2003)
35. Sanderson, C., Bengio, S., Gao, Y.: On Transforming Statistical Models for Non-frontal Face Verification. Journal Pattern Recognition (February 2006)
36. Shan, T., Lovell, B.C., Chen, S.: Face Recognition Robust to Head Pose from One Sample Image. In: 18th International Conference on Pattern Recognition, pp. 515–518 (2006)
37. Sanderson, C., Shang, T., Lovell, B.C.: Towards Pose-Invariant 2D Face Classification for Surveillance. In: Proc. of the 3rd International Conference on Analysis and Modeling of Faces and Gestures (2007)
38. Cardinaux, F., Sanderson, C., Bengio, S.: User Authentication via Adapted Statistical Models of Face Images. IEEE Trans. on Signal Processing, 361–373 (2006)
39. Sanderson, C., Lovell, B.C.: Multi-Region Probabilistic Histograms for Robust and Scalable Identity Inference. In: International Conference on Biometrics, pp. 199–208 (2009)
40. Dempster, A.P., Laird, N.M., Rubin, D.B.: Maximum Likelihood from Incomplete Data via the EM Algorithm. J. R. Stat. Soc. Ser., 1–38 (1977)
41. Grgic, M., Delac, K., Grgic, S.: SCface - Surveillance Cameras Face Database. Multimedia Tools and Applications Journal, 863–879 (2011)
42. Zhen, L., Ahonen, T., Pietikainen, M., Li, S.Z.: Local Frequency Descriptor for Low-resolution Face Recognition. In: Automatic Face & Gesture Recognition and Workshops, pp. 161–166 (2011)

Classifying Plant Leaves from Their Margins Using Dynamic Time Warping

James S. Cope and Paolo Remagnino

Digital Imaging Research Centre, Kingston University, London, UK
{j.cope,p.remagnino}@kingston.ac.uk

Abstract. Most plant species have unique leaves which differ from each other by characteristics such as the shape, colour, texture and the margin. Details of the leaf margin are an important feature in comparative plant biology, although they have largely overlooked in automated methods of classification. This paper presents a new method for classifying plants according to species, using only the leaf margins. This is achieved by utilizing the dynamic time warping (DTW) algorithm. A margin signature is extracted and the leaf's insertion point and apex are located. Using these as start points, the signatures are then compared using a version of the DTW algorithm. A classification accuracy of over 90% is attained on a dataset of 100 different species.

1 Introduction

In the field of comparative biology, novel sources of data are continuously being sought to enable or enhance research varying from studies of evolution to generating tools for taxon identification. Leaves are especially important in this regard, because in many applied fields, such as studies of ecology or palaeontology, reproductive organs, which may often provide an easier form of identification, are unavailable or present for only a limited season. Leaves are present during all seasons when plants are in growth. There are also millions of dried specimens available in herbaria around the world, many of which have already been imaged. While these specimens may possess reproductive organs, the main character features are often concealed in images through being internal or due to poor preparation. However, almost all specimens possess well-preserved and relatively easily imaged leaf material.

The leaf margin, its outer edge, often contains a pattern of "teeth" - small serrated portions of leaf (see figure 1 for examples). Alternatively, it may feature small hairs, or be undulated. These margin features are very useful for botanists when describing leaves, with typical descriptions including details such as the tooth spacing, number per centimetre and qualitative descriptions of their flanks (for example convex or concave). Information about the teeth on leaves is particularly useful as it can indicate the plant's climate and growth patterns. Indeed, the teeth on fossilised leaves have even been used to make inferences about prehistoric climates [13].

J. Blanc-Talon et al. (Eds.): ACIVS 2012, LNCS 7517, pp. 258–267, 2012.

Traditional methods employed by botanists for describing leaves rely on terminology and are largely qualitative and open to some level of interpretation [7]. In recent decades plant science has begun to use a range of quantitative morphometric methods in comparative studies [12,9]. However, such data currently exist for a small minority of plant taxa, largely due to the limitations imposed by manual data capture.

In this paper we present a method for the automated classification of plants by species from their margin data, using dynamic time warping. Section 2 outlines previous work carried out in this area. Our methodology is described in section 3, with results given in section 4.

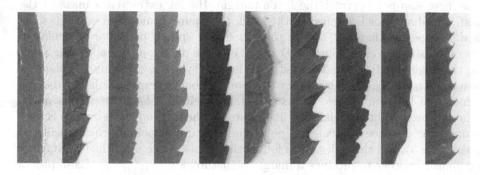

Fig. 1. Examples of leaf margins

2   Previous Work

Although the leaf margin is of great importance to botanists, there has been surprisingly little work towards its automated analysis. This may be due to the fact that not all plant species leaves feature teeth, although in these cases classification could still be aided by quantitative descriptors of the margin, which in many of these cases are still not entirely smooth. Another reason could be the difficulty in successfully acquiring meaningful measurements, particularly if it's assumed that these descriptors should match those currently used by botanists. Indeed, it has been claimed that "no computer algorithm can reliably detect leaf teeth" [14] as yet. Instead, most work in automated plant classification has concentrated on either leaf shape [9,8,21,11] or texture [1,2,5].

McLellan and Endler [10] used a single value measure of margin roughness, calculated by summing the angles between the lines connecting adjacent points around the contour. This was then combined with a selection of single-parameter shape descriptors. An angle code histogram - histogram of the angles at point around the leaf - were used by Wang et al [20], alongside the centroid-contour distance method of shape description. A number of authors, such as Clark [3] [4] and Rumpunen [15], have taken manual tooth measurements and used them in computer-based analysis.

3   Methodology

The method involves first extracting the leaf's margin, as described in section 3.1. We then use the Dynamic Time Warping algorithm (described in section 3.2) for two purposes. The first is to locate the insertion point and apex of the leaf (section 3.3), before using these as reference points for comparing the margin with those in the training set (section 3.4) in order to perform the classification.

3.1   Extracting the Margin

The first step is to extract the leaf's margin. Having extracted a mask of the leaf, a median filter is applied to the mask to acquire a smoothed version of the leaf's shape (see figure 2). From this, m evenly spaced points are calculated, encompassing the entire outline. For each of these points, a corresponding point on the original outline is calculated. This is done by first estimating the line that is normal to the edge of the leaf at this point as being perpendicular to the line which runs between the two points at distance k either side of the current point. The sub-pixel point at which this line intersects the original leaf's outline is then found. The distance between this point and the current point is then calculated (see figure 3), and these distances for all the points in the smoothed outline are combined in order to produce a margin signature, $\mathbf{s} = \langle s_1, ..., s_m \rangle$. Examples of extracted margin signatures are given in figure 4.

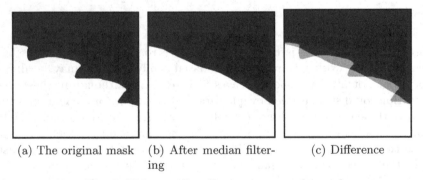

(a) The original mask   (b) After median filtering   (c) Difference

Fig. 2. Using median filters to extract the teeth

The extracted margin is partitioned into n overlapping windows, $\mathbf{x} = \langle x_1, ..., x_n \rangle$, of equal size and spacing (in this case $n = \frac{m}{8}$ and the window size used is $\frac{m}{128}$). For each window, 6 features are calculated. This is done for a number of reasons. Firstly, the exact number of teeth will vary between leaves of the same species, which may cause problems when attempting to align their margins. By using windows, each window will provide a description for the area of the margin

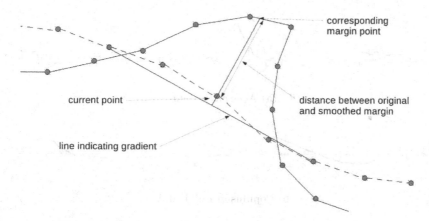

Fig. 3. Calculating a point on the margin signature

within it, and so be more robust to this. Furthermore, This allows for an adequate description of the margin whilst using a much smaller number of datapoints, and so greatly reducing computation time. By overlapping the windows, sensitivity to their exact position in **s** is reduced.

For each point within a window, x_i, 3 values are calculated:

1. Magnitude - This is the signed distance between the smoothed margin point and its corresponding point in the original margin, where the sign is determined by whether the original margin point lines inside or outside of the smoothed margin.
2. Gradient - The signed difference between the current point in the margin signature and the next point.
3. Curvature - The angle at the current point between the previous point and the next point.

For each of these, 2 features are then calculated for the window:

- Average positive value

$$\sum_{\substack{s_j \in x_i \\ s_j \geq 0}} \frac{s_j}{|x_i|}$$

- Average negative value

$$\sum_{\substack{s_j \in x_i \\ s_j \leq 0}} \frac{s_j}{|x_i|}$$

Where x_i is the current window, s_j is the value at a point within the signature, and $|x_i|$ is the size of the window.

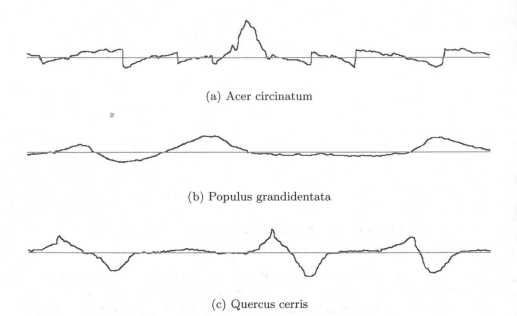

(a) Acer circinatum

(b) Populus grandidentata

(c) Quercus cerris

Fig. 4. Examples of segments from extracted margin signatures

3.2   Dynamic Time Warping

Dynamic time warping (hereon DTW) [16] is a technique for measuring the similarity between two different sequences. During the comparison, it allows parts of the signals to be stretched or compressed to a certain extent, thereby accounting for the sequences being of different lengths (for instance, due to differences in speed) or containing natural distortions. A typical application for DTW is speech recognition, where people may speak at different speeds, or elongate different sounds. It has also seen use for a number of computer vision problems, including face detection [19] and action recognition [18].

Given two sequences $\mathbf{x} = \langle x_1, ..., x_m \rangle$, $\mathbf{y} = \langle y_1, ..., y_n \rangle$ an $m \times n$ cost matrix $\mathbf{C}$ is calculated, whereby value c_{ij} is the distance between points x_i and y_j. Under the assumption that point x_1 corresponds to point y_1 (i.e. the same starting points), and x_m to y_n, a monotonic path through $\mathbf{C}$ is found, beginning at c_{00} and ending at c_{mn}, such that the accumulated value of the nodes visited is minimized. This path then represents the optimal alignment of points in $\mathbf{x}$ to those in $\mathbf{y}$. This can be calculated relatively efficiently (quadratic complexity) by recursively accumulating the costs in a matrix $\mathbf{D}$. The value d_{ij} is calculated as follows:

$$d_{ij} = \begin{cases} c_{ij} & \text{if } (i = 1 \wedge j = 1) \\ \infty & \text{if } (i = 1 \wedge j > 1) \vee (j = 1 \wedge i > 1) \\ c_{ij} + \min \begin{pmatrix} d_{i-1,j} \\ d_{i,j-1} \\ d_{i-1,j-1} \end{pmatrix} & \text{otherwise} \end{cases} \tag{1}$$

Once all the values in **D** have been calculated, the measure of the similarity between the two sequences is given by d_{mn}.

There are a number of extensions to the standard DTW algorithm that have been proposed in the literature [16,17]. Calculating d_{ij} by using equation 1 results in a path which travels monotonically between adjacent cells, either horizontally, vertically or diagonally. Since a continued horizontal or vertical movement represents the compression of a subsequence to unit length, or the stretching of a single point to a much longer length, this could result in unrealistic distortions. To counter this we add the condition that a every step that is made horizontally or vertically must also be accompanied by a diagonal step (see figure 5). This restricts the maximum distortion of a subsequence to a level that is realistic for this type of data, whilst ensuring that distortions carry an additional cost due to resulting in longer paths.

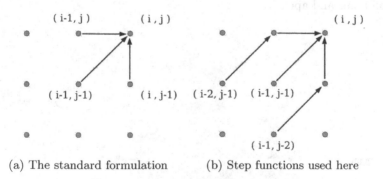

(a) The standard formulation   (b) Step functions used here

Fig. 5. Legal steps for path when calculating DTW

If two sequences are similar, the optimal DTW path will be close to the diagonal of the cost matrix, where $i = j$. If the optimal path diverges from this by more than a certain amount, it is unlikely that the two sequences are from the same class. This allows a constraint to be added to improve the speed of the algorithm. By only calculating d_{ij} for when $|i - j| \le k$, the complexity can be reduced from $\mathcal{O}(n^2)$ to $\mathcal{O}(kn)$ where $k \ll n$, without risking finding a sub-optimal path, when the two sequences are from the same class [17]. With these improvements included, the equation for calculating d_{ij} becomes:

$$
d_{ij} = \begin{cases}
\infty & \text{if } |i - j| > k \\
c_{ij} & \text{if } (i = 1 \wedge j = 1) \\
\infty & \text{if } (i = 1 \wedge j > 1) \vee (j = 1 \wedge i > 1) \\
c_{ij} + \min \begin{pmatrix} d_{i-2,j-1} + c_{i-1,j}, \\ d_{i-1,j-2} + c_{i,j-1}, \\ d_{i-1,j-1} \end{pmatrix} & \text{otherwise}
\end{cases}
$$

$$(2)$$

3.3 Locating the Insertion Point and Apex

In order to align two margins, a common start point must first be found. In the case of leaves, the only two landmarks in the shape which consistently exist are the 'insertion point' - where the petiole, or stem, attaches to the leaf - and the apex - the tip of the leaf (see figure 6). To locate these two points, potential candidate points are first identified by selecting the local maxima from the margin signature which have an absolute magnitude greater than 25% of the global maximum. Based on the principle that both sides of a leaf - from insertion point to apex - will be approximately a reflection of each other, dynamic time warping can be used to identify the two points on the margin for which the difference between the two sides is minimised, and so are most likely to be the insertion point and apex.

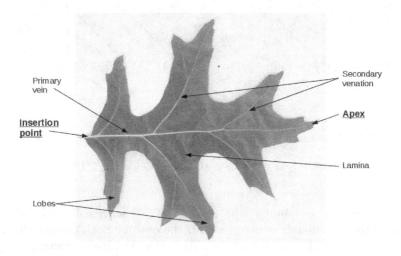

Fig. 6. Some of the key features of a leaf

For a given candidate point, the corresponding window, x_i is identified from the circular sequence of windows $\mathbf{x} = \langle x_1, ..., x_n \rangle$ for the leaf. Two sequences, $\mathbf{a} = \langle a_1, ..., a_{\frac{n}{2}+w} \rangle$, $\mathbf{b} = \langle b_1, ..., b_{\frac{n}{2}+w} \rangle$ are generated, where $a_1 = b_1 = x_i$, $a_j =$

x_{i+j}, $b_k = x_{i-k}$ and n is the total number of windows. Since the insertion point and apex may not lie directly opposite each other, the sequences $\mathbf{a}$ and $\mathbf{b}$ are continued for a distance of w beyond the mid-point $x_{i+\frac{n}{2}}$, such that the ends of the sequences are overlapping. A value of $w = \frac{n}{8}$ was used.

The accumulated cost matrix $\mathbf{D}$ is generated as described in section 3.2. Because the last w points in the two sequence are the reverse of each other, similarity is calculated as the minimum d_{jk} where $j + k = n$. Using this method, the insertion point and apex were correctly identified in 97.75% of test cases, with one or the other correctly found in 99.25% of cases.

3.4   Comparing Margins

Whilst the apices and insertion points have been identified, it is not known which is which. When comparing two margins, all four combinations for sequence start points are therefore used. Some species' leaves have a degree of asymmetry. Whilst the details along the margin in these cases will be similar on either side of the leaf, the distance between insertion point and apex may be quite different. To account for this, the margins are oriented so that they always procede along the shortest side first. The DTW algorithm is applied for all four configurations, and the smallest measurement is selected.

Following the assumption in section 3.3 that the maximum difference between the lengths of the two sides of the leaf will be $2w$, where $w = \frac{n}{8}$, the value of k used in formula 2 is also set to $\frac{n}{8}$, as this is the point in the sequences where the most distortion is expected to occur.

4   Results

The method is evaluated on a dataset containing 16 leaves from each of 100 different species. A 16-fold cross-validation is performed, such that one leaf from each species is used each time in the testing set, whilst the remaining leaves are used as the training set. Classification is performed using the k-nearest-neighbour technique, with $k = 5$. For comparison, two other techniques are also used on the same data:

- Cross-correlation:
  For two sequences, $\mathbf{a}, \mathbf{b}$, the distance between the two is calculated for every possible offset of one sequence against the other. The lowest distance calculated is used for the classification.

$$distance = \min_{0 \leq i < n} \sum_{j=0}^{n} \|a_j - b_{j+i \bmod n}\|$$

- Bag-of-Words:
  A large number of feature vectors are sampled from the entire training set, and a clustering is performed on these. The cluster centroids are used as the 'codewords' in a 'dictionary' used to perform a quantization of the data, by assigning each data-point to its nearest 'codeword'. A margin sequence can

then be described as the frequency of occurrence of each 'codeword' [6]. For classification, the distance between two sequences if then calculated as the Jeffrey-divergence metric for their two histograms.

The results for the three methods are shown in table 1.

Table 1. Results for the three methods

Method	Result (%)
Cross-Correlation	57.12
Bag-of-Words	74.51
Proposed Method	91.32

As the results show, the proposed method performed significantly better than the other two. The cross-correlation method conserves the order of the sequence but is too rigid to account for the variations that occur in leaves, for example in the exact positions of the tips of lobes, which appear as peaks in the signature. By ignoring the order of the sequence, the bag-of-words method describes only the content of the margin, and loses valuable information. By using the DTW algorithm, the proposed method can utilize the order of the sequence, whilst having enough flexibility to deal with the variation inherent to natural data.

5   Conclusion

In this paper it has been demonstrated that, whilst leaf margins have been largely ignored as feature for use in automated plant classification, it is possible to accurately classify plants using margin features alone. A classification rate of 91.32% was acheived on a large dataset of 100 different species. The dynamic time warping algorithm was used both for locating the apices and insertion points, and for comparing leaves, utilizing how the margin pattern may alter along the sequence, whilst allowing for the variability often present in this type of data. Accurate indentification of the insertion point and apex may furthermore be useful when considering other leaf features, for example in extracting the venation. The proposed method was found to perform significantly better than a number of alternative methods.

References

1. Backes, A.R., Bruno, O.M.: Plant Leaf Identification Using Multi-scale Fractal Dimension. In: Foggia, P., Sansone, C., Vento, M. (eds.) ICIAP 2009. LNCS, vol. 5716, pp. 143–150. Springer, Heidelberg (2009)
2. Casanova, D., de Mesquita Sá Junior, J.J., Bruno, O.M.: Plant leaf identification using Gabor wavelets. International Journal of Imaging Systems and Technology 19, 236–243 (2009)
3. Clark, J.Y.: Plant identification from characters and measurements using artificial neural networks. In: MacLeod, N. (ed.) Automated Taxon Identification in Systematics: Theory, Approaches and Applications, pp. 207–224. CRC (2007)

4. Clark, J.Y.: Neural networks and cluster analysis for unsupervised classification of cultivated species of *Tilia* (Malvaceae). Botanical Journal of the Linnean Society 159, 300–314 (2009)
5. Cope, J.S., Remagnino, P., Barman, S., Wilkin, P.: Plant Texture Classification Using Gabor Co-occurrences. In: Bebis, G., Boyle, R., Parvin, B., Koracin, D., Chung, R., Hammound, R., Hussain, M., Kar-Han, T., Crawfis, R., Thalmann, D., Kao, D., Avila, L. (eds.) ISVC 2010. LNCS, vol. 6454, pp. 669–677. Springer, Heidelberg (2010)
6. Csurka, G., Dance, C.R., Fan, L., Willamowski, J., Bray, C.: Visual categorization with bags of keypoints. In: Workshop on Statistical Learning in Computer Vision, ECCV 2004, pp. 1–22 (2004)
7. Ellis, B., Daly, D.C., Hickey, L.J., Johnson, K.R., Mitchell, J.D., Wilf, P., Wing, S.L.: Manual of Leaf Architecture. Cornell University Press (2009)
8. Hearn, D.J.: Shape analysis for the automated identification of plants from images of leaves. Taxon 58, 934–954 (2009)
9. Jensen, R.J., Ciofani, K.M., Miramontes, L.C.: Lines, outlines, and landmarks: Morphometric analyses of leaves of Acer rubrum, Acer Saccharinum (Aceraceae) and their Hybrid. Taxon 51(3), 475–492 (2002)
10. McLellan, T., Endler, J.A.: The relative success of some methods for measuring and describing the shape of complex objects. Systematic Biology 47, 264–281 (1998)
11. Pauwels, E.J., de Zeeum, P.M., Ranguelova, E.B.: Computer-assisted tree taxonomy by automated image recognition. Engineering Applications of Artificial Intelligence 22(1), 26–31 (2009)
12. Plotze, R.D., Falvo, M., Padua, J.G., Bernacci, L.C., Vieira, M.L.C., Oliveira, G.C.X., Martinez, O.: Leaf shape analysis using the multiscale Minkowski fractal dimension, a new morphometric method: A study with *Passiflora* (Passifloraceae). Canadian Journal of Botany 83(3), 287–301 (2005)
13. Royer, D.L., Wilf, P.: Why do toothed leaves correlate with cold climates? Gas exchange at leaf margins provides new insights into a classic paleotemperature proxy. International Journal of Plant Sciences 167(1), 11–18 (2006)
14. Royer, D.L., Wilf, P., Janesko, D.A., Kowalski, E.A., Dilcher, D.L.: Correlations of climate and plant ecology to leaf size and shape: potential proxies for the fossil record. American Journal of Botany 92(7), 1141–1151 (2005)
15. Rumpunen, K., Bartish, I.V.: Comparison of differentiation estimates based on morphometric and molecular data, exemplified by various leaf shape descriptors and RAPDs in the genus *Chaenomeles*. Taxon 51, 69–82 (2002)
16. Sakoe, H., Chiba, S.: Dynamic programming algorithm optimization for spoken word recognition. IEEE Transactions on Acoustics, Speech and Signal Processing 26(1), 43–49 (1978)
17. Salvador, S., Chan, P.: Toward accurate dynamic time warping in linear time and space. Intelligent Data Analysis 11(5), 561–580 (2007)
18. Sempena, S., Maulidevi, N.U., Aryan, P.R.: Human action recognition using dynamic time warping. In: International Conference on Electrical Engineering and Informatics. IEEE (2011)
19. Turkan, M., Dulek, B., Onaran, I., Cetin, A.: Human face detection in video using edge projections. In: Visual Information Processing. SPIE (2006)
20. Wang, Z., Chi, Z., Dagan, F.: Shape based leaf image retrieval. Vision, Image And Signal Processing 150, 34–43 (2003)
21. Ye, L., Keogh, E.: Time series shapelets: A new primitive for data mining. In: IEEE International Conference on Knowledge Discovery and Data Mining, pp. 947–956. ACM (2009)

Utilizing the Hungarian Algorithm for Improved Classification of High-Dimension Probability Density Functions in an Image Recognition Problem

James S. Cope and Paolo Remagnino

Digital Imaging Research Centre, Kingston University, London, UK
{j.cope,p.remagnino}@kingston.ac.uk

Abstract. A method is presented for the classification of images described using high-dimensional probability density functions (pdfs). A pdf is described by a set of n points sampled from its distribution. These points represent feature vectors calculated from windows sampled from an image. A mapping is found, using the Hungarian algorithm, between the set of points describing a class, and the set for a pdf to be classified, such that the distance that points must be moved to change one set into the other is minimized. The method uses these mappings to create a classifier that can model the variation within each class. The method is applied to the problem of classifying plants based on images of their leaves, and is found to outperform several existing methods.

1   Introduction

For many machine learning problems, an object of data, e.g. an item to be classified, can be described as a single point within a feature space. Many different methods exist for classifying such objects, from simple methods, such as k-nearest-neighbour, to more sophisticated methods, such as support vector machines. However it is sometimes more appropriate to describe an object as a distribution within a feature space. In the case of image recognition, this might a be set of feature vectors calculated for different points within an image.

A number of methods also exist for classifying data of this type. When described using histograms, the difference between two probability density functions (pdfs) can be calculated using bin-by-bin methods, such as the Jeffrey-divergence metric, however these methods encounter problems when the data has a high dimensionality, where a large number of bins makes the calculation expensive, whilst the sparse population of bins causes poor results. The earth mover's distance (EMD) [8] deals this by using signatures, and provides an accurate and intuitive measurement. These 'signatures' are weighted points within the feature space. This is akin to clustering data points drawn from the distribution, and weighting each cluster centroid by the number of points in the cluster. Another method is to use kernel density estimation [7] to estimate a

J. Blanc-Talon et al. (Eds.): ACIVS 2012, LNCS 7517, pp. 268–277, 2012.

probability density function using points sampled from a distribution, and then to use this estimation to predict the probability of another sampling of points belonging to the same distribution. More recently, 'bag-of-words' methods have enjoyed increasing usage for this problem, particularly in the guise of 'bag-of-visual-words' [9] for image retrieval.

In this paper we utilize information generated in the calculation of the earth mover's distance in order to allow for more robust classification of pdfs, particularly when there is high intra-class variation. Our method is applied to the problem of plant leaf recognition, with each leaf being described by features calculated at windows sampled randomly from the surface of the leaf.

In section 2 we describe the EMD method in more detail before formally defining the problem in section 3. In section 4 a method is described in which the EMD is used to aid modelling of the intra-class variation to enable for improved classification. A comparison of this method with other common methods, using empirical results, is given in section 5.

2 The Hungarian Algorithm and the Earth Mover's Distance

The earth mover's distance (EMD) [8] is a measure of the difference between two pdfs. The analogy is that, to reform one mound of earth as another, the effort required would depend on the sum the of distances that each unit of dirt must be moved. Whilst bin-by-bin methods only consider the amount of 'earth' in each location, the EMD considers how far it must be moved. There are two forms of pdf descriptions that allow the EMD to be calculated, histogram binning, and the aforementioned signatures. Since the binning is analogous to using evenly spaced signatures, we need only consider the latter.

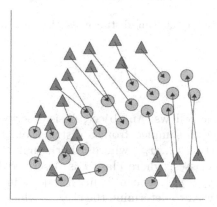

Fig. 1. The mapping via the Hungarian algorithm between two sets of points

Whilst there may be many ways of reforming one pdf into another, the EMD is calculated as being the one that requires the minimum total movement (see figure 1). The standard way of determining this is to model it as the transportation problem. There are a number of methods for solving the transportation problem, but by reforming the data so that each signature has an equal weight, it becomes equivalent to the simpler assignment problem, which can be solved using the Hungarian algorithm [6]. Whilst the original Hungarian algorithm was $O(n^4)$, an $O(n^3)$ version has since been found by [4].

The EMD typically only uses the minimum cost calculated by the Hungarian algorithm, but in our usage here we will also record the corresponding mapping between signatures, as it provides not only a measurement of the difference between the pdfs, but also information about in what way they are different. The EMD normally uses the Euclidean distance as the cost of moving 'earth' between two points, but here the squared Euclidean distance is used, as this helps to preserve the topology (figure 2).

(a) Euclidean distance

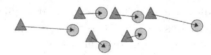

(b) Squared Euclidean distance

Fig. 2. Using the squared Euclidean distance as the cost function preserves the topology

3   Notation

We define the problem as follows. An object, X, is described by a set of n data points, $X = \{\bar{x}_1, \bar{x}_2, ... \bar{x}_n\}$, sampled from a distribution. Each data point $\bar{x}$ is a feature vector, $\bar{x} = [x_1, x_2, ..., x_d]$, where d is the number of features. Given a number of different classes, where class i is described by another set of n data points, $C_i = \{\bar{y}_1, \bar{y}_2, ... \bar{y}_n\}$, drawn from all objects in the training set that belong to the class, we wish to determine the class to which object X most likely belongs. This is calculated using Bayes theorem:

$$c^* = \arg\max_i P(C_i|X) \tag{1}$$

$$= \arg\max_i P(X|C_i)P(C_i)/P(X) \tag{2}$$

$$= \arg\max_i P(X|C_i)P(C_i) \tag{3}$$

4   Methodology

The method attempts to improve reliability by modelling the variation within each class. Each class object's data points are separated into a number of clusters. We model the movement within each of these clusters under the mapping between the class object and its training examples (figure 3). This essentially aims to describe how each portion of the distribution typically varies for that class. These models are then used to determine to which class another object most likely belongs.

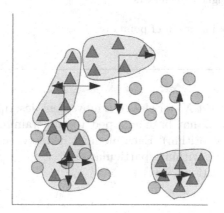

Fig. 3. Descriptors are generated to model the movement between the class object and another object in terms of each cluster

4.1   Training the Classifier

For each class, a class object is produced by randomly selecting n points from the class's example in the training set. For each training object, a mapping is found from its data points to those its class object using the Hungarian algorithm. This mapping pairs the points in one object to those in the other, such that the sum of the squared Euclidean distances between paired points is minimised (see figure 1). We define the point in the class object C_i to which point $\bar{x}$ is paired as $M(\bar{x}, C_i)$.

Next a small number, k, of cluster centroids are found, for each class, using the clustering algorithm described in figure 4. This method of clustering creates clusters of equal size, and thereby helps to ensure the centroids are appropriately spread thoughout the distribution. Any clustering algorithm with similar properties could also be used. All the points in the class object are then assigned to the cluster of their nearest centroid. The change between objects will be measured relative to these clusters. The jth cluster for class i is denoted as K_{ij}.

Fig. 4 Clustering algorithm

Initialise cluster centroids at randomly picked data points
repeat
    for all clusters **do**
       Sort points according to distance from centroid
    end for
    repeat
       for all clusters **do**
          Assign next nearest unassigned point to cluster
       end for
    until all points assigned to clusters
    for all clusters **do**
       Calculate centroid as mean of points in cluster
    end for
until converged

For each training object X_i^t for class i, a movement descriptor F_i^t is generated, after the class object C_i has been mapped to the training object (as before, using the Hungarian algorithm). Each element in the descriptor is the sum of the movements of points within a particular cluster, for a particular dimension and in a particular direction.

$$F_i^t = \{\bar{f}_{ab}^t | 0 < a < k; 0 < b < d\} \qquad (4)$$

$$\bar{f}_{ab}^t = [f_{ab+}^t, f_{ab-}^t] \qquad (5)$$

$$f_{ab+}^t = \frac{k}{|X_i^t|} \sum_{\substack{\bar{x} \in X_i^t \\ x_b - M(\bar{x}, C_i)_b > 0 \\ M(\bar{x}, C_i) \in K_{ia}}} x_b - M(\bar{x}, C_i)_b \qquad (6)$$

$$f_{ab-}^t = \frac{k}{|X_i^t|} \sum_{\substack{\bar{x} \in X_i^t \\ x_b - M(\bar{x}, C_i)_b < 0 \\ M(\bar{x}, C_i) \in K_{ia}}} x_b - M(\bar{x}, C_i)_b \qquad (7)$$

where d is the number of dimensions, k is the number of clusters, and t is the training instance. $\bar{x} \in K_{ia}$ indicates that point $\bar{x}$ is assigned to the ath cluster for class i, and x_b refers to the value in $\bar{x}$ corresponding to the bth feature (likewise for $M(\bar{x}, C_i)_b$).

Equations 6 and 7 calculate the elements of the descriptor for cluster a, in the positive and negative directions, respectively, along dimension b. These are calculated as being the sum of the distances between training points and their mapped class points, where the mapped point is in the given cluster. These are normalized by multiplying by the number of clusters, divided by the number of points in the training object.

4.2 Classification

To classify an object X, for each potential class, the mapping and generation of a movement descriptor, F_i, is performed as per the training stage. We then use a Parzen window method [7] with a Gaussian kernel to calculate the likelihoods for each class, and determine the classification.

$$c^* = \arg\max_i P(X|C_i)P(C_i) \tag{8}$$

$$P(X|C_i) = P(F_i|C_i) \tag{9}$$

$$= \prod_{a=0}^{a<d} \prod_{b=0}^{b<k} P(\bar{f}_{ab}|C_i) \tag{10}$$

$$P(\bar{f}_{ab}|C_i) = \frac{1}{T_i} \sum_{t=0}^{T_i} P(\bar{f}_{ab}|\bar{f}_{ab}^t) \tag{11}$$

$$P(\bar{f}_{ab}|\bar{f}_{ab}^t) = \phi(||\bar{f}_{ab}^t - \bar{f}_{ab}||) \tag{12}$$

where T_i is the number of training examples for class i and $\phi(x)$ is a normal distribution function with mean, $\mu = 0$ and standard deviation, $\sigma = 0.002$.

5   Experiments

In this section the new algorithm is empirically evaluated by comparing it to a selection of other techniques. For these experiments we have 32 different classes, with 16 examples of each, performing a 16-fold cross validation. Each example's object has 1024 data-points.

5.1   Test Data

To test the algorithm we apply it to a visual computing problem, the classification of plant species from images of their leaves. This is a problem which has received much interest recently [5,1,2]. For each leaf image in the database, we randomly select 1024 small windows from the surface of the leaf. For each window we calculate 20 features based on the responses from different filters applied to all the pixels in the window. The set of features for each window becomes one of the object's data-points in a 20-dimension feature space.

The filters used are a variation of the Gabor filter, made to be rotational invariant:

$$g(x,y) = \exp \frac{r^2}{2\sigma^2} \cos \frac{2\pi r}{\lambda}$$

where $r = \sqrt{x^2 + y^2}$ is the distance from the centre of the filter, σ is the standard deviation, and λ is the wavelength, set to be $\lambda = 3\sigma$. Five different scale filters are used, produced by varying σ. Each filter is convolved with the window and four features are then calculated for that filter for the window:

1. Average positive value

$$\sum_{\substack{(i,j)\in W \\ s_j \geq 0}} \frac{f_{ij}}{|W|}$$

2. Average negative value

$$\sum_{\substack{(i,j)\in W \\ s_j \leq 0}} \frac{f_{ij}}{|W|}$$

3. Energy

$$\sum_{(i,j)\in W} \frac{f_{ij}^2}{|W|}$$

4. Entropy

$$-\sum_{(i,j)\in W} \frac{|f_{ij}|}{|W|} \log \frac{|f_{ij}|}{|W|}$$

Where W is the current window, f_{ij} is the response for the current filter at pixel (i,j), and $|W|$ is the size of the window.

5.2   Methods for Comparison

The three methods we use for comparison are kernel density estimation, the earth mover's distance, and a bag-of-words method using a Naive-Bayes classifier.

Fig. 5. Examples of images in the test dataset

Kernel Density Estimation. Kernel density estimation is used to predict the probability density function for each class. This estimate of the pdf is then used to calculate the likelihood of the object belonging to that class.

$$P(X|C_i) = \prod_{\bar{x} \in X} P(\bar{x}|C_i)$$

$$= \prod_{\bar{x} \in X} \sum_{\bar{y} \in C_i} \frac{\phi(||\bar{y} - \bar{x}||)}{|C_i|}$$

where $\phi(x)$ is a normal distribution function with mean, $\mu = 0$ and standard deviation, $\sigma = 0.1$. This kernel function was used as it appeared to give the best results for the dataset.

Earth Mover's Distance. The pure value calculated by the earth mover's distance is used, instead of utilizing the mapping between objects. Each object is classified as belonging to the class whose object is closest to it according to the EMD metric.

Naive-Bayesian Bag-of-Words. A large number of points are sampled from the training distributions and then a clustering is performed on these. The cluster centroids are used as the 'codewords' in a 'dictionary' used to perform a quantization of the data, by assigning each data-point to its nearest 'codeword'. A set of points from a distribution can then be described as the frequency of occurrence of each 'codeword' [3]. Naive-Bayes classifier is then used to perform the classification.

5.3   Results

Table 1 give the results for the proposed method, using different numbers of data points, and different numbers of clusters. The overall results of the experiments are given in table 2.

Table 1. Results for the proposed method, varying object size and number of clusters (in %)

	$n = 256$	$n = 512$	$n = 1024$
$k = 8$	69.73	80.08	86.33
$k = 16$	83.79	90.63	92.97
$k = 32$	91.21	93.75	98.05
$k = 64$	94.73	96.48	98.05

Table 2. Overall results, using best parameter values for each method (in %)

Method	$n = 256$	$n = 512$	$n = 1024$
Proposed Method	94.73	96.48	98.05
Kernel Density Estimation	69.73	73.83	77.73
Earth Mover's Distance	73.83	79.88	85.35
Bag-of-Words	77.15	79.30	80.27

As the results show, the new method performed far better than the traditional method. The kernel density estimation and earth mover's distance methods both performed the worst. These methods both directly compare samplings from distributions, and so are susceptible to noise produced by the sampling. The bag-of-words method eliminates much of this noise, by quantisation via assignment to codewords, as does the new method, by using the behaviour of different parts of the distribution.

The proposed method performs best because it deals better with the variation within each class, which for this type of data may be quite high, due to varying levels of damage or disease present on the leaves, and slight differences in lighting conditions.

Given that the EMD must be calculated in performing the new methods, it may be possible to improve the results by incorporating the EMD metric. In our experience, however, doing so produced no change in the results. As would be expected, increasing the number of points used to describe objects increases the quality of the classification, but the new method still performs better than the other methods when a smaller number of points are used, making it particularly suitable when larger samplings are not practicle.

6   Conclusion

The accurate classification of probability density functions is useful in many different domains. In this paper we have proposed a new method for this, which outperforms a number of existing methods. This method utilizes the Hungarian algorithm to calculate a mapping between pdfs, and in doing so encapsulate the variation that is present within a class, thereby allowing more robust classification. For a visual object recognition problem the algorithm was found to perform significantly better than a number of existing techniques, achieving over 98% accuracy.

Due to $O(n^3)$ nature of the Hungarian algorithm, the method presented here can be quite slow compared to some other methods, requiring approximately 6 seconds in our tests, with $n = 1024$. Despite this, for many applications the additional time required is entirely acceptable given the improvement in accuracy, and the cost can be mitigated to some extent, for example, by using a faster, less reliable method to eliminate the least likely classes first. Furthermore, our method still performed better than the other methods tested here when $n = 256$, greatly reducing the time required, and allowing accurate classification even when less data is available.

References

1. Backes, A.R., Bruno, O.M.: Plant Leaf Identification Using Multi-scale Fractal Dimension. In: Foggia, P., Sansone, C., Vento, M. (eds.) ICIAP 2009. LNCS, vol. 5716, pp. 143–150. Springer, Heidelberg (2009)
2. Cope, J.S., Remagnino, P., Barman, S., Wilkin, P.: Plant Texture Classification Using Gabor Co-occurrences. In: Bebis, G., Boyle, R., Parvin, B., Koracin, D., Chung, R., Hammound, R., Hussain, M., Kar-Han, T., Crawfis, R., Thalmann, D., Kao, D., Avila, L. (eds.) ISVC 2010. LNCS, vol. 6454, pp. 669–677. Springer, Heidelberg (2010)
3. Csurka, G., Dance, C.R., Fan, L., Willamowski, J., Bray, C.: Visual categorization with bags of keypoints. In: Workshop on Statistical Learning in Computer Vision, ECCV 2004, pp. 1–22 (2004)
4. Edmonds, J., Karp, R.M.: Theoretical improvements in algorithmic efficiency for network flow problems. Journal of The ACM 19, 248–264 (1972)
5. Gu, X., Du, J.-X., Wang, X.-F.: Leaf Recognition Based on the Combination of Wavelet Transform and Gaussian Interpolation. In: Huang, D.-S., Zhang, X.-P., Huang, G.-B. (eds.) ICIC 2005. LNCS, vol. 3644, pp. 253–262. Springer, Heidelberg (2005)
6. Kuhn, H.W.: The Hungarian method for the assignment problem. Naval Research Logistics Quarterly 2, 83–97 (1955)
7. Parzen, E.: On estimation of a probability density funstion and mode. Annals of Mathematical Statistics 33, 1065–1076 (1962)
8. Rubner, Y., Guibas, L.J., Tomasi, C.: The earth mover's distance, multi-dimensional scaling, and color-based image retrieval. In: ARPA Image Understanding Workshop, pp. 661–668 (1997)
9. Sivic, J., Zisserman, A.: Google video: A text retrieval approach to object matching in videos. In: International Conference on Computer Vision, vol. 2, pp. 1470–1477 (2003)

Classification of Hyperspectral Data over Urban Areas Based on Extended Morphological Profile with Partial Reconstruction

Wenzhi Liao[1,2], Rik Bellens[1], Aleksandra Pižurica[1],
Wilfried Philips[1], and Youguo Pi[2]

[1] Ghent University, TELIN-IPI-IBBT, Ghent, Belgium
wenzhi.liao@telin.ugent.be
[2] School of Automation Science and Engineering,
South China University of Technology, 510640 Guangzhou, China

Abstract. Extended morphological profiles with reconstruction are widely used in the classification of very high resolution hyperspectral data from urban areas. However, morphological profiles constructed by morphological openings and closings with reconstruction can lead to some undesirable effects. Objects expected to disappear at a certain scale remain present when using morphological openings and closings by reconstruction. In this paper, we apply extended morphological profiles with partial reconstruction (EMPP) to the classification of high resolution hyperspectral images from urban areas. We first used feature extraction to reduce the dimensionality of the hyperspectral data, as well as reduce the redundancy within the bands, then constructed EMPP on features extracted by PCA, independent component analysis and kernel PCA for the classification of high resolution hyperspectral images from urban areas. Experimental results on real urban hyperspectral image demonstrate that the proposed EMPP built on kernel principal components gets the best results, particularly in the case with small training sample sizes.

Keywords: Morphological profiles, classification, urban hyperspectral image, high resolution, feature extraction.

1 Introduction

Recent advances in sensors technology have led to an increased availability of remote sensing data from urban areas at very high both spatial and spectral resolutions. Many techniques are developed to explore the spatial information of the high resolution remote sensing data, in particular, mathematical morphology [1] is one of the most popular methods. Classical morphological openings and closings degrade the object boundaries and deform the object shapes, which may result in losing some crucial information and introducing fake objects in the image. To avoid this problem, one often uses morphological openings and closings by reconstruction to construct morphological profile (MP)

J. Blanc-Talon et al. (Eds.): ACIVS 2012, LNCS 7517, pp. 278–289, 2012.
© Springer-Verlag Berlin Heidelberg 2012

[15,2,17,6,12,11,16,4,13,14]. The approach of [2] proposed the use of morpho-logical transformations to build a MP, and then used these MPs as the input of a neural network for the classification of panchromatic data (a single-band image). The approach of [17] extended the method in [2] by using feature extraction to reduce the redundancy in the morphological profile, and made a significant improvement in the classification accuracy of the panchromatic high resolution images. Benediktsson *et al.* [6] extended the method in [17] for hyperspectral data with high spatial resolution by using principal component analysis (PCA) [19] to reduce the high dimensionality of the data. The resulting method built MPs on the first principal components (PCs) extracted from a hyperspectral image, leading to the definition of extended morphological profile (EMP). Palmason *et al.* [12] built MPs on the first features extracted from original hyperspectral data by independent component analysis (ICA) [7], with an improvement in the classification results. In [4], features extracted by kernel PCA (KPCA) [10] are used to construct the EMP, with significantly improvement in terms of classi-fication accuracies compared with the conventional EMP built on PCs. In [13], the morphological attribute profiles were applied to the first PCs extracted from a hyperspectral image, generating an extended morphological attribute profiles (EAP). Mura *et al.* [14] improved the classification results by building the EAP on the first independent components (ICs) comparing to the results of those built on PCs [13].

With reconstruction, morphological openings and closings can reduce some shape noise in the image. However, morphological openings and closings by re-construction leads to some unexpected results for remote sensing images, such as over-reconstruction, as was discussed in [5]. Objects which are expected to dis-appear at a certain scale remain present when using morphological openings and closings by reconstruction. The approach of [5] proposed a partial reconstruction for the classification of very high-resolution panchromatic urban imagery. Mor-phological openings and closings by partial reconstruction can solve the problem of over-reconstruction while preserving the shape of objects as much as possible.

In this paper, we applied morphological profile by partial reconstruction from panchromatic urban imagery [5] to hyperspectral imagery, leading to the defi-nition of extended morphological profiles with partial reconstruction (EMPP). We first extract features from the original hyperspectral data by PCA, ICA and KPCA, then build extended morphological profiles on the extracted features with morphological openings and closings by partial reconstruction. Finally, we use the EMPP as the inputs of SVM classifiers to do classification.

2   Feature Extraction (FE)

The high dimensionality of hyperspectral data as well as the redundancy within the bands, make the generation of an MP based on each spectral band seem not feasible. To overcome this problem, feature extraction (FE) is firstly used to reduce the dimensionality of these hyperspectral data, and then morphological processing is applied on each extracted feature band independently. The effect of different FE methods on extracting features from the hyperspectral data to build MPs has been discussed in several studies [6,12,4,14].

2.1   Principal Component Analysis (PCA)

Principal Component Analysis (PCA) [19] performs feature extraction through analyzing the covariance matrix of the original data. Due to its low complexity and the absence of parameters, PCA has been widely used for feature extraction in hyperspectral images [6,11,16]. Let $\{\mathbf{x}_i\}_{i=1}^{N}$, $\mathbf{x}_i \in R^d$ denote high-dimensional data, $\{\mathbf{z}_i\}_{i=1}^{N}$, and $\mathbf{z}_i \in R^r$ the low-dimensional representations of the high-dimensional data $r \leq d$. In our application, d is the dimensionality of the original hyperspectral data sets, and r is the dimensionality of the extracted features. The goal of PCA feature extraction is to find a $d \times r$ transformation matrix $\mathbf{W}$, which can map every high-dimensional data $\mathbf{x}_i$ to $\mathbf{z}_i = \mathbf{W}^T\mathbf{x}_i$ into a much lower dimensional feature space.

$$\mathbf{S}\mathbf{w} = \lambda\mathbf{w} \tag{1}$$

where $\mathbf{S} = \frac{1}{N-1}\mathbf{X}\mathbf{X}^T = \frac{1}{N-1}\sum_{i=1}^{N}\mathbf{x}_i\mathbf{x}_i^T$, and $\mathbf{X}$ is centered data. The transformation matrix $\mathbf{W} = (\mathbf{w}_1, \mathbf{w}_2, \cdots, \mathbf{w}_r)$ is made up by the r eigenvectors of the matrix $\mathbf{S}$ associated with the largest r eigenvalues $\lambda_1 \geq \lambda_2 \geq \cdots \geq \lambda_r$.

2.2   Independent Component Analysis (ICA)

Independent Component Analysis (ICA) [7] has been largely studied during the past years for linear blind source separation. Its application to feature extraction for hyperspectral data sets has been found in [8,12,9,14]. ICA assumes that data are linearly mixed and separates them into a set of statistically independent components (ICs). ICA finds a $d \times r$ separating matrix $\mathbf{W}$ to generate r ICs as:

$$\mathbf{Z} = \mathbf{W}_{ICA}^T\mathbf{X} \tag{2}$$

Commonly, PCA is used as a pre-processing step to sphere and reduce the dimensionality of the original data sets. In this paper, ICs are extracted from the r most important principal components with the accumulative variance of 99%, the $d - r$ rest of the PCs are not used. FastICA algorithm [7], which uses the absolute value of kurtosis to measure the non-gaussianity, is selected to implement the ICA.

2.3   Kernel Principal Component Analysis (KPCA)

Kernel Principal Component Analysis (KPCA) [10] is an extension of PCA using techniques of kernel methods. Its application to reducing the dimensionality of hyperspectral data sets has been investigated in [3,4,18]. KPCA solves the eigenvectors by performing eigen decomposition on Gram matrix. There exists a function φ which can map the original data into a higher or infinite dimensional Hilbert space.

A new data set can be obtained in the feature space $\boldsymbol{\Phi} = (\varphi(\mathbf{x}_1), \varphi(\mathbf{x}_2), \cdots,$ $\varphi(\mathbf{x}_n))$. φ is an implicit function, which cannot be calculated directly, but some kernel functions can be used by performing inner product between the two samples $\mathbf{x}_i$ and $\mathbf{x}_j$ in the original space, $\kappa_{ij} = \kappa(\mathbf{x}_i, \mathbf{x}_j) = \varphi^T(\mathbf{x}_i)\varphi(\mathbf{x}_j)$. The most widely used Mercer kernels [10] include Gaussian kernel and polynomial kernel. The covariance matrix is defined in the feature space as follows:

$$\mathbf{C} = \frac{1}{n} \sum_{i=1}^{n} \varphi(\mathbf{x}_i)\varphi^T(\mathbf{x}_i) \tag{3}$$

It satisfies the secular equation:

$$\mathbf{C}\mathbf{v} = \lambda\mathbf{v} \tag{4}$$

where $\mathbf{v}$ and λ are the eigenvectors and eigenvalues of the covariance matrix $\mathbf{C}$, and $\mathbf{v}$ can be described in the span of the data set $\boldsymbol{\Phi} = (\varphi(\mathbf{x}_1), \varphi(\mathbf{x}_2), \cdots, \varphi(\mathbf{x}_n))$:

$$\mathbf{v} = \sum_{i=1}^{n} \alpha_i \varphi(\mathbf{x}_i) \tag{5}$$

From equations 3, 4 and 5, we get

$$\frac{1}{n}\mathbf{K}\boldsymbol{\alpha} = \lambda\boldsymbol{\alpha} \tag{6}$$

where $\boldsymbol{\alpha} = (\alpha_1, \alpha_2, \cdots, \alpha_n)$, $\mathbf{K}$ is $n \times n$ Gram matrix, $\mathbf{K} = \boldsymbol{\Phi}^T(\mathbf{X})\boldsymbol{\Phi}(\mathbf{X})$, with elements $\kappa_{ij} = \kappa(\mathbf{x}_i, \mathbf{x}_j)$. Then for each testing sample $\mathbf{x}$, its kernel principal component can be calculated as follows:

$$(\mathbf{v}, \varphi(\mathbf{x})) = \sum_{i=1}^{n} \alpha_i(\varphi(\mathbf{x}_i) \cdot \varphi(\mathbf{x})) = \sum_{i=1}^{n} \kappa(\mathbf{x}_i, \mathbf{x}) \tag{7}$$

It is assumed that the Gram matrix $\mathbf{K}$ is zero-mean, otherwise, it can be centered as:

$$\overline{\mathbf{K}} = \mathbf{K} - \mathbf{I}_n\mathbf{K} - \mathbf{K}\mathbf{I}_n + \mathbf{I}_n\mathbf{K}\mathbf{I}_n \tag{8}$$

where $\mathbf{I}_n = \frac{1}{n}\mathbf{I}_{n \times n}$, and $\mathbf{I}_{n \times n}$ is the identity matrix of size $n \times n$.

3 Extended Morphological Profiles with Partial Reconstruction (EMPP)

Morphological operators act on the shape of the objects represented in an image. The basic operators are dilation and erosion [1]. These operators are applied to an image with a set of known shapes, called the structuring elements (SEs). In the case of erosion, a pixel takes the minimum value of all the pixels in its neighborhood, defined by the SE. By contrast, dilation takes the maximum

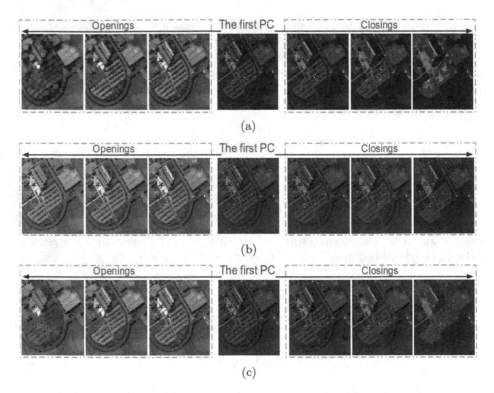

Fig. 1. The scales of SEs vary from 2 to 6, with step size increment of 2. The image processed is part of the first PC extracted from *University Area* data set in Figure 3a: (a) Morphological Profiles without reconstruction, (b) Morphological Profiles with reconstruction, (c) Morphological Profiles with partial reconstruction.

value of all the pixels in its neighborhood. Dilation and erosion are usually employed in pairs, either dilation of an image followed by erosion of the dilated result, or erosion of an image followed by dilation of the eroded result. These combinations are known as opening and closing. Each opening and closing results in a transformation of the original image in which objects smaller than the SE are deleted. By increasing the size of the SE, more and more objects are removed. We will use the term scale of an opening or closing to refer to this size. A vector containing the pixel values in openings and closings of different scales is called the morphologic profile (MP). The MP carries information about the size and the shape of objects in the image.

The morphological openings and closings with disk-shaped SEs are the most popular methods used in current literature [6,16,18]. Objects with a width smaller than $2 \times R$ (R is the radius of the disk SE) are deleted from the image. Aside from deleting objects smaller than the SE, morphological openings and closings also deform the objects which are still present in the image, see Fig. 1a. As the size of the SE increases, more and more bright objects disappear in the dark background in the opening profile, and more and more dark objects disappear

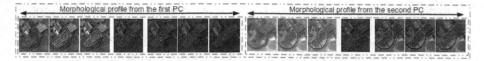

Fig. 2. EMPP built on the first two PCs with 3 openings and 3 closings. Disk SEs are used with radius vary from 2 to 6, with step size increment of 2.

in the bright background in the closing profile, but the corners of rectangular objects are rounded. To preserve the shapes of objects, morphological openings and closings by reconstruction are generally the tool of choice [15,16]. This process reconstructs the whole object if at least one pixel of the object survives the opening or closing. We can see the results in Fig. 1b, the shapes of the objects are well preserved, and some small objects disappear as the scale increases. However, an MP with reconstruction will lead to some undesirable effects (such as over-reconstruction), a lot of objects that disappeared in the MP without reconstruction remain present in the MP with reconstruction. Objects with a width smaller than $2 \times R$ are expected to disappear in the image when the radius of the disk SE is larger than R, but they still present at even higher scales, as shown in Fig. 1b.

The approach of [5] proposed a partial reconstruction to solve the problem of over-reconstruction while preserving the shape of objects as much as possible, and applied to the classification of very high-resolution panchromatic urban imagery with a great improvement. In the partial reconstruction process, a pixel is only reconstructed if it is connected to a pixel that was not erased, and this second pixel lies within a certain geodesic distance from the pixel. The geodesic distance between two pixels is the length of the shortest path between the two pixels that lies completely within the object. Fig. 1c shows the results of MP with partial reconstruction. The shapes of objects are better preserved with partial reconstruction compared to the MP with no reconstruction. On the other hand, a lot of small objects which remain present in the MP with reconstruction, now disappear in the case with partial reconstruction. For more details on MP with partial reconstruction, the readers should consult [5].

3.1 Extended Morphological Profiles with Partial Reconstruction

A morphological profile (MP) consists of the opening profile (OP) and the closing profile (CP). For the panchromatic image, MP is built on the original single band image directly. The OP with p scales at pixel $\mathbf{x}$ forms p-dimensional vector, and so as the CP. By incorporating the OP and the CP, the morphological profile of pixel $\mathbf{x}$ is defined as $(2p + 1)$-dimensional vector. When applying MP to the hyperspectral data, feature extraction is used as a pre-processing to reduce the dimensionality of the high-dimensional original data, as well as reduce the redundancy within the bands. Then an extended MP is constructed on the extracted features. Extended morphological profile with reconstruction (EMP) built on different features has been discussed in several studies [6,12,4].

Motivated by the construction of EMP [6], we applied morphological profile with partial reconstruction to hyperspectral data, leading to the definition of extended morphological profile with partial reconstruction (EMPP). The resulting method applies morphological openings and closings with partial reconstruction [5] to construct morphological profile on each extracted feature independently, an EMPP is formed as a stacked vector which is constructed from all the morphological profiles. Suppose r features are extracted from the original hyperspectral data to construct the EMPP, then the EMPP of pixel $\mathbf{x}$ is a $r(2p+1)$-dimensional vector. Fig. 2 shows an EMPP built on the first two PCs.

4   Experimental Results

Experiments were run on '*University Area*' from urban area in the city of Pavia, Italy. The data were collected by the ROSIS (Reflective Optics System Imaging Spectrometer) sensor, with 115 spectral bands in the wavelength range from 0.43 to 0.86μm and very fine spatial resolution of 1.3 meters by pixel. The data contains 103 spectral channels after removal of noisy bands, with 610×340 pixels. It has 9 land cover/use classes, Fig. 3 shows its false color composite and test set.

To construct EMPP, feature extraction was first applied to to reduce the dimensionality of the original hyperspectral data. For PCA and ICA, the first 3 principal components (PCs) were selected (representing almost 99% of the cumulative variance) to construct the EMPP, which is the same as the construction of EMP in [6,16]. For KPCA, the number of extracted kernel principal components which represent 99% of the cumulative variance depends on the the number of total training samples and the parameters in the selected kernel function, as was also discussed in [4,18]. In our experiments, 5000 samples were randomly selected to train and construct the training kernel matrix, Gaussian kernel function $(\kappa(\mathbf{x}_i, \mathbf{x}_j) = exp(-\frac{\|\mathbf{x}_i - \mathbf{x}_j\|^2}{2\delta^2}))$ with $\delta = \frac{4}{n \times n}\sqrt{\sum_{i=1}^{n}\sum_{j=1}^{n}\kappa_{ij}^2}$, where n is the total number of the training samples, $\kappa_{ij} = \kappa(\mathbf{x}_i, \mathbf{x}_j)$ is the element of the kernel matrix. To achieve more than 99% of the cumulative variance, 12 KPCs are needed in the data. Morphological profiles with 4 openings and closings (ranging from 2 to 8 with step size increment of 2) were then computed for each extracted features, which is the same scales as [16,4]. We represent extended morphological profile with no reconstruction as EMPN. EMPP built on features extracted by PCA, ICA and KPCA are denoted as $EMPP_{PCA}$, $EMPP_{ICA}$ and $EMPP_{KPCA}$, respectively.

We used one of the most popular classifiers: support vector machines (SVM) [10], as it performs well even with a limited number of training samples, which can overcome the Huges phenomenon. The SVM classifier with radial basis function (RBF) kernels and linear kernels in Matlab SVM Toolbox, LIBSVM [20], is applied in our experiments. SVM with RBF kernels has two parameters: the penalty factor C and the RBF kernel widths γ. While SVM with linear kernels has only one parameter (the penalty factor C). We apply a grid-search on C and γ using 5-fold cross-validation to find the best C within the given set

Table 1. *University Area.* Overall accuracy (%) in a classification with spectral features compared to classifications with EMPN, EMPR and EMPP built on different features (*# bands*)

FE	Methods	Classifier	Training Set Size				
			10	50	100	150	All
Spectral only	Raw (103)	Linear	66.4	74.1	76.8	77.2	78.2
		RBF	63.5	75.5	78.8	79.9	80.2
	PCA (3)	Linear	58.6	69.3	73.2	71.6	73.6
		RBF	61.3	64.1	66	66.4	66.5
	ICA (3)	Linear	61.8	69.3	73	71.5	73.6
		RBF	63.5	66	66.1	65.7	66.9
	KPCA (12)	Linear	62.7	75.1	78.8	79.4	81.3
		RBF	64.3	73.2	77.7	77.9	80.3
EMPN	PCA (27)	Linear	82.6	86	85.4	85	86.3
		RBF	82.1	85.2	84.5	85	85.8
	ICA (27)	Linear	80.1	85.6	84.7	84.3	84.9
		RBF	80.3	86.3	84.7	85.5	85.2
	KPCA (108)	Linear	84.4	91	91.4	91.5	91.3
		RBF	84.2	91	91.5	91.8	91.5
EMPR	PCA (27)	Linear	76.9	81.1	82.2	80.8	82.6
		RBF	74.1	80.4	81.6	80.4	80.3
	ICA (27)	Linear	75.4	84.3	87.5	86.5	84
		RBF	73.7	82	84	82.8	83.1
	KPCA (108)	Linear	71.2	88.9	92.7	93.2	**95.7**
		RBF	71.7	89	93	92.6	94.8
EMPP	PCA (27)	Linear	81.9	88	87.8	87.4	87.8
		RBF	82.5	89.1	89.2	89	88.7
	ICA (27)	Linear	81.4	87.9	87.8	87.5	88.9
		RBF	80.5	89.3	89.3	89.7	89.2
	KPCA (108)	Linear	86	**93.9**	**94.5**	**94.7**	94.4
		RBF	**86.2**	93	94	94.2	94.3

$\{10^{-1}, 10^0, 10^1, 10^2, 10^3\}$ and the best γ within the given set $\{10^{-3}, 10^{-2}, 10^{-1},$ $10^0, 10^1\}$. The training data sets for classifier were randomly subsampled to create samples whose sizes corresponded to five distinct cases: 10, 50, 100, 150 samples per class, respectively. The classifiers were evaluated against the testing sets, the results were averaged over five runs.

4.1   Results

Table 1 displays the classification accuracies of testing data in different sample size. The best accuracy in each sample size (in column) is highlighted in bold font. From the tables, we have the following findings:

(1) Morphological features can improve the classification results. The results using morphological features are much better than those using the original

hyperspectral data and the spectral features only. By building the extended morphological profiles on the first few extracted features, the results can be improved a lot. Compared to the situation with the original hyperspectral data and the spectral features only in each training sample size, the OA with morphological profiles built on features extracted by PCA, ICA and KPCA have 0.5%-20%, 2.9%-20% and 2.9%-20% improvements, respectively.

(2) The classification results with the features (representing almost 99% of the cumulative variance) extracted by KPCA are better than those with features extracted by PCA and ICA. The OA with KPCs has 1.4%-14.4% and 0%-14.7% improvements, compared to the results with features extracted by PCA and ICA in each training sample size.

(3) It is better not to use morphological openings and closings with reconstruction in some cases. By using EMPP built on PCA and ICA, the results can be improved a lot. Compared to the results with EMP built on PCs, the OA of EMPP built on PCs with training sample size of 10, 50, 100, 150 and all has 5%-8.7%, 6.9%-8.7%, 5.6%-7.6%, 5.6%-8.6% and 5.2%-8.4% improvements, respectively. For EMPP built on ICs, the improvements are 5.1%-7.7%, 3.6%-7.3%, 0.3%-5.3%, 1%-6.9% and 4.9%-6.1%, respectively. For $EMPP_{KPCA}$, these improvements are obvious in small sample size, with 14.3% improvements when using 10 training samples per class.

(4) EMPN, EMP and EMPP built on nonlinear features (KPCs) perform better than those built on linear features (PCs and ICs), the improvements are 2%-5% and 3%-7%.

(5) As the number of training samples increases, the OA will increase, this is obvious when the training samples size increases from 10 to 50. When the training samples size is larger than 50, the performances using EMPN and EMPP keep stable. When 50 training samples per class were used, we get 93.9% OA by using $EMPP_{KPCA}$. To achieve similar OA, the EMP_{KPCA} in this case requires more than three times training samples.

(6) When using $EMPP_{KPCA}$, we get almost the highest OA in different training sample size. The highest OA with the training samples size of 10, 50, 100, 150 and all are 86.2% ($EMPP_{KPCA}$ and SVM classifier with RBF kernel), 93.9% ($EMPP_{KPCA}$ and SVM classifier with linear kernel), 94.5% ($EMPP_{KPCA}$ and SVM classifier with linear kernel), 94.7% ($EMPP_{KPCA}$ and SVM classifier with linear kernel) and 95.7% (EMP_{KPCA} and SVM classifier with linear kernel), respectively.

In order to compare the classified maps visually, we generate classification maps using the best combinations of SVM classifiers when 10 training samples per class are used, displayed in Fig. 3.

From the figure, we can find that the EMPN, EMP and EMPP can preserve well spatial information on hyperspectral images. The classification maps with morphological features produce much smoother homogeneous regions than those with the raw data, which is particularly significant when using EMPN and EMPP. The classification maps using the EMP looks much noisy because of the over reconstruction problems, see Fig. 3e, Fig. 3h and Fig. 3k. The EMPN

(a) False color RGB   (b) Test set   (c) Raw data   (d) $EMPN_{PCA}$

(e) EMP_{PCA} (f) $EMPP_{PCA}$ (g) $EMPN_{ICA}$ (h) EMP_{ICA}

(i) $EMPP_{ICA}$ (j) $EMPN_{KPCA}$ (k) EMP_{KPCA} (l) $EMPP_{KPCA}$

Fig. 3. Classification maps for using the best combinations of SVM classifiers when 10 training samples per class are used

deform the objects, see Fig. 3d, Fig. 3g and Fig. 3j, the borders of some objects are deformed. The shapes of objects are better preserved with EMPP. Simultaneously, the spatial information are better preserved with EMPP, which can be seen in Fig. 3f, Fig. 3i and Fig. 3l.

5   Conclusion

In this study, we investigated the influence of morphological features with different reconstruction (including with no reconstruction, with reconstruction and with partial reconstruction) for the classification of high resolution hyperspectral images from urban areas. To apply morphological profiles on hyperspectral data, we first reduced the dimensionality of hyperspectral data by feature extraction, then built the extended morphological profiles on the extracted features. Experimental results show that KPCA is more efficient to extract features for constructing EMP. In many cases, the most widely used EMP with reconstruction can not get a satisfied result, because of over-reconstruction problems. EMP with partial reconstruction built on KPCs is more competitive than those of EMP with no reconstruction and with reconstruction built on other different features. However, the high dimensionality of $EMPP_{KPCA}$ may create a new challenge for the conventional classifiers which are not robust to the Hughes phenomenon. Additional experiments on reducing the dimensionality of $EMPP_{KPCA}$ will be further considered in future work.

Acknowledgment. The authors would like to thank Prof. Paolo Gamba from the University of Pavia, Italy, for kindly providing University Area data set.

References

1. Soille, P.: Morphological Image Analysis, Principles and Applications, 2nd edn. Springer, Berlin (2003)
2. Pesaresi, M., Benediktsson, J.A.: A new approach for the morphological segmentation of high-resolution satellite imagery. IEEE Trans. Geosci. Remote Sens. 39(2), 309–320 (2001)
3. Fauvel, M., Chanussot, J., Benediktsson, J.A.: Kernel principal component analysis for feature reduction in hyperspectrale images analysis. In: Proceedings of the 7th Signal Processing Symposium, pp. 238–241 (2006)
4. Fauvel, M., Chanussot, J., Benediktsson, J.A.: Kernel principal component analysis for the classification of hyperspectral remote-sensing data over urban areas. EURASIP Journal on Advances in Signal Processing, 14 pages (2009)
5. Bellens, R., Gautama, S., Martinez-Fonte, L., Philips, W., Chan, J.C.-W., Canters, F.: Improved classification of VHR images of urban areas using directional morphological profiles. IEEE Trans. Geosci. Remote Sens. 46(10), 2803–2812 (2008)
6. Benediktsson, J.A., Palmason, J.A., Sveinsson, J.R.: Classification of hyperspectral data from urban areas based on extended morphological profiles. IEEE Trans. Geosci. Remote Sens. 43(3), 480–491 (2005)
7. Hyvarinen, A., Oja, E.: Independent component analysis: algorithms and applications. Neural Networks 13, 411–430 (2000)
8. Varshney, P.K., Arora, M.K.: Advanced Image Processing Techniques for Remotely Sensed Hyperspectral Data. Springer, Berlin (2003)
9. Wang, J., Chang, C.-I.: Independent component analysis-based dimensionality reduction with applications in hyperspectral image analysis. IEEE Trans. Geosci. Remote Sens. 44(6), 1586–1600 (2006)
10. Scholkopf, B., Smola, A., Muller, K.-R.: Nonlinear component analysis as a Kernel eigenvalue problem. Neural Computation 10(5), 1299–1319 (1998)
11. Plaza, A., Martinez, P., Plaza, J., Perez, R.: Dimensionality reduction and classification of hyperspectral image data using sequences of extended morphological transformations. IEEE Trans. Geosci. Remote Sens. 43(3), 466–479 (2005)

12. Palmason, J.A., Benediktsson, J.A., Sveinsson, J.R., Chanussot, J.: Classification of hyperspectral data from urban areas using morphological preprocessing and independent component analysis. In: IEEE Proceedings of International Geoscience and Remote Sensing Symposium (IGARSS 2005), pp. 147–156 (2005)
13. Mura, M.D., Benediktsson, J.A., Waske, B., Bruzzone, L.: Extended profiles with morphological attribute filters for the analysis of hyperspectral data. Int. J. Remote Sens. 48(10), 3747–3762 (2010)
14. Mura, M.D., Villa, A., Benediktsson, J.A., Chanussot, J., Bruzzone, L.: Classification of Hyperspectral Images by Using Extended Morphological Attribute Profiles and Independent Component Analysis. IEEE Trans. Geosci. Remote Sens. Lett. 8(3), 541–545 (2011)
15. Crespo, J., Serra, J., Shafer, R.: Theoretical aspects of morphological filters by reconstruction. Signal Process. 47(2), 201–225 (1995)
16. Fauvel, M., Benediktsson, J.A., Chanussot, J., Sveinsson, J.R.: Spectral and Spatial Classification of Hyperspectral Data Using SVMs and Morphological Profile. IEEE Trans. Geosci. Remote Sens. 46(11), 3804–3814 (2008)
17. Benediktsson, J.A., Pesaresi, M., Arnason, K.: Classification and feature extraction for remote sensing images from urban areas based on morphological transformations. IEEE Trans. Geosci. Remote Sens. 41(9), 1940–1949 (2003)
18. Castaings, T., Waske, B., Benediktsson, J.A., Chanussot, J.: On the influence of feature reduction for the classification of hyperspectral images based on the extended morphological profile. Int. J. Remote Sens. 31(22), 5921–5939 (2010)
19. Hotelling, H.: Analysis of a complex of statistical variables into principal components. Journal of Educational Psychology 24, 417–441 (1933)
20. Chang, C. C. and Lin, C. J., LIBSVM: A Library for Support Vector Machines (2001), http://www.csie.ntu.edu.tw/~cjlin/libsvm

Saliency Filtering of SIFT Detectors: Application to CBIR

Dounia Awad, Vincent Courboulay, and Arnaud Revel

L3I-University of La Rochelle, Av Michel Crepeau 17000 La Rochelle, France

Abstract. The recognition of object categories is one of the most challenging problems in computer vision field.It is still an open problem , especially in content based image retrieval (CBIR).When using analysis algorithm, a trade-off must be found between the quality of the results expected, and the amount of computer resources allocated to manage huge amount of generated data. In human, the mechanisms of evolution have generated the visual attention system which selects the most important information in order to reduce both cognitive load and scene understanding ambiguity. In computer science, most powerful algorithms use local approaches as bag-of-features or sparse local features. In this article, we propose to evaluate the integration of one of the most recent visual attention model in one of the most efficient CBIR method. First, we present these two algorithms and the database used to test results. Then, we present our approach which consists in pruning interest points in order to select a certain percentage of them (40% to 10%). This filtering is guided by a saliency map provided by a visual attention system. Finally, we present our results which clearly demonstrate that interest points used in classical CBIR methods can be drastically pruned without seriously impacting results. We also demonstrate that we have to smartly filter learning and training data set to obtain such results.

1 Introduction

The recognition of object categories is one of the most challenging problems in the field of computer vision. One of the main reasons that explains such a challenging task is that images can present many variations [Marszaek2006]. For instance, the changes that the image may submit can be: clean vs. cluttered background; stereotypical vs. multiple views; degree of scale change; amount of occlusion [Everingham2009]. To manage these tasks, most of recent existing recognition or retrieval processes are based on local approach that uses sparse local features or bag-of-features [Everingham2009], using interest point detectors [Tuytelaars2007] such as Harris, Harris-Laplace or SIFT[Lowe2004] to describe images. Although these approaches have demonstrated a high efficiency in this domain, some weaknesses may be mentioned.

The first limitation relies on interest point detectors themselves. Most of these detectors are based on geometric forms as corners, blobs or junctions and consider that the interest of the image is directly correlated with the presence of such features. This constraints is well known as semantic gap[Santini2001].

J. Blanc-Talon et al. (Eds.): ACIVS 2012, LNCS 7517, pp. 290–300, 2012.

The second constraint mentioned in literature concerns especially the popular SIFT descriptor [Lowe2004]. Although SIFT shows a high efficiency, scalability remains an important problem due to the large number of features generated for each image [Santini2007]. Many of them are outliers.

Nevertheless, some researchers have proposed solutions to overcome these constraints. For instance, Foo et al. [Santini2007] proposed a pruning strategy that reduces the number of SIFT features by changing the threshold applied to discard candidate local peaks in Lowe's algorithm, mainly for the low contrast (intensity) threshold. This approach performed well, with average recall close to the original approach: they demonstrate that by reducing the number of SIFT key points to 10% have a little effect on the performance of a near-duplicate image matching algorithms. Nevertheless, the main weakness of this method is that it is precisely devoted to duplicate or near-duplicate images, and was not tested in a content based image retrieval context. Besides it only used a very simple saliency measure.

The main objective of this pasper is to present convincing results of an original approach that proposes a first step to solve previous problems. We proposed to combine an efficient CBIR method with a recent and a convincing saliency detection system. The objectives of such an approach is extracting the regions of interest that attract our attention in a bottom-up way (salient regions) according to some features. These features must be sufficiently discriminative with respect to the surrounding features[Frintrop2010]. Based on these objectives, we hypothesize that these systems can be used as filter to reduce the number of points of interests and either equal or improve classical results presented in literature. We demonstrate this proposal on a large and well known database VOC [VOC2005].

This article is classically organized as follow. In the following section, we present the related communities and the reference algorithms chosen. In section [sec:Our-approach], we present our method. Experimental results are given in section [sec:Experiments].

2   Context

2.1   Content Based Image Retrieval (CBIR)

Content based image retrieval has seen considerable progress over the past years. Many challenges have been proposed to test the efficiency and robustness of the recognition methods. One of the most popular challenges is the Visual Object Classes Challenge.

Visual Object Classes Challenge (VOC). VOC was proposed for the first time in 2005 with one objective: recognizing objects from number of visual object classes in realistic scenes [Everingham2009]. Since then, it has been organized every year and integrates new constraints in order to provide a standardized database to the researchers.

As mentioned before, the main challenge started in 2005, and was taken as a standard for reference works. In addition, this challenge offers a database well designed to fit to the objectives of this paper, for instance, the images in this challenge were manually selected to avoid the duplicate and near-duplicate images. As a consequence, the selected images were only those which contained objects at different scales and in different contexts.

Concerning its composition, the dataset used in this challenge was actually composed by two sub-databases. The first one allows to validate proposed methods, and it consists of two subsets. The training set (L) contains 684 images and the test set (T) contains 689 images. The second sub-database was composed by images randomly selected in Google Image and by the way less structured than the first one, we have decided not to consider this database for our test.

In 2005, twelve algorithms have been proposed to compete for winning the challenge; it is interesting to mention that all these algorithms were based on local feature detection. We propose a taxonomy in table [tab:taxonomy-VOC2005].

Finally, INRIA-Zhang appeared to be the most efficient method. We decide to take it as the reference algorithm for object recognition. The next section is dedicated to its presentation.

Table 1. Taxonomy of methods proposed in VOC2005

Category	Description
Distribution of local image feature	Images are represented by probability distributions over the set of descriptors, basing on two methods. Bags of words [Sivic2006] in which image is represented by a histogram over a dictionary, recording either the presence of each word. Alternative way is based on kernel as Bhattacharyya kernel [Kondor2003] Finally, the model is learned using classification methods as SVM.
Recognition of individual local feature	In this approach, interest points detector are used to focus the attention on a small number of local patches. Then each patch in each image is associated with a binary label. Vectors are built by grouping these labels. A parametric model of the probability that the patch belongs to a class is built. Finally the output is the posterior class probability for a patch feature vector.
Recognition based on segmented regions	This method combines the features extracted from the image and the regions obtained by an image segmentation algorithm.the Self Organizing Maps (SOM) [Laaksonen2000] are defined on the different feature spaces that were used to classify the descriptors resulting from the segmented regions and the whole image
Classifications by detection	It extracts patches in an image using interest points detector. A codebook is built using a clustering method. A new object class is detected using matching method. Then a hypothesis on which accept or refusal is defined.

INRIA-Zhang Algorithm. In this part, we briefly present this algorithm which mainly consists of extracting an invariant image representation and classifying this data with non-linear support vector machines (SVM) with a χ^2 kernel. As shown in Figure 1, algorithm can be divided in 3 parts:

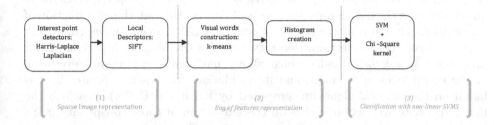

Fig. 1. Architecture of Zhang algorithm

1. Sparse image representation: this part extract a set of SIFT keypoints $K_{Zhang}(I)$ from an image $I(x,y)$ which was provided before as input. It consists of two steps :
   - Interest points detectors: Zhang uses two complementary local region detectors to extract *interesting* image structures: Harris-Laplace detector [Mikolajczyk2004], dedicated to corner-like region and Laplacian detector [Lindeberg1998] dedicated to blob-like regions. These two detectors have been designed to be scale invariant.
   - Local descriptor: To compute appearance-based descriptor on the extracted patches , Zhang used the SIFT descriptor [Lowe2004] . it computes descriptors less sensitive to scale variations and invariant to illumination changes .
2. Bag-of-features representation: Zhang builds a visual vocabulary by clustering the descriptors from the training set. Each image is represented as a histogram of visual words drawn from the vocabulary. He randomly selects a set of descriptors for each class extracted from the training set and he clusters these features using k-means to create 1000-elements vocabulary. Finally, each feature in an image is assigned to the closest word and a histogram that measures the frequency of each word in an image is built for each image.
3. Classification: Zhang uses a non-linear SVM in which the decision function has the following form :

$$g(x) = \sum \alpha_i y_i k(x_i, x) - b \qquad (1)$$

with $k(x_i, x)$ the kernel function value for the training sample x_i and the test sample x. α_i is the learned weighted coefficient for the training sample x_i , and b is the learned threshold. Finally, to compute the efficiency of the algorithm, thenSVM score has been considered as a confidence measure for a class.

In the following section, we present the salient region detection method that we use to prune SIFT keypoints.

2.2   Saliency Based Region Selection

As mentioned before, our main objective is to integrate perceptual constraints and to decrease the huge number of points of interest through the introduction of a new approach that combine two communities: CBIR previously described, and saliency based region selection. Recenlty, Perreira Da Silva et al. [Perreira2011] proposes a new hybrid model which allows modeling the temporal evolution of the visual focus of attention and its validation. As shown in figure 2, it is based on the classical algorithm proposed by Itti in ([Itti1998]), in which the first part of its architecture relies on the extraction of three conspicuity maps based on low level characteristics computation. These three conspicuity maps are representative of the three main human perceptual channels: color, intensity and orientation. Perreira Da Silva et al. propose to substitute the second part

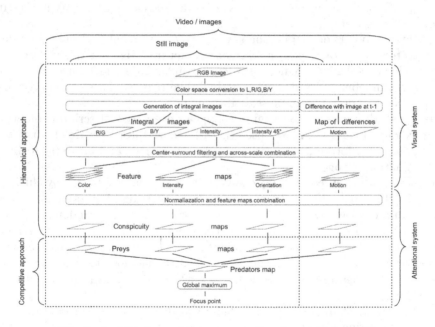

Fig. 2. Architecture of the computational model of attention

of Itti's model by an optimal competitive approach: a preys / predators system. They have demonstrated that it is an optimal way of extracting information. Besides, this optimal criteria, preys / predators equations are particularly well adapted for such a task:

- preys / predators systems are dynamic, they include intrinsically time evolution of their activities. Thus, the visual focus of attention , seen as a predator, can evolve dynamically;
- without any objective (top-down information or pregnancy), choosing a method for conspicuity maps fusion is hard. A solution consists in developing a competition between conspicuity maps and waiting for a natural balance in the preys / predators system, reflecting the competition between emergence and inhibition of elements that engage or not our attention;
- discrete dynamic systems can have a chaotic behavior. Despite the fact that this property is not often interesting, it is an important one in this case. Actually, it allows the emergence of original paths and exploration of visual scene, even in non salient areas, reflecting something like curiosity.

[PerreiraDaSilva2010] shows that despite the non deterministic behavior of preys / predators equations, the system exhibits interesting properties of stability, reproducibility and reactiveness while allowing a fast and efficient exploration of the scene. We applied the same optimal parameters used by Perreira Da Silva in [PerreiraDaSilva2010] to evaluate our approach. The output of this algorithm is a saliency map $S(I, t)$, computed by a temporal average of the focalization computed through a certain period of time t. In this context, we propose to merge

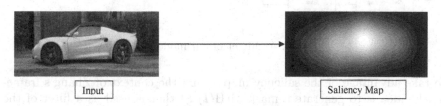

Fig. 3. saliency map generated

the two previous algorithms in order to reduce the number of points provide by the SIFT method and to introduce perceptual consideration. We present our approach in the next section.

3   Our Approach

As pointed out in section 2, we choose Zhang's algorithm as the reference of our developments since it performed the best in VOC 2005. Analyzing the different steps of the algorithm, it can be noticed that the first step consists in using the SIFT detector. As mentioned before, such a method usually extracts a huge number of keypoints. Our hypothesis is that not all of those points are useful to categorize the images. On the contrary, we assume the idea that non relevant "noisy" information can also be detected. Following Foo [Santini2007], the idea we develop is that an attentional system can be used to select among all the keypoints only those which are the most salient. For that purpose, we choose to refer to Perreira Da Silva's attentional system. Given the selection of salient keypoints, the rest of Zhang's algorithm could stay unchanged for a CBIR application (see figure 4).

Practically speaking, the process we propose consists in providing both Zhang's and Perreira Da Silva's systems the same image $I(x,y)$. After step 2 of Zhang's framework, a first set $K_{Zhang}(I)$ of keypoints is obtained. In parallel, for the same image $I(x,y)$., Perreira Da Silva's system provides a saliency map $S_{map}(I,t)$ which evolves with time. In order to emphasize the visual regions the system mainly focuses on, $S_{map}(I,t)$ is integrated along the time axis to get what is usually known as a "heatmap"'. Formally, the heatmap can be defined as : $H(I) = \int_0^T \mathcal{S}_{map}(I,t).dt$, with T the integration window.

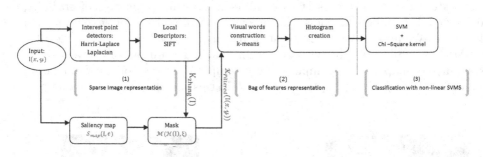

Fig. 4. Architect of our model

To take advantage of the saliency map within the context of Zhang's framework, the idea is to generate a mask $M(H(I),\xi)$ that is used as a filter of the SIFT keypoints set, with ξ the minimum level of saliency considered in the image. Formally, the generated mask could be defined as:

$$M(H(I),\xi) = \begin{cases} 1 \ if \ H(x_h,y_h) > \xi \\ 0 \ otherwise \end{cases} \quad (2)$$

The filtering process by itself consists in selecting the subset $K_{Filtered}(I)$ of keypoints in $K_{Zhang}(I)$ for which the mask $M(H(I),\xi)$ is on:

$$\begin{aligned} K_{Filtered}(I(x,y)) = \\ \{Key_j \in K_{Zhang}(I(x_h,y_h)) \mid M(H(I),\xi) = 1\} \end{aligned} \quad (3)$$

This subset $K_{Filtered}(I)$ serves as input for the next parts of Zhang algorithm for object recognition. In the following sections, we evaluate our approach on VOC 2005 dataset with an intention to validate our hypothesis mentioned in 1.

4 Results and Discussion

In order to measure the performances of our approach, we compare its result on the VOC2005 learning database with Zhang's nominal implementation. As mentioned in section 2.1, the VOC challenge proposed 2 images subsets , the subset S_1 with selected images and another subset S_2 with Google images randomly selected. In our test, we only focused on the first subset S_1. Moreover , this subset is itself splitted un two databases : the learning base L and the test base T. For simplicity reasons, we choose to use only the L database. Finally, as the categories were not equally represented in L , we choose to discard some images in over represented categories so as to obtain statistically equivalent learning sets, keeping 168 images in each category.

Practically, a re-implementation of Zhang's method was performed and evaluated on the L database. L was splitted with a ratio of 2/3 for training and 1/3 for test. As a consequence, 112 images of each class were used for training and 56 images of each class for the test set. The learning set being smaller, we obtained little loss of performance between our re-implemented method and the result reported in the challenge.

As it can be seen in the previous section, the value of the threshold parameter ξ has a great impact on the decimation of the keypoints: the higher it is , the least number of keypoints are kept. As the number of the keypoints depends on the images, we have chosen to adapt the parameter to the ration ρ between the number of remaining keypoints $Card(\mathrm{K}_{\mathrm{Filtered}}(I))$ and the number of keypoints in the image $Card(\mathrm{k}_{\mathrm{Zhang}}(I))$.

ρ was varied $\{10\%, 20\%, 30\%, 40\%\}$. We were not able to vary ρ over 40%, since with the minimum value $\xi = 0$ (the whole heatmap is considered) , 60% of the keypoints were already filtered.

The filtering of the keypoints can be performed independently during learning and for the test process. Therefore, ρ was varied on both the learning set (ρ_L) and the training set (ρ_T): our idea was to determine whether more or less keypoints during training or test may affect the effectiveness of our approach. We evaluate the binary classification using Receiver Operating Characteristic (ROC) [Fawcett2006]. We performed also quantitative evaluation of ROC curves computing the Area Under Curve (AUC) and the Equal Error Rate (EER) [Fawcett2006] following the procedure defined for the challenge.

4.1 Results

The results are summarized in Tables 2, 3, 4, 5 which present the result for each class with,respectively, Zhang'original score as reported in the challenge summary, our implementation of Zhang' algorithm without filtering and several couples of (ρ_L,ρ_T) keypoints filtering, Observing the results shows that reducing by about 60% the number of keypoints does not affect the performances sensibly except for cars for which minimal performance(2% loss only). the corresponding ROC curves are presented in Figure 5. For reason of clarity , we dont't present the tests we did exhausively : we selected only the "best" and "worst" curves.

Table 2. AUC /EER values for Persons class

AUC/ EER	Zhang	Reimpl.of Zhang	40%,40%	20%,10%
	0.97/ 0.91	0.95/ 0.85	0.95/ 0.85	0.87/ 0.79

Table 3. AUC /EER values for cars class

AUC/ EER	Zhang	Reimpl.of Zhang	40%,40%	10%,40%
	0.98/ 0.93	0.95/ 0.90	0.93/ 0.93	0.70/ 0.84

Table 4. AUC /EER values for bikes class

AUC/ EER	Zhang	Reimpl.of Zhang	40%,40%	20%,40%
	0.98/ 0.93	0.90/ 0.93	0.90/ 0.89	0.83/ 0.81

Table 5. AUC /EER values for motorbikes class

AUC/ EER	Zhang	Reimpl.of Zhang	20%,30%	40%,10%
	0.99/ 0.96	0.96/ 0.88	0.96/ 0.88	0.84/ 0.77

4.2 Discussion

The results above seems to validate our initial hypothesis concerning the fact that not all the keypoints extracted by a SIFT detector are needed to recognize an object since by discarding 60% of the keypoints the recognition performances stay practically unchanged. It is a first step to solve the memory and time constraints involved by the use of SIFT extractor in recognition systems. Indeed the consumption of memory constitute a serious problem in object recognition since SIFT generates huge sets of keypoints. These keypoints are usually used as bags-of-features, codebooks or dictionaries that consume a large quantity of memory. Concerning recognition, it is classically performed by a SVM classifier whose computation time is directly linked with the dimension of the input space. Therefore, the time needed for learning the classifier can be very long. More problematic is the fact that for huge databases, the time spent to answer a query is very long too. By reducing the number of keypoints so dramatically, we can hope both accelerating the retrieval algorithms and make it possible the use of very large databases.

Furthermore, we suggest that by using a saliency-based detection systems, we select SIFT keypoints that are relevant not only for human perception but also for artificial systems. In this implementation, the saliency system has just been

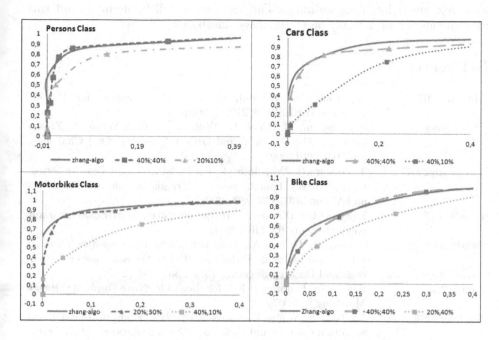

Fig. 5. ROC curve with and without our filter approach for the different classes

used to filter a classical detector. The SIFT characterization of the keypoints was unchanged. However, we think that the saliency system can also be used to characterize the keypoints. In the future, we intend not only to use this system to detect interesting points but also to characterize them. As the attentional system is intrinsically dynamic, we also intend to apply our framework to videos.

5   Conclusion

In this paper, we proposed a new approach for selecting the most relevant SIFT keypoints according to the human perception. For that purpose, we suggested to use Perreira Da Silva's saliency based region detection systems as it extract the most salient regions based on the three main human perceptual channels: intensity, color and orientation. We tested this approach on VOC2005, a popular dataset in the object recognition domain. We demonstrated that we can maintain approximately the same performance by selecting only 40% of SIFT keypoints. Based on this result, we propose this approach as a first step to solve many problems related to the management of memory and query run-time when using SIFT detectors. In the future, it would be interesting to build a new hybrid object recognition algorithm that merge the two communities: CBIR and saliency based region detection. We think it can be done by replacing the interest point detectors by a saliency-based detector as these two systems reach to extract the most relevant points from an image. Furthermore, it will be useful to test this idea on videos and not only on static image databases .

References

[Marszaek2006]   Marszaek, M., Schmid, C.: Spatial Weighting for Bag-of-Features. IEEE, 2118–2125 (2006)
[Everingham2009]   Everingham, M., Gool, L., Williams, C.K.I., Winn, J., Zisserman, A.: The Pascal Visual Object Classes (VOC) Challenge, pp. 303–338 (2009)
[Tuytelaars2007]   Tuytelaars, T., Mikolajczyk, K.: Local Invariant Feature Detectors: A Survey. Foundations and Trends in Computer Graphics and Vision 3(3), 177–280 (2008)
[Lowe2004]   Lowe, D.G.: Distinctive Image Features from Scale-Invariant Keypoints, pp. 91–110 (2004)
[Santini2001]   Santini, S., Gupta, A., Jain, R.: Emergent Semantics Through Interaction in Image Databases. IEEE Transactions on knowledge and Data Engineering 13(3), 337–351 (2001)
[Santini2007]   Foo, J.J.: Pruning SIFT for Scalable Near-Duplicate Image Matching 9 (2007)
[Frintrop2010]   Frintrop, S., Rome, E., Christensen, H.I.: Computational visual attention systems and their cognitive foundations. ACM Transactions on Applied Perception 7(1), 1–39 (2010)
[VOC2005]   VOC, VOC 2005 (2005)
[Sivic2006]   Sivic, J., Russell, B.C., Efros, A.A., Zisserman, A., Freeman, W.T.: Discovering objects and their location in images. Russell The Journal of The Bertrand Russell Archives
[Kondor2003]   Kondor, R., Jebara, T.: A Kernel Between Sets of Vectors (2003)
[Laaksonen2000]   Laaksonen, J.: PicSOM content based image retrieval with self organizing maps, pp. 1199–1207 (2000)
[Mikolajczyk2004]   Mikolajczyk, K.: Scale and Affine Invariant Interest Point Detectors, pp. 63–86 (2004)
[Lindeberg1998]   Lindeberg, T.: Feature Detection with Automatic Scale Selection 96 (1998)
[Itti1998]   Itti, L., Koch, C., Niebur, E., et al.: A model of saliency-based visual attention for rapid scene analysis. IEEE Transactions on Pattern Analysis and Machine Intelligence 20(11), 1254–1259 (1998)
[PerreiraDaSilva2010] Perreira da Silva, M., Courboulay, V., Prigent, A., Estraillier, P.: Evaluation of preys / predators systems for visual attention simulation, in VISAPP, - International Conference on Computer Vision Theory and Applications Angers: INSTICC, pp. 275–282 (2010)
[Fawcett2006]   Fawcett, T.: An introduction to ROC analysis, 861–874 (2006)
[Perreira2011]   Perreira da Silva, M., Courboulay, V., Estraillier, P., Rochelle, L., Cedex, L.R.: Objective validation of a dynamical and plausible computational model of visual attention. In: EUVIP, Paris (2011)

Detection of Near-Duplicate Patches in Random Images Using Keypoint-Based Features

Andrzej Śluzek[1] and Mariusz Paradowski[2]

[1] Khalifa University, Abu Dhabi, UAE
andrzej.sluzek@kustar.ac.ae
[2] Wroclaw University of Technology, Poland
mariusz.paradowski@pwr.wroc.pl

Abstract. Detection of similar fragments in unknown images is typically based on the *hypothesize-and-verify* paradigm. After the keypoint correspondences are found, the configuration constraints are used to identify clusters of similar and similarly transformed keypoints. This method is computationally expensive and hardly applicable to large databases. As an alternative, we propose novel affine-invariant TERM features characterizing geometry of groups of elliptical keyregions so that similar patches can be found by feature matching only. The paper overviews TERM features and reports experimental results confirming their high performances in image matching. A method combining visual words based on TERM descriptors with SIFT words is particularly recommended. Because of its low complexity, the proposed method can be prospectively used with visual databases of large sizes.

Keywords: configurations of keypoints, keypoint correspondences, near-duplicate areas, local features, feature descriptors, affine invariance, object detection.

1 Introduction

Keypoint matching is one of the most fundamental techniques in modern machine vision. However, individual keypoint matches are usually incorrect in a global context. Numerous methods have been proposed to solve this problem, but in the area of near-duplicate fragments retrieval (e.g., detection of similar objects on random backgrounds) the popular approaches follow basically the same two-step scheme. First, the most credible keypoint correspondences are hypothesized and, subsequently, configuration constraints are applied to identify groups of similar keypoints related by approximately the same transformation (affine geometry is typically used).

In this paper, we discuss an alternative methodology where configurations of several elliptical keypoints are invariantly represented by individual features. Novel features and their affine-invariant descriptors are proposed for this purpose. Thus, algorithms for fast detection of similar patches in random images can be built upon matching individual descriptors only. This approach could be

J. Blanc-Talon et al. (Eds.): ACIVS 2012, LNCS 7517, pp. 301–312, 2012.
© Springer-Verlag Berlin Heidelberg 2012

particularly suitable for the identification of the same/similar objects randomly located within scenes of unpredictable contents and complexities.

We can use any affine-invariant keypoint detectors (i.e. the returned keypoints are represented by ellipses) but we focus only on two popular detectors, i.e. Harris-Affine, [11] and MSER, [10]. In Harris-Affine, the shapes of ellipses approximate the local image anisotropy, while MSER-generated ellipses are the best-fit approximations of the detected uniform regions. As explained later in the paper, Harris-Affine is eventually the preferred choice.

SIFT [9] is the keypoint descriptor of our choice but the actual selection of keypoint descriptors is not critical in the proposed approach. Similarly to numerous works, descriptors (of features and keypoints) can be quantized into a finite set of visual words, e.g. [14,3].

Keypoint correspondences are established using two typical schemes, i.e. *one-to-one* (O2O) and *many-to-many* (M2M). M2M schemes (its simplest variant is based on the visual word matching) often return unacceptably large numbers of correspondences (depending primarily on the size of the visual vocabulary) while O2O schemes (e.g., the *mutual nearest neighbour*) are computationally expensive but they generally return more credible correspondences.

From keypoint correspondences, similar images or images fragments (patches) are found using diversified approaches. Whole images can be matched by simple voting schemes, histogram-based approaches (bag of words), e.g. [13,14] or RANSAC-related methods. Unfortunately, in sub-image retrieval (or detection of similar patches) keypoint correspondences are usually incorrect in the wider context so that semi-local *configuration constraints* (typically modeled by affine transformations) are additionally used. Similar fragments are identified as groups of keypoints for which a consensus exists between the visual similarities and the configuration model. Several approaches have been proposed for such a task. Some solutions are based on the Hough transform (e.g. [8], [12]) other are based on hashing (e.g. [7], [2]), etc. Nevertheless, all these approaches exploit the *hypothesize-and-verify* paradigm. Thus, in spite of the recent improvements in the configuration constraints analysis (e.g. weak geometrical consistency in [6]) the numbers of images that can be reasonably quickly matched are, therefore, limited. The objective of this paper is to introduce a mechanism which does not need this paradigm.

1.1 Overview of the Paper

In Section 2 of the paper, we introduce affine-invariant features (and their descriptors) formed by tuples of several ellipses. The acronym TERM (**T**uples of **E**llipses **R**epresented by **M**oments) is proposed because their descriptors are built from the moment invariants computed over shapes defined by the properties of ellipses within a tuple. The number of such features in an image grows exponentially with the number of ellipses in a feature, so that we focus only on TERM3 and (supplementarily) on TERM2 features, i.e. features built from 3 or 2 ellipses. Other steps are also undertaken to further restrict the numbers of these features.

In Section 3, a family of matching algorithms based on TERM descriptors is incrementally built and their performances are discussed. We focus on the task for which TERM features are particularly suitable, i.e. detection of near-duplicate patches (fragments) in random images. It is shown that although TERM descriptors alone do not perform better than SIFT, a combination of TERM and SIFT is a powerful mechanism. The major experiment is conducted on a publicly available dataset which contains images of various objects within diversified scenes; exemplary results for images from other popular databases are also provided. Section 4 concludes the paper and highlights the suggested directions of the future researches.

2 TERM Features and Their Descriptors

2.1 TERM3

Assume E_0 ellipse with p_0 centre, and an external point p_1. Two intersection points r_{01A} and r_{01B} are uniquely defined by the direction of tangent line at t_{01} point (details in Fig. 1a). If the same operation is performed using another point p_2, a trapezoid $Q_{0(1,2)}$ is unambiguously defined (see Fig. 1b) by the geometry of the ellipse and the locations of p_1 and p_2 points, which should not be collinear with the ellipse centre.

Similar trapezoids $Q_{1(0,2)}$ and $Q_{2(0,1)}$ can be built for other ellipses located around points p_1 and p_2 (see Fig. 2). The set of these three trapezoids will be referred to as **TERM3** feature built over three ellipses. In order to avoid ambiguities, we order the ellipses in a tuple according to their area.

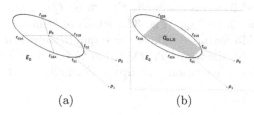

(a)   (b)

Fig. 1. Building a trapezoid in an ellipse in the context of two other points

When a set of three ellipses is transformed by an affine mapping, the configuration of Q trapezoids is transformed by the same mapping, see Fig. 2d. Thus, the affine covariance of two three-ellipse configurations can be verified by comparing affine-invariant shape descriptors of TERM3. Because the shapes or interest are very simple, we propose to build TERM3 descriptors using the least complex affine moment invariant (e.g. [16]) $Inv = \frac{\mu_{20}\mu_{02}-\mu_{11}^2}{m_{00}^4}$, where μ_{pq} indicates a central moment of $(p+q)^{th}$ order and m_{00} is the moment of 0th order. More sophisticated invariant descriptors can be alternatively used, but we do expect any significant improvements for such simple shapes.

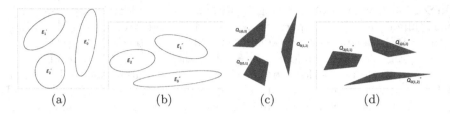

Fig. 2. Two affine-related configurations of three ellipses (a,b) and the corresponding TERM3 feature

Formally, the TERM3 descriptor is built as follows:

- Let $\{E_0, E_1, E_2\}$ be a tuple of three ellipses.
- Build the trapezoids $\{Q_{0(1,2)}, Q_{1(0,2)}, Q_{2(0,1)}\}$ (Figs 1 and 2). Let $\{f_0, f_1, f_2\}$ be their characteristic functions (i.e. 1 inside and 0 outside).
- Create TERM3 descriptor as a 7D vector of the Inv invariant values:

$$TERM3 = [I_0, I_1, I_2, I_{01}, I_{02}, I_{12}, I_{012}], \tag{1}$$

where $I_0 = Inv(f_0)$, $I_{01} = Inv(f_0 + f_1)$, $I_{012} = Inv(f_0 + f_1 + f_2)$, etc.

It should be noted that TERM3 descriptors can be algebraically computed from the corner coordinates of the Q trapezoids (very low computational complexity!).

2.2 TERM2

TERM2 features are built over two ellipses. Given a pair of ellipses (ordered by the area) three quadrilaterals are built: the "top" Q_T, Fig. 3b, the "bottom" Q_B, Fig. 3c, and the "large" Q_L, Fig. 3d (details of building the quadrilaterals are similar to TERM3 features). These three quadrilaterals define the TERM2 feature. Obviously, the shapes of TERM2 change under affine transformations covariantly with the configurations of ellipses. Formally, TERM2 descriptor is a

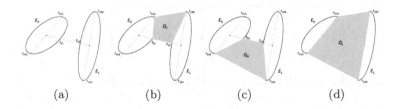

Fig. 3. Building Q quadrilaterals for TERM2 features

3D vector of the Inv invariant values computed over the characteristic functions of Q_T, Q_B and Q_L quadrilaterals:

$$T2 = [Inv(f_T), Inv(f_B), Inv(f_L)]. \tag{2}$$

2.3 Limiting the Number of TERM Features

The numbers of keypoints in typical images can be high (e.g., over 1000) which results in prohibitively large numbers of TERM features. Thus, similarly to other works where configurations of keypoints are analyzed (e.g. [13,17,12]), only neighboring keypoints are considered to build TERM's. However, we use a non-standard concept of neighborhood which takes into account both the distance between keypoints and their sizes. It can be argued that: (1) if ellipses are very small compared to the distance between their centers, the keypoints most probably belong to unrelated fragments of the image and (2) if the distance is very short compared to the size of ellipses, the keypoints are just slightly different representations of the same visual contents (e.g., a discussion in [12]).

Therefore, a pair of ellipses E_0 and E_1 (with p_0 and p_1 centers) is used for TERM3 building only if

$$\frac{1}{\alpha} max\left(\lambda_0, \lambda_1\right) \leq dist\left(p_0, p_1\right) \leq \alpha min\left(\Lambda_0, \Lambda_1\right), \tag{3}$$

where λ and Λ are the lengths of minor and major half-axes of the ellipses, while α is the parameter to further control the range of acceptable distances between ellipse centers.

Results obtained using over 1000 diversified images (keypoints extracted by MSER and Harris-Affine detectors) indicate that $\alpha = 2.0$ is a recommended choice. For such a value, typical neighborhoods of keypoints seldom contain more than $10 - 15$ other keypoints, i.e. the number of formed TERM features is reasonable. If, however, the neighborhood is unusually large, we limit it to 30 neighbors only. In TERM3 building, we additionally exclude configurations for which the triangle of ellipse centers is too acute (the minimum angle is $15°$).

The further reduction of TERM features is obtained by limiting the number of keypoints (we have found that images with more than 300 keypoints typically generate too many TERMs). Thus, for MSER we keep at most the largest 300 keypoints, while in Harris-Affine we adaptively modify the acceptance threshold to get a similar number of keypoints. Eventually, the images from the database used in the main experiments (see Subsection 3.1) contain 28-300 MSER keypoints and 12-252 Harris-Affine keypoints. The resulting numbers of TERMs are more diversified. For MSER, the images contain between 30 and 1354 TERM2 and from 3 to 7339 TERM3 (for Harris-Affine the ranges are between 3 and 1697, and from 3 to 16518, correspondingly).

2.4 Visual Words from TERM3 and TERM2 Descriptors

Discretization schemes (vocabulary building) are often based on the assumption that probabilities of all discrete values should be approximately the same, e.g. [4]. When the number of samples is relatively small, this is usually approximated by clusterization (e.g. K-means). However, if the probability distributions of the process values are available (or can be estimated) discretization can be performed by partitioning the process space into sub-areas of the same probability.

Over $30,000,000$ TERM3 features (and the corresponding number of TERM2) have been extracted from over 1000 diversified images (keypoints detected by both MSER and Harris-Affine). Since the dimensionality of the feature space is rather low (7 for TERM3 and 3 for TERM2), we have obtained a sufficiently dense coverage of the whole space to estimate the probabilistic model of the TERM descriptors. Because practically the same model has been obtained using separately MSER and Harris-Affine keypoints (which are highly different) we assumed a normal distribution of TERM3 and TERM2 descriptors.

Subsequently, we investigated correlations between individual dimensions of the descriptors. The experimentally obtained matrix of correlation coefficients confirms the intuitive expectation that individual dimensions of TERM3 are uncorrelated:

$$\begin{bmatrix} 1 & 0.009 & -0.010 & -0.002 & 0.009 & 0.000 & 0.006 \\ 0.009 & 1 & -0.004 & -0.003 & 0.000 & -0.003 & 0.018 \\ -0.010 & -0.004 & 1 & -0.001 & -0.003 & -0.003 & 0.003 \\ -0.002 & -0.003 & -0.001 & 1 & -0.000 & -0.000 & 0.002 \\ 0.009 & 0.000 & -0.003 & -0.000 & 1 & 0.000 & 0.022 \\ 0.000 & -0.003 & -0.003 & -0.000 & 0.000 & 1 & 0.003 \\ 0.006 & 0.018 & 0.003 & 0.002 & 0.022 & 0.003 & 1 \end{bmatrix} . \tag{4}$$

For TERM2, the correlation between individual dimensions is also very low.

Therefore, the visual vocabulary is generated by partitioning Gaussian distributions of individual dimensions into areas of equal probabilities, and taking the Cartesian products of such partitions. Thus, the number of words would be 2^7, 3^7, 4^7, etc. for the TERM3 vocabulary and 2^3, 3^3, 4^3, etc. for TERM2 vocabulary. Alternative algorithms can be used (e.g. K-means) but in our opinion the proposed method is more general, in particular for handling collections of images with unpredictable contents.

3   Experimental Verification

3.1   Methodology

As mentioned earlier, TERM3 and TERM2 features could be primarily used to detect similarly looking patches in random images of unpredictable complexity and content. Therefore, the major experiment has been conducted using a publicly available[1] VISIBLE dataset which seems particularly suitable for preliminary experiments. The set consists of 100 images containing diversified views of 1, 2 or 3 objects from over 30 classes of objects (each class defined by the same physical object or its nearly identical copies) on varying backgrounds (indoor and outdoor images, varying quality of images, etc.). Because the objects are locally planar, some pairs of images share near-duplicate patches (i.e. object views). Manually outlined shapes of all objects are considered the ground truth (see examples in Fig. 4). The objective is to verify how effectively such patches can be detected/matched regardless the wider image context.

With 100 images, 4950 image pairs exist altogether and all of them are matched in the experiments. 512 of these pairs, i.e. slightly more than 10%, share at least one near-duplicate patch.

---

[1] http://www.ii.pwr.wroc.pl/~visible/data/upload/FragmentMatchingDB.zip

Fig. 4. Exemplary images (and the outlines of objects they contain) from VISIBLE dataset

Almost one thousand of images from other popular databases (Caltech101, 15 Scenes, INRIA, Pascal2007) have been tested as well, but these datasets do not provide ground truth in the form we require (although Pascal2007 provides outlines of *the-same-class* objects, but they do not have to be *visually* similar). Thus, the results from those databases are not used for a systematic analysis of performances.

In all images, MSER and Harris-Affine keypoints are extracted using publicly available executables; limited numbers of TERM2 and TERM3 features (as explained in Subsection 2.3) are built from these keypoints.

All descriptors are precomputed off-line. We use SIFT descriptor to characterize individual keypoints, and TERM3 (TERM2) to describe triplets (pairs) of keypoints. Visual vocabularies are also precomputed. TERM words are built according to Subsection 2.4. The SIFT vocabulary of 500 words has been built (separately for MSER and Harris-Affine keypoints) using randomly selected 600 images from all databases used. The vocabularies are fixed and we do not plan to change them when more images are added (or if other datasets are used).

Because the proposed approach uses keypoint extraction as the fundamental mechanism, we use the numbers (relative or absolute) of correct keypoint correspondences as the measure of performance (note that a match between TERM2 features contributes two correspondences, and TERM3 - three). For a large number of image matches, it is impossible to manually verify correctness of all such correspondences. Thus, we use an approximate method where a keypoint match is considered a true correspondence if in both images the keypoints belong to the outlines of the same class objects. This assumption may generate some false positives (matching different parts of the same object) and false negatives (visually similar patches from outside the outlined objects) but, in general, it has been found reliable enough.

In contrast to almost all published methods we are aware of, detection of near-duplicate patches is based on matching individual descriptors only, i.e. no semi-local configuration constraints are analyzed. Under such assumptions, there are very few alternative approaches that can be compared to the proposed method.

3.2 Main Experiments

Initially, the image correspondences have been found using the following methods:

- **Method** M_1. O2O keypoint matching using SIFT descriptors (mutual nearest neighbors).
- **Method** M_2. M2M keypoint matching using SIFT vocabulary (the same word).

- **Method** M_3. O2O matching of keypoint pairs using pairs of SIFT descriptors.
- **Method** M_4. M2M matching of keypoint pairs using pairs of SIFT words.
- **Method** M_5. O2O TERM2 matching (mutual nearest neighbors).
- **Method** M_6. O2O TERM3 matching (mutual nearest neighbors).

It can be noted that M_3 and M_4 methods are almost identical to the concepts outlined in [1,5] (which are the first attempts to build features from combinations of keypoints).

Table 1 shows that all these methods are virtually useless in detection of near-duplicate patches in random images. However, performances of TERM-based

Table 1. The numbers of keypoint correspondences found in VISIBLE dataset (all image pairs matched). M = MSER, HA = Harris-Affine.

Method	M_1 (M)	M_1 (HA)	M_2 (M)	M_3 (M)	M_4 (M)	M_5 (HA)	M_6 (M)	M_6 (HA)
Total	556898	139394	9027281	2210352	2361800	1629682	5852349	5780451
Correct	14155	4183	60145	51028	56789	33093	57904	162756
Correct %	2.54%	2.98%	0.67%	2.31%	2.40%	2.03%	0.99%	2.82%

matching can be dramatically improved if we accept only correspondences between TERMs which additionally have the identical corresponding SIFT words. Such a modification is symbolically denoted as $M_6 \cap 3M_2$ (i.e. we accept O2O matches between TERM3 only if three SIFT words are also the same). The results are given in Table 2. Slightly inferior results have been obtained for TERM2 features (which are eventually used in a different way as explained later). Fig. 5 illustrates differences between methods based on either SIFT or TERM only, and between $M_6 \cap 3M_2$ method.

Table 2. The numbers of keypoint correspondences when O2O TERM3 matching is supported by the verification of SIFT words (M_2 method)

Method	Total	Correct	Correct %
$M_6 \cap 3M_2$ (MSER)	1569	1412	89.99%
$M_6 \cap 3M_2$ (HarrAff)	2241	2042	91.12%

Unfortunately, the numbers of matches returned by $M_6 \cap 3M_2$ method are very small (see Table 2). Actually, in VISIBLE database most of these matches are concentrated in about 15-20 pairs of images, while the majority of pairs with similar objects remain undetected (i.e. high *precision* of keypoint matching and low *recall* of image matching). Detailed analysis of unsuccessful cases revealed two main causes of such a low recall. First, too few keypoints are detected at the corresponding locations (or too many are discarded when the number of keypoint is reduced) and, secondly, dissimilarities exist between affine mappings modeling

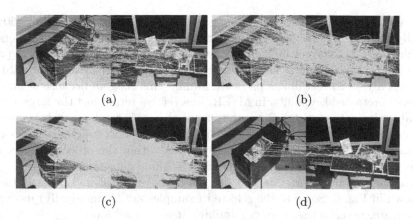

(a) (b)

(c) (d)

Fig. 5. Exemplary results of image matching by M_1 (a), M_5 (b), M_6 (c) and $M_6 \cap 3M_2$ (d) methods. MSER keypoints are used.

Table 3. The numbers of keypoint matches for M_7 method supported by SIFT words and (the last two columns) by TERM2 words. **M** = MSER, **HA** = Harris-Affine.

Method	$M_7(2^7 w) \cap 3M_2$: M	$M_7(6^7 w) \cap 3M_2$: M	M_8 : M	M_8 : HA
Total	58131	41838	2589	14523
Correct	9098	8177	2311	13599
Correct %	15.65%	19.54%	89.26%	93.64%

the image distortions and mappings modeling the keypoint deformations (i.e. the *actual* affine invariance of the keypoint detectors is not satisfactory).

While the solution of the first problems is partially outside the scope of this paper, we attempted to rectify the second one. Instead of O2O matching of TERM3 features, we use M2M matching based on TERM words (this is referred to as M_7 method) . In accordance with Subsection 2.4, we use TERM3 vocabularies of $2^7 = 128$, $3^7 = 2187$, etc. words. As a result, the number of matched keypoints grows significantly (see Table 3) but, at the same time, the percentage of correct matches significantly lowers. However, when we additionally match TERM2 words (using a simple vocabulary of $3^3 = 27$ words) for keypoint pairs within each TERM3, the number of keypoint matches is still relatively high and most of them are correct (the last two columns of Table 3; note that only 128 TERM3 words are used there). Therefore, we define the ultimate matching method (referred to as M_8) as an intersection of word-based TERM3, SIFT and TERM2 matches. Formally:

$$M_8 = M_7(128 words) \cap 3M_2 \cap 3TERM2(27 words). \tag{5}$$

Not only the credibility of keypoint matching is high for M_8 method, but also the number of detected image pairs is reasonable. For the Harris-Affine variant,

248 image pairs sharing the same objects are identified (*recall* of approx. 50%). Actually, the effective recall is even higher because with the limited numbers of keypoints only 311 correct image pairs can be retrieved (the other correct pairs do not share any matching keypoints within the outlined areas). For MSER, however, only 86 correct image pairs are found. This is again because of limited numbers of retained keypoints. In MSER, howver, we retain just the largest ones (no viable alternative exists). Since the size of objects is random, their keypoints are often too small to be retained. In Harris-Affine, the most prominent keypoints are retained so that the changes that keypoints within the objects survive are higher. Thus, we suggest the use of the Harris-Affine detector.

Exemplary results of M_8 method images from VISIBLE and other datasets are shown in Fig. 6. Some of the selected examples are (semantically) incorrect but they are, nevertheless, correct (similar) at the visual level.

Fig. 6. Exemplary results of M_8 method. The last row shows (semantically) incorrect matches. The outlines indicate locations of matched features.

4   Conclusions

4.1   Summary

The paper presents a novel method for detection of near-duplicate patches in images of unknown and unpredictable contents. Instead of typical keypoint matching followed by the analysis of configuration constraints, we use a one-step matching of precomputed feature descriptors. New types of features (TERM3 and, supplementarily, TERM2) characterizing semi-local geometric configurations of elliptical keypoints are proposed and tested. The affine-invariant descriptors of these features are based on a low-complexity moment invariant.

It is shown that in detection of similar patches TERM descriptors alone do not perform better than standard keypoint descriptors (e.g. SIFT). However, when the feature description combines TERM3, TERM2 and SIFT words, the results are very encouraging. Although slightly similar ideas have been reported in [1,5], the proposed method is apparently the first solution providing so high performances at so low computational costs (simple word-matching).

Since the numbers of TERM3 features built in a single image (after the reduction procedure described in Subsection 2.3) seldom reach 10, 000, the memory footprint is acceptably compact. Using a relatively inefficient Matlab implementation and a naive matching by exhaustive search, hundreds of image pairs can be matched within a few seconds. We can expect, therefore, thousands of matches in a second for the optimized Java (or C++) implementations. With more sophisticated matching strategies and/or efficiently organized databases (e.g. [15,4]) the method can be prospectively used with large visual databases. For an independent performance verification, Java source codes for TERM descriptors are available on request (please contact the authors).

4.2   Future Works

The presented method, although supported by experimental verification, cannot be considered fully mature. In particular, the conflict between the number of retained keypoints (data completeness) and the number of resulting TERM3 features (memory usage) should be optimally compromised. Keypoint ranking (which is currently defined for Harris-Affine but not for MSER) and adaptive modifications of keypoint neighborhoods are the recommended directions. As the ultimate solution, however, we envisage the method where semi-local characteristics of images are represented by descriptions of *individual* keypoints.

References

1. Chum, O., Matas, J.: Geometric hashing with local affine frames. In: Proc. IEEE Conf. CVPR 2006, New York, pp. 879–884 (2006)
2. Chum, O., Perdoch, M., Matas, J.: Geometric min-hashing: Finding a (thick) needle in a haystack. In: Proc. IEEE Conf. CVPR 2009, pp. 17–24 (2009)

3. Csurka, G., Bray, C., Dance, C., Fan, L., Willamowski, J.: Visual categorization with bags of keypoints. In: Proc. 8th ECCV 2004, Workshop on Statistical Learning in Computer Vision, Prague, pp. 1–22 (2004)

4. Fayyad, U., Irani, K.: Multi-interval discretization of continuous-valued attributes for classification learning. In: Proc. 13th Int. Joint Conf. on Art l. Int. IJCAI 1993, pp. 1022–1029 (1993)

5. Forssén, P.E., Lowe, D.G.: Shape descriptors for maximally stable extremal regions. In: Proc. IEEE Conf. ICCV 2007, pp. 1–8, Rio de Janeiro (2007)

6. Jegou, H., Douze, M., Schmid, C.: Improving bag-of-features for large scale image search. International Journal of Computer Vision 87(3), 316–336 (2010)

7. Ke, Y., Sukthankar, R., Huston, L.: Efficient near-duplicate detection and sub-image retrieval. In: Proc. ACM Multimedia Conf., pp. 869–876 (2004)

8. Lowe, D.G.: Object recognition from local scale-invariant features. In: Proc. 7th IEEE Int. Conf. Computer Vision, vol. 2, pp. 1150–1157 (1999)

9. Lowe, D.G.: Distinctive image features from scale-invariant keypoints. International Journal of Computer Vision 60(2), 91–110 (2004)

10. Matas, J., Chum, O., Urban, M., Pajdla, T.: Robust wide baseline stereo from maximally stable extremal regions. In: British Machine Vision Conference, pp. 384–393 (2002)

11. Mikolajczyk, K., Schmid, C.: Scale and affine invariant interest point detectors. International Journal of Computer Vision 60, 63–86 (2004)

12. Paradowski, M., Śluzek, A.: SC I339, chap. Local Keypoints and Global Affine Geometry: Triangles and Ellipses for Image Fragment Matching. In: Innovations in Intelligent Image Analysis, pp. 195–224. Springer (2011)

13. Schmid, C., Mohr, R.: Local grayvalue invariants for image retrieval. IEEE Trans. PAMI 19(5), 530–535 (1997)

14. Sivic, J., Zisserman, A.: Video google: A text retrieval approach to object matching in videos. In: Proc. 9th IEEE Conf., ICCV 2003, Nice, vol. 2, pp. 1470–1477 (2003)

15. Sivic, J., Zisserman, A.: Efficient visual search of videos cast as text retrieval. IEEE PAMI 31(4), 591–606 (2009)

16. Śluzek, A.: Zastosowanie metod momentowych do identyfikacji obiektów w cyfrowych systemach wizyjnych. WPW, Warszawa (1990)

17. Yang, D., Śluzek, A.: A low-dimensional local descriptor incorporating tps warping for image matching. Image and Vision Computing 28(8), 1184–1195 (2010)

The Mean Boundary Curve of Anatomical Objects

Keiko Morita[1], Atsushi Imiya[2], Tomoya Sakai[3], Hidekata Hontan[4],
and Yoshitaka Masutani[5]

[1] School of Advanced Integration Sciences, Chiba University, Japan
Yayoi-cho 1-33, Inage-ku, Chiba, 263-8522, Japan
[2] Institute of Media and Information Technology, Chiba University, Japan
Yayoi-cho 1-33, Inage-ku, Chiba, 263-8522, Japan
[3] Department of Computer and Information Science, Nagasaki University
Bunkyo-cho 1-44, Nagasaki, 852-8521, Japan
[4] Department of Computer Science, Nagoya Institute of Technology, Gokiso,
Showa-ku, Nagoya 466-8555, Aichi, Japan
[5] Department of Radiology, The University of Tokyo Hospital
Division of Radiology and Biomedical Engineering,
Graduate School of Medicine, The University of Tokyo
Hongo 7-3-1, Bunkyo-ku 113-8655, Tokyo, Japan

Abstract. In this paper, we develop an algorithm to compute the mean
shape of a collection of planar curves for the computation of the mean
shape of a collection of organs. We first define the relative distortion of
a pair of curves using curvatures of curves. Then, we derive the mean of
curves as the curve which minimises the total distortion of a collection
of shapes.

1 Introduction

We define the variational mean [3] of a collection of planar curves, which are
derived as the contour curves of planar slices of anatomical organs. In medical
image registration, the establishment of relations between different images is the
main issue in researches. This registration process between images clarifies the
difference between images which is used for medical diagnosis. This registration
process is mainly achieved by the matching process, which is an established
fundamental idea in pattern recognition. In computational anatomy, statistical
mean shape, which is computed using principal component analysis of shape
descriptor, is well defined [12, 15]. In both structure pattern recognition [4, 5]
and variational registration [1, 3], the mean shape of a collection of given shapes
is interested.

In medical image diagnosis and retrieval [1, 2], the mean image and shape
of individual organs provides essential properties for the general expression of
organs. Shape retrieval categorises and classifies shapes, and finds shapes from
portions of shapes. In shape retrieval, the matching of shapes based on the defo-
morphism of shapes [8, 9, 16, 19–21] and descriptor of shape boundary contours

J. Blanc-Talon et al. (Eds.): ACIVS 2012, LNCS 7517, pp. 313–324, 2012.

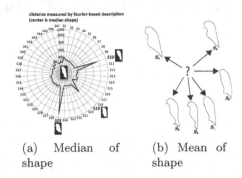

(a)   Median   of shape   (b) Mean of shape

Fig. 1. The mean and median shape of planar simple curve. Although the median of the shape is selected from elements of a collection of shapes (a), the mean is computed from a collection of shapes (b).

[10] are used. In the matching process for discrete shapes, the string edit-distance [4, 6] computed by dynamic programming is a fundamental tool. Moreover, in the matching process of images, the variational registration strategy [1, 2] is a typical tool. Since, in registration of grey-valued images, the deformation is assumed to be relatively small, the point correspondences between the target and reference images are estimated as a local deformation of images [1–3]. For the matching of planar curves, we are required to estimate both alignments and local deformation of curves. In this paper, we separate this problem into alignment estimation [16, 17] in the normalised set of curves and deformation of curves. Furthermore, since for the computation of the mean of curves, we are required to establish multiple alignments of curves, we introduce the total distortion of a collection of curves and estimate alignments by minimising this distortion.

2   The Mean and Median of Normal Curves

Mean and Median in Metric Space. Setting $d(S_i, S_j)$ to be a distance measure [9] between shapes S_i and S_j over the shape space $\mathbb{S}$, the mean and median in a shape subset $\{S_i\}_{i=1}^n = \mathbb{S}_n \subset \mathbb{S}$ are

$$\text{mean}(\mathbb{S}_n) = \arg\left(\min_{S \in \mathbb{S}} \sum_{i=1}^n d(S_i, S) \right), \tag{1}$$

$$\text{median}\,(\mathbb{S}_n) = \arg\left(\min_{S \in \mathbb{S}_n} \sum_{i=1}^n d(S_i, S) \right). \tag{2}$$

We establish a variational method to compute the mean of simple planar curves, which are derived as the boundary curves of biological organs. Figure 1 illustrates a computational property of the mean shape. The median of the shape is selected from elements of the collection of shapes, though the mean is note required to be selected from a collection of shapes.

For a pair of planar curves $c(s) = (c_1(s), c_2(s))^\top$ and $\bar{c}(s) = (\bar{c}_1(s), \bar{c}_2(s))^\top$, whose lengths are C and $\bar{C}$, respectively, assuming $c(s+C) = c(s)$ and $\bar{c}(s+\bar{C}) = \bar{c}(s)$, the alignment of curves is obtained as

$$\text{Align}(c, \bar{c}) = \min_{t,\psi} \int_0^C |\bar{c}(\psi(s) - t) - c(s)|^2 ds, \tag{3}$$

where $\psi(\tau)$ is a monotone function from the interval $[0, C]$ to the interval $[0, \bar{C}]$ [13, 14, 16]. The function $\tau = \psi(s)$ and the displacement t define the correspondences of points on a pair of curves $c(s)$ and $\bar{c}(\tau)$.

The dynamic time warping (DTW) is a fundamental procedure to achieve curve alignment employing dynamic programming [13]. The time warping sometimes maps a point on a curve to a relatively long interval of another curve. The derivative dynamic time warping technique (DDTW) [14], which computes alignment of derivative curves, solves this pathological mapping. Therefore, we can also use

$$\text{Align}(c, \bar{c}) = \min_{t,\psi} \int_0^C |\dot{\bar{c}}(\psi(s) - t) - \dot{c}(s)|^2 ds, \tag{4}$$

for the derivative of curves [14] $\dot{c}$ and $\dot{\bar{c}}$.

Using an appropriate transform [1] Θ, we introduce the criterion

$$\text{Align}(c, \bar{c}) = \min_t \int_0^1 |\Theta[\dot{\bar{c}}(s - t)] - \Theta[\dot{c}(s)]|^2 ds \tag{5}$$

for the pair of curves whose lengths are normalised to unity [11], since this transform allows the symmetry relation

$$\text{Align}(c, \bar{c}) = \text{Align}(\bar{c}, c). \tag{6}$$

Distance of Normal Curves. Distances between a pair of planar curves are desired to be invariant for scaling and Euclidean motion. Therefore, we first normalise the length of curves to unity. Then, for the normalised curves, we construct a distance which is invariant for Euclidean motion.

For a planar curve S_i, the normal curve s_i is the curve whose length are normalised to unity is a normalised curve. For the normal curve $x(s)$ the unit normal vector is $n(s) = (-\sin\theta(s), \cos\theta(s))^\top$, if $\dot{x}(s)/|\dot{x}(s)| = (\cos\theta(s), \sin\theta(s))^\top$. We call $\theta(s)$ the p-expression of the curve. The normalised curve is reconstructed from the p-expression $\theta(s)$ as

$$x(s) = \int_0^s |\dot{x}(s)| \begin{pmatrix} \cos\theta(\tau) \\ \sin\theta(\tau) \end{pmatrix} d\tau, \tag{7}$$

---

[1] The L_2 Gromov-Hausdorff distance [7] between a pair of planar curves is

$$d_{GH}^{L_2}(S_1, S_2) = \left(\min_{\psi_1, \psi_2, t_1, t_2} \int_0^1 |c_1(\psi_1(s) - t_1) - c_2(\psi_2(s) - t_2)|^2 ds \right)^{\frac{1}{2}}$$

for the invertible functions $\psi_1(s)$ from $[0, C_1]$ to $[0, 1]$ and $\psi_2(s)$ from $[0, C_2]$ to $[0, 1]$, where C_1 and C_2 is the lengths of S_1 and S_2, respectively.

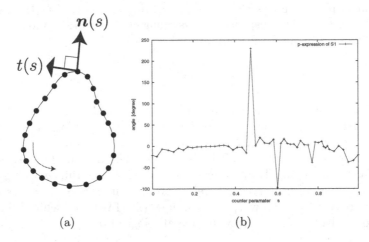

(a)   (b)

Fig. 2. Geometric property of the image boundary of curve. (a) Configuration of the normal and tangent vectors on a planar simple curve. (b) The phase (p-) expression of a planar simple curve.

and the original curve is reconstructed as $p(s) = x(Ls)$, where L is the total length of the curve, since $n(s) = \dot{x}(s)/|\dot{x}(s)|$. In refs. [9] and [10], the tangent expression $T(s)$ of the normal curves is introduced. Since $\theta(s) = T_s(s)(T(s) = \int_0^s \theta(\tau)d\tau)$, the p-expression is invariant for Euclidean motion, that is, for curve $x(s)$, $y(s) = x(s) + a$ derives the same p-expression. Figures 2(a) and (b) show geometry of the tangent vector and the p-expression of a curve.

Since a rotation of $x(s)$ derives a sift for $\theta(s)$, that is, the p-expressions of $Rx(s)$ is $\theta(s-t)$ for an appropriate t. The p-distance of a pair of simple polygonal curve S_i and S_j is defined by

$$D(S_i, S_j) = \left(\min_t \int_0^1 |\theta_i(s - t) - \theta_j(s)|^2 ds \right)^{\frac{1}{2}}. \tag{8}$$

where θ_i and θ_j are the p-expressions of the normalised curve s_i and s_j of S_i and S_j, respectively.

The p-expression $\theta(k)$ of a normalised polygonal curve, whose vertices are $\{x_k\}_{k=1}^n$, is computed as

$$\frac{x_k - x_{k-1}}{|x_k - x_{k-1}|} = (\cos \theta(k), \sin \theta(k))^\top. \tag{9}$$

Furthermore, setting $\theta_i^k = \theta_i(k\Delta)$, the distance between a pair of normalised curves is approximately computed by

$$d_{ij} \approx \min_p \sum_{k=1}^m |\theta_i^k - \theta_j^{k-p}|^2 \tag{10}$$

for an appropriately large m such that $\Delta m = 1$.

Multiple Curve Alignment by Distortion. We define the log measure between two normal curves as

$$H(\theta_1, \theta_2) = \int_0^1 \left| \ln \frac{\exp(i\theta_1(s - t_1))}{\exp(i\theta_2(s - t_2))} \right|^2 ds, \tag{11}$$

using p-expression of each curve of a pair. Then, for eq. (8), we have the relation

$$D(S_1, S_2) = (\min_{t_1, t_2} H(\theta_1, \theta_2))^{\frac{1}{2}}. \tag{12}$$

Using the relative distortion, we define the total distortion of $S_m \in \mathbb{S}_n = \{S_i\}_{i=1}^n$ as

$$\text{Dist}(\mathbb{S}_n) = \sum_{k=1}^n \left\{ \min_{t_m} \int_0^1 \left| \ln \frac{\exp(i\theta_k(s - t_k))}{\exp(i\theta_m(s))} \right|^2 ds \right\}. \tag{13}$$

We adopt the minimiser of $\text{Dist}(\mathbb{S}_n)$ as the median in $\mathbb{S}_n$, that is,

$$\text{median}(\{S_k\}_{k=1}^n) = \arg\left(\min_{\theta_k} \left[\sum_{k=1}^n \left\{ \min_{t_m} \int_0^1 \left| \ln \frac{\exp(i\theta_k(s - t_k))}{\exp(i\theta_m(s))} \right|^2 ds \right\} \right] \right). \tag{14}$$

Therefore, if we set

$$d_{ij} = \min_{t_i} \int_0^1 |\theta_i(s - t_i) - \theta_j(s)|^2 ds, \tag{15}$$

we can have the relation

$$\text{median}(\{S_i\}_{i=1}^n) = \arg\left\{ \min_j \sum_{i=1}^n d_{ij} \right\} = \arg\left\{ \min_i \sum_{j=1}^n d_{ij} \right\}. \tag{16}$$

3   The Mean of Normal Curves

We define the mean $\phi_{ij}(s)$ of a pair of p-expressions $\theta_i(s)$ and $\theta_j(s)$ as the minimiser of the functional

$$J(\phi_i, \phi_j, \phi_{ij}, t_i, t_j) = \int_0^1 \left\{ |(\theta_i(s - t_i) - \phi_i(s)) - \phi_{ij}(s)|^2 \right.$$
$$+ |(\theta_j(s - t_2) - \phi_j(s)) - \phi_{ij}(s)|^2$$
$$\left. + \lambda |\dot{\theta}_{ij}(s)|^2 + \mu |\dot{\phi}_i(s)|^2 + \mu |\dot{\phi}_j(s)|^2 \right\} ds. \tag{17}$$

Setting

$$t_{ij} = \arg\left(\min_t (\int_0^1 |\theta_i(s - t_{ij}) - \theta_j(s)|^2 ds \right), \tag{18}$$

Equation (17) is converted to the problem,

$$J_2(\phi_{ij}) = \int_0^1 \left\{ |(\theta_i(s - t_{ij}) - \phi_i(s) - \phi_{ij}(s))|^2 \right.$$
$$+ |(\theta_j(s) - \phi_j(s) - \phi_{ij}(s)|^2$$
$$\left. + \lambda|\dot\phi_{ij}(s)|^2 + \mu|\dot\phi_i(s)|^2 + \mu|\dot\phi_j(s)|^2 \right\} ds. \tag{19}$$

Since t_{ij} aligns a pair of p-expressions, for a generalisation of eq. (19), the initial points of a collection of curves are required to be aligned. Using the minimisers $t_i{}_{i=1}^n$ for $t_m = 0$ of eq. (13), we define the multiple aligned p-expression $\{\theta_i^*(s) = \theta_i(s - t_i)\}_{i=1}^n$ Using $\{\theta_i^*(s)\}_{i=1}^n$, we define the mean $\phi_{n+1}(s)$ of $\{\theta_i(s)\}_{i=1}^n$ as the minimiser of the criterion

$$J(\phi_{n+1}) = \sum_{i=1}^n \left[\int_0^1 \left\{ (\theta_i(s - t_i) - \phi_i(s) - \phi_{n+1}(s))^2 \right.\right.$$
$$\left.\left. + \lambda|\dot\phi_{n+1}(s)|^2 + \mu|\dot\phi_i(s)|^2 \right\} ds \right], \tag{20}$$

where

$$t_i = \arg\min_t \int_0^1 |\theta_i(s - t) - \theta_0(s)| ds \tag{21}$$

for the median θ_0 of $\{\theta_i\}_{i=1}^n$.

Setting

$$\phi = (\phi_1, \phi_2, \cdots, \phi_n, \phi_{n+1})^\top, \quad \theta = (\theta_1^*, \theta_2^* \cdots, \theta_n^*, \theta_{n+1})^\top \tag{22}$$

for $\theta_{n+1} = \sum_{i=1}^n \theta^*$, the Euler-Lagrange equation of eq. (20) is

$$M\ddot\phi = A\phi - \theta, \tag{23}$$

where

$$N = \begin{pmatrix} I_n & e \\ e^\top & n \end{pmatrix}, \quad M = Diag(\underbrace{\mu, \cdots, \mu}_n, \lambda), \tag{24}$$

for $e = (1, 1, \cdots, 1)^\top \in \mathbb{R}^n$.

Since the associated diffusion equation of the Euler-Lagrange equation is

$$\frac{\partial}{\partial t}\phi = \ddot\phi - M^{-1}N\phi + M^{-1}\theta, \tag{25}$$

we have the semi-explicit discretisation

$$\frac{f^{(k+1)} - f^{(k)}}{\tau} = (I_n \otimes D)f^{(k)} - I_m \otimes M^{-1}N f^{(k+1)} + I_m \otimes M^{-1}t, \tag{26}$$

for $m \times m$ matrix

$$D = \frac{1}{2} \begin{pmatrix} -2 & 1 & 0 & \cdots & 0 & 1 \\ 1 & -2 & 1 & 0 & \cdots & 0 \\ \vdots & & & & & \\ 1 & 0 & \cdots & 0 & 1 & -2 \end{pmatrix}, \tag{27}$$

and

$$\boldsymbol{f} = (f_1, f_2, \cdots, f_{n+1})^\top \quad \boldsymbol{t} = (t_1, t_2, \cdots, t_{n+1})^\top, \tag{28}$$

where

$$f_i = (\phi_i(\Delta), \phi_i(2\Delta), \cdots, \phi_i(m\Delta)), \quad t_i = (\theta_i(\Delta), \theta_i(2\Delta), \cdots, \theta_i(m\Delta)). \tag{29}$$

Therefore, we have the iteration form

$$\boldsymbol{A}\boldsymbol{f}^{(k+1)} = \boldsymbol{B}\boldsymbol{f}^{(k)} + \boldsymbol{c}, \tag{30}$$

where

$$\boldsymbol{A} = \boldsymbol{I}_{m \times n} + \tau \boldsymbol{I}_m \otimes \boldsymbol{M}^{-1}\boldsymbol{N}, \quad \boldsymbol{B} = \boldsymbol{I}_{m \times n} + \tau \boldsymbol{I}_m \otimes \boldsymbol{D}, \quad \boldsymbol{c} = \tau \boldsymbol{I}_m \otimes \boldsymbol{M}^{-1}\boldsymbol{t}. \tag{31}$$

4   The Mean of Polygonal Curves

Assuming that the correspondence of the vertices of curves $\{S_i\}_{i=1}^n$ are established by minimising eq. (8), we define the distance between a pair of polygonal curves $\boldsymbol{f}_{ik} = (x_{ik}, y_{ik})^\top$, for $k = 1, 2, \cdots, m$ with the condition $\boldsymbol{f}_{im+k} = \boldsymbol{f}_{ik}$, as

$$\begin{aligned}
D(S_i, S_j) &= \min_{\boldsymbol{u}_k^{ij}} \left\{ \sum_{k=1}^m \{(\boldsymbol{f}_{ik} - \boldsymbol{u}_k^{ij}) - \boldsymbol{f}_{jk}\}^2 + \mu \sum_{k=1}^m (\overline{\nabla}\boldsymbol{u}_k^{ij})^2 \right\} \\
&= \min_{\boldsymbol{u}_k^{ij}} \left\{ \sum_{k=1}^m \{\boldsymbol{f}_{ik} - (\boldsymbol{f}_{jk} - \boldsymbol{u}_k^{ji})\}^2 + \mu \sum_{k=1}^m (\overline{\nabla}\boldsymbol{u}_k^{ji})^2 \right\} \\
&= D(S_j, S_i), \tag{32}
\end{aligned}$$

where $\boldsymbol{u}_k^{ij} = -\boldsymbol{u}_k^{ji}$ is the displacement between $\boldsymbol{f}_{ik}$ and $\boldsymbol{f}_{jk}$ and $\overline{\nabla}$ stands for the discrete differential operation along a polygonal curve [2]. Using this distance, we compute the mean shape of polygonal curves. We adopt the minimiser $\boldsymbol{g}$ of the discrete variational form

$$\begin{aligned}
J(\boldsymbol{f}_{n+1}) &= \sum_{i=1}^n \left\{ \sum_{k=1}^m \{(\boldsymbol{f}_{ik} - \boldsymbol{u}_{ik}) - \boldsymbol{g}_k\}^2 + \mu \sum_{k=1}^m \overline{\nabla}\boldsymbol{u}_{ik})^2 + \lambda \sum_{k=1}^m (\overline{\nabla}\boldsymbol{g}_k)^2 \right\} \\
&= \sum_{i=1}^n \left\{ \sum_{k=1}^m \{\boldsymbol{f}_{ik} - (\boldsymbol{g}_k + \boldsymbol{u}_{ik})\}^2 + \mu \sum_{k=1}^m (\overline{\nabla}\boldsymbol{u}_{ik})^2 + \lambda \sum_{k=1}^m (\overline{\nabla}\boldsymbol{g}_k)^2 \right\} \tag{33}
\end{aligned}$$

where $\boldsymbol{u}_{ik}$ is deformation of the vertex $\boldsymbol{f}_{ik}$ of the shape S_i.

Setting the same matrix in the previous section, we have the matrix equation

$$(\boldsymbol{I}_n \otimes \boldsymbol{D})\boldsymbol{s} = (\boldsymbol{I}_n \otimes \boldsymbol{M}^{-1}\boldsymbol{N})\boldsymbol{s} - (\boldsymbol{I}_n \otimes \boldsymbol{M}^{-1})\boldsymbol{c} \tag{34}$$

as the Euler-Lagrange equation of eq. (33), where

$$\boldsymbol{s} = (\boldsymbol{u}_1^\top, \cdots, \boldsymbol{u}_n^\top, \boldsymbol{g}^\top)^\top, \quad \boldsymbol{c} = (\boldsymbol{f}_1^\top, \cdots, \boldsymbol{f}_{n+1}^\top)^\top, \tag{35}$$

for $\boldsymbol{f}_{n+1} = \sum_{i=1}^n \boldsymbol{f}_i$. We can solve this problem using the numerical scheme introduced in the previous section.

---

[2] $\overline{\nabla}\boldsymbol{g}_k = \boldsymbol{g}_{k+\frac{1}{2}} - \boldsymbol{g}_{k-\frac{1}{2}}$ and $\overline{\nabla}^2\boldsymbol{g}_k = \frac{1}{2}(\boldsymbol{g}_{k+1} - 2\boldsymbol{g}_k + \boldsymbol{g}_{k-1})$.

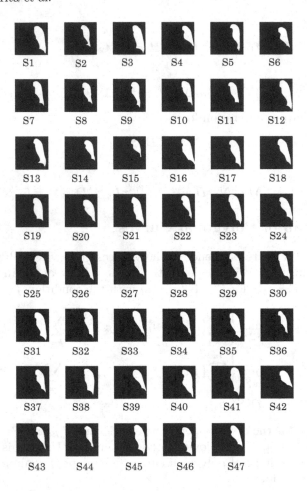

Fig. 3. Images of the boundary curves of lungs

5 Numerical Examples

We have evaluated geometrical and analytical properties of the median of polygonal curves. Setting $\boldsymbol{u}$ and $\boldsymbol{J}$ to be the deformation and its Jacobian between to curves, respectively, We define the following three measures

$$H^{ij} = \sum_{k=0}^{n-1} tr(\boldsymbol{J}_k \boldsymbol{J}_k^{\top}), \;\; L_2^{ij} = \sum_{k=0}^{n-1} |\boldsymbol{u}_k|^2, \;\; S^{ij} = \sum_{k=0}^{n-1} \Delta_k, \;\; \Delta_k = det(\boldsymbol{u}_{k+1}^{ij}, \boldsymbol{u}_k^{ij})$$

(36)

Here, H^{ij} is the constrain for the computation of distance and L_2^{ij} is the energy of the deformation. Moreover, S^{ij} is the area measure of deformation. The algorithm decides the S_{45} is the median of shapes in Fig. 3. Radar charts in Fig. 4 show the distribution of the organ boundaries in the shape space. These charts show that the shapes distribute around the median uniformly. Therefore,

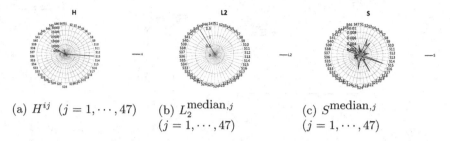

(a) H^{ij} $(j = 1, \cdots, 47)$ (b) $L_2^{\text{median},j}$ $(j = 1, \cdots, 47)$ (c) $S^{\text{median},j}$ $(j = 1, \cdots, 47)$

Fig. 4. Geometric property of the image boundary of lungs in Fig. 3I

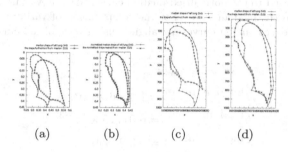

(a)   (b)   (c)   (d)

Fig. 5. Geometric property of the image boundary of lungs in Fig. 3II. (a) The median shape is superimposed to the most further curve for normalised curves. (b) The median shape is superimposed to the most nearest curve for normalised curves. (c) The median shape is superimposed to the most further curve. (d) The median shape is superimposed to the most nearest curve.

these examples show the validity of our definition of the median of organs using the boundary curves. In Fig. 5, the median curve and curves are compared by superimposing the median to the nearest and most further curves. (a) The median shape is superimposed to the most further curve for normalised curves. (b) The median shape is superimposed to the most nearest curve for normalised curves. (c) The median shape is superimposed to the most further curve. (d) The median shape is superimposed to the most nearest curve.

Figure 6(a) shows the variational mean of the the boundary curves of lungs in Fig. 3. Figure 6(b) shows multi dimensional scaling (MDS) of the boundary curves using the distance matrix. This MDS implies that in 47 polygonal curves, there exist four outliers. Figures 6(c) and 6(d) show the normalised variational mean curve superimposed to the normalised median curve, and the variational mean curve is superimposed to the median curve. The measure H, T, and L_2 between the variational mean curve is superimposed to the median curve are

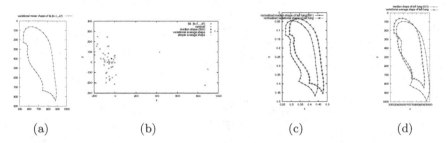

(a)   (b)   (c)   (d)

Fig. 6. Geometric property of the image boundary of lungs in Fig. 3III. (a) The variational mean of the boundary curves of lungs in Fig. 3. (b) Multi dimensional scaling of the boundary curves using the distance matrix. (c) The normalised variational mean curve is superimposed to the normalised median curve. (d) The variational mean curve is superimposed to the median curve. For the computation of variational mean curve, vertex-correspondences among curves are aligned using normalised curves.

$$H^{\text{median mean}} = 1.4696 \times 10^4,$$
$$L_2^{\text{median mean}} = 6.07715 \times 10^{-32},$$
$$S^{\text{median mean}} = -9.27359^{-5}.$$

For the computation of variational mean curve, vertex-correspondences among curves are aligned using normalised curves. These results show that variational mean is smoother than the median in the shape space.

6   Conclusions

Using the distance of the normal curves, we develop a method to compute mean shape of the normal curves. Furthermore, using the matching procedure of the normal curves, we also develop a method to compute the mean shape of planar polygonal curves.

For curves $\{c_i\}_i^n$, $c_i(s) = (c_{i1}(s), c_{i2}(s))^\top$, whose lengths are C_i assuming $c_i(s + C_i) = c_i(s)$ we can define the median as the minimiser of D_i for

$$D_i(\psi_{ji}, t_{ji}) = \sum_{j=1}^{n} \int_0^{C_i} |c_j(\psi_{ij}(s) - t_{ij}) - c_i(s)|^2 ds, \qquad (37)$$

were $\psi_{ij}(\tau)$ is a monotone function from the interval $[0, C_j]$ to the interval $[0, C_i]$. We are required to compute $n \times n$ functions ϕ_{ij} and $n \times n$ parameters t_{ij}, since the alignment based on eq. (3) is asymmetry. However, our method based on eq. (5) needs to compute n parameters for the computation of the median. Furthermore, for $c_j^*(s) = c_i(\psi_{ij}(s) - t_{ji})$, we can write the mean of curves as the minimiser of the criterion

$$J(\boldsymbol{c}, \phi_i, C) = \sum_i^n \Delta_i + \gamma \Gamma \qquad (38)$$

for

$$\Delta_i = \oint_C (|\boldsymbol{c}_i(\phi_i(s)) - \boldsymbol{c}(s)|^2 + \mu |\dot{\phi}_i(s)|^2) ds, \qquad (39)$$

$$\Gamma = \oint_C (\alpha |\dot{\boldsymbol{c}}(s)|^2 + \frac{1}{2} \beta |\ddot{\boldsymbol{c}}(s)|^2) ds, \qquad (40)$$

where Δ_i and Γ are the deformation energy between a curve and the average, and the energy of the boundary curve for deformation of the mean curve [18–21]. For the estimation of the length of the mean curve, we are required additional information. However, our method based on eq. (5) does not require to this estimation process [3].

Definitions of the mean and median of eqs. (1) and (2), respectively, are valid for shapes S_i $i = 1, 2, \cdots, n$ expressed as arrays of symbols, such as strings and graphs, if an appropriate distance measure is defined for symbols [4–6]. Semi-landmark description of shapes adopts combination of vectors and symbols. If shapes descriptor is a combination of vectors and symbols, we use the distance such that

$$d(S_i, S_j) = \alpha d_n(S_i, S_j) + (1 - \alpha) d_s(S_i, S_j), \ 0 \le \alpha \le 1, \qquad (41)$$

where $d_n(S_i, S_j)$ and $d_s(S_i, S_i)$ are the numeric and symbolic parts of the distance between pair of shapes S_i and S_j.

This research was supported by "Computational anatomy for computer-aided diagnosis and therapy: Frontiers of medical image sciences" funded by the Grant-in-Aid for Scientific Research on Innovative Areas, MEXT, Japan, the Grants-in-Aid for Scientific Research funded by Japan Society of the Promotion of Sciences and the Grant-in-Aid for Young Scientists (A), NEXT, Japan.

References

1. Hill, D.L.G., et al.: Medical image registration. Phys. Med. Biol. 46, R1–R45 (2001)
2. Fischer, B., Modersitzki, J.: Ill-posed medicine- an introduction to image registration. Inverse Problem 24, 1–17 (2008)

---

[3] If the length of the mean curve is pre-estimated, the circle integrals $\oint_C$ of eqs. (39) and (40) are converted to the interval integral $\int_0^C$, that is, we can have the equation

$$J_2(\boldsymbol{c}, \phi_i) = \sum_{i=1}^n \left\{ \int_0^C \left(|\boldsymbol{c}_i(\phi_i(s)) - \boldsymbol{c}(s)|^2 + \mu |\dot{\phi}_i(s)|^2 \right) ds \right\}$$

A possible estimation of the curve length C are $C = \sum_i^n C_i$ and the length of the median curve computed by eq. (37).

3. Rumpf, M., Wirth, B.: A nonlinear elastic shape averaging approach. SIAM Journal on Imaging Sciences 2, 800–833 (2009)

4. Sebastian, T.B., Klein, P.N., Kimia, B.B.: On aligning curves. IEEE Trans. PAMI 25, 116–125 (2003)

5. Baeza-Yates, R., Valiente, G.: An image similarity measure based on graph matching. In: Proc. 7th Int. Symp. String Processing and Information Retrieval, pp. 8–38 (2000)

6. Riesen, K., Bunke, H.: Approximate graph edit distance computation by mean s of bipartite graph matching. Image and Vision Computing 27, 950–959 (2009)

7. Mémoli, F.: Gromov-Hausdorff distances in Euclidean spaces. In: NORDIA-CVPR (2008)

8. Arrate, F., Tilak Ratnanather, J., Younes, L.: Diffeomorphic active contours. SIAM J. Imaging Sciences 3, 176–198 (2010)

9. Grigorescu, C., Petkov, N.: Distance sets for shape filters and shape recognition. IEEE Trans. IP 12, 1274–1286 (2003)

10. Tănase, M., Veltkamp, R.C., Haverkort, H.J.: Multiple Polyline to Polygon Matching. In: Deng, X., Du, D.-Z. (eds.) ISAAC 2005. LNCS, vol. 3827, pp. 60–70. Springer, Heidelberg (2005)

11. Arkin, E.M., Chew, L.P., Huttenlocher, D.P., Kedem, K., Mitchell, J.S.B.: An Efficiently Computable Metric for Comparing Polygonal Shapes. IEEE Trans. PAMI 13, 209–216 (1991)

12. Stegmann, M.B., Gomez, D.D.: A brief introduction to statistical shape analysis, Informatics and Mathematical Modelling, Technical University of Denmark (2002), http://www2.imm.dtu.dk/pubdb/p.php?403

13. Müller, M.: Information Retrieval for Music and Motion, ch. 4. Springer (2007)

14. Keogh, E.J., Pazzani, M.J.: Derivative dynamic time warping. In: First SIAM International Conference on Data Mining, SDM 2001 (2001), http://www.cs.ucr.edu/~eamonn/

15. Srivastava, A., Joshi, S., Mio, W., Liu, X.: Statistical shape analysis: Clustering, learning, and testing. IEEE Trans. PAMI 27, 590–602 (2005)

16. Sebastian, T.B., Klein, P.N., Kimia, B.B.: On aligning curves. PAMI 25, 116–125 (2003)

17. Marques, J.S., Abrantes, A.J.: Shape alignment? optimal initial point and pose estimation. Pattern Recognition Letters 18 (1997)

18. Kass, M., Witkin, A., Terzopoulos, D.: Snakes: Active contour models. IJCV 1, 321–331 (1988)

19. Sharon, E., Mumford, D.: 2D-shape analysis using conformal mapping. IJCV 70, 55–75 (2006)

20. Mumford, D., Shah, J.: Boundary detection by minimizing functionals. In: Proc. CVP 1985, pp. 22–26 (1985)

21. Mumford, D., Shah, J.: Optimal approximations by piecewise smooth functions and associated variational problems. Comm. on Pure and Applied Math. bXLII, 577–684 (1989)

3D Parallel Thinning Algorithms Based on Isthmuses

Gábor Németh and Kálmán Palágyi

Department of Image Processing and Computer Graphics,
University of Szeged, Hungary
{gnemeth,palagyi}@inf.u-szeged.hu

Abstract. Thinning is a widely used technique to obtain skeleton-like shape features (i.e., centerlines and medial surfaces) from digital binary objects. Conventional thinning algorithms preserve endpoints to provide important geometric information relative to the object to be represented. An alternative strategy is also proposed that preserves isthmuses (i.e., generalization of curve/surface interior points). In this paper we present ten 3D parallel isthmus-based thinning algorithm variants that are derived from some sufficient conditions for topology preserving reductions.

Keywords: Shape analysis, Feature extraction, Skeletons, Thinning algorithms, Topology preservation.

1 Introduction

A skeleton is a region-based shape descriptor which represents the general shape of objects. Skeleton-like shape features (i.e., centerlines and medial surfaces) extracted from volumetric binary images play an important role in various applications in image processing, pattern recognition, and visualization [25].

Parallel thinning algorithms use parallel reduction operations: some object points in a binary image that satisfy certain topological and geometric constraints are deleted simultaneously, and an iteration step is repeated until stability is achieved [6]. Thinning has a major advantage over the alternative 3D skeletonization methods: it can produce both skeleton-like shape features. Surface-thinning algorithms can extract medial surfaces and curve-thinning algorithms can produce centerlines. Medial surfaces are generally extracted from general shapes and 3D tubular structures can be represented by their centerlines.

Conventional 3D thinning algorithms preserve some points that provide relevant geometrical information with respect to the shape of the object. These points are called curve-endpoints or surface-endpoints. Bertrand and Couprie proposed an alternative strategy by accumulating some curve/surface interior points that are called isthmuses [4]. Characterizations of these isthmuses (for curve-thinning and surface-thinning) were defined first by Bertrand and Aktouf [3]. There are dozens of endpoint-based 3D thinning algorithms, but only five existing 3D algorithms use an isthmus-based thinning scheme [3,4,24].

J. Blanc-Talon et al. (Eds.): ACIVS 2012, LNCS 7517, pp. 325–335, 2012.

Topology preservation [7] is an essential requirement for skeletonization algorithms. In order to verify that a given parallel 3D thinning algorithm preserves the topology, some sufficient conditions for topology preservation have been proposed [9,21]. Verifying these conditions usually means checking several configurations of points. Some previous algorithms [10,11] claim to be topology preserving, but they made a mistake in the proof. That is why Palágyi et al. [23] proposed a safe technique for designing topologically correct parallel 3D thinning algorithms. It is based on some sufficient conditions for topology preservation that consider individual points (instead of point configurations). The alternative sufficient conditions were combined with various parallel thinning strategies and various endpoint characterizations [23]. In this paper we present ten new algorithm variants that are based on our sufficient conditions for topology preservation and the isthmus-preserving thinning approach. Five of the new algorithms are capable of producing centerlines, and the remaining five are surface-thinning algorithms.

This paper is organized as follows: Section 2 reviews the basic notions and results of 3D digital topology, and we present our sufficient conditions for topology preservation. In Section 3, we introduce the ten new parallel 3D isthmus-based thinning algorithms. Some illustrative results are presented in Section 4, and the new isthmus-based algorithms are compared with their corresponding variants that preserve endpoints. Finally, we round off the paper with some concluding remarks.

2   Basic Notions and Results

In this section, we outline some concepts of digital topology and related key results that will be used in the sequel.

Let p be a point in the 3D digital space $\mathbb{Z}^3$. Let us denote $N_j(p)$ (for $j = 6, 18, 26$) the set of points that are j-adjacent to point p and let $N_j^*(p) = N_j(p) \backslash \{p\}$ (see Fig. 1a).

The sequence of distinct points $\langle x_0, x_1, \ldots, x_n \rangle$ is called a j-path (for $j = 6, 18, 26$) of length n from point x_0 to point x_n in a non-empty set of points X if each point of the sequence is in X and x_i is j-adjacent to x_{i-1} for each $1 \leq i \leq n$. Note that a single point is a j-path of length 0. Two points are said to be j-connected in the set X if there is a j-path in X between them ($j = 6, 18, 26$). A set of points X is j-connected in the set of points $Y \supseteq X$ if any two points in X are j-connected in Y ($j = 6, 18, 26$).

A *3D binary* (26,6) *digital picture* $\mathcal{P}$ is a quadruple $\mathcal{P} = (\mathbb{Z}^3, 26, 6, B)$ [8]. Each element of $\mathbb{Z}^3$ is called a *point* of $\mathcal{P}$. Each point in $B \subseteq \mathbb{Z}^3$ is called a *black point* and has a value of 1 assigned to it. Each point in $\mathbb{Z}^3 \backslash B$ is called a *white point* and has a value of 0 assigned to it. An *object* is a maximal 26-connected set of black points, while a *white component* is a maximal 6-connected set of white points. In a finite picture there is a unique infinite white component, which is called the *background*. A finite white component is called a *cavity*.

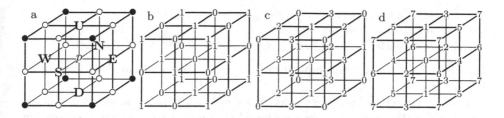

Fig. 1. Frequently used adjacencies in $\mathbb{Z}^3$. The set $N_6(p)$ contains point p and the six points marked **U**, **D**, **N**, **E**, **S**, and **W**. The set $N_{18}(p)$ contains $N_6(p)$ and the twelve points marked by "○". The set $N_{26}(p)$ contains $N_{18}(p)$ and the eight points marked by "●".

The usual divisions of $\mathbb{Z}^3$ into 2 (b), 4 (c), and 8 (d) subfields. If partitioning into k subfields is considered, then points marked "i" are in the subfield $SF_k(i)$ ($k = 2, 4, 8$, $i = 0, 1, \ldots, k - 1$).

A black point is called a *border point* in $(26, 6)$ pictures if it is 6-adjacent to at least one white point. A border point is called a **U**-*border point* if the point marked **U** in Fig. 1a is a white point. We can define **D**-, **N**-, **E**-, **S**-, and **W**-border points in the same way. A black point is called an *isolated point* if it is not 26-adjacent to any other black point.

The *lexicographical order relation* "$\prec$" between two distinct points $p = (p_x, p_y, p_z)$ and $q = (q_x, q_y, q_z)$ in $\mathbb{Z}^3$ is defined as follows:

$$p \prec q \quad \Leftrightarrow \quad (p_z < q_z) \vee (p_z = q_z \wedge p_y < q_y) \vee (p_z = q_z \wedge p_y = q_y \wedge p_x < q_x).$$

Let $X \subseteq \mathbb{Z}^3$ be a set of points. Point $p \in X$ is the *smallest element* of X if for any $q \in X \backslash \{p\}$, $p \prec q$.

A *unit lattice square* is a set of four mutually 18-adjacent points in $\mathbb{Z}^3$, while a *unit lattice cube* is a set of eight mutually 26-adjacent points in $\mathbb{Z}^3$. An object is called a *small object* if it is contained in a unit lattice cube, but it is not contained in a unit lattice square.

A *reduction operation* transforms a binary picture only by changing some black points to white ones (which is referred to as the deletion of black points). A reduction operation does *not* preserve topology [7] if any object in the input picture is split (into several ones) or is completely deleted, any cavity in the input picture is merged with the background or another cavity, or a cavity is created where there was none in the input picture. There is an additional concept called *hole* (which doughnuts have) in 3D pictures [8]. Topology preservation implies that eliminating or creating any hole is not allowed.

A black point is *simple* in a $(26, 6)$ picture if and only if its deletion is a topology preserving reduction operation [8]. A useful characterization of simple points on $(26, 6)$ pictures is stated as follows:

Theorem 1. [14] *A black point p is simple in picture $(\mathbb{Z}^3, 26, 6, B)$ if and only if all of the following conditions hold:*

1. *The set $N_{26}^*(p) \cap B$ contains exactly one 26–component.*
2. *The set $N_6(p) \setminus B$ is not empty.*
3. *Any two points in $N_6(p) \setminus B$ are 6–connected in the set $N_{18}(p) \setminus B$.*

Based on Theorem 1, the simplicity of a point p can be decided by examining the set $N_{26}(p)$.

Parallel reduction operations delete a set of black points and not just a single simple point. Hence we need to consider what is meant by topology preservation when a number of black points are deleted simultaneously. Palágyi et al. gave some sufficient conditions for topology preservation as a basis for designing 3D parallel thinning algorithms [23].

Theorem 2. [23] *The parallel reduction operation $\mathcal{T}$ is topology preserving for $(26, 6)$ pictures if all of the following conditions hold for any black point p in any picture $(\mathbb{Z}^3, 26, 6, B)$ such that p is deleted by $\mathcal{T}$.*

1. *Let $Q \subseteq B$ be any set of simple points in $(\mathbb{Z}^3, 26, 6, B)$ such that p is the smallest element of Q, and Q is contained in a unit lattice square. Then point p is simple in picture $(\mathbb{Z}^3, 26, 6, B \setminus (Q \setminus \{p\}))$.*
2. *Point p is not the smallest element of any small object.*

In this paper we present ten parallel thinning algorithms that are based on the sufficient conditions of Theorem 2 combined with parallel thinning strategies and isthmus preservation. Our algorithms use the following characterizations of isthmuses.

Definition 1. *A border point p in a picture $(\mathbb{Z}^3, 26, 6, B)$ is an $\mathcal{I}_C$-isthmus (for curve-thinning) if the set $N_{26}^*(p) \cap B$ contains more than one 26–component (i.e., Condition 1 of Theorem 1 is violated).*

Definition 2. *A border point p in a picture $(\mathbb{Z}^3, 26, 6, B)$ is an $\mathcal{I}_S$-isthmus (for surface-thinning) if p is not a simple point (i.e., Condition 1 of Theorem 1 or Condition 3 of Theorem 1 is violated).*

We can state that no isthmus point is simple. Note that these two characterizations correspond to the isthmuses proposed by Bertrand and Aktouf [3], with the exception that isolated (non-simple) points, which are not isthmuses by the terminology used in [3], are $\mathcal{I}_S$-isthmuses by Definition 2. Raynal and Couprie [24] used $\mathcal{I}_C$-isthmuses in their curve-thinning algorithm, but they consider an additional type of isthmuses: a border point is an isthmus in their surface-thinning algorithm if Condition 3 of Theorem 1 is violated. We want to produce medial surfaces that contain curves (i.e., 1D patches) for tubular parts. Hence we consider that each $\mathcal{I}_C$-isthmus point is an $\mathcal{I}_S$-isthmus, too.

3   Isthmus-Based Parallel 3D Thinning Algorithms

In this section, ten isthmus-based parallel 3D thinning algorithm variants are presented. These algorithms are composed of topology preserving parallel reduction operations, hence all algorithms are topologically correct.

3.1 Fully Parallel Algorithms

In fully parallel [6] algorithms, the same parallel reduction operation is applied in each iteration step [1,10,11,15,19,22,23].

The scheme of the proposed two isthmus-based fully parallel thinning algorithms 3D-FP-$\mathcal{I}_C$ and 3D-FP-$\mathcal{I}_S$ are sketched in Algorithm 1.

Algorithm 1. Algorithm 3D-FP-$\mathcal{I}$ ($\mathcal{I} \in \{\mathcal{I}_C, \mathcal{I}_S\}$)

1: *Input*: picture $(\mathbb{Z}^3, 26, 6, X)$
2: *Output*: picture $(\mathbb{Z}^3, 26, 6, Y)$
3: $Y = X$
4: $I = \emptyset$
5: **repeat**
6:     // *one iteration step*
7:     $I = I \cup \{\, p \mid p \in Y \setminus I$ and p is an $\mathcal{I}$-isthmus $\}$
8:     $D = \{\, p \mid p \in Y \setminus I$ and p is *3D-FP-deletable* in $Y\}$
9:     $Y = Y \setminus D$
10: **until** $D = \emptyset$

3D-FP-deletable points are defined as follows:

Definition 3. *A black point is 3D-FP-deletable if all conditions of Theorem 2 hold.*

Deletable points of the proposed fully parallel algorithms (see Definition 3) are derived directly from conditions of Theorem 2. Hence, both algorithms 3D-FP-$\mathcal{I}_C$ and 3D-FP-$\mathcal{I}_S$ are topology preserving.

3.2 Subiteration-Based Algorithms

In subiteration-based (or frequently referred to as directional) thinning algorithms, an iteration step is decomposed into k successive parallel reduction operations according to k deletion directions [6]. If the current deletion direction is d, then a set of d-border points can be deleted by the parallel reduction operation assigned to it. Since there are six kinds of major directions in 3D cases, 6-subiteration algorithms were generally proposed [2,5,18,20,23,24,26,27].

In what follows, we present two parallel 3D 6-subiteration thinning algorithms 3D-6-SI-$\mathcal{I}_C$ and 3D-6-SI-$\mathcal{I}_S$. These isthmus-based algorithms are described by Algorithm 2.

The ordered list of deletion directions $\langle \mathbf{U}, \mathbf{D}, \mathbf{N}, \mathbf{E}, \mathbf{S}, \mathbf{W} \rangle$ [5,20] is considered in the proposed algorithms 3D-6-SI-$\mathcal{I}_C$ and 3D-6-SI-$\mathcal{I}_S$. Note that subiteration-based thinning algorithms are not invariant under the order of deletion directions (i.e., choosing different orders may yield various results).

In the first subiteration, the set of *3D-6-SI-$\mathbf{U}$-deletable* points are deleted simultaneously, and the set of *3D-6-SI-$\mathbf{W}$-deletable* points are deleted in the last (i.e., the 6th) subiteration. Now we define *3D-6-SI-$\mathbf{U}$-deletable* points.

Algorithm 2. Algorithm 3D-6-SI-$\mathcal{I}$ ($\mathcal{I} \in \{\mathcal{I}_C, \mathcal{I}_S\}$)

1: *Input*: picture $(\mathbb{Z}^3, 26, 6, X)$
2: *Output*: picture $(\mathbb{Z}^3, 26, 6, Y)$
3: $Y = X$
4: $I = \emptyset$
5: **repeat**
6:    // *one iteration step*
7:    **for** each $d \in \{\mathbf{U}, \mathbf{D}, \mathbf{N}, \mathbf{E}, \mathbf{S}, \mathbf{W}\}$ **do**
8:       // *subiteration for deleting some d-border points*
9:       $I = I \cup \{ p \mid p \in Y \setminus I$ and p is an $\mathcal{I}$-isthmus $\}$
10:      $D(d) = \{ p \mid p \in Y \setminus I$ and p is *3D-6-SI-d-deletable* in $Y\}$
11:      $Y = Y \setminus D(d)$
12:   **end for**
13: **until** $D(\mathbf{U}) \cup D(\mathbf{D}) \cup D(\mathbf{N}) \cup D(\mathbf{E}) \cup D(\mathbf{S}) \cup D(\mathbf{W}) = \emptyset$

Definition 4. *A black point is 3D-6-SI-$\mathbf{U}$-deletable if it is a $\mathbf{U}$-border point, and all conditions of Theorem 2 hold.*

It can be readily seen that both subiteration-based algorithms 3D-6-SI-$\mathcal{I}_C$ and 3D-6-SI-$\mathcal{I}_S$ are topology preserving. Note that conditions of Theorem 2 can be simplified if d-border points ($d \in \{\mathbf{U}, \mathbf{D}, \mathbf{N}, \mathbf{E}, \mathbf{S}, \mathbf{W}\}$) are taken into consideration as potential deletable points [23].

3.3   Subfield-Based Algorithms

The third kind of parallel thinning algorithm applies a subfield-based technique [6]. In existing subfield-based parallel 3D thinning algorithms, the digital space $\mathbb{Z}^3$ is partitioned into two [12,16,23], four [13,17,23], and eight [3,17,23] subfields which are alternatively activated. At a given iteration step of a k-subfield algorithm, k successive parallel reduction operations associated with the k subfields are performed. In each of them, some border points in the active subfield can be designated for deletion.

Let us denote $SF_k(i)$ the i-th subfield if $\mathbb{Z}^3$ is partitioned into k subfields ($k = 2, 4, 8$; $i = 0, \ldots, k-1$). The considered divisions are illustrated in Fig. 1b-d.

In order to reduce the noise sensitivity and the count of skeletal points, Németh et al. introduced a new subfield-based thinning scheme [16]. The iteration level border detection strategy takes the border points into consideration at the beginning of iteration steps as potential deletable points within the entire iteration.

Next, we present our six new parallel 3D subfield-based thinning algorithms. The scheme of the subfield-based parallel thinning algorithm 3D-k-SF-$\mathcal{I}$ ($k = 2, 4, 8$; $\mathcal{I} \in \{\mathcal{I}_C, \mathcal{I}_S\}$) with iteration-level checking is sketched in Algorithm 3.

The 3D-k-SF-i-deletable points are defined as follows ($k = 2, 4, 8$; $i = 0, \ldots, k-1$):

Algorithm 3. Algorithm 3D-k-SF-$\mathcal{I}$ ($k = 2, 4, 8$; $\mathcal{I} \in \{\mathcal{I}_C, \mathcal{I}_S\}$)

1: *Input*: picture $(\mathbb{Z}^3, 26, 6, X)$
2: *Output*: picture $(\mathbb{Z}^3, 26, 6, Y)$
3: $Y = X$
4: $I = \emptyset$
5: **repeat**
6:     // *one iteration step*
7:     $E = \{\, p \mid p$ is a border point in $Y \,\}$
8:     $I = I \cup \{\, p \mid p \in E$ and p is an $\mathcal{I}$-isthmus $\}$
9:     **for** $i = 0$ **to** $k - 1$ **do**
10:         // *subfield* $SF_k(i)$ *is activated*
11:         $D(i) = \{\, q \mid q \in E \setminus I$ and is *3D-k-SF-i-deletable* in $Y \,\}$
12:         $Y = Y \setminus D(i)$
13:     **end for**
14: **until** $D(0) \cup D(1) \cup \ldots \cup D(k - 1) = \emptyset$

Definition 5. *A black point p is 3D-k-SF-i-deletable if $p \in SF_k(i)$ and all conditions of Theorem 2 hold.*

It is easy to see that all of the six subfield-based algorithms 3D-k-SF-$\mathcal{I}$ ($k = 2, 4, 8; \mathcal{I} \in \{\mathcal{I}_C, \mathcal{I}_S\}$) are topology preserving. Note that conditions of Theorem 2 can be simplified if elements of a subfield are considered as potential delatable points [23].

4   Results

In experiments the proposed algorithms were tested on objects of various images. Due to the lack of space, here we present two illustrative examples below (see Figs. 2-3). The new algorithms were compared with the corresponding endpoint-preserving 3D parallel thinning algorithms presented in [23]. We can state that the isthmus-based algorithms produce fewer unwanted side branches or surface patches than the thinning algorithms that preserve curve-endpoints of type **CE** or surface-endpoints of type **SE** [23]. Figure 2 presents ten kinds of centerlines produced by the five new isthmus-based curve-thinning algorithms (3D-FP-$\mathcal{I}_C$, 3D-6-SI-$\mathcal{I}_C$, 3D-2-SF-$\mathcal{I}_C$, 3D-4-SF-$\mathcal{I}_C$, and 3D-8-SF-$\mathcal{I}_C$) and the corresponding five algorithms (3D-FP-**CE**, 3D-6-SI-**CE**, 3D-2-SF-**CE**, 3D-4-SF-**CE**, and 3D-8-SF-**CE**) that use curve-endpoints as geometrical constraint [23]. Ten kinds of medial surfaces are presented in Fig. 3: five of them are produced by the proposed isthmus-based surface-thinning algorithms (3D-FP-$\mathcal{I}_S$, 3D-6-SI-$\mathcal{I}_S$, 3D-2-SF-$\mathcal{I}_S$, 3D-4-SF-$\mathcal{I}_S$, and 3D-8-SF-$\mathcal{I}_S$), and these medial surfaces can be compared with the results of the five endpoint-preserving surface thinning algorithms (3D-FP-**SE**, 3D-6-SI-**SE**, 3D-2-SF-**SE**, 3D-4-SF-**SE**, and 3D-8-SF-**SE**) [23].

Note that the reported algorithms are not time consuming and it is easy to implement them on conventional sequential computers by adapting the efficient implementation method presented in [22]. Centerlines and medial surfaces can be extracted from large 3D shapes within one second on a usual PC.

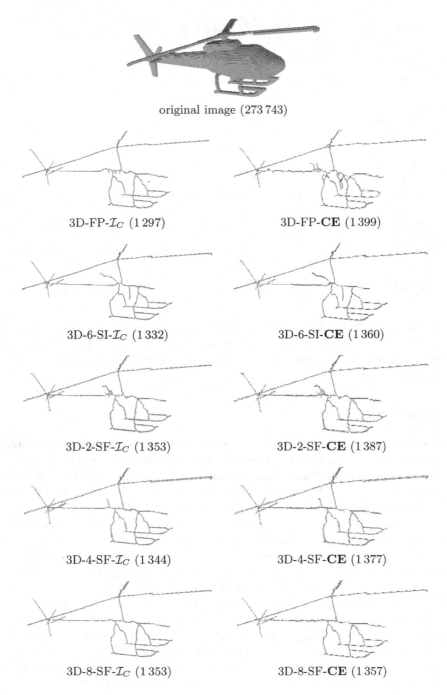

original image (273 743)

3D-FP-$\mathcal{I}_C$ (1 297)   3D-FP-**CE** (1 399)

3D-6-SI-$\mathcal{I}_C$ (1 332)   3D-6-SI-**CE** (1 360)

3D-2-SF-$\mathcal{I}_C$ (1 353)   3D-2-SF-**CE** (1 387)

3D-4-SF-$\mathcal{I}_C$ (1 344)   3D-4-SF-**CE** (1 377)

3D-8-SF-$\mathcal{I}_C$ (1 353)   3D-8-SF-**CE** (1 357)

Fig. 2. A $102 \times 381 \times 255$ image of a helicopter and its centerlines produced by the five new isthmus-based curve-thinning algorithms (left column) and the centerlines produced by the five existing endpoint-based curve-thinning algorithms (right column). (Numbers in parentheses mean the count of black points.)

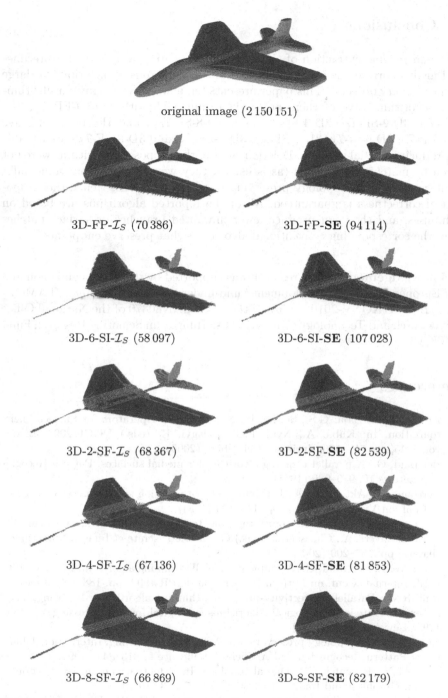

original image (2 150 151)

3D-FP-$\mathcal{I}_S$ (70 386)   3D-FP-**SE** (94 114)

3D-6-SI-$\mathcal{I}_S$ (58 097)   3D-6-SI-**SE** (107 028)

3D-2-SF-$\mathcal{I}_S$ (68 367)   3D-2-SF-**SE** (82 539)

3D-4-SF-$\mathcal{I}_S$ (67 136)   3D-4-SF-**SE** (81 853)

3D-8-SF-$\mathcal{I}_S$ (66 869)   3D-8-SF-**SE** (82 179)

Fig. 3. A $515 \times 455 \times 110$ image of an airplane and its medial surfaces produced by the five new isthmus-based surface-thinning algorithms (left column) and the medial surfaces produced by the five existing endpoint-based surface-thinning algorithms (right column). (Numbers in parentheses mean the count of black points.)

5   Conclusions

Fast and reliable extraction of skeleton-like 3D shape features (i.e., centerlines and medial surfaces) is extremely important in numerous applications for large shapes (binary objects). This paper presents ten new variations for parallel thinning algorithms: five of them are curve-thinning algorithms (3D-FP-$\mathcal{I}_C$, 3D-6-SI-$\mathcal{I}_C$, 3D-2-SF-$\mathcal{I}_C$, 3D-4-SF-$\mathcal{I}_C$, and 3D-8-SF-$\mathcal{I}_C$), and the remaining five (3D-FP-$\mathcal{I}_S$, 3D-6-SI-$\mathcal{I}_S$, 3D-2-SF-$\mathcal{I}_S$, 3D-4-SF-$\mathcal{I}_S$, and 3D-8-SF-$\mathcal{I}_S$) are capable of producing medial surfaces. Deletion rules of the proposed algorithms were not given by matching templates (as is usual), they were derived from some sufficient conditions for topology preserving parallel reductions. Hence their topological correctness is guaranteed. All of the reported algorithms are based on isthmuses, and they can produce fewer unwanted branches or surface patches than the corresponding conventional algorithms that preserve endpoints.

Acknowledgements. This research was supported by the European Union and the European Regional Development Fund under the grant agreement TÁMOP-4.2.1/B-09/1/KONV-2010-0005, and the grant CNK80370 of the National Office for Research and Technology (NKTH) & the Hungarian Scientific Research Fund (OTKA).

References

1. Arcelli, C., di Baja, G.S., Serino, L.: New Removal Operators for Surface Skeletonization. In: Kuba, A., Nyúl, L.G., Palágyi, K. (eds.) DGCI 2006. LNCS, vol. 4245, pp. 555–566. Springer, Heidelberg (2006)
2. Bertrand, G.: A parallel thinning algorithm for medial surfaces. Pattern Recognition Letters 16, 979–986 (1995)
3. Bertrand, G., Aktouf, Z.: A 3D thinning algorithm using subfields. In: SPIE Proc. of Conf. on Vision Geometry, pp. 113–124 (1994)
4. Bertrand, G., Couprie, M.: Transformations topologiques discrètes. In: Coeurjolly, D., Montanvert, A., Chassery, J. (eds.) Géométrie Discrète et Images Numériques, Hermès, pp. 187–209 (2007)
5. Gong, W.X., Bertrand, G.: A simple parallel 3D thinning algorithm. In: Proc. 10th IEEE Internat. Conf. on Pattern Recognition, ICPR 1990, pp. 188–190 (1990)
6. Hall, R.W.: Parallel connectivity-preserving thinning algorithms. In: Kong, T.Y., Rosenfeld, A. (eds.) Topological Algorithms for Digital Image Processing, pp. 145–179. Elsevier Science (1996)
7. Kong, T.Y.: On topology preservation in 2–d and 3–d thinning. International Journal of Pattern Recognition and Artificial Intelligence 9, 813–844 (1995)
8. Kong, T.Y., Rosenfeld, A.: Digital topology: Introduction and survey. Computer Vision, Graphics, and Image Processing 48, 357–393 (1989)
9. Ma, C.M.: On topology preservation in 3D thinning. CVGIP: Image Understanding 59, 328–339 (1994)
10. Ma, C.M.: A 3D fully parallel thinning algorithm for generating medial faces. Pattern Recognition Letters 16, 83–87 (1995)

11. Ma, C.M., Sonka, M.: A fully parallel 3D thinning algorithm and its applications. Computer Vision and Image Understanding 64, 420–433 (1996)
12. Ma, C.M., Wan, S.Y., Chang, H.K.: Extracting medial curves on 3D images. Pattern Recognition Letters 23, 895–904 (2002)
13. Ma, C.M., Wan, S.Y., Lee, J.D.: Three-dimensional topology preserving reduction on the 4-subfields. IEEE Transaction on Pattern Analysis and Machine Intelligence 24, 1594–1605 (2002)
14. Malandain, G., Bertrand, G.: Fast characterization of 3D simple points. In: Proc. 11th IEEE Internat. Conf. on Pattern Recognition, ICPR 1992, pp. 232–235 (1992)
15. Manzanera, A., Bernard, T.M., Prêteux, F., Longuet, B.: Medial faces from a concuise 3D thinning algorithm. In: Proc. 7th IEEE Int. Conf. on Computer Vision, pp. 337–343 (1999)
16. Németh, G., Kardos, P., Palágyi, K.: Topology preserving 2-subfield 3D thinning algorithms. In: Proc. 7th IASTED Int. Conf. Signal Processing, Pattern Recognition and Applications, pp. 310–316 (2009)
17. Németh, G., Kardos, P., Palágyi, K.: Topology Preserving 3D Thinning Algorithms Using Four and Eight Subfields. In: Campilho, A., Kamel, M. (eds.) ICIAR 2010. LNCS, vol. 6111, pp. 316–325. Springer, Heidelberg (2010)
18. Németh, G., Kardos, P., Palágyi, K.: A Family of Topology-Preserving 3D Parallel 6–Subiteration Thinning Algorithms. In: Aggarwal, J.K., Barneva, R.P., Brimkov, V.E., Koroutchev, K.N., Korutcheva, E.R. (eds.) IWCIA 2011. LNCS, vol. 6636, pp. 17–30. Springer, Heidelberg (2011)
19. Palágyi, K.: A 3D fully parallel surface-thinning algorithm. Theoretical Computer Science 406, 119–135 (2008)
20. Palágyi, K., Kuba, A.: A 3D 6–subiteration thinning algorithm for extracting medial lines. Pattern Recognition Letters 19, 613–627 (1998)
21. Palágyi, K., Kuba, A.: A parallel 3D 12-subiteration thinning algorithm. Graphical Models and Image Processing 61, 199–221 (1999)
22. Palágyi, K., Németh, G.: Fully Parallel 3D Thinning Algorithms Based on Sufficient Conditions for Topology Preservation. In: Brlek, S., Reutenauer, C., Provençal, X. (eds.) DGCI 2009. LNCS, vol. 5810, pp. 481–492. Springer, Heidelberg (2009)
23. Palágyi, K., Németh, G., Kardos, P.: Topology preserving parallel 3D thinning algorithms. In: Barneva, R., Brimkov, V. (eds.) Digital Geometry Algorithms. Theoretical Foundations and Applications to Computational Imaging, pp. 165–188. Springer (2012)
24. Raynal, B., Couprie, M.: Isthmus-based 6-directional parallel thinning algorithms. In: Domenjoud, E. (ed.) DGCI 2011. LNCS, vol. 6607, pp. 175–186. Springer, Heidelberg (2011)
25. Siddiqi, K., Pizer, S. (eds.): Medial representations – Mathematics, algorithms and applications. Computational Imaging and Vision, vol. 37. Springer, New York (2008)
26. Tsao, Y.F., Fu, K.S.: A parallel thinning algorithm for 3–D pictures. Computer Graphics and Image Processing 17, 315–331 (1981)
27. Xie, W., Thompson, R.P., Perucchio, R.: A topology-preserving parallel 3D thinning algorithm for extracting the curve skeleton. Pattern Recognition 36, 1529–1544 (2003)

Approximate Regularization for Structural Optical Flow Estimation

Aless Lasaruk

FORWISS, Universität Passau, 94030 Passau, Germany
lasaruk@uni-passau.de

Abstract. We address the problem of maximum a posteriori (MAP) estimation of optical flow with a geometric prior from gray-value images. We estimate simultaneously the optical flow and the corresponding surface – the structural optical flow (SOF) – subject to three types of constraints: intensity constancy, geometric, and smoothness constraints. Our smoothness constraints restrict the unknowns to locally coincide with a set of finitely parameterized admissible functions. The geometric constraints locally enforce consistency between the optical flow and the corresponding surface. Our theory amounts to a discrete generalization of regularization defined in terms of partial derivatives. The point-wise regularizers are efficiently implemented with linear run-time complexity in the number of discretization points. We demonstrate the applicability of our method by example computations of SOF from photographs of human faces.

Keywords: Optical flow, Approximation theory, Bayesian model.

1 Introduction

Precise estimation of optical flow and the corresponding rigid scene geometry is one of the most challenging problems in image processing [1, 2]. It is also an important benchmark problem for comparison of different algorithmic paradigms including variational [3–6], pure differential [7], and statistical [8, 9] methods. In this paper we address the problem of simultaneous maximum a posteriori (MAP) estimation of optical flow and the corresponding surface from the viewpoint of a reference camera given a pair of gray-value images. Our practical application is high-precision three-dimensional printing of human faces (see Figure 2) reconstructed from a small number of photographs. This requires a precise geometric and statistical model of the problem in contrast to the related work, which mainly focuses on computational efficiency.

Let $\Omega = [0, w] \times [0, h] \subseteq \mathbb{R}^2$ for $w, h \in \mathbb{N}$ be our *image domain*. *Optical flow* is an image deformation $f : \Omega \to \mathbb{R}^2 \cup \{\infty\}$, which maps a pixel $\mathbf{x} \in \Omega$ in one photographic image $I : \Omega \to \mathbb{R}$ to its corresponding pixel $f(\mathbf{x})$ (if such exists) in the other image $I' : \Omega \to \mathbb{R}$ taken from a different perspective. We speak of *structural optical flow* (SOF) if the notion of correspondency is defined in terms of two cameras $K, K' : \mathbb{R}^3 \to \mathbb{R}^2 \cup \{\infty\}$ corresponding to I and I'

J. Blanc-Talon et al. (Eds.): ACIVS 2012, LNCS 7517, pp. 336–348, 2012.

respectively and a three-dimensional surface $d : \Omega \to \mathbb{R}^3$, which are connected by the *triangulation constraint*

$$f(K(d(\mathbf{x}))) = K'(d(\mathbf{x})). \tag{1}$$

To summarize the above, a SOF instance comprises two cameras K and K', an optical flow f, and the corresponding surface d, which satisfy Equation (1). In particular, this definition implies the rigidity of the observed scene.

State of the art approaches model the problem of optical flow estimation as a minimization of an energy function with respect to the unknown f [3, 4, 9]. Most of the methods essentially impose two types of constraints: intensity constancy and regularization constraints. *Intensity constancy* observation constraints typically have the form $l(I)(\mathbf{x}) = l(I')(f(\mathbf{x}))$ for some $\mathbb{R}^m$-valued linear form l. Such constraints are in general only necessary for (structural) optical flow even under idealized conditions, so an additional *regularization constraint* is introduced to resolve ill-posedness. The continuous nature of the problem seems to prescribe the calculus of variations with a regularizer of the form $\nabla^k f(\mathbf{x}) = 0$, where ∇^k is a derivative operator for a $k \in \mathbb{N}$ [3, 4]. However, this approach has several drawbacks. Already in [3] the authors discuss a lack of geometric consistency of the gradient-based regularization. The above regularization constraint favors polynomial functions, while the optical flow is a fractional function even under simplified assumptions of a pinhole camera viewing a plane in space [2]. Last decades have brought a variety of variational solutions to the above problem, which essentially vary the observation constraints [5, 10] based on the ideas of Lucas and Kanade [7] or change the metric for regularization [6]. In parallel, the statistically motivated idea of working with "the most accurate" estimates rapidly becomes popular in the vision community [8, 11, 12]. A major discomfort of the variational framework arises when trying to add statistical considerations to the problem. To our knowledge, practical realizations of statistical optical flow estimation appear merely in the discrete context [8, 9, 13]. In most of the above approaches the presence of a regularizer amounts to a smoothing process which does not increase the accuracy of the optical flow [8]. Finally, most of the successors [4, 5, 10] to [3] solve a discretized version of Euler-Lagrange equations derived from the variational energy in practice.

The above observations motivate us to consider SOF estimation as a MAP problem in the discrete Bayesian setting. We choose the intensity constraints proposed in [4]. To involve geometric information inherent to the definition of SOF we enrich our model by the triangulation constraint, thus, introducing the surface d as an additional unknown. This general idea of correspondence correction in parallel to triangulation is classified as the *gold standard principle* of reconstruction [2]. In order to overcome the problems sketched above, we propose a systematic approach to obtain a set of common geometric regularization constraints for the optical flow and the corresponding surface. We start with a set of purely problem-motivated assumptions about d formalized as a set of locally admissible functions. From this we obtain a corresponding set of locally admissible functions for the optical flow f. The triangulation constraint, as it does not depend on the gray-value observations, works as an additional regularizer. It penalizes unlikely admissible functions with regard to the observed surface. Our approach yields an iterated MAP procedure, which simultaneously estimates the optical flow and the corresponding surface. In view of the fractional form of the constraints, our approach might at a first glance appear infeasible in practice. In this paper we present efficient approximate solutions for the arising questions.

The original contributions of the paper are the following. We formalize the problem of SOF estimation as a non-linear MAP problem involving approximation during regularization. This result is an application of approximation [14] and statistical perturbation theory [8, 9, 15]. We discuss a series of approximations of our model in order to obtain a computationally efficient algorithm. Our theory amounts to an iterative method, which reduces the latter infeasible problem to a sequence of approximately linear problems with Gaussian priors. Our regularizers have a point-wise optimal computational complexity of a local filter.

The outline of the paper is as follows. Section 2 discusses an example setup of an optical system, a surface model, and the corresponding SOF model. In Section 3 we formalize our observations introduced by example in a general setting and derive a Bayesian model of SOF. In Section 4 we apply approximation theory to derive a simplified approximate parameterization of SOF. Section 5 discusses computational details of an algorithm to solve our problem. Section 6 then experimentally compares the results with and without the proposed method. Section 7 summarizes our work and points to future development.

2   Example of an Optical System and Geometric Constraints

As sketched in the introduction, a model of SOF goes hand in hand with a model of the optical system and the geometry of the visible surface. Prior to discussing our theory in general terms, we give one complete example of our model. We start by defining the cameras, which are assumed to be precisely calibrated. We restrict for simplicity to finite pinhole cameras without distortions. Formally, the reference camera $K : \mathbb{R}^3 \to \mathbb{R}^2 \cup \{\infty\}$ is defined for each $\mathbf{p} \in \mathbb{R}^3$ as

$$K(\mathbf{p}) = \pi(\mathbf{P}\mathbf{R}(\mathbf{p} - \mathbf{c})) \tag{2}$$

with an upper-diagonal regular $\mathbf{P} \in \mathbb{R}^{3\times3}$, an orthogonal $\mathbf{R} \in \mathbb{R}^{3\times3}$, and a $\mathbf{c} \in \mathbb{R}^3$. Here, we denote by $\pi : \mathbb{R}^3 \to \mathbb{R}^2 \cup \{\infty\}$ the perspective projection $\pi(x, y, z) = (x/z, y/z)$ for $z \neq 0$ and $\pi(x, y, z) = \infty$ otherwise. Our K projects entire rays through its *camera center* $\mathbf{c}$ and a fixed pixel $\mathbf{x} \in \Omega$ to $\mathbf{x}$. For each $z \in \mathbb{R} \setminus \{0\}$ we have

$$K(K^{-1}(z, \mathbf{x})) = \mathbf{x}, \tag{3}$$

where $K^{-1}(z, \mathbf{x}) = z\mathbf{R}^t\mathbf{P}^{-1}(\mathbf{x}, 1)^t + \mathbf{c}$. Intuitively, $\mathbf{R}^t\mathbf{P}^{-1}(\mathbf{x}, 1)^t$ is the point in the $\{z = 1\}$-plane in the local coordinates of K corresponding to $\mathbf{x}$. Without loss of generality we assume that K is fixed in the origin. In other words, $\mathbf{R} = \mathbf{I}_3$

is the 3×3-identity matrix, and $\mathbf{c} = 0$. For K' we assume the same *intrinsic parameters* $\mathbf{P}$ but a different pose $\mathbf{R}' \in \mathbb{R}^{3\times3}$ and $\mathbf{c}' \in \mathbb{R}^3$. In other words, $K'(\mathbf{p}) = \pi(\mathbf{PR}'(\mathbf{p} - \mathbf{c}'))$.

We consider a parameterization of d tied to K by imposing the constraint $K(d(\mathbf{x})) = \mathbf{x}$ for all $\mathbf{x} \in \Omega$. According to Equation (3) we consider the function $z : \Omega \to \mathbb{R}$, which for an $\mathbf{x} \in \Omega$ and a surface point $\mathbf{p} = d(\mathbf{x})$ satisfies

$$d(\mathbf{x}) = K^{-1}(z(\mathbf{x}), \mathbf{x}) = \mathbf{p}. \tag{4}$$

Then z returns the z-depth of the corresponding space point $\mathbf{p}$ with respect to the local coordinate system of K. Following [16] we call z a *range image* of d.

Suppose that for some fixed $\mathbf{x}^* \in \Omega$ our surface d is parallel to the image plane of K around $d(\mathbf{x}^*)$. The above assumption is purely problem-motivated in the sense that it origins from the assumed geometry of the viewed objects. Consequently, there exists a neighborhood $U(\mathbf{x}^*) \subseteq \Omega$ of $\mathbf{x}^*$ such that we have $z(\mathbf{x}) = \alpha \in \mathbb{R}$ for all $\mathbf{x} \in U(\mathbf{x}^*)$. Formally, we have introduced a set of admissible functions $\mathcal{L}$ describing the local form of d in $U(\mathbf{x}^*)$ with

$$\mathcal{L} = \{z : U(\mathbf{x}^*) \to \mathbb{R} \mid z(\mathbf{x}) = \alpha, \alpha \in \mathbb{R}\}. \tag{5}$$

We view $\mathcal{L} = \mathcal{L}(b_z)$ as a one-dimensional linear subspace of functions $z : \Omega \to \mathbb{R}$ spanned by the basis $b_z = (\mathbb{1})$, where $\mathbb{1} : \Omega \to \mathbb{R}$ is the constant "one"-function. Clearly, an interpretation of $\mathcal{L}(b_z)$ does only make sense over $U(\mathbf{x}^*)$.

After $\mathcal{L}(b_z)$ is fixed as a set of admissible functions for the range image z of d, the triangulation constraint defines the corresponding admissible functions for the optical flow in $U(\mathbf{x}^*)$. An explicit form of the triangulation constraint is obtained by substitution of our assumptions, the definition of K', and the depth parameterization in Equation (4) into Equation (1) as

$$f(\mathbf{x}) = f(K(d(\mathbf{x}))) = \pi(z(\mathbf{x})\mathbf{PR}'\mathbf{R}^t\mathbf{P}^{-1}(\mathbf{x}, 1)^t - \mathbf{PR}'\mathbf{c}'). \tag{6}$$

A short revision of the right hand side shows that all the three components of the resulting "homogeneous optical flow" prior to application of π are affine functions in $\mathbf{x}$. Without loss of generality we can assume $f(\mathbf{x}) \neq \infty$ for all $\mathbf{x} \in U(\mathbf{x}^*)$. With that we obtain

$$\mathcal{Q} = \left\{ f : U(\mathbf{x}^*) \to \mathbb{R}^2 \mid f(\mathbf{x}) = \frac{1}{r(\mathbf{x})} \begin{pmatrix} p(\mathbf{x}) \\ q(\mathbf{x}) \end{pmatrix}, p, q, r \in \mathcal{L}(\mathbb{1}, \mathbf{x}, \mathbf{y}) \right\}, \tag{7}$$

where $\mathcal{L}(\mathbb{1}, \mathbf{x}, \mathbf{y})$ denotes the set of affine functions. Unfortunately, the set $\mathcal{Q}$ of *homography-induced* rational fractions is finitely parameterized but not a finite-dimensional affine space of functions. Notice that this is a representative picture for the most perspective camera models. The approximation theory in the following Section 4 does not admit to straight-forwardly work with the above class of functions as well [14]. A comprehensive discussion of our theory for $\mathcal{Q}$ goes out of scope of this paper.

To simplify the presentation we assume that $r(\mathbf{x})$ in Equation (7) is constant for $\mathbf{x} \in U(\mathbf{x}^*)$. Substitution of $r(\mathbf{x}) = 1$ into Equation (7) renders the admissible functions for the two components x and y of the optical flow $f = (x, y)$ affine. More formally, $x \in \mathcal{L}(b_x)$ and $y \in \mathcal{L}(b_y)$ with $b_x = b_y = (1, \mathbf{x}, \mathbf{y})$. The above definition reduces the model with finitely parametrized fractions to a model with finite-dimensional linear spaces of polynomials. Latter step on its own is common to optical flow models and corresponds to choosing $\nabla^2 f(\mathbf{x}) = 0$ as a regularizer [9]. However, as we have an additional regularization constraint, not all functions from $\mathcal{L}(b_x)$ and $\mathcal{L}(b_y)$ have the same occurrence likelihood. Latter observation is discussed in more general terms in the following section.

3   Bayesian Model of Structural Optical Flow

With the above example in mind, we now give a Bayesian model of SOF. To do this, we have to specify a prior and an observation distribution. The prior distribution reflects the application-dependent belief about the occurrence likelihood of admissible realizations of visible geometry and the corresponding image deformations. The observation model defines the conditional likelihood of observing image data for a particular given SOF instance. We generally regard any deviations of our random variables from their unknown true values as noise. For instance, ∞ is regarded as an arbitrary fixed value with a large noise level.

We start with the prior distribution. We assume that our optical system comprises two piece-wise smooth cameras K and K'. We denote by $K^{-1} : \mathbb{R} \times \Omega \to \mathbb{R}^3$ the *inverse camera* to K with the defining property $K(K^{-1}(z, \mathbf{x})) = \mathbf{x}$ for each $\mathbf{x} \in \Omega$ and $z \in \mathbb{R} \setminus \{0\}$. As exemplified earlier, we use a range image parameterization $z : \Omega \to \mathbb{R}$ for the surface with

$$d(\mathbf{x}) = K^{-1}(z(\mathbf{x}), \mathbf{x})$$

in the sequel and consider a SOF as a map $s : \Omega \to \mathbb{R}^3$ with $s(\mathbf{x}) = (f(\mathbf{x}), z(\mathbf{x}))$. Our special surface parameterization is tied to K, which imposes $K(d(\mathbf{x})) = \mathbf{x}$ for all $\mathbf{x} \in \Omega$. With the defining Equation (1) this yields a simplified triangulation constraint

$$f(\mathbf{x}) = f(K(d(\mathbf{x}))) = K'(d(\mathbf{x})) = K'(K^{-1}(z(\mathbf{x}), \mathbf{x})). \tag{8}$$

We assume, furthermore, that z is piece-wise smooth. From the above assumptions and with Equation (8) it follows that f is piece-wise smooth and uniquely defined by the surface and the optical system in regions of I, which are not occluded in I'. We generally discard influences of perspective occlusions.

As we work in a discrete setting, we fix a set of points of interest $\mathbf{x}_1, \ldots, \mathbf{x}_n \in \Omega$ in the reference image I, which in the implementation will be chosen as a regular grid $\mathbf{x}_i = (u - 1/2, v - 1/2)$ for $(u, v) \in \{1, \ldots, w\} \times \{1, \ldots, h\}$. In the following we will tacitly denote variables with index i as ranging over $i = 1, \ldots, n$, if not explicitly stated otherwise. From the smoothness properties of s it follows that s can be approximated by suitable function spaces of low dimension around the points $\mathbf{x}_i$ of interest. In order to define admissible instances of s, we fix a set of basis families b_{x_i}, b_{y_i}, and b_{z_i} for the components of $s : \Omega \to \mathbb{R}^3$ respectively and define the block-diagonal basis evaluation matrices.

$$B_i(\mathbf{x}) = \begin{pmatrix} b_{x_i}(\mathbf{x})^t & 0 & 0 \\ 0 & b_{y_i}(\mathbf{x})^t & 0 \\ 0 & 0 & b_{z_i}(\mathbf{x})^t \end{pmatrix}. \tag{9}$$

As discussed earlier, a particular choice of basis functions is problem-dependent. With that, we associate to each $\mathbf{x}_i$ a function $s_i : \Omega \to \mathbb{R}^3$ with

$$s_i(\mathbf{x}) = (x_i(\mathbf{x}), y_i(\mathbf{x}), z_i(\mathbf{x}))^t = B_i(\mathbf{x})\alpha_i.$$

for $x_i \in \mathcal{L}(b_{x_i})$, $y_i \in \mathcal{L}(b_{y_i})$, and $z_i \in \mathcal{L}(b_{z_i})$. In the sequel we also use the abbreviation $f_i = (x_i, y_i)$ for the optical flow component defined by s_i. Here,

$$\mathcal{L}(b) = \{g : \Omega \to \mathbb{R} \mid g(\mathbf{x}) = b(\mathbf{x})^t \alpha, \alpha \in \mathbb{R}^d\} \tag{10}$$

for a linear independent function family b. A function $g \in \mathcal{L}(b)$ is uniquely defined by the basis b and the corresponding coefficient vector $\alpha \in \mathbb{R}^d$. Hence, an instance of SOF s is uniquely defined by a family $\alpha = (\alpha_1, \ldots, \alpha_n)$ of the corresponding linear coefficients $\alpha_i \in \mathbb{R}^{d_i}$, where $d_i \in \mathbb{N}$ is the column number of B_i. Notice that as a consequence we merely restrict to a finite parameterization of s. Latter, however, is still considered as a function $s : \Omega \to \mathbb{R}^3$. For an arbitrary partition function $\varphi : \Omega \to \{1, \ldots, n\}$ with the property $\varphi(\mathbf{x}_i) = i$ we have the *simple evaluation* $\bar{s} : \Omega \to \mathbb{R}^3$ of s with

$$\bar{s}(\mathbf{x}) = s_{\varphi(\mathbf{x})}(\mathbf{x}),$$

which piece-wise inherits the smoothness properties of the basis functions. Intuitively, in a neighborhood of each $\mathbf{x}_i$ the SOF s is defined by the corresponding s_i. Each instance of $s = (s_1, \ldots, s_n)$ (independently of a particular choice of φ) specifies by $s(\mathbf{x}_i) = s_i(\mathbf{x}_i)$ an admissible value of s at our points of interest. Notice that given the s_i there are several ways to obtain a continuous or even smooth evaluation of s, for instance by Krigging [17]. In the following we tacitly associate $s = (s_1, \ldots, s_n)$ with its simple evaluation $\bar{s}$.

The model defined so far is highly flexible, so we impose additional constraints. Our triangulation constraint in Equation (8) enforces

$$f_i(\mathbf{x}_i) = K'(K^{-1}(z_i(\mathbf{x}_i), \mathbf{x}_i)). \tag{11}$$

We call the latter constraints *geometric constraints*, since they involve the surface structure. Observe that our geometric constraints are in general non-linear in the parameters of z_i due to a perspective transformation in the right hand side of Equation (11), which is common to most camera models. To obtain a linearized version of the constraints we consider a true SOF s^* with the components $s_i^* = (f_i^*, z_i^*)$. Then, Taylor expansion around the true value $z_i^* = z_i^*(\mathbf{x}_i)$ yields the linearized constraint

$$f_i(\mathbf{x}_i) = \mathbf{t}_i^* + \nabla_z t_i^* (z_i(\mathbf{x}_i) - z_i^*), \tag{12}$$

where $\mathbf{t}_i^* = K'(K^{-1}(z_i^*, \mathbf{x}_i))$ and $\nabla_z t_i^* = \nabla_z (K' \circ K^{-1})(z_i^*, \mathbf{x}_i)$.

Let $N(i) \subseteq \{1, \ldots, n\}$ denote the neighbors of $\mathbf{x}_i$. We assume that the neighborhood system N is symmetric with $i \in N(j)$ if and only if $j \in N(i)$. We make use of the overlapping definition domains of the $s_1, \ldots, s_n$ and enforce

$$s_i(\mathbf{x}_j) = s_j(\mathbf{x}_j) \tag{13}$$

for all $j \in N(i)$, which has a clear intuitive interpretation of surface patches coinciding over the intersections of their domains. We call our second type of constraints *smoothness constraints*, since they effectively prescribe smoothness of s. Due to symmetry of N latter constraints are equivalently rewritten as $s_i(\mathbf{x}_i) = s_j(\mathbf{x}_i)$ for all $j \in N(i)$.

We use the constraints in Equations (11) and (13) to define a prior for our SOF model. We define the occurrence probability density of an instance s as $p(\boldsymbol{\alpha}) = c_r \cdot \exp(-\sum_{i=1}^{n} r_i(\boldsymbol{\alpha})/2)$, where $c_r \in \mathbb{R}$ is a normalization constant and

$$r_i(\boldsymbol{\alpha}) = \|\mathbf{T}_i s_i(\mathbf{x}_i) - \mathbf{t}_i\|_{\Sigma_{\mathbf{t}_i}}^2 + \sum_{j \in N(i)} \|s_i(\mathbf{x}_i) - s_j(\mathbf{x}_i)\|^2, \tag{14}$$

where $\mathbf{T}_i = \left(-\mathbf{I}_2 \mid \nabla_z t_i^*\right) \in \mathbb{R}^{2 \times 3}$ and $\mathbf{t}_i = \nabla_z t_i^* z_i^* - \mathbf{t}_i^*$. As usual $\|\mathbf{x}\|_\Sigma = \mathbf{x}^t \Sigma^- \mathbf{x}$ denotes the Mahalanobis norm with respect to a square Σ, where Σ^- denotes the pseudo-inverse of Σ. The matrices $\Sigma_{\mathbf{t}_i} \in \mathbb{R}^{2 \times 2}$ express our belief in the precision of the estimated structure and depend besides the optical system as well on the unknown true value z_i^*. We postpone the definition of the $\Sigma_{\mathbf{t}_i}$ to Section 5.

We consider the evaluation process for our image data $I, I' : \Omega \to \mathbb{R}$ at discrete locations being subject to Gaussian noise. With this, for any $\mathbb{R}^m$-valued linear form l we have identically and independently distributed Gaussian random variables $l(I)(\mathbf{x})$ and $l(I')(\mathbf{x})$ with unknown mean and covariance matrices $\Sigma_{l(I)(\mathbf{x})} \in \mathbb{R}^{m \times m}$ and $\Sigma_{l(I')(\mathbf{x})} \in \mathbb{R}^{m \times m}$ respectively. A discussion about reliable estimation of the latter quantities is out of scope of the current paper. An interested reader might have a look at [18]. According to our intensity constancy constraints for a given SOF s we observe an image I', which is (partially) defined by $I'(f(\mathbf{x})) = I(\mathbf{x})$. Then for the $\mathbf{x}_i$ we have the constraint equations

$$l(I')(f_i(\mathbf{x}_i)) = l(I)(\mathbf{x}_i). \tag{15}$$

In general, the left hand side of Equation (15) is non-linear in $f(\mathbf{x}_i)$ and its parameters $\boldsymbol{\alpha}_i$. A linearized version of the intensity constancy constraint around the true value $\mathbf{f}_i^* = f_i^*(\mathbf{x}_i)$ is given by

$$l(I')(\mathbf{f}_i^*) + \nabla l(I')(\mathbf{f}_i^*)(f(\mathbf{x}_i) - \mathbf{f}_i^*) = l(I)(\mathbf{x}_i).$$

Notice that our image data $\mathbf{d} = (\mathbf{d}_1, \ldots, \mathbf{d}_n)$ defined by $\mathbf{d}_i = \nabla l(I')(\mathbf{f}_i^*)\mathbf{f}_i^* - l(I')(\mathbf{f}_i^*) + l(I)(\mathbf{x}_i)$ is approximately a Gaussian random variable with unknown mean and covariance matrix $\Sigma_{\mathbf{d}_i} = \Sigma_{l(I)(\mathbf{x}_i)} + \Sigma_{l(I')(\mathbf{f}_i^*)} \in \mathbb{R}^{m \times m}$. We define the conditional observation distribution $p(\mathbf{d} \mid \boldsymbol{\alpha}) = c_d \cdot \exp(-\sum_{i=1}^{n} d_i(\mathbf{d}, \boldsymbol{\alpha})/2)$ where $c_d \in \mathbb{R}$ is a normalization constant and

$$d_i(\mathbf{d}, \boldsymbol{\alpha}) = \|\mathbf{D}_i s_i(\mathbf{x}_i) - \mathbf{d}_i\|_{\Sigma_{\mathbf{d}_i}}^2, \tag{16}$$

where $\mathbf{D}_i = \left(\nabla l(I')(\mathbf{f}_i^*) \mid 0\right) \in \mathbb{R}^{m \times 3}$.

Given a particular unknown true SOF s^* and the matrices $\Sigma_{\mathbf{t}_i}$ our Bayesian model is fully specified by $p(\boldsymbol{\alpha})$ and $p(\mathbf{d} \mid \boldsymbol{\alpha})$. Since we have used our linearized constraints, the above Gibbs distributions are in fact Gaussian. Our SOF model can be viewed as a Gaussian *Gibbs random field spline* model with overlapping domains for the loosely connected spline patches.

4   Approximation Theory for Smoothness Constraints

The general model introduced in the previous section is not tractable for computations in practice as it involves a large number of redundant parameters. To simplify our SOF model, Equations (14) and (16) suggest to parameterize a particular instance s by a vector $\mathbf{s} = (\mathbf{s}_1, \ldots, \mathbf{s}_n)$ by defining $\mathbf{s}_i = (\mathbf{f}_i, z_i)$ with $\mathbf{s}_i = s_i(\mathbf{x}_i)$. For the observation model in Equation (16) we redefine the observation distribution as $p(\mathbf{d} \mid \mathbf{s}) = c_d \cdot \exp(-\sum_{i=1}^{n} d_i(\mathbf{d}, \mathbf{s})/2)$, where $c_d \in \mathbb{R}$ is a normalization constant and

$$d_i(\mathbf{d}, \mathbf{s}) = \|\mathbf{D}_i \mathbf{s}_i - \mathbf{d}_i\|_{\Sigma_{\mathbf{d}_i}}^2 \tag{17}$$

with other parameters left unchanged. Unfortunately, the above substitution does not eliminate all the occurrences of the old parameterization in Equation (14), since expressions of the type $s_i(\mathbf{x}_j)$ do not evaluate s_i in the corresponding points $\mathbf{x}_i$ of interest. For the weak membrane model [9] the equation $s_i(\mathbf{x}_j) = s_i(\mathbf{x}_i)$ is true per definition. In our general case latter approximation is invalid.

To estimate $s_i(\mathbf{x}_j)$ we use the constraints in Equation (13) to approximately estimate the coefficients $\boldsymbol{\alpha}_i$, which, in turn, give us by Equation (10) the required $s_i(\mathbf{x}_j)$. Our technical tool is the theory of function approximation to the given data with respect to a suitable metric [14]. With this idea we can parametrize a practically relevant subset of our SOF model defined in the previous section.

The defining property of s_i together with Equation (9) gives us an explicit form of the smoothness constraints

$$B_i(\mathbf{x}_j)\boldsymbol{\alpha}_i = \mathbf{s}_j$$

for all $j \in N(i)$. Recall now that for a particular true instance s^* of SOF, the parameter vector $\boldsymbol{\alpha}$ is a Gaussian random variable. Consequently, the family $\mathbf{s} = (\mathbf{s}_1, \ldots, \mathbf{s}_n)$ is a Gaussian random variable as well. For the purpose of approximating the $s_i(\mathbf{x}_j)$ we consider the components $\mathbf{s}_1, \ldots, \mathbf{s}_n$ as independent Gaussian random variables with unknown mean and a covariance matrix $\Sigma_{\mathbf{s}_i} \in \mathbb{R}^{3\times3}$, which we will approximately derive in Section 5.

Given the observations $\mathbf{s}_j$ for $j \in N(i)$, a maximum likelihood (ML) estimate of the conditional mean of $\boldsymbol{\alpha}_i$ and its covariance matrix $\Sigma_{\boldsymbol{\alpha}_i}$ are given by

$$\boldsymbol{\alpha}_i = \Sigma_{\boldsymbol{\alpha}_i} \sum_{j \in N(i)} B_i(\mathbf{x}_j)^t \Sigma_{\mathbf{s}_j}^- \mathbf{s}_j, \quad \text{and} \quad \Sigma_{\boldsymbol{\alpha}_i}^- = \sum_{j \in N(i)} B_i(\mathbf{x}_j)^t \Sigma_{\mathbf{s}_j}^- B_i(\mathbf{x}_j). \tag{18}$$

The estimate $\boldsymbol{\alpha}_i$ is computed in linear time in the size of $N(i)$ and in quadratical time in the (small) dimension d provided that B_i is evaluated in constant time [15]. This establishes the point-wise complexity of our method.

The evaluation of s_i in any $\mathbf{x} \in \Omega$ results in a conditional estimate $s_i(\mathbf{x})$ of $s(\mathbf{x})$ with the corresponding covariance matrix $\Sigma_{s_i(\mathbf{x})}$ with

$$s_i(\mathbf{x}) = B_i(\mathbf{x})\boldsymbol{\alpha}_i, \quad \text{and} \quad \Sigma_{s_i(\mathbf{x})} = B_i(\mathbf{x})\Sigma_{\boldsymbol{\alpha}_i}B_i(\mathbf{x})^t. \tag{19}$$

Equation (19) defines now for each s_j the required $s_{ij}^* = s_i(\mathbf{x}_j)$ in the definition of our prior. As we are merely approximating the values $s_i(\mathbf{x}_j)$, we can assume that the distribution characteristics of our regularizer do not change with this approximation. With that we arrive at our final approximated prior $p(\mathbf{s}) = c_r \cdot \exp(-\sum_{i=1}^{n} r_i(\mathbf{s})/2)$ with the normalization constant $c_r \in \mathbb{R}$ and

$$r_i(\mathbf{s}) = \|\mathbf{T}_i\mathbf{s}_i - \mathbf{t}_i\|_{\Sigma_{\mathbf{t}_i}}^2 + \sum_{j \in N(i)} \|\mathbf{s}_i - \mathbf{s}_{ji}^*\|^2. \tag{20}$$

Notice that even in its approximated form and without the triangulation constraint Equation (20) is a generalization of the weak membrane [9].

5   Estimation of Structural Optical Flow

A MAP solution to our problem is obtained by maximizing the posterior density $p(\mathbf{s} \mid \mathbf{d})$. Latter is equivalent (see [9] for a comprehensive introduction) to minimizing the likelihood energy

$$e_{s^*}(\mathbf{d}, \mathbf{s}) = \sum_{i=1}^{n}(d_i(\mathbf{d}, \mathbf{s}) + r_i(\mathbf{s})). \tag{21}$$

Equation (21) is merely a theoretical expression, since it involves the true unknown value s^* and looses its linearity by considering s^* as an unknown. To overcome this difficulty, we define a sequence of Bayesian models with the corresponding likelihood energy $e_{s^{(k)}}$. Each $e_{s^{(k)}}$ uses a guess $s^{(k)}$ of the true value of s^*. Each $s^{(k)}$ is, in turn, approximately parametrized by $\mathbf{s}^{(k)}$ as defined in Section 4. According to the Bayesian principle, the first estimate $\mathbf{s}^{(0)}$ is guessed. After an optimal solution $\mathbf{s}$ in iteration k is computed by minimizing the energy $e_{s^{(k)}}$ as defined in Equation (21), the value $\mathbf{s}$ is used as $\mathbf{s}^{(k+1)}$ in the next iteration. The above algorithm essentially resembles a gradient descent method with convex objectives in each step. If the initial guess is sufficiently close to the true solution s^* the $\mathbf{s}^{(i)}$ converge to an approximation $\mathbf{s}^*$ of s^*. To assure latter assumption we propose a coarse-to-fine procedure described in [4].

An iterative solution for the conditional mean $\mathbf{s}^{(k+1)}$ for the observed data in iteration k is obtained by computing the conditional expectations given the estimates of the previous iteration $\mathbf{s}^{(k)}$ as

$$\mathbf{s}_i^{(k+1)} = \mathbf{s}_i^{(k)} - \Sigma_{\mathbf{s}_i^{(k+1)}} \left(\mathbf{D}_i^t \Sigma_{\mathbf{d}_i}^- (\mathbf{D}_i \mathbf{s}_i^{(k)} - \mathbf{d}_i) \right.$$
$$\left. + \mathbf{T}_i^t \Sigma_{\mathbf{t}_i}^- (\mathbf{T}_i \mathbf{s}_i^{(k)} - \mathbf{t}_i) + \sum_{j \in N(i)} (\mathbf{s}_i^{(k)} - \mathbf{s}_{ji}^*) \right), \quad (22)$$

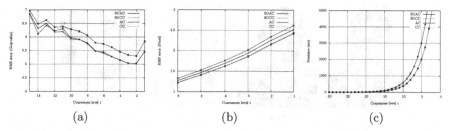

Fig. 1. Comparison of the root mean squared residual magnitudes of the constraints (a) in Equation (15) and (b) Equation (11) of our method at the last iteration on each coarseness level for the different SOF models (c) and runtime of our method

where we have dropped the superscript (k) for the values of $\mathbf{D}_i$, $\mathbf{T}_i$ etc. computed from $\mathbf{s}^{(k)}$. The covariance matrix $\Sigma_{\mathbf{s}_i^{(k+1)}}$, which we have used in Equation (18), is given by

$$\Sigma_{\mathbf{s}_i^{(k+1)}}^- = \mathbf{D}_i^t \Sigma_{\mathbf{d}_i}^- \mathbf{D}_i + \mathbf{T}_i^t \Sigma_{\mathbf{t}_i}^- \mathbf{T}_i + |N(i)| \mathbf{I}_3.$$

Although we consider it as a rough approximation, we use the heuristic $\Sigma_{\mathbf{t}_i} = \sigma_{z_i}^2 (\nabla_z t_i^*)^t \nabla_z t_i^*$, where $\sigma_{z_i}^2$ is the $(3,3)$-entry of $\Sigma_{\mathbf{s}_i^{(k)}}$. Latter is obtained by applying the linear covariance propagation law for the right hand side of Equation (12) to $\mathbf{s}_i^{(k)}$ and the corresponding covariance matrix $\Sigma_{\mathbf{s}_i}^{(k)}$.

6   Experimental Results

In this section we demonstrate the applicability of our method on practical examples with four SOF models derived from the model in Section 2. As we do not propose a particular model or algorithm, we only briefly compare the results of our implementations with and without the methods introduced in this paper.

For all methods we use the $\mathbb{R}^3$-valued linear form $l(I) = (I, \nabla_x I, \nabla_y I)^t$ proposed in [4]. Furthermore, we choose the coarse-to-fine factor 0.85 and perform 20 iterations of Equation (22) on each coarseness level. For all experiments we use the 5×5-pixel neighborhood system N with $|N(i)| = 25$. The pictures have the size of 1024×768-pixels. The computations have been performed on an Intel® Core™ i7-2600K CPU with 3.40 GHz by using only one core.

The piece-wise affine SOF model (SOAC) results by choosing $b_{x_i} = b_{y_i} = (\mathbb{1}, \mathbf{x}, \mathbf{y})$ and $b_{z_i} = (\mathbb{1})$ as discussed in detail in Section 2. The constant model (SOCC) results by restricting to $b_{x_i} = b_{y_i} = b_{z_i} = (\mathbb{1})$. The methods CC and AC are derived from SOCC and SOAC respectively by discarding the triangulation constraint in the prior Equation (20). Hence, they require an additional triangulation step, which is implemented by estimating the range image from the optical flow by minimizing (20) with respect to z_i for a fixed $\mathbf{f}_i$. The method BC is closely related to the discretization of optical flow estimation method in [4].

Figure 1 illustrates the convergence rates of the methods for the test data set depicted in Figure 2 in the first row. Notice that the errors are measured over

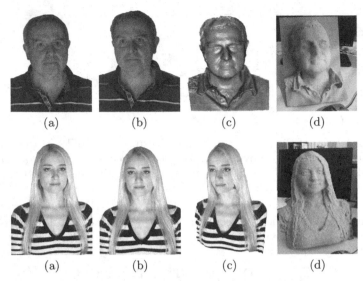

(a)   (b)   (c)   (d)

(a)   (b)   (c)   (d)

Fig. 2. Examples (a)-(b) of two input pictures with removed background for face reconstruction, (c) three-dimensional model recovered from the pictures with and without texture, and (d) its print. The model in the second row is printed with a lower resolution than the model in the first row.

the complete image and so the results describe merely the overall performance of the method. Single outliers are not well represented by the above diagram. Because of image resizing artifacts the values in Figure 1 (a) do not show a strictly decreasing behavior. Furthermore, the values in Figure 1 (b) grow with the increasing image resolution, since the size of the image plane in space remains constant while the pixel size changes. All the methods perform well, since they are essentially extensions of the discretized algorithm in [4]. However, constant models CC and SOCC explain the image data with less precision, while their reconstruction and runtime are superior to AC and SOAC. The slower affine models AC and SOAC explain the image data better but have larger errors in reconstruction, since they are more sensitive to noise. SOAC outperforms the others in the sense that it has a small observation and reconstruction error.

7   Conclusions and Future Work

Approximate regularization discussed in the current work is a powerful method to introduce geometric assumptions into Bayesian methods for SOF estimation. We have demonstrated the performance of our method on practical examples. As a part of future work we target extensions of the class of admissible functions for which the computational complexity is still feasible. Our discrete approach generalizes the algorithmic discretized part of variational methods without addressing the calculus of variations at any point. We claim that the adherer of the latter approach should motivate its need more explicitly in their publications.

Acknowledgments. This work is partially funded by the ZIM project "Büstenrekonstruktion". We would like to thank Thomas Müller-Gronbach and his team at the University of Passau for fruitful discussions, in which we have obtained a better intuition about Bayesian statistics. Finally, we are grateful to our industry partner voxeljet technology GmbH for providing three-dimensional prints of our models.

References

1. McCane, B., Novins, K., Crannitch, D., Galvin, B.: On Benchmarking Optical Flow. Computer Vision and Image Understanding 84(1) (2001)
2. Hartley, R., Zisserman, A.: Multiple View Geometry in Computer Vision. Cambridge University Press (2000)
3. Horn, B.K., Schunck, B.G.: Determining optical flow. Technical report, Massachusetts Institute of Technology, Cambridge, MA, USA (1980)
4. Brox, T., Bruhn, A., Papenberg, N., Weickert, J.: High Accuracy Optical Flow Estimation Based on a Theory for Warping. In: Pajdla, T., Matas, J(G.) (eds.) ECCV 2004. LNCS, vol. 3024, pp. 25–36. Springer, Heidelberg (2004)
5. Bruhn, A., Weickert, J., Schnörr, C.: Lucas/kanade meets horn/schunck: combining local and global optic flow methods. Int. J. Comput. Vision 61, 211–231 (2005)
6. Zach, C., Pock, T., Bischof, H.: A Duality Based Approach for Realtime TV-L1 Optical Flow. In: Hamprecht, F.A., Schnörr, C., Jähne, B. (eds.) DAGM 2007. LNCS, vol. 4713, pp. 214–223. Springer, Heidelberg (2007)
7. Lucas, B.D., Kanade, T.: An Iterative Image Registration Technique with an Application to Stereo Vision. In: IJCA 1981, vol. 81, pp. 674–679 (1981)
8. Kanatani, K.: Statistical Optimization for Geometric Computation: Theory and Practice. Elsevier Science Inc., New York (1996)
9. Li, S.Z.: Markov random field modeling in image analysis. Springer-Verlag New York, Inc., Secaucus (2001)
10. Nir, T., Bruckstein, A.M., Kimmel, R.: Over-parameterized variational optical flow. Int. J. Comput. Vision 76, 205–216 (2008)
11. Lamovsky, D.V., Lasaruk, A.: Calibration and Reconstruction Algorithms for a Handheld 3D Laser Scanner. In: Blanc-Talon, J., Kleihorst, R., Philips, W., Popescu, D., Scheunders, P. (eds.) ACIVS 2011. LNCS, vol. 6915, pp. 635–646. Springer, Heidelberg (2011)
12. Corrochano, E.B., Förstner, W.: Uncertainty and projective geometry. In: Handbook of Geometric Computing, pp. 493–534. Springer, Heidelberg (2005)
13. Hoeffken, M., Oberhoff, D., Kolesnik, M.: Temporal Prediction and Spatial Regularization in Differential Optical Flow. In: Blanc-Talon, J., Kleihorst, R., Philips, W., Popescu, D., Scheunders, P. (eds.) ACIVS 2011. LNCS, vol. 6915, pp. 576–585. Springer, Heidelberg (2011)
14. Cheney, E.: Introduction to approximation theory. AMS Chelsea Publishing Series. AMS Chelsea Pub. (1982)
15. Björck, Å.: Numerical Methods for Least Squares Problems. SIAM, Philadelphia (1996)

16. Salvi, J., Matabosch, C., Fofi, D., Forest, J.: A review of recent range image registration methods with accuracy evaluation. Image Vision Comput. 25, 578–596 (2007)
17. Wackernagel, H.: Multivariate Geostatistics: An Introduction With Applications. Springer (2003)
18. Liu, C., Freeman, W.T., Szeliski, R., Kang, S.B.: Noise estimation from a single image. IEEE Computer Vision and Pattern Recognition 1, 901–908 (2006)

Semi-variational Registration of Range Images by Non-rigid Deformations

Denis Lamovsky

FORWISS, Universität Passau, 94032 Passau, Germany
lamouski@forwiss.uni-passau.de

Abstract. We present a semi-variational approach for accurate registration of a set of range images. For each range image we estimate a transformation composed of a similarity and a free-form deformation in order to obtain a smoothly stitched surface. The resulting three-dimensional model has no jumps or sharp transitions in the place of stitching. We use the presented approach for accurate human head reconstruction from a set of facets subsequently captured from different views and computed independently. A joint energy for both types of transformations is formulated, which involves several regularization constraints defined according to a specification of the resulting surface. A strategy for reweighting the impact of correspondences is presented to improve stability and convergence of the approach. We demonstrate the applicability of our method on several representative examples.

1 Introduction

Reconstruction of three-dimensional structure from multiple view observations of an object of interest is a challenging problem and has received a considerable attention in recent years. State of the art approaches of structure estimation use camera-based laser scanners [1,2], structured light scanners [3], and multi-view reconstruction from images [4]. These methods are based on camera-like sensors and return the reconstructed three-dimensional surface as a two-dimensional perspective parameterization, called a *range image*. A range image typically describes the reconstructed surface only from one point of view. Therefore, only parts of the observed object are captured at once and have to be stitched together later on. As for any measuring device, the resulting surfaces are subject to errors. These errors can be subdivided into a (non-systematic) noise of the sensor hardware and systematic deformations caused for example by inprecise camera calibration, inhomogeneous light sources, or by inaccuracy of the reconstruction method. In the later case the reconstructed parts of the surface can not be joined together by a simple change of coordinates without additional processing.

Numerous registration methods for range images have been developed in the recent decades. An excelent overview over the existing methods can be found in [5]. Just as the classification of errors, the algorithms of registration are subdivided into two general classes. The coordinate transformation methods compute a global coordinate transformation for each of the parts of the three-dimensional

J. Blanc-Talon et al. (Eds.): ACIVS 2012, LNCS 7517, pp. 349–360, 2012.

structure in order to position them in a common coordinate system. The second class of algorithms compute a free-form deformation between the coarsly positioned parts to compensate for systematic distortions.

One of the most popular methods for range image registration is the Iterative Closed Points (ICP) algorithm which was described by Besl and McKay [6]. They proposed the iterative approach for estimation of rigid motion transformation $T = (R, t)$ by minimizing an objective function

$$f(R, t) = \sum_i^N \omega_i \|Rx_i + t - C_i\|^2, \tag{1}$$

where C_i is a closest point on a destination surface for the point x_i and N is a number of correspondence points. It is considered that all points x_i have correspondences and the correspondences are equivalent ($\omega_i = 1$). A numerous variations of the ICP algorithm involves correspondences weighting and filtering were presented later on [7,8,9,10]. Schütz proposed a simple method for outliers elimination based on a threshold which depends on the distance between centers of mass of two surfaces [8]. Zhang developed statistical outlier classifier [9] which uses a threshold obtained from a normal distribution of the point pairs distances. A distance between a point and a normal to the target surface in a corresponding point is used in [10] for weighting of correspondences. Appropriate weights allow first of all using ICP for partially overlapped surfaces registration and improve the stability and convergence of the algorithm.

Correction of the distortions is another challenging task in surface registration. In [11] systematic deformation is corrected by considering whole surface as a set of connected piecewise rigid sections. Rigid transformation is then computed for each of such parts. Cheng and others [12] use cubic B-splines to recover non-rigid deformation parameters for two pieces of a deformed object which are initially rigidly registered. We consider a so called *scene flow* as a prominent way for distortion correction. A scene flow is a three dimensional vector field which shows the movement of points in space. It is usually computed for fixed camera and is a three dimensional analogue of optical flow. Most common approach for scene flow computation is based on the variational methods [13]. We adopt this idea for correction of the deformations.

In this paper we address the problem of range images registration which are subject to a complex deformation. We consider this problem as a problem of estimation of a combination of rigid and non-rigid transforms. An appropriate energy functional is formulated for joined estimation of both transformations. A semi-variational approach is then applied to find transformation parameters which minimize the energy. Additional regularization is used to achieve required properties of transformations. For example the requirement of minimal non-rigid transformation is considered.

The paper is organized as follows: In Section 2 our object reconstruction setup is briefly described and the problem of reconstructed surfaces stitching is defined. In Section 3 we formulate the energy functional for pair-wise stitching and multi-view stitching problems. A solution of the semi-variational problem for the registration will be considered in Section 4. Section 5 will describe a weighting strategy used in our algorithm. A short formal description of the algorithm is presented in Section 6. Evaluation of the presented method and experimental results will be presented in Section 7.

2   Problem Statement

We concentrate our attention on the application of human head reconstruction with the aim to print obtained model using a 3D printing technology. We obtain range images by consequently capturing of the object of interest from different views. Each range image is reconstructed separately using a vision based semi-variational reconstruction method. An example of reconstructed parts for registration is presented in Figure 1.

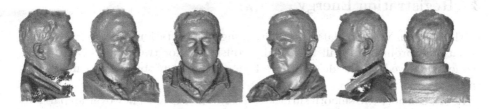

Fig. 1. Reconstructed parts of the object of interest

Detailed description of the reconstruction method is not presented here, being beyond the scope of this paper. We just mention that the method simultaneously optimises optical flow, camera positions and depth map. Due to the complexity of the reconstruction algorithm resulting surfaces are subject to distortions. These distortions are caused first off all by errors in reconstruction process due to a big amount of reconstruction parameters. Another source of the distortions is non-rigidity of the object of interest. It means that the captured human can move his had relative to his body between shootings. This influence dramatically on the process of stitching because the face part of the bust have different positions relatively to the body part in different views.

Our aim is to stitch the parts together by matching and distortions correction. We consider $\Omega = [0, w] \times [0, h] \subseteq \mathbb{R}^2$, where $w, h \in \mathbb{N}$, as an *image domain*. The range image is then a three-dimensional surface $q : \Omega \to \mathbb{R}^3$. Function q maps the pixel $x \in \Omega$ to a point on the range image using the depth map $d : \Omega \to \mathbb{R}$ and the corresponding inverse projection camera matrix $P \in \mathbb{R}^{3\times3}$. Each range image is supplied also by the rigid motion $H = (R, t)$ which defines the position of the surface in space.

We consider the stitching process as a process of estimation of the combined transformations set $T = (T_1, \ldots, T_n)$ for a given set of range images

$q = (q_1, \ldots, q_n)$. Here n is the amount of parts for stitching. Transformed surfaces $(h_1, \ldots, h_n)$ should form smooth surface without jumps or sharp transitions in the place of stitching. Such range images can be strait forwardly transformed to a mesh by using for example the marching cube [14] algorithm.

We will formulate the problem of range images stitching in terms of variation, which is commonly used for scene flow computation. Variational approach requires an appropriate energy functional in the form:

$$\xi = \int_\Omega D(q, T, x) + \alpha r(T, x) dx, \qquad (2)$$

where D is the data constraint, r is the regularization constraint. A regularization gain α determines the influence of regularisation term on the result.

Each range image is supplied with a quality characteristic $\omega : \Omega \to \mathbb{R}$ which describes the accuracy of the surface estimation in each point. It is used in our weighting strategy which will be described in Section 5.

3   Registration Energy

In this section we formulate the range images registration problem as a semi-variational problem. It will be initially considered for two range images registration, followed by the description of an expanded problem for a multi-view case.

Let us consider two smooth surfaces $f \in \mathbb{R}^3$ and $q \in \mathbb{R}^3$. They overlap partially and don't fit together. We want to estimate a pair of non-rigid transformations T_f and T_q for both surfaces respectively. The transformed surfaces $h_f = T_f(f)$ and $h_q = T_q(q)$ should smoothly flow one in another.

Because of unknown distortions of the source surfaces we don't formulate a problem of registration as aligning of the surface f on q but as aligning them to some *mean surface*. Let's consider one direction of the registration, i.e. searching the transformation of f. Inverse problem for q is symmetric to the direct one.

The transformed surface h_f has to be similar to both source surfaces in the area of their overlapping. This leads us to the following constraint

$$D(f, q, T_f, x) = \omega_{f(x)} \|h_f(x) - f(x)\|^2 + \omega_{C_{fq}(x)} \|h_f(x) - C_{fq}(x)\|^2, \qquad (3)$$

where $C_{fq}(x)$ is the correspondence point for $f(x)$ on q. Weights $\omega_{f(x)}$ and $\omega_{C_{fq}(x)}$ determine the influence of each surface on the registration result. Although all ω are functions $\Omega \to \mathbb{R}$ we will further discard the notation (x) from weights to simplify the representation.

Equation 3 can be easily transformed by rearranging to

$$D(f, q, T_f, x) = (\omega_f + \omega_{C_{fq}}) \left\| h_f(x) - \frac{\omega_f f(x) + \omega_{C_{fq}} C_{fq}(x)}{\omega_f + \omega_{C_{fq}}} \right\|^2 + \varsigma. \qquad (4)$$

The constant part $\varsigma = \omega_f \omega_{C_{fg}} \|f(x) - C_{fg}(x)\|^2 / (\omega_f + \omega_{C_{fq}})$ can be discarded from the constraint.

Equation (4) shows that in contrast to classical ICP our algorithm matches a range image not with another range image but with some *expecting* surface $g_f = \frac{\omega_f f(x) + \omega_{C_{fq}} C_{fq}(x)}{\omega_f + \omega_{C_{fq}}}$, which is a weighted mean of matching surfaces. The surface g_f is defined in the same domain as f.

In a multi-view case we have a set of partially overlapping surfaces $q = (q_1, \ldots, q_n)$. The weighted mean surface which corresponds to a *base* range image $f \in q$ is estimated using the following equation:

$$g_f(q, x) = \frac{\sum_i^n \omega_{C_{fq_i}} C_{fq_i}(x)}{\sum_i^n \omega_{C_{fq_i}}(x)}. \tag{5}$$

Last equation can be also obtained by minimisation of the following *consistency constraint*:

$$\sum_i^n \omega_{C_{fq_i}} \|g_f(x) - C_{fq_i}(x)\|^2. \tag{6}$$

As it was discussed in the previous section we estimate a transformation which is a combination of global rigid and local non-rigid transformations. We define it as

$$T(f, x) = M f(x) + S(x) = \alpha R f(x) + t + S(x), \tag{7}$$

where M is a similarity transformation of the coordinate system and S is a scene flow.

The similarity $M = (\alpha, R, t)$ includes scale factor, rotation matrix and translation respectively. The similarity is intended for bringing patches together as close as possible only by transformations of theirs coordinate systems.

The scene flow $S : \Omega \to \mathbb{R}^3$ is defined at the same parametrization domain as transforming (base) range image. The scene flow blends surfaces in order to impose them smoothly to the mean surface. The scene flow is required for correction of source patches inconsistencies. It should not describe any global space transformation. Therefore the scene flow should be as small as possible. The latter can be formulated using Tikchonov regularization constraint for minimization problem $r_S = \int_\Omega \|S(x)\|^2$. Additionally we impose a smoothness constraint $r_{\nabla S} = \int_\Omega \|\nabla S(x)\|^2$ in order to have smooth non-rigid transformation of the surface. The last constraint, in cooperation with requirements of source surfaces smoothness, guarantee smoothness of the transformed surface.

Similarly to [15] we incorporate the function $\psi(x) = \sqrt{x^2 + \epsilon^2}$ (with $\epsilon = 0.001$) as the energy penalization function for the data constraint. This makes the minimisation more robust with respect to outliers in the data term.

Now error energy functional can be formulated as follows:

$$\xi(M, S) = \int_\Omega \omega_c \psi(M f(x) + S(x) - g_f(x)) \\ + \alpha \omega_t \|S(x)\|^2 + \beta \omega_r \|\nabla S(x)\|^2 dx, \tag{8}$$

where α and β are regularization gains for r_S and $r_{\nabla S}$ respectively. The last equation includes *data constraint* weight ω_c, *Tikhonov regularisation* constraint weight ω_t and *smoothnes* constraint weight ω_r. They are involved to make registration process stable and convergent. In the Section 5 we consider equations for weights estimation and define all mentioned weights in explicit form.

4   Solving the Semi-variational Problem

Extremum of the energy functional $\xi(M, S)$ is computed according to the variational approach by solving the Euler-Lagrange equation.

First of all, we linearise the energy functional in some fixed S^*. Considering $\Delta S = 0$ and discarding constant terms we can write the energy minimization problem as following

$$\xi(M) = \int_\Omega \omega_c \psi \Big(M f(x) - \big(g_f(x) - S^*(x)\big) \Big) dx. \tag{9}$$

This is the L^1 minimization problem in parameters of the rigid transformation M. After discretisation it can be strait forwardly solved. We drop the description of the solution because of the restriction of the paper space. The result M^* of the minimization of (9) is an intermediate optimal solution with respect to S^*.

We use the intermediate optimal solution M^* for formulation of the variational problem for computation of optimal S. The energy functional is then represented as

$$\xi(S) = \int_\Omega \omega_c \psi \Big(S(x) - \big(g_f(x) - M^* f(x)\big) \Big) \\ + \alpha \omega_t \|S(x)\|^2 + \beta \omega_r \|\nabla S(x)\|^2 dx. \tag{10}$$

We denote the data term $Mf(x) + S(x) - g_f(x)$ further as $D_{MS}(x)$ to simplify equations representation.

Minimization of energy functional by S is done by using the Euler-Lagrange equation and leads us to a system of non-linear equations

$$\omega_c \psi'(D_{M^*S}(x))D_{M^*S}(x) + \alpha \omega_t S(x) - \beta \omega_r div(\nabla S(x)) = 0, \tag{11}$$

where $\psi'(x) = {}^1 / \sqrt{x^2 + \epsilon^2}$ is a derivative of the penaliser.

Linearisation of the last equation allows writing a solution for ΔS in an explicit form

$$\Delta S(x) = \frac{\omega_c(g_f(x) - M^* f(x))\psi^* - (\omega_c \psi^* + \alpha \omega_t)S^*(x) + \beta \omega_r div(\nabla S^*(x))}{\omega_c \psi^* + \alpha \omega_t}. \tag{12}$$

Here $\psi^* = \psi'(D_{M^*S^*}(x))$ is an additional weight factor, which appears due to the using of the penalizer.

The solution (12) leads to an incremental algorithm for computation of $S(x) = S^*(x) + \Delta S(x)$, where S^* is the estimation the scene flow from previous iteration. As most successors of Horn and Shunk algorithm [16] we minimize the discussed functional on a discrete grid of image points. Discretisation allows us using weighting strategy presented in next section.

5 Weights and Consistency

As it was mentioned in Section 2 that each source depth image q is supplied by weights ω_q. We consider this weights as an approximation of $1/\sigma_q^2$, where σ_q^2 is a noise level of the surface estimation error [1].

Quality properties of other data terms involved in our computation, are represented in the same way. They are estimated based on weights of source surfaces and depend on a way of data fusion in a corresponding equation. We consider two ways of interconnection between data terms. In the case of equation (5) the data terms *compete* with each other, i. e. at least one should be valid in order to obtain consistent result. Another case is a fusing process where data terms *cooperate* with each other. It means that all data terms should be valid for consistent result estimation. We can see such relations, for example, in both parts of the data constraint (3). Considering the relations we can estimate weights involved in the energy function (8).

Let's now consider the data constraint $D_{MS}(x)$, defined in Section 4, as simplest case of data fusion with the cooperation of data terms. It includes two data terms: f and g_f. Notice that the term S^* is intermediate estimation of the minimising function parameter and it should not be considered in the weighting strategy. The weight of the data constraint is estimated using the uncertainty propagation rule as

$$\sigma_c^2 = \sigma_f^2 + \sigma_{q_f}^2 \quad \Rightarrow \quad \omega_c = \frac{\omega_f \omega_{g_f}}{\omega_f + \omega_{g_f}}. \tag{13}$$

The weight ω_{g_f} in the last equation is the quality measure of the corresponding mean surface. It is seen from (4) that the weighted mean surface g has weight $\omega_g = \omega_f + \omega_q$. Considering in the same way the equation (5) we can write a common rule for new quality measures estimation for the competition of data terms

$$\frac{1}{\sigma_c^2} = \frac{1}{\sigma_{q_1}^2} + \cdots + \frac{1}{\sigma_{q_n}^2} \quad \Rightarrow \quad \omega_{g_f} = \sum_i^n \omega_{q_i}. \tag{14}$$

Here g_f denotes a function $g(q_1, \ldots, q_n, x)$, where $f = q_j : j \in (1 \ldots n)$, and ω_{q_i} is the quality measure of the corresponding surface point.

The weight of the mean surface should describe also the realisation of the consistency constraint (6). This is done by the weight correction procedure which estimates corrected weight using the residual of the constraint (6) as follows:

$$\omega_g = \frac{\omega_{g_f}}{\sum_i^n \omega_{q_i} \|g_f - q_i\|^2}. \tag{15}$$

The denominator of the last equation wouldn't be equal to zero. In other case we set weight ω_{g_f} to a defined value ω_{max} which corresponds to maximum of the weights value.

---

[1] We assume that all data terms have errors which are i.i.d. Gaussian variables with zero mean value and a covariance matrix in the form $\sigma_e^2 \Sigma_e$. Here σ_e^2 is a noise level and Σ_e is a base known covariance matrix.

It is not easy to estimate the weight ω_r of the smoothness constraint in a proper way because of complexity of the regularization term. For appropriate weight computation we assume by analogy with [16] that $\nabla S(x)$ is approximated by $S(x) - \overline{S}$, where $\overline{S}$ is mean value of function S in the neighbourhood of x. Computation of $\overline{S}$ involves competition of the S values in a window $m \times m$. Hence correspondent equations for weight and consistency are

$$\omega_r = \sum_i^{m^2} \omega_{S_i}, \tag{16}$$

where ω_{S_i} is weights of scene flow values in the regularisation window.

The weight ω_t of the Tikhonov regularisation constraint in (10) defines places where estimating scene flow should not grow. These places correspond to the points where source surface is estimated with hight precision. Therefore we use the weight of the base surface ω_f as the weight for the Tikhonov regularisation.

The value of scene flow is computed based on energy functional minimization where all terms compete with each other. Therefore the update of the scene flow quality measurement is done using following equations

$$\omega_S = \frac{\omega_c + \omega_t + \omega_r}{J}, \tag{17}$$

where J is the residual of the energy function (8) in the current point.

Algorithm 1. Computation of the set of complex transformations $T = (M, S)$ for the given set $q = (q_i, \ldots, q_n)$ of range images.

---

for $i = 1, \ldots, n$ **do**
    Initialize $S_i := (0.0, 0.0, 0.0)$ with constant weights $\omega_S := 10e - 7$
    Initialize $M_i := (1.0, I, (0.0, 0.0, 0.0))$
repeat
    for $i = 1, \ldots, n$ **do**
        Compute g_i using equation (5)
        Estimate weights of g_i according to Equation (15)
    for $i = 1, \ldots, n$ **do**
        Let $S_i^* = S_i$
        repeat
            Compute M_i by the minimization of Equation (9)
        until *convergence or a number of iterations*
        Let $M_i^* = M_i$
        repeat
            Compute $S_i = S_i^* + \Delta S_i$ using Equation (12)
        until *convergence or a number of iterations*
        Update ω_{S_i} using Equation (17)
until *convergence or a number of iterations*
return $T = (T_1, \ldots, T_n)$ where $T_i = (M_i, S_i)$

---

6   Algorithm Description

A short formal description of the proposed registration procedure is presented in this section (see Algorithm 1).

The algorithm includes two steps: the step of mean surfaces computation and the step of energy functional minimisation.

A correspondence estimation procedure is a part of the mean surface g_i computation step. We use *Bounding Volume Hierarchy* (BVH) structure for fast closes point search on giving surface.

The two internal circles for computation of M and S are included due to reweighing by ψ^* and regularisation of scene flow.

Notice that ICP recalculates closest points at each iteration. Our algorithm does this only after convergence in the internal circle.

7   Results

In this section we present the results of range image registration by our algorithm. We compare it with weighting version of ICP algorithm and show the advantage of using the scene flow for consistent stitching.

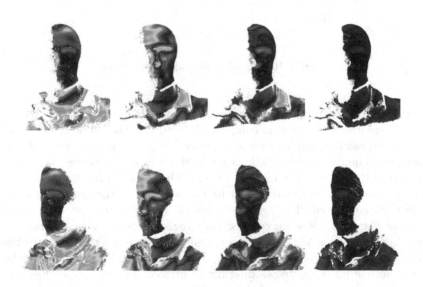

Fig. 2. Distance maps between frontal and half right views. From left to right: initial solution, the result of ICP, the result of proposed algorithm without scene flow, the result of proposed algorithm with scene flow. (black color correspondents to zero value, white - to infinity or undefined value)

We take two range images f and q for comparison of the algorithms. They have been obtained by front camera and by camera rotated by approximately 45 degree. The surfaces overlap each other at approximately 50%. A visual evaluation of the quality of the registration is done by using a *distance map*. A distance map is an image where each point represents a distance from a giving surface point to its correspondence at another surface. A distance map is calculated for a pair of range images and has the same domain as the first image in the pair. Distance maps for initial match are presented in Figure 2 (left column).

In order to estimate the registration quality we calculate *mean distance to expected surface* (MD), which is a weighted sum of lengths of the correspondence vectors between the given surface and the expected mean surface. This measure is calculated at the correspondence estimation step in tests of the both algorithms. In Figure 3 the result of MD measure estimation is presented.

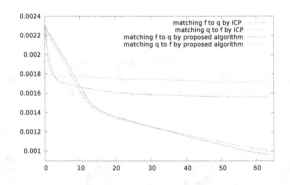

Fig. 3. Results of rigid body registration

In the test of the weighted ICP algorithm, weights ω_f, ω_g and penalization weight ψ' are involved to obtain comparable results. It should be noted that ICP calculates transformation for only one range image in the pair. In contrast our algorithm computes transformations for both surfaces. Distance maps after 65 iterations of ICP is presented in the second column of Figure 2.

The proposed algorithm is tested in two stages. At the fist stage only the similarity is computed. The result of this operation is presented in the third column of Figure 2. Here we can see that registration is more accurate in the place where correspondences between range images are inverse. It means that in notation of Equation (3) $C_{fg}(x) = q(x' + \delta)$ and $C_{qf}(x') = f(x + \delta)$, where δ is less than one pixel. Corresponding mean surfaces g_f and g_q are close to each other and consistent (because of the consistency constraint (6)) in such case. We see that the depth images come together in the face area there surface is not changed from one view to another. Opposite the fields of a breast where surface is subject to deformations are automatically ignored. ICP algorithm searches the optimal solution for registration for whole range image which leads to inaccuracy in our case.

The resulting distance maps after applying the algorithm with scene flow computation are presented in right column of Figure 2. The distance between the surfaces is close to zero in all places there correspondences can be obtained.

The main advantage of scene flow is a possibility to blend surface on to others where local distortions can not be corrected by rigid transformation. We use the set of four range images in order to reconstruct the object of interest. Source patches intersect at approximately 30% of their surface. We use in this case a strategy when rigid registration is made until convergence. Scene flow is applied at final step. The result of stitching is presented in Figure 4.'

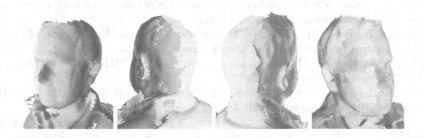

Fig. 4. Resulting stitching of a bust

We consider the presented approach as a useful solution for deformed range image stitching. Registration step can be effectively used instead of ICP algorithm for accurate matching of distorted surfaces. Scene flow computation step is prominent solution for local deformation in order to have consistent surface.

Acknowledgements. This work is partially funded by the ZIM project "Büstenreconstruction".

References

1. Arthaya, B., Gunawan, I., Gunawan, H.: Point clouds construction algorithm from a home-made laser scanner. In: 8th International Conference on Intelligent Systems Design and Applications, ISDA 2008, vol. 1, pp. 570–575 (November 2008)
2. Lamovsky, D., Lasaruk, A.: Calibration and Reconstruction Algorithms for a Hand-held 3D Laser Scanner. In: Blanc-Talon, J., Kleihorst, R., Philips, W., Popescu, D., Scheunders, P. (eds.) ACIVS 2011. LNCS, vol. 6915, pp. 635–646. Springer, Heidelberg (2011)
3. Lanman, D., Crispell, D., Taubin, G.: Surround structured lighting for full object scanning. In: Proceedings of the Sixth International Conference on 3-D Digital Imaging and Modeling, 3DIM 2007, pp. 107–116. IEEE Computer Society, Washington, DC (2007)
4. Furukawa, Y., Ponce, J.: Accurate, dense, and robust multiview stereopsis. IEEE Trans. Pattern Anal. Mach. Intell. 32(8), 1362–1376 (2010)

5. Salvi, J., Matabosch, C., Fofi, D., Forest, J.: A review of recent range image registration methods with accuracy evaluation. Image Vision Comput. 25, 578–596 (2007)
6. Besl, P., McKay, N.: A method for registration of 3-d shapes. IEEE Transactions on Pattern Analysis and Machine Intelligence 14, 239–256 (1992)
7. Turk, G., Levoy, M.: Zippered polygon meshes from range images. In: Proceedings of the 21st Annual Conference on Computer Graphics and Interactive Techniques, SIGGRAPH 1994, pp. 311–318. ACM, New York (1994)
8. Schütz, C., Jost, T., Hügli, H.: Semi-Automatic 3d Object Digitizing System Using Range Images. In: Chin, R., Pong, T.-C. (eds.) ACCV 1998. LNCS, vol. 1352, pp. 490–497. Springer, Heidelberg (1997)
9. Zhang, Z.: Iterative point matching for registration of free-form curves and surfaces. Int. J. Comput. Vision 13, 119–152 (1994)
10. Coudrin, B., Devy, M., Orteu, J.-J., Brèthes, L.: Precise Registration of 3D Images Acquired from a Hand-Held Visual Sensor. In: Blanc-Talon, J., Kleihorst, R., Philips, W., Popescu, D., Scheunders, P. (eds.) ACIVS 2011. LNCS, vol. 6915, pp. 712–723. Springer, Heidelberg (2011)
11. Ikemoto, L.: A hierarchical method for aligning warped meshes. In: Proc. Intl. Conf. on 3D Digital Imaging and Modeling, pp. 434–441 (2003)
12. Cheng, Z.Q., Jiang, W., Dang, G., Martin, R.R., Li, J., Li, H., Chen, Y., Wang, Y., Li, B., Xu, K., Jin, S.: Non-rigid registration in 3d implicit vector space. In: Proceedings of the 2010 Shape Modeling International Conference, SMI 2010, pp. 37–46. IEEE Computer Society, Washington, DC (2010)
13. Vedula, S., Baker, S., Rander, P., Collins, R., Kanade, T.: Three-dimensional scene flow. IEEE Transactions on Pattern Analysis and Machine Intelligence 27(3), 475–480 (2005)
14. Lorensen, W.E., Cline, H.E.: Marching cubes: A high resolution 3d surface construction algorithm. SIGGRAPH Comput. Graph. 21(4), 163–169 (1987)
15. Brox, T., Bruhn, A., Papenberg, N., Weickert, J.: High Accuracy Optical Flow Estimation Based on a Theory for Warping. In: Pajdla, T., Matas, J(G.) (eds.) ECCV 2004. LNCS, vol. 3024, pp. 25–36. Springer, Heidelberg (2004)
16. Horn, B.K.P., Schunck, B.G.: Determining optical flow. Artifical Intelligence 17, 185–203 (1981)

Active Visual-Based Detection and Tracking of Moving Objects from Clustering and Classification Methods

David Márquez-Gámez and Michel Devy

CNRS, LAAS, Université de Toulouse
7 avenue du Colonel Roche, F-31077 Toulouse Cedex, France
{dmarquez,michel}@laas.fr

Abstract. This paper describes a method proposed for the detection, the tracking and the identification of mobile objects, detected from a mobile camera, typically a camera embedded on a robot. A global architecture is presented, using only vision, in order to solve simultaneously several problems: the camera (or vehicle) Localization, the environment Mapping and the Detection and Tracking of Moving Objects. The goal is to build a convenient description of a dynamic scene from vision: what is static? What is dynamic? where is the robot? how do other mobile objects move? It is proposed to combine two approaches; first a Clustering method allows to detect static points, to be used by the SLAM algorithm and dynamic ones, to segment and estimate the status of mobile objects. Second a classification approach allows to identify objects of known classes in image regions. These two approaches are combined in an active method based in a Motion Grid in order to select actively where to look for mobile objects. The overall approach is evaluated with real data acquired indoor and outdoor from a camera embedded on a mobile robot.

Keywords: Moving Objects, Detection, Tracking, Clustering, Classification.

1 Introduction

This work copes with the detection and the tracking of moving objects from a camera embedded on a mobile robot, navigating in an unknown and dynamic environment. The goal is to provide a convenient description of the world, and especially of the moving objects: position, speed and, when possible, type (pedestrian, vehicle, bike. . .). Indeed in order to build such a model for moving objects, it is required in the same time, to characterize the robot position and speed with respect to static components of the environment.

This last problem is solved by a SLAM algorithm, for Simultaneous Localization and Mapping; thanks to the convergence between Structure From Motion in Vision, and SLAM in Robotics it exists now efficient methods (PTAM, iSAM2. . .) able of estimating both a vehicle trajectory and the world structure. But all SLAM algorithms assume that the world is static, so that landmark position estimates can be iteratively refined, and can be used as external references for robot localization.

J. Blanc-Talon et al. (Eds.): ACIVS 2012, LNCS 7517, pp. 361–373, 2012.

If the robot moves in a dynamic world, the SLAM algorithm must avoid landmarks to be selected on moving objects. This paper proposes a complete system to solve the SLAM with Detection and Tracking of Moving Objects (*SLAM+DATMO*) using only vision. Here visual SLAM based on point landmarks is supposed to be solved, using the EKF-SLAM algorithm developed in [9]. This paper is focused on the Moving Objects Detection problem, i.e. how to initially *detect* moving objects or features. Taking into account robustness, safety and real time constraints, one difficult issue arises from the impossibility to exhaustively analyze the whole image surface at every single frame. It is proposed first an active method that exploits knowledge extracted from previous images in order to anticipate where potential moving objects may appear in the image, thus focusing the detecting procedure to those areas. Second a framework is proposed in order to combine several detection algorithms, on the basis of a probabilistic Motion Grid, in which every detection result is recorded. Once the robot position is known and moving features are detected, the MOT problem is solved by filtering techniques.

Outline: previous works are detailed in section 2. Initial moving object model definition and representation is presented in section 3. The proposed *SLAM+DATMO* system is described in section 4. Section 5 presents some experimental results using real image sequences. Finally, section 6 summarizes our contribution and presents future works.

2   Related Works

Simultaneous localization, mapping and moving object tracking (SLAMMOT) involves both the SLAM execution in dynamic environments and the detecting and tracking of dynamic objects. The first remarkable work on SLAMMOT is due to Wang [13]. The system takes 2D laser-based SLAM and incorporates tracking of moving objects. These objects are detected by isolating portions of the current laser scan that do not show sufficiently good match with respect to the current SLAM map. The whole system relies on high speed, long range, laser range finders. The most impressive aspect resides in its ability to perform large area SLAM at high speeds with long loop-closing in urban, dense-traffic conditions.

An alternative interesting approach is due to Agrawal et al. [1]. Dense disparity images are produced by means of a calibrated stereo rig. Visual odometry is proposed to determine the camera egomotion. Then an Inverse Perspective Mapping method, allows to compare the appearance of each pixel to the appearance it should have based on the previous image. Pixels that show sufficiently large appearance variation are classified as candidates to have suffered independent rigid motion, hence belonging to moving objects. Some blob grouping and spurious rejection are performed; finally a Kalman filter in 3D space with a constant-speed model, allows to estimate to the trajectory and speed for each moving object.

Sola [10], did an observability analysis in order to isolate moving objects from static ones. Some contextual rules allow to make simpler the detection problem. Tracking was done separately and individually for each moving object in a robocentric representation.

In [14], a 3D object tracker runs in parallel with monocular SLAM for tracking a predefined moving object. This prevents the visual SLAM framework from incorporating moving features extracted on the moving object. But the proposed approach does not cope with moving object detection.

Migliore et al. [8], proposed monocular SLAMMOT approach; moving objects are detected by a simple statistic test and tracked by separated bearing only trackers. The main drawback of their system is the poor accuracy on estimates of the moving objects, due to the fact that they maintain separate filters for tracking each individual moving feature.

Gate and al [6] proposes a multisensor system based on a laser-based hypothesis generation, and in a vision-based classification approach to make the Object Detection function more robust.

All the presented approaches, propose original methods to compute SLAM with MOT. Indeed, these systems can arguably and mostly be seen as a juxtaposition of a SLAM algorithm and a MOT algorithm that share limited information. There are still important boundaries between *localization and mapping* on the first hand and *detection and tracking* on the other hand, besides, only a small number of possible interactions between SLAM and MOT is exploited.

3 Moving Objects: Model and Representation

In this section, we described the initial model definition and representation of moving objects for understanding the proposed *BiCam SLAM-DATMO* approach described in next section.

3.1 Moving Objects Model

The model of a single point is defined as a generic $3D$ point in space. A moving point, is a point which is intended to be tracked by the robot. The moving points, $o_j^{O_i}$, are considered punctual, defined by their position and linear velocities.

An object, O_i, is defined as a set of nearby points with coherent motion (very similar velocities) that are rigidly linked together, defining a fixed structure. This structure, is a characteristic of the object and can be specified by all moving points in a certain object frame. A moving object keeps the fixed structure but its frame varies with time giving, $o_j^{O_i} = o_j^{O_i}(t)$ and $O_i = O_i(t)$. The notation of time (t) is considered implicit and omitted in the formulation.

We write then the initial representations of *moving points* and *moving objects* states as follows:

$$o_j^{O_i} = \begin{bmatrix} m_j^{O_i} & v_j^{O_i} \end{bmatrix}^T, \quad O_i = \begin{bmatrix} o_1^{O_i} \dots o_n^{O_i} \end{bmatrix}^T \tag{1}$$

where $o_j^{O_i}$, is the state of *moving point* j, containing their position, $m_j^{O_i}$, and linear velocity $v_j^{O_i}$, respectively. The set of moving points $(o_j^{O_i})$, defines the *moving object* i (O_i). Any moving point can be expressed in world frame W $(o_j^{O_i^W})$, robot frame R $(o_j^{O_i^R})$ or camera frame C $(o_j^{O_i^C})$, with the usual frame transformation functions.

3.2 Moving Objects Representation

In a classic SLAM system, landmarks are usually static in order to guarantee proper localization, the presence of moving objects avoids us to consider for localization: the measurements that the robot will make on them must not contribute to modify its belief on its own localization. This approach, allows to a moving objects representation completely independent from the map, which in our case is accomplished by de-correlating moving objects states from robot and landmarks states. The only link between the robot pose, the mapped moving objects and their past positions are described by the current measurements and the moving object's motion model. Finally the *BiCam SLAM-DATMO* map consists of the main BiCam SLAM state and a set of stochastic vectors, updated by EKF, one per moving object, thus:

$$X^T = \begin{bmatrix} C_L^T & C_R^T & L_1^T & \dots & L_M^T \end{bmatrix}, \quad \mathcal{O}_i^T = \begin{bmatrix} \mathbf{o}_1^{\mathcal{O}_i T} \dots \mathbf{o}_n^{\mathcal{O}_i T} \end{bmatrix} \tag{2}$$

where $C_{L/R}^T = [\mathbf{r}_{L/R}^T, \mathbf{q}_{L/R}^T] \in \mathbb{R}^7$, is the camera state Left or Right respectively, given by its position and orientation quaternion plus the set of landmarks $L_j = i_j \in \mathbb{R}^6$ (inverse depth) or $L_j = p_j \in \mathbb{R}^3$ (euclidean coordinates) and $\mathbf{o}_j^{\mathcal{O}_i T} = (\mathbf{m}_j^{\mathcal{O}_i}, \mathbf{v}_j^{\mathcal{O}_i})$, is the moving point state given by its position and motion model (velocity). Motion model is initially considered constant-velocity model.

4   System Description

We have developed a complete system for SLAM-DATMO, using a BiCam-vision bench as the only sensor. The major processing blocks of our system are depicted in Figure 1. Hereafter functions related to the two detection approached, are commented; the SLAM function execute a classical vision-based SLAM, either from a monocular system or using from several cameras using the Bi-Cam strategy presented in [10].

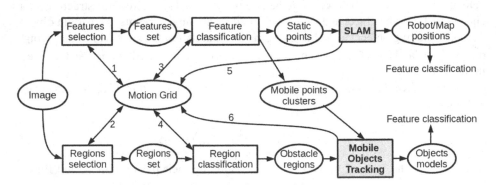

Fig. 1. The major processing blocks in our system and their connections, executed for each frame of a video sequence

4.1   Feature Selection

The Feature Selection function must profit from all knowledge already found on previous images, or from contextual or application-dependant knowledge. So every time points have to be selected, it exploits a *Motion Grid*, built from a discretization of the image space; this map gives the probability on every image cell, to find a dynamic point. Initially this probability is uniform; then it is updated according to several criteria discussed in section 4.2. New points are detected in cells which have the higher probability; initially these points are uniformly distributed in the image. Then as one goes along the method, points are replaced once they have been either lost by the point tracker, or identified as static, while dynamic points are kept in the points set and tracked continuously.

4.2 Motion Grid

In our system, it is important to add new points that make the model of the detected moving object denser, and at the same time detect new incoming moving objects, thus, it is required to actively select points or regions to be classified as obstacle or as mobile; especially features tracks will be searched only in regions where the occurrence of a moving object is the more probable. To describe the behavior of this occurrence, the concept of *Motion Grid* was introduced in [2]. A Motion Grid acts as an occupancy grid, in the sense that higher probabilities represent occupied (moving) zones and lower probabilities free (statio) ones, where to monitor the arrival of new moving points.

The motion grid is modified or exploited by a function on every labelled edge on figure 1. On the edges 1 and 2, the *Features selection* and *Regions selection* functions select features or regions on the more probable areas where to detect mobile obstacles. It will allow to confirm or not a previous detection. It has been found that the feature-based method could generate false alarms on the ground in regions close to the camera because here, the apparent motion is important; the region-based method could remove these false alarms. But it is possible that it exist really here a mobile object, the class of which has not been learnt (for example an animal); so one detector can be efficient while the other one fails. For example, the region-based approach is able to detect static objects belonging to the learnt classes; even if static, these objects could move, so that (1) features selected on these regions must be monitored to detect when these objects move, and (2) SLAM must avoid to select features on these areas.

On the edge 3 and 4, the *Feature classification* and *Region classification* functions update the motion grid. As a set of features tracked during N_{im} successive images, are grouped in a mobile feature cluster, the motion grid must be updated. The probability values in the map are modified by a bidimensionnal Gaussian function centered on every mobile point (u, v), with σ_u and σ_v, parameters to be tuned. The probability that a pixel belongs to a moving object, is inversely proportional to its distance to the closer detected moving point. The same method is applied around a static point, using the inverse of a bidimensionnal Gaussian function, so that the probability that a point is static is also inversely proportional to its distance to the closer detected static point. So every pixel in the Motion Grid receives the influence of closer points labelled static or dynamic. The method is detailed in [2]. For a region, the uncertainty given by the classification method is directly transferred to every pixel of the region, whatever the label.

Finally, for the edge 5 and 6, the *SLAM* and *MOT* functions update the motion grid. For SLAM, if a landmark is not observed, it could be interpreted that it is occluded by a new obstacle. So probabilities around the predicted position of its observation, are updated using the Gaussian function. Reciprocally, if a landmark is observed, it means that the surrounding area is static, so probabilities are updated using the inverse Gaussian function. For MOT, probabilities are updated according to the object tracking results: features will be selected inside and around regions already detected as mobile in the previous images. It will allow to densify the object models, to select features behind an object track (perhaps the tracked object occludes another one),.

4.3   Feature Classification

We need to classify new features as dynamic or static before using them to estimate the robot pose, the moving objects pose and the map. Based on [2], a solution to detect moving objects is proposed, we call this procedure *Feature classification*, the goal of which is recalled on Figure 2.

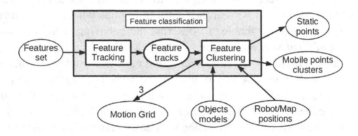

Fig. 2. The *Feature classification* process

In this point, N_p initial feature points are selected. Feature locations in next image are searched by a KLT tracker, based on correlation and optimization functions. This process loops on N_{Im} successive images. This set of N_{Im} processed images, are the number of images used to accumulate positions and apparent velocities of tracked features. Only moving KLT features are selected for being grouped by the a contrario clustering method [11]. Thus, this function generates a list of static points and a list of M_i clusters or potential moving objects, each one defined by a list of points and by characteristics: the cluster barycenter and the mean points apparent velocity. This function requires the Robot position or the motion estimation between the last acquisitions, in order to remove false positives by an EgoMotion compensation. It needs also the current Object models, in order to try to fuse new clusters to existing objects, before creating new ones.

4.4   Object Hypotheses: Classification Based Approach

Object hypotheses, are created from the output of a detector based classification. The system we propose is independent of a particular detector choice [5], [12]. Nevertheless in our experiments for practical purposes we use the AdaBoost algorithm [12]. This algorithm is based on the idea that a series of trained weak classifiers can build a strong and efficient classifier. The algorithm described here is specifically and only intended to classify a region as being a pedestrian or a car.

Each cluster or group candidate noted M_i sent by the *Feature classification* function, produces a region of interest in the corresponding image. Only these regions of interest will be processed by the *Object Hypotheses* algorithm to accelerate the search-detection of the classification algorithm inside the image.

Thus, the region of interest M_i is decomposed into n different regions, $(M_i^k)_{1 \leq k \leq n}$, each one of these n regions is processed by the classification algorithm and is given a value λ_i^k corresponding to the sum of the weighted combination of the N weak classifiers, $(w_l)_{1 \leq l \leq N}$

$$\lambda_i^k = \sum_{1 \leq l \leq N} \alpha_l w_l(M_i^k) \tag{3}$$

Finally, for each cluster M_i a global classification score is computed as follow:

$$\Theta_i^c = \max_{1 \leq k \leq n} \lambda_i^k \tag{4}$$

As the algorithm described above is only trained to compute a classification probability for a given region to be a pedestrian or a car, no detection or tracking information can be deduced from such result. However, as explained above every cluster region is given a new classification score Θ_i^c.

For any given cluster-object i at time k, this classification score is independent and different from the uncertainty score already computed by the *Motion Grid*. The fusion rule to combine those different scores is detailed below.

Final Object Hypotheses Fusion Rule. In order to finally detect correctly moving objects, the estimation of the *Motion Grid* has to be combined with the estimation of the *Object Hypotheses classification based approach*. Two different estimates of the same probabilities, $P(\mathcal{O}_i|A_j)$, the probability of the event $\mathcal{O}_i$ (to be a moving object) given A_j. These estimates have been computed by algorithms that are subject to uncertainties. Thus, each estimate can be rewritten as follows:

$$P(\mathcal{O}_i|A_1) = \Theta_i^{pm} \tag{5}$$

$$P(\mathcal{O}_i|A_2) = \Theta_i^c \tag{6}$$

where $P(\mathcal{O}_i|A_1)$ is the estimation of the *Motion Grid* and $P(\mathcal{O}_i|A_2)$ is the estimation of the *classification based approach*. Assuming that A_1 and A_2 are independent, the following fusion rule can be derived from basic Probability rules:

$$\begin{aligned}
P(\mathcal{O}_i) &= P(\mathcal{O}_i \cap (A_1 \cup A_2)) + P(\mathcal{O}_i \cap (\overline{A_1 \cup A_2})) \\
&= P(\mathcal{O}_i|A_1)P(A_1)P(\overline{A_2}) + P(\mathcal{O}_i|A_2)P(\overline{A_1})P(A_2) \\
&\quad + P(\mathcal{O}_i|A_1 \cap A_2)P(A_1)P(A_2) + P(\mathcal{O}_i|\overline{A_1} \cap \overline{A_2})P(\overline{A_1})P(\overline{A_2})
\end{aligned} \tag{7}$$

where $P(A_j)$ refers to the probability for the subsystem j (motion grid or classification based approach) to return wrong estimation. $P(\mathcal{O}_i|\overline{A_1} \cap \overline{A_2})$ can be approximated to ξ, a priory classification probabilities. Thus, the fusion rule is approximated as a weighted sum:

$$\begin{aligned}
\Phi_{\mathcal{O}_i} &= \Theta_i^{pm}P(A_1)P(\overline{A_2}) + \Theta_i^c P(\overline{A_1})P(A_2) \\
&\quad + \frac{\Theta_i^{pm}P(A_1) + \Theta_i^c P(A_2)}{P(A_1) + P(A_2)} P(A_1)P(A_2) + \xi P(\overline{A_1})P(\overline{A_2})
\end{aligned} \tag{8}$$

At this point, final estimate for the detection probability is available. The final Moving Object detection is done based on a threshold. Thus, for each region of interest M_i,

$$M_i = \begin{cases} Moving\ Object & \text{if } \Phi_{\mathcal{O}_i} \geq \text{threshold} \\ NOT\ Moving\ Object & \text{if } \Phi_{\mathcal{O}_i} < \text{threshold} \end{cases}$$

Our fusion strategy is based on the combination of the estimates of two algorithms of different nature that are contributing, the *Motion Grid* and the *Object Hypotheses classification based approach* algorithms.

4.5 Moving Objects Tracking

Moving Points and Objects Creation. Upon each moving object detection an EKF is created to host its state's *pdf*. The mobile state vector is hence the Gaussian $\mathcal{O} \sim \mathcal{N}\{\bar{\mathcal{O}}; \mathbf{P}_{\mathcal{O}}\}$. For its creation we will follow the IDP initialization method like in [3]. Initial mean and covariances matrix for moving points positions $\mathbf{m}_j^{\mathcal{O}_i}$, belonging to moving object $\mathcal{O}_i$, are determined from the inverse depth parametrization from the left camera

$$\mathbf{m}_j^{\mathcal{O}_i} = \mathbf{d}_L(C_L, \mathbf{h}_L, \rho) \tag{9}$$

where $\mathbf{d}_L(\cdot)$ is a function of $C_L^T = [\mathbf{x}_L^T, \mathbf{q}_L^T]$ the left camera state containing current position and orientation, $\mathbf{h}_L \sim \mathcal{N}\{\mathbf{y}_L; \mathbf{R}\}$ the Gaussian observation from the left camera and $\rho \sim \mathcal{N}\{\bar{\rho}; \sigma_\rho^2\}$ the inverse of the Euclidean distance from C_L to the moving point position. After the first observation with the left camera, all parameters of $\mathbf{m}_j^{\mathcal{O}_i}$ except ρ are immediately observable, and their values and covariances are obtained by proper inversion and linearization of the observation functions.

Thus, moving point position's, $\mathbf{m}_j^{\mathcal{O}_i}$, initial mean and covariances matrix are then

$$\bar{\mathbf{m}}_j^{\mathcal{O}_i} = \mathbf{d}_L(C_L, \bar{\mathbf{h}}_L, \bar{\rho}) \tag{10}$$

$$\mathbf{P_{mm}} = \mathbf{D}_{Lh}\,\mathbf{R}\,\mathbf{D}_{Lh}^T + \mathbf{D}_{L\rho}\,\sigma_\rho^2\,\mathbf{D}_{L\rho}^T \tag{11}$$

where $\mathbf{R}$ is the rotation matrix and the Jacobian matrices are

$$\mathbf{D}_{Lh} = \left.\frac{\partial \mathbf{d}_L}{\partial \mathbf{h}^T}\right|_{(\bar{C}_L, \bar{\mathbf{h}}, \bar{\rho})}, \quad \mathbf{D}_{L\rho} = \left.\frac{\partial \mathbf{d}_L}{\partial \rho^T}\right|_{(\bar{C}_L, \bar{\mathbf{h}}, \bar{\rho})} \tag{12}$$

Initial mean and covariances matrix for the moving points's velocity $\mathbf{v}_j^{\mathcal{O}_i} \sim \mathcal{N}\{\bar{\mathbf{v}}_j^{\mathcal{O}_i}; \mathbf{P_{vv}}\}$ are heuristically determined like in [7].

Finally, the full moving object's Gaussian *pdf* is the specified by the couple

$$\bar{\mathcal{O}}_i = \begin{bmatrix} \bar{\mathbf{m}}_j^{\mathcal{O}_i} \\ \bar{\mathbf{v}}_j^{\mathcal{O}_i} \end{bmatrix}, \quad \mathbf{P}_{\mathcal{O}_i} = \begin{bmatrix} \mathbf{P_{mm}} & 0 \\ 0 & \mathbf{P_{vv}} \end{bmatrix}, \tag{13}$$

Immediately after creation, this EKF is updated with the observation from the right camera. The observation function from the right camera is the simple pin-hole camera projection function expressed in right-frame, generically written as

$$\mathbf{y}_R = \mathbf{h}_R(C_R, \mathbf{m}_j^{\mathcal{O}_i}) + v_R \tag{14}$$

where $v_R \sim \mathcal{N}\{0; \mathbf{R}\}$ is independent white Gaussian observation noise.

Thus, upon observation from right camera, with uncertainty pose $C_R \sim \mathcal{N}\{\bar{C}_R; \mathbf{P}_{C_R}\}$, the moving object's pdf is update following the EKF equations. The linearity test in [4] is regularly evaluated. If passed, the object position can be safely transformed into a 3-D Euclidean parametrization.

Moving Objects and Robot Motion Compensation. The robot time-evolution model is considered an odometry model, this, can be generically written as $R^+ = \mathbf{f}_R(R, \mathbf{u})$ where $\mathbf{u}$ is a vector of robots controls or odometry data

$$\mathbf{u} = \begin{bmatrix} \delta\mathbf{x} \\ \delta\mathbf{e} \end{bmatrix} = [\delta x, \delta y, \delta z, \delta\phi, \delta\theta, \delta\psi]^T \in \mathbb{R}^6 \tag{15}$$

with Gaussian pdf $\mathbf{u} \sim \mathcal{N}\{\bar{\mathbf{u}}; \mathbf{U}\}$. Upon robot motion, moving objects must change their coordinates from the old robot frame-position to the new one, thus

$$\mathcal{O}_i^+ = \mathbf{j}_{\mathcal{O}}(\mathcal{O}_i, \mathbf{u}) \tag{16}$$

which is a frame transformation that is specified by the odometry parameters $\mathbf{u}^T = [\delta\mathbf{x}^T, \delta\mathbf{e}^T]$, we can then write the moving objects as

$$\mathbf{m}_j^{\mathcal{O}_i+} = \mathbf{R}^T \delta(e) \cdot (\mathbf{m}_j^{\mathcal{O}_i} - \delta x) \tag{17}$$

$$\mathbf{v}_j^{\mathcal{O}_i+} = \mathbf{R}^T \delta(e) \cdot \mathbf{v}_j^{\mathcal{O}_i} \tag{18}$$

where $\mathbf{R}^T \delta(e)$ is the rotation matrix from the Euler angles increment $\delta(e)$.

Thus, with the new (compensated) positions and velocities, the moving object's pdf is update following the EKF equations.

Moving Objects Motion. Constant velocity motion models produce more or less smooth trajectories depending on the amount of noise introduced in the system. For example, the motion of a pedestrian can be modeled with a constant velocity model in the 2D plane. If we consider it cannot stop abruptly, a single, relatively small Gaussian will do. A larger Gaussian could be used to accommodate for sudden stops and goes, but that would reduce the motion's smoothness and eliminate the difference between the states go and stop. The better suited model is a two hypotheses model with associated transition probabilities. Nevertheless, in this work, for practical purposes, motion model is considered constant-velocity model. Therefore, moving object's time-evolution model is written as

$$\mathcal{O}_i^+ = \mathbf{f}_{\mathcal{O}}(\mathcal{O}_i, \omega) \tag{19}$$

which responds to the constant-velocity model with no rotational part defined by

$$\mathbf{m}_j^{\mathcal{O}_i+} = \mathbf{m}_j^{\mathcal{O}_i} + T_s \mathbf{v}_j^{\mathcal{O}_i} \tag{20}$$

$$\mathbf{v}_j^{\mathcal{O}_i+} = \mathbf{v}_j^{\mathcal{O}_i} + \omega \tag{21}$$

where T_s is the filter's sampling time and $\omega = [\omega_x, \omega_y, \omega_z]^T \in \mathbb{R}^3$ is a white Gaussian velocity perturbation $\omega \sim \mathcal{N}\{0, \mathbf{Q}\}$.

5   Experimental Results

We present preliminary results with a ground robot: a Segway platform equipped with a calibrated stereo-vision bench made of two 1024 x 768 cameras with a baseline of 0.35 m. We demonstrate the BiCam SLAM-DATMO system operation in two real data experiment with various number and type of moving objects.

5.1   Indoor Experiment: 2D Detection and Tracking Task

The robot with the two cameras looking forward is run in straight line inside the robotic lab at LAAS. Two moving objects are presented in the scene, first, a single pedestrian traversing from left to right appears and then a second pedestrian with a caddy traversing from right to left.

Figure 3, shows results for this experiment. The result showed that effectively moving objects are successfully detected clustered and tracked by the proposed approach. The left image of Figure 3 shows the bounding box on two moving objects, $\mathcal{O}_1$ which enters from the left side of the image and $\mathcal{O}_2$ on the right side; all detected points inside this box are used to initialize the object model. Object region could grow at each time when new clusters are detected, thanks to the cluster fusion mechanism. An example of this behavior is shown in the center image of Figure 3, where we clearly see that the bounding box of $\mathcal{O}_2$ was enlarged.

Fig. 3. Detection clustering and tracking objects. In the image view, *cyan* and *blue* features are static points to be used by the SLAM process; *yellow* features are updated moving points; *red squares* are moving objects. The result show that two moving objects are detected and tracked simultaneously in 2D space.

Fig. 4. Outdoor experiment results: image plane and top views of the produced 3D map. In the image view, *red* features are updated IDP landmarks; *magenta* features are predicted IDP landmarks; *cyan* features are update euclidean landmarks; *blue* features are predicted euclidean landmarks; *yellow* features are updated moving points; *3D bounding box* are moving objects (yellow: O_1; green: O_2; magenta: O_3). The moving objects has been successfully detected and tracked in 3D space as can be seen in the views.

5.2 Outdoor Experiment: BiCam SLAM-DATMO

We tested our system in outdoor environment. For this experiment, the robot with the two cameras looking forward is run in the *Canal du Midi*. A simple 2D odometry model is used for robot-motion predictions. Three moving objects can be observed (O_1, O_2, O_3): three persons riding bicycle traversing the scene, moving in all directions and occluding each other. Figure 4, shows the results for this experiment. As can be seen, the system is able to detect and track moving objects and to accurately predict their future motion in 3D space. The bounding boxes are colored to show objects identities. Below each image, we show the map in a overhead view, static landmarks used by the SLAM process are marked in blue. In the first row, the three first images show the evolution of a moving object O_1 (with bounding box yellow) which enters from the left side; in the first image of the third row, a second moving object O_2 (with bounding box green) which enters from the right side is detected. The system ability to track through occlusion is demostrated in the third row: note how the person entering from the left with bounding box magenta (O_3), temporarily occludes the person entering from the right with bounding box green (O_2). Still, the system manages to pick up the trajectory of the person on the right again.

The performance of robot localization, mapping and tracking of moving objects verify that the proposed BiCam SLAM-DATMO approach is feasible in dynamic environments. Videos illustrating the results, can be can be seen at:

`http://homepages.laas.fr/dmarquez/slammot`

6   Conclusions

This paper presents a system that enables a practical solution to the SLAM problem with Detection and Tracking of Moving Objects that is based only on visual exteroceptive perception. The detection of moving objects is performed by a method that allows selection of interesting regions in the image in order to anticipate eventual moving objects apparition in the next few frames. The different functions in the system were integrated to perform visual SLAM and detection and tracking of moving objects, and we presented, how each function interact with other. Experiments on various real indoor and outdoor sequences shows the efficacy of the system.

References

1. Agrawal, M., Konolige, K., Iocchi, L.: Real-time detection of independent motion using stereo. In: Proceedings IEEE Workshop on Visual Motion (2005)
2. Almanza-Ojeda, D.L., Devy, M., Herbulot, A.: Active method for mobile object detection from an embedded camera, based on a contrario clustering. In: Informatics in Control, Automation and Robotics, vol. 89, pp. 267–280 (2011)
3. Civera, J., Davison, A.J., Montiel, J.M.M.: Inverse depth parametrization for monocular slam. IEEE Trans. on Robotics 24 (2008)
4. Civera, J., Davison, A.J., Montiel, J.M.M.: Inverse depth to depth conversion for monocular slam. In: International Conference on Robotics and Automation, pp. 2778–2783 (2007)

5. Dalal, N., Triggs, B.: Histograms of oriented gradients for human detection. In: Proceedings of the 2005 IEEE Computer Society Conference on Computer Vision and Pattern Recognition (CVPR 2005), Washington, DC, vol. 01, pp. 886–893 (2005)

6. Gate, G., Breheret, A., Nashashibi, F.: Fast pedestrian detection in dense environment with a laser scanner and a camera. In: IEEE 69th Vehicular Technology Conference, VTC Spring 2009, pp. 1–6 (April 2009)

7. Lin, K.H., Wang, C.C.: Stereo-based simultaneous localization, mapping and moving object tracking. In: IEEE/RSJ International Conference on Intelligent Robots and Systems (IROS), Taipei, Taiwan (October 2010)

8. Migliore, D., Rigamonti, R., Marzorati, D., Matteucci, M., Sorrenti, D.: Use a single camera for simultaneous localization and mapping with mobile object tracking in dynamic environments. In: Proceedings of International Workshop on Safe Navigation in Open and Dynamic Environments Application to Autonomous Vehicles (May 2009)

9. Sola, J., Monin, A., Devy, M., Vidal-Calleja, T.: Fusing monocular information in multicamera slam. IEEE Trans. on Robotics 24(5), 958–968 (2008)

10. Sola, J.: Towards Visual Localization, Mapping and Moving Objects Tracking by a Mobile Robot: a Geometric and Probabilistic Approach. Ph.D. thesis, Institut National Politechnique de Toulouse, Toulouse (February 2007)

11. Veit, T., Cao, F., Bouthemy, P.: Space-time a contrario clustering for detecting coherent motions. In: 2007 IEEE International Conference on Robotics and Automation, pp. 33–39 (April 2007)

12. Viola, P., Jones, M.: Robust real-time object detection. International Journal of Computer Vision 57(2), 137–154 (2002)

13. Wang, C.C.: Simultaneous Localization, Mapping and Moving Object Tracking. Ph.D. thesis, Robotics Institute, Carnegie Mellon University, Pittsburgh, PA (April 2004)

14. Wangsiripitak, S., Murray, D.: Avoiding moving outliers in visual slam by tracking moving objects. In: IEEE International Conference on Robotics and Automation, ICRA 2009, pp. 375–380 (May 2009)

Recovering Projective Transformations
between Binary Shapes

József Németh

Department of Computer Algorithms and Artificial Intelligence, University of Szeged
H-6701 Szeged, P.O. Box 652., Hungary
nemjozs@inf.u-szeged.hu

Abstract. Binary image registration has been addressed by many authors recently however most of the proposed approaches are restricted to affine transformations. In this paper a novel approach is proposed to estimate the parameters of a general projective transformation (also called homography) that aligns two shapes. Recovering such projective transformations is a fundamental problem in computer vision with various applications. While classical approaches rely on established point correspondences the proposed solution does not need any feature extraction, it works only with the coordinates of the foreground pixels. The two-step method first estimates the perspective distortion independently of the affine part of the transformation which is recovered in the second step. As experiments on synthetic as well on real images show that the proposed method less sensitive to the strength of the deformation than other solutions. The efficiency of the method has also been demonstrated on the traffic sign matching problem.

1   Introduction

In most of the image processing applications a key step is the registration of images *i.e.* the estimation of the transformation which aligns one image to the other (see [17] for a good survey). The overlapped images can be then combined or compared. The estimation of the parameters of a projective transformation (also known as planar homography) between two views of the same planar object has a fundamental importance in computer vision.

Classical landmark based (or correspondence based) methods usually trace back the problem into the solution of a system of linear equations set up using the coordinates of point pairs [7]. These point pairs are usually established by matching the intensity value patterns around the points[9]. On the other hand featureless methods estimate the transformation parameters directly from image intensity values over corresponding regions[10].

In many cases, however, the images do not contain suffcient variety of graylevel values (*e.g.* images of traffic signs or letterings), or suffered from intensity value distortions (*e.g.* X-ray images). Although there are some time consuming methods to cope with brightness change across image pairs [8], these conditions make the classical brightness-based methods unreliable. In [5], Francos *et al.* propose a method for the estimation of a homeomorphism between graylevel images. They showed how to

J. Blanc-Talon et al. (Eds.): ACIVS 2012, LNCS 7517, pp. 374–383, 2012.

transform the problem into the solution of a linear system of equations, however they assumed that the intensity values differ only by a zero mean Gaussian noise.

When the segmentations are available it is reasonable to solve the registration problem using the binary versions of the images [13,6]. Most of the current approaches are restricted to affine transformations. For example Domokos *et al.* showed that it is possible to trace back the affine matching problem to an exactly solvable polynomial system of equations [2]. Affine moments and invariants can also been used to recover linear transformation [15]. In [16] Yezzi *et al.* proposed a variational framework that uses active contours to simultaneously segment and register features from multiple images. Belongie *et al.* proposed a nonlinear shape matching algorithm in [1]. The method first establish point correspondences between the binary shapes using a novel similarity metric, called *shape context*, which consists in constructing a log-polar histogram of surrounding edge pixels. Then it uses the generic thin plate spline model to align the shapes.

In [11], Nemeth *et al.* proposed a method to estimate the parameters of projective transformations between binary shapes and later it has been extended by Domokos *et al.* [3] to more general nonlinear transformations *e.g.* polynomial and thin plate spline. This method has been proved to be efficient in case of many real applications *e.g.* matching handwritten characters or aligning multimodal prostate images. Altough this approach proved to be very robust against the strength of the deformation, in some cases (*e.g.* when the shapes are rotated more than 90 degrees), it could not find the right solution due to the iterative minimization involved.

In this paper we propose a novel method to estimate the parameters of projective transformations between shapes. The perspective and the affine parts of the transformation are recovered in two sequential steps. It does not need any feature extraction or established correspondences, it works only with the coordinates of the foreground pixels. The performance of the method has been examined on synthetic as well as on real images.

2 The Registration Method

We are looking for a two dimensional projective transformation (also called *planar homography*) $\varphi : \mathbb{R}^2 \to \mathbb{R}^2$, $\varphi(\mathbf{x}) = [\varphi_1(\mathbf{x}), \varphi_2(\mathbf{x})]^T$ that aligns a pair of binary shapes, so that for any corresponding point pair $\mathbf{y} = [y_1, y_2]^T$ and $\mathbf{x} = [x_1, x_2]^T$ on the *template* and *observation* shapes:

$$\mathbf{y} = \varphi(\mathbf{x}). \tag{1}$$

A projective transformation in 2D is given by

$$y_1 = \varphi_1(\mathbf{x}) = \frac{h_{11}x_1 + h_{12}x_2 + h_{13}}{h_{31}x_1 + h_{32}x_2 + 1}$$
$$y_2 = \varphi_2(\mathbf{x}) = \frac{h_{21}x_1 + h_{22}x_2 + h_{23}}{h_{31}x_1 + h_{32}x_2 + 1}, \tag{2}$$

where h_{ij} are the elements of the $\mathbf{H}_{3\times3}$ matrix (for more details on planar homography transformations see [7]). Since $\mathbf{H}$ is defined up to scale (it has only 8 degree of freedom), one of its elements can be fixed (herein $h_{33} = 1$). Furthermore we represent the template and the observation shapes by their foreground regions $\mathcal{F}_t \subset \mathbb{R}^2$ and $\mathcal{F}_o \subset \mathbb{R}^2$. Thus we can simply write

$$\mathcal{F}_t = \varphi(\mathcal{F}_o). \tag{3}$$

The parameters h_{31} and h_{32} are responsible for the *perspective* distortion, while the others effect *affine* transformation (translation, rotation, scaling and shearing). These two parts of the transformation can be performed one after the other, so thus φ can be decomposed as follows:

$$\varphi = \varphi^a \circ \varphi^p \tag{4}$$

where $\varphi^p : \mathbb{R}^2 \to \mathbb{R}^2$, $\varphi^p(\mathbf{x}) = [\varphi_1^p(\mathbf{x}), \varphi_2^p(\mathbf{x})]^T$ is a nonlinear transformation:

$$\varphi_1^p(\mathbf{x}) = \frac{x_1}{p_1 x_1 + p_2 x_2 + 1}$$
$$\varphi_2^p(\mathbf{x}) = \frac{x_2}{p_1 x_1 + p_2 x_2 + 1}, \tag{5}$$

resulting only perspective distortion. and $\varphi^a : \mathbb{R}^2 \to \mathbb{R}^2$, $\varphi^a(\mathbf{x}) = [\varphi_1^a(\mathbf{x}), \varphi_2^a(\mathbf{x})]^T$ is an affine transformation:

$$\varphi_1^a(\mathbf{x}) = a_{11} x_1 + a_{12} x_2 + a_{13}$$
$$\varphi_2^a(\mathbf{x}) = a_{21} x_1 + a_{22} x_2 + a_{23}, \tag{6}$$

Thus we can write the relationship between the shapes as follows:

$$\mathcal{F}_t = (\varphi^a \circ \varphi^p)(\mathcal{F}_o) = \varphi^a(\varphi^p(\mathcal{F}_o)) \tag{7}$$

The proposed method estimates the p_i parameters of the perspective component φ^p and the a_i parameters of the affine component φ^a in two distinct steps, then using Eq. (4) we can get the h_{ij} parameters of φ as follows:

$$h_{11} = a_{11} + p_1 a_{13}, \quad h_{12} = a_{12} + p_2 a_{13},$$
$$h_{21} = a_{21} + p_1 a_{23}, \quad h_{22} = a_{22} + p_2 a_{23},$$
$$h_{13} = a_{13}, \quad h_{23} = a_{23}, \quad h_{31} = p_1, \quad h_{32} = p_2 \tag{8}$$

2.1   Step 1: Estimation of the Perspective Distortion

If Eq. (7) stands then there is only an affine transformation between $\mathcal{F}_t$ and $\varphi^p(\mathcal{F}_o)$, thus for any affine-invariant function $I : \mathbb{R}^2 \to \mathbb{R}$:

$$I(\mathcal{F}_t) = I(\varphi^p(\mathcal{F}_o)). \tag{9}$$

Note that the unknowns of this equation are the p_i parameters of φ^p. Moreover as we will show for given values of p_1 and p_2 using traditional moment-based affine invariants the right hand side of the equation can be efficiently estimated using only the jacobian of φ^p, so it is not necessary to actually generate the image $\varphi^p(\mathcal{F}_o)$ which would be very time-consuming.

The basic idea of the proposed method is that given a set of independent affine invariant functions $I_i : \mathbb{R}^2 \to \mathbb{R}$, $i = 1 \ldots n$ we obtain a system of equations:

$$I_i(\mathcal{F}_t) = I_i(\varphi^p(\mathcal{F}_o)). \tag{10}$$

The parameters of φ^p are obtained as the solution of this system of equations. It is clearly a highly nonlinear system and thus do not have exact solution. However as experimental results show it can be efficiently solved by a general nonlinear solver.

Although any set of affine invariant functions could be appropriate, herein we use affine moment invariants [4], because it allows a very efficient numerical estimation of the system of equations in Eq. (10). The left hand sides of the system of equations Eq. (10) do not depend on the parameters of φ^p so can be estimated directly using the point coordinates of the template image. The geometric moment m_{rs} of order $(r + s)$ of a shape $\mathcal{F}$ is defined as

$$m_{rs}(\mathcal{F}) = \int_{\mathcal{F}} x_1^r x_2^s \mathrm{d}x. \tag{11}$$

The affine moment invariants I_i of a shape are rely on the so called central moments that are defined as follows:

$$\mu_{rs}(\mathcal{F}) = \int_{\mathcal{F}} (x_1 - c_1)^r (x_2 - c_2)^s \mathrm{d}x \tag{12}$$

where the coordinates of the center of mass of the shape is given by using the geometric moments:

$$c_1 = \frac{m_{10}(\mathcal{F})}{m_{00}(\mathcal{F})} \quad \text{and} \quad c_2 = \frac{m_{01}(\mathcal{F})}{m_{00}(\mathcal{F})}. \tag{13}$$

The affine moment invariants $I_i(F)$ then are obtained using these central moments. For example the first two affine moment invariants are given as follows:

$$
\begin{aligned}
I_1 &= (\mu_{20}\mu_{02} - \mu_{11}^2)/\mu_{00}^4 \\
I_2 &= (-\mu_{30}^2\mu_{03}^2 + 6\mu_{30}\mu_{21}\mu_{12}\mu_{03} - 4\mu_{30}\mu_{12}^3 \\
&\quad -4\mu_{21}^3\mu_{03} + 3\mu_{21}^2\mu_{12}^2)/\mu_{00}^{10}.
\end{aligned} \tag{14}
$$

For more on affine moment invariants see [4].

Given fixed parameters of φ^p we show how to compute the right hand side of the equations Eq. (10) avoiding the generation of the image $\varphi^p(\mathcal{F}_o)$ by making use of the Jacobian J_{φ^p} of the transformation. For a shape $\mathcal{F}$ that is distorted by φ^p the geometric moment can be estimated as follows:

$$m_{rs}(\varphi^p(\mathcal{F})) = \int_{\mathcal{F}} [\varphi_1^p(\mathbf{x})]^r [\varphi_2^p(\mathbf{x})]^s J_{\varphi^p}(\mathbf{x})\mathrm{d}x \tag{15}$$

where the Jacobian of the perspective distortion is given by

$$J_{\varphi^p}(\mathbf{x}) = \frac{1}{(p_1 x_1 + p_2 x_2 + 1)^3},$$

(for more details on the usage of the Jacobian and mathematical derivation of such equations see [5] and [3]). On the perspectively distorted shape $\varphi^p(\mathcal{F})$ the central moments are given by

$$\mu_{rs}(\varphi^p(\mathcal{F})) = \int_{\mathcal{F}} [\varphi_1^p(\mathbf{x}) - c_1]^r [\varphi_2^p(\mathbf{x}) - c_2]^s J_{\varphi^p}(\mathbf{x})d\mathbf{x}, \tag{16}$$

where

$$c_1 = \frac{m_{10}(\varphi^p(\mathcal{F}))}{m_{00}(\varphi^p(\mathcal{F}))} \quad \text{and} \quad c_2 = \frac{m_{01}(\varphi^p(\mathcal{F}))}{m_{00}(\varphi^p(\mathcal{F}))}. \tag{17}$$

For fixed values of the parameters p_1 and p_2 the affine moment invariants $I(\varphi^p(F))$ in the right hand side of the system Eq. (10) can be obtained using the central moments in Eq. (16) that can be estimated using only the foreground points of the shape $\mathcal{F}$. Thus we avoid to generate the $\varphi^p(\mathcal{F})$ images which would be very time consuming.

2.2   Step 2: Estimation of the Affine Transformation

After the perspective distortion is recovered (*i.e.* its parameters p_1 and p_2 are determined) the affine transformation φ^a should be estimated between shapes $\mathcal{F}_t$ and $\varphi^p(\mathcal{F}_o)$. For that purpose we used the approach proposed in [2] and, as in the previous section, in order to avoid the generation of $\varphi^p(\mathcal{F}_o)$ we modified the method by making use of the Jacobian J_{φ^p} of the perspective part. The following system of equations

$$\int_{F_t} y_k^n d\mathbf{y} = J_{\varphi^a} \sum_{i=1}^{n} \binom{n}{i} \sum_{j=0}^{i} \binom{i}{j} a_{k1}^{n-i} a_{k2}^{i-j} a_{k3}^j \int_{F_o} \varphi_1^p(\mathbf{x})^{n-i} \varphi_2^p(\mathbf{x})^{i-j} J_{\varphi^p}(\mathbf{x})d\mathbf{x} \tag{18}$$

for $n = 1, 2, 3$ and $k = 1, 2$ can be written for the a_{ij} parameters of the affine transformation. This system contains six polynomial equations up to order three which is enough to solve for all unknowns.

The Jacobian of an affine transformation is constant over the whole plane, thus it can be simply estimated as the ratio of the areas of the shapes:

$$J_{\varphi^a} = \frac{\int_{\mathcal{F}_t} d\mathbf{y}}{\int_{\mathcal{F}_o} J_{\varphi^p}(\mathbf{x})d\mathbf{x}} \tag{19}$$

However the system Eq. (18) may have many solutions, we can select the real root which gives the same determinant as what we computed in Eq. (19). Note that the solution is not unique if the shape is affine symmetric.

Putting together the projective transformation φ^p and the affine transformation φ^a using Eq. (8) we get the h_{ij} parameters of the aligning planar homography transformation φ.

2.3   Implementational Issues

Altough the two unknowns of the perspective part φ^p would necessitate only two equations *i.e.* two invariants in system Eq. (10), the independence of the chosen set of affine

Algorithm 1. Pseudo code of the proposed algorithm

Input   : Binary images: *template* and *observation*
Output: The h_{ij} parameters of the aligning planar homography
1   Choose a set of affine invariants $I_i : \mathbb{R}^2 \rightarrow \mathbb{R}$ $(i = 1, \ldots, n)$
2   The solution of the system of equations Eq. (10) gives the perspective parameters p_1 and p_2
3   Solve the system of equations Eq. (18) to determine the affine parameters a_{ij}
4   Use Eq. (8) to obtain the h_{ij} parameters of the aligning planar homography

moment invariants is not garanteed. Accordingly we obtained better results with overdetermined systems. The results shown in Section 3 was attained using the $\{I_3, I_4, I_5, I_6\}$ set of invariants. Since the system is clearly nonlinear we found that it could be solved effenciently using nonlinear optimization methods. We used the standard differential evolution [14] method in the tests presented in Section 3. The equations are constructed in the continuum but in practice we only have a limited precision digital image. Consequently, the integrals over the continuous domains $\mathcal{F}_t$ and $\mathcal{F}_o$ can only be approximated by discrete sums over the set of foreground pixels denoted by F_t and F_o.

The pseudo code of the proposed algorithm can be found in Algorithm 1 while Fig. 1 shows example result images after the two subsequent steps of the method.

Template	Observation	Step 1	Step 2

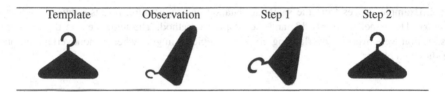

Fig. 1. The registration process: The first step removes only the perspective distortion from the observation image while the second step restores the affine transformation and thus align it to the original template image

3   Experiments

The performance of the proposed method has been tested on a large synthetic dataset consist of 35 different template shapes and their projectively distorted versions as observations a total of ≈ 1100 images of size 300×300. The applied projective transformations were randomly composed of $0.5, \ldots, 1.5$ scalings; $-\frac{\pi}{4}, \ldots, \frac{\pi}{4}$ rotations along the x and y axes and $-\pi, \ldots, \pi$ along the z axe; $-1, \ldots, 1$ translations along both x and y axis and $0.5, \ldots, 2.5$ along the z axis; and a random focal length chosen from the $[0.5, 1.5]$ interval.

Registration results were quantitatively evaluated using two kind of error measures. The first one (δ) measures the percentage of the non-overlapping area of the template

Template	Observation	Shape Context	Domokos *et al.*	Proposed

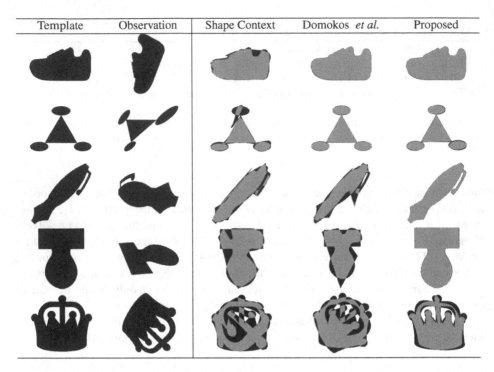

Fig. 2. Example images from the synthetic data set and registration results obtained by Shape Context [1], Domokos *et al.* [3] and the proposed method. The template and the registered observation were overlaid, overlapping pixels are depicted in gray whereas nonoverlapping ones are shown in black.

and the registered observation while ϵ measures the distance (in pixels) between the true φ and the estimated $\hat{\varphi}$ transformation:

$$\delta = \frac{|F_r \bigtriangleup F_t|}{|F_r| + |F_t|} \cdot 100\%, \quad \epsilon = \frac{1}{|F_o|} \sum_{\mathbf{x} \in F_o} \|\varphi(\mathbf{x}) - \hat{\varphi}(\mathbf{x})\|,$$

where F_r denote the set of foreground pixels of the registered template respectively. The summary of the results is shown in Table 1.

For comparison we examined the results of Domokos *et al.* [3] on the same dataset. It provided weaker results since could not cope with cases when the images were rotated more than 90 degrees. We have also compared the performance of our method to that of *Shape Context* [1], a more general shape matching algorithm developed for nonlinear registration of binary images. For testing, we used the program provided by the authors, its parameters were set empirically to their optimal value (*beta_init* = *30*, *n_iter* = *30*, annealing rate $r = 1$).

The average running time of the Domokos *et al.* and the proposed method (C implementations) were 4.75 sec. and 12.86 sec. respectively. The runtime of the Matlab implementation of Shape Context (68.87 sec.) is not authoritative.

Table 1. Test results on the synthetic dataset of Shape Context, Domokos *et al.* and the proposed method. m, μ, and σ denote the median, mean, and deviation.

	$\delta(\%)$			ϵ (pixel)		
	m	μ	σ	m	μ	σ
Shape Context	10.10	13.36	11.02	-	-	-
Domokos *et al.*	10.54	14.31	13.99	151.60	122.72	87.21
Proposed	2.38	6.23	12.34	1.88	23.46	53.00

3.1 Traffic Signs

The recognition of traffic signs has an increasing importance in the car industry. The orientation of the sign is also important to decide wether it should be taken into consideration and it can be determined by registering the projectively distorted sign to a template. Herein we used classical thresholding however automatic detection and segmentation is also possible [12]. Fig. 3 shows some registration results of the proposed method. Recently, in [11] it has been shown that Shape Context[1] and SIFT[9] are unsuitable to extract point correspondences between traffic sign image pairs.

Fig. 3. Registration results on traffic signs. The images used as *observations* are shown in the first row, and below them the corresponding *templates* with the overlayed contours of the registration results.

4 Conclusion

We have proposed a novel approach to recover projective transformations of planar shapes. The two-step solution first estimates the perspective distortion independently of the affine part of the transformation which is recovered in the second step. While classical image registration algorithms use feature correspondences our method works with invariant moments estimated using the point coordinates of the whole object. The efficiency of our method has been demonstrated on synthetic dataset as well as on real traffic sign images. Comparative test showed that our algorithm outperform other methods, especially in the case of strong deformations *e.g.* when the shapes are rotated more than 90 degrees. The examination of the robustness of the method against different level of segmentation errors will be the subject of future research.

Acknowledgements. This research was supported by the European Union and the European Regional Development Fund under the grant agreements TÁMOP-4.2.1/B-09/1/KONV- 2010-0005 and TÁMOP-4.2.2/B-10/1-2010-0012.

References

1. Belongie, S., Malik, J., Puzicha, J.: Shape matching and object recognition using shape context. IEEE Transactions on Pattern Analysis and Machine Intelligence 24(4), 509–522 (2002)
2. Domokos, C., Kato, Z.: Parametric estimation of affine deformations of planar shapes. Pattern Recognition 43(3), 569–578 (2010)
3. Domokos, C., Nemeth, J., Kato, Z.: Nonlinear shape registration without correspondences. IEEE Transactions on Pattern Analysis and Machine Intelligence 34(5), 943–958 (2012)
4. Flusser, J., Suk, T., Zitová, B.: Moments and Moment Invariants in Pattern Recognition. Wiley & Sons (October 2009)
5. Francos, J., Hagege, R., Friedlander, B.: Estimation of multidimensional homeomorphisms for object recognition in noisy environments. In: Proceedings of Conference on Signals, Systems and Computers, vol. 2, pp. 1615–1619. Pacific Grove, California (2003)
6. Guo, H., Rangarajan, A., Joshi, S., Younes, L.: Non-rigid registration of shapes via diffeomorphic point matching. In: Proceedings of International Symposium on Biomedical Imaging: From Nano to Macro, vol. 1, pp. 924–927. IEEE, Arlington (2004)
7. Hartley, R.: In defense of the eight-point algorithm. IEEE Transactions on Pattern Analysis and Machine Intelligence 19(6), 580–593 (1997)
8. Kaneko, S., Satohb, Y., Igarashi, S.: Using selective correlation coefficient for robust image registration. Pattern Recognition 36, 1165–1173 (2003)
9. Lowe, D.G.: Distinctive image features from scale-invariant keypoints. International Journal of Computer Vision 60(2), 91–110 (2004)
10. Mann, S., Picard, R.W.: Video orbits of the projective group a simple approach to featureless estimation of parameters. IEEE Transactions on Image Processing 6(9), 1281–1295 (1997)
11. Nemeth, J., Domokos, C., Kato, Z.: Recovering planar homographies between 2d shapes. In: Proceedings of International Conference on Computer Vision, pp. 2170–2176. IEEE, Cairo, Egypt (2009)
12. Paulo, C.F., Correia, P.L.: Automatic detection and classification of traffic signs. In: Proc. of Workshop on Image Analysis for Multimedia Interactive Services, Santorini, Greece, pp. 11–14 (June 2007)
13. Simonson, K.M., Drescher, S.M., Tanner, F.R.: A statistics-based approach to binary image registration with uncertainty analysis. IEEE Transactions on Pattern Analysis and Machine Intelligence 29, 112–125 (2007)
14. Storn, R., Price, K.: Differential evolution - a simple and efficient heuristic for global optimization over continuous spaces. Journal of Global Optimization 11(4), 341–359 (1997)

15. Suk, T., Flusser, J.: Affine Normalization of Symmetric Objects. In: Blanc-Talon, J., Philips, W., Popescu, D.C., Scheunders, P. (eds.) ACIVS 2005. LNCS, vol. 3708, pp. 100–107. Springer, Heidelberg (2005)
16. Yezzi, A., Zöllei, L., Kapurz, T.: A variational framework for joint segmentation and registration. In: Proceedings of IEEE Workshop on Mathematical Methods in Biomedical Image Analysis, pp. 44–51. IEEE, Kauai (2001)
17. Zitová, B., Flusser, J.: Image registration methods: A survey. Image and Vision Computing 21(11), 977–1000 (2003)

Hand Posture Classification by Means of a New Contour Signature

Nabil Boughnim, Julien Marot, Caroline Fossati, and Salah Bourennane

Institut Fresnel, D. U. de Saint Jérôme Av. Normandie-N.,
13397, Marseille, France
julien.marot@fresnel.fr

Abstract. This paper deals with hand posture recognition. Thanks to an adequate setup, we afford a database of hand photographs. We propose a novel contour signature, obtained by transforming the image content into several signals. The proposed signature is invariant to translation, rotation, and scaling. It can be used for posture classification purposes. We generate this signature out of photographs of hands: experiments show that the proposed signature provides good recognition results, compared to Hu moments and Fourier descriptors.

Keywords: contour description, antenna array, hand posture classification.

1 Introduction

Gesture and posture classification yield many applications in human-computer interaction. We focus on hand posture characterization. Some descriptors have been proposed, which exhibit invariance properties, but skip some details of the hand contour to ensure a low computational load. To overcome this limitation, we seek for a method exhibiting a resolution of one pixel.

1.1 Overview on Hand Posture and Gesture Classification

Systems that employ hand driven human-computer communication interpret hand gestures and postures in different modes of interaction depending on the application domain. Previous works have concentrated on hand gesture classification [1,2], where gesture command is based on slow movements with large amplitude (see for instance in [2] the twelve types of hand gesture). To our knowledge, future applications should concern the classification of hand posture, for the purpose of automated sign language decoding for instance. Contrary to hand gesture, hand posture describes the hand shape and not its movement. Hand posture recognition is a difficult task: the number of 2000 signs is commonly reached in a sign dictionary, so some postures may be very similar.

The main approach for hand posture characterization is based Hu moments [3] and on Fourier descriptors [4]. The advantages of Hu moments and Fourier

J. Blanc-Talon et al. (Eds.): ACIVS 2012, LNCS 7517, pp. 384–394, 2012.

descriptors is their intrinsic invariance to rotation and scaling. For instance, Fourier descriptors were applied for the first time to hand posture recognition in [1]. The illustrations therein show that a large the drawbacks of Hu moments and Fourier descriptors in the context of hand recognition is that a large number of coefficients is required to get an accurate representation of an object. The Fourier descriptors proposed therein provide elevated recognition rates for most of the 11 postures of the considered database. However, Table 4 shows that the algorithm mistakes postures which are visually close. This is due to the low number of used Fourier coefficients -which ensures a low computational load. We wish to distinguish more accurately similar postures, such as the postures 8 and 11. That is why we apply the proposed non star-shaped contour characterization method to distinguish between very similar posture. We predict that the signature provided by the proposed method should yield better classification results than Fourier descriptors, which do not characterize contours with a resolution of one pixel.

1.2 State of the Art on Contour Description and Limitations of Existing Methods

The description of closed contours is a major topic in computer vision. Several features have been proposed: moment invariants in general [5] which aim at extracting shape characteristics independently of scaling, translation and rotation, especially Hu Moment invariants [3], and Fourier descriptors [4]. The main advantage of Fourier descriptors is their invariance to scaling, translation and rotation. Also, their stability has been improved (see [6] and references therein). They involve a regular sampling of the considered contour, the sampling points delimiting arcs of same length. The drawbacks of Fourier descriptors are the following: they are not invariant to the initial description point [6], and a large number of Fourier coefficients, obtained through Fourier transform of the contour coordinates, may be required to distinguish two similar contours (see illustrations in [1]).

Original methods for contour retrieval rely on signal generation on an antenna [7]: A set of virtual sensors forming an antenna, is associated with the image to turn its content into a 1-D signal. These methods were recently improved to detect strongly distorted star-shaped contours [8]. Their main advantages are as follows. First, as opposed to Fourier descriptors, the sampling of the contour does not depend on its shape, but on the chosen directions for signal generation. Refer to [8] for details about signal generation out of the image on a circular antenna. Antenna-based methods permit to distinguish close concentric circles, and their computational load does not depend on the noise level. The main drawback of these antenna-based methods is that they are limited to one-pixel wide star-shaped contours. This prevents the method from fitting various applications like hand posture characterization, considered in this paper.

The limitations cited above lead to the purpose of this paper: we aim at describing a planar free-form contour which may be non star-shaped with a resolution of one pixel.

1.3   Outline of the Paper and Overview of the Proposed Method

For this, we propose a novel scan of the image, inspired from [8] but also from [9]. Various signatures can be associated with contours, for instance distance to the center of mass, complex coordinates, curvature function, or cumulative angles. The image scan in [9] provides a contour signature as a matrix involving the contour polar coordinates. However, it does not offer a pixel-by-pixel description of the contour: its provides the number of pixels in bins which are regularly spaced using some concentric circles and equal interval angle. hence the impossibility to distinguish details which are smaller than the bins. And, the more precise the description, the smaller the regions, but the higher the computational load and the storage place. On the contrary, we propose a contour signature which offers a resolution of one pixel.

The proposed method for image content retrieval splits the image into several rings centered on a reference point. The requirements on the location of this reference point are low, contrary to the condition imposed by the method in [8]. We apply the proposed method to a practical case of non star-shaped contour characterization: hand posture characterization. We aim at distinguishing very similar postures with a computational load which is lower than what the generally used Fourier descriptors would require.

The rest of the paper is organized as follows: in section 3, we define the new representation of contours which is adapted to non star-shaped contours. In section 4, we give a detailed description of the proposed approach for hand posture characterization and report promising results. Concluding remarks and future works are in section 5.

2   Image Acquisition Setup

This setup contains a CMOS camera. Its has the size of a webcam, see Fig. 1 and could further be integrated in an embedded system.

The camera is placed over the desk surface, it axis is orthogonal to the desk surface. Wide angle optics (90°) are used so that the field of vision is wide enough. The acquisition format can be either CIF, or VGA. The video stream is transmitted to the computer by a USB connection in RGB format. The USB connection has a limited stream and requires part of the CPU ressources of the computer.

However at this point, we do not need a high video stream transmission rate. Each video is split into a series of images. The set of images forms our database. Our database contains images with various types of hand postures, which will be described further in detail.

3   A Novel Signature for Non Star-Shaped Contours

A size $N \times N$ image is considered, whose pixels are referred to, starting from the top left corner of the image, as $I_{l,m}$ (see Fig. 2(a)). The 1-valued pixels

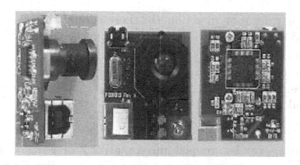

Fig. 1. Camera

compound the expected contour. The contour pixels are located in a system of polar coordinates with pole $\{l_c, m_c\}$ (see Fig. 2(a)). Contrary to the methods proposed in [8], where the center must be chosen in such a way that the contour is star-shaped, the computation of the center coordinates is not essential. What we call signature in this paper is a set of data which characterizes the corresponding contour and permit to reconstruct it. The novel signature that we propose in this paper is based on the generation of signals out of an image. We get inspired from [8] and [9]: as in [8], a circular array of sensors is associated with the image. The sensor array is supposed to be placed along a circle centered on the pole $\{l_c, m_c\}$. The number of sensors is denoted by Q and one sensor corresponds to one direction for signal generation D_i, which makes an angle θ_i with the vertical axis. See for instance the ith and the Qth sensors in Fig. 2(b). The other sensors are not represented for sake of clarity. The method proposed in [8] is valid only for contours exhibiting at most one pixel for one direction D_i. We wish to overcome this limitation and characterize non star-shaped contours. To separate the influence of each pixel located along a given direction D_i, we no longer generate one 1-D signal, but a number L of 1-D signals on the antenna. Each signal corresponds to one 'ring' represented on Fig. 2.

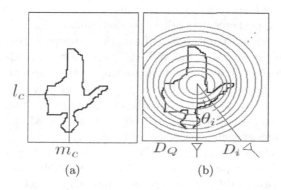

Fig. 2. Image and edge model (a); signal generation process (b)

We assume that, for each direction D_i, there is only one pixel in each of the L intervals. L differs from one direction D_i to another. Its maximum value is, for instance, $\frac{N}{\sqrt{2}}$, if $l_c = N/2$ and $m_c = N/2$.

So, we generate L signal vectors for each direction D_i. For the lth interval $(l = 1, \ldots, L)$ and the direction D_i $(i = 1, \ldots, Q)$, the signal component $z_{l,i}$ is computed as follows:

$$z_{l,i} = I_{l_{l,i}, m_{l,i}} \sqrt{l_{l,i}^2 + m_{l,i}^2} \tag{1}$$

The components $z_{l,i}$ can be grouped into a matrix $\mathbf{Z}$ of size $L \times Q$. All columns of $\mathbf{Z}$ should have the same number of rows, so for the directions D_i for signal generation which cross less than L intervals, 0-valued components are set in $\mathbf{Z}$ for the corresponding column indices i. If the width of the intervals is chosen such that there is at most one pixel per direction D_i and per interval, this matrix permits to reconstruct exactly the contour: it contains the radial coordinates of the contour in the system of pole $\{l_c, m_c\}$.

4   Hand Posture Characterization

In this section, we detail the process of hand posture classification: out of a database coming from our acquisition setup, we afford a set of images corresponding to 11 postures (see subsection 4.1). The database is split into a learning database and a test database. But the images cannot be directly exploited: they require a preprocessing which provides the hand contour (see subsection 4.2), so that we can obtain the contour signature as described in section 3. We present the classification process and the two distances that we use for this purpose in subsection 4.3. We provide the results obtained by the proposed method and comparative methods in terms of recognition rates (see subsection 4.4).

4.1   Hand Posture Database

A hand can exhibit a great variety of postures, and it is extremely difficult to recognize all possible configurations of the hand starting from its projection on a 2-D image. Indeed, some parts of the hand can be hidden. It is necessary to consider subsets of postures depending on the application.

There exist some reference databases of specific hand postures, such as the Triesch database [10], available on the Web [11]. This database exhibits limitations: the number of images is low, the viewing angle, the size and the orientation of the hand is always the same, the images are in grey level and contain only the hand. That is why a database made in our research team has been used for experiments in this paper. This database was also used in [12] and in [1]. It contains 11 postures, which are displayed in Fig. 3.

These postures have been chosen to be easily performed by any person. They get inspired from the 8 postures of the completed spoken language presented in [13]. These postures differ from the sign language which aims at easing lip reading. Some postures have been added to test the discrimination performances

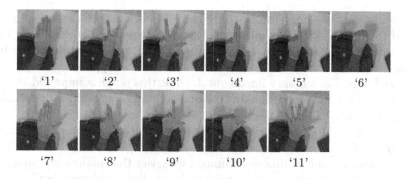

Fig. 3. Postures of the database (cropped images)

of the proposed and comparative methods: they are visually very close, such as postures 4 and 5, as well as postures 8 and 9. The images of the database were obtained as follows: an expert user shoots a movie containing the 11 postures. Then the frames of the video are split to get the images in the RGB color space. These images compound the learning database. Other users which are not the expert user shoot a movie containing the 11 postures. The same process as for the learning database is adopted to get a set of image. These images compound the test set.

In Fig. 4, we display 4 images of the learning database, corresponding to postures 4, 5, 8, and 9.

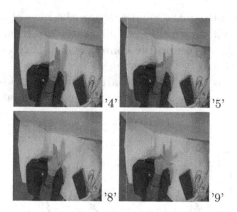

Fig. 4. Images 4, 5, 8, 9 of the database

4.2   Preprocessing

To get images which are fit for hand contour retrieval and posture recognition, we have to get rid of the background and, in the best case, conserve solely the hand contour. In [14], Soriano et al. propose a dynamic skin color model, for a segmentation purpose. Their method copes with changes in illumination. However, their method is applied to faces and not to hands.

We apply the following preprocessing steps to each frame: the color image is mapped to the YC_bC_r space and we select C_b component, where the contrast between hand and background is the largest. We remove the non-moving background from each frame, and an Otsu threshold [15] is applied to the resulting difference frame. Each binary image obtained at this point is impaired by noise; morphological filtering operations of erosion and dilation are applied to eliminate isolated pixels and fill out holes [2].

Before getting the image I which is fed to the method proposed in section 3, we apply two further preprocessings.

Firstly, from the initial processed image, we select the smallest subimage containing the expected contour. This subimage is called "enclosing box". The enclosing box is obtained in the following way: the image content is projected onto the left and the bottom sides (it could be also the right and the top sides). We get two signals, $\mathbf{z}^{left}$ and $\mathbf{z}^{bottom}$, from this projection: Their components are obtained as follows: $z_l^{left} = \sum_{m=1}^{N} I_{l,m} \ l = 1, \cdots, N$ and $z_m^{bottom} = \sum_{l=1}^{N} I_{l,m} \ m = 1, \cdots, N$. For each signal, a non-zero section indicates the presence of the expected feature. The l and m indices of the non-zeros sections yield a box enclosing the contour. Extracting this box reduces the computational load of the signature generation.

Secondly, we rotate several times the enclosing box and generate each time $\mathbf{z}^{left}$ and $\mathbf{z}^{bottom}$. We stop when the non zero section length is the largest in $\mathbf{z}^{left}$ and the smallest in $\mathbf{z}^{bottom}$. The hand contour is then straightened up.

Eventually, through the following remarks (•) we can assess that the rows of matrix $\mathbf{Z}$ compose a complete set of invariant features:

• Matrix $\mathbf{Z}$ describes entirely the hand contour: the rows of matrix $\mathbf{Z}$ compose a complete set of invariant features. Fig. 5 illustrates this by showing a segmented hand posture (see Fig. 5(a)), and the contour which is reconstructed out of its signature $\mathbf{Z}$ (see Fig. 5(b)).
• They are invariant to translation: whatever the hand position in the initial image, the box which encloses the contour is blindly estimated.

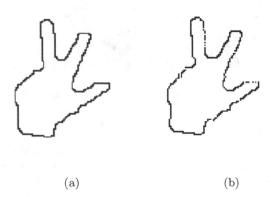

(a)   (b)

Fig. 5. Segmented contour (a); contour reconstructed from the signature $\mathbf{Z}$ (b)

• They are invariant to scaling: whatever the size of the subimage (small number of pixels if the camera is far from the hand, large number of pixels if the camera is near to the hand), the number of intervals for the radial coordinate values L is always the same. Also, the number of directions for signal generation is always the same. This makes the method invariant to scaling. Hence, the signature depends on the shape of the hand, not on its size.

• They are invariant to rotation: whatever the initial orientation of the hand, straightening up the hand contour makes the proposed method invariant to rotation.

Matrix $\mathbf{Z}$ can then be used for classification issues.

4.3   Classification Process

Let's consider H classes of hand postures. For the purpose of hand posture classification, we compare two distances: the Bayesian and the Euclidian distance. For this, we turn any matrix $\mathbf{Z}$ characterizing a posture into a vector $\mathbf{z}$ of size $L * Q$ where $*$ denotes simple multiplication. For each class h, a subset of hand photographs is available. The H subsets compose the learning set. The learning set was created by an expert who knows exactly what position his fingers should have to fit each posture in Fig. 3. A mean invariant vector μ_h and a covariance matrix Λ_h are computed using the learning set for each class. Even if there are small variations from one posture provided by the expert to another, these variations are smoothed through the computation of the mean invariant vector μ_h. Any image coming from the test set and characterized by vector $\mathbf{z}$ is classified by minimizing the Mahalanobis distance:

$$\mathcal{D}_m = (\mathbf{z} - \mu_h)^T \Lambda_h^{-1} (\mathbf{z} - \mu_h) \tag{2}$$

We also provide a study where the distance used for classification is the Euclidian distance: any image coming from the test set and characterized by matrix $\mathbf{Z}$ is classified by minimizing the distance $||\mathbf{Z}_c - \mathbf{Z}||$, where $||.||$ denotes Frobenius norm: $||\mathbf{Z}|| = \sqrt{\sum_{p=1}^{P} \sum_{i=1}^{Q} z_{p,i}^2}$.

The Mahalanobis distance usually provides better classification results, but the Euclidean distance is easier to implement.

4.4   Results and Discussion

We process images of size 320×240 with a 2-core processor @3.2 GHz, using Matlab®. A value $L = 24$ pixels is large enough to get an exclusive signature for each posture and small enough to get a reasonable computational load. To ensure the invariance to scaling, the number of sensors depends only on the maximum size of the enclosing box. The maximum size of the enclosing box is 120×120, so the number of sensors is $Q = \lceil \sqrt{2}\pi 120 \rceil = 534$, large enough to detect the pixels which are the farthest from the image center.

The learning set is composed of 3300 images, and the test set is composed of 440 images.

Table 1 presents the results obtained with either Hu moments, Fourier descriptors, or the proposed method, using Euclidian distance. The results concerning Hu moments and Fourier descriptors are extracted from [1].

Table 1. Recognition rates per posture with internal database and Euclidian distance, on the test set

	'1'	'2'	'3'	'4'	'5'	'6'	'7'	'8'	'9'	'10'	'11'	Mean value
HU	79.2	60.3	64.5	60.0	90.8	100	45.3	62.4	62.4	40.6	67.5	66.6
FD1	92.8	75.3	78.4	92.4	93.8	94.5	89.1	70.7	85.5	75.9	76.2	84.1
Proposed method	97.7	89.5	79.1	88.6	75.7	100	86.1	74.4	85.6	87.2	97.0	87.4

Hu moments method exhibits the worst results among the three methods. This methods encounters difficulties with postures 4, 7, and 10. Fourier descriptors exhibit quite good results, but have difficulties for postures 2, 8, and 11.

The recognition rates of Fourier descriptors and the proposed method (see Table 1) confirms the superiority of the proposed method over Fourier descriptors for all postures except postures 4, 5 and 7. So the proposed method outperforms Fourier descriptors for 8 postures out of 11. The mean recognition rate is also higher (87.4 % against 84.1 % for Fourier descriptors). Postures 4, 5 are very similar: if the segmentation is not performed correctly, for instance if the parameters of the mathematical morphology operations are not perfectly tuned, the segmentation of the two joint fingers in posture 4 is very similar to the segmentation of a single finger. Fourier descriptors cannot be used with an acceptable computational time with more than 6 invariant features [12]. So they miss the concave section corresponding to one finger. This is not the case for the proposed method: it yields a pixel-to-pixel precision with a constant computational load, whatever the considered processed image.

Table 2 provides the recognition results obtained while using the Bayesian distance.

Table 2. Recognition rates per posture with internal database and Bayesian distance, on the testing set

	'1'	'2'	'3'	'4'	'5'	'6'	'7'	'8'	'9'	'10'	'11'	Mean value
HU	82.3	68.3	66.5	65.0	93.8	89.0	48.3	65.4	82.8	74.4	40.6	70.6
FD1	86.6	90.8	96.4	60.8	97.8	94.3	80.6	64.8	88.6	73.4	96.2	84.6
Proposed method	98.2	92.7	94.1	89.9	84.2	100	88.1	76.4	85.6	97.4	96.9	91.2

Results concerning Hu moments and Fourier descriptors are extracted from [12]. We notice that using the Bayesian distance improves significantly the results obtained by Hu moments. It also slightly improves the results obtained by Fourier descriptors and by the proposed method. Fourier descriptors still get better recognition results for postures 3, 5, and 9. It has to be privileged for further developments involving the proposed method. While performing our experiments, we noticed that some images from the database yield bad segmentation results, and that these images are particularly concerned with false classification. Sorting and removing these bad segmented images from the learning database could further improve the classification rates. Also, improving the preprocessing step, by changing the mathematical morphology operators for instance, may improve the final recognition results.

Table 3. Proposed and comparative methods, comparison of performances. a) Gabor filtered + PCA + SVM; b) FD1 + Bayesian; c) Proposed method

	'Processing time'	'System performance'	'Interface'	'Recognition rate (%)'
a)	4 frames/sec	3.4 GHz	C language	93.7
b)	20 frames/sec	2 GHz	C language	84.6
c)	5 frames/sec	3.1 GHz	Matlab	91.2

Table 3 shows that we must find a compromise between the recognition rate and the computational load. For our method this compromise is satisfactory. It can even be improved in terms of computational load, if we implement our algorithm in C/C++ language, instead of Matlab. In terms of recognition rates, we could get inspired by the comparative method a). It is based on a preprocessing with Gabor filters. Using Gabor filters to ensure invariance to rotation was proposed in [16] and further developed in [17]. We could also adapt Gabor filtering to improve the preprocessing and thus the recognition rates. Meanwhile, we should pay attention to the compromise between computational load and recognition rate, depending on the final application.

5   Conclusion and Future Works

This paper deals with hand posture classification. A camera acquires photographs of hand postures with a wide viewing angle. We propose a novel signature for the characterization of hand posture. This signature is made of several 1-D signals. Each signal contains radial coordinates of the pixels in an image region which has the shape of a ring. This signature permits to reconstruct the corresponding contour with a precision of one pixel. By applying two preprocessings, we ensure that this signature forms a complete set of features which are invariant to translation, scaling and rotation. This makes this signature fit for hand posture recognition: we associate the proposed signature generation method with Euclidian and Bayesian distances to get recognition results. We reach promising results which outperform the results obtained by Hu moments and Fourier descriptors, for 8 postures out of 11 while comparing with Fourier descriptors. Prospects for this work are as follows: we could use two cameras or a set of cameras, to have access to the parts of the hand which are hidden; also, the preprocessing step could be improved to get a better segmentation result before generating the signature.

Acknowledgements. This work was financially supported by the "Conseil régional Provence Alpes Côte d'Azur", and by the firm Intuisens, to which we are very grateful.

References

1. Bourennane, S., Fossati, C.: Comparison of shape descriptors for hand posture recognition in video. Signal, Image and Video Processing, August 14 (2010) (online First)
2. Zhu, Y., Xu, G., Kriegman, D.J.: A real-time approach to the spotting, representation, and recognition of hand gestures for Human-Computer Interaction. Computer Vision and Image Understanding 85, 189–208 (2002)
3. Hu, M.-K.: Visual pattern recognition by moment invariants. IEEE Trans. on Information Theory 8, 179–187 (1962)
4. Persoon, E., Fu, K.: Shape discrimination using fourier descriptors. IEEE Trans. on Pattern Analysis and Machine Intelligence 8(3), 388–397 (1986)
5. Xu, D., Li, H.: Geometric moment invariants. Pattern Recognition 41, 240–249 (2008)
6. Charmi, M.-A., Derrode, S., Ghorbel, F.: Fourier-based geometric shape prior for snakes. Pattern Recognition Letters 29(7), 897–904 (2008)
7. Aghajan, H.K., Kailath, T.: Sensor array processing techniques for super resolution multi-line-fitting and straight edge detection. IEEE Trans. on IP 2(4), 454–465 (1993)
8. Jiang, H., Marot, J., Fossati, C., Bourennane, S.: Strongly concave star-shaped contour characterization by algebra tools. Elsevier Signal Processing (January 2012)
9. Shu, X., Wu, X.-J.: A novel contour descriptor for 2D shape matching and its application to image retrieval. Image and Vision Computing 29, 286–294 (2011)
10. Triesch, J., von der Malsburg, C.: Robust classification of hand postures against complex backgrounds. In: Proc. of the IEEE Int. Conf. on Automatic Face and Gesture Recognition, pp. 170–175 (1996)
11. http://www.idiap.ch/resource/gestures/
12. Conseil, S., Bourennane, S., Martin, L.: Comparison of Fourier descriptors and Hu moments for hand posture recognition. In: EUSIPCO 2007, Poznan, Poland (2007)
13. Caplier, A., Bonnaud, L., Malassiotis, S., Strintzis, M.: Comparison of 2D and 3D analysis for automated cued speech gesture recognition. In: SPECOM (September 2004)
14. Soriano, M., Martinkauppi, B., Huovinen, S., Laaksonen, M.: Skin detection in video under changing illumination conditions. In: Procs. of the 15th ICPR, vol. 1, pp. 839–842 (2000)
15. Otsu, N.: A threshold selection method from gray level histograms. IEEE Trans. on Systems, Man, and Cybernetics 9, 62–66 (1979)
16. Amin, M.A., Yan, H.: Sign language finger alphabet recognition from Gabor- PCA representation of hand gestures. In: Proceedings of the 6th International Conference on Machine Learning and Cybernetics, Hong Kong, pp. 2218–2223 (2007)
17. Huang, D.-Y., Hu, W.-C., Chang, S.-H.: Gabor filter-based hand-pose angle estimation for hand gesture recognition under varying illumination. Expert Systems with Applications 38, 6031–6042 (2011)

Kernel Similarity Based AAMs for Face Recognition

Yuyao Zhang[1], Younes Benhamza[2], Khalid Idrissi[1], and Christophe Garcia[1]

[1] University de Lyon, CNRS
INSA-Lyon, LIRIS, UMR CNRS 5205, F-69621, France
{Yuyao.Zhang,khalid.Idrissi,Christophe.garcia}@insa-lyon.fr
[2] Laboratoire LARATIC, INTTIC Oran Algrie
ybenhamza@ito.dz

Abstract. Illumination and facial pose conditions have an explicit effect on the performance of face recognition systems, caused by the complicated non-linear variation between feature points and views. In this paper, we present a Kernel similarity based Active Appearance Models (KSAAMs) in which we use a Kernel Method to replace Principal Component Analysis (PCA) which is used for feature extraction in Active Appearance Models. The major advantage of the proposed approach lies in a more efficient search of non-linear varied parameter under complex face illumination and pose variation conditions. As a consequence, images illuminated from different directions, and images with variable poses can easily be synthesized by changing the parameters found by KSAAMs. From the experimental results, the proposed method provides higher accuracy than classical Active Appearance Model for face alignment in a point-to-point error sense.

Keywords: AAMs, Kernel methods, dimension reduction.

1 Introduction

Face recognition has been a well investigated topic the in image processing and computer vision communities. In the last decade, large efforts have been done in searching for a face recognition system that is capable of working with "real-world" faces. Among these efforts, Active Appearance Model, first proposed in [1], is a non-linear, generative, and parametric model of a certain visual phenomenon [2]. AAMs is quite well-known and widely used in the face recognition field. The aim of the algorithm is to "explain" novel images by generating synthetic images that are as similar as possible, using a parameterized model of appearance. There are several major unsolved problems existing in AAMs like position variations of the faces and directions of the sources of illumination.

Within the last years, the problems of illumination independence and complex pose fitting have been addressed by different approaches. A common method to deal with variations of illumination is to supplement additional parameters

J. Blanc-Talon et al. (Eds.): ACIVS 2012, LNCS 7517, pp. 395–406, 2012.

during the construction of the model. As demonstrated explicitly in [3] , this approach directly increase computational complexity and is more time consuming. R. Navarathna et al. proposed to employ Gabor filter on data to gain a invariance condition for AAMs. But with the increasing responses of multiple filter, AAMs became computationally prohibitive. In order to get a computationally efficient AAM fitting, [4] posed fitting procedure in the Fourier domain that affords invariance to both expression and illumination. D. Pizarro et al. introduced an AAMs fitting based on the invariant space in [5], the idea to avoid from the effect of illumination or shadow in similar with [4]. Two major problems are contained in such method. First, we can hardly define a illumination free image. Second, the filters eliminate both shadow effect but also detail information from recognition image, such algorithms can hardly synthesize faces with variations of illumination during the fitting procedure. Meanwhile, the pose problems are equally complex because of the non-linear variation caused by the rotation of the head and different positions of the camera. In particular, a single AAMs is able to cope with shape variations from a narrow range of face poses (turning and nodding of 20). It utilizes PCA to model shape and appearance variation across pose, expression, illumination and identity. But the linear assumption does not hold true when large rotations of the face exist. Several works [6, 7] applied the non-linear statistic tool, Kernel-PCA instead of PCA to build shape models of wide range of face rotations. But these methods all suffered from the rough approximation reconstruction problem of kernel PCA.

In this paper, a non-linear statistic approach is supposed to build the shape, texture and appearance model of AAMs. It benefits from kernel similarity matrix, but avoids the reconstruction problem of kernel PCA. Our method efficiently functions with the face reconstruction in complex illumination environments, and works much more efficiently with the wide range face rotation case comparing with AAMs.

The organization of this paper is as follows. Section 2 presents the classical Active Appearance Models algorithm. Section 3 introduces how the proposed KSAAMs algorithm works. Section 4 presents results of the performance of the proposed algorithm and a statistical comparison with AAMs. Section 5 concludes the paper.

2   Active Appearance Model

Active Appearance Model is an algorithm which allows generating a synthetic image as close as possible to a particular target image by making use of constraints of the appearance models. An appearance model is combined by two linear subspaces, one for the object shape and one for the object texture which are both learnt from a labeled set of training images [11].

Interpreting a novel image is an optimization problem in which the method minimizes the difference between a new image and one synthesized by the appearance model. The difference vector δI can be defined as:

$$\delta I = I_{\text{i}} - I_{\text{m}} \tag{1}$$

where I_{i} is the vector of grey-level values in the image, I_{m} is the vector of grey-level values for the current model parameters.

This method proceeds in three steps:

I) A Principal Component Analysis (PCA) is applied respectively on the shape training base and a shape-free texture training base. PCA created the statistical shape and texture model as the follows.

$$s = \bar{s} + Q_{\text{s}}b_{\text{s}} \tag{2}$$

$$t = \bar{t} + Q_{\text{t}}b_{\text{t}} \tag{3}$$

where $\bar{s}$ is the mean shape; $\bar{t}$ the mean texture in a mean shape patch; Q_{s} and Q_{t} are the matrices of eigenvectors of the shape and texture covariance matrices; b_{s} and b_{t} are vectors of coefficients in the Q_{s} and Q_{s} spaces which control the synthesis of shape and texture.

Another PCA is then applied on the samples of vector b, which is combined by b_{s} so as to construct the appearance parameter c:

$$b = Qc \tag{4}$$

with Q the matrix of PCA eigenvectors c is a vector controlling both b_{s} and b_{t} at the same time.

II) An experiment matrix creating procedure in which each control parameter c is disturbed from a known value and the residuals of each displacement in each image is measured to build a relationship between the parameter and the image variations. This relationship can be presented by:

$$\delta c = R * \delta I \tag{5}$$

Here R is the experiment matrix build in this step, δc and δI represent the parameter and the image variations respectively.

III) The fitting procedure in which by varying the model parameter c, the magnitude of the difference vector $\Delta = (\delta I)^2$ is minimized in order to find the best match between model and image.

3   Kernel Simlarity AAMs

A standard Active Appearance Model explains novel images by linear combination of statistic models which are build by applying Principle Component Analysis on training data. Therefore, PCA is not designed to extract non-linear features from the shape and texture of the non-frontal or non-uniformly illuminated faces. In general, both illumination and pose variations remain difficult to handle in face recognition.

In this paper, a non-linear component analysis method is considered to be more appropriate for handling the multiple variations which are caused by the changes of the light source. In this respect, a kernel method component analysis is employed instead of PCA to search more efficient components for generating new images in complex illumination and pose conditions. The following subsection aims at presenting the the proposed Kernel Similarity Active Appearance Model method.

3.1   PCA Trick in Feature Space

Consider a $N \times M$ observation matrix A, where each column is an observation and each row is the dimension of the observation. For example, in the context of this paper, each column is an image and each row are the image pixels. One observation is denoted as x_k, $k = 1, 2, \ldots\ldots, M$, $x_k \in R^N$, and $\sum_{k=1}^{M} x_k = 0$, which means that the data is centered. Normally, PCA diagonalizes the covariance matrix as shown in Eqn.(6).

$$C = \frac{1}{M} \sum_{j=1}^{M} x_j x_j^T \qquad (6)$$

In some special case, for example the case in our paper we have much more dimensions than faces, that $N >> M$, so finding the eigenvectors of the large $N \times N$ matrix is computationally difficult. We apply a PCA trick: instead of (6), Eqn (7) is more computationally tractable.

$$\tilde{C} = \frac{1}{N} \sum_{i=1}^{N} y_i y_i^T \qquad (7)$$

where y_i is the vector of each element of the observation x_j, N is the dimension of observation x_j.

To diagonalize it, one has to solve the following eigenvalue equation:

$$\tilde{\lambda} u = \tilde{C} u. \qquad (8)$$

where $\tilde{\lambda} = \lambda$ represent to the eigenvalues of the matrix $\tilde{C}$; the eigenvectors $u = A^T v = \sum_{i=1}^{N} y_i v_i$.

The previous part of this section is devoted to a straightforward translation to a non-linear scenario. We shall now describe this computation in a Hilbert space H, which is introduced via a mapping Φ.

$$\Phi : R^N \rightarrow H, x \rightarrow X. \qquad (9)$$

In the feature space H, we assume that $\Phi(x)$ has an arbitrarily large, possibly infinite dimensionality. Again, in feature space, the data should be centered, $\sum_{k=1}^{M} \Phi(x_k) = 0$. Applying the PCA trick in feature space H,

$$\bar{C} = \frac{1}{N} \sum_{i=1}^{N} \Phi(y_i)\Phi(y_i)^T \qquad (10)$$

Now one has to extract eigenvalues satisfying

$$\bar{\lambda}U = \bar{C}U \tag{11}$$

The solutions U lies in the span of $\Phi(y_1), \Phi(y_2), \cdots, \Phi(y_N)$. As shown in [13], this has two useful consequences: first, we can consider the equivalent equation

$$\bar{\lambda}(\Phi(y_k)^T U) = (\Phi(y_k)^T \bar{C}U) \tag{12}$$

for all $k = 1, 2, \cdots, N$ and second, there exist coefficients α_i $(i = 1, \cdots, N)$ such that

$$U = \sum_{i=1}^{N} \alpha_i \Phi(y_i) \tag{13}$$

Combining (12) and (13), we get

$$\bar{\lambda} \sum_{i=1}^{N} \alpha_i(\Phi^T(y_k) \cdot \Phi(y_i)) = \frac{1}{M} \sum_{i=1}^{N} \alpha_i(\Phi^T(y_k) \cdot \sum_{j=1}^{N} \Phi(y_j))(\Phi^T(y_j) \cdot \Phi(y_i)) \tag{14}$$

Defining a $N \times N$ matrix K by

$$K_{i,j} = (\Phi^T(y_i) \cdot \Phi(y_j)) \tag{15}$$

which lead (13) to:

$$M\bar{\lambda}K\alpha = K^2\alpha \tag{16}$$

where α denotes the column vector with entries $\alpha_1, \cdots, \alpha_N$. As K is symmetric,

$$M\bar{\lambda}\alpha = K\alpha \tag{17}$$

Note that K is positive semi-definite, which can be seen by noticing that it equals

$$K_{i,j} = k(y_i, y_j) = e^{-\frac{\|y_i - y_j\|^2}{2\delta^2}} \tag{18}$$

Then, for the extraction of eigenvalues in feature space, we therefore only need to diagonalize the kernel similarity matrix $K_{i,j}$. Let $\bar{\lambda}_1 \geq \bar{\lambda}_2 \geq \cdots \geq \lambda_N$ denote the eigenvalues, and $\alpha^1, \alpha^2, \cdots, \alpha^N$ the corresponding complete set of eigenvectors.

3.2   Parameter Estimation

As described previously, kernel method component analysis deals with nonlinear transformation via nonlinear kernel functions. In kernel the functions, there is a parameter σ that must be predetermined, knowing that it has a significant impact on image representation in feature space. As the kernel function is defined with the Gaussian function $k(a, b) = e^{-\frac{d(a,b)^2}{2\delta^2}}$, in which $d(a, b)^2$ represent Euclidean distances between elements contained in each vector; $k(a, b)$ can be considered as a zero mean Gaussian distribution of $d(a, b)^2$. So if $d(a, b)^2$ follows

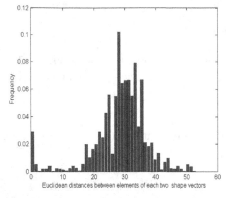
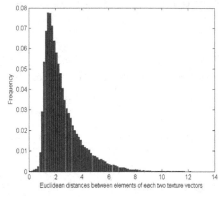

(a)Histogram of Euclidean distances between elements of shape vectors

(b)Histogram of Euclidean distances between elements of texture vectors

Fig. 1. Histogram of Euclidean distances between elements of vector of illumination database

Gaussian distribution, then σ represented the variance of $d(a,b)^2$. With respect to this assumption, we built histograms of the Euclidean distances between elements contained in each vector to study the distribution of observed variables. As illustrated in Figure 1, for shape vectors and texture vectors from the illumination database (described in the Experiment result section), the Euclidian distances between each observed variable follows a Gaussian distribution. The parameters σ is estimated.

3.3   Feature Extraction

In classical AAMs, we seek a parameterized model (the parameter c) used to control variations if both shape and texture, which is extracted by Principal Component Analysis. In our work, the kernel similarity matrix $K_{i,j} = k(y_i, y_j) = e^{-\frac{\|y_i - y_j\|^2}{2\delta^2}}$ replaces the covariance matrix (used in PCA).

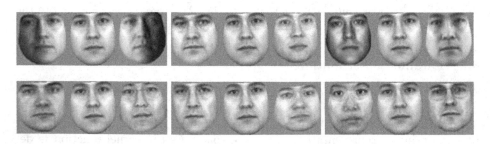

Fig. 2. Variations in the appearance parameter c; the first row presents the first three modes learnt by KSAAMs; the second row presents the first three modes learnt by PCA)

As explained in section 2., features are extracted to control variation on shape, texture and appearance. The parameter c, which represents the parameter of appearance is build to control both shape and texture variation simultaneously. Figure 2 illustrates the first three modes of variations of c for classical AAMs and the proposed method. One can observe that the model built by kernel similarity matrix is able to take into account more efficiently the variations of illumination.

4   Experimental Results

We evaluated the proposed method on the CMU Pose, Illumination, and Expression (PIE) database of human faces [14]. For the experiments on the variation of illumination and pose, the training database is built from a subset of the CMU database as illustrated in Figure 3. The test set is built from the images of the persons shown in the last row of Figure 3. We manually labeled 1200 images of size 640×486 pixels. To train the models, 58 landmarks were placed on each face image: 8 points for the mouth, 11 points for the nose, 16 points for both eyes, 10 points for both eyebrows, and 13 points for the chin. The warped images have approximately 7325 pixels inside the facial mask. To evaluate the performance of the proposed algorithm, the manually annotated landmarks are considered as the ground truth shape information. For each image the landmarks re-labeled by the methods are compared with the ground truth landmarks. A distance measure, $D(x_{gt}, x)$, gives a interpretation of the fit between two shapes, the ground truth, x_{gt} and the actual shape x. Point-to-point error E_{pt-pt} is defined as the Euclidean distance between each corresponding landmark in Eqn.(19). To interpret a novel image, an optimization is performed in which the method minimizes the error between the pixels contained in a new image and the pixels synthesized by the appearance model. The pixel-to-pixel error $E_{pix-pix}$ can be defined as in Eqn. (20).

$$E_{pt-pt} = \frac{1}{n} \sum \sqrt{(x_i - x_{gt,i})^2 + (y_i - y_{gt,i})^2} \tag{19}$$

$$E_{pix-pix} = |\delta I|^2 = |I_i - I_m|^2 \tag{20}$$

Fig. 3. Persons in the training and test databases; the first two rows present the persons in the training database; the last row present the persons in the test database (not present in the training database)

where (x_i, y_i) are the coordinates of the re-labeled landmarks, I_i is the vector of grey-level values in the image and I_m is the vector of grey-level values for the current model parameters.

To evaluate the superiority of the proposed method, Eqn.(21) is used to compute the gain in precision.

$$gain\% = \frac{E_{pt-pt}(AAMs) - E_{pt-pt}(kernel)}{E_{pt-pt}(AAMs)}\%$$ (21)

4.1   Sensitivity to the Illumination

The database for training is built by all the frontal faces which are captured by camera number 27. Each person involved in the training set (shonw in Figure 3) has 20 frontal face images under 20 different illumination conditions. The training database contains 16 people and the test database contains 10 people as shown in Figure 3.

In figure 4(a), images in the left column are synthesized by the proposed method, and compared with fitting results of Standard AAMs in the central column. An increased precision has been obtained due to the extraction of non-linear features. The gain in precision on point-to-point errors is reported in table 1, computed by eqn. (19)-(21).

Figure 5 show the errors obtained in the "Standard AAMs experiment" (square dotted curve) and "Kernel Similarity AAMs experiment" (asterisk curve) on both training (subfigure (a)) and test (subfigure (b)) databases. Errors are normalized by the Euclidian distance between the eyes ($E_{pt-pt}/Deye$, where E_{pt-pt} represented point-to-point error, and $Deye$ represented the distance between the centre of the eyes of each person). This normalization is done to eliminate

(a) Fitting results on different for the different illuminations

(b)Fitting results for different poses

Fig. 4. Fitting result on the PIE facial images with the proposed method in left column, classical AAMs in middle column, and Input images in the right column

the effect of varying size of faces on the point-to-point error. Each curve point in Figure 5 is the mean error made by the model in the database under the same illumination conditions. The number of illumination from 1 to 20 are the 20 different illuminations contained in database. Illuminations from numbers 1 to 4 correspond to a light source from the left side of the face, illuminations from 12 to 17 correspond to a light source from the right side of the face. The other illuminations (from number 5 to 11 and number 18 to 20) correspond to different light sources in front of the face. The error curves depict the robustness of the KSAAMs method since it makes it possible to find non-linear facial features.

We can see that with the proposed method, some errors are still made, but not as strong as with the standard method with an increased robustness to side illuminations. Figure 6 present the average pixel-to-pixel error for each illumination condition.

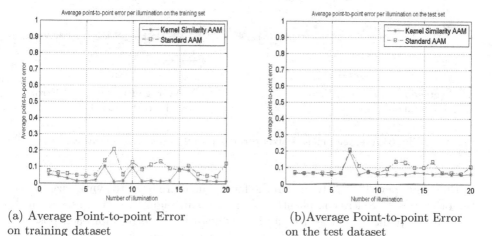

(a) Average Point-to-point Error on training dataset

(b) Average Point-to-point Error on the test dataset

Fig. 5. Average point-to-point error versus illumination variations

4.2   Sensitivity to the Poses

The training set is built with the same 16 persons, each person having 11 different pose captured by different cameras, the test set containing images from 10 persons.

As presented in Figure 4(b), images in the left column are synthesized by the proposed method, compared with fitting results of classical AAMs in the central column. An increased precision has been obtained due to the extraction of non-linear features. The gain in precision on point-to-point errors is reported in table 2, computed by eqn. (19)-(21).

Table 1. Gain in percentage for the KSAAMs method for the illumination problem (Eqn.(21))

	$E_{pt-pt}gain\%$	$E_{pix-pix}gain\%$
Training database	87.85%	61.23%
Test database	76.76%	27.02%

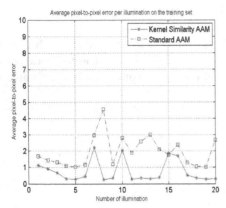
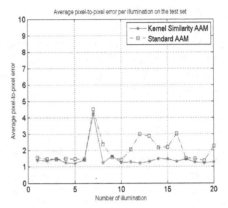

(a) Average Pixel-to-pixel Error on the training dataset

(b)Average Pixel-to-pixel Error on the test dataset

Fig. 6. Average pixel-to-pixel error versus illumination conditions

Poses numbers 1, 6, 7, 10 are profile faces which are hard to synthesize, while the other poses are less complicated. The curves in Figure 7 and Figure 8 which present the point-to-point errors and the pixel-to-pixel errors for each pose respectively give a consistent result. As illustrated by the curves, for the test on the training database, the proposed method is more efficient except for poses number 1, 7 and 10. On the test set, the results of poses number 1, 7 and 10 are missing, because the fitting procedures have problem to converge for both KSAAMs and AAMs. As a consequence, the proposed kernel method gives better fitting results in the conditions that the out-of-plane rotations of face are in a the range of ±60°. The problem of the complete profile faces is still waiting to be solved.

Table 2. Gain in percentage for the KSAAMs method for the variation of pose problem (Eqn.(21))

	$E_{pt.-pt.}Avd\%$	$E_{pix.-pix.}Avd\%$
Training database	16.63%	14.05%
Test database	22.44%	18.67%

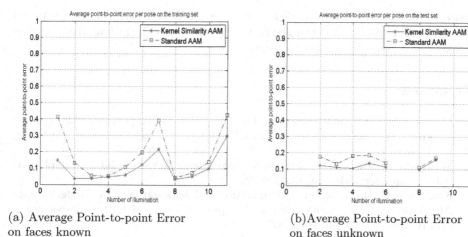

(a) Average Point-to-point Error
on faces known

(b) Average Point-to-point Error
on faces unknown

Fig. 7. Average point-to-point error per pose

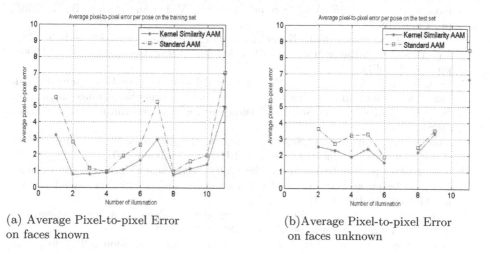

(a) Average Pixel-to-pixel Error
on faces known

(b) Average Pixel-to-pixel Error
on faces unknown

Fig. 8. Average Pixel-to-pixel error per pose

5   Conclusion

In this study, we have proposed a Kernel method combined with the AAMs fitting algorithm that is robust to illumination and pose changes of face images. Instead of the covariance matrix used in Principal Component Analysis of classical Active Appearance Model, we use eigenvectors of the kernel similarity matrix to build the deformable model.

It is shown that the model build by the proposed kernel method is less sensitive to the illumination variations. With this novel method, the fitting procedure can accurately synthesize faces semi-bright-semi-dark affected by the illumination.

Meanwhile, conditions with a variety of poses also benefit from the proposed algorithm; the ability of synthesizing faces with shape variations from a wide range of face poses has been improved.

References

1. Cootes, T.F., Edwards, G.J., Taylor, C.J.: Active Appearance Models. In: Burkhardt, H., Neumann, B. (eds.) ECCV 1998. LNCS, vol. 1407, p. 484. Springer, Heidelberg (1998)
2. Matthews, I., Baker, S.: Active Appearance Models Revisited. International Journal of Computer Vision 60, 135–164 (2003)
3. Kahraman, F., et al.: An Active Illumination and Appearance (AIA) Model for Face Alignment. In: IEEE Conference on Computer Vision and Pattern Recognition, CVPR 2007, vol. 60, pp. 1–7 (2007)
4. Navarathna, R., Sridharan, S., Lucey, S.: Fourier Active Appearance Models. In: International Conference on Computer Vision, ICCV 2011, pp. 1919–1926 (November 2011)
5. Pizarro, D., Peyras, J., Bartoli, A.: Light-invariant fitting of active appearance models. In: 2008 IEEE Conference on Computer Vision and Pattern Recognition, pp. 1–6 (2008)
6. Twining, C.J., Taylor, C.J.: Kernel Principal Component Analysis and the Construction Of Non-Linear. In: The British Machine Vision Conference, BMVC 2001, pp. 23–32 (2001)
7. De la Torre, F., Nguyen, M.H.: Parameterized Kernel Principal Component Analysis: Theory and applications to supervised and unsupervised image alignment. In: IEEE Conference on Computer Vision and Pattern Recognition, pp. 1–8 (June 2008)
8. Cootes, T.F., Taylor, C.J.: Statistical models of appearance for computer vision. World Wide Web Publication. Technical Report (February 2004)
9. Sim, T., Hal, S.: Combining visual dictionary, kernel-based similarity and learning strategy for image category retrieval. Computer Vision and Image Understanding 110(3), 403–417 (2008)
10. Scholkopf, B., Smola, A.: Nonlinear component analysis as a kernel eigenvalue problem. Neural Computation 10(5), 1299–1319 (1998)
11. Baker, Bsat, M.: The CMU Pose, Illumination, and Expression (PIE) database. In: Proceedings of Fifth IEEE International Conference on Automatic Face and Gesture Recognition, pp. 46–51. IEEE (2002)

Real-Time Dance Pattern Recognition Invariant to Anthropometric and Temporal Differences

Meshia Cédric Oveneke, Valentin Enescu, and Hichem Sahli

Vrije Universiteit Brussel Department of Electronics and Informatics (ETRO)
Pleinlaan 2, 1050 Brussels, Belgium
coveneke@vub.ac.be,
{venescu,hichem.sahli}@etro.vub.ac.be

Abstract. We present a cascaded real-time system that recognizes dance patterns from 3D motion capture data. In a first step, the body trajectory, relative to the motion capture sensor, is matched. In a second step, an angular representation of the skeleton is proposed to make the system invariant to anthropometric differences relative to the body trajectory. Coping with non-uniform speed variations and amplitude discrepancies between dance patterns is achieved via a sequence similarity measure based on Dynamic Time Warping (DTW). A similarity threshold for recognition is automatically determined. Using only one good motion exemplar (baseline) per dance pattern, the recognition system is able to find a matching candidate pattern in a continuous stream of data, without prior segmentation. Experiments show the proposed algorithm reaches a good trade-off between simplicity, speed and recognition rate. An average recognition rate of 86.8% is obtained in real-time.

Keywords: dance motion recognition, real-time, similarity measure, threshold determination, DTW.

1 Introduction

With the emergence of low-cost and reliable depth sensing cameras capable of body tracking, such as Microsoft Kinect, human motion analysis has attracted much attention recently and remains one of the most active research topics in Computer Vision. Recent work has explored many applications such as gesture recognition, human-computer interaction, human activity surveillance, computer animations and special effects for movies and video games, which require the spatio-temporal analysis of motion patterns. Recently, a considerable amount of research has been done on topics related to dance pattern recognition. Most of them are using sequence similarity measures based on DTW. In [11], the focus is on a gesture recognition approach using a feature weighting within the DTW framework. Their sample similarity measure is based on a weighted euclidean distance between normalized point-based skeletal models. However, the feature weighting approach is not well-suited for dance patterns since we assume each part of the body has an equal contribution to a certain dance pattern. In [7], a DTW-based comparison is used for the detection of dance patterns. Although they explicitly target dance patterns as we do, the motion data is segmented by computing the beat

J. Blanc-Talon et al. (Eds.): ACIVS 2012, LNCS 7517, pp. 407–419, 2012.

timestamps for the corresponding audio track beforehand. A custom threshold clustering algorithm is then used for subsequent unsupervised classification of movements. A
slightly different approach than the ones mentioned above is presented in [1,9]. There,
2D video data is used to match motion patterns under view-point, anthropometric and
temporal transforms. Their sample similarity measure is based on the epipolar geometry between correspondent 2D anatomical landmarks. Totally different approaches, not
DTW-based, have also been proposed for research related to dance pattern recognition. In [16], a hypercube sweeping algorithm that efficiently matches subsequences
between a query motion to a motion database is presented. Their method uses a polar
angle representation for the motion and generates indices on the multi-dimensional data
as multiple 1-D signals. A histogram is then used to keep track of how many dimensions
of each frame are matched. In [3,14] spatio-temporal self-similarities are used to perform action recognition under view changes. Finally, the combination of an angle-based
skeletal model and an invariant similarity measure has been investigated in [10], which
is similar to our approach. However, a classifier that requires musical beat information
is used in [10] to simplify the template matching process.

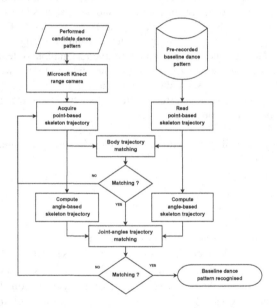

Fig. 1. Structure of the dance pattern recognition system

In this work, we focus on *dance pattern recognition* using skeletal information coming from a Microsoft Kinect range camera, and propose an easy-to-implement algorithm
that can solve this problem in real-time. The main difficulties such a problem poses
include *anthropometric and temporal variations* [1]. Although these variations are in-
evitable when acquiring human motion data, we mitigate their impact on recognition
performance by:

- using an *angle-based skeletal model* that eliminates the anthropometric dependence, while it reduces the dimensionality of the originally acquired joint-based
  skeleton model without loss of information.
- introducing a *sequence similarity measure* based on DTW to eliminate temporal
  transformations (speed variations). This similarity measure is bounded, thereby being invariant to the length and category of the analyzed dance pattern. In this in-
  carnation, DTW relies on a similarity measure between temporal samples using the
  normalized inner product between two feature vectors, which is immune to the case
  where one feature vector is the scaled version of the other (amplitude differences).

The proposed recognition system is developed as part of an application for teaching
children to dance with a humanoid robot. A dance pattern is split in several atomic
motions that can be demonstrated/repeated by the robot until the child correctly executes the motion. Since we are interested in assessing whether the child's motion approaches an 'ideal' motion, we prerecord only one exemplar per dance pattern (referred
to as baseline) with the help of a dance professional. Hence, we do not adopt a statistical recognition method, such as Hidden Markov Models [8], which entails a large set
of data to extract statistically meaningful parameters. Moreover, using more than one
recording per pattern would result in integrating out the variation in execution, thereby
departing our goal of assessment with respect to an 'ideal' motion.

The structure of the system is illustrated in Figure 1. It consists of four major modules: i) a Microsoft Kinect range camera for skeletal tracking at a rate of 30Hz [15], ii)
a body trajectory comparison module for matching body displacements relative to the
depth-sensing camera, iii) a module converting the 3D point-based skeleton trajectories
into angle-based skeleton trajectories, and iv) an angle-based skeleton-trajectory comparison module, which is, along with module ii), the main contribution of our work. It
is the output of this comparison, along with a similarity threshold and a pair of tolerance factors, that will determine if a dance pattern is recognized or not. An important
feature is that, unlike the majority of sequence matching algorithms, ours does not need
to segment a candidate pattern in the incoming motion data prior to recognition. Only
one good motion exemplar (baseline) is required to perform the recognition on any
candidate sequence.

The sequel of the paper is structured as follows. Section 2 presents the point-based
and angle-based skeletal models required for the body and joint-angles trajectory matching respectively. Section 3 describes the DTW-based recognition algorithm. Experimental results are included in Section 4. Finally, Section 5 concludes the paper.

2   Dance Pattern Representation

2.1   Joint-Angles Trajectory

For the representation of the dance pattern, we start from a *point-based skeletal model*,
as provided by the Microsoft Kinect range camera. This model consists of a set of
24 joints, $\mathcal{J} = \{1, 2, \ldots, 24\}$, depicted by dots in Figure 2. Each joint position is
represented by a point $\mathbf{x}_j \in \mathbb{R}^3$ relative to camera coordinate system, where $\mathbf{x}_j = (x_j, y_j, z_j)^T$ and $j \in \mathcal{J}$. Thus we can represent the skeleton as a set $\mathcal{S} = \{\mathbf{x}_1, \ldots, \mathbf{x}_{24}\}$

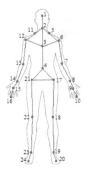

Fig. 2. Frontal view of the 3D point-based skeletal model of the human body

of 3D joint positions. Although this representation can describe every pose of a human body, it is heavily dependent on body size and proportions (anthropometric) differences among people. One way to eliminate the influence of body size is working with joint angles instead of 3D joint positions. To this end, we define a function f by

$$f(\mathbf{a}, \mathbf{b}, \mathbf{c}, \mathbf{d}) := \arccos \frac{\langle \mathbf{b} - \mathbf{a}, \mathbf{d} - \mathbf{c} \rangle}{\|\mathbf{b} - \mathbf{a}\| \|\mathbf{d} - \mathbf{c}\|} \qquad \forall \mathbf{a}, \mathbf{b}, \mathbf{c}, \mathbf{d} \in \mathcal{S} \qquad (1)$$

where $\langle \cdot, \cdot \rangle$ is the inner product and $\| \cdot \|$ the norm. Using this function, we can construct a *angle-based skeletal model* consisting of a feature vector of 13 angles,

$$\mathbf{v} = \begin{pmatrix} \theta_{ler} \\ \theta_{ley} \\ \theta_{lsr} \\ \theta_{lsp} \\ \theta_{rer} \\ \theta_{rey} \\ \theta_{rsr} \\ \theta_{rsp} \\ \theta_{lhp} \\ \theta_{lkr} \\ \theta_{rhp} \\ \theta_{rkr} \\ \theta_{tor} \end{pmatrix} = \begin{pmatrix} f(\mathbf{x}_7, \mathbf{x}_6, \mathbf{x}_7, \mathbf{x}_9) \\ f(\mathbf{x}_6, \mathbf{x}_2, \mathbf{x}_7, \mathbf{x}_9) \\ f(\mathbf{x}_6, \mathbf{x}_{17}, \mathbf{x}_6, \mathbf{x}_7) \\ f(\mathbf{x}_{17}, \mathbf{x}_{21}, \mathbf{x}_6, \mathbf{x}_7) \\ f(\mathbf{x}_{13}, \mathbf{x}_{12}, \mathbf{x}_{13}, \mathbf{x}_{24}) \\ f(\mathbf{x}_{12}, \mathbf{x}_2, \mathbf{x}_{13}, \mathbf{x}_{24}) \\ f(\mathbf{x}_{12}, \mathbf{x}_{21}, \mathbf{x}_{12}, \mathbf{x}_{13}) \\ f(\mathbf{x}_{21}, \mathbf{x}_{17}, \mathbf{x}_{12}, \mathbf{x}_{13}) \\ f(\mathbf{x}_{18}, \mathbf{x}_{17}, \mathbf{x}_2, \mathbf{x}_4) \\ f(\mathbf{x}_{18}, \mathbf{x}_{17}, \mathbf{x}_{18}, \mathbf{x}_{20}) \\ f(\mathbf{x}_{22}, \mathbf{x}_{21}, \mathbf{x}_2, \mathbf{x}_4) \\ f(\mathbf{x}_{22}, \mathbf{x}_{21}, \mathbf{x}_{22}, \mathbf{x}_{24}) \\ f(\mathbf{x}_{21}, \mathbf{x}_{17}, \mathbf{x}_{12}, \mathbf{x}_6) \end{pmatrix} \qquad (2)$$

which is a reduction of the original point-based skeletal model $\mathcal{S}$, without loss of useful information. The physical meaning of each angle is given by a three-letter code. The first letter can be l(left) or r(right). The second letter can be e(elbow), s(shoulder), h(hip) or k(knee). Finally we have a third letter standing for r(roll), p(pitch) or y(yaw) angle. Note that the last angle θ_{tor} is an exception to that three-letter code. There, *to* stands for torso and r for roll angle. At this stage, we can define any dance pattern of N time samples as a *angle-based skeleton trajectory* as a set $\mathcal{V}$ of N feature vectors:

$$\mathcal{V} = \{\mathbf{v}_1, \mathbf{v}_2, \ldots, \mathbf{v}_N\}. \qquad (3)$$

2.2 Body Trajectory

The angle-based skeletal model does not provide information on the global displacement of the body with respect to the sensor coordinate system. As such, we describe the global displacement of the skeleton by the trajectory of its *center of mass* in the 3D-space. At each time step, the center of mass is computed using the positions of the hips and waist (joints 17, 21 and 4). This results in a trajectory in the 3D-space:

$$\mathcal{P} = \{\mathbf{p}_1, \mathbf{p}_2, \ldots, \mathbf{p}_N\} \tag{4}$$

where, for each sample i, $\mathbf{p}_i = \frac{1}{3}((\mathbf{x}_4)_i + (\mathbf{x}_{17})_i + (\mathbf{x}_{21})_i)$ and N is the number of time samples. Finally, we decide to use just the x and z coordinates to make $\mathcal{P}$ immune to corruption by articulated motion generating vertical displacements, i.e. along the y-axis. The recognition system will then process both the joint-angles and the body motion sequences. In the rest of the paper, we will use the symbols $\mathcal{B}$ and $\mathcal{C}$ as baseline and candidate patterns, respectively. Both patterns consists of their joint-angles and body trajectories.

3 Dance Pattern Recognition

As illustrated in Figure 1, the goal of the system is to recognize a baseline skeleton trajectory $\mathcal{B} = \{\mathbf{b}_1, \mathbf{b}_2, \ldots, \mathbf{b}_M\}$ in a candidate skeleton trajectory $\mathcal{C} = \{\mathbf{c}_1, \mathbf{c}_2, \ldots, \mathbf{c}_N\}$, captured in real-time. The recognition implies both the corresponding joint-angles and body trajectories must match. To achieve this, we make the following assumptions about the baseline and candidate trajectories [13]:

- there is no *a priori* knowledge about which parts of the candidate trajectory $\mathcal{C}$ contain important information.
- the difference in length between a matching subsequence of the candidate trajectory and the baseline trajectory is bounded.

3.1 Similarity Measure

Before applying the DTW algorithm, we first need to define a sample similarity measure between feature (angle/position) vectors defining the skeleton pose. An obvious candidate is the Euclidean distance. However, to accommodate differences in amplitude between feature vectors without affecting the similarity, we propose to formulate it based on the *normalized inner product* of the two feature vectors. We define the sample similarity measure ρ for skeleton poses as

$$\rho(\mathbf{v}, \mathbf{w}) := 1 - \frac{\langle \mathbf{v}, \mathbf{w} \rangle}{\|\mathbf{v}\| \|\mathbf{w}\|} \tag{5}$$

This measure has the important property that it is bounded, which is important in the process of finding the recognition threshold. Using this measure in combination with DTW, we can now formulate a sequence similarity measure. To this end, we shortly introduce the classical DTW approach based on the definitions in [13] and [4].

Let the baseline motion trajectory $\mathcal{B} = \{\mathbf{b}_1, \mathbf{b}_2, \ldots, \mathbf{b}_M\}$ of length M and the candidate motion trajectory $\mathcal{C} = \{\mathbf{c}_1, \mathbf{c}_2, \ldots, \mathbf{c}_N\}$ of length N be the two motion sequences to be matched by DTW. To compare two feature vectors $\mathbf{b}$ and $\mathbf{c}$, we use the sample similarity measure ρ, introduced in the previous subsection as local similarity measure. By evaluating the local cost measure for each pair of elements of the sequences $\mathcal{B}$ and $\mathcal{C}$, we obtain the cost matrix $\mathbf{R} \in [0, 2]^{M \times N}$ defined by

$$
\mathbf{R} = \begin{pmatrix}
\rho(\mathbf{b}_1, \mathbf{c}_1) & \rho(\mathbf{b}_1, \mathbf{c}_2) & \cdots & \rho(\mathbf{b}_1, \mathbf{c}_N) \\
\rho(\mathbf{b}_2, \mathbf{c}_1) & \rho(\mathbf{b}_2, \mathbf{c}_2) & \cdots & \rho(\mathbf{b}_2, \mathbf{c}_N) \\
\vdots & \vdots & \ddots & \vdots \\
\rho(\mathbf{b}_M, \mathbf{c}_1) & \rho(\mathbf{b}_M, \mathbf{c}_2) & \cdots & \rho(\mathbf{b}_M, \mathbf{c}_N)
\end{pmatrix}
\tag{6}
$$

Then the goal is to find an alignment (or a *warping path*) between $\mathcal{B}$ and $\mathcal{C}$ having a minimal total cost. We first define a (N, M)-warping path as a sequence $\mathcal{T} = \{\mathbf{t}_1, \mathbf{t}_2, \ldots, \mathbf{t}_K\}$ with $\mathbf{t}_k = (i_k, j_k) \in [1, M] \times [1, N]$ for $k \in [1, K]$ satisfying the following three conditions:

- Boundary condition: $\mathbf{t}_1 = (1, 1)$ and $\mathbf{t}_K = (M, N)$.
- Monotonicity condition: $i_1 \leq i_2 \leq \ldots \leq i_K$ and $j_1 \leq j_2 \leq \ldots \leq j_K$.
- Step size condition: $\mathbf{t}_{k+1} - \mathbf{t}_k \in \{(1, 0), (0, 1), (1, 1)\}$ for $k \in [1, K-1]$.

The warping path $\mathcal{T}$ defines an alignment between $\mathcal{B}$ and $\mathcal{C}$ by assigning the element $\mathbf{b}_{i_k}$ of $\mathcal{B}$ to the element $\mathbf{c}_{j_k}$ of $\mathcal{C}$. The boundary condition enforces that the alignment refers to the entire sequences $\mathcal{B}$ and $\mathcal{C}$. The monotonicity condition reflects the requirement that if an element in $\mathcal{B}$ precedes a second one this should also hold for the corresponding elements in $\mathcal{C}$, and vice versa. Finally, the step size condition expresses a kind of continuity condition, i.e. no element in $\mathcal{B}$ and $\mathcal{C}$ can be omitted and there are no replications in the alignment. We can now define the total cost $d_{\mathcal{T}}(\mathcal{B}, \mathcal{C})$ over a warping path $\mathcal{T}$ between $\mathcal{B}$ and $\mathcal{C}$ with respect to the local cost measure ρ as

$$
d_{\mathcal{T}}(\mathcal{B}, \mathcal{C}) := \frac{1}{K} \sum_{k=1}^{K} \rho(\mathbf{b}_{i_k}, \mathbf{c}_{j_k}).
\tag{7}
$$

where we divide by K (the number of points on the warping path) to make sure it is a *normalized total cost*. Finally, we define the *optimal warping path* between $\mathcal{B}$ and $\mathcal{C}$ as a warping path $\mathcal{T}^*$ having minimal total cost among all possible warping paths. The total cost over the optimal warping path is then defined as:

$$
DTW(\mathcal{B}, \mathcal{C}) := d_{\mathcal{T}^*}(\mathcal{B}, \mathcal{C})
\tag{8}
$$

It is this cost that will be used as *sequence similarity measure* for the trajectory recognition. Note that $DTW(\mathcal{B}, \mathcal{C})$ is *bounded*, since it is a normalized sum of the sample similarity measure defined in equation (5). This property will determine the sequence similarity thresholds of various baselines to be grouped in a relatively narrow interval.

3.2 Skeleton Trajectory Recognition

Now that we have a sequence similarity measure, we can use this to recognize parts of a candidate dance pattern C that are similar to the baseline pattern B. Therefore, we need a *sequence similarity threshold* th_B to decide whether there is a match or not. Before that we discuss some important drawbacks of the classical DTW algorithm and several improvements we have devised.

Trajectory Variance Test. A first drawback of the classical DTW algorithm is the matching of flat signals, i.e. signals with very small variations. In this case, DTW has the tendency to match any pair of signals, which increases the number of false positives. Consider, for instance, only the joint-angles trajectories of B and C. We first make the strong assumption that the baseline signals are not flat, then we use the two-tailed F-test to test the equality of the variances of each angle k of the two trajectories. The hypothesis test (with a significance level of $\alpha = 0.05$) is then defined as:

$$H_0 : (\sigma_k)^2_B = (\sigma_k)^2_C \qquad H_1 : (\sigma_k)^2_B \neq (\sigma_k)^2_C \qquad (9)$$

where $k = 1, \ldots, 13$. As test statistic, we have the ratio $r := \frac{(s_k)^2_B}{(s_k)^2_C}$, where $(s_k)^2_B$ and $(s_k)^2_C$ are the sample variances. The more this ratio deviates from one, the stronger the evidence for unequal population variances. To determine whether or not the candidate trajectory C is a possible false positive, we calculate the weighted percentage of angles that have a significant equality. We define the weight of each angle w_k by:

$$w_k = \frac{(s_k)_B}{\sum_{k=1}^{13} (s_k)_B} \qquad (10)$$

Let us consider now the set $\mathcal{L} \subseteq \{1, \ldots, 13\}$ as the set of angles for which the hypothesis H_0 is accepted, we then define the weighted percentage π_C as:

$$\pi_C = \frac{\sum_{l \in \mathcal{L}} w_l}{\sum_{k=1}^{13} w_k} \qquad (11)$$

If $\pi_C < 0.7$, then the joint-angles sequence of C is classified as a non-matching skeleton trajectory. Note that the same test is applied to the body trajectories of B and C.

Automatic Threshold Determination. Another drawback of the classical DTW algorithm is the empirical determination of the matching threshold. In this section, we propose a discriminative solution to automate the process of finding an optimal threshold for a specific baseline B. To this end, we generate positive and negative sets of candidate sequences. The positive set comprises the baseline as well as perturbed versions of it, obtained by adding Gaussian noise to the feature vectors composing the baseline, over-sampling and sub-sampling the baseline, and combinations thereof. Let us denote by $p_+(d)$ the probability distribution function (pdf) of the sequence similarity measure values returned by the DTW algorithm when taking as parameters the baseline and a positive sequence. In the negative set, we include any motion sequence which is different from the baseline under consideration: perturbed versions of other baseline motions and sequences that represent random motions acquired to this purpose. Let $p_-(d)$ denote the pdf of the sequence similarity measure values returned by the DTW algorithm with the baseline and a negative sequence as parameters. Then we can find the threshold th by minimizing the probability of matching error $P_{error}(th)$:

$$
\begin{aligned}
P_{error}(th) &= P_{fn}(th) + P_{fp}(th) \\
&= P_+(d > th) + P_-(d < th) \\
&= \int_{th}^{\infty} p_+(d)dd + \int_{-\infty}^{th} p_-(d)dd \\
&= 1 - \int_{-\infty}^{th} p_+(d)dd + \int_{-\infty}^{th} p_-(d)dd \\
&= 1 - \text{cdf}_+(th) + \text{cdf}_-(th),
\end{aligned}
\tag{12}
$$

where P_{fp} and P_{fn} are the probabilities of false positives and false negatives, respectively, while cdf is the cumulative distribution function. Approximating the pdf's of positive and negative classes by normalized histograms, the optimal threshold corresponding to $\mathcal{B}$, $th_\mathcal{B}$, can be found with a precision of half bin. In this way, we can compute two thresholds for each baseline: one for global motion matching and the other for articulate motion matching. In our experiments, we have observed a very good correspondence between the empirically-found thresholds and the optimal ones.

On-Line Candidate Subsequence Matching. Having an automatic way to determine a sequence similarity threshold and eliminate potential false positives, we still have to deal with the fact that we don't know in advance the start and end points of the matching candidate sequence. If there is a matching candidate subsequence $\mathcal{C}_{match} \subseteq \mathcal{C}$, it must have a difference in length (with respect to the baseline pattern) lying in a certain interval. We formulate this condition by

$$
\tau_{min} \leq \frac{|\mathcal{C}_{match}|}{|\mathcal{B}|} \leq \tau_{max}
\tag{13}
$$

where $\tau_{min} \in (0, 1]$, $\tau_{max} \in [1, +\infty)$ and $|.|$ is the length of the sequence. In this way the system has more flexibility in terms of tolerance against length differences. The more τ_{min} and τ_{max} are closer to 1, the more the system is severe. In short, we say that a candidate subsequence $\mathcal{C}_{match}$ that matches a baseline sequence $\mathcal{B}$ is recognized if and only if $DTW(\mathcal{B}, \mathcal{C}_{match}) \leq th_\mathcal{B}$ and $\mathcal{C}_{match}$ satisfies condition (13), given a sequence similarity threshold $th_\mathcal{B}$ and the tolerance factors τ_{min} and τ_{max}. These tests along with a circular buffer technique enable us to handle the sequence matching from a continuous stream of motion data. Thus, our DTW implementation does not require the segmentation of a candidate sequence beforehand. Algorithm 1 illustrates the recognition process. The circular-buffer based DTW approach has a computational time-complexity of $\mathcal{O}(\tau_{max}M^2)$.

Algorithm 1 $C^* = OnlineDancePatternRecognition(\mathcal{B}, th_\mathcal{B}, \tau_{min}, \tau_{max})$

Require: A baseline dance pattern $\mathcal{B} = \{b_1, b_2, \ldots, b_M\}$, a sequence similarity threshold $th_\mathcal{B}$ and tolerance factors τ_{min} and τ_{max}.

Ensure: Each returned candidate subsequence C_{match} of collection C^* satisfies $DTW(\mathcal{B}, C_{match}) \leq th_\mathcal{B}$ and condition (13).

$C^* = \emptyset$ //C^* = collection of matching candidate subsequences.
$C_{temp} = \emptyset$ //C_{temp} = circular buffer of current candidate sequence.
$k = 0$ //initialize the length of the current candidate in the circular buffer C_{temp}.
$\mathcal{D} = \emptyset$ //initialize the set of sequence similarity scores.
while !$StopRecognition$ **do**
  $\mathcal{S} = CaptureSkeleton()$
  $\mathbf{c} = ComputeAngles(\mathcal{S})$
  $C_{temp} = C_{temp} \cup \{\mathbf{c}\}$
  $k = k + 1$ //update length in the circular buffer C_{temp}.
  if $\tau_{min}|\mathcal{B}| \leq k \leq \tau_{max}|\mathcal{B}|$ **then**
    $d = 2.0$ //set d to maximal value of sequence similarity score.
    $\pi_{C_{temp}} = BodyTrajectoryFTest(\mathcal{B}, C_{temp})$ //using eq. (3.2)
    if $\pi_{C_{temp}} \geq 0.7$ **and** $BodyTrajectoryMatch(\mathcal{B}, C_{temp})$ **then**
      $\pi_{C_{temp}} = JointAnglesTrajectoryFTest(\mathcal{B}, C_{temp})$ //using eq. (3.2)
      if $\pi_{C_{temp}} \geq 0.7$ **then**
        $d = DTW(\mathcal{B}, C_{temp})$
      end if
    end if
    $\mathcal{D} = \mathcal{D} \cup \{d\}$ //save the current sequence similarity score.
  else if $k > \tau_{max}|\mathcal{B}|$ **then**
    $j = \text{argmin } \mathcal{D}$
    if $d_j \leq th_\mathcal{B}$ **then**
      $C_{match} = \{c_1, \ldots, c_j\}$
      $C^* = C^* \cup C_{match}$ //add matching candidate subsequence to collection C^*.
    else
      $C_{match} = C_{temp}$
    end if
    $C_{temp} = C_{temp} \setminus C_{match}$ //extract the best matching subsequence.
    $k = |C_{temp}|$ //update length in the circular buffer C_{temp}.
    $\mathcal{D} = \emptyset$ //reset the set of sequence similarity scores.
  end if
end while
return C^* //return collection of matching candidate subsequences.

---

4 Experimental Results

For the experiments, we implemented algorithm 1 on a Linux-platform using C++. We use the OpenNI [6] library for the acquisition of Microsoft Kinect range data. Using this library we can acquire the point-based skeletons at 30Hz. The data set used for recognition consists of pre-recorded baseline patterns. Those patterns have been recorded using the same Microsoft Kinect range camera. Different categories of patterns have been chosen, going from simple gestures (*clap*, *wave* and *bend*) to more complicated dance patterns (*Swing left to right* and the famous *YMCA* dance).

4.1 Automatic Threshold Determination

A first experiment is the automatic determination of the sequence similarity threshold. As explained in previous section, the determination is done by processing positive and negative examples using DTW and looking at the distribution of the outcome. An example for the joint-angles trajectory of the dance *YMCA* is shown in the Figure 3. This example was obtained by automatically generating 150 positive examples by adding a perturbation of maximum 30 degrees on each feature element of the baseline. For the negative examples, 312 different patterns were randomly chosen from a set of baselines that were known to be significantly different from the tested baseline patterns.

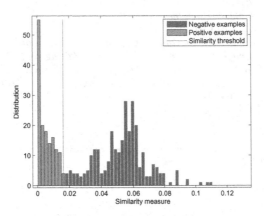

Fig. 3. Threshold determination for the joint-angles trajectory of the dance *YMCA* using distribution of positive and negative examples. Number of positive examples = 150 and number of negative examples = 312. Similarity threshold = 0.015241.

4.2 Body Trajectory Matching

In a second experiment we test the body trajectory matching process. Two baseline patterns were used for this experiment. A first baseline consisted of two steps to the left side of the actor. The second baseline consisted of two steps to the right of the actor. The goal of this experiment is to test if the sequence similarity measure, along with its threshold determination and trajectory variance test, is able to distinguish both patterns. We therefore used a candidate sequence consisted of four alternations of the two baseline patterns. Figure 4 shows the evolution of the sequence similarity measure in function of the possible candidate start frame. The left graph corresponds to the recognition first baseline and the second graph to the second baseline. Note that both were processed on the same candidate sequence. We can clearly see the four repetitions in both graphs. Furthermore we can see the alternation of both baselines by looking at the extrema of both graphs. The minima of the left graph correspond to the maxima of the second one and vice-versa. We can therefore conclude that there is a clear distinction of the two baseline patterns.

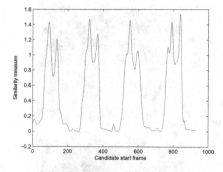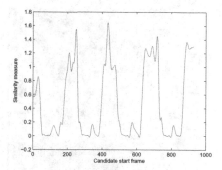

Fig. 4. Body trajectory matching. Left graph: recognition of *Two steps left*. Right graph: recognition of *Two steps right*. Both baselines are processed on the same candidate sequence. Minima corresponds to matches.

4.3 On-Line Candidate Subsequence Matching

To test the quantitative performance of the recognition system explained in Algorithm 1, we test 5 different baseline patterns separately. We used 4 actors to make sure there are anthropometric and temporal differences. The tolerance factors used during the tests are $\tau_{min} = 0.8$ and $\tau_{max} = 1.2$. The similarity thresholds have been automatically predetermined.

Table 1. Recognition rate (in percentage) over a set of baseline dance patterns of different length and category. Tolerances $\tau_{min} = 0.8$ and $\tau_{max} = 1.2$.

Motion pattern	Number of frames	Recognition rate
Clap	11	92.5%
Wave	16	85.0%
Bend	26	90.5%
Swing left to right	34	80.7%
YMCA	81	85.4%

In a second experiment, we test the real-time qualitative performance of the system. We therefore test 4 different baseline patterns in parallel. The same 4 actors as in the previous quantitative experiment were used to perform. Figures 5 and 6 illustrate the recognition of the baseline patterns *Wave* and *YMCA* respectively. For each process, the recognition score was rendered in a bar. The higher the score, the more the bar was filled (in blue) until it reached the recognition threshold (orange). A counter was updated each time a baseline pattern was recognized, to keep track of the matching candidate sub-sequences. The system is therefore able to handle periodical patterns.

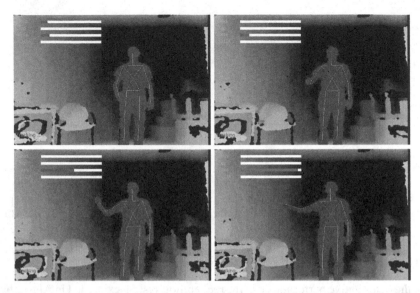

Fig. 5. Four key-frames of the *Wave* baseline pattern, performed by subject 1. The orange bar corresponds to the recognition of the baseline pattern.

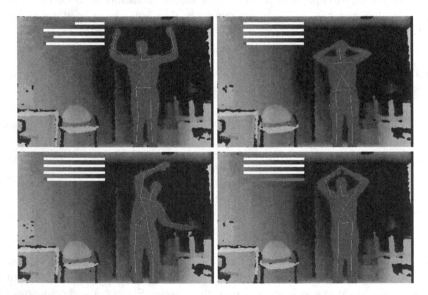

Fig. 6. Four key-frames of the *YMCA* baseline pattern, performed by subject 3. The orange bar corresponds to the recognition of the baseline pattern.

5   Conclusion and Future Work

We presented a real-time dance pattern recognition system, based on an enhanced DTW approach. First, a twofold representation was adopted for the human body motion: i) global motion trajectory of the body and ii) joint angles trajectory accounting for the articulated motion of the limbs relative to the body. Decoupling the articulated motion from the body motion using an angular representation renders the system invariant to anthropomorphic differences throughout dance performers. Moreover, using a cascade of two DTW matchers for global and articulated motions guarantees the early discarding of the non-resembling patterns. Second, we proposed a discriminative approach for automatic similarity threshold predetermination, thereby avoiding the cumbersome, classical empirical procedure. Third, a signal variance test was introduced to guard the system against flat signals resulting in false positives. Fourth, we used a circular buffer to collect motion samples and extract pattern candidates. This allows the system to take in a continuous motion stream, obviating the need for pattern segmentation. The experimental results show a high recognition rate. However, some improvements can still be made to increase the performance. A first step will be to leverage the inverse kinematics techniques [5,2] for the angle-based skeletal model, to recognize more complex patterns. It is also interesting to investigate whether more sophisticated DTW approaches [4,12] could increase the performance of the system.

References

1. Gritai, A., Sheikh, Y., Rao, C., Shah, M.: Matching trajectories of anatomical landmarks under viewpoint, anthropometric and temporal transforms. IJCV 84(3), 325–343 (2009)
2. Heise, R., MacDonald, B.A.: Kinematics of an elbow manipulator with forearm rotation: the Excalibur (1988), http://hdl.handle.net/1880/45573
3. Junejo, I.N., Dexter, E., Laptev, I., Perez, P.: View-independent action recognition from temporal self-similarities. IEEE Trans. PAMI 33(1), 172–185 (2011)
4. Muller, M.: Information Retrieval for Music and Motion. Springer, Heidelberg (2007)
5. Murray, R.M., Sastry, S.S., Zexiang, L.: A Mathematical Introduction to Robotic Manipulation, 1st edn. CRC Press, Inc., Boca Raton (1994)
6. OpenNI (March 2012), http://www.openni.org/
7. Pohl, H., Hadjakos, A.: Dance pattern recognition using dynamic time warping. In: Sound and Music Computing (2010)
8. Rabiner, L.R.: A tutorial on hidden markov models and selected applications in speech recognition. Proc. of the IEEE 77(2), 257–286 (1989)
9. Rao, C., Gritai, A., Shah, M., Syeda-Mahmood, T.: View-invariant alignment and matching of video sequences. In: International Conference on Computer Vision (ICCV), Los Alamitos, USA, vol. 2, pp. 939–945 (2003)
10. Raptis, M., Kirovski, D., Hoppe, H.: Real-time classification of dance gestures from skeleton animation. ACM SIGGRAPH, 147–156 (2011)
11. Reyes, M., Dominguez, G., Escalera, S.: Feature weighting in dynamic time warping for gesture recognitionin depth data. In: 1st IEEE Workshop on Consumer Depth Cameras for Computer Vision, Barcelona, Spain, pp. 1182–1188 (2011)
12. Riedel, D.E., Venkatesh, S., Liu, W.: Threshold dynamic time warping for spatial activity recognition. International Journal of Information and Systems Sciences 3(3), 392–405 (2007)
13. Sakoe, H., Chiba, S.: Dynamic programming algorithm optimization for spoken word recognition. IEEE Trans. ASSP 26(1), 43–49 (1978)
14. Shechtman, E., Irani, M.: Matching local self-similarities across images and videos. In: Computer Vision and Pattern Recognition (CVPR), pp. 1–8. IEEE (2007)
15. Shotton, J., Sharp, T.: Real-time human pose recognition in parts from single depth images. In: Computer Vision and Pattern Recognition (CVPR), pp. 1297–1304. IEEE (2011)
16. So, C.K.F., Baciu, G.: Hypercube sweeping algorithm for subsequence motion matching in large motion databases. In: VRCIA 2006, pp. 221–228. ACM, New York (2006)

Entropy Based Supervised Merging for Visual Categorization

Usman Farrokh Niaz and Bernard Merialdo

EURECOM, 2229 Route des Cretes, 06560 Sophia Antipolis, France

Abstract. Bag Of visual Words (BoW) is widely regarded as the standard representation of visual information present in the images and is broadly used for retrieval and concept detection in videos. The generation of visual vocabulary in the BoW framework generally includes a quantization step to cluster the image features into a limited number of visual words. This quantization achieved through unsupervised clustering does not take any advantage of the relationship between the features coming from images belonging to similar concept(s), thus enlarging the semantic gap. We present a new dictionary construction technique to improve the BoW representation by increasing its discriminative power. Our solution is based on a two step quantization: we start with k-means clustering followed by a bottom-up supervised clustering using features' label information. Results on the TRECVID 2007 data [8] show improvements with the proposed construction of the BoW.

We equally give upperbounds of improvement over the baseline for the retrieval rate of each concept using the best supervised merging criteria.

1 Introduction

The codebook or Bag of Words (BoW) model is a histogram representation used for scene description that is proven to be promising for large scale image and video retrieval. It is usually obtained through vector quantization performed on a number of keypoints or robust descriptors gathered from images. Each image is in turn coded by this histogram representation.

For the generation of visual vocabulary in the BoW framework, keypoints or Local Interest Points (LIPs) containing rich local information from images are identified. These keypoints are described using local image descriptors such as Scale Invariant Feature Transformation (SIFT) [5] resulting in a 128 dimensional feature vector and are clustered to form the visual codebook. This quantization is usually performed using any unsupervised clustering algorithm, like e.g. k-means. The clustering process divides the feature space into adjacent Voronoi cells where the cluster centers are the words of the visual vocabulary. After quantization of the feature space an image can be represented by a histogram where the bins of this histogram count the number of visual words in each cell. This histogram is then used for training the classifier; typically the two class Support Vector machines (SVM).

J. Blanc-Talon et al. (Eds.): ACIVS 2012, LNCS 7517, pp. 420–430, 2012.

Image description in the BoW framework generally faces two important issues. The first is that generating the visual vocabulary through unsupervised quantization from tens of thousands of low level descriptors does not capture semantic context as category information is not accounted for during clustering. Doing so the expressive or discriminative power of the vocabulary is affected as only overall distortion is minimized and category information is not used increasing the semantic gap between the concept and the mid-level BoW feature. This category information should be used in the vocabulary generation to build class specific visual words. The other problem with codebook representation is choosing the vocabulary size. Typical size of visual vocabulary ranges from 200 to 5000 words. The categorization performance usually increases with the dictionary size but this affects the retrieval efficiency and also the generalization ability of the vocabulary over noisy descriptors. There is therefore a need to find a compromise between the dictionary size and its discrimination ability. We present a dictionary construction method in this paper, to address these issues, for generating discriminative codebooks to improve retrieval results.

The problem of increasing the discriminative power of BoW model has been attacked by many authors in the recent years. Wang [9] builds a multi-resolution codebook by adding a new codeword at each step using hierarchical clustering and a selection criterion based on Boosting. This is done to find a compromise between a small codebook that lacks discriminative power and a large one that may result in overfitting. Perronnin et al. [7] represent each image with a bipartite histogram by building universal and class specific vocabularies using maximum likelihood estimation. Lin et al. [4] use a similar principle to bridge the semantic gap between the concept(s) depicted in the image and the low level features. k-means is used to generate separate class specific vocabularies followed by an agglomerative clustering on class codebooks to get the uinversal vocabulary. In both these works an image is represented by a set of histograms, one per class, using the amalgamated codebooks. Hao and Jie [3] present an improved BoW algorithm for scene recognition exploring discriminative power of codewords when representing different scene categories. They obtain a weighted histogram to code every image that highlights the discriminative capabilities of each codeword for each category.

For generating a discriminative codebook we follow a two step clustering framework as proposed by Winn et al. [10], where they compress an initial large dictionary by optimizing a statistical measure of discrimination that finds a compromise between low intra-class variance and inter-class discrimination. Moosmann et al. [6] build a set of randomized decision trees using the class labels with the leaf of a tree representing a spatial code (visual word). They calculate information gain of the split at each step of tree growing and use it as a threshold to split the tree based on the descriptor dimension at that level. Similarly, we use en entropy measure to merge clusters, achieved through an initial clustering, by minimizing information loss.

We use a clustering method with only a few k-means' mean shift iterations using a better centers initialization based on [1] to generate a larger than required number of clusters before doing a supervised mapping significantly reducing the number of clusters (visual words). We initially merge neighboring clusters based on entropy minimization criteria that allows the generation of non-convex connex clusters. We present three such merging criteria in order to increase the discriminative power of BoW with an increase in the retrieval performance over the baseline. We then relax certain constraints in our merging criteria to allow the generation of non-connex clusters. We have used SIFT descriptors [5] calculated on keypoints extracted from images, contrary to dense sampling [10,6], labeled with one or more classes rather than segmented hand-labeled images [10].

We also show that using our dictionary construction from supervised merging a smaller dictionary gives the performance comparable to the retrieval performance given by a dictionary upto 8 times its size.

The rest of this paper is organized as follows. Section 2 gives the detailed description of the two step supervised clustering algorithm and its three variants. In Sect. 3 we discuss detailed experimentation and present the results with the improvements proposed. Finally Sect. 4 concludes the paper.

2 Supervised Clustering Based on Entropy Minimization

In the two step clustering paradigm, Fig. 1, first of all the nearest neighbors are quantized into a large number of visual words using k-means. The number of initial visual words (k-means clusters) is $p * D$, where D is the size of the desired dictionary. In the second step the number of clusters is reduced by $1/p$ by merging neighboring clusters repeatedly based on entropy driven information loss minimization criterion.

2.1 Concept Distribution Entropy Minimization

For deriving this minimization criterion we have the m concepts $X_l \in \mathbf{X}$, $l = 1 \ldots m$ and we know with what concept(s) is each image I labeled. Thus we know what concept is represented by each descriptor (keypoint). Now suppose as a result of the initial clustering we have $p * D$ clusters, and for each cluster $C_i \in \mathbf{C}, i = 1 \ldots p * D$ we know the labels of the keypoints assigned to it (we are only treating keypoints coming from labeled shots). For finding the number of keypoints belonging to a concept X_k in the cluster C_i we consider that there may exist shots that are labeled with more than one concept. Also generally keypoints extracted from a shot are assigned to different centers. Thus we compute the number of occurences of concept X_k in the cluster C_i as:

$$|X_k \in C_i| = \sum_{I labeled with X_k} \frac{|Keypoints(I) \in C_i|}{|Keypoints(I)|} \tag{1}$$

We find next the conditional probability of the concept X_k given the cluster C_i:

$$p(X_k/C_i) = \frac{|X_k \in C_i|}{\sum_l |X_l \in C_i|} \tag{2}$$

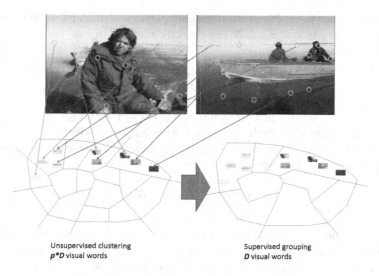

Fig. 1. Supervised merging of visual words

The set $Nb\{i\}$ contains the neighbors of the cluster C_i where two clusters are neighbors if the midpoint between their centers is closer to those two centers than to any other center. When joining two neighboring clusters C_i and C_j, where $j \in Nb\{i\}$, all the keypoints in C_j are assigned to C_i, and all the neighbors of C_j are added to those of C_i. C_j is then deleted from the set of clusters i.e. $C = C \backslash C_j$.

The entropy of the concept distribution given a clustering is given by:

$$H(X/C) = -\sum_C p(C) \sum_X p(X/C) \log p(X/C) \qquad (3)$$

which is increased (or stays the same) when any two clusters are merged.

The combination $C_i \cup C_j$ that minimizes the increase in entropy is our target combination and those two clusters are merged together.

$$\underset{C_i \cup C_j, j \in Nb\{i\}}{\operatorname{argmin}} \quad H(X/C) \qquad (4)$$

Thus the entropy $H(X/C)$ is calculated for a given clustering C. This step is repeated $p * D - D$ times until the desired number of clusters D is reached.

2.2   Concept Dependent Entropy Minimization

The entropy minimization principle can be equally used to find a merge of clusters independently for each concept using entropy of only that concept. This way we shall have one combination of clusters per concept and thus we will end up with a different BoW representation for each semantic concept. Using the above notation, for the concept $X_k \in \mathbf{X}$ the entropy is given by:

$$H^{cd}(X_k/C) = -\sum_{C \in \mathbf{C}} \left[p(X_k, C) \log p(X_k/C) + p(\overline{X_k}, C) \log p(\overline{X_k}/C) \right] \quad (5)$$

where $p(\overline{X_k}, C) = p(C) - p(X_k, C)$ and $p(\overline{X_k}/C) = 1 - p(X_k/C)$.

Now for each possible combination of two neighboring clusters we will calculate the entropy to find the best merge by choosing the two clusters that result in minimum entropy increase, given by:

$$\underset{C_i \cup C_j, j \in Nb\{i\}}{\operatorname{argmin}} \quad H^{cd}(X_k/C) \quad (6)$$

This step is repeated, reducing the total number of clusters by one each time, until the desired number of clusters is reached. This whole process is repeated for each concept resulting in a different clustering for each concept as well as a different bag of words model. An image is thus represented by a set of histograms, one per concept.

2.3   Average Concept Entropy Minimization

Another possibility to obtain a clustering combination is by combining the output of the concept dependent clusterings. This is done by taking the sum of entropy of all concepts for a merge of two clusters and then minimizing that sum for every possible combination of clusters. This clustering of average over all concepts is given by:

$$\underset{C_i \cup C_j, j \in Nb\{i\}}{\operatorname{argmin}} \sum_{X_k \in \mathbf{X}} H^{cd}(X_k/C) \quad (7)$$

where $H^{cd}(X_k/C)$ is the concept dependent entropy as given in (5).

2.4   Relaxing Constraints

Based on the results shown in Sect. 3 we select the best entropy minimization based clustering criterion and make few changes. To reduce the bias of the labeled keframes over the unlableled ones we include all the keypoints in the second step of clustering. This is done by including all the unlabeled keypoints as the $(m+1)^{th}$ concept during the calculation of the entropy of the concept distribution and recalculating the mapping based on entropy minimization. Furthermore we relax the constraint of merging only neighboring clusters where any two clusters (not necessarily neighbors) can be mapped together in the high dimensional disjoint clustering space. This allows the generation of a non-connex BoW model. These alterations are further explored in the Sect. 3 discussing the experiments and results.

Table 1. Mean Average Precision for 20 concepts using three entropy minimization based mapping criteria

Dictionary Size	K-means	Min Ent	Av Cd	Cd
500	0.0739			
1000 to 500		0.0795	0.0792	0.0757
2000 to 500		0.0801	0.0791	0.0758
4000 to 500		0.0813	0.0775	0.0727

3 Experiments

We present here experiments carried out on the TRECVID 2007 Sound and Vision database comprising 219 videos [8]. The training corpus consists of 110 videos and the other half is used for tests. Twenty semantic concepts are used to demonstrate the results. We have used 1 vs all SVM classifiers with chi-square kernel of degree 2 using the LIBSVM [2] package for each concept.

3.1 Supervised Clustering Results

Initially we evaluate the performance of supervised clustering for a resulting dictionary of 500 visual words using the three types of entropy minimization criteria. In our experiments the maximum value of p, as described in Sect. 2, is 8. That is the maximum size of initial visual dictionary obtained through k-means is 8 times the size of the desired supervised dictionary. To obtain a large initial dictionary we have used **k-means++** algorithm [1] for a better initialization in order to avoid a large number of k-means iterations, which is costly for a large number of centers. K-means++ is an initialization method that selects initial seeds far from each other while minimizing the effects of outliers. This is done by chosing a new cluster centers with a probability propotional to its distance to the closest center already chosen. After the initialization 10 normal k-means iterations are performed to generate initial visual dictionaries.

Using these large dictionaries supervised mappings are done from clustering space with 1000, 2000 and 4000 centers to 500 centers by merging neighboring clusters using entropy minimization criteria. In all three cases the final dictionary generated is always 500-word big which is then used to represent images as histograms. SVM classifiers are trained for each concept and independently for each set of histograms obtained through entropy minimization based mappings. The Mean Average Precision (MAP) for all 20 concepts is shown in the Table 1 for the 3 mapping criteria and for the 3 initial cluster sizes, along with the MAP obtained using 500 visual words achieved directly through k-means (baseline).

As the number of initial centers increases the individual concept dependent entropy minimization criteria for mapping suffers from overfitting as it generates dictionaries for each concept independently. The image level labeling does not translate well to increase the discriminative power of the BoW model built for each concept separately. This effect is carried on to the average (of concept dependent) entropy minimization as the retrieval performance is adversely affected with the increase in the number of initial cluster centers in the first step of clustering.

Contrarily, merging neighboring clusters using minimization of the entropy of concept distribution given clustering improves retrieval performance with the increase in the size of the initial number of centers. Thus this merging criterion is used for evaluating the retrieval performance of 1000 word dictionaries obtained from larger dictionaries and we see improved performances as the initial dictionary size increases. Figure 2 shows concept-wise Average Precision (AP) results along with the MAP for the two baselines of 500 and 1000 visual words and entropy minimization based mappings with the value of p selected from 2, 4 and 8. Concepts like *Airplane Flying* and *Person Playing Soccer* that have a very low number of positives in the training set are adversely affected in their performance as the number of initial centers is increased. The MAP for 1000-words dictionary increases from 0.0796 (baseline) to 0.0831 with 8000 initial centers.

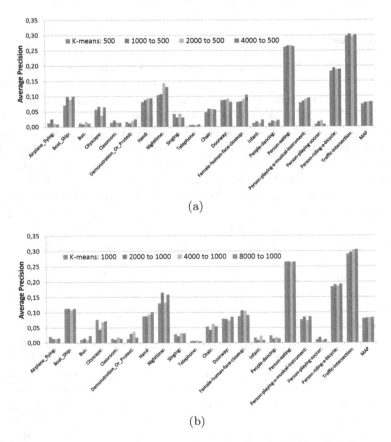

(a)

(b)

Fig. 2. Supervised clustering scores for 20 concepts using the first (best) entropy minimization criterion for (a) 500 and (b) 1000 visual words dictionaries

3.2   Alternative Mappings

We test retrieval performance for three simple modifications in the clustering criterion. To see the effect of including the unlabeled examples in the second step of our clustering framework we include all keypoints coming from the unlabeled keyframes as a new concept making the total number of concepts $m + 1$. The rest of the method remains the same which is the best performing entropy minimization criterion from the previous sub-section.

The second alternative is the relaxation of the constraint that only neighboring clusters can be merged, and the third version includes the unlabeled features while merging clusters over the whole clustering space. The MAP scores for a final dictionary of 500 words are presented in Table 2. Here we see good performance for the merging of 1000 initial clusters into 500 for the three alternatives and then a decline in the performance as the number of initial clusters is increased. This may be due to some overtraining as the number of choices for merging clusters are increased with the relaxation of constraints. However the performance is still better than the baseline results in each case.

Table 2. Mean Average Precision for 20 concepts using three alternatives of the concept distribution entropy minimization based mapping

Dictionary Size	Unlab	All Space	Unlab All Space
1000 to 500	0.0803	0.0805	0.0794
2000 to 500	0.0788	0.0795	0.0795
4000 to 500	0.0777	0.0755	0.0780

Finally we give upper bounds of improvement for each concept with highest average precision score selected from the retrieval results of different initial dictionary sizes for concept distribution entropy minimization with (i) neighboring constraint, (ii) inclusion of unlabeled features, (iii) relaxing the neighbor constraint and (iv) the inclusion of unlabeled features with the relaxation of neighbor constraint. Tables 3-(a) and 3-(b) shows the upper bounds of improvements for the two step clustering performed with its alternatives showing significant increase in the individual score for each concept for 500 and 1000 word final dictionary sizes. Individual scores for each concept improve significantly with only the concepts *Person eating* and *Traffic intersection* showing little improvement as their performance is already quite high. An exception is the concept *Airplane flying* which shows a decrease in performance with supervised merging for 1000 words dictionaries as shown in Table 3-(b).

3.3   Small and Informative vs Large Dictionaries

In the previous subsections we have shown results of our technique for building a visual dictionary and compared them to retrieval results of the baseline using

Table 3. Upperbounds of concept-wise improvements for dictionaries of (a) 500 visual words and (b) 1000 visual words

(a)

Semantic Concept	k-means	Entropy	Unlabeled	All-space	Unlab All	improvment
Airplane flying	0.0126	0.0257	**0.0266**	0.0266	0.0212	111%
Boat/Ship	0.0709	0.1005	0.1041	**0.1149**	0.1015	62%
Bus	0.0123	0.0170	0.0140	**0.0248**	0.0168	103%
Cityscape	0.0564	**0.0661**	0.0522	0.0652	0.0660	17%
Classroom	0.0132	0.0211	0.0265	**0.0463**	0.0197	250%
Demonstration	0.0158	0.0249	0.0239	**0.0325**	0.0168	106%
Hand	0.0809	0.0938	**0.0962**	0.0879	0.0872	19%
Nighttime	0.1037	0.1430	0.1487	**0.1545**	0.1460	49%
Singing	0.0415	0.0423	0.0399	0.0367	**0.0435**	5%
Telephone	0.0055	0.0072	0.0072	**0.0074**	0.0071	34%
Chair	0.0476	0.0581	**0.0618**	0.0576	0.0553	30%
Doorway	0.0865	**0.0915**	0.0857	0.0840	0.0810	6%
Female face closeup	0.0809	**0.1045**	0.1040	0.0959	0.0984	29%
Infant	0.0110	**0.0233**	0.0131	0.0170	0.0158	111%
People dancing	0.0116	0.0219	0.0218	**0.0301**	0.0196	159%
Person eating	0.2612	0.2664	0.2653	**0.2714**	0.2683	4%
Playing music	0.0779	0.0945	0.0926	**0.0949**	0.0884	22%
Person playing soccer	0.0081	**0.0203**	0.0179	0.0137	0.0138	151%
Person riding bicycle	0.1820	0.1926	0.1980	0.1949	**0.2100**	15%
Traffic intersection	0.2971	0.3036	0.3065	0.2947	**0.3096**	4%
MAP	**0.0739**	0.0859	0.0853	0.0875	0.0843	

(b)

Semantic Concept	k-means	Entropy	Unlabeled	All-space	Unlab All	improvment
Airplane flying	**0.0208**	0.0147	0.0130	0.0197	0.0178	-5%
Boat/Ship	0.1136	0.1129	0.1016	**0.1167**	0.1080	3%
Bus	0.0107	0.0235	0.0194	0.0212	**0.0317**	198%
Cityscape	0.0765	0.0720	**0.1042**	0.0697	0.0591	36%
Classroom	0.0140	0.0181	0.0177	**0.0394**	0.0197	181%
Demonstration	0.0130	**0.0366**	0.0339	0.0335	0.0332	181%
Hand	0.0876	0.1014	0.0997	**0.1023**	0.0959	17%
Nighttime	0.1297	0.1585	**0.1912**	0.1712	0.1570	47%
Singing	0.0282	0.0317	0.0397	**0.0405**	0.0367	44%
Telephone	0.0058	**0.0074**	0.0066	0.0059	0.0063	29%
Chair	0.0534	**0.0616**	0.0571	0.0581	0.0579	15%
Doorway	0.0792	**0.0855**	0.0825	0.0757	0.0777	8%
Female face closeup	0.0877	**0.1049**	0.1038	0.0957	0.1014	20%
Infant	0.0173	**0.0231**	0.0107	0.0151	0.0139	33%
People dancing	0.0238	0.0174	**0.0295**	0.0191	0.0181	24%
Person eating	0.2643	0.2643	0.2668	**0.2694**	0.2657	2%
Person playing music	0.0758	0.0860	**0.0890**	0.0830	0.0790	17%
Person playing soccer	0.0109	0.0111	**0.0129**	0.0120	0.0119	18%
Person riding bicycle	0.1839	0.1923	0.1875	0.1912	**0.2069**	13%
Traffic intersection	0.2967	**0.3045**	0.3014	0.2978	0.3024	3%
MAP	0.0796	0.0864	0.0884	0.0869	0.0850	

a dictionary obtained through sufficient number of k-means iterations. In those cases the sizes of the baseline and supervised dictionaries were same (500 words and 1000 words). We claimed that the retrieval performance of using dictionary obtained through supervised merging matches that of using a larger dictionary which is evident from the results in the Table 4.

Table 4. Comparing MAP for 20 concepts using three large dictionaries vs corresponding smaller supervised dictionaries of (a) 500 and (b) 1000 visual words

(a)

1000		2000		4000	
k-means	500	k-means	500	k-means	500
0.0796	0.0795	0.0814	0.0801	0.0830	0.0813

(b)

2000		4000		8000	
k-means	1000	k-means	1000	k-means	1000
0.0814	0.0806	0.0830	0.0816	0.0847	0.0831

SVM classifiers were trained for larger dictionaries containing 1000, 2000, 4000 and 8000 visual words. These are the dictionaries obtained in the first stage of the supervised merging using k-means. The training time for these larger BoWs is much higher and the performance is comparable to the smaller supervised BoW models. For example the 8 times smaller dictionary only results in 2% performance decrease as can be seen in the last two columns of the Table 4-(a) and less than 2% performance decrease as evident in the last two columns of the Table 4-(b).

The difference in performance will increase as the size of the first step dictionary increases as it becomes richer and richer. While merging helps to capture important semantic information the performance of the resulting supervised dictionary will be limited as the smaller dictionary will always be a coarser representation of the visual space.

As far as the computation overhead for supervised clustering is concerned it only uses the information from the image labels. Thus it does not perform any direct computation on the image features. The time complexity of supervised clustering is $O(n^3)$, with $n = p*D$, which is the cost borne once at the clustering stage during training phase giving a mapping from $p*D$ visual words to D visual words. After the two step clustering the costs of baseline and supervised dictionary for the remaining stages of video retrieval are similar.

4   Conclusions

We have seen that the discriminative ability of the Bag of Words model increases when performing the two step supervised clustering. The performance of a much smaller dictionary obtained through supervised merging reaches that of larger dictionaries obtained through k-means. The merging step is fast and incorporates already available label knowledge for calculation of the entropy. Although class specific merging of clusters overfits the BoW representation the performance is high as long as the initial number of clusters is kept low.

References

1. Arthur, D., Vassilvitskii, S.: k-means++: the advantages of careful seeding. In: Proceedings of the Eighteenth Annual ACM-SIAM Symposium on Discrete Algorithms, SODA 2007, Philadelphia, PA, USA, pp. 1027–1035 (2007), http://portal.acm.org/citation.cfm?id=1283383.1283494
2. Chang, C.C., Lin, C.J.: LIBSVM: A library for support vector machines. ACM Transactions on Intelligent Systems and Technology 2, 27:1–27:27 (2011), http://www.csie.ntu.edu.tw/~cjlin/libsvm
3. Hao, J., Jie, X.: Improved bags-of-words algorithm for scene recognition. In: 2010 2nd International Conference on Signal Processing Systems (ICSPS), vol. 2, pp. V2-279 –V2-282 (2010)
4. Lin, C., Li, S., Su, S.: Image classification using adapted codebook. In: ITIME 2009, vol. 1, pp. 1307–1312 (2009)
5. Lowe, D.G.: Distinctive image features from scale-invariant keypoints. Int. J. Comput. Vision 60, 91–110 (2004), http://portal.acm.org/citation.cfm?id=993451.996342
6. Moosmann, F., Triggs, B., Jurie, F.: Fast discriminative visual codebooks using randomized clustering forests. In: NIPS (2006), http://lear.inrialpes.fr/pubs/2006/MTJ06
7. Perronnin, F., Dance, C.R., Csurka, G., Bressan, M.: Adapted Vocabularies for Generic Visual Categorization. In: Leonardis, A., Bischof, H., Pinz, A. (eds.) ECCV 2006. LNCS, vol. 3954, pp. 464–475. Springer, Heidelberg (2006), http://dx.doi.org/10.1007/1174408536
8. Smeaton, A.F., Over, P., Kraaij, W.: Evaluation campaigns and trecvid. In: MIR 2006, pp. 321–330 (2006), http://doi.acm.org/10.1145/1178677.1178722
9. Wang, L.: Toward a discriminative codebook: Codeword selection across multi-resolution. In: CVPR (2007), http://dx.doi.org/10.1109/CVPR.2007.383374
10. Winn, J., Criminisi, A., Minka, T.: Object categorization by learned universal visual dictionary. In: ICCV 2005, pp. 1800–1807 (2005)

Selective Color Image Retrieval
Based on the Gaussian Mixture Model

Maria Luszczkiewicz-Piatek[1] and Bogdan Smolka[2]

[1] University of Lodz, Faculty of Mathematics and Computer Science,
Department of Applied Computer Science, Banacha 22, 90-238 Lodz, Poland
`mluszczkiewicz@math.uni.lodz.pl`
[2] Silesian University of Technology, Department of Automatic Control, Akademicka 16 Str,
44-100 Gliwice, Poland
`bogdan.smolka@polsl.pl`

Abstract. In this paper a novel technique of color based image retrieval is proposed. The image is represented by Gaussian mixtures of the set of histograms corresponding to the spatial location of the color regions within the image. The proposed approach enables to express user's needs concerning the specified color arrangements of the retrieved images, in form of the colors belonging to the eleven basic color groups along with their spatial locations. The solution proposed in this paper utilizes the mixture modeling of the information of each set of the color channels. Experimental results show that the proposed method is efficient and flexible, when specific user's requirements are considered.

Keywords: color image retrieval, mixture modeling, spatial information, color categorization, color selection.

1 Introduction

The advances in information technology are the result of explosive growth of the number of images being captured, stored in large databases, shared and processed via World Wide Web. However, this unimaginable amount of information needs effective and efficient tools which allow users to manage those large collections, [1, 2]. In general, there are three main categories of image retrieval methods: text based retrieval, content based and semantic based retrieval.

The approach presented in this paper falls into the second group of methods. At the beginning of the image retrieval systems development, images were annotated manually, but along with the expansion of the image collection sizes, this highly effort consuming task became ineffective, not to mention that the quality of annotation is highly correlated with the subjective perception of the operator. There is lot of effort put into automatization of this process. The other approach related to image retrieval is searching for the similarity between images on the basis of their low-level visual features such as color, texture etc. Image indexes are computed only on the basis of image content without any need for incorporation of the semantic annotations. This group of retrieval methods continuously attract much attention due to their effectiveness and independence of any subjective influences on the retrieval process. Spatial organization of colors has been recently explored in form of spatial statistics between color pixels, such

J. Blanc-Talon et al. (Eds.): ACIVS 2012, LNCS 7517, pp. 431–443, 2012.
© Springer-Verlag Berlin Heidelberg 2012

as correlograms [3] or some filter outputs [4–7]. Related approaches use points of interest similarly to classic object recognition methods [8] and many other retrieval methods rely on segmentation as a basis for image indexing [9–12]. Mutual arrangements of regions in images are also the basis of the retrieval, however the representation of the relationship can be non-symbolic [13].

The third group of retrieval methods reflects the semantic concepts conveyed by analyzed images. Semantic based image retrieval is associated with the advances in cognitive science and artificial intelligence, and thus their limitations severely influences the effectiveness of this type of retrieval methods.

The proposed method, operating on the color image, takes into account spatial arrangements of the chosen group of colors. The very common approach to deal with the spatial distribution of the image color information is the use of grid-like image partition associated with the color categorization, which is the basis for image matching providing the information about the similarity of the specified image regions in the color domain. Although this approach is very appealing due its intuitive accuracy, there are few major disadvantages questioning is practical usability. Firstly, it needs to be specified whether the grid mask determining the image regions is rectangular, octagonal or has other shape. Secondly, it should be determined if regions are overlapping and at what rate. Finally, the size or sizes of the grid regions should be provided. If image is analyzed with mask of various (e.g. growing) and overlapping regions sizes, the computational cost increases enormously. In contradiction to the mentioned above scheme, we propose a convenient method overcoming this problems. The proposed solution evaluates the information about color localization and its "density" (higher if the color forms a large homogenous region) in the image on the basis of the Gaussian Mixture Modeling [14, 15] of set of the histograms reflecting the localization of the key colors and the coherence of regions of their occurrence.

The paper is organized as following. Firstly, the idea of multichannel image representation is discussed, then the method for color information modeling is presented along with the image indexing scheme. Finally, the experimental results are presented and the future work is discussed.

2   Multichannel Color Image Representation

The most popular representation of image color information is the global color histogram. It describes the overall distribution of colors in the image, thus providing general clue about the similarity between images due the relatively high robustness to object distortions, image rotations, translations, scaling. However, the main weakness of this type of image descriptor is the fact that it does not take into account any spatial distribution of image color. Although there are numerous schemes designed to integrate the color and spatial information for retrieval purposes, the most common approach to incorporate the spatial information into retrieval process is to divide an image into regions and evaluate the color descriptors for these regions, [16–18]. The next step is the comparison of the descriptors of the corresponding regions for analyzed images. The efficiency of such defined retrieval scheme is greatly influenced, as mentioned before, by choice of the regions size, shape and rate of their possible overlapping. In this paper we present a novel approach to color image retrieval taking into account the spatial organization of the colors conveyed by the image. The proposed scheme enables the user to retrieve images not only sharing similarity in terms of the overall color distribution, but also in terms of localization of chosen color or color groups. Thus it is possible to successfully evaluate queries concerning request of finding e.g. portraits regardlessly of the background composition. In order to achieve this functionality it is necessary to decompose color image into color channels corresponding with spatial occurrence of pixels of certain groups of colors. As a representative colors we understand a set of following colors: red, green, blue, white, black, gray, yellow, brown, orange, pink, purple. Thus each of image colors can be classified into one of the following categories according to perceptual model proposed in [19]. This scheme was evaluated on the basis of the experimental setup consisting of categorization of given colors to one of the basic 11 categories according to subjective sensation of the human subjects. On the basis of this experiments the nonlinear transformation between colors of HSI system to 11 basic color set was established.

Having color image categorized, as shown in Fig. 1 (in form of a of the binary images reflecting the membership to one of the color group), the next step is to build a map of weights reflecting spatial color distribution and the size of the homogenous color regions. In details, each pixel indicated by color categorization process is represented in the weight map by associated coefficient reflecting its similarity to color of neighboring pixels with relation to the spatial distance between them, precisely if neighboring pixels are of the same color category or not. Therefore, the pixels located in the center of the homogenous region tend to have larger weights than those scattered over entire image. In consequence, such approach assigns significantly larger weights to large color regions than to small ones, often reflecting unimportant details, artifacts or even noise. It is worth underlining that the proposed approach concentrates on more profound image scene features, neglecting those of potentially lesser importance. The second mechanism providing this effect is the nature of the applied mixture modeling, which will be discussed in next Section.

The weighting process for the pixel at position (x, y) for g-th color group is evaluated according to the formula:

$$w_{x,y}^{(g)} = \frac{1}{n} \sum_{(i,j) \in W} \exp\left(-\frac{\| c_{x,y} - c_{i,j} \|}{h}\right)^{k_1} \cdot \exp\left(-\frac{d_{i,j}}{\delta}\right)^{k_2}, \quad (1)$$

where $c_{i,j}$ and $c_{x,y}$ denote the membership of the pixels color to color category (g) at positions (i, j) and (x, y) respectively, h is the color difference scaling parameter, $d_{i,j}$ is the Euclidean distance between the pixel at position (i, j) and (x, y), which is the center of the filtering window W and δ is a spatial normalizing parameter equal to the diameter of the square filtering window. The number of pixels n in W was set to be equal to 10% of the total number of pixels in the image and we assumed $k_1 = k_2$. Thus, if analyzed pixel and its neighbor belong to the same color category (g) they contribute to the overall pixel weight. Therefore, the pixels located at the centers of the homogenous color regions tend to have associated higher weights, than those located on the borders of the region. This phenomenon can be noticed in Fig. 2, where spectral histograms approximations are illustrated. The centers of the homogenous regions have associated larger weights, with values also in close relation to the size of the regions.

These distribution modes indicate also the centers of presumable objects depicted the image scene.

It is worth mentioning that the great advantage of the incorporation of this model into creation of color channels is the fact that each channel conveys only relevant color information based on perceptual measurements in contrast to any arbitrarily chosen quantization scheme which not necessarily reflects the perceptual similarity among colors in the same category, or cause dispersion of color information to many channels. At this stage of the algorithm, the original color image is transformed into multichannel image consisting of 11 binary images indicating the spatial occurrence of group of colors. For each of this binary images the map of pixel weights is computed.

Fig. 1. Exemplary results (right) of the original color image (left) categorization technique [19] for 11 base colors evaluated for 2 images of the database of Wang [9]

3   Multichannel Histogram Modeling

Next stage of the proposed scheme is the modeling of the evaluated weighting map associated with color channels. Thus, each map is treated as a histogram reflecting the spatial distribution of each color. Moreover, higher weights generally represent the higher "concentration" or "density" of color, i.e. such values are present for pixels belonging to centers of homogenous color regions. If there are few, scattered pixels of analyzed color, the weights associated with these pixels are distinctively lower. Let us note, that this mechanism enables to weaken the influence of the unimportant and very small regions, whose presence may be caused by e.g. noise. Taking into account this reasoning, it is recommended to built a model which will only reflect the "important" information omitting that of lower significance. Therefore, the model chosen for further analysis is the one approximating the given data using the mixture of distributions. Such a model seems to be very well suited to this task as it enables to decide about how well the data is reflected by the model. This important feature is obtained by the choice of the number of model components, and results in possible omission of the less pronounced data. Let us note, that if more profound modeling would be evaluated, all the questionable data also would be incorporated into the model, which is undesirable. Thus, the preferred model should be of rather low to medium complexity. Moreover, it is recommended that the model offers the compact form of color information summarization. This feature is provided by mixture models family. Let us note that the histogram based or region matching method mentioned earlier lack this compact form of color information representation. Therefore, for the information conveyed by the color channels the *Gaussian Mixture Models* (GMM) were chosen. As shown in [14] the model parameters are defined as:

$$\alpha_m^{k+1} = N^{-1} \sum_{i=1}^{N} p(m|x_i, \Theta^k), \quad \mu_m^{k+1} = \frac{\sum_{i=1}^{N} x_i \cdot p(m|x_i, \Theta^k)}{\sum_{i=1}^{N} p(m|x_i, \Theta^k)}, \qquad (2)$$

$$\upsilon_m^{k+1} = \frac{\sum_{i=1}^{N} p(m|x_i, \Theta^k)(x_i - \mu_m^{k+1})(x_i - \mu_m^{k+1})^T}{\sum_{i=1}^{N} p(m|x_i, \Theta^k)}, \qquad (3)$$

where μ and υ denote the mean and variance. N is the number of samples (i.e. image pixels), m is the index of the model component and Θ^k is the set of model parameters in k-th iteration evaluated on the basis of the related probability denoted as p. The E (Expectation) and M (Maximization) steps [20] are performed simultaneously, according to (2) and (3) and in each iteration, as the input data we use parameters obtained in the previous one.

On the basis of the previous Author's research [21, 22], as the most desirable model complexity was chosen a model of 7 components evaluated using E-M algorithm with 75 iterations. Thus, for each analyzed color image a GMM model is composed and represented as 11 collections of maximum 7 sets of GMM parameters, i.e. mean and the covariance matrix for each normal distribution with the associated mixing coefficient p. Due to varying image sizes mixture parameters are recalculated to percentage scale of the image.

4   Image Indexing and Similarity Measures

In order to test the efficiency of the proposed methodology, we indexed color images using the information about their similarity to the others. One approach is related to the "point to point" similarity, using Minkowskis norm such as L_1. However, it is more suitable to generalize this concept toward "distribution to distribution" similarity. Thus, as the spatial arrangement of the information in each color channel can be expressed by a set of mixture parameters (image signatures). It is possible to compare these signatures using a measure taking into account distribution features as not only the position of the center of mass of each distribution but also whether they are more or less compact, which indicates the concentration of the color pixels in that particular region of the image. For that purpose we applied the Earth Mover's Distance [23], which is based on the assumption that one of the histograms reflects "hills" and the second represents "holes" in the ground of a histogram. The measured distance is defined as a minimum amount of work needed to transform one histogram into the other using a "soil" of the first histogram. As a measure of the distance between two distributions in EMD framework we used the Kullback-Leibler divergence, which is a measure of the dissimilarity between two probability distributions:

$$D_{KL}(G_i, G_j) = (\mu_i - \mu_j)^T \Sigma^{-1}(\mu_i - \mu_j) + \mathrm{TR}(\Sigma_i \Sigma_j^{-1} + \Sigma_i^{-1} \Sigma_j) \qquad (4)$$

where G_i and G_j denotes normal distributions with mean values μ_i and μ_j, and covariance matrices Σ_i and Σ_j respectively.

In details, let us assume that a user is interested in retrieval of images similar to a given query, having regions of the perceptually similar colors in corresponding locations. All images are subjected to the color categorization, mixture modeling of weighted maps, and similarity-to-query index construction. The exact value of the image index is bounded to the number of chosen colors, in terms of which, images are being compared. For image retrieval based on Gaussian mixture approach to color localization, each pair of the corresponding spectral images (of the query and the analyzed images) their mutual similarity is evaluated. Knowing that each spectral image is represented by a mixture model, the similarity evaluation resolves to the calculation of the similarity between evaluated GMMs for a corresponding color. The similarity indices for each spectral level are then combined to create the overall similarity-to-query index η for each image in the analyzed database. For the user choice of colors, the index η, representing each database image, is constructed in relation to query image. The evaluated index also depends on the number of chosen colors, according to:

$$\eta_i = \sum_{k=1}^{m} d(Q_k, I_{i,k}) \tag{5}$$

where m denotes the number of spectral images (colors) taken into account during retrieval process, Q and I represent query and analyzed image from the database, indexed by i respectively. The distance between the spectral images Q_k and $I_{i,k}$ can be defined as Minkowski distance (in this approach L_1).

On the basis of those indices of the candidate images, the most similar to given query are selected. Let us note that when only a small set of basis color is chosen, the retrieved images will be similar only in terms of those colors, that can lead to the perceptual sensation that candidate images are in fact dissimilar when the overall image composition is taken into account. Moreover, not only the the undesirable data (as noise) can be omitted in the modeling process, but also the relatively small regions, in comparison to overall image size, can be not included into the mixture model. The ratio of data which is modeled to overall image data, depends on the complexity of the used mixture model. Thus, increasing the model complexity, on the one hand, leads to more accurate reflection of the given data, but on the other hand, there is a possibility that redundant data will be taken into consideration.

5   Image Retrieval Experiments

In order to test the efficiency of the proposed methodology we conducted experiments on a database of Wang [9] and database of Webmuseum (http://www.ibiblio.org/wm/) consisting of 1000 and 1303 color images respectively. These databases consist of set of images representing various color arrangements, thus they are very well suited for selective color image comparison. The main idea behind the experiment's design was to obtain an answer whether the proposed methodology is capable to select images corresponding to the given query only in aspect of only one or few selected colors representing specified objects within the analyzed images, not taking into account the remaining image content. In case of such a problem, the key step is to determine the color composition of the object of interest, expressed in terms of basic colors. Having this information gathered, it is possible to launch a retrieval process which should produce a set of candidate images sharing the desired color composition in the same locations as visible on the query image. Let us note, that when the retrieval process is based only on a single color there is a chance that the overall similarity sensation can

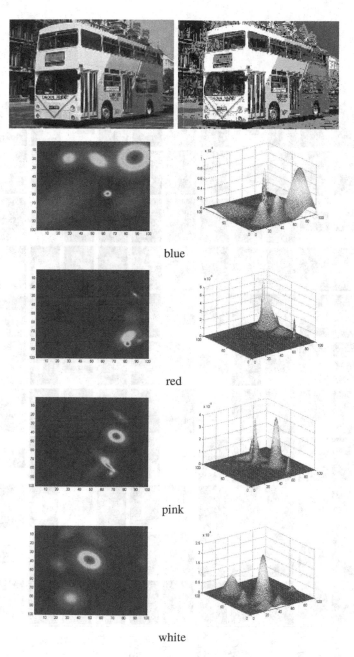

blue

red

pink

white

Fig. 2. The construction of the set of GMM models for each spectral image, which is a basis for the proposed image retrieval. The original image (upper row left) was subjected to color categorization technique [19](upper row right) and each of the transformed spectral images corresponding to one of the 11 basic colors are modeled using GMM approach. The subsequent rows illustrate the result of mixture modeling of the weighted spectral image (2D model left and 3D model right).

Fig. 3. The comparison of the retrieval results for the proposed methodology, MTH method [24], cooccurence histogram (CH) [3], Spatial Color Layout Desciptor (SpCD) [25] and Color Layout Descriptor (CLD) [25, 26], using the of database of Wang [9] for 3 query images (left) when 10 first candidate images (right) are chosen on the basis of their similarity to query in terms of spatial distribution, red (first), white (second).

Fig. 4. The comparison of the retrieval results for the proposed methodology, MTH method [24], cooccurence histogram (CH) [3], Spatial Color Layout Descriptor (SpCD) [25] and Color Layout Descriptor (CLD) [25, 26], using the of database of WebMuseum for 3 query images (left) when 10 first candidate images (right) are chosen on the basis of their similarity to query in terms of spatial distribution of yellow (first) and, red (second).

be different than those suggested by multiple color comparisons. However, proposed experiments prove the efficiency of the proposed methodology.

The proposed method was evaluated for L_1 and EMD similarity measures as representative for the vast amount of other commonly used measures producing comparable results. We also compared the proposed scheme with the method operating on multi-texton based histogram (MTH), taking into account the spatial arrangement of the image colors as shown in [24], representing the attribute of co-occurence matrix. This method was chosen as it does not operate on any subblocks sliding through the image. It also enables a search on the basis of the chosen group of colors as it operates on quantized RGB color space. This approach provides the constant set of colors in comparison to other well known methods (such as Dominant Color Descriptor (DCD) of MPEG-7 standard) which represent each image with different set of representative colors. The MTH [24] is a histogram constructed as an image representation consisting of textons (masks representing various configurations of adjacent pixels) count for each of one of 64 color groups evaluated as a partition of the RGB color space and 12 bins representing textural image features, not taken into account in this comparison. The main disadvantages of any non-perceptual based division of color space is the fact that some colors are represented by more than one histogram bin. In order to precisely specify the retrieval criteria, it is necessary to look through all color categories to choose the most relevant one. Moreover, it is also possible that one arbitrarily quantized category can consist of colors which can be perceived as distinct by human spectator. Thus, the application of the proposed color categorization scheme greatly facilitates the expression of the users needs. On the other hand, the vast choice of available color categories especially for highly distinct colors can be an advantage in some applications. We compared the proposed method with retrieval approach based on correlograms (CH) [3] because it

Table 1. The average precision at 1,5,10 and 20 retrieved images and average recall at 1,5,10 and 20 retrieved images for sets for 31 randomly chosen queries of database of Wang (upper table) and Webmuseum (bottom table) for the proposed methodology, MTH method [24], cooccurence histogram (CH) [3], Spatial Color Layout Desciptor (SpCD) [25] and Color Layout Descriptor (CLD) [25, 26]

Method	P_1	P_5	P_{10}	P_{20}	R_1	R_5	R_{10}	R_{20}
GMM (L_1)	0.81	0.78	0.71	0.69	0.036	0.039	0.041	0.042
GMM (EMD)	0.81	0.79	0.76	0.72	0.029	0.031	0.039	0.041
MTH	0.61	0.54	0.45	0.4	0.030	0.024	0.023	0.019
CH	0.6	0.48	0.46	0.42	0.028	0.030	0.032	0.039
SpCD	0.4	0.52	0.5	0.4	0.026	0.032	0.033	0.036
CLD	0.6	0.76	0.56	0.47	0.039	0.045	0.047	0.051
Method	P_1	P_5	P_{10}	P_{20}	R_1	R_5	R_{10}	R_{20}
GMM (L_1)	0.78	0.75	0.71	0.70	0.016	0.019	0.033	0.036
GMM (EMD)	0.81	0.79	0.76	0.69	0.022	0.039	0.0	0.036
MTH	0.49	0.45	0.29	0.24	0.022	0.023	0.029	0.031
CH	0.45	0.41	0.32	0.24	0.014	0.022	0.027	0.03
SpCD	0.42	0.28	0.26	0.23	0.017	0.019	0.021	0.031
CLD	0.44	0.24	0.28	0.24	0.018	0.021	0.028	0.03

enables the color specified comparisons. The Spatial Color Layout Descriptor (SpCD) and Color Layout Descriptor (CLD), [25] were also applied for comparison.

Let us closely examine the evaluated results depicted in Figs. 3 and 4. For each of these Figures three queries were given. The first retrieval experiment, evaluated on Wang database, was expected to produce images which share the spatial color composition of the query in the aspect of red (1) and white (2) colors. The first query is concerned on the red object in the center of the image regardlessly of the background composition. It can be seen that other retrieval schemes produce relevant results but these methods provide candidate images presenting more scattered objects of desired color and not always occupying the entire region of interest. The second query expects the central white object to be comprised in the candidate images. It can be seen that the proposed method better satisfies the user's expectations.

The second group of experiments was evaluated on Webmuseum database for 2 query images when 10 first candidate images are chosen on the basis of their similarity to the query in terms of spatial distribution of yellow (1) and red (2). It can be seen that the proposed method also outperforms the other approaches. Table 1 summarizes the retrieval efficiency of the analyzed methods. The precision and recall values evaluated for 1, 5, 10 and 20 retrieved images is presented as usually user is more interested in relevance of the highly ranked candidate images than the overall efficiency of the retrieval system.

In general, the proposed method produce more accurate results, which in this case, is manifesting as the retrieved images convey more homogenous color regions, as the given query. In contrary, the compared methods produce images which present more scattered and smaller regions of color of interest. This is due to the fact that the compared methods (especially MTH and CH) do not preserve exact information about the position of the large homogenous color regions but rather overall spatial relationship among regions.

6 Conclusions and Future Work

The proposed retrieval scheme enables to express user's needs concerning the spatial arrangements of user specified set of colors. This solution utilizes the mixture modeling of the information of each set of the color channels along with the incorporated spatial information concerning the color "density". Thus, this approach can reflect better spatial color distribution of the image. This phenomena can be seen in Figs. 3 and 4 revealing that proposed approach produces candidate images reflecting more the spatial structure of the given query than the other methods also utilizing the overall image color information. The comparison with the retrieval methods utilizing the color spatial information prove that the proposed methodology is very well suited for this type of task. The future work will comprise more detailed comparison with other retrieval methods, evaluated on more numerous image collections. The analysis of the usefulness of the other color categorization methods for the proposed methods will also be explored.

Acknowledgments. *This work has been supported by The National Science Centre under SONATA grant no. 2011/01/D/ST6/04554.

References

1. Datta, R., Joshi, D., Li, J., Wang, J.Z.: Image Retrieval: Ideas, Influences, and Trends of the New Age. ACM Computing Surveys 40(2), 1–60 (2008)
2. Zhou, X.S., Rui, Y., Huang, T.S.: Exploration of Visual Data. Kluwer (2003)
3. Huang, J., et al.: Spatial Color Indexing and Applications. International Journal of Computer Vision 35(3), 245–268 (1999)
4. Pass, G., Zabih, R.: Comparing images using joint histograms. Journal of Multimedia Systems 7(3), 234–240 (1999)
5. Ciocca, G., Schettini, L., Cinque, L.: Image Indexing and Retrieval Using Spatial Chromatic Histograms and Signatures. In: Proc. of CGIV, pp. 255–258 (2002)
6. Lambert, P., Harvey, N., Grecu, H.: Image Retrieval Using Spatial Chromatic Histograms. In: Proc. of CGIV, pp. 343–347 (2004)
7. Hartut, T., Gousseau, Y., Schmitt, F.: Adaptive Image Retrieval Based on the Spatial Organization of Colors. Computer Vision and Image Understanding 112, 101–113 (2008)
8. Heidemann, G.: Combining Spatial and Colour Information For Content Based Image Retrieval. Computer Vision and Image Understanding 94, 234–270 (2004)
9. Wang, J.Z., Li, J., Wiederhold, G.: SIMPLIcity: Semantics-Sensitive Integrated Matching for Picture Libraries. IEEE Trans. Patt. Anal. Mach. Intel. 9, 947–963 (2001)
10. Rugna, J.D., Konik, H.: Color Coarse Segmentation and Regions Selection for Similar Images Retrieval. In: Proc. of CGIV, pp. 241–244 (2002)
11. Dvir, G., Greenspan, H., Rubner, Y.: Context-Based Image Modelling. In: Proc. of ICPR, pp. 162–165 (2002)
12. Jing, F., Li, M., Zhang, H.J.: An Effective Region-Based Image Retrieval Framework. IEEE Trans. on Image Processing 13(5), 699–709 (2004)
13. Berretti, A., Del Bimbo, E.: Weighted Walktroughs Between Extended Entities for Retrieval by Spatial Arrangement. IEEE Trans. on Multimedia 3(1), 52–70 (2002)
14. Bilmes, J.: A Gentle Tutorial on the EM Algorithm and its Application to Parameter Estimation for Gaussian Mixture and Hidden Markov Models, University of Berkeley, ICSI-TR-97-021 (1997)
15. McLachlan, G., Peel, D.: Finite Mixtures Models. John Wiley & Sons (2000)
16. Ediz, S., Ugur, G., Ulusoy, O.: A histogram-based approach for object-based query-by-shape-and-color in image and video databases. Image and Vis. Comp. 23, 1170–1180 (2005)
17. Stricker, M., Dimai, A.: Color indexing with weak spatial constraints. In: SPIE Proc., vol. 2670, pp. 29–440 (1996)
18. Xuelong, L.: Image retrieval based on perceptive weighted color blocks. Pattern Recognition Letters 24(12), 1935–1941 (2003)
19. Van den Broek, E.L., Schouten, Th.E., Kisters, P.M.F.: Modeling human color categorization. Pattern Recogn. Lett. 29(8), 1136–1144 (2008)
20. Dempster, A., Laird, N., Rubin, D.: Maximum Likelihood from incomplete data. J. Royal Stat. Soc. 39B, 1–38 (1977)
21. Luszczkiewicz, M., Smolka, B.: Spatial Color Distribution Based Indexing and Retrieval Scheme. Advances in Soft Computing 59, 419–427 (2009)
22. Luszczkiewicz, M., Smolka, B.: Application of Bilateral Filtering and Gaussian Mixture Modeling for the Retrieval of Paintings. In: Proc. of ICIP, pp. 77–80 (2009)
23. Rubner, Y., Tomasi, C., Guibas, L.J.: A Metric for Distributions with Applications to Image Databases. In: Proc. of ICCV, pp. 59–66 (1998)

24. Liu, G.H., Zhan, L., Hou, Y.H., Li, Z.Y., Yang, J.Y.: Image retrieval based on multi-texton histogram. Pattern Recognition 7(43), 2380–2389 (2010)
25. Chatzichristofis, S.A., Boutalis, Y.S., Lux, M.: IMG(RUMMAGER): An Interactive Content Based Image Retrieval System. In: Proc. of the 2nd International Workshop on Similarity Search and Applications (SISAP), pp. 151–153 (2009)
26. Manjunath, B.S., Ohm, J.R., Vasudevan, V., Yamada, A.: Color and Texture Descriptors. IEEE Trans. Cir. Sys. Video Technology 11, 703–715 (1998)

Water Region Detection Supporting Ship Identification in Port Surveillance

Xinfeng Bao[1], Svitlana Zinger[1], Rob Wijnhoven[2], and Peter H.N. de With[1]

[1] Video Coding and Architectures Research Group,
Electrical Engineering Faculty, Eindhoven University of Technology,
P.O. Box 513, 5600 MB Eindhoven, The Netherlands
[2] ViNotion B.V., Horsten 1, 5600 CH Eindhoven, The Netherlands

Abstract. In this paper, we present a robust and accurate water region detection technique developed for supporting ship identification. Due to the varying appearance of water body and frequent intrusion of ships, a region-based recognition is proposed. We segment the image into perceptually meaningful segments and find all water segments using a sampling-based Support Vector Machine (SVM). The algorithm is tested on 6 different port surveillance sequences and achieves a pixel classification recall of 97.5% and precision of 96.4%. We also apply our water region detection to support the task of multiple ship detection. Combined with our cabin detector, it successfully removes 74.6% false detections generated in the cabin detection process. A slight decrease of 5% in the recall value is compensated by a significant improvement of 15% in precision.

Keywords: Water Detection, Multiple Ship Detection, Autonomous Port Surveillance.

1 Introduction

Autonomous port surveillance is currently an emerging research area, which aims at monitoring and controlling ship traffic coming from or leaving for the sea. Automating ship detection techniques based on video cameras is a promising tool for port surveillance. However, due to the large variations of shapes, texture and the varying number of ships passing by, it is difficult to achieve robust and accurate ship detection. Considering the fact that ships always travel within the water region, it is expected that false detections of ships can be significantly reduced if the water region is detected simultaneously and provided as contextual information. Therefore, the problem we want to solve is to automatically find the water region in port surveillance videos, such that it supports the ship identification.

Although some work on this topic has been performed, water region detection still remains challenging and relatively unexplored. The difficulty is that the appearance of water varies considerably, influenced by the intensity of sunlight (different weather conditions), the reflection of surrounding objects and areas

J. Blanc-Talon et al. (Eds.): ACIVS 2012, LNCS 7517, pp. 444–454, 2012.

(sky, vegetation and man-made infrastructures) and the surface disturbance by wind, rain and moving ships. Fig. 1 shows some examples of the large variation of water appearance. A straightforward method for water detection is described in [4]. Fefilatyev *et al.* generate a horizon line to separate the sea pixels from sky pixels, using an SVM classifier based on color features. The idea is later improved in [1], where a self-supervised segmentation method is established to find the river path. The horizon line gives strong hints for adaptive training of a classifier, which solves the problem of spatio-temporal variation of water. However, adaptive appearance models fail when non-water objects (e.g. boats and birds) appear below the horizon line. Moreover, water detection results become unpredictable when the geometric assumption [1][4] that the water region is situated below a distinct horizon line, is not satisfied. Recently, several pub-

Fig. 1. Examples of water regions with different appearances

lications report on detecting water hazards for autonomous navigation. Some researchers successfully realize automatic water detection making use of a variety of passive non-visible sensors such as thermal infrared, polarization imaging and hyperspectral imagery [7][8][13]. However, these solutions always come with high costs of sensors and their maintenance. Conventional low-cost video cameras are also used [9][10][11][14]. The work in [9][11][14] uses multiple features, such as color, texture and spatio-temporal statistics of camera images to form a feature vector. The feature vector is then used to train a supervised classifier to perform the pixel-based water detection. However, such methods operate at the pixel level, by labeling each pixel as belonging to the water region or not. The previous proposals have two main drawbacks: (a) time-costly processing for Standard Definition (SD) port surveillance images; (b) inability to generate a connected water region. Since water is a highly variable region, it is difficult to correctly label every pixel inside the region, even if multiple cues are employed and classifiers are carefully trained. In [10], a new model is proposed to distinguish the water area from the surrounding terrain. However, this model cannot depict a water region having a serious surface disturbance caused by passing ships, which is a common situation in port surveillance.

In this paper, instead of labeling the water directly on pixel basis, we propose region-based recognition by combining a fast graph-based segmentation with a sampling-based SVM classification. The algorithm involves two main steps.

First, surveillance images are pre-processed using a graph-based segmentation. As a result, water region is coarsely distinguished from other objects (sky, vegetation, ships etc.) and the water region itself is kept as coherent as possible. Second, random sampling is performed to pick out a certain amount of pixels from each segment. The sampled pixels are evaluated whether they belong to the water region using an off-line trained SVM. The segment is labeled as water if 60% of its sampled pixels are classified as water. The water region is detected after all water segments are labeled. It will be shown that our water detection technique improves the reliability of ship detection and contributes to multiple ship detection.

The paper is organized as follows. Section 2 discusses the water detection algorithm including pre-processed segmentation and the region-based classification. Section 3 presents our water detection results and the corresponding ship detection results using the contextual information generated by water detection. Section 4 draws conclusions.

2   Water Detection Algorithm

This section presents our two-step region-based water detection. Firstly, graph-based segmentation is performed on the original image. Secondly, an off-line trained SVM classifier labels pixels sampled from each segment. The flowchart of the algorithm is depicted in Fig. 2. In the following subsections, details of the algorithm are provided.

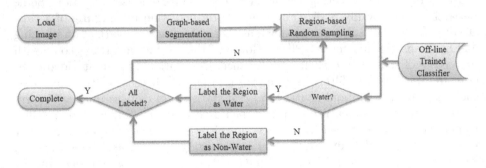

Fig. 2. Flowchart of our water region detection algorithm

2.1   Segmentation as Pre-processing

Efficient graph-based segmentation [5] is employed as pre-processing in our water detection to achieve two objectives: (a) distinguish water regions from other objects while preserving the overall actual characterization of the water region itself; (b) perform fast segmentation to support real-time application in port surveillance systems.

In graph-based segmentation, a key element that affects the quality of segmentation is the edge weight $w_{i,j}$, which measures the difference between two neighboring pixels i and j in a specified feature space. In our approach, the weight $w_{i,j}$ is defined as:

$$w_{i,j} = \sqrt{\left(\frac{R_i}{L_i} - \frac{R_j}{L_j}\right)^2 + \left(\frac{G_i}{L_i} - \frac{G_j}{L_j}\right)^2 + \left(\frac{B_i}{L_i} - \frac{B_j}{L_j}\right)^2} + \alpha \cdot \left|\frac{L_i}{M_i} - \frac{L_j}{M_j}\right|, \quad (1)$$

where R_i, G_i, B_i are the RGB color values of the pixel i (or j when indicated). Likewise, L_i represents the brightness of the pixel i, giving:

$$L_i = \begin{cases} (R_i + G_i + B_i)/3, & \text{if } R_i + G_i + B_i \neq 0; \\ 1, & \text{otherwise.} \end{cases} \quad (2)$$

A further parameter M_i is used to normalize the brightness component, representing the maximum component value of the pixel i:

$$M_i = \begin{cases} \max(R_i, G_i, B_i), & \text{if } R_i + G_i + B_i \neq 0 \\ 1, & \text{otherwise.} \end{cases} \quad (3)$$

In the first summation term of Equation (1), the color value is normalized by the corresponding brightness to reduce the influence of brightness. This is motivated by considering that parts of the water region with strong disturbances or reflections usually differ a lot from other parts of water, in terms of brightness [11]. Reducing the influence of brightness will ensure that the segmentation does not divide the water region into too many segments. However, the brightness is an important feature to distinguish water region from other objects, so that the influence of the brightness cannot be fully reduced, because otherwise the vegetation and ships also merge into the water region. Therefore, in the second term of Equation (1), the brightness difference is measured and weighted by the weighting factor α.

2.2   Region-Based Classification

After obtaining the segmented image, we need to find all segments representing water and merge them into the water region. In our algorithm, we employ a supervised learning approach to train a classifier based on set of representative surveillance images. In order to obtain robust detection, multiple features are employed to design the classifier. Considering its high performance on high-dimensional feature spaces, the Support Vector Machine (SVM) classifier is selected to perform classification in our system.

Selection of Features for Classification. To train a reliable and robust SVM classifier, the feature vector X needs to be well constituted so that it can discriminate the local appearance of water and non-water regions.

Color is the most important feature for water detection [9][11][14]. However, the color of water depends significantly on the lighting conditions, and therefore, texture features are also used in our method to improve the robustness. We apply two texture descriptors: a group of Gabor filters with 3 scales and 4 orientations and Laws' mask with 14 rotationally invariant kernels.

Detection of Water Region. For each segment C of the image, we randomly select a group of pixels C_G, according the following criterion:

$$C_G = \begin{cases} \{\text{randomly sampled pixels, 5\% of the total}\}, & \text{if } |C_G| > 2000; \\ \{\text{randomly sampled set of 100 pixels}\}, & \text{otherwise.} \end{cases} \quad (4)$$

In the above, $|C_G|$ is the total number of pixels in segment C. Instead of using all the pixels in a segment, 5% of the total pixels is randomly selected, which are capable of representing the nature of the regions, according to our experiments. Afterwards, the off-line trained SVM is applied to each pixel in C_G and the number of pixels labeled as water are counted as $|C_W|$. We define the probability $P(C)$ that the segment C is a segment of the water region, giving

$$P(C) = \frac{|C_W|}{|C_G|}. \quad (5)$$

In this equation, $|C_G|$ is the total number of sampled pixels in segment C. The segment is then labeled with label $L(C)$ as follows:

$$L(C) = \begin{cases} 1, & \text{if } P(C) > 0.6; \\ 0, & \text{otherwise.} \end{cases} \quad (6)$$

The threshold for labeling is set empirically to 0.6 and used for all our test sequences.

3 Implementation Results

3.1 Water Region Detection Results

To measure the performance of our water region detection method, we use real-life video sequences recorded in the harbor of Rotterdam, the Netherlands, with different PTZ camera positions and zoom-in/out factors. The videos are recorded between 9:00 AM and 7:00 PM during sunny weather, including sunrise and sunset moments. The captured video sequences have an SD resolution of 720×576 pixels. We select 60 typical frames from 10 sequences to train a two-cluster (water and non-water) SVM classifier. The 60 frames are representative for various scenarios: water region with/without passing ship, water region with smooth/rippled surface and water region with low/high reflections.

We first explore the segmentation process in our water region detection. In equation (1), the weighting factor α adjusts the influence ratio of brightness

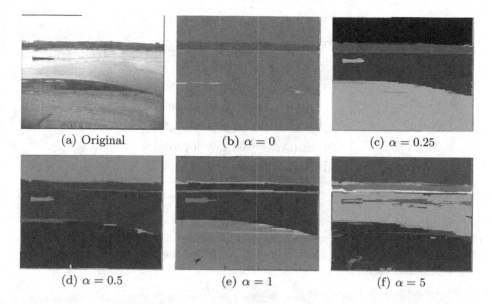

Fig. 3. (a) the original image; (b) - (f) the influence of the weighting factor α on segmentation

and normalized RGB, which is essential to the segmentation. Fig. 3 shows the results of segmentation when changing α from 0 to 5. When $\alpha = 0$, the water is represented as single region. However, the vegetation and ships also merge with water region, which leads to failures in the classification process. When α increases, the segmentation method is more sensitive to the brightness and water is successfully separated from other objects. When $\alpha > 1$, water region tends to be segmented into patches with different levels of disturbances or reflections. In our tests, we set α to 0.8 to separate water from other objects while keeping it as integral as possible.

We then test our region-based classification. Since we are looking for the optimal feature vector, 5 specific classifiers are trained with different features: RGB color, Gabor texture, Laws' texture, a combination of color and Gabor features (COLOR-GABOR) and a combination of color and Laws' features (COLOR-LAWS). As discussed in section 2.2, we use a Gabor filter bank with 3 scales (defined by radial frequencies of $4\sqrt{2}$, $8\sqrt{2}$ and $16\sqrt{2}$ cycles/image-width) and 4 orientations (with values of $0°$, $45°$, $90°$ and $135°$) [6] and Laws' mask with 14 rotationally invariant kernels. The testing set is composed as follows: we choose 6 sequences different from the training sets and take 20 frames from each sequence (totally 120 frames). We measure the classification results by calculating the recall and precision, which is commonly used in evaluating classifications and object detections [3]. For comparison, we implement the water detection algorithm of Rankin *et al.* [11] and measure it with the same metrics. The test results are listed in Table 1. From the numerical test analysis, both the COLOR-GABOR features and COLOR-LAWS features yield good water detec-

Table 1. Water Region Detection Results

Methods	Precision	Recall
COLOR	93.99%	91.33%
GABOR	85.15%	98.73%
LAWS	98.02%	93.06%
COLOR-GABOR	99.29%	96.05%
COLOR-LAWS'	96.43%	97.51%
Rankin *et al.* [11]	99.31%	77.40%

tion results. However, the classification based on COLOR-LAWS has a lower computational complexity which is more suitable for a possible real-time implementation. Therefore, the feature vector X in our method is constructed as a 17 dimensional vector:

$$X = \{X_C, X_L\}, \tag{7}$$

where X_C is a three-dimensional vector of R, G, B values and X_L is a 14 dimensional vector of rotationally invariant Laws' texture measures.

When compared to a typical pixel-based water region detection algorithm [11], our region-based water detection demonstrates a much better performance. Fig. 4 shows some examples of our water detection results based on the above-defined feature vector X and the corresponding results obtained by the algorithm of Rankin *et al.* [11] for a visual comparison. From the test results, when the water region is relatively smooth, as in the left image of Fig. 4(a), both our region-based algorithm and Rankin's *et al.* pixel-based algorithm work well. The latter has incorrect classification only in the rippled regions. When the water regions have strong light reflections and disturbances, as in the middle and right images of Fig. 4(a), our algorithm can still capture the region-level characteristics of water and provide good results. However, in these cases, the algorithm of Rankin *et al.* fails.

3.2   Multi-ship Detection Implementation and Results

In a port surveillance system, most of the monitoring should be focused on the water region. The detected water region can provide very important cues for various applications. For this purpose, we have designed a two-step multi-ship detection system using our water detection algorithm. In the first step, a Histogram of Oriented Gradients (HOG) based cabin detector [2][12] is applied to the input image. Parameters are tuned to enable an aggressive ship detection: the algorithm should detect as many presented ships as possible, at the cost of introducing false detections of ships.

In the second step, the verification process is designed based on an intuitive fact that the detected regions should contain mostly ship pixels rather than water pixels. Therefore, we perform the water detection for the same image to create

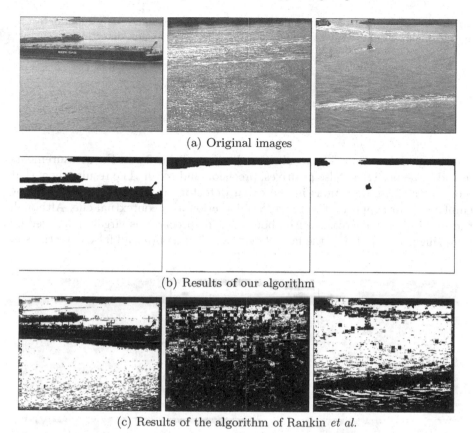

(a) Original images

(b) Results of our algorithm

(c) Results of the algorithm of Rankin *et al.*

Fig. 4. Water detection results: white color represents the water regions and black indicates non-water regions

a binary water map. The water map is then applied to the detection results. Within each detected region D, the number of water pixels $|D_W|$ is counted and $P_F(D)$, the probability of false detection of a ship in region D, is defined as follows:

$$P_F(D) = \frac{|D_W|}{|D|}. \tag{8}$$

Parameter $|D|$ denotes the total amount of pixels inside the detected region D. We recognize the region D to be a false detection if $P_F(D) > T$. The threshold T is set as 0.65 for all the testing sequences. The final ship detection results are then obtained by removing all false detections using the previous criterion for $P_F(D)$.

To measure the performance of the multi-ship detection system, we use 3 video sequences from the test set described in Section 3.1. The selected frames contain 240 ships in total. We test the ship detection with only applying the cabin detector first and then compare it with the detection when combined with our

Table 2. Multi-ship detection results of the algorithms "Cabin" (only cabin detector) and algorithm "Cabin-Water" (cabin detector with water region detection).

Algorithm	True Pos.	False Pos.	Precision	Recall
Cabin	225	67	77.05%	93.75%
Cabin-Water	213	17	92.61%	88.75%

water region detection. The results are shown in Table 2 and the measurements include true positives, false positives, precision and recall. The results show that most of the false detections in the cabin detector are successfully removed by employing our supporting water region detection as a contextual cue. Although the recall slightly decreases with about 5%, the precision is largely improved by removing nearly 74.6% of the false detections. In Fig. 5(a), all false detections in

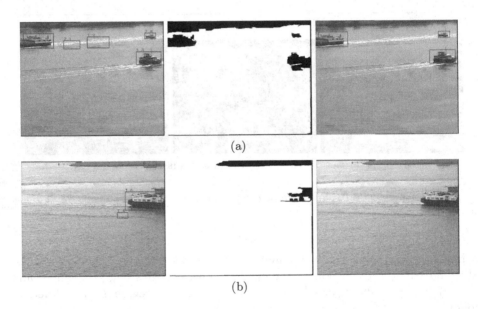

(a)

(b)

Fig. 5. Examples of multiple ship detection: left column contains the results generated by cabin detector, middle column - binary maps generated by water region detection and right column - results after verification process. Bounding boxes delimit the areas of detected ships.

the water region are successfully removed by verification. In Fig. 5(b), although the false detection in the water region is removed, the correct ship detection is also removed because the water detection incorrectly labels part of the ship as water. Also, this false detection removal cannot deal with the false detections in non-water regions, so that the false detection in a vegetation area is still considered to be a correct ship detection.

4 Conclusions

This paper has shown that the detection of water supports the correct detection of ships in port surveillance. We have presented a water region detection algorithm, combining segmentation with region-based classification. Segmentation is carried out as a pre-processing step to increase the accuracy and decrease the computation complexity of the complete detection. The edge weight in segmentation is carefully defined by combining the following properties of the water region: normalized color components while preserving a certain but reduced influence of the brightness. We have empirically optimized this weighted influence of the brightness feature in order to preserve the overall characterization of water region while separating it from other objects in the image.

The classification is performed at a region level with an off-line trained SVM. A random sampling is applied for each segment obtained in the pre-processing and the SVM classification is used to calculate the probability of the segment to be a water region. The reason for modeling a region-level appearance is that the water varies considerably depending on environmental influences. Even in a single image, the water pixels tend to have large distances in the feature space, which leads to a low performance of an off-line trained SVM. However, grouping of water pixels can have more stable appearance when fusing multiple features. We have selected the color combined with Laws' texture as the key features. In our experiments, water detection at region level has proven to be more robust and accurate. We have obtained a precision of 96.4% and a recall of 97.5%.

In order to show the importance of water region detection in a port surveillance scenario, we have also implemented a multi-ship detection system by providing water region detection results as contextual information to a cabin detector. The test shows that introducing water region detection improves the reliability of the detection of multiple ships in the same scene by removing 74.6% of the false detections at the cost of 5% decrease in the recall.

References

1. Achar, S., Sankaran, B., Nuske, S., Scherer, S., Singh, S.: Self-supervised segmentation of river scenes. In: Proc. IEEE International Conference on Robotics and Automation, pp. 6227–6232 (2011)
2. Dalal, N., Triggs, B.: Histograms of oriented gradients for human detection. In: Proc. IEEE Computer Society Conference on Computer Vision and Pattern Recognition, pp. 886–893 (2005)
3. Everingham, M., Gool, L., Williams, Ch.K., Winn, J., Zisserman, A.: The pascal visual object classes (voc) challenge. International Journal of Computer Vision 88(2), 303–338 (2010)
4. Fefilatyev, S., Smarodzinava, V., Hall, L.O., Goldgof, D.B.: Horizon detection using machine learning techniques. In: International Conference on Machine Learning and Applications, pp. 17–21 (2006)
5. Felzenszwalb, P.F., Huttenlocher, D.P.: Efficient graph-based image segmentation. International Journal of Computer Vision 59, 167–181 (2004)

6. Jain, A.K., Farrokhnia, F.: Unsupervised texture segmentation using gabor filters. In: Proc. IEEE International Conference on Systems, Man and Cybernetics, pp. 14–19 (1990)
7. Kwon, H., Rosario, D., Gupta, N., Thielke, M., Smith, D., Rauss, P., Gillespie, P., Nasrabadi, N.: Hyperspectral imaging and obstacle detection for robotics navigation, Tech. Report ARL-TR-3639, U.S. Army Research Laboratory (2005)
8. Pandian, A.: Robot navigation using stereo vision and polarization imaging. Master's thesis, Institut Universitaire de Technologie IUT Le Creusot, Universite de Bourgogne (2008)
9. Rankin, A., Matthies, L.: Daytime water detection and localization for unmanned ground vehicle autonomous navigation. In: Proc. Army Science Conference (2006)
10. Rankin, A., Matthies, L.: Daytime water detection based on color variation. In: Proc. IEEE International Conference on Intelligent Robots and System, pp. 215–221 (2010)
11. Rankin, A., Matthies, L., Huertas, A.: Daytime water detection by fusing multiple cues for autonomous off-road navigation. In: Proc. Army Science Conference (2004)
12. Wijnhoven, R., van Rens, K., Jaspers, E.G.T., de With, P.H.N.: Online learning for ship detection in maritime surveillance. In: Symposium on Information Theory in the Benelux (2010)
13. Xie, B., Pan, H., Xiang, Z., Liu, J.: Polarization-based water hazard detection for autonomous off-road navigation. In: Proc. IEEE/RSJ International Conference on Intelligent Robots and Systems, pp. 3186–3190 (2007)
14. Yao, T., Xiang, Z.Y., Liu, J.L., Xu, D.: Multi-feature fusion based outdoor water hazards detection. In: Proc. IEEE Conference on Mechatronics and Automation, pp. 652–656 (2007)

Hand Posture Recognition with Multiview Descriptors

Jean-François Collumeau[1], Hélène Laurent[1], Bruno Emile[2], and Rémy Leconge[3]

[1] ENSI de Bourges, Laboratoire PRISME 88 bd Lahitolle
18020 Bourges Cedex, France
[2] Laboratoire PRISME, Université d'Orléans, 2 av F. Mitterrand
36000 Châteauroux, France
[3] Laboratoire PRISME, Université d'Orléans, 12 rue de Blois, BP 6744
45067 Orléans cedex 2, France

Abstract. Preservation of asepsis in operating rooms is essential for limiting the contamination of patients by hospital-acquired infections. Strict rules hinder surgeons from interacting directly with any sterile equipement, requiring the intermediary of an assistant or a nurse. Such indirect control may prove itself clumsy and slow up the performed surgery. Gesture-based Human-Computer Interfaces show a promising alternative to assistants and could help surgeons in taking direct control over sterile equipements in the future without jeopardizing asepsis.

This paper presents the experiments we led on hand posture feature selection and the obtained results. State-of-the-art description methods classified in four different categories (i.e. local, semi-local, global and geometric description approaches) have been selected to this end. Their recognition rates when combined with a linear Support Vector Machine classifier are compared while attempting to recognize hand postures issued from an *ad-hoc* database. For each descriptor, we study the effects of removing the background to simulate a segmentation step and the importance of a correct hand framing in the picture. Obtained results show all descriptors benefit to various extents from the segmentation step. Geometric approaches perform best, followed closely by Dalal et al.'s Histogram of Oriented Gradients.

Keywords: Human-Computer Interface, Gesture Recognition, Geometry-Based Hand Description.

1 Introduction

With the development of computer systems and their evergrowing embedded presence into our daily life, the question of convenient and natural types of human-computer-interaction becomes crucial. If user-computer relationships have already evolved in that sense, going from cumbersome text-based command lines to dedicated devices such as mouse or pen, they still remain restrictive. One way to simplify the means of interacting with computers consists in using voice or hand gesture interfaces as people do in their daily life while speaking to one another. Two ways exist to make hand gestures interpreted by computers. The first one relies on the use of extra sensors, such as magnetic ones or data gloves. If these instruments often help in collecting accurate information

J. Blanc-Talon et al. (Eds.): ACIVS 2012, LNCS 7517, pp. 455–466, 2012.

on hand configuration and motion, they also act as a brake upon free movements. The load of cables connected to the computer, induced by this approach, indeed hinders the ease of the user interaction. A less intrusive solution resorts to vision-based systems. Even though it is difficult to intend a generic interface using this technique, this approach has many appealing advantages. The most interesting among these is undoubtly the naturalness of interaction, which results in a much more intuitive communication between human and computers.

Many application domains take interest in gesture interaction, one can quote among others : computer games development, virtual reality, robots control or sign language interpretation [1]. Our work takes place in the specific context of the $CORTECS$ project. This project focuses on intelligent operating rooms (OR) allowing to improve the working conditions of the medical staff including nurses, assistants, surgeons... One objective is to give the operating team the capacity to directly master its environment. Due to asepsis preservation, the interaction with the entire equipment of the OR is restricted for surgeons and assistants who apply for nurse assistance to manipulate non-sterile devices. This results in a paradoxical situation where more and more performing equipments surround the medical staff (as shown in figure 1) while remaining non directly accessible for most of them for fear of contamination. The objective of the project is to make the transition between sterile and non-sterile worlds easier without jeopardizing asepsis preservation.

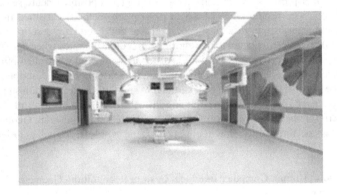

Fig. 1. Example of operating room design with varied and complex equipments, including mobile lights, fixed or mobile screens and cameras

Due to the OR's noisy environment, voice-controlled systems, as proposed in [2], seem to be less competitive than vision-based ones. First attempts to design remote non-contact OR equipment controls concerned tools for sterile browsing of MRI or CT scan images [3,4], with hand-based commands. The principal drawback of these systems is their low flexibility which forces the surgeon to be positioned in front of the controlled device and consequently to move away from the patient. Within the $CORTECS$ project, the foreseen system should allow the surgeon to interact with various equipments and to choose parameters settings or positions of mobile devices by performing various hand postures. After a preliminary survey conducted with several personnel from various medical branches, it appears that most of time surgeons can easily free one hand in non-urgent situations during both pre-operative and operative stages. Moreover they are used to wearing medical equipment. Using a camera embedded in the protagonist's kit would therefore not be awkward for the user while allowing the camera to stay at the heart of the operating theater. Thereby we aim at avoiding attention loss from the user by allowing him to remain close to the patient. On the other hand, due to the use of a mobile camera, the system will thus have to be tolerant to disparities in acquisition points of view and in lighting conditions.

We focus in this paper on the hand posture recognition step. Selecting pertinent features is crucial for the whole process' performance. In a preliminary study conducted in [5], we compared the performances of classical object recognition approaches in this specific context where objects, i.e. postures, could only slightly differ in finger positioning. In this article, we complete this study by comparing several global, semi-local, local and geometrical approaches. The corresponding descriptors are presented in section 2. In order to work in more application-dependant conditions, we created an ad-hoc database using surgical materials. Section 3 is dedicated to the presentation of the created database and the test protocol. Relative performances of tested descriptors are compared. The influence of background substraction and object texture are also studied. Indeed these may impact descriptor performance. Finally, first considerations in combining different descriptors are introduced and hand positioning aspects in posture vocabulary definition are considered. Section 4 presents the conclusions and perspectives of this study.

2   Presentation of the Tested Descriptors

In order to characterize an object (here, various hand postures) that can appear at different scales and orientations, an invariant descriptor must be used. The descriptors can be divided into four classes: the global descriptors that work on the entire image, semi-local descriptors that work on a set of sub-images representing cuts of the complete image, local descriptors that combine interest points detection and characterization of the neighborhood of each detected keypoint and geometric descriptors that utilize low level features to express object shape. In the following paragraphs, we detail some descriptors for each class. For this study, these descriptors have been combined with a linear Support Vector Machine *SVM*.

2.1   Global Approach

Zernike Moments (Zer). The Zernike descriptor is among the most used in the literature. It is built from a set of Zernike polynomials. This set is complete and orthonormal in the interior of the unit circle. The Zernike moments have shown their performance in terms of noise resistance and near zero value in redundancy of information. The Zernike moments formulation is given below [6]:

$$A_{mn} = \frac{m+1}{\pi} \sum_{x} \sum_{y} I(x,y)[V_{mn}(x,y)] \tag{1}$$

with $x^2 + y^2 < 1$.

$I(x, y)$ is the pixel gray-level of the image I ; m and n are the values defining the moment order. Zernike polynomials $V_{mn}(x, y)$ are expressed in the radial-polar form:

$$V_{mn}(r, \theta) = \sum_{s=0}^{\frac{m-|n|}{2}} \frac{(-1)^s (m - s)! r^{m-2s}}{s! (\frac{m+|n|}{2} - s)! (\frac{m-|n|}{2} - s)!} e^{-jn\theta} \tag{2}$$

These moments respect translation, scale and rotation invariance. They have been used by [7] for recognizing hand postures in a human-robot interaction context.

Hu Moments (Hu). The seven Hu moments are invariant under translation, rotation and scaling [8] and are calculated from the normalized moments :

$$\mu_{p,q} = \frac{v_{p,q}}{v_{0,0}^{1+(p+q)/2}} \tag{3}$$

with

$$v_{p,q} = \int_{\mathbb{R}^2} x^p y^q I(x + x_0, y + y_0) dx dy \tag{4}$$

(x_0, y_0), centroid of I, is defined by : $x_0 = \frac{m_{1,0}}{m_{0,0}}$ and $y_0 = \frac{m_{0,1}}{m_{0,0}}$. Such moments have been used for hand recognition application [9].

2.2   Semi-local Approach

Histogram of Oriented Gradient Descriptors (HOG). Histogram of Oriented Gradient (HOG) descriptors are features widely used by the object detection and object recognition community. They have been shown to be distinctive and robust under small affine transformations and illumination changes. They are constructed by dividing the image into a dense grid of uniformly spaced cells and then computing the orientation histograms of the image gradient values on each cell. The illumination and contrast changes are taken into account by local normalization of the gradient strengths which requires grouping the cells together into larger, spatially-connected blocks. The HOG descriptor is then the vector of the components of the normalized cell histograms for all the block regions. Dalal et al. [10] have proposed Histogram of Oriented Gradients in the case of human detection. They have also been used for hand posture recognition [11] and gesture recognition [12].

2.3   Local Approach

Scale Invariant Feature Transform ($SIFT$). The Scale Invariant Feature Transform ($SIFT$) is a well known local descriptor created in 1999 by Lowe, allowing to detect and extract features which are invariant to rotation and scale and robust to some variations of illuminations, viewpoints and noise. The $SIFT$ descriptor is computed in four steps [4]. The two first stages correspond to the choice of keypoints, first identifying potential interest points that are scale and rotation invariant and then rejecting the ones that have low contrast and stability. The two last stages correspond to the descriptor vector computation, assigning one or more orientations to each elected keypoint based on local image gradient directions and using a 4*4 location Cartesian grid to compute the gradient on each location bin on the patch around the keypoint. The $SIFT$ descriptor gives good results in the case of object recognition when it can find relevant keypoints. It has been used by Wang et al. [13] for hand posture recognition with the objective of human-robot interaction.

Speeded Up Robust Feature ($SURF$). Speeded Up Robust Feature $SURF$ was first presented by Bay et al. in 2006. Partly inspired by the $SIFT$ descriptor, $SURF$ also consists in interesting points localization followed by feature descriptors computation. In both cases, the output is a representation of the neighbourhood around an interest point as a descriptor vector. $SURF$ is based on the distribution of first order Haar wavelet responses [14]. One of the principal advantages of $SURF$ is to be several times faster than $SIFT$ while stating to have more discriminative power. It uses the integral images to simplify and to accelerate the computations. Yielding a lower dimensional feature descriptor, it reduces the time for feature computation and matching. In [15], a fast multi-scale feature detection, $SURF$-inspired, and a description method for hand gesture recognition is proposed.

2.4 Geometrical Approach

Varied Form Descriptor (Var). Full reconstruction of the hand is not essential for gesture recognition. Many approaches have instead used the extraction of low-level image measurements for that purpose [16]. Being fairly robust to noise, these characteristics can be extracted quickly. In this approach we created a geometry-based feature vector by gathering simple geometrical characteristics described hereunder :

$$\text{Isometric rate} = \frac{hand's\ perimeter^2}{hand's\ area * 4 * \pi} \tag{5}$$

$$\text{Lengthening} = \frac{radius\ of\ the\ biggest\ hand\ inscribed\ circle}{radius\ of\ the\ smallest\ hand\ circumscribed\ circle} \tag{6}$$

$$\text{Concavity} = \frac{perimeter\ of\ the\ hand's\ convex\ hull}{hand's\ perimeter} \tag{7}$$

$$\text{Elongation} = \frac{major\ axis\ of\ the\ hand's\ smallest\ elliptical\ hull}{minor\ axis\ of\ the\ hand's\ smallest\ elliptical\ hull} \tag{8}$$

3 Comparative Study

3.1 Test Database

In order to come closer to operating room conditions, a 6000 pictures database has been acquired by dressing the hand of speakers with surgical gloves. A surgical sheet is used as background and the lighting is provided by a LED dome placed above the operating table. The illuminance measured near the hand varies from 150 to 300 lux.

The prototype used for these acquisitions is presented in figure 2 along with a gray-level image (640 x 480 pixels) extracted from the video captured by the image acquisition system, which is located on the speaker. Because of the important illumination variation of surgical workplaces depending on the performed surgery, colors may fade away or become saturated. Therefore color was regarded as an extra source of uncertainty and a gray-level camera was chosen for the speaker-embedded acquisition system in order to discard it.

Fig. 2. View of the prototype designed for the database creation using surgical equipments. Picture example acquired through the speaker-embedded camera.

Four speakers have been involved in this experiment. They were asked to reproduce 6 hand postures: 'Y', 'OK', 'Open hand', 'Fist', 'Thumbs up' and 'U'. The postures are presented in figure 3. This posture vocabulary has been selected in order to induce various situations with possible confusions. One can note variations in scale, rotations and lighting conditions. Moreover differences appear between speakers in the vocabulary realization with more or less tensed or spaced fingers. The objectives leading to the creation of such a database are first to test the descriptors' performances to geometrical alterations (i.e. rotations and scaling), and to assert their robustness to both simple and more complicated scenarii (e.g. sparse lighting conditions or inter-speaker posture variability). The final vocabulary will be defined afterwards, drawing lessons from these experiments and being extended or customized to the user's affinity. For each posture, 50 views have been acquired. This was repeated three times for two speakers and twice for the two others. To validate the best hand orientation, the above procedure was realized twice in order to obtain two subsets of 3000 pictures presenting respectively palmar and dorsal aspects of hands. Ground truths were extracted manually for every picture of the database.

3.2 Experiments

The final goal of our work is to enable each surgeon to intervene in the definition of his own vocabulary, resulting in a necessary specific training for each surgeon. As mentioned previously, this results from the various ways different speakers may effect a posture. We decided accordinlgy to train speaker-dependant Support Vector Machine (*SVM*) classifiers. According to Chang and Lin's recommandations on kernel selection [17] in the case of a low ratio between the database's size and the amount of descriptors

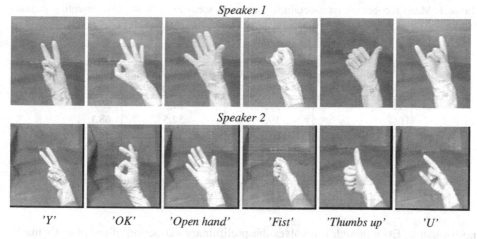

Fig. 3. Examples of the 6 postures constituting the gesture vocabulary for two speakers

involved for describing each of the pictures, we chose a linear kernel. The classifiers were trained using 50 pictures of each posture; 50 other pictures were used to test the classifier performances and compute the recognition rate. Each descriptor was tested using different images as input data: a gray-level image containing both hand and background ($GL\_H\&B$), a gray-level image of the extracted hand on a black background (GL_H) and a binary image containing the mask or contour of the extracted hand (B_M or B_C). Figure 4 presents examples of the images used as input data for the descriptors' computation for a single picture issued from the database.

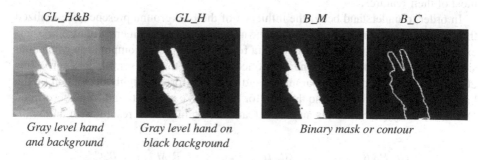

Fig. 4. Input pictures for the computation of the tested descriptors

Table 1 presents the global performances of each descriptor over the whole database corresponding to palmar pictures. The values represent mean recognition rates of the 6 postures for the 4 speakers using different subsets of images for the training and the recognition steps. They are computed averaging sixteen different tests.

Best results are obtained using extracted masks or contours of hands as input images for the descriptors' computation, emphasizing the need for a segmentation step to remove the background in order to achieve satisfactory results. One can observe that the geometrical approach provides an interesting compromise between complexity and

Table 1. Mean recognition rates obtained over the 4 speakers with images presenting palmar aspect

Palmar aspect			
Recognition rates (%)	Gray-level hand and background	Gray-level hand on black background	Binary object
Zer	21,1	24,9	25,6
Hu	19,7	52,5	**68,1**
HOG	33,2	**44,3**	38,2
SIFT	58,1	60,3	63,5
SURF	51,5	60,1	**66,8**
Var	-	-	76,4

performance. Even though it involves the preliminary extraction of the object's mask or contour, this approach supplies the best mean recognition rate while requiring very few features. Also depicting the object's geometry, Hu moments arrive second and outperform *HOG* and *SIFT/SURF* features. Both features from the semi-local and local approaches probably suffer in these tests from the relatively large background of the tested images. This can result in the consideration of a few erroneous interest points by *SIFT/SURF* keypoint detectors when full images are taken as input, hence characterizing partly the hand and partly the background. Such confused characterization may lead to confusions between the different hand postures and hinder recognition. Moreover, the poor performances obtained by the local approach may also result from the relative similarity of the objects (i.e. the hand in different configurations) considered in our application. Indeed, many hand postures differ only slightly and share several to most of their features.

In order to understand better the influence of the background presence, we realized the same tests using images restricted to the nearest hand environment. Figure 5 presents examples of the images used as input data for the descriptors' computation when considering reduced background. One can notice in table 2 that the semi-local approach is effectively influenced by this parameter and will therefore by highly dependant on the hand detection step. This is also the case for the Zernike moments and *HOG* descriptor. On the contrary, Hu moments and local features obtain similar results with and with-

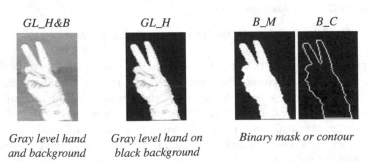

GL_H&B   GL_H   B_M   B_C

Gray level hand   Gray level hand on   Binary mask or contour
and background   black background

Fig. 5. Input images for the computation of the tested descriptors - Reduced background

Table 2. Mean recognition rates obtained over the 4 speakers with images presenting palmar aspects - Reduced background

Palmar aspect			
Recognition rates (%)	Gray-level hand and background	Gray-level hand on black background	Binary object
Zer	41,5	35,5	43,3
Hu	27,6	52,1	**68,2**
HOG	56,9	68,5	**70,4**
SIFT	63,4	64,7	58,5
SURF	57,0	57,4	**67,9**
Var	-	-	**76,4**

out reducing the background. As expected, the geometrical approach's results remain stable.

We were also interested in studying the influence of the point of view under which the hand is seen. In order to check whether using a frontal or a dorsal view of the hand influences the descriptors performances, we reproduced the comparative study conducted with reduced background, on a second set of images presenting dorsal aspects of hand. The corresponding results are gathered in table 3. In comparison to the ones presented in table 2, one can observe that results corresponding to dorsal views are generally similar or poorer than the ones on palmar views. This comment is particularly true when considering gray-level images as input data for the descriptors' computation. This can be explained by the presence of particular folds on glove appearance for some of the selected hand postures. Each palmar posture including tucked fingers will present typical areas with highly structured gray-level contrasts likely to represent potential significant zones or points of interest, whereas dorsal pictures lack these areas. Best results being obtained on palmar images, further developments have been realized considering this situation which also corresponds to more ergonomic-friendly positions.

Table 3. Mean recognition rates obtained over the 4 speakers with images presenting dorsal aspects - Reduced background

Dorsal aspect			
Recognition rates (%)	Gray-level hand and background	Gray-level hand on black background	Binary object
Zer	38,5	34,8	42,9
Hu	22.8	47.3	**69,8**
HoG	50.3	62.2	**68.7**
SIFT	55,0	**61,0**	48,0
SURF	53,8	56,1	**61,0**
Var	-	-	**76,0**

Table 4. Example of confusion matrix obtained for speaker 1, with Hu descriptor, on images with reduced background

			Palmar aspect			
Confusion matrix *Speaker 1* Hu *descriptor*	'Y'	'OK'	'Open hand'	'Fist'	'Thumbs up'	'U'
'Y'	**50**	1	0	9	0	12
'OK'	0	**43**	0	0	0	0
'Open hand'	0	2	**50**	0	0	0
'Fist'	0	0	0	**41**	0	0
'Thumbs up'	0	0	0	0	**1**	0
'U'	0	4	0	0	49	**38**

Table 5. Example of confusion matrix obtained for speaker 1, with Var descriptor, on images with reduced background

			Palmar aspect			
Confusion matrix *Speaker 1* Var *descriptor*	'Y'	'OK'	'Open hand'	'Fist'	'Thumbs up'	'U'
'Y'	**6**	0	0	0	0	6
'OK'	0	**44**	13	0	0	1
'Open hand'	0	0	**37**	0	0	0
'Fist'	2	0	0	**50**	1	0
'Thumbs up'	0	0	0	0	**49**	1
'U'	42	6	0	0	0	**42**

Table 6. Example of confusion matrix obtained for speaker 1, with Hu-Var combination, on images with reduced background

			Palmar aspect			
Confusion matrix *Speaker 1* $Hu - Var$ *combination*	'Y'	'OK'	'Open hand'	'Fist'	'Thumbs up'	'U'
'Y'	**48**	1	0	2	0	10
'OK'	0	**42**	1	0	0	0
'Open hand'	0	4	**49**	0	0	0
'Fist'	2	0	0	**48**	0	0
'Thumbs up'	0	0	0	0	**44**	2
'U'	0	3	0	0	6	**38**

Finally, a promising lead would consist in joining various descriptors together in order to improve the recognition rates through descriptor cooperation. Tables 4 and 5 present the confusion matrices obtained for speaker 1 with respectively Hu and Var

descriptors considered individually. We still consider here images with reduced background. 50 images were used as a training set while a second set of 50 images was used for the recognition characterization. Columns correspond to the real hand posture, while rows correspond to the SVM classification output. Confusions occur between postures using both Hu and Var approaches, but the two descriptors misclassify different postures. In order to get some idea on the benefit which could be expected from descriptors combinations, we present in table 6 the confusion matrix obtained on the same data combining Hu and Var descriptors. An interesting gap in the global performances can be noticed – 89.7% recognition rate when using the combination versus 74.3% and 76.0% using respectively Hu and Var independently – thanks to the removal of many confusions. Remaining misclassifications are mainly due to the relative similarity of 'Y' and 'U' postures when seen under specific angles. To better exploit the capacity of existing features, further investigations on descriptors' complementarity in differentiating postures will be conducted. If performed for every speaker, such studies may in addition help adapting the process and the chosen vocabulary to each users' specificity.

4 Conclusion

In this paper, we introduced the non-contact Human-Computer Interface part of the $CORTECS$ project. An extensive *ad-hoc*-created picture database including various speakers effecting multiple hand postures is used as a benchmark for computing geometric, global, semi-global and local descriptors' performances when associated to a linear SVM and comparing them. Geometrical approach Var and geometry-based global approach Hu moments perform best with respectively 76.4% and 68.2% recognition rates but require a segmentation step prior to their computation. They are followed by keypoint-based local methods ($SIFT$, $SURF$) whose performance is little enhanced by the segmentation step. HOG proved to be especially dependant on the correct framing of the hand, performing poorly when facing a large background-enclosed hand but achieving second best recognition rate (70.4%) when the hand is well-framed. Although less improved than Hu moments by the segmentation step, HOG's performance nevertheless suffers from its lack. Zernike moments come last with a less than 25% recognition rate.

These results outline the worthiness of simple, geometrical descriptors for describing a single object, namely the user's hand, displayed in various configurations. Predominance of such descriptors conveying the hands' shape will therefore focus future research on descriptors whose relevance have been established when dealing with shapes. Descriptor cooperation showed promising prospects and will be studied in greater depth in future works. To this end, data fusion between such descriptors through various means, like *a priori* descriptor concatenation or confidence-based *a posteriori* label decision fusion, will be investigated.

Acknowledgment. The authors would like to thank the Regional Council of the Centre and the French Industry Ministry for their financial support within the framework of the Cortecs project through the Competitiveness Pole S2E2.

References

1. Murthy, G.R.S., Jadon, R.S.: A review of vision based hand gestures recognition. International Journal of Information Technology and Knowledge Management 2(2), 405–410 (2009)
2. Hansen, T.R., Bardram, J.E.: ActiveTheatre - a Collaborative, Event-based Capture and Access System for the Operating Theatre. In: Beigl, M., Intille, S.S., Rekimoto, J., Tokuda, H. (eds.) UbiComp 2005. LNCS, vol. 3660, pp. 375–392. Springer, Heidelberg (2005)
3. Wachs, J.P., Stern, H.I., Edan, Y., Gillam, M., Handler, J., Feied, C., Smith, M.: A gesture-based tool for sterile browsing of radiology images. Journal of the American Medical Informatics Association 15(3), 321–323 (2008)
4. Lowe, D.: Distinctive image features from scale-invariant keypoints. International Journal of Computer Vision 60(2), 91–110 (2004)
5. Collumeau, J.-F., Leconge, R., Emile, B., Laurent, H.: Hand-gesture recognition: comparative study of global, semi-local and local approaches. In: Proc. International Symposium on Image and Signal Processing and Analysis (ISPA), pp. 247–252 (2011)
6. Khotanzad, A., Hong, H.: Invariant image recognition by Zernike moments. IEEE Transactions on Pattern Analysis and Machine Intelligent 12(5), 489–497 (1990)
7. Gu, L., Su, J.: Natural hand posture recognition based on Zernike moments and hierarchical classifier. In: Proc. IEEE International Conference on Robotics and Automation (ICRA), pp. 3088–3093 (2008)
8. Hu, M.K.: Visual pattern recognition by moments invariants. IEEE Transaction on Information Theory 8, 179–187 (1962)
9. Gowtham, P.N.V.S.: An Interactive Hand Gesture Recognition System on the Beagle Board. In: International Proceedings of Computer Science and Information Technology, vol. 20, pp. 113–118 (2011)
10. Dalal, N., Triggs, B., Schmid, C.: Human Detection Using Oriented Histograms of Flow and Appearance. In: Leonardis, A., Bischof, H., Pinz, A. (eds.) ECCV 2006. LNCS, vol. 3952, pp. 428–441. Springer, Heidelberg (2006)
11. Fang, Y., Cheng, J., Wang, J., Wang, K., Liu, J., Lu, H.: Hand posture recognition with co-training. In: Proc. International Conference on Pattern Recognition (ICPR) (2008)
12. Kaâniche, M.B., Brémond, F.: Tracking HOG descriptors for gesture recognition. In: Proc. IEEE International Conference on Advanced Video and Signal Based Surveillance (AVSS) (2009)
13. Wang, C.-C., Wang, K.-C.: Hand posture recognition using adaboost with SIFT for human robot interaction. In: Proc. International Conference on Advanced Robotics (ICAR) (2007)
14. Bay, H., Ess, A., Tuytelaars, T., Van Gool, L.: SURF: Speeded-Up Robust Features. In: Computer Vision and Image Understanding (CVIU), vol. 110(3), pp. 346–359 (2008)
15. Fang, Y., Cheng, J., Wang, K., Lu, H.: Hand gesture recognition using fast multi-scale analysis. In: Proc. International Conference on Image and Graphics (ICIG), pp. 694–698 (2007)
16. New, J.R., Hasanbelliu, E., Aguilar, M.: Facilitating User Interaction with Complex Systems via Hand Gesture Recognition. In: Proc. Southeastern ACM Conference (2003)
17. Chang, C.-C., Lin, C.-J.: LIBSVM: a library for support vector machines (2001) Software, http://www.csie.ntu.edu.tw/cjlin/libsvm

State-Driven Particle Filter
for Multi-person Tracking

David Gerónimo Gomez[1], Frédéric Lerasle[2,3], and Antonio M. López Peña[1]

[1] Computer Vision Center and Department of Computer Science
Edifici O, 08193 Campus Universitat Autònoma de Barcelona, Bellaterra, Spain
{dgeronimo,antonio}@cvc.uab.es
[2] CNRS-LAAS, 7 avenue du Colonel Roche, F-31077 Toulouse, France
[3] Université de Toulouse (UPS), F-31077 Toulouse, France
lerasle@laas.fr

Abstract. Multi-person tracking can be exploited in applications such as driver assistance, surveillance, multimedia and human-robot interaction. With the help of human detectors, particle filters offer a robust method able to filter noisy detections and provide temporal coherence. However, some traditional problems such as occlusions with other targets or the scene, temporal drifting or even the lost targets detection are rarely considered, making the systems performance decrease. Some authors propose to overcome these problems using heuristics not explained and formalized in the papers, for instance by defining exceptions to the model updating depending on tracks overlapping. In this paper we propose to formalize these events by the use of a state-graph, defining the current state of the track (e.g., *potential*, *tracked*, *occluded* or *lost*) and the transitions between states in an explicit way. This approach has the advantage of linking track actions such as the online underlying models updating, which gives flexibility to the system. It provides an explicit representation to adapt the multiple parallel trackers depending on the context, i.e., each track can make use of a specific filtering strategy, dynamic model, number of particles, etc. depending on its state. We implement this technique in a single-camera multi-person tracker and test it in public video sequences.

1 Introduction

Human detection and tracking has been one of the most relevant research topics in computer vision for almost two decades. Nowadays, it is still an important subject of investigation due to the difficulty to develop techniques capable of reliably performing this task in many contexts. Humans are one of the most challenging classes in computer vision: they are dynamic, deformable, unpredictable, their variability in size and clothings is big and they can be affected by changing illumination. Furthermore, they can often be occluded, appear in groups or isolated. Some of the applications of human detection and tracking are surveillance [1], advanced driver assistance systems [2], human-robot interaction [3], etc. All these applications require multi-target detection and tracking of people from single camera, which is the focus of this paper.

J. Blanc-Talon et al. (Eds.): ACIVS 2012, LNCS 7517, pp. 467–478, 2012.
© Springer-Verlag Berlin Heidelberg 2012

The detection is defined as the process of providing information about objects in images in a frame-by-frame basis, hence the task of a detector if mainly restricted to just localizing the objects. The tracking identifies and follows these objects through a sequence of images, enlarging the tasks to the initialization of tracks, updating their state, managing the occlusions, reinitializing the tracks after occlusions, data association, etc. During the last decades, Particle Filters [4,5] have become popular in the visual tracking literature thanks to their capability to provide a simple while robust framework to tackle some tracking process. Nowadays, the most successful approaches make use of the so-called tracking-by-detection approach, which takes advantage of the output of an object detector to (re)initialize and provide evidences through the frames [6,7].

In spite of the plethora of tracking strategies, which are more or less efficient depending on the context, few papers address traditional difficulties such as occlusions with other targets or with the scene, temporal drifts of the tracks, lost tracks, etc., which can lead to typical tracking problems like target hijacking or track model drifting. These problems not only decrease the system performance but also result in misinterpretations of the scene. The traditional approach is to manage occlusions or lost targets by heuristics not detailed in the papers. For instance, in the well-known approach in [6], the authors just update the classifiers when tracks are not overlapped and terminate tracks with no associated detections during several frames. In this case, an optimization algorithm that makes use of an online classifier, a gait function and the particles position, is used to match the current detections and tracks at each frame without explicitly reasoning about the state of the targets. One of the approaches adapting the tracker strategies to occlusions is presented in [8], in which the authors propose different trackers for a multi-view object tracking system. Depending on whether the targets are viewed from different cameras or not and on whether they are isolated or not, the algorithms can be: Interactively Distributed Multi-Object Tracking, Bayesian Multiple Camera Tracking or Multiple Independent Particle Filter. However, apart from being addressed specifically to multi-camera systems, it does only exploit geometrical cues such as isolation and camera projection, not taking advantage of the possible cues that the target model can provide in a single camera. In [9], Zhou et al. propose an event analysis stage that identifies presence of targets in the scene and inter-object occlusion. In this case, contrary to our proposal, this reasoning is made as a posterior process to the filtering to provide high-level event information.

Based on a Particle Filter tracker, we propose a novel approach for multi-person tracking that defines a state for each track (*potential*, *tracked*, *occluded* or *lost*), represented in a graph. The nodes of a graph are used to depict the states (context), which define a specific tracking strategy, while the arcs represent the conditions that trigger the state transitions. As conditions we employ a traditional bounding box overlapping approach to detect non-isolated tracks, together with a Kalman Filter and Generalized Likelihood Ratio Test [10] to detect tracker failures. The benefits of this state-graph compared to the conventional implementation are clear. It provides an explicit representation to adapt the multiple parallel trackers to the context, i.e., each track could make use of a specific filtering strategy, dynamic model, number of particles, sampling strategy, etc. depending on its state. For example, it allows to use different simultaneous filtering approaches like Condensation and ICondensation in the same scene, or to restrict the update of the track model to non-occluded targets, which ammends the problem of model drifting but it is still more flexible than fixing a constant model. Furthermore, recent approaches dealing with occlusions [11] or tracker failures [12] can be embedded in the framework. We test the tracker combined with a HOG-SVM detector [13] in public sequences with multiple persons in real situations.

The structure of the manuscript is as follows. Section 2 recalls the conventional particle filtering algorithm. Section 3 presents our state-based approach. We first define the states of the graph, with the associated actions and adapted filtering strategy, and then describe the transition conditions. The experimental results are presented in Section 4. Finally, the conclusions and perspectives are summarized in Section 5.

2   Original Particle Filtering Formulation

In this section we first recall the main concepts and components of a conventional ICondensation particle filter [14]. Let us define a set of N particles representing hypotheses of the position and scale of a person (track). Each particle has an associated state vector $\mathbf{x}_k^{(i)} = <x, y, s, w>$, where $i \in 1, \ldots, N$ is the particle index, x,y,s are image coordinates and scale of the track bounding box at frame k, and w its weight. When a track is initialized at $k = 0$, we set $w_k^{(i)} = 1/N$ and draw particles according to a prior $p_0(\mathbf{x})$. Next, at each frame a process of prediction and correction is carried out following the next steps:

1. Prediction (Importance function), which propagates particles from $k-1$ to k according to dynamics from a predefined probability density function (*pdf*) p and/or measurements z_k (from current image), defined as:

$$q(\mathbf{x}_k^{(i)}|\mathbf{x}_{k-1}^{(i)}, z_k) = \alpha\pi(\mathbf{x}_k^{(i)}|z_k) + \beta p(\mathbf{x}_k^{(i)}|\mathbf{x}_{k-1}^{(i)}) + (1 - \alpha - \beta)p_0(\mathbf{x}_k^{(i)}) \ , \quad (1)$$

where $\pi(\mathbf{x}_k^{(i)}|z_k) \in [0..1]$ corresponds to an intermittent image cue (e.g., a human detector [13]), $p(\mathbf{x}_k^{(i)}|\mathbf{x}_{k-1}^{(i)})$ is the dynamics *pdf* and p_0 is the prior. $\alpha, \beta \in [0..1]$ represent the proportion of particles according to observations and dynamics, respectively.

2. Correction (Weighting), which assigns a weight $w_k^{(i)}$ to each particle according to:

$$w_k^{(i)} \propto w_{k-1}^{(i)} \frac{p(z_k|\mathbf{x}_k^{(i)})p(\mathbf{x}_k^{(i)}|\mathbf{x}_{k-1}^{(i)})}{q(\mathbf{x}_k^{(i)}|\mathbf{x}_{k-1}^{(i)}, z_k)} \ , \quad (2)$$

where $p(z_k|\mathbf{x}_k^{(i)})$ is the likelihood of the measurement z_k with respect to the particle state $\mathbf{x}_k^{(i)}$.

3. Resampling, in which the particles are redrawn according to $w_k^{(i)}$.

3   State-Driven Particle Filtering

In any Particle Filtering approach, the propagation and weighting is made independently of the state of the track, e.g., the particles in an occluded track are propagated according to the same equation as in a non-occluded one. This can lead to an inefficient particles distribution and even a target loss if the target does not re-appear as the dynamics predict, which often derive in the aforementioned problems enumerated in Section 1. We propose a three-noded graph to maintain the state of the tracks, with an additional one for the detections that can potentially become tracks, that modulates the strategy and parameters of the filtering.

Figure 1 illustrates the model. Each node defines a track state (*potential*, *tracked*, *occluded* and *lost*) while each arc defines the conditions to move from one state to another (i.e., tracks overlapping or confidence).

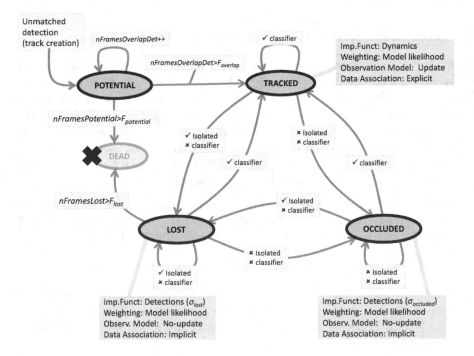

Fig. 1. Proposed state-graph

In the following subsections we detail the state-actions and the state-transitions proposed in our graph.

3.1   State-Actions (Nodes)

The track state is represented as a node, which defines the corresponding actions on the tracking process of the specific target. For example, with this approach a *tracked* track can make use only of dynamics in the importance function without taking into account the detections (setting $\alpha = 0, \beta = 1$ in Equation (1) as in Condensation [4]), while an *occluded* track can depend both on detections and dynamics (i.e., $\alpha, \beta \neq 0$ in Equation (1) as in ICondensation [5]). In terms of implementation this can be represented by a weighted importance function that uses different sampling methods, which are adjusted for each state. As can be seen, the state-graph provides an explicit representation capable of working with two different trackers in the same image depending on the context. Figure 2 illustrates the different tracker strategies, which depend on the state of the track.

Potential Track. A *potential* track is created for each detection that does not match any of the current tracks. The matching is made if the overlapping between two detections in two consecutive frames exceeds a given threshold, and a counter is used to store the number of frames a track has been in this state. After $F_{overlap}$ frames in which the *potential* track matches a detection, it is upgraded to *tracked*. On the contrary, if the track stands for $F_{potential}$ frames as *potential* without enough matching detections, it is killed. Of course, this procedure is suited for the standard tracking test videos focused on surveillance or driver assistance. For other kind of applications, this procedure must be adapted to the specific video frame rate and the object detector performance of each case.

Tracked Track. Once a track has earned the state *tracked*, it can not return to the *potential* one, so from this frame a track model is used (initialized at this frame) and a complete particle filter process is carried out. The filtering process for this state is as follows:

- **Importance Function:** It is completely based on dynamics. In our proposal, we set $\alpha = 0$ and

$$p(\mathbf{x}_k^{(i)}|\mathbf{x}_{k-1}^{(i)}) = \mathbf{x}_{k-1}^{(i)} + R(\mathbf{x}_{k-1}^{(i)}, \Sigma_{dyn}) \qquad (3)$$

  is used, where R is a Gaussian random walk function with covariance matrix Σ_{dyn} centered at $\mathbf{x}_{k-1}^{(i)}$.
- **Weighting Function:** The particles are weighted according to $p(z_k|\mathbf{x}_k^{(i)})$, i.e., the likelihood of the track model applied to their current position and scale in the image.
- **Data Association:** Explicit and carried out after the importance function and weighting. It matches the current detections with the *tracked* tracks, aimed at both discarding these detections to be used by *potential*, *occluded* or *lost* tracks and to compute the scale of the track as the average of the last

three detections. We construct a distance matrix with each tracked track t and each detection d using the equation:

$$Cost(t,d) = p(d|t) \cdot \mathcal{N} \left(\frac{1}{N} \sum_{i=0}^{N} dist(\mathbf{x}_k^{(i)}, d); 0, \sigma_{dist}^2 \right) , \qquad (4)$$

where $p(d|t)$ is the matching probability of the track t model applied to d (see Sect. 4); $dist(\mathbf{x}_k^{(i)}, d)$ is the Euclidean distance between a particle $\mathbf{x}_k^{(i)}$ from t and the center of the detection d; and $\mathcal{N}$ is a Gaussian function with mean 0 and variance σ_{dist}^2. This cost function rewards detections that are similar to the track model and near the track particles. Finally, an optimization algorithm like Munkres or a greedy approach [6] is used to compute the best matching.

The data association is applied according to a state-based preference, i.e., first *tracked*, then *occluded* and finally *lost* tracks (as will be seen, their association is implicit). This approach is based on the assumption that *tracked* tracks are independent from detections, so the process is focused on explaining the scene status as better as possible with the last known data. Then, the algorithm tries to explain the unmatched detections with the *occluded* or *lost* tracks, whose confidence is lower than the *tracked* ones.

Occluded Track. An occluded track is a target which is significantly occluded by another one and whose track confidence decreases (these concepts will be detailed later in Sect. 3.2). In this case, the filtering is as follows:

- **Importance Function:** We draw particles in all the near unmatched detections weighted by their distance to the track ($\beta = 0$ in Equation (1)):

$$q(\mathbf{x}_k^{(i)}|z_k) = \pi(\mathbf{x}_k^{(i)}|z_k) \qquad (5)$$

  If there are not unmatched detections in the current frame, the particles are not sampled and the state is not changed.
- **Weighting Function:** The same equation as in *tracked* is used.
- **Data Association:** In this case, the association is implicit, i.e., no optimization is made. We assume that each *occluded* track provides the best possible matching with a detection, and we just make the matches track-detection according to the highest weighted particle. If a detection is matched by two occluded tracks, just the one with highest weight is taken while the other is left as unmatched.

Lost Track. A *lost* track is often the result of an occlusion with the scene or a sudden change in its appearance, which prevents the model to be updated on time, which make the maximum likelihood decrease suddenly. In this case, as explained later, the track is isolated from other tracks in the scene.

As importance function in this case we use the same as in *occluded*, however, the Gaussian used to draw the particles in the nearby detections is bigger since we understand that an occlusion is local while a *lost* track can be found anywhere in the image if the sufficient number of frames has passed (e.g., could be occluded by a vehicle or street furniture) and appear in the other side of the image. In the case of weighting function and data association, we use the same as in the *occluded* state.

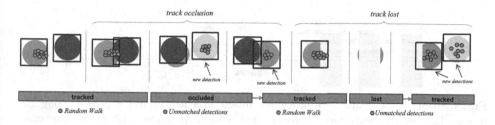

Fig. 2. Example of a track (blue) through the different states. Note: black boxes represent detections, blue, red and yellow circles represent objects. The figure can be seen as evolving from left to right.

3.2   State-Transitions (Arcs)

In order to go from one state to another, state-transitions depend on conditions of the tracks. In our proposal, the conditions are based on the classifier confidence output of each track and on the overlapping between tracks.

Classifier Matching. The classifier confidence of each track is computed as the maximum likelihood of its particles $C(\mathbf{x}_k|z_k) = \max(w_k^{(i)}) \; \forall i \in 0, \dots, N$. In order to detect track model failures, we propose to use a 1D Kalman Filter and the Generalized Likelihood Ratio Test (GLRT) to filter the confidence of an online classifier (Sect. 4). The GLRT is a statistical test used to compare two models that extends the Neyman-Pearson lemma [15] for hypotheses testing in a sub-optimal way. It involves the computation of the ratio $\frac{l_{H_1}}{l_{H_0}}$, where l_{H_0} is the log-likelihood of a null hypothesis and l_{H_1} is the log-likelihood of an alternative one. Whenever this ratio is greater than a threshold defined *a priori*, the test fails. In [10], Willsky and Jones proposed to filter the residual of a KF, i.e., the difference between actual measure and its prediction, with the GLRT to determine if a change in a signal has occurred.

In our proposal we set H_0 as no confidence change and H_1 as a confidence decrease. In Fig. 3 we illustrate the behaviour of the confidences in two tracks, one occluded and another non-occluded. As can be seen, depending on the state of the Kalman Filter, the GLRT is able to detect if a jump has been produced in the confidence signal.

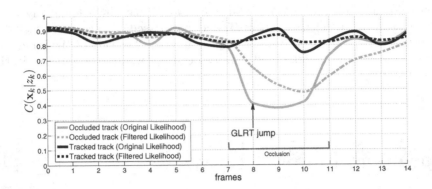

Fig. 3. In black, the confidence of a color model in a non-occluded person along 15 frames. In blue, the confidence of an occluded person. At frame 8, the GLRT successfully detects the decrease in the confidence.

Isolated Track. The isolated condition is computed by using the Jaccard overlapping criterion between two tracks:

$$J(t_0, t_1) = \frac{|t_0 \cap t_1|}{|t_0 \cup t_1|} > J_T \qquad (6)$$

where $J(t_0, t_1) \in [0, 1]$, t_0 and t_1 are the areas of two given tracks and J_T is a fixed overlapping threshold (e.g., 0.5).

4   Experimental Results

In this section we evaluate the performance of the proposed approach in comparison with the original not state-based version. The public datasets used are TUD-Crossing, TUD-Campus[1] [16], with 201 and 71 frames, respectively; and PETS2009-S2L1 View1[2] with 795 frames. Video results can be found at http://www.cvc.uab.es/~dgeronimo/projects/ACIVS12.

The detector used as input is the well-known HOG/LinearSVM person detector by Dalal and Triggs [13], which is a current standard in the field. The particle filter uses 150 particles in the TUD sequences and 300 the PETS, all in a distributed filtering fashion. The online model of the track is based on a rgI color histogram of the torso region quantized into 16 bins per channel (in our experiments rgI works slightly better than RGB color space). The likelihood is based on the histograms difference, assumed to be normally distributed. As evaluation metrics, we make use of CLEARMOT [18], which defines an

---

[1] http://www.mis.tu-darmstadt.de/node/382
[2] http://www.cvg.rdg.ac.uk/PETS2009/ (groundtruth annotations from [17]).

evaluation protocol specific for multi-object tracking in terms of precision (MOTP[3]) and accuracy (MOTA[4]). The matching between detections and annotations is defined as in Eq. (6) with $J_T > 0.5$. For the sake of completeness, in addition to the CLEARMOT metrics, we also specify the number of total identity switches a long a full track (not only to the consecutive ones in the original formulation), the false negative rate FNR and the false positives per image $FPPI$.

Table 1 summarizes the performance of the system in the video sequences. As can be seen, the precision of both approaches is similar given that always a target is detected, it is based on the same detector and the likelihood model is the same in both cases. On the contrary, in the case of the accuracy, the state-driven approach improves the results AROUND A 7% in all cases. The FNR improvement is around $3 - 5\%$ depending on the sequence; and the FPPI significantly improves $(11 - 28\%)$, this latter thanks to the reduction in the number of track drifts. In the case of ID switches, the improvement can be clearly appreciated in TUD-Crossing, in which there are many pedestrians and occlusions along the sequence. The improvement in FPPI is also significant in all the sequences.

Table 1. Performance comparison between the traditional approach (Original) and our proposal (State-based). In parentheses, global ID switches for full tracks.

Dataset	MOTP	MOTA	FNR	FPPI	IDSw.
TUD Crossing (Original)	77.8%	51.1%	36.7%	0.61	0 (12)
TUD Crossing (State-based)	77.7%	58.8%	33.7%	0.37	0 (5)
TUD Campus (Original)	78.6%	27.1%	64.9%	0.34	0 (1)
TUD Campus (State-based)	76.0%	34.8%	59.9%	0.23	0 (0)
PETS2009-S2L1 (Original)	73.9%	43.5%	48.0%	0.49	2 (40)
PETS2009-S2L1 (State-based)	75.0%	51.1%	45.2%	0.21	0 (27)

Fig. 4(a) illustrates the evolution of a track from *potential* to *tracked* (the brighter the particle, the higher its weight). Blue bounding boxes correspond to tracks (with their associated numeric id at the corner) and yellow boxes correspond to detections. Fig. 4(b) shows the algorithm behaviour after an inter-person occlusion, in which the foreground person is labeled as *tracked* while the person in the background is labeled as *occluded*. Fig. 4(c) shows an occlusion with an object of the scene.

Fig. 5 shows a detailed reinitialization process after an occlusion with an undetected person. During the occlusion, the algorithm unsuccessfully tries to

---

[3] MOTP$=\frac{\sum_{i,t} dst_t^i}{\sum_t c_t}$, where dst_t^i is the Euclidean distance between the annotation i and the corresponding detection and c_t is the number of matches, all in frame t.

[4] MOTA$= 1 - \frac{\sum_t m_t - fp_t - mme_t}{\sum_t g}$, where m_t are object misses, fp_t are false positives, mme_t are missmatches and g_t are groundtruth objects at frame t.

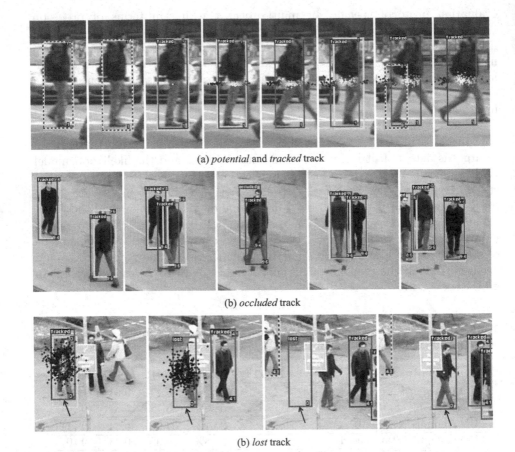

(a) *potential* and *tracked* track

(b) *occluded* track

(b) *lost* track

Fig. 4. Examples of the tracker behaviour (a) in TUD-Crossing and (b,c) in PETS2009. Track particles in sequence (b) are not shown for visualization clarity. Note: detections in yellow, tracks in blue, potential track in dashed blue.

match the *lost* track with a near unmatched detection. After the occlusion, a new detection matches the online model and the track is reinitialized maintaining the same id. Without the proposed approach, a new track (with a new id) is created for the new detection resulting in an identity switch (counted in our full track switch criterion noted inside the parentheses in Table 1). These experiments demonstrate that even with simple components our proposal already provides improvement.

The errors in the tracking are mainly a result of the simple online track model used (based on the color histogram of the torso). For example, when persons are very similar in clothes and shapes, *lost* or *occluded* tracks can be misassigned after reinitialization. In addition, when the tracks change in scale, particles at different scales but centered in the torso region are equally weighted, leading to a wrong

Fig. 5. Detailed reinitialization process of a track after an occlusion with an undetected person

track scale estimation. These problems could be ammended by a more complex observation model exploiting shape in addition to color [6]. Other improvements such as a more elaborated occlusion manager [17,11] or track failure detector [12] are likely improve the overall performance.

Finally, it is worth to mention that our proposal is not limited to distributed particle filters. In fact, it can be potentially applied in a centralized filtering approach by including the track state and the potential matched detections in the state vector, and in other filters such as Kalman or Mean-shift by adapting the actions and transitions of the state-graph.

5   Conclusion

In this paper we have presented a novel approach based on a state-graph able to deal with some problems of tracking like hijacking, occlusions or drifting. The main contribution is the formalization of the target state in a graph, with associated parameters and actions in the nodes and track-based conditions as node transitions. In our implementation, we demonstrate the benefits of our approach by switching between filtering strategies depending on the target status. The experimental results have proven that this representation is capable of overcoming the aforementioned problems in realistic complex video sequences.

As future work, in addition to improving the current components of the system as explained in the previous section, we plan to use state-dependent model cues (e.g., more complex appearance or color models if the track is lost), balance the number of particles according to the state, and perform graph interactions in order to provide a more robust state estimation.

Acknowledgements. This work was developed during D. Gerónimo stay at LAAS-CNRS, supported by the post-doctoral mobility grant AIRE-CTP 2010 CTP 00009 of the Generalitat de Catalunya, and the Spanish Ministry of Education and Science projects TRA2011-29454-C03-00 and Consolider Ingenio 2010: MIPRCV (CSD200700018).

References

1. Negre, A., Tran, H., Gourier, N., Hall, D., Lux, A., Crowley, J.L.: Comparative study of people detection in surveillance scenes. In: International Workshop on Structural and Syntactic Pattern Recognition, Kyoto, Japan (2006)
2. Gerónimo, D., López, A., Sappa, A., Graf, T.: Survey of pedestrian detection for advanced driver assistance systems. TPAMI 32(7), 1239–1258 (2010)
3. Germa, T., Lerasle, F., Ouadah, N., Cadenat, V.: Vision and RFID data fusion for tracking people in crowds by a mobile robot. Computer Vision and Image Unterstanding 114(6), 641–651 (2010)
4. Isard, M., Blake, A.: CONDENSATION – conditional density propagation for visual tracking. IJCV 29(1), 5–28 (1998)
5. Isard, M., Blake, A.: ICONDENSATION: Unifying low-level and high-level tracking in a stochastic framework. In: ICCV, Freiburg, Germany, pp. 893–908 (1998)
6. Breitenstein, M.D., Reichlin, F., Leibe, B., Koller-Meier, E., Van Gool, L.: Online multi-person tracking-by-detection from a single, uncalibrated camera. TPAMI 33(9), 1820–1833 (2010)
7. Okuma, K., Taleghani, A., de Freitas, N., Little, J.J., Lowe, D.G.: A Boosted Particle Filter: Multitarget Detection and Tracking. In: Pajdla, T., Matas, J(G.) (eds.) ECCV 2004. LNCS, vol. 3021, pp. 28–39. Springer, Heidelberg (2004)
8. Qu, W., Schonfeld, D., Mohammed, M.: Distributed bayesian multiple-target tracking in crowded environments using multiple collaborative cameras. EURASIP Journal on Advances in Signal Processing (2007)
9. Zhou, Y., Benois-Pineau, J., Nicolas, H.: Multi-object particle filter tracking with automatic event analysis. In: ACM International Workshop on Analysis and Retrieval of Tracked Events and Motion in Imagery Streams (2010)
10. Willsky, A., Jones, H.: A generalized likelihood ratio approach to the detection and estimation of jumps in linear systems. IEEE Trans. on Automatic Control AC-21(1), 108–112 (1976)
11. Wang, F., Yu, S., Yang, J.: Robust and efficient fragments-based tracking using mean shift. Int. Journal of Electronics and Communications 64, 614–623 (2010)
12. Di Caterina, G., Soraghan, J.: An improved mean shift tracker with fast failure recovery strategy after complete occlusion. In: 8th IEEE Int. Conf. on Advanced Video and Signal-Based Surveillance (2011)
13. Dalal, N., Triggs, B.: Histograms of oriented gradients for human detection. In: CVPR, San Diego, CA, USA, vol. 1, pp. 886–893 (2005)
14. Pérez, P., Vermaak, J., Blake, A.: Data fusion for visual tracking with particles. Proceedings of the IEEE 92(3), 495–513 (2004)
15. Neyman, J., Pearson, E.: On the problem of the most efficient tests of statistical hypotheses. Philosophical Transactions of the Royal Society of London, Series A, Containing Papers of a Mathematical or Physical Character 231, 289–337 (1933)
16. Andriluka, M., Roth, S., Schiele, B.: People-tracking-by-detection and people-detection-by-tracking. In: Int. Conf. on Computer Vision and Pattern Recognition, Anchorage, AK, USA (2008)
17. Andriyenko, A., Roth, S., Schindler, K.: An analytical formulation of global occlusion reasoning for multi-target tracking. In: 11th IEEE International Workshop on Visual Surveillance (at ICCV), Barcelona (2011)
18. Bernardin, K., Stiefelhagen, R.: Evaluating multiple object tracking performance: the clear mot metrics. EURASIP Journal on Image and Video Processing (2010)

Particle Swarm Optimization with Soft Search Space Partitioning for Video-Based Markerless Pose Tracking

Patrick Fleischmann[1], Ivar Austvoll[2], and Bogdan Kwolek[3]

[1] Institute for Communication Systems ICOM,
University of Applied Sciences of Eastern Switzerland,
8640 Rapperswil, Switzerland
patrick.fleischmann@hsr.ch
[2] Dept. of Electrical and Computer Engineering,
University of Stavanger, N-4036 Stavanger, Norway
ivar.austvoll@uis.no
[3] Rzeszów University of Technology, 35-959 Rzeszów, Poland
bkwolek@prz.edu.pl

Abstract. This paper proposes a new algorithm called soft partitioning particle swarm optimization (SPPSO), which performs video-based markerless human pose tracking by optimizing a fitness function in a 31-dimensional search space. The fitness function is based on foreground segmentation and edges. SPPSO divides the optimization into two stages that exploit the hierarchical structure of the model. The first stage only optimizes the most important parameters, whereas the second is a global optimization which also refines the estimates from the first stage. Experiments with the publicly available Lee walk dataset showed that SPPSO performs better than the annealed particle filter at a frame rate of 20 fps, and equally well at 60 fps. The better performance at the lower frame rate is attributed to the explicit exploitation of the hierarchical model structure.

Keywords: Video Processing, Particle Swarm Optimization, Motion Capture.

1 Introduction

Pose tracking, also known as motion capture, is the process of sequentially estimating the pose and position of a human subject in a sequence of images. The applications of video-based markerless human pose tracking range from computer games to medical gait analysis. The ubiquitous presence of computer vision hardware in our environment offers many opportunities for video based human motion capture.

Markerless pose tracking is a hard problem due to ambiguities and self-occlusions arising from the mapping of 3D body poses to 2D images. The high dimensionality of the parameter space is another major problem in all approaches

J. Blanc-Talon et al. (Eds.): ACIVS 2012, LNCS 7517, pp. 479–490, 2012.
© Springer-Verlag Berlin Heidelberg 2012

that use articulated body models. The required number of parameters for a full body model is often over 30, even for coarse models. The most successful pose tracking algorithms are interacting simulated annealing (ISA) [5] and the annealed particle filter (APF) [4]. They are both optimization algorithms that aim to find the maximum of the posterior probability for tracking.

Particle Swarm Optimization (PSO) [9] is well suited for parameter optimization problems like pose estimation. It was first applied to markerless pose estimation by Ivekovic and Trucco in 2006 [7]. They only performed static pose estimation of the upper body in this work. In two recent papers, Ivekovic et al. describe a hierarchical approach using PSO for full body pose tracking [7,8]. They use the articulated human model of the Lee walk dataset [1] and divide the 31-dimensional parameter space into 12 hierarchical subspaces to overcome the problem of high dimensionality. This approach has some shortcomings because the optimization cannot escape from local maxima found in preceding hierarchical levels. Moreover the final solution tends to drift away from the true pose, especially at low frame rates [8].

Krzeszowski et al. propose a global local PSO (GLPSO) [10] where the PSO-based optimization is divided into two stages. The first stage is a global optimization of the pose and the second stage is a local refinement of the limb configuration. This is done for the legs and arms separately. Kwolek et al. [11] combine the global-local approach with a modified PSO named global local annealed PSO (GLAPSO). The most notable property of this variant of PSO is the quantization of the fitness function. Instead of one global best particle, the algorithm maintains a pool of candidates, which improves the algorithm's ability to explore the search space. This modification improves the tracking performance and allows the use of fewer fitness evaluations.

Robertson and Trucco use an approach where the number of optimized parameters is iteratively increased so that a superset of the previously optimized parameters is optimized at every hierarchical stage [13]. This approach, like SPPSO, exploits the hierarchical structure of the body model while avoiding the error accumulation problem of other hierarchical approaches. The main difference to SPPSO is that they use 3D observations in contrast to 2D for SPPSO and they require 6 optimization stages for an upper body model, whereas SPPSO requires only two stages for a full body model.

Hierarchical optimization, as well as global local PSO, divides the optimization into multiple stages, in which a subset of the parameters is optimized while the rest of the parameters are fixed. This is a hard partitioning of the search space. The term soft partitioning was introduced by Deutscher et al. to describe the way the annealed particle filter automatically adjusts the sampling variance of individual parameters [4]. In contrast to hard partitioning, soft partitioning means that some parameters are allowed more variance than others, but no parameters are completely fixed. The annealed particle filter adjusts the variance fully automatic. It uses no prior information about the hierarchical structure of the body model and is therefore a very general approach. SPPSO on the other hand, explicitly exploits the hierarchical structure.

SPPSO belongs to the class of direct model use (generative) algorithms. That means it incorporates a 3D model of the human body in an analysis-by-synthesis fashion [12]. The kinematic structure is modelled by a kinematic tree with the joint angles as the variable parameters during tracking. A kinematic tree for a full body model requires around 30 parameters. Such a high number of degrees of freedom (DoF) makes pose estimation and tracking a very hard problem. Examples of direct model use algorithms can be found in [2,6,14]. When the type of motion (e.g. walking) is known, a strong (action specific) motion model can be used to predict possible poses in the next frame. When the motion is arbitrary, a weak motion model must be used. SPPSO uses a zero motion model, which is suitable for any type of motion as long as it is not too fast. Algorithms that use a weak motion model generally require multiple camera views to alleviate the ambiguities and self-occlusion problems [12]. SPPSO was evaluated using four camera views.

In this work, human pose tracking is achieved by Particle Swarm Optimization. The major contribution is a novel PSO with soft search space partitioning for markerless human pose tracking in multi-view videos. The algorithm has been compared with the state-of-the-art annealed particle filter in qualitative and quantitative evaluations using the Lee walk dataset which includes multi-view video and ground truth poses.

2   SPPSO-Based Human Pose Tracking

2.1   Body Model

The body model used by SPPSO is a modified version of the publicly available model used by Balan et al. [1]. It uses a kinematic tree with 31 parameters to describe a human pose. The first six parameters determine the global position and orientation of the model and the remaining parameters are relative joint angles. The outer shape of the body is modelled with ten truncated cones (henceforth called cylinders), which are fixed to the kinematic tree. Figure 1 shows the kinematic tree and the cylinder model. The dimensions of the cylinders were determined by Balan et al. using marker-based motion capture and are kept constant during tracking. The cylinder model is used to project the silhouettes and edges to the four camera views, where they are compared to the silhouettes and edges that were extracted from the four videos using image processing.

2.2   Fitness Function

The body model described above is used to compute the fitness of candidate poses, defined by the parameters $x_1 - x_{31}$. The fitness indicates how well a candidate pose matches the observations, i.e. the images from all four views at the time instant. The fitness $f = f_s + f_e$ is the sum of two terms: the *silhouette fitness* f_s and the *edge fitness* f_e. Both terms are normalized to lie in the range

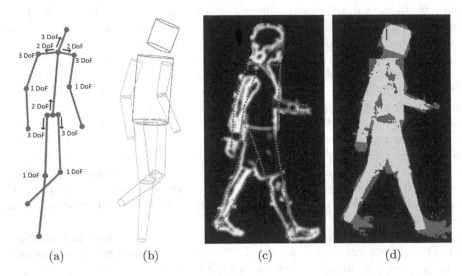

(a)   (b)   (c)   (d)

Fig. 1. (a) Kinematic tree of the body model with 31 degrees of freedom. (b) Cylinder model with ten cylinders (right limbs in yellow, left limbs in cyan). (c) Sampling points for the edge fitness function, overlaid on the edge map. (d) Image segmentation for the silhouette fitness. Red: in observed silhouette but not in projected, blue: in projected but not in observed, yellow: overlap of both silhouettes.

between 0 and 1, where 0 means no match and 1 means complete match. Both partial fitness terms are defined on a single observed image. The total fitness is computed by first averaging the partial fitness values of all four views and then summing the two averaged partial fitness values.

Edges are a robust image feature and human subjects usually produce strong edges along the outline of the body and individual limbs. Edges are therefore a valuable feature for pose tracking [4]. The edge map is obtained by edge detection, blurring, and rescaling to the range between 0 and 1. The edge fitness f_e is then computed by sampling the edge map at discrete points along the visible edges of the candidate pose, similar to the *edge likelihood* used by Balan et al. [1]. The edge fitness can be computed for all, or for individual cylinders. At the first stage of SPPSO, only the torso cylinder is considered for the edge fitness. Except for the torso cylinder, only the edges parallel to the cylinder axes of the model are considered. The upper edge of the torso is also sampled because it provides a valuable hint for the z-location of the model. The head cylinder is never used for the edge fitness because the cylindrical shape is only a very crude approximation of the head's shape. Figure 1c depicts the sampling points for the edge fitness overlaid on the edge map.

The silhouette fitness f_s measures the overlap of the observed silhouette and the projected silhouette. The *observed silhouette* is a binary image, obtained by foreground-background segmentation of the observed image. The *projected silhouette* is obtained by projecting the cylinders of the candidate pose into the respective view.

A good silhouette fitness must be bidirectional [14]. This means that it must measure how much of the projected silhouette falls into the observed, as well as how much of the observed silhouette falls into the projected. This is necessary to prevent unreasonably high fitness values for poses that have overlapping limbs. SPPSO uses a silhouette fitness based on the bidirectional silhouette log-likelihood used by Sigal et al. [14]. It is computed as follows: Let R be the area that lies in the observed, but not in the projected silhouette, B the area that lies in the projected, but not in the observed silhouette, and Y the overlap area of both silhouettes (See Fig. 1d for an illustration of this segmentation.). The silhouette fitness is then computed as $f_s = \frac{1}{2}\frac{Y}{B+Y} + \frac{1}{2}\frac{Y}{R+Y}$. Hence, f_s is 1 when the two silhouettes are identical, and 0 when there is no overlap.

2.3 Optimization

SPPSO maximizes the fitness for every new frame with a particle swarm optimization. The estimated pose from the previous frame is used to initialise the optimization. Hence, the tracking process is a series of static optimizations. These optimizations are divided into two hierarchical stages and both stages use a constricted PSO, as introduced by Clerc and Kennedy [3].

Each particle in the PSO constitutes a candidate pose. Its position vector consists of the variable parameters of the body model (i.e. the position and angles of the kinematic tree). The initial particle positions x_i^t are sampled from a multivariate normal distribution, centred around the estimated pose from last frame $\widehat{x}^{t-1}$.

$$x_i^t \leftarrow \mathcal{N}(\widehat{x}^{t-1}, \Sigma), \quad \Sigma = \begin{pmatrix} \sigma_1^2 & & 0 \\ & \ddots & \\ 0 & & \sigma_{31}^2 \end{pmatrix}, \quad \sigma = \begin{pmatrix} \sigma_1 \\ \vdots \\ \sigma_{31} \end{pmatrix} \tag{1}$$

Σ is the same diagonal covariance matrix as used for the first annealing layer in the annealed particle filter of Balan et al. [1]. The standard deviations σ_d in Σ, where d stands for dimension, are equal to the maximum absolute inter-frame differences of the parameters in a training set of motion capture data at 60 fps. For example: σ_4 (x-translation) is 13.7 mm and σ_{10} (left knee angle) is 0.093 rad. Therefore, the distribution $\mathcal{N}(\widehat{x}^{t-1}, \Sigma)$ can be interpreted as a prior probability for the parameters at time t and it is reasonable to sample the initial particle set from this distribution.

The used training set focuses primarily on walking motions. Therefore, this covariance matrix can be regarded as a weak model for walking motions. This bias towards walking motions could be removed by using a training set with more diverse motions. But this would enlarge the search space and therefore make the tracking of a walking subject more difficult. For experiments at slower frame rates than 60 fps, σ is always upscaled accordingly. For example, σ is multiplied by three when tracking at a frame rate of 20 fps.

The particle velocity is limited to two times the standard deviation in every dimension to prevent unreasonable poses. The initial particle velocities are sampled from a uniform distribution in the interval $[-\sigma, +\sigma]$.

The optimization is subject to two constraints: (i) The angles must remain inside anatomical joint limits and (ii) the limbs may not inter-penetrate. These constraints are equal to the *hard priors* of Balan et al. [1]. They were found to improve the tracking performance significantly by Balan et al. because they reduce the search space. The constraints are enforced by resampling the particle velocity until either the constraints are met or the maximum number of 10 attempts is exceeded.

Algorithm 1 shows the PSO that is used at the two stages of SPPSO. The coefficients $c_1(k)$ and $c_2(k)$ are linearly increased from 2.05 to 2.15 during the optimization to gradually increase the algorithm's tendency to converge. Consequently, the constriction factor $\chi(k)$ is adapted according to (3) for every iteration to ensure convergence [3]. This can be seen as an annealing scheme which was introduced to enforce swarm convergence even with a limited number of iterations N.

$$c_1(k) = c_2(k) = \frac{0.1}{N-2}(k-2) + 2.05 \tag{2}$$

$$\chi(k) = \frac{2}{\left| 2 - \varphi(k) - \sqrt{\varphi(k)^2 - 4\varphi(k)} \right|}, \quad \varphi(k) = c_1(k) + c_2(k) \tag{3}$$

Algorithm 1. Constricted PSO with enforced constraints for one stage of the SPPSO algorithm

---

sample particle positions $x_i \leftarrow \mathcal{N}(\hat{x}^{t-1}, \Sigma)$
sample particle velocities $v_i \leftarrow \mathcal{U}(-\sigma, \sigma)$
calculate particle fitness: $f(x_i) = f_s(x_i) + f_e(x_i)$
update particle best p_i and global best p_g
for each iteration $k = 2$ **to** N **do**
   for each particle i **in the swarm do**
      repeat
         for each dimension d **do**
           $v_{id} = \chi(k)(v_{id} + c_1(k)\epsilon_1(p_{id} - x_{id}) + c_2(k)\epsilon_2(p_{gd} - x_{id}))$
         end for
         limit abs(v_i) **to** 2σ
         $x_i = x_i + v_i$
      until x_i **meets constraints**
      calculate particle fitness: $f(x_i) = f_s(x_i) + f_e(x_i)$
      update particle best p_i **and global best** p_g
   end for
end for

2.4   Soft Partitioning Stages

The optimization of the pose is divided into two hierarchical stages. Both stages are complete optimizations with the above described PSO and the estimated pose from the first stage is used as the initialisation for the second stage.

Pose estimation which is divided into hierarchical stages with hard partitions suffers from error accumulation. This happens because the fitness function for one stage cannot be evaluated completely independently from subsequent stages. SPPSO uses a soft partitioning scheme to avoid error accumulation. Figure 2 illustrates the principle of soft partitioning compared to hard (hierarchical) partitioning. As in hierarchical schemes, the search space is partitioned according to the model hierarchy. The most important parameters are optimized first, while the less important are kept constant. The crucial difference to hard partitioning is that the previously optimized parameters are allowed some variation in the following stage. Soft partitioning reduces the search space not as much as hard partitioning but the search space is much smaller than in a global optimization. This allows a much more efficient search for the optimal pose.

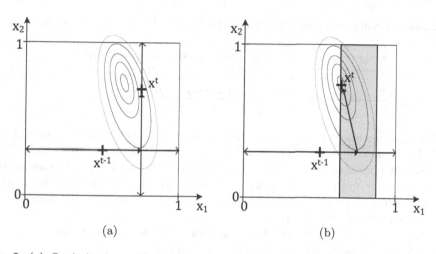

(a)   (b)

Fig. 2. (a) Optimization with hard partitioning. At the first stage, x_1 is optimized while x_2 is kept constant. At the second stage, x_1 is kept constant while x_2 is optimized. Consequently, the optimizer cannot correct the suboptimal estimate of x_1 from the first stage. (b) Soft partitioning. The first stage is identical to the hierarchical scheme, but x_1 is allowed some variation at the second stage. Therefore, the optimizer finds a better estimate.

SPPSO has two hierarchical stages, where only the first six parameters $x_1 - x_6$ (global orientation and position) are optimized in the first stage. The second stage is a global optimization of all parameters where the standard deviations for $x_4 - x_6$ (global position) are divided by an empirically determined factor of ten. Experiments showed that the tracking performance is not significantly increased when the optimization is further divided into three stages. However, the soft partitioning scheme performs much better than global optimization or hard partitioning.

3   Experimental Results

This section presents the experimental evaluation of SPPSO. After showing general results and establishing the maximum obtainable tracking accuracy with the used body model, SPPSO is compared to the annealed particle filter (APF), which is the benchmark algorithm of the HumanEva framework [1,14]. Finally, the computation time for different parts of the SPPSO algorithm is analysed.

Table 1 shows the number of particles and iterations per optimization stage as well as the used fitness functions for the experiments with 1000 fitness evaluations. Keeping the number of evaluations fixed allows a fair comparison to other algorithms because fitness evaluations (including rendering) dominate the total processing time. 1000 evaluations per frame is the standard number of evaluations in the HumanEva framework [14].

Table 1. Configuration of SPPSO for experiments with 1000 fitness evaluations

Stage	Particles	Iterations	Edge fitness	Silhouette fitness
1	10	20	only torso	full body
2	20	40	full body	full body

The experiments were performed on the Lee walk dataset which contains video at 60 fps from four views, showing a human subject that walks in a circle. The ground truth poses contained in the dataset were obtained using a marker-based motion capture system. All reported tracking errors are computed using the standard error measure of Balan et al. [1], which is the average 3D-distance of 15 marker joints to the ground truth positions. Figure 4 shows that the tracking has some errors at 20 fps, but it can generally follow the body configuration. However, at 60 fps the tracking is accurate enough.

Generally, the tracking gets more accurate with higher frame rates and more evaluations per frame. This is also illustrated by Table 2, which shows the mean and maximum tracking error of several tracking runs that were performed to establish the minimal obtainable tracking error. The minimal mean error is reached at about 35 mm and is limited by two factors: First, the ground truth poses are not perfectly accurate. Second, the body model is very coarse.

Figure 3 shows error plots produced by SPPSO with 1000 evaluations per frame at 60 fps and 20 fps. The mean error is a little smaller at 60 fps and the tracking is generally more stable. The outliers in the graph at 60 fps come from a temporarily lost arm. At 20 fps, the maximum error is much higher because SPPSO often loses track of the legs around frame 250 and also loses arms frequently. Figure 5 illustrates how SPPSO loses multiple limbs but reacquires

Table 2. Tracking error of SPPSO at 60 fps with different evaluation rates. The table shows mean and maximum 3D error on the first 450 frames of the Lee walk sequence

evaluations/frame	1000	2000	4000
runs	5	3	1
mean error [mm]	38.0	37.3	35.7
max error [mm]	86.4	82.3	56.7

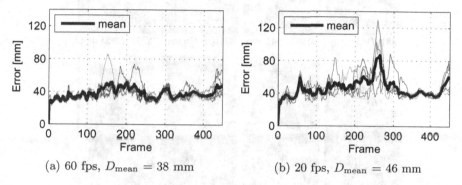

(a) 60 fps, $D_{mean} = 38$ mm   (b) 20 fps, $D_{mean} = 46$ mm

Fig. 3. 3D tracking error of SPPSO with 1000 evaluations per frame for the Lee walk sequence. The graphs show five individual runs and the mean error.

them after some frames at 20 fps. The ability to recover from tracking failures is an important feature for pose tracking algorithms. As expected, the tracking is always very good during the period when the subject stands still (frame 330 to 430).

3.1 Comparison to the Annealed Particle Filter

SPPSO was compared to the annealed particle filter, which currently is the state-of-the-art algorithm for human pose tracking. It is also the benchmark algorithm of the HumanEva framework [14]. Figure 6 shows the results of an experiment with 1000 evaluations per frame at 60 fps and 20 fps, with the same body model and fitness function for both algorithms. Furthermore, both algorithms used the same parameter covariance Σ. SPPSO performs significantly better at 20 fps and equally well at a frame rate of 60 fps. The better performance of SPPSO at the lower frame rate is attributed to the direct exploitation of the hierarchical model. The APF on the other hand, relies on an automatic soft partitioning [4].

3.2 Computation Time

SPPSO is based on the HumanEva framework [1,14] and therefore almost completely implemented in Matlab, including the rendering of the 3D model. Consequently, the algorithm needs 20 seconds to process one frame (1000 evaluations)

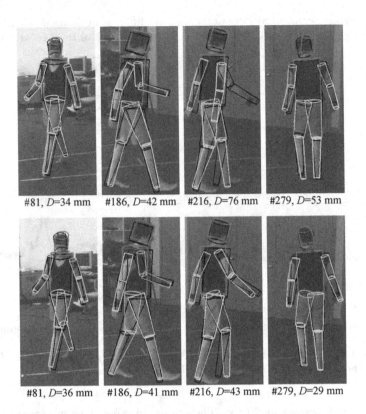

Fig. 4. (top) SPPSO tracking results with 1000 evaluations per frame at 20 fps. (bottom) Tracking with 1000 evaluations per frame at 60 fps. Ground truth cylinders are shown in black, estimated cylinders are coloured to distinguish left and right limbs. Results are shown at frames 81, 186, 216, and 279. D denotes the tracking error at the depicted frame.

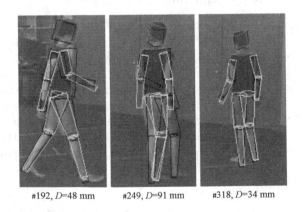

Fig. 5. SPPSO tracking results with 1000 evaluations per frame at 20 fps. The tracker temporarily loses the legs and one arm but can recover in later frames.

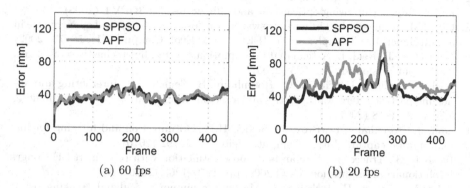

Fig. 6. Tracking error of SPPSO and APF with 1000 evaluatins per frame for the Lee walk sequence. The graphs show mean errors from five individual runs.

and is therefore far from being real-time, which would be necessary for many applications. The most processor-intensive tasks in SPPSO are model rendering and fitness evaluation, which account for 50% and 39% of the processing time. These tasks could be performed very fast by graphics processing hardware.

4 Summary and Conclusions

This paper proposes the SPPSO algorithm for human pose tracking, which has been evaluated on the publicly available Lee walk dataset. These experiments showed that SPPSO performs better than APF at a frame rate of 20 fps with the same number of fitness evaluations.

PSO is a relatively new optimization method for pose tracking (The first source known to the authors is [7]). And there exist only few, more or less successful, attempts to video-based *full body* tracking [8,10]. It seems that the methods which use a hard partitioning require more fitness evaluations to minimize the problem of error accumulation.

All of the algorithms discussed in the introduction use different hierarchical approaches to overcome the problem of high dimensionality and none of them seems to be clearly superior. With the soft partitioning scheme, SPPSO proposes a novel approach for full body tracking and it has been shown to perform well. In contrast to the similar approach by Robertson and Trucco [13], SPPSO uses fewer optimization stages for a body model with more parameters.

A further development of SPPSO could add a local refinement stage to the algorithm to achieve a better accuracy with less computational power. This approach has been proven successful for pose tracking by recent research [15,6].

References

1. Balan, A., Sigal, L., Black, M.: A quantitative evaluation of video-based 3d person tracking. In: 2nd It. IEEE Int. Workshop on Visual Surveillance and Performance Evaluation of Tracking and Surveillance 2005, pp. 349–356 (2005)

2. Ballan, L., Cortelazzo, G.M.: Marker-less motion capture of skinned models in a four camera set-up using optical flow and silhouettes. In: 3DPVT (2008)
3. Clerc, M., Kennedy, J.: The particle swarm - explosion, stability, and convergence in a multidimensional complex space. IEEE Trans. Evol. Comput. 6(1), 58–73 (2002)
4. Deutscher, J., Reid, I.: Articulated body motion capture by stochastic search. Int. J. Comput. Vision 61, 185–205 (2005)
5. Gall, J., Potthoff, J., Schnörr, C., Rosenhahn, B., Seidel, H.P.: Interacting and annealing particle filters: Mathematics and a recipe for applications. J. Math. Imaging Vision 28, 1–18 (2007)
6. Gall, J., Rosenhahn, B., Brox, T., Seidel, H.P.: Optimization and filtering for human motion capture. Int. J. Comput. Vision 87, 75–92 (2010)
7. Ivekovic, S., Trucco, E.: Human body pose estimation with pso. In: IEEE Congr. Evolutionary Computation, CEC 2006, pp. 1256–1263 (2006)
8. John, V., Trucco, E., Ivekovic, S.: Markerless human articulated tracking using hierarchical particle swarm optimisation. Image Vision Comput. 28(11), 1530–1547 (2010)
9. Kennedy, J., Eberhart, R.: Particle swarm optimization. In: Proceedings of the IEEE Int. Conf. on Neural Networks 1995, vol. 4, pp. 1942–1948 (1995)
10. Krzeszowski, T., Kwolek, B., Wojciechowski, K.: Model-Based 3D Human Motion Capture Using Global-Local Particle Swarm Optimizations. In: Burduk, R., Kurzyński, M., Woźniak, M., Żołnierek, A. (eds.) Computer Recognition Systems 4. AISC, vol. 95, pp. 297–306. Springer, Heidelberg (2011)
11. Kwolek, B., Krzeszowski, T., Wojciechowski, K.: Swarm Intelligence Based Searching Schemes for Articulated 3D Body Motion Tracking. In: Blanc-Talon, J., Kleihorst, R., Philips, W., Popescu, D., Scheunders, P. (eds.) ACIVS 2011. LNCS, vol. 6915, pp. 115–126. Springer, Heidelberg (2011)
12. Moeslund, T., Hilton, A., Krüger, V.: A survey of advances in vision-based human motion capture and analysis. Comput. Vision Image Understanding 104(2-3), 90–126 (2006)
13. Robertson, C., Trucco, E.: Human body posture via hierarchical evolutionary optimization. In: BMVC 2006, vol. 3, p. 999 (2006)
14. Sigal, L., Balan, A., Black, M.: HumanEva: Synchronized video and motion capture dataset and baseline algorithm for evaluation of articulated human motion. Int. J. Comput. Vision 87, 4–27 (2010)
15. Sminchisescu, C., Triggs, B.: Covariance scaled sampling for monocular 3d body tracking. In: IEEE Computer Soc. on Conf. Computer Vision and Pattern Recognition, CVPR, vol. 1, pp. I:447–I:454. IEEE (2001)

Estimation and Prediction of the Vehicle's Motion Based on Visual Odometry and Kalman Filter

Basam Musleh[1], David Martin[1], Arturo de la Escalera[1],
Domingo Miguel Guinea[1], and Maria Carmen Garcia-Alegre[2]

[1] Intelligent Systems Lab, University Carlos III, Leganes, Madrid 28911, Spain
`bmusleh,dmmartin,escalera,dguinea@ing.uc3m.es`
[2] Center for Automation and Robotics (CAR), Spanish Council for Scientific
Research (CSIC), 28500 Arganda del Rey. Madrid
`maria@iai.csic.es`

Abstract. The movement of the vehicle is an useful information for different applications, such as driver assistant systems or autonomous vehicles. This information can be known by different methods, for instance, by using a GPS or by means of the visual odometry. However, there are some situations where both methods do not work correctly. For example, there are areas in urban environments where the signal of the GPS is not available, as tunnels or streets with high buildings. On the other hand, the algorithms of computer vision are affected by outdoor environments, and the main source of difficulties is the variation in the ligthing conditions. A method to estimate and predict the movement of the vehicle based on visual odometry and Kalman filter is explained in this paper. The Kalman filter allows both filtering and prediction of vehicle motion, using the results from the visual odometry estimation.

Keywords: Stereo vision, Visual odometry, Kalman filter.

1 Introduction

Various applications of Intelligent Transportation Systems (ITS), such as Advanced Driver Assistance Systems (ADAS) or autonomous vehicles need to have information about the movement of the vehicle. This information is usually supplied by a GPS, but there are some areas where the signal is not available in urban environments. This is because the signal is affected by high buildings or tunnels. Another option in order to know the movement of the vehicle is using the visual odometry. On the other hand, the visual odometry is affected by other kind of problems, mainly the light conditions make errors or do not allow to obtain the information about the vehicle's motion. A method to estimate the movement of the vehicle is presented in this paper, based on the visual odometry and whose results are filtered by using Kalman filter. Furthermore, if the method of visual odometry does not supply any estimation in a period of time, the Kalman filter can be used in order to predict the trajectory of the vehicle.

J. Blanc-Talon et al. (Eds.): ACIVS 2012, LNCS 7517, pp. 491–502, 2012.
© Springer-Verlag Berlin Heidelberg 2012

The visual odometry is one of the most active field in computer vision. Different solutions have made use of monocular cameras [18], stereo systems [4] and omnidirectional cameras [15]. Monocular sensors have the problem of scalar factor, but its implementation is easier than stereo systems which present a complex calibration step. Stereo systems achieve the most accurate results in long distances, because 3D information is avalaible, although they present great uncertainty in depth estimation [3]. Several methods have been presented, working in the disparity space in order to solve the uncertainty [2]. Finally, omnidirectional cameras allow to track the feature points along more frames than other sensors[16]. On the other hand, the distorsion makes difficult the feature matching. The presented method is based on a stereo vision system [12]. The visual odometry estimation is normally performed by means of detecting and tracking feature points between consecutive frames [14]. This visual odometry estimation makes use of the dense disparity map [17] to detect the road in front of the vehicle. Once the road has been detected, it is possible to only use the feature points that belong to the road, avoiding feature points of obstacles which can be a source of outliers if the obstacles are moving [20]. Another interesting result of using only feature points that belong to the road is the unnecessary search of feature points in the whole image, thus the developed algorithm only needs to process a lower third of the image.

The information of the road profile [8] is used to obtain the world coordinates of the road feature points. Besides the road profile, it is only necessary to know the position of the feature points on the left image in order to obtain the world coordinates, in constrast to most of the visual odometry algorithms, which need to perform a matching between the images of the stereo pair in order to obtain the disparity for each feature point. Moreover, the used feature points are close to the vehicle, reducing the uncertainty in depth estimation. Kalman filtering [7] has been applied to many situations in engineering, such as radio communication signals or applications to navigation. The filtering approach of the algorithm is applied in this work to raw data in order to smooth undesirable fluctuations in visual odometry. An acquisition of raw data from a GPS is synchronized with the capture of images in order to compare the results of the visual odometry with the GPS. The GPS is based on a Novatel receiver [5] that has been configured to work with Satellite-Based Augmentation Systems (SBAS) for sub-meter positioning. The solution has been calculated specifically with the European Geo-Stationary Navigation System (EGNOS), which is a type of geo-stationary satellite system that improves the accuracy of the basic GPS signals. Accuracy is enhanced through the use of wide area corrections for GPS satellite orbits and ionospheric errors. EGNOS consists of a series of reference stations, master stations, ground uplink stations and geostationary satellites (GEOs).

2 Obstacles and Road Detection

Two equal and parallel cameras can be used to obtain the depth (Z) for a point $P = (X, Y, Z)$ in world's coordinates by using (1), where the projections of point

P over the image planes are (u_L, v_L) and (u_R, v_r) for the left camera and the right one respectively.

$$Z = \frac{f \cdot B}{u_L - u_R} = \frac{f \cdot B}{d} \tag{1}$$

Where d is the disparity, f is the focal length and B is the baseline between both cameras. The disparity map is obtained by using the rectified images supplied by the stereo system, being the disparity (d) represented in the disparity map for every pixel of the image. Once the disparity map has been created, the u-v disparity [6] can be obtained. The v-disparity [8] expresses the histogram over the disparity values for every image row (v coordinate), whereas the u-disparity does the same, but for every column (u coordinate).

The dense disparity map and the u-v disparity are developed in order to detect obstacles in front of the vehicle. The method for detecting obstacles and the free space in front of the vehicle has been presented in [11]. This method obtains, as a result, two different dense disparity maps. The first one is the obstacle map (Fig.1(c)) and the second one, the free map (Fig.1(d)). The obstacle map is a disparity map where only the obstacles appear, whereas the free map is the opposite to the obstacle map, where only the empty space ahead of the vehicle appears. The obstacle detection has to detect every obstacle which blocks the movement of the vehicle, but it must not detect as an obstacle some possible elements which do not avoid the movement, for example a speed bump. Althought the free map usually corresponds to the road, theoretically, is the empty whole space. This information can be used by a system of detection and localization of obstacles, as shown in [10].

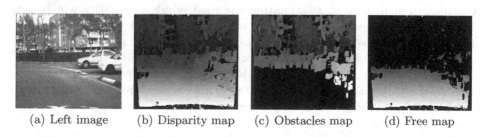

(a) Left image   (b) Disparity map   (c) Obstacles map   (d) Free map

Fig. 1. Example of the obstacles and road detection

2.1 Estimation and Use of the Road Profile

As commented before, the depth (Z) for a point P can be calculated by means of (1), where the depth (Z) is a function of the disparity d, but the range of the disparity is low. This range is a function of the extrinsic and intrisic parameters of the cameras, (for the results presented in this work, the range of disparity is $d = \{0, 25\}$). Thus, the resolution of (1) is sparse. The road profile [8] can be used in order to increase this resolution of the depth. The road appears as an oblique line in the v-disparity (road profile), which can be expressed as a straight line

(2) if a flat ground assumption is performed. Where v is the vertical coordinate of the image and b is the theoretical value of the horizon of the stereo system. Furthermore, once the road profile has been estimated, it is possible to know the pitch α between the stereo rig and the road [8] for each frame, by means of the (3) where C_v is the vertical coordinate of the optical center.

$$v = m \cdot d + b \tag{2}$$

$$\alpha = \arctan \frac{b - C_v}{f} \tag{3}$$

The road profile (2) shows the relationship between the vertical coordinate of the image v and the disparity d, then it is possible to obtain a new expression (4) merging the stereo equation (1) and the road profile (2), where now the depth (Z) is a function of the vertical coordinate of the image v. This new expression to calculate the depth Z is only for points belonging to the road. Moreover, in order to calculate the depth to the vehicle instead of the depth to the camera, it is necessary to use the information about the pitch α (3). Once the depth (Z) for a point belonging to the road has been calculated, it is possible to obtain its world coordinate X, which is a function of Z as (5) shows. Where C_u is the horizontal coordinate of the optical center.

$$Z = \frac{m \cdot f \cdot B}{v - b} \cdot \cos \alpha \tag{4}$$

$$X = \frac{Z \cdot (u - C_u)}{f} = \frac{m \cdot B \cdot (u - C_u)}{v - b} \tag{5}$$

It is important to note that estimating the road profile v-disparity which has been generated by using the disparity map, can be a difficult task in urban environments, so the detection of the oblique line corresponding to the road profile is difficult. An extended explanation of the solution to this problem is presented in [11]. For this reason, it is better to use the free map in order to generate the v-disparity because the obstacles are removed from the v-disparity, so it is easier to estimate the road profile.

3   Raw Visual Odometry Estimation

The visual odometry estimation is based on tracking feature points between consecutive frames of the left camera. In opposition to the usual methods of visual ego motion estimation or visual odometry [12], this method does not have to match up the feature points between both images of the stereo system to locate the points in world coordinates, because the method only uses the points belonging to the road. This points can be located on world coordinates by using (4) and (5) with the coordinates of points on the left image. An implementation of the Scale-Invariant Transform Feature (SIFT) detector and descriptor [9] developed for the MATLAB environment [19] is used in order to detect the feature points of the images.

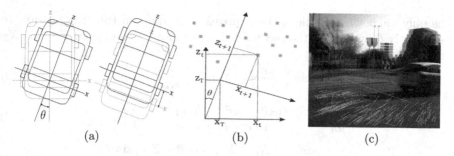

Fig. 2. (a) Schema of the movement of the vehicle. On the left, rotation stage. On the right, translation stage. (b) Schema of the movement of the cartesian coordinate system between consecutives frames. (c) Example of feature points detecting and matching between consecutives frames.

The chosen model for the kinematic motion of the vehicle is the Ackerman's sterring model [1] [13]. In order to simplify the visual odometry estimation, it is necessary to make some assumptions: firstly, the movement of the vehicle between two consecutive frames can be divided into two stages, whose velocity is constant in each one (Fig.2(a)): a rotation around the center of the motion of the rear axle and a forward translation after the rotation. The second assumption is that there is no slip in any direction.

3.1   Estimation of the Visual Odometry between Consecutive Frames

The vehicle odometry estimation between two consecutive frames (t and $t+1$) is perfomed in two steps. Firstly, the feature points have to be detected on the two left images of the stereo pair, in the instants t and $t+1$. Then, a correspondence between the two sets of feature points (t and $t+1$) is done in order to know the displacement of the feature points within the images. As commented before, the method only makes use of points of the road which are situated at the bottom of the image. For this reason, it is possible to detect only the feature points at the bottom of the image, determining what feature points belong to the road by means of the free map. Besides the reduction of the computing time, using only the closest points to the vehicle, the flat ground assumption is improved. Once the image coordinates of the feature points have been obtained, it is possible to calculate the world coordinates $\{X, Z\}$ of these feature points in the instants t and $t+1$ by means of (4) and (5).

Secondly, the estimation of the vehicle movement between two consecutives frames (t and $t+1$) can be calculated by using the different locations in the instant t and $t+1$ of the points detected in the previous step. As Fig.2(b) shows, the rotation angle θ of the vehicle can be calculated by means of (6), where Z_T and X_T represent the translation after the rotation. Besides, it is possible to express Z_T and X_T as a function of θ and the locations of a road point, in the instant t and $t+1$ by using (7). On the other hand, the angle θ

is the only unknown variable of the expression in equation (8). It is possible to obtain firstly θ by solving the second order equation (9) and then Z_T and X_T by using (7).

$$\theta = \arctan\left(\frac{X_T}{Z_T}\right) \Rightarrow \tan\theta = \frac{\sin\theta}{\cos\theta} = \frac{X_T}{Z_T} \tag{6}$$

$$\begin{bmatrix} X_t \\ Z_t \end{bmatrix} = \begin{bmatrix} \cos\theta & \sin\theta \\ -\sin\theta & \cos\theta \end{bmatrix} \begin{bmatrix} X_{t+1} \\ Z_{t+1} \end{bmatrix} + \begin{bmatrix} X_T \\ Z_T \end{bmatrix} \tag{7}$$

$$\frac{X_T}{Z_T} = \frac{\sin\theta}{\cos\theta} = \frac{X_t - X_{t+1}\cos\theta - Z_{t+1}\sin\theta}{Z_t - Z_{t+1}\cos\theta + X_{t+1}\sin\theta} \tag{8}$$

$$(X_t^2 + Z_t^2)\sin^2\theta + (2 \cdot X_{t+1} \cdot Z_t)\sin\theta + (X_{t+1}^2 - X_t^2) = 0 \tag{9}$$

In this way, a set of solutions $\{\theta, Z_T, X_T\}$ for the visual odometry estimation is obtained, where a solution $\{\theta, Z_T, X_T\}_k$ has been calculated for each pair of points $\{X_t, Z_t\}_k$ and $\{X_{t+1}, Z_{t+1}\}_k$. Different methods can be used in order to choose a unique solution $\{\theta, Z_T, X_T\}$ from the set of solutions, as a result of the visual odometry between the two consecutive frames. The algorithm uses a solution from the set by means of the median because it is robust to possible outliers.

4 Description of the Kalman Filter Implementation

The visual odometry estimation uses Kalman algorithm to solve filtering and prediction problem. The filtering approach of the algorithm is applied to raw data in order to smooth out undesirable fluctuations of visual odometry variables $\{\theta, Z_T, X_T\}$. Moreover, the Kalman algorithm is used if it is necessary to predict the evolution of the former variables in case of raw data loss.

4.1 Model Using in Kalman Filter

The process model is implemented by a linear time-varying (LTV) model in discrete time. That is, the process is described by a linear system. In this work, the system is a vehicle driving along a road at constant velocity. This linear system is a process, which can be described by the following two equations:

$$x_{t+1} = A_t \cdot x_t + w_t \tag{10}$$

$$y_t = B \cdot x_t + z_t \tag{11}$$

Where, t is the time index, x is the state of the system and y is the measured output. The variable w is the process noise and z is the measurement noise. The matrix A is the state transition matrix and B is the measurement matrix, which are obtained to model a simple vehicle moving with constant velocity.

Then, the state vector x consists of the vehicle location $p = [X, Z, \theta]$ and velocity v: $x_t = \begin{bmatrix} p_t \\ v_t \end{bmatrix}$, and the linear system equations are:

$$x_{t+1} = \begin{bmatrix} 1 & T_t \\ 0 & 1 \end{bmatrix} \cdot x_t + w_t \qquad (12)$$

$$y_t = [1\ 0] \cdot x_t + z_t \qquad (13)$$

The Kalman filter combines the measurements from the system (variables for the visual odometry estimation $\{\theta, Z_T, X_T\}$), with the information provided by the motion model in order to obtain an optimal estimate of the system state. In this work, the measurement noise covariance matrix has been selected as the square of standard deviation of measurement (such as, 1^2 if we estimate Z_T), and the process noise covariance matrix uses process noise variance of 0.01.

4.2   Utilities of the Kalman Filter

The Kalman algorithm has been applied for filtering and prediction of visual odometry variables. Both utilities of the Kalman algorithm are displayed in Fig. 3, where three graphs represent the same example of a curve trajectory of the vehicle. The example shows only one of the three variables corresponding to odometry estimation, that is the angle θ. The example of the angle sequence starts at 20 second when the curve trajectory appears. The red circles of the graphs are visual odometry angles and blue circles are obtained solution with Kalman algorithm.

The first solution is the graph of Fig. 3(a), which presents the angle without fluctuations of the real data. The result allows to follow a smooth curve trajectory and eliminate outliers. In the graph can be observed that there are close measurements of 0.1 seconds where the algorithm smoothes correctly the curve trajectory. However, the most useful result appears when there is a gap of more than 0.1 seconds and an outlier is obtained by the visual odometry estimation, this outlier is usually caused by the shutter of the camera. In this special case, the Kalman filter obtains good results again as can be observed in the graph, smoothing the curve trajectory of the vehicle.

The second utility is prediction, where the Kalman algorithm is used to predict a solution when visual odometry cannot be calculated. Then, it is necessary to predict the evolution of the variables. We continue using the same curve trajectory as example and it is presented in (b) and (c) graph of Fig. 3. The experiment consists of requesting to Kalman algorithm an prediction of 100 measurements of odometry angle with a time interval of 100 milliseconds. The entire interval of 10 seconds is requested in two cases, first case when the vehicle is in the middle of the curve trajectory (Fig. 3(b)), and second case when the vehicle is reaching the end of the curve trajectory (Fig. 3(c)). Both prediction results are according to curve trajectory. In the right graph (Fig. 3(b)), the predicted angle presents an overshoot and finishes the estimated curve trajectory at 35 second. The third graph (Fig. 3(c)) shows the vehicle finishing again the estimated curve trajectory at 40 second and displays after a small overshoot. Both estimations reach a steady-state angle of 0 degrees.

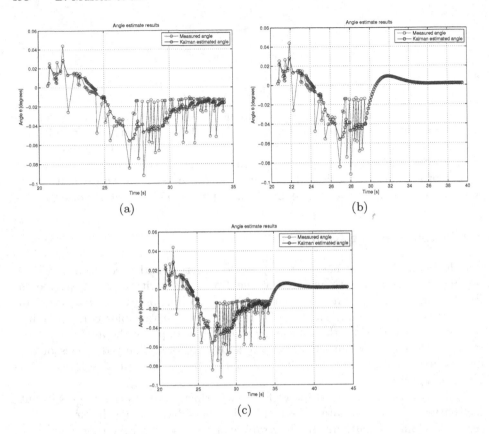

Fig. 3. Example of filter (a) and prediction ((b) and (c)) of θ raw data

5   Evaluation

Several tests have been performed in urban environments in order to evaluate the goodness of the algorithm of the visual odometry estimation. The results of a sequence, where the vehicle performs a closed loop in a urban environment, are presented in this section. The sequence has 1 minute and 38 seconds' duration and it is composed of 982 stereo images. Two different methods are used in order to evaluate the degree of accuracy of the visual odometry estimation. Firstly, it is possible to compare the difference between the initial and final location (position and orientation) of the vehicle. Due to the vehicle performes a closed loop, this two locations should be the same. Secondly, aerial imagery can be also used to overlay the resulting trajectory of the visual odometry estimation, and GPS raw data.

5.1   Results of the Visual Odometry Estimation

The first evaluation result is based on a comparison between the median and the mean, that has been performed in order to evaluate the robustness of the median

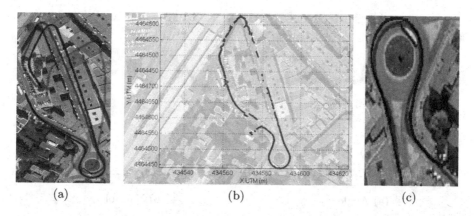

(a)   (b)   (c)

Fig. 4. Comparison between the different trajectories of the visual odometry estimation and GPS overlay in an aerial imagery. (a) Trajectory using obstacles in blue, mean in green and final visual odometry estimation (median) in red. (b) Raw data of the GPS overlay over an aerial imagery (c) Detail for comparison between the visual odometry estimation and the GPS raw data.

when it is used to choose the final solution $\{\theta, Z_T, X_T\}$. Fig. 4(a) presents the resulting trajectory of the visual odometry using both methods: the trajectory calculated by the mean appears in green and the median in red. The trajectory is deformed due to use the mean, in comparison with the obtained one with the median. The effect of not to use the feature points from the obstacles has been also studied. Fig. 4(a) shows the obtained trajectory using the feature points from the obstacles (blue colour). The fact that using feature points from the obstacles ahead of the vehicle produce a 50% position error higher than the visual odometry estimation without obstacles, whereas the rotation error is similar. Regarding to the trajectory, the deviation is more prominent in the entire trajectory as Fig. 4(a) shows.

Following, the raw data resulting from the visual odometry estimation are filtered in order to smooth fluctuations, Fig. 5 shows the results of filtering each variable $\{\theta, Z_T, X_T\}$. It is possible to observe the improvement of the smoothness in the three variables. The Fig. 5(a) displays the visual odometry estimated angle in red colour and Kalman filtered angle in blue colour. That is, Kalman algorithm estimates next angle using former angles of the time series. The results of the filter is appropriate in linear and curve trajectories, as can be observed in Fig.5(a), which first displays a linear trajectory followed by a curve to the left and so on. It is interesting to compare Fig.5(a) and Fig. 4(a) to observe the overall trajectory of the experiment, for example, when the vehicle is in the roundabout and how the Kalman filter smoothes continuously the curve trajectory to the left. The Fig.5(b) displays the X position and the behaviour of the filter is accurate obtaining again a smooth trajectory. It can be observed again the equivalence between Fig.5(b) and Fig. 4(a). The third graph is the Z position where the Kalman algorithm filters fluctuations of approximately 0.8 meters. The algorithm smoothes efficiently the Z variable.

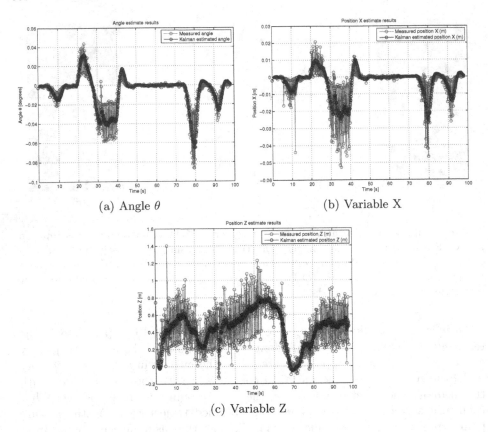

(a) Angle θ

(b) Variable X

(c) Variable Z

Fig. 5. Results of the raw data filtering from visual odometry estimation

5.2 Comparision between Visual Odometry Results and GPS

The second evaluation result is based on GPS. The GPS raw data of the followed trajectory by the vehicle is displayed in Fig 4(b). Raw data is shown in Universal Transverse Mercator (UTM) geographic coordinate system to compare visual odometry estimation data and GPS raw data in meters. The trajectory start, which is followed by the vehicle, is marked with a red dot in Fig. 4(b), and each blue dot stands for a GPS point. The accuracy of overall trajectory is less than one meter when GPS + EGNOS is active, and if the receiver uses single point L1 solution the accuracy is 1.5 meters. Moreover, if the receiver is working in single point L1 solution and the number of GPS satellites is insufficient to calculate an optimum solution, then the accuracy of the solution can be increased more than 1,5 meters, resulting in a lateral displacement of the blue dots close to the real trajectory of the vehicle. The trajectory shows some gaps, where the receiver cannot compute the solution caused by the loss of GPS satellites. The loss of satellite signals is caused by obstructions from close buildings in the right and left side of the road. The comparison between visual odometry estimation results and GPS raw data can be observed in Fig. 4(c). The visual odometry trajectory is indicated in red colour and GPS raw data in blue colour. This comparison is the tool that allows to establish the performance of the visual odometry estimation. Considering the accuracy of the GPS receiver, explained in former paragraph, the results establish that visual odometry has better performance that GPS raw data. It is possible to observe wrong data at the bottom-right of the Fig.4(c) due to the receiver cannot compute the solution caused by the loss of GPS satellites. The loss of satellite signals is caused by a close building in the right of the road. The red trajectory matches exactly with the cars in the aerial image, as can be observed at the beginning of the roundabout where appears a car that is waiting for entering in the roundabout. A second example is in the middle of the roundabout, where a bus is performing a curve trajectory.

6   Conclusions

The 2D visual odometry estimation has been explained and applied in urban environments. The advantages of the smart algorithm have been shown comparing GPS raw data with visual odometry results. The robust visual odometry estimation ensures safe trajectory in case of GPS raw data loss caused by buildings, trees, tunnels, among other solid elements around the vehicle. The GPS drawbacks have been solved with proposed algorithm. The visual estimation has reached the accuracy for curve and linear trajectories of the vehicle, avoiding outliers from dynamic obstacles. The results display a position error of 3.2% and a rotation error of 2.6% in a close loop, which accomplishes the goal of the estimation algorithm. In addition, the use of the road profile and free map information allow to search feature points only in the lower third of the left images, and reduce the uncertainly in depth estimation because these points are close to the vehicle. Kalman filter has been used as a great asset for smoothing out undesirable fluctuations of visual odometry variables, and if necessary the Kalman algorithm can predict the variables of the vehicle's movement in case of raw data loss.

Acknowledgments. This work was also supported by Spanish Government through the CICYT projects FEDORA (Grant TRA2010-20255-C03-01), Driver Distraction Detector System (Grant TRA2011-29454-C03-02) and by CAM through the projects SEGVAUTO-II.

References

1. Borenstein, J., Everett, H., Feng, L.: Where am i? sensors and methods for mobile robot positioning. University of Michigan 119, 120 (1996)
2. Demirdjian, D., Darrell, T.: Motion estimation from disparity images. In: Proceedings of Eighth IEEE International Conference on Computer Vision, ICCV 2001, vol. 1, pp. 213–218. IEEE (2001)
3. Hernández, A., Nieto, J., Vidal Calleja, T., Nebot, E., et al.: Large scale visual odometry using stereo vision (2011)

4. Howard, A.: Real-time stereo visual odometry for autonomous ground vehicles. In: IEEE/RSJ International Conference on Intelligent Robots and Systems, IROS 2008, pp. 3946–3952. IEEE (2008)
5. NovAtel Inc., Calgary (2012), http://www.novatel.com
6. Hu, Z., Lamosa, F., Uchimura, K.: A complete uv-disparity study for stereovision based 3d driving environment analysis. In: Fifth International Conference on 3-D Digital Imaging and Modeling, 3DIM 2005, pp. 204–211. IEEE (2005)
7. Kalman, R.: A new approach to linear filtering and prediction problems. Journal of basic Engineering 82(Series D), 35–45 (1960)
8. Labayrade, R., Aubert, D., Tarel, J.: Real time obstacle detection in stereovision on non flat road geometry through v-disparity representation. In: Intelligent Vehicle Symposium, vol. 2, pp. 646–651. IEEE (2002)
9. Lowe, D.: Distinctive image features from scale-invariant keypoints. International Journal of Computer Vision 60(2), 91–110 (2004)
10. Musleh, B., Escalera, A., Armingol, J.: Real-time pedestrian recognition in urban environments. In: Advanced Microsystems for Automotive Applications, pp. 139–147 (2011)
11. Musleh, B., de la Escalera, A., Armingol, J.: U-v disparity analysis in urban environments. In: Moreno-Díaz, R., Pichler, F., Quesada-Arencibia, A. (eds.) EUROCAST 2011, Part II. LNCS, vol. 6928, pp. 426–432. Springer, Heidelberg (2012)
12. Nistér, D., Naroditsky, O., Bergen, J.: Computer Vision and Pattern Recognition. In: Proceedings of the 2004 IEEE Computer Society Conference on CVPR 2004 , vol. 1, p–652. IEEE (2004)
13. Nourani-Vatani, N., Roberts, J., Srinivasan, M.: Practical visual odometry for car-like vehicles. In: IEEE International Conference on Robotics and Automation, ICRA 2009, pp. 3551–3557. IEEE (2009)
14. Parra, I., Sotelo, M., Llorca, D., Ocana, M.: Robust visual odometry for vehicle localization in urban environments. Robotica 28(3), 441–452 (2010)
15. Scaramuzza, D., Fraundorfer, F., Siegwart, R.: Real-time monocular visual odometry for on-road vehicles with 1-point ransac. In: IEEE International Conference on Robotics and Automation, ICRA 2009, pp. 4293–4299. IEEE (2009)
16. Scaramuzza, D., Siegwart, R.: Appearance-guided monocular omnidirectional visual odometry for outdoor ground vehicles. IEEE Transactions on Robotics 24(5), 1015–1026 (2008)
17. Scharstein, D., Szeliski, R.: A taxonomy and evaluation of dense two-frame stereo correspondence algorithms. International Journal of Computer Vision 47(1), 7–42 (2002)
18. Stein, G., Mano, O., Shashua, A.: A robust method for computing vehicle ego-motion. In: Proceedings of the IEEE Intelligent Vehicles Symposium, IV 2000, pp. 362–368. IEEE (2000)
19. Vedaldi, A.: An open implementation of the SIFT detector and descriptor. Tech. Rep. 070012, UCLA CSD (2007)
20. Wangsiripitak, S., Murray, D.: Avoiding moving outliers in visual slam by tracking moving objects. In: IEEE International Conference on Robotics and Automation, ICRA 2009, pp. 375–380. IEEE (2009)

Detection of HF First-Order Sea Clutter and Its Splitting Peaks with Image Feature: Results in Strong Current Shear Environment

Yang Li[1], Zhenyuan Ji[1], Junhao Xie[1], and Wenyan Tang[2]

[1] Department of Electronic Engineering, [2] Institute of Automatic Testing and Control
Harbin Institute of Technology
Harbin 150001, China
li.yang@hit.edu.cn

Abstract. Strong current shear environment always results in the twisty and splitted sea clutter along the range dimension in the range-Doppler spectral map. A sea clutter detection method with image feature is proposed. With 2-D image features in range-Doppler spectrum, the trend of first-order sea echoes is extracted as indicative information by a multi-scale filter. Detection rules for both single and splitting first-order sea echoes are given based on the characteristic knowledge combining the indicative information with the global characteristics such as amplitude, symmetry, continuity, etc. Compared with the classical algorithms, the proposed method can detect and locate the first-order sea echo in the HF band more accurately especially in the environment with targets/clutters smearing. Experiments with real data in strong current shear environment verify the validity of the algorithm.

Keywords: sea state remote sensing; first-order sea clutter; image feature; Bragg peak splitting; high frequency radar.

1   Introduction

In the application of sea state remote sensing, High Frequency Surface Wave Radar (HFSWR) acquires the sea state information by estimating the parameters of the first order and second order sea echo/clutter. On the other hand, in the surveillance of moving target such as ship and iceberg, it will result in the false alarm and missing alarm for not recognizing targets and sea clutter when the speed of them is equal or close. Thus, it is a key and useful technique to detect the first-order sea echo (clutter/backscatter) spectra (Bragg Peak) contaminated with clutter/noise not only for sea state sensing but also for long range target detection [1,2]. In most surveillance space for HFSWR, the Bragg peaks near the coast are always dominant in local Doppler spectrum. Thus Hickey and Gill proposed a local peak detection method [3]. And Barrick gave the statistical location of the first-order sea echo by estimating the centroid of spread spectrum peaks [4]. However, if there are ships, ionosphere

J. Blanc-Talon et al. (Eds.): ACIVS 2012, LNCS 7517, pp. 503–514, 2012.

interference[5] and other clutters around the Bragg peak, the performances of those algorithms will be degraded rapidly [6]. To solve the problems, clutter canceling methods are proposed using space-time characteristics to eliminate/extract first-order sea clutters from interferences [7-9]. To get a better detection performance, Ji analyzed characteristics and mechanism of first-order sea clutters systematically [10]. And Tong studied a ship target CFAR detection method in a strong sea clutter background with the amplitude characteristic and background distribution information [11]. In literature [12], four detection rules for Bragg peak location were proposed based on multidimensional characteristics such as amplitude, SNR (signal-to-noise ratio), continuity, symmetry, etc., which solved the Bragg peak detection problem to some extent. Recent researches [13,14] found that Bragg peak spectrum would be migrated, spread or splitting when there was strong current shear, eddy or some other interrupted current changes. In such circumstances, sea environment parameters estimation and target detection performances will be decreased if there is no way to identify them.

In this paper, a method with image feature is proposed to detect HF first-order sea echoes. After the theory of the first-order sea clutter in the HF band is introduced, the trend of Bragg peaks in range-Doppler map is extracted by image feature in multi-scale space. Combining the trend information with the experiential knowledge, rules for detecting both single and splitting Bragg peaks are given. Then the flow chart shows the procedure of the algorithm. In the experiments, real data Strong current shear environment is used for verifying the validity of the proposed method

2   First-Order Sea Echo in the HF Band

Lots of experiments show that the backscatter of sea surface has specific Doppler shift correlating with sea state by HF irradiation when the sea is fully developed. Crombie observed the phenomena and deduced first-order interaction between HF electromagnetic wave and ocean wave with Bragg scattering model [15]. This theory indicates that the dominant symmetrical spikes (namely first-order Bragg peaks of sea clutter) in Doppler spectrum are generated by double sets of sea wave trains with $\lambda/2$ (where λ is the radar wavelength) moving forward and receding from the radar. In deep water, the predicted position of the first-order Bragg peak is

$$f_B = \pm\sqrt{\frac{g}{\pi\lambda}} = \pm\sqrt{\frac{gf_c}{\pi c}} \tag{1}$$

Here, f_c is the radar carrier frequency, g is the gravitational constant, and c is the velocity of light. Considering the shallow sea, the above formula can be modified as

$$f_B = \pm\sqrt{\frac{gf_c}{\pi c}\tanh(\frac{4\pi h f_c}{c})} \tag{2}$$

Here, h is the water depth, $\tanh(\cdot)$ is the hyperbolic tangent function. Simulation shows that if $f_c > 2\text{MHz}$ and $h<30\text{m}$, the results from (1) and (2) tend to be uniform [13].

From the actual measurements, it can be found that the locations of first-order peaks often departure from the theoretical values (see Figure1(a)). The reason is that the waves causing first-order scattering are superimposed on a sea surface which are physically moving due to surface currents [16]. The radial component of this surface-current vector can thus be calculated in terms of the offset of the Bragg peak.

Under normal conditions, the effect on the position of the Bragg peak by the surface-current is stable. In that case, the surface current field is homogenous in radar target spatial resolution, and the Bragg peak is shown as a narrow-band single spike. Heron and Gill [16] found that Bragg peak splitting was induced by the non-uniform velocity field within the target cell resulting from strong current shear and eddy. A typical example is shown in Figure1(a).

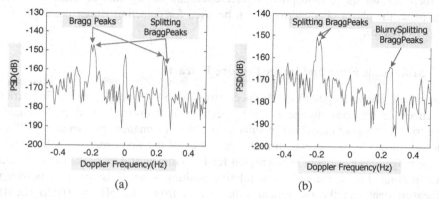

Fig. 1. Doppler spectrum of HFSWR: (a) Typical Doppler spectrum, (b) Blurry splitting Bragg peaks

What's more, ship echoes, ionosphere interference, radio frequency interference and second-order continuum, etc. can also contaminate the first-order spectrum. It's obvious that the actual situation for Bragg peaks is more complicated than the case in which the amplitude is dominant and the position is predictable. We can conclude that, to locate the first-order sea echo spectrum accurately in such a changeable environment, invariant features making the Bragg peak distinctive from other echoes should be found firstly.

3   Location of the Bragg Peak

3.1   Spectral Characteristics of the Bragg Peak

Experimental measurements show that the first-order sea echoes have these features in stable ocean surface current in the distance not far from the coast (usually less than 200km):

1) The offset range between the theoretical value and the actual measurement is predictable [4].

2) The offset directions of the positive/negative Bragg peaks in a same range bin are same [16].
3) The Bragg peak is dominant in Doppler spectrum which is presented as local maximal or the 2nd major amplitude. The windowing Bragg peak usually occupies 3-5 spectral lines.
4) Because the motion of sea surface is continuous, the position of the Bragg peak is changing slowly and continuously along the range direction.
5) The SNR being used for estimating the radial surface current is above 5-10dB [12].

If there are no ships, ionosphere interference and strong current shear near the Bragg peak, the above characteristics can be used for detecting Bragg peaks with a good performance.

If there are no ships, ionosphere interference and strong current shear near the Bragg peak, the above characteristics can be used for detecting Bragg peaks with a good performance.

3.2   Multi-scale Filter and Image Feature Extraction

In Amplitude-Range-Doppler (ARD) spectrum of HFSWR (see Figure2), first-order sea echoes in the gray image of RD spectrum is presented as two dominant, symmetrical and smooth curves. It results from Bragg resonance and symmetry effect to the sea surface by the ocean current. The offset of the first-order sea echo varies with the range bins especially in the region far from the coast. Let's take the real data shown in Figure2 as an example. The relative position offset of Bragg peak between the measurement and the theoretical value varies from -0.026Hz to 0.026 Hz. If searching range centering at the theoretical value is $[-\Delta_{max}, \Delta_{max}]$ (where Δ_{max} is the velocity offset causing by the maximal radial ocean current, and $\Delta_{max}=0.026$Hz in that example), it will lead to too much candidate peaks that results in error detection or false alarms. It's obvious that the two Bragg lines along the range are presented as ridges in the gray image of RD spectrum. Thus a certain image processing method is proposed to help extract Bragg peaks in the rang-Doppler plane.

First of all, multi-scale filter is used for filtering the high frequency noise in ARD map. Given any image $f : R^2 \times \to R$, its scale-space representation $L : R^2 \times R_+ \to R$ is defined by [17]

$$L(\cdot;t) = g(\cdot;t) * f \tag{3}$$

Where * denotes convolution, $g : R^2 \times R_+ \to R$ denotes the Gaussian kernel given by

$$g(x, y; t) = \frac{1}{2\pi t} e^{-(x^2+y^2)/(2t)} \tag{4}$$

and t is the scale parameter, (x, y) denotes the Cartesian coordinates of a certain point in the 2-D image. From this representation, scale-space derivatives are then defined by

$$L_{x^\alpha y^\beta}(\cdot;t) = \partial_{x^\alpha y^\beta} L(\cdot;t) = g_{x^\alpha y^\beta}(\cdot;t) * f \tag{5}$$

Here (α, β) is the order of differentiation. It's easy to find that filtering results vary from different t.

Then use a ridge detection method for extracting Bragg peaks from filtered ARD image. We can give a relative wider range for ridge detection according to the maximal offset by ocean current in radar detection area. And calculate the 1st and the 2nd order differentiation $L_{x^1 y^0}(v, r; t)$ and $L_{x^2 y^0}(v, r; t)$ at (v, r) along the Doppler dimension (where v is the Doppler bin number and r is the range bin number). If

$$\begin{cases} L_{v^1 r^0}(v, r; t) L_{v^1 r^0}(v, r+1; t) < 0 \\ L_{v^2 r^0}(v, r; t) < 0 \end{cases} \quad \text{or}$$

$$\begin{cases} L_{v^1 r^0}(v, r; t) L_{v^1 r^0}(v, r-1; t) < 0 \\ L_{v^2 r^0}(v, r; t) < 0 \end{cases} \tag{6}$$

The point (v, r) is defined as a ridge. The above processing results sometimes involve both Bragg peaks and other interference (such as ionosphere, ships, etc.). Because the interference is relative positional independent in RD map, we can use one of morphologic processing methods, called erosion [18], for filtering them.

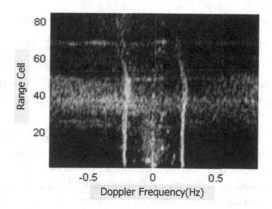

Fig. 2. ARD spectrum

Figure3 is the processing result which takes Figure2 as the original input data. Let $t=22$. We can summarize the characteristics of Bragg peaks in strong current shear environment:

1) In range bin 70-80 being far from the coast, because those positive Bragg peaks are smeared by the effect of surface wave attenuation and ionosphere interference.
2) The positions of Bragg peaks deviate from the theoretical in strong current shear environment. And such bias shows the irregular trend along the range dimension in RD map.

3) Splitting peaks appear (from No.37-70 range cells) in high frequency as a result of the effect of strong current shear.

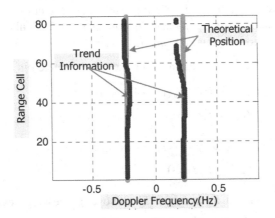

Fig. 3. Trend of Bragg peaks

3.3   Global Rules for Bragg Peak Extraction

Based on the former results, rules for Bragg peak extraction is given as

1) Spectral characteristic criterion Set detection band $[v_0 - \Delta_{max}, v_0 + \Delta_{max}]$ in Doppler region at (v_0, r_i). Select local peaks in the detection band as candidate Bragg peaks. The number of reference cells can be 2-4. The initial screening position (v_0, r_i) is determined by the trend information of Bragg peaks that has been got in Section 2.2.

2) Symmetry criterion Compare the positions of positive with negative candidate peaks at a same range bin, and pick up the ones that offset symmetrically.

3) Continuous and smooth criterion As the simplest smooth curve, cubic spline is used for getting secondary indicative information of Bragg peaks from candidate peaks. In this way, continuous and smooth indicative information can be got in the range direction.

4) SNR criterion Use the SNR estimation method which is able to eliminate interference, clutters, etc. in reference cells. Then reject the target of which SNR is less than 6dB.

3.4   Global Rules for Bragg Peak Extraction Splitting Bragg Peak

In middle Doppler resolution (integrating time is about 100-200s), as well-known phenomena for HFSWR, Bragg peak splitting is resulted from a transient change of a surface current field within a target cell. In this paper a Bragg peak with bigger amplitude in any side of zero Doppler is called primary peak; a smaller one near the primary peak is called splitting peak which still satisfies most characteristics in

Section 2.1. The amplitude difference between primary peak and splitting peak at the same side of zero Doppler in the same range bin (usually 0-20dB) varies with the relative position between the current shear and the target cell. We also found that the smaller the SNR of splitting peak is, the more seriously the detection performance is affected by interference. In this paper, it's called blurry splitting Bragg peaks, which are presented as visible on the positive/negative side but invisible on the other side of zero Doppler(see Figure1(b)).

Basing on the observation and mechanism of splitting Bragg peaks, detection rules are given as

1) *Second largest criterion*

In local area Splitting Bragg peak is dominant in local area in Doppler region except for the primary peak.

2) *Offset range prediction criterion*

The distance between a primary peak a the splitting peak should be no more than Δ'_{max} (where Δ'_{max} is the maximal Doppler offset of Bragg peaks causing by the stable/transient current). Thus the searching range for splitting Bragg peaks is $[f_m - \Delta'_{max}, f_m + \Delta'_{max}]$, where f_m is the Doppler position of the primary peak.

3) *Symmetry criterion*

Because current shear acts on both sides of Bragg peaks symmetrically, the offset directions of the positive/negative splitting Bragg peaks in the same range bin are same. Considering resolution, system error, etc., let one Doppler cell be the tolerable error in middle Doppler resolution.

4) *Amplitude difference criterion*

The amplitude difference between primary peak and splitting peak at the same side of zero Doppler in the same range bin, usually 0-20dB. If the difference exceeds this range, the corresponding targets will be determined as interference.

5) *Blurry splitting Bragg peak identify criterion*

Interference sometimes makes a splitting peak be visible on only one side of zero Doppler. In this case, it's necessary for us to study the spectrum around the primary peak on the invisible side. If the spectral structure is presented as characteristics interfered by adjacent cells, it can be determined as blurry splitting Bragg peak. The broadening degree of the primary peak can help to identify the phenomena.

6) *SNR criterion*

Supporting by the SNR estimation algorithm with wild value and identified clutter elimination, a splitting peak should satisfy a specified SNR (for example, 5-10dB). Peaks with too lower SNR are meaningless for current estimation and surface target detection as well.

3.5   Flow Chart of the Algorithm

A simplified detection algorithm flow chart of Bragg peak is shown in Figure4 based on Section 3.1-3.4. Each node in the figure corresponds to the above-mentioned algorithms or rules. Main difference between widely used methods and the proposed method is marked with dashed frames. On the one hand, the ridge detection algorithm followed by multi-scale filtering gives trend information of Bragg peak in RD map; on the other hand, the splitting Bragg peak detection method provides more accurate and precise sea state information and helps decrease false alarms and missing alarms for sea surface moving target detection.

It must be noted that, being affected by strong clutters and noise, the trend information sometimes cannot locate the position of Bragg peaks accurately. In addition, splitting peaks increase the emergence risk of the false alarm. Thus "blind area" and "global characteristic confirmation" blocks are added to the flow chart. The former aims at investigating the area without indicative trend information and confirm the candidate Bragg peak by symmetry. The latter is aided by both symmetry and smooth criterion to control the false alarm rising from splitting peaks detection, high order sea clutter and ships. Other processes in the algorithm flow diagram can also help get better performances.

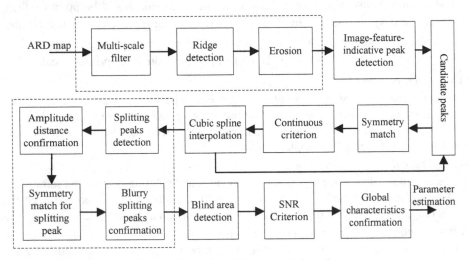

Fig. 4. Flow chart of Bragg peak detection

4   Experiments and Result Analysis

To verify the advantage of the proposed algorithm, three methods have been operated on the same real data from HFSWR. The carrier frequency is 4.9MHz, and the integrated period of Doppler process is 120s. Considering the resolution of HFSWR and the maximal offset by radial current in the detected sea area, select 5 positive/negative Doppler cells as searching area to select candidate Bragg peaks. The positions of the Bragg peaks shown in Figure5 are estimated by the methods in literature [19] after detection.

Figure5 shows the results of the experiments in strong current environment. Method 1 uses criterion 1 in Section 3.3 and local maximal rule to select the maximal

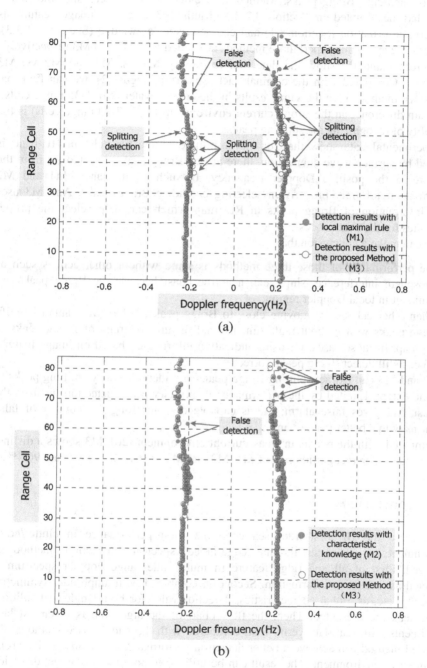

Fig. 5. Results of detection of Bragg peaks: (a) M1 vs. M3, (b) M2 vs. M3

peak as candidate Bragg peaks. Method 2 is aided with characteristic knowledge which has been noted in Section 3.2-3.3. Method 3 uses the image feature as indicative information (Section 3.1) and characteristic knowledge (Section 3.2-3.3). For convenience in this paper, those methods are called M1, M2 and M3 respectively.

Figure5(a) and (b) show the detection results by M1 vs. M3 and M2 vs. M3 separately. Compared with the original ARD spectrum (Figure 2), we can find that these three methods give the same results in the coastal water (No. 1-35 range cells). The main difference in the strong current environment (No. 37-70 range cells) is the capability of recognizing the splitting peaks.

Experimental data show that for the amplitude of the sea echo in HF band is affected by surface wave attenuation, there are no Bragg peaks detected far from the seashore in the positive Doppler frequency. In such circumstance, M1 and M2 perform their arbitrary property in selecting candidate Bragg peaks. And M3 uses trend information of Bragg peaks in RD map which can help select the proper candidates for the post-process.

We can make a conclusion that

1) The performance of those three methods is same without other echoes such as ionosphere interference, ships, etc. near the coast because the Bragg peaks are dominant in local Doppler region.
2) When other echoes are moving close to Bragg peaks, M1 or M2 cannot identify Bragg peaks well without multi-dimensional features or trend of Bragg peaks in RD map. In those cases, for using indicative information based on image feature, M3 can still detect Bragg peaks correctly.
3) M2 and M3 can extract splitting Bragg peaks and identify blurry splitting peaks to some extent. Limited by the performance of primary peaks detection far from the coast, M2 gives false alarm; M3 is capable of controlling the number of false alarms with a better performance.
4) Compared with the results in weak current environment [20], M3 shows a distinct advantage. The recognition rate of M1, M3 and M3 are 61.9%, 79.8% and 96.4%.

5   Conclusions

To increase the HF first-order sea echo detection performance in clutter/noise environment, a characteristic-knowledge-aided spectrum detection method is proposed. First of all, the ridge feature in multi-scale range-Doppler spectrum is extracted as indicative information. Secondly, combined with amplitude, symmetry, continuity, etc. as global characteristics, detection rules for both single and splitting Bragg peak are presented. Then, the flow chart of the algorithm is given. At last, experiments with real data verify that, compared with the widely used methods, the proposed method can achieve a better detection performance especially in the strong current shear environment. The result can be utilized in both moving target detection and sea state remote sensing.

Acknowledgment. The project is supported by the National Natural Science Foundation of China (Grant No. 61102158), the State Key Program of the National Natural Science Foundation of China (Grant No. 61132005), General Financial Grant from the China Postdoctoral Science Foundation (Grant No. 2011M500667) and the Fundamental Research Funds for the Central Universities (Grant No. HIT.NSRIF.2012022).

References

1. Wyatt, L.R., Green, J.J., Middleditch, A., et al.: Operational Wave, Current, and Wind Measurements With the Pisces HF Radar. IEEE Journal of Oceanic Engineering 31(4), 819–834 (2006)
2. Sevgi, L., Ponsford, A., Chan, H.C.: An Integrated Maritime Surveillance System Based on High-Frequency Surface-Wave Radars, Part 1: Theoretical Background and Numerical Simulations. IEEE Antennas and Propagation Magazine 43(4), 28–43 (2001)
3. Hickey, K.J., Gill, E.W., Helbig, J.A., et al.: Measurement of ocean surface currents using a long-range, high-frequency ground wave radar. IEEE Journal of Oceanic Engineering 19(4), 549–554 (1994)
4. Barrick, D.E.: Accuracy of parameter extraction from sample-averaged sea-echo Doppler spectra. IEEE Transactions on Antennas and Propagation 28(1), 1–11 (1980)
5. Shang, S., Zhang, N., Li, Y.: Research of Ionospheric Clutter Statistical Properties in HFSWR. Chinese Journal of Radio Science 26(3), 521–527 (2011)
6. Wyatt, L.R., Green, J.J., Middleditch, A.: Wave, Current and Wind Monitoring using HF Radar. In: Proc. of the IEEE/OES Eighth Working Conference on Current Measurement Technology, pp. 53–57. IEEE Press, New York (2005)
7. Khan, R., Power, D., Walsh, J.: Ocean Clutter Suppression for An HF Ground Wave Radar. In: IEEE 1997 Canadian Conference on Electrical and Computer Engineering, pp. 512–515. IEEE Press, New York (1997)
8. Wang, J., Lynn, R.K.: Improvement of high frequency ocean surveillance radar using subspace methods based on sea clutter suppression. In: Sensor Array and Multichannel Signal Processing Workshop Proceedings, pp. 557–560. IEEE Press, New York (2002)
9. Xing-Bin, G., Cheng-Ge, Z., Ye-Shu, Y.: Sea-Clutter-Canceling for HF Ground-Wave Shipborne OTH Radar. Dian Zi Xue Bao 28(3), 5–8 (2000)
10. Ji, Z., Meng, X., Zhou, H.: Analysis of Sea Clutters in HF Ground Wave Over-the-Horizon Radar. System Engineering and Electronics 22(5), 12–16 (2000)
11. Tong, J., Wen, B., Wang, S.: Ship Target Detection in Strong Sea Clutter Background. Journal of Wuhan University (Natural and Science Edition) 51(3), 370–374 (2005)
12. Qiang, Y.: Research of Detector in High Frequency Ground Wave Radar, Harbin Institute of Technology (August 2002)
13. Parkinson Murray, L.: Observations of the broadening and coherence of MF lower HF surface-radar ocean echoes. IEEE Journal of Oceanic Engineering 2(2), 347–363 (1997)
14. Heron, M.L., Gill, E.W., Prytz, A.: An Investigation of Double-peaked HF Radar Spectra via A Convolution/De-convolution Algorithm. In: OCEANS 2008, pp. 1–5. IEEE Press, New York (2008)
15. Crombie, D.D.: Doppler Spectrum of Sea Echo at 13. 56MHz. Nature 175, 681–682 (1955)
16. Barrick, D.E., Headrick, J.M., Bogle, R.W., et al.: Sea Backscatter at HF: Interpretation and Utilization of the Echo. Proceedings of the IEEE 62(6), 673–680 (1974)

17. Lindeberg, T.: Edge Detection and Ridge Detection with Automatic Scale Selection. International Journal of Computer Vision 30(2), 107–153 (1998)
18. Yujin, Z.: Image Engineering (II): Image Analysis, 2nd edn., pp. 369–376. Tsinghua University Press, Beijing (2005)
19. Yang, L., Ning, Z., Qiang, Y.: A Fast, Accurate Spectral Peak Location Estimator. Journal of Harbin Institute of Technology 40(S1), 160–163 (2008)
20. Yang, L., Ning, Z., Qiang, Y.: Characteristic-Knowledge-Aided Spectral Detection of High Frequency First-Order Sea Echo. Journal of Systems Engineering and Electronics 20(4), 718–725 (2009)

Object Recognition Using Radon Transform-Based RST Parameter Estimation

Nafaa Nacereddine[1], Salvatore Tabbone[2], and Djemel Ziou[3]

[1] DTSI, Centre de Recherche en Soudage et Controle, 16002 Algiers, Algeria
nafaa.nacereddine@enp.edu.dz
[2] Université Nancy 2-Loria, BP 239, 54506 Vandoeuvre-lès-Nancy, France
tabbone@loria.fr
[3] Dépt. d'informatique, Univ. de Sherbrooke, Qc., Canada J1K 2R1
djemel.ziou@usherbrooke.ca

Abstract. In this paper, we propose a practical parameter recovering approach, for similarity geometric transformations using only the Radon transform and its extended version on $[0, 2\pi]$. The derived objective function is exploited as a similarity measure to perform an object recognition system. Comparison results with common and powerful shape descriptors testify the effectiveness of the proposed method in recognizing binary images, RST transformed, distorted, occluded or noised.

Keywords: RST parameters, Radon transform, object recognition.

1 Introduction

The shape is an important visual feature for object description, unavoidable in object recognition and image retrieval tasks. Object description techniques are extensively studied in literature (e.g. [1]) and broadly divided in two groups: contour-based and region-based shape descriptors. Within this last category, an increasing and recent interest is devoted to shape descriptors using the Radon transform (e.g. [2],[3],[4],[5]), because of its richness in information. The Radon transform (RadTr), since its introduction in the beginning of the last century, has long been studied and applied by researchers in great number of applications, especially in the biomedical imaging field, where the obtained raw data are often sinograms. By using the Radon transform properties regarding usual geometric transformations of rotation, scaling and translation (RST), it is question to recover the parameters of such transformations, by handling only the image projections assuming no access to the spatial domain of image. In [6], the authors present a method for the transformation parameter recovering of a binary object subjected to reflection, scaling, translation and rotation using only the Radon projections. Nevertheless, the objective function used for the computation of the rotation angle is not valid for any angle of rotation belonging to the range $[0, 2\pi]$, as it will be shown in Sect. 3. In [7], the authors use the results obtained in [6] but develop a novel method for parameter decoupling and an improved phase correlation method for accurate shift estimation, resulting in a

J. Blanc-Talon et al. (Eds.): ACIVS 2012, LNCS 7517, pp. 515–526, 2012.

fast matching algorithm. However, the rotation angle estimation is slightly less accurate compared to [6]. In this paper, in Sect. 4., we develop a step-by-step method with the aim to estimate the RST transform parameters brought into play between to unknown images, where we construct a 2π-based Radon transform to deal with the problem of rotation by any angle comprising in $[0, 2\pi]$. Results of this part are given in Sect. 5.1. Moreover, at Sect. 5.2., an object recognition system is proposed, using the Radon-based paradigm developed in the previous section.

2   Object Subjected to RST Transformations

Assume f an image in $x - y$ plane, subjected to a sequence of geometric transformations of rotation R_{ϕ_0}, scaling S_α and translation T_{x_0, y_0}, where ϕ_0 (in $[0, 2\pi]$), α (in $\mathbb{R}_+$) and (x_0, y_0) (in $\mathbb{R}^2$) are, respectively, the rotation angle, the scaling factor and the translation vector components. The result is a transformed image, noted g with coordinates x', y', as shown in Fig. 1. This composition of transformations can be formulated as

$$\begin{cases} x' = \alpha(\cos\phi_0 x - \sin\phi_0 y) + x_0 \\ y' = \alpha(\sin\phi_0 x + \cos\phi_0 y) + y_0 \end{cases} \tag{1}$$

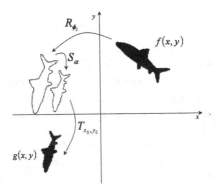

Fig. 1. A binary image rotated, scaled and translated

3   Radon Transform and Its Properties

Let L be a straight line in the $x - y$ plane and ds be an increment of length along L, the Radon transform [8] of a real valued function f, denoted $f^\vee$, is defined by its integral as

$$f^\vee(p, \phi) = \int_L f(x, y) ds \tag{2}$$

$f^{\vee}(p, \phi)$ is then determined by integration of all lines $L_{p,\phi}$, in the $x - y$ plane, $p \in \mathbb{R}, \phi \in [0, \pi]$. From Fig. 2, the equation of L is written as $p = x \cos \phi + y \sin \phi$. If we rotate the coordinate system by an angle ϕ, and label the new axes p and s, we obtain $x = p \cos \phi - s \sin \phi$, $y = p \sin \phi + s \cos \phi$. Then, $f^{\vee}$ is defined by

$$f^{\vee}(p, \phi) = \int_{-\infty}^{\infty} f(p \cos \phi - s \sin \phi, p \sin \phi + s \cos \phi)ds \qquad (3)$$

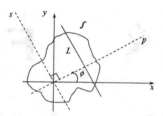

Fig. 2. Definition of the Radon transform

The Radon transform has several useful properties [8]. We give here those that are relevant for our application :

- *Periodicity:* $f^{\vee}(p, \phi) = f^{\vee}(p, \phi \pm 2k\pi)$, $k \in \mathbb{Z}$
- *Symmetry:* $f^{\vee}(p, \phi) = f^{\vee}(-p, \phi \pm (2k + 1)\pi)$, $k \in \mathbb{Z}$
- *Translation by a vector* $\boldsymbol{u} = (x_0, y_0)$: Let $g = T_{\boldsymbol{u}}(f)$ then $g^{\vee}(p, \phi) = f^{\vee}(p - x_0 \cos \phi - y_0 \sin \phi, \phi)$
- *Rotation by an angle* ϕ_0: Let $g = R_{\phi_0}(f)$ then $g^{\vee}(p, \phi) = f^{\vee}(p, \phi - \phi_0)$
- *Scaling by a factor* α ($\alpha > 0$): Let $g = S_{\alpha}(f)$ then $g^{\vee}(p, \phi) = \alpha f^{\vee}(p/\alpha, \phi)$

Before going any further, let us examine in details the rotation properties where modifications will be brought to make the algorithm proposed in the next section efficient in the object recognition task.

Let be f_r the function representing the rotated object by an angle ϕ_0 ($\phi_0 \in [-\pi, \pi]$), i.e. for any (x, y) belonging to $\mathbb{R}^2$,

$$f_r(x, y) = f(\cos \phi_0 x - \sin \phi_0 y, \sin \phi_0 x + \cos \phi_0 y) \qquad (4)$$

In the rest of this section, we assume that the object is centered, i.e. the object is translated so that its centroid coincides with the $x - y$ plan origin O. This assumption is taken to avoid the translation effect introduced by the rotation, since only the rotation property, properly named, will be examined. It can be shown that the rotation property of the Radon transform displayed on $[0, \pi]$ obeys to the following equations
for $\phi_0 \in [-\pi, 0]$

$$f_r^{\vee}(p, \phi) = \begin{cases} f^{\vee}(-p, \phi - \phi_0 - \pi) & \text{if} \quad \phi \geq \phi_0 + \pi \\ f^{\vee}(p, \phi - \phi_0) & \text{if} \quad \phi \leq \phi_0 + \pi \end{cases} \qquad (5)$$

for $\phi_0 \in [0, \pi]$

$$f_r^\vee(p, \phi) = \begin{cases} f^\vee(-p, \phi - \phi_0 + \pi) & \text{if} \quad \phi \leq \phi_0 \\ f^\vee(p, \phi - \phi_0) & \text{if} \quad \phi \geq \phi_0 \end{cases} \tag{6}$$

In Fig. 3, an example explaining the above equations is given. Then, as it can be seen, the rotation property of the Radon transform often given in the literature $(f_r^\vee(p, \phi) = f^\vee(p, \phi - \phi_0))$ is only valid if $\phi_0 \leq \phi \leq \phi_0 + \pi$.

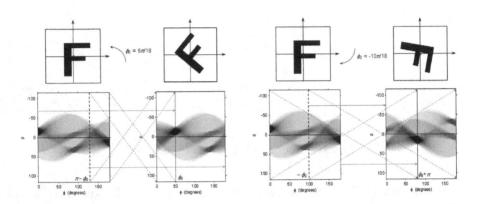

Fig. 3. Rotation property of Radon transform defined on π: if $\phi_0 \in [-\pi, 0]$ then $f_r^\vee(p, 0 : \phi_0 + \pi) = f^\vee(p, -\phi_0 : \pi)$ and $f_r^\vee(p, \phi_0 + \pi : \pi) = f^\vee(-p, 0 : -\phi_0)$; however, if $\phi_0 \in [0, \pi]$ then $f_r^\vee(p, 0 : \phi_0) = f^\vee(-p, \pi - \phi_0 : \pi)$ and $f_r^\vee(p, \phi_0 : \pi) = f^\vee(p, 0 : \pi - \phi_0)$

Besides its circular shifting in the variable ϕ, the complete rotation property of Radon transform will be related to the symmetry property of this latter. For this reason, an extended version of Radon transform (see Fig. 4) is proposed in (7) which is derived from the above equations so that, the rotation property of the new version of Radon transform will be simply and globally defined of any object rotation angle belonging to $[0, 2\pi]$

$$f_{2\pi}^\vee(p, \phi) = \begin{cases} f^\vee(p, \phi) & \text{if} \quad \phi \in [0, \pi] \\ f^\vee(-p, \phi) & \text{if} \quad \phi \in]\pi, 2\pi] \end{cases} \tag{7}$$

and the 2π-based Radon transform of the rotated object is expressed as

$$f_{r2\pi}^\vee(p, \phi) = \begin{cases} f_{2\pi}^\vee(p, \phi - \phi_0) & \text{if} \quad \phi \geq \phi_0 \\ f_{2\pi}^\vee(p, \phi - \phi_0 + 2\pi) & \text{if} \quad \phi \leq \phi_0 \end{cases} \tag{8}$$

which can be written as $f_{r2\pi}^\vee(p, \phi) = f_{2\pi}^\vee(p, \phi - \phi_0)$, since Radon transform is 2π periodic. As shown in Fig. 4, the rotation is transformed in circular shifting on $[0 \ 2\pi]$. Consequently, the 2π-based Radon transform will be employed in the next section in the computation of the objective function leading to the estimation of the rotation angle between two compared images via their sinograms. According to the Radon transform definition and the symmetry property, the part of transform below to zero can be omitted.

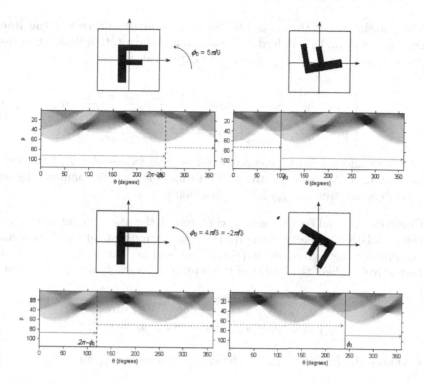

Fig. 4. Rotation property of RadTr represented on 2π: A rotation of the image by an angle ϕ_0 implies a shifting of the 2π-based Radon transform of ϕ_0 modulo 2π

4   Recover RST Parameters Using Radon Transform

To be useful, a shape recognition framework should allow explicit invariance under RST operations. To measure the similarity between the Radon matrix of two shapes, it is necessary to know the underlying geometric transformations from one shape into the other. We can see from the Radon transform properties that if a given shape is RST transformed, it will be difficult to recover all the RST parameters using only the quoted transform. To circumvent this situation, we propose a step-by-step RST parameter recovering, handling only the source and target object Radon projections.

(a) **Input data**: Source image f and target image g.

(b) **Output**: Transform parameters α, $u(x_0, y_0)$, ϕ_0^* and similarity measure $F(\phi_0^*)$.

(c) Compute the RadTrs $f^\vee$ and $g^\vee$. Deduce the scaling parameter α as in [6]

$$\alpha = \left| \frac{\int_{-\infty}^{+\infty} g^\vee(p, \phi) dp}{\int_{-\infty}^{+\infty} f^\vee(p, \phi) dp} \right|^{1/2} \tag{9}$$

for any angle, ϕ.

(d) The coordinates of the centroids can be computed in terms of the Radon transforms $f^\vee$ and $g^\vee$. Indeed, by using (3) and the rotation Radon transform property for $\phi_0 = \pi/2$, (x_f, y_f) can be expressed, for any ϕ, by

$$
\begin{cases}
x_f = \dfrac{\int_{-\infty}^{+\infty} p f^\vee(p,\phi)dp}{\int_{-\infty}^{+\infty} f^\vee(p,\phi)dp} \cos\phi - \dfrac{\int_{-\infty}^{+\infty} p f^\vee(p,\phi+\pi/2)dp}{\int_{-\infty}^{+\infty} f^\vee(p,\phi)dp} \sin\phi \\
y_f = \dfrac{\int_{-\infty}^{+\infty} p f^\vee(p,\phi)dp}{\int_{-\infty}^{+\infty} f^\vee(p,\phi)dp} \sin\phi + \dfrac{\int_{-\infty}^{+\infty} p f^\vee(p,\phi+\pi/2)dp}{\int_{-\infty}^{+\infty} f^\vee(p,\phi)dp} \cos\phi
\end{cases}
\tag{10}
$$

where x_f and y_f can be computed for several values of ϕ and the results are averaged. Analogously, the above formula is used to compute the mass center coordinates (x_g, y_g) for the function g.

(e) Compute the RadTrs of f and g, centered at the axes system origin, using the translation property of the RadTr. The components of the displacement vectors are then given by $\mathbf{u}_f(-x_f, -y_f)$ and $\mathbf{u}_g(-x_g, -y_g)$ for f and g, respectively. Then, the RadTr of the centered images f_c and g_c are given by:

$$
\begin{cases}
f_c^\vee(p,\phi) = f^\vee(p + x_f \cos\phi + y_f \sin\phi, \phi) \\
g_c^\vee(p,\phi) = g^\vee(p + x_g \cos\phi + y_g \sin\phi, \phi)
\end{cases}
\tag{11}
$$

(f) Compute the RadTr on 2π for the centered images $f_{c2\pi}^\vee$ and $g_{c2\pi}^\vee$ using (7).

(g) Compute $f_{c2\pi}^\vee$ normalized in size to $g_{c2\pi}^\vee$

$$
f_{c2\pi}^{\vee s}(p,\phi) = \alpha f_{c2\pi}^\vee\left(\frac{p}{\alpha}, \phi\right)
\tag{12}
$$

(h) Compute the optimal rotation angle ϕ_0^* (in $[0, 2\pi]$) given by the minimal value of the following objective function

$$
F(\phi_0) = \int_0^{2\pi} \int_{-\infty}^{\infty} |g_{c2\pi}^\vee(p,\phi) - f_{c2\pi}^{\vee s}(p, \phi - \phi_0)| \, dp \, d\phi
\tag{13}
$$

and then, $\phi_0^* = \arg\min_{\phi_0} F$.

(i) Deduce from (1) the coordinates of the translation vector $\mathbf{u}(x_0, y_0)$

$$
\begin{cases}
x_0 = x_g - \alpha \cos\phi_0^* x_f + \alpha \sin\phi_0^* y_f \\
y_0 = y_g - \alpha \sin\phi_0^* x_f - \alpha \cos\phi_0^* y_f
\end{cases}
\tag{14}
$$

5 Experiments

The first experiment will consist in the implementation of the proposed algorithm to recover the parameters of RST operation sequence applied on a real binary image. The second experiment will be conducted using such algorithm, for an object recognition purpose.

5.1 RST Parameters Recovering

The implementation of the proposed algorithm on the 200×200 fish image of Fig. 1 can be summarized in Fig. 5 where real RST transform parameters are: $\phi_0 = 5\pi/9$, $\alpha = 0.7$, $u(x_0, y_0) = (-10, -30)$, and the estimated ones are: $\hat{\phi}_0 = 5\pi/9$, $\hat{\alpha} = 0.701$, $\hat{u}(x_0, y_0) = (-10.09, -29.98)$. In Table 1, we compare the proposed algorithm with that of [7] on recognizing the Shepp-Logan head phantom test image [9] (Fig. 6). The symbol s in [7] represents $1/\alpha$ in this paper.

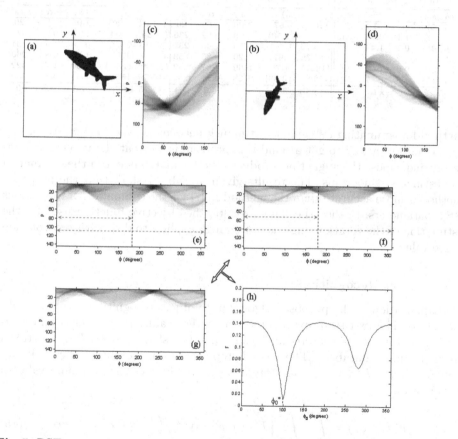

Fig. 5. RST parameter compuation using Radon transform. (a) Original fish image f. (b) The RST transformed image g with $\phi_0 = 5\pi/9$, $\alpha = 0.7$, $u(-10, -30)$. (c) and (d) f and g RTs, resp. (e),(f) and (g) 2π-based RadTr of f centered, g centered and f centered and scaled, resp. (h) Objective function F where $\phi_0^* = 100° \sim 5\pi/9$.

Contrary to the proposed method, where the rotation angle estimate $\hat{\phi}_0$ (in $[0, 2\pi]$) can be obtained directly by (13), we note that for the work in [7], the

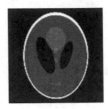

Fig. 6. Shepp-Logan head phantom test image of size 128×128

Table 1. Performance comparison between the algorithm in [7] and the proposed algorithm

Initial parameters				Algorithm in [7]				Proposed algorithm			
(x_0, y_0)	s	α	ϕ_0	$(\hat{x}_0, \hat{y}_0)$	$\hat{s}$	$\hat{\alpha}$	$\hat{\phi}_0$	$(\hat{x}_0, \hat{y}_0)$	$\hat{s}$	$\hat{\alpha}$	$\hat{\phi}_0$
(11 -5)	1	1	20	(10.32 -4.87)	1.00	1	20	(11.04 -4.99)	1.00	1	20
(-3 -12)	1.1	0.91	236	(-2.61 -11.50)	1.09	0.92	236	(-3.04 -12.04)	1.10	0.91	236
(-6 -2)	0.7	1.43	231	(-5.79 -1.76)	0.70	1.43	231	(-6.13 -2.12)	0.70	1.43	231
(-1 11)	1.2	0.83	260	(-0.75 11.67)	1.20	0.83	259	(-1.67 11.19)	1.20	0.83	260
(13 -12)	0.6	1.67	322	(12.82 -11.75)	0.60	1.67	322	(12.90 -11.74)	0.60	1.67	322
(-11 -15)	1.3	0.77	236	(-10.83 -13.89)	1.28	0.78	235	(-10.79 -15.36)	1.30	0.77	236
Mean error ($\times 10^{-3}$)				(3.13 4.88)	4.1	4.0	8.1	(1.15 1.63)	0.3	0.6	0

method for estimating ϕ_0 cannot distinguish between ϕ_0 and $\phi_0 + \pi$. According to the author, a way to get around this problem is to treat the two cases separately and choose the angle that produce a better match between the original an the estimated sinograms. The results given in Table 1 show that the proposed method is more accurate than the method in [7] for the estimation of the various RST parameters. In the other hand, for [6], the objective function used for the estimation of the rotation angle is not enough explicit to deal with any rotation angle value.

5.2   Object Recognition

The application of the proposed algorithm to object recognition is divided into two steps. The first step involves recovering the scaling parameter α and computing RadTrs of the centered images for any two shape images I and J, taken from the image database. The second step consists in measuring the similarity between I and J by computing the distance which gives the minimum value of F versus ϕ_0.

$$F(I, J, \phi_0) = \int_0^{2\pi} \int_0^{\infty} \left| J_{c2\pi}^{\vee}(p, \phi) - \alpha I_{c2\pi}^{\vee} \left(\frac{p}{\alpha}, \phi - \phi_0 \right) \right| dp \, d\phi \qquad (15)$$

and then,

$$dist(I, J) = \min_{\phi_0} F(I, J, \phi_0) \qquad (16)$$

In order to demonstrate the effectiveness of the proposed descriptor, named RST-$\Re$, in object recognition, two experiments have been carried out on two binary image databases. Firstly, RST-$\Re$ is implemented and compared with other descriptors on Shapes99 database [10] (Fig. 7), which is composed of 99 shapes, grouped in 9 categories with 11 shapes per category, and which is used to evaluate its robustness to occlusion, variations in form, missing parts and elastic deformation. Moreover, some samples are scaled and rotated. Secondly, the robustness to noise of the proposed descriptor is tested on the a set of datasets generated from the UMD Logo dataset [11] by adding noise of different levels to its images (Fig. 8). Each of these six logo datasets has 80 images of 10 categories, each of them contains 8 images generated by randomly scaling, rotating, translating the corresponding logo image. The "salt & peeper" noise density, noted d, consists in the percentage of the corrupted pixel in the image. This noise is added to each image with different densities ranging from 0 (noiseless image) to 0.20 with an increment of 0.04. For both shape image databases, RST-$\Re$ is compared to five region-based shape descriptors: Hu moments [12], Zernike moments [13], Generic Fourier Descriptor (GFD) [14], Radon Composite Features (RCF) [4] and Wavelet $\Phi\Re$-signature (W$\Phi\Re$) [5]. The criterion used for comparison among descriptors is the precision-recall curve used in the information retrieval context. In their simplest definition, precision (Pr) is the proportion of retrieved images that are relevant, and recall (Re) is the proportion of relevant images that are retrieved. To compute the precision-recall curve for each database, in the experiment, each of the images in the database is used as a query to which all the images in the database are compared with. The comparison is carried out using the similarity measure for RST-$\Re$ given by (16); whereas, for the other descriptors and for any two shape images I and J, the similarity measure is defined, as the ℓ_1-norm distance

$$dist(I, J) = \|D(I) - D(J)\|_1 \tag{17}$$

where D is the shape descriptor to which RST-$\Re$ is compared with.

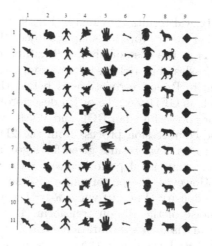

Fig. 7. Images of database "Shapes99"

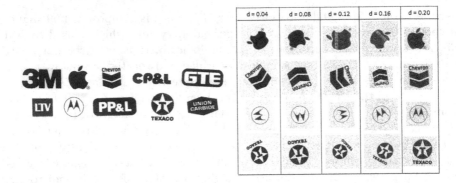

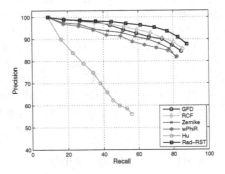

Fig. 8. (Left) Ten logo images from the UMD Logo database (noise-free images representing the first dataset). (Right) Sample of noisy images generated with d = 0.04, 0.08, 0.12, 0.16, 0.20 corresponding to the five noisy datasets.

Fig. 9. $Pr - Re$ curves of comparison descriptors on the "Shapes99" database

According to the retrieval results provided in Fig. 9, it appears that $\Re$-RST outperforms all the other descriptors for shapes subjected to distortion, occlusion and deformation as in the case of Shapes99 database. Indeed, the Radon transform is not only lossless but rich in information, the reason for which $\Re$-RST exploiting the entire Radon projections is better than descriptors using spatial information such as GFD, Zernike or Hu descriptors. Moreover, the proposed descriptor is more powerful than RCF and W$\Phi\Re$ which may have loss of information due to the compression process from the 2D Radon image to 1D signatures. According to retrieval results given for logo datasets in Fig. 10, we note that all descriptors have ideal performance for the noiseless dataset, i.e. d=0 (top-left graph). However, the performance of other descriptors decreases proportionally to noise density (Fig. 10) while $\Re$-RST performs well due to robustness to additive noise of the Radon transform (Refer to [15] for detailed proof). Another important issue is computational complexity. The major part of computational time of $\Re$-RST is spent in the minimization of the similarity measure which may be high; however, it is largely dependent on how big the image

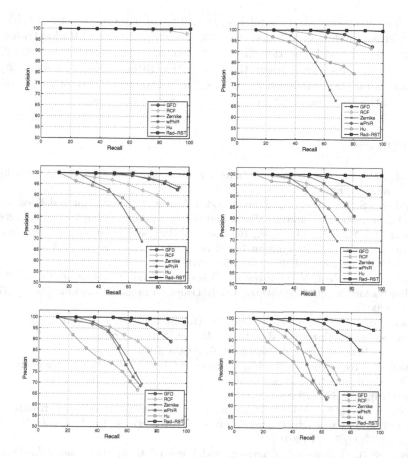

Fig. 10. $Pr - Re$ curves of comparison descriptors on the six logo datasets. Noise densities vary from d = 0 to d = 0.20 with an increment of 0.04 for the six figures from left to right and from top to bottom.

Table 2. Average running time for each descriptor and similarity measure computation for a single pair of shape images in Shapes99 database

	GFD	RCF	Zernike	W$\varPhi\Re$	Hu	$\Re$-RST
Runtime (sec.)	0.87	0.32	1.97	0.85	0.15	3.15

is. As far as concern to computational cost, the observed average running time (including descriptor and similarity measure computation times) for all methods and for one pair of images is provided in Table 2.

6 Conclusion

In this paper, we have developed a method of finding RST parameters from Radon projections. This is of particular interest in domains where only image projections are provided, as in medical or industrial computed tomography. We have described in details and motivated the extended version of Radon transform on $[0, 2\pi]$ to deal with rotation in $[-\pi, \pi]$. We have also used this method for a pattern recognition task where the recognition rates testify its superiority to well known and powerful descriptors. Extension of the method to other geometric transformations are interesting topics for further investigations.

References

1. Zhang, D., Lu, G.: Review of shape representation and description techniques. Pattern Recognition 37(1), 1–19 (2004)
2. Tabbone, S., Wendling, L., Salmon, J.-P.: A new shape descriptor defined on the Radon transform. Computer Vision and Image Understanding 102, 42–51 (2006)
3. Wang, X., Xiao, B., Ma, J.-F., Bi, X.-L.: Scaling and rotation invariant analysis approach to object recognition based on Radon and Fourier-Mellin transforms. Pattern Recognition 40(12), 3503–3508 (2007)
4. Chen, Y.W., Chen, Y.Q.: Invariant Description and Retrieval of Planar Shapes using Radon Composite Features. IEEE Trans. on Signal Processing 56(10), 4762–4771 (2008)
5. Nacereddine, N., Tabbone, S., Ziou, D., Hamami, L.: Shape-based image retrieval using a new descriptor based on the Radon and wavelet transforms. In: 20th Intern. Conf. on Pattern Recognition, pp. 1997–2000 (2010)
6. Hjouj, F., Kammler, D.W.: Identification of Reflected, Scaled, Translated, and Rotated Objects from their Radon Projections. IEEE Trans. on Image Processing 17(3), 301–310 (2008)
7. Wan, Y., Wei, N.: A Fast Algorithm for Recognizing Translated, Rotated, Reflected, and Scaled Objects from only their Projections. IEEE Signal Processing Letters 17(1), 71–74 (2010)
8. Deans, S.R.: The Radon Transform and Some of its Applications. John Wiley & Sons, New York (1983)
9. Shepp, L.A., Logan, B.F.: Fourier reconstruction of a head section. IEEE Trans. Nuclear Sci. 21(3), 21–44 (1974)
10. Sebastian, T.B., Klein, P.N., Kimia, B.B.: Recognition of Shapes by Editing Shock Graphs. In: 8th Intern. Conference on Computer Vision, pp. 755–762 (2001)
11. Doermann, D.S., Rivlin, E., Weiss, I.: Applying algebraic and differential invariants for logo recognition. Machine Vision and Applications 9(2), 73–86 (1996)
12. Teh, C.H., Chin, R.T.: On image analysis by the method of moments. IEEE Trans. on Pattern Analysis and Machine Intelligence 10(4), 496–513 (1988)
13. Khotanzad, A., Hong, Y.H.: Invariant image recognition by Zernike moments. IEEE Trans. on Patt. Anal. and Mach. Intell. 12(5), 489–497 (1990)
14. Zhang, D., Lu, G.: Shape-based image retrieval using generic Fourier descriptor. Signal Processing: Image Communication 17(10), 825–848 (2002)
15. Jafari-Khouzani, K., Soltanian-Zadeh, H.: Rotation-invariant multiresolution texture analysis using Radon an wavelet transforms. IEEE Trans. on Image Processing 14(6), 783–795 (2005)

Multi-view Gait Fusion for Large Scale Human Identification in Surveillance Videos

Emdad Hossain and Girija Chetty

Faculty of Information Science and Engineering, University of Canberra
emdad.hossain@canberra.edu.au

Abstract. In this paper we propose a novel multi-view feature fusion of gait biometric information in surveillance videos for large scale human identification. The experimental evaluation on low resolution surveillance video images from a publicly available database [1] showed that the combined LDA-MLP technique turns out to be a powerful method for capturing identity specific information from walking gait patterns. The multi-view fusion at feature level allows complementarity of multiple camera views in surveillance scenarios to be exploited for improvement of identity recognition performance.

Keywords: multi view images, LDA, MLP, identification, feature fusion.

1 Introduction

Human identification from arbitrary views is a very challenging problem, especially when one is walking at a distance. Over the last few years, recognizing identity from gait patterns has become a popular area of research in biometrics and computer vision, and one of the most successful applications of image analysis and understanding. Also, gait recognition is being considered as a next-generation recognition technology, with applicability to many civilian and high security environments such as airports, banks, military bases, car parks, railway stations etc. For these application scenarios, it is not possible to capture the frontal face, and is of low resolution. Hence most of traditional approaches used for face recognition fail; however, several studies have shown that it is possible to identify human from a distance from their gait or the way they walk. Even if frontal face is not visible, it is possible to establish the identity of the person using certain static and dynamic cues such as from face, ear, walking style, hand motion during walking etc. If automatic identification systems can be built based on this concept, it will be a great contribution to surveillance and security area.

However, each of these cues or traits captured from long range low resolution surveillance videos on its own are not powerful enough for ascertaining identity, A combination or fusion of each of them, along with an automatic processing technique can result in satisfactory recognition accuracies. In this paper, we propose usage of full profile silhouettes of persons without frontal faces acquired from multiple views, for capturing complementarity or inherent multi-modality available from the gait patterns of the walking human. This also addresses the problems with frontal faces, such as vulnerability to pose, illumination and expression variations. In addition, one of the

J. Blanc-Talon et al. (Eds.): ACIVS 2012, LNCS 7517, pp. 527–537, 2012.
© Springer-Verlag Berlin Heidelberg 2012

biggest shortcomings of frontal face is user cooperation - a mandatory requirement for establishing identity. On other hand, long range biometric information from surveillance videos captures several biometric traits such as side face, ear, body shape, and gait, which are a combination of physiological and behavioral biometrics, and this rich complementary information can be used in development of robust identification approaches. Further, by using certain automatic processing techniques for extracting salient features based on subspace or kernel methods, multivariate statistical techniques and learning classifiers, it is possible to enhance the performance in real world operating scenarios. In this paper we propose use of complementary information available from multiple views, and simple feature extraction technique based on linear discriminant analysis (LDA) along with a learning classifier based on "MultiLayerPerceptron" (MLP) for establishing identity. Further, we propose a feature level fusion of multiple views as fusing information at an early stage, is more effective than at later stages (score level fusion or late fusion), because features extracted from different biometrics at feature level can retain inherent multimodality much better at feature level and much more information than those in other fusion stages [2]. The experimental evaluation of the proposed multi-view fusion scheme on a publicly available (CASIA [1]) database shows promising performance for real world video surveillance scenarios. Rest of the paper is organised as follows. The background on the role of gait biometric for establishing identity is described in next section. The details of the proposed multimodal identification scheme is described in Section 3. Section 4 describes the experimental setup and results, and Section 5 concludes the paper with some plans for further research.

2   Background

Current state-of-the-art video surveillance systems, when used for recognizing the identity of the person in the scene, cannot perform very well due to low quality video or inappropriate processing techniques. Though much progress has been made in the past decade on visual based automatic person identification through utilizing different biometrics, including face recognition, iris and fingerprint recognition, each of these techniques work satisfactorily in highly controlled operating environments such as border control or immigration check points, under constrained illumination, pose and facial expression variations. To address the next generation security and surveillance requirements for not just high security environments, but also day-to-day civilian access control applications, we need a robust and invariant biometric trait [3] to identify a person for both controlled and uncontrolled operational environments. In this case, trait selection can play vital role. According to authors in [4], the expectations of next generation identity verification involve addressing issues related to application requirements, user concern and integration. Some of the suggestions made to address these issues were use of non-intrusive biometric traits, role of soft biometrics or dominant primary and non-dominant secondary identifiers and importance of novel automatic processing techniques. To conform to these recommendations; often there is a need to combine multiple physiological and behavioral biometric cues, leading to so called multimodal biometric identification system.

Each of the traits, physiological or behavioral have distinct advantages, for example; the behavioral biometrics can be collected non-obtrusively or even without the knowledge of the user. Behavioral data often does not require any special hardware (other than low cost off the shelf surveillance camera), so, it is very much cost effective. While most behavioral biometrics is not unique enough to provide reliable human identification they have been proved to be sufficiently accurate [5]. Gait, is such a powerful behavioral biometric, but on its own it cannot be considered as a strong biometric to identify a person. But, if we combine some other equally non-intrusive biometric with gait; it is expected to be strong combination for human identification. This could be profile (side) images containing side face or ear biometric traits and used with gait. Here side-face and ear images form the physiological component. Both can be collected unobtrusively without user involvement which is very much important in the public surveillance scenarios. It is possible to capture some or all of these multimodal components, if we use gait image information from multiple camera views, which can capture static and dynamic gait profile of a person from one view, with clear side face and ear from other views. This could be extremely applicable and reliable, as most of security infrastructure in public surveillance scenarios currently use multiple cameras. A multi-modal scheme based on such novel approach using multiple camera views can result in establishing identity from long range video images, which is otherwise difficult because face is not clearly visible in such scenarios. Further, it can also address shortcomings of unimodal biometric systems, which perform person recognition based on a single source of biometric, and are often affected by problems such as noisy sensor data and non-universality. Thus, due to these practical problems, the error rates associated with unimodal biometric systems are quite high and consequently it makes them unacceptable for deployment in security critical applications [6] like public surveillance.

Researchers found that one of the most promising techniques is use of multimodality or combination of biometric traits. Using PCA on combined image of ear and face, researchers in [7, 8] have found that multimodal recognition results in significant improvement over either individual biometrics. But most of these schemes work on highly controlled environment which is not quite the case for real world surveillance scenarios. Recently, few attempts have been expended on combining various biometrics in a bid to improve upon the recognition accuracy of classifiers that are based on a single biometric. Some biometric combinations which have been experimented include face, fingerprint and hand geometry [9]; face, fingerprint and speech [10]; face and iris [11]; face and ear [12]; and face and speech [13]. The multi-view fusion in gait profile however, did not attract much attention from the research community. This could be due to difficulty in processing and shortage of multi-view surveillance data. Next Section presents the proposed multi-view gait fusion scheme.

3   Multiview Gait Fusion Scheme

For experimental evaluation of the proposed multiview gait fusion schems, we used CASIA Gait Database collected by Institute of Automation, Chinese Academy of Sciences [1]. It is a large multi-view gait database, which is created in January 2005.

There are more than 300 subjects. We used three (3) different datasets known as dataset A (36 degree view point) dataset B (90 degree view point) and Dataset C (126 degree view point). All data was captured with normal video camera in 11 different views know as view angles. It takes into account four walking conditions: normal walking, slow walking, fast walking, and normal walking with a bag. All of our data here in this experiment taken from normal walking with free hand. The videos were all captured at night. Figure 1 shows the sample images in different view angles.

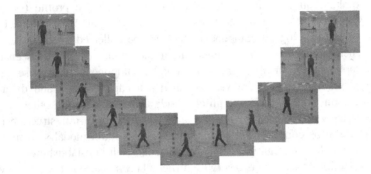

Fig. 1. Sample images

For all the experiments, we used 50 subjects from each of the dataset. It means, we used 50 subjects of extracted silhouettes from Dataset A, 50 subjects from B and 50 subjects from C. Each subject consists of 16 images and in total 2400 images for 150 subjects. Figure 2 shows the extracted silhouettes from dataset B and C.

Fig. 2. Extracted silhouettes

For each of the images in these data sets, we extracted the feature vectors in lower dimensional subspaces separately by using PCA (principal component analysis) and Linear Discriminant Analysis (LDA), and used a learning classifier based on well know multi-layer perceptron (MLP) for classifying each person ID. Our multiview fusion experiments involved identity recognition in LDA-MLP subspace for dataset (unimodal) and fusion of multiple views. The details of LDA subspace for extracting discriminating features is described next.

3.1   Linear Discriminant Analysis

The Linear Discriminent Analysis (LDA) similar to principal component analysis (PCA) and factor analysis, looks for linear combinations of variables which can best explain the data. LDA explicitly attempts to model the difference between the classes of data. PCA on the other hand does not take into account any difference in class, and factor analysis builds the feature combinations based on differences rather than similarities. Discriminant analysis is also different from factor analysis in that it is not an interdependence technique: a distinction between independent variables and dependent variables (also called criterion variables) must be made. LDA works when the measurements made on independent variables for each observation are continuous quantities. When dealing with categorical independent variables, the equivalent technique is discriminant correspondence analysis [15]. In our experiment LDA shows very promising as LDA model the difference between class and data.   Figure 3 shows the extracted feature using LDA

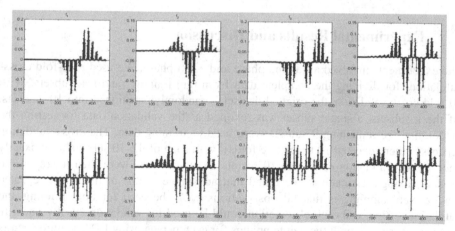

Fig. 3. LDA values extracted from silhouettes

3.2   Multi Layer Perceptron

Multi Layer perceptron (MLP) is a feedforward neural network with one or more layers between input and output layer. Feedforward means that data flows in one direction from input to output layer (forward). This type of network is trained with the backpropagation learning algorithm. MLPs are widely used for pattern classification, recognition, prediction and approximation. Multi Layer Perceptron can solve problems which are not linearly separable 16]. In our experiments we had 49 input layer, 800 hidden layer (for each data set) and 50 output layer. This is basically based on dimensions, instances and the classes of the dataset. Figure 4 shows the network architecture with MLP, where the green baton to very left; represents dimensions of LDA feature vector, the yellow baton in very right; represents each class (person). The details of the experiments is described in the next Section.

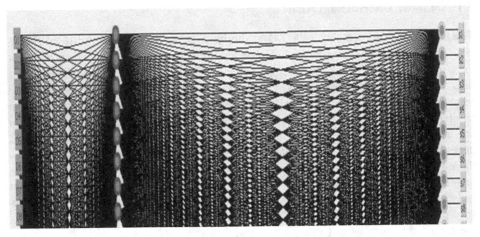

Fig. 4. MLP network architecture for the proposed scheme

4   Experimental Results and Discussion

The experiments involved a training phase and a test phase. We used a 10-fold cross-validation for dividing the complete data from tnto training and test subsets. With 10-fold cross-validation, the original dataset is randomly partitioned into 10 subsets. Of the k subsets, a single subset was retained as the validation data for testing the model, and the remaining 9 subsets were used as training data. The cross-validation process is then repeated 10 times (the folds), with each of the 10 subsets used exactly once as the validation data. The 10 results from the folds were then averaged to produce a single estimation. We found that advantage of this method over repeated random sub-sampling is that all observations could be used for both training and validation/testing, and each observation could be used for validation exactly once. In training phase, we built the gait templates for each person using LDA feature vectors for each of the dataset images (Dataset A, B and C) and trained the MLP classifier. In test phase the LDA feature vectors from unseen images in training set were classified with MLP classifier for each of the datasets separately(dataset A, B, C) and by fusion of multiple views. Figure 5 shows the rate of identification in 36 degree view point.

The figure shows high level of accuracy with the proposed scheme, for data captured in 36 degree view point. We achieved 98% correct identification by using LDA-MLP approach. And only 2% has been identified with wrong/incorrect identification. On the other hand, the data captured in 90 degree view point resulted in poor results as compare to the data from 36 degree view point. This could be due to

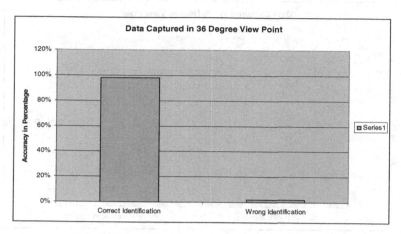

Fig. 5. Rate of Identification in 36 degree view point

difficulty in capturing the identity specific information from 90 degree view point as compared to 36 degrees. Figure 6 shows the results achieved with the data from 90 degree view point.

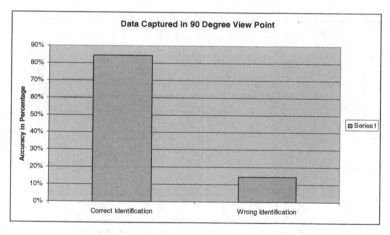

Fig. 6. Rate of Identification in 90 degree view point

The result shows, we received 84.5% correct identification for a large data set which has captured in 90 degree view point. And wrong/incorrect identification rate is around 14.5% which is quite large for real world scenario. Figure 7 represents the identification for dataset C (126 degree view point). It can be seen from this figure that it was possible to achieve 88.88% correct identification with the data captured in 123 degree view point. And 11.12% identified were wrongly identified.

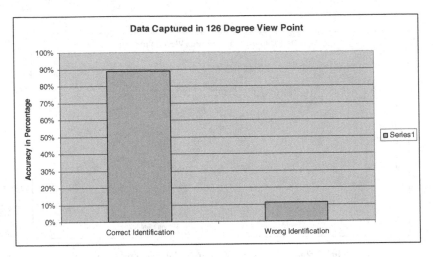

Fig. 7. Rate of Identification in 126 degree view point

After three (3) successful single mode experiments we combined data from all views. We performed feature level fusion of all three extracted set of LDA features, and Figure 8 shows the results of multi-view feature fusion based on gait images from surveillance videos.

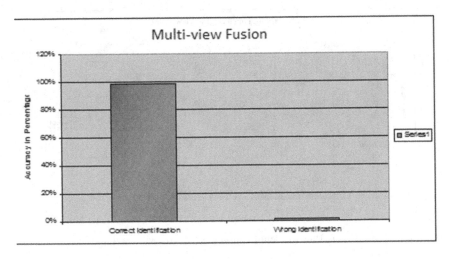

Fig. 8. Result of 3-D fusion

As can be seen from Figure 8, feature level fusion of multiple views results in a significant improvement in correct identification rate as compared to singe views, with 99 % accuracy for fusion of multiple views. Further, accuracy of each class individually was also good with excellent true positive (TP) rates. The figure for details accuracy is shown in the appendix after the references section. As mentioned earlier, each class in the table in the appendix represents each individual or person.

=== Detailed Accuracy By Class ===

TP Rate	FP Rate	Precision	Recall	F-Measure	ROC Area	Class
1	0	1	1	1	1	s1
1	0	1	1	1	1	s2
1	0	1	1	1	1	s3
0.875	0.003	0.875	0.875	0.875	0.994	s4
1	0	1	1	1	1	s5
0.875	0.003	0.875	0.875	0.875	0.998	s6
1	0	1	1	1	1	s7
1	0	1	1	1	1	s8
0.938	0	1	0.938	0.968	1	s9
0.938	0.001	0.938	0.938	0.938	1	s10
0.938	0	1	0.938	0.968	1	s11
1	0	1	1	1	1	s12
1	0	1	1	1	1	s13
1	0.001	0.941	1	0.97	1	s14
1	0	1	1	1	1	s15
1	0	1	1	1	1	s16
1	0.001	0.941	1	0.97	1	s17
1	0	1	1	1	1	s18
1	0	1	1	1	1	s19
0.938	0	1	0.938	0.968	1	s20
1	0	1	1	1	1	s21
1	0	1	1	1	1	s22
1	0	1	1	1	1	s23
1	0	1	1	1	1	s24
1	0	1	1	1	1	s25
1	0.001	0.941	1	0.97	1	s26
1	0	1	1	1	1	s27
1	0	1	1	1	1	s28
1	0.001	0.941	1	0.97	1	s29
0.938	0	1	0.938	0.968	1	s30
1	0.003	0.889	1	0.941	1	s31
1	0	1	1	1	1	s32
0.875	0	1	0.875	0.933	1	s33
1	0	1	1	1	1	s34
0.941	0	1	0.941	0.97	0.951	s35
1	0.001	0.938	1	0.968	0.999	s36
1	0	1	1	1	1	s37
0.938	0	1	0.938	0.968	1	s38
0.938	0	1	0.938	0.968	1	s39
1	0	1	1	1	1	s40
1	0	1	1	1	1	s41
1	0	1	1	1	1	s42
1	0	1	1	1	1	s43
1	0	1	1	1	1	s44
1	0	1	1	1	1	s45
0.938	0	1	0.938	0.968	1	s46
1	0	1	1	1	1	s47
0.938	0.004	0.833	0.938	0.882	0.999	s48
1	0.001	0.941	1	0.97	1	s49
1	0	1	1	1	1	s50

Figure: Detail accuracy by class (person to person)

Finally, to summarize our experimental validation we can say that; by using multiple views of surveillance video footage with long range videos (without detailed face images), it is possible to perform large scale identification with high level of accuracy, using simple subspace features (LDA) and classifier techniques(MLP). Such simple approaches can lead to real time and real world intelligent video surveillance systems - the beginning of a new dimension of security systems in public surveillance. Our small experimental efforts reported here shows the importance of multiview images from several cameras and feature level fusion of multiple views as an efficient gait biometric identification.

5   Conclusions and Further Plan

In this paper we proposed a novel multi view feature fusion from low resolution surveillance video for large scale human identification. We applied three (3) different camera views of image data captured with visible cameras. The experimental results shows the multi view fusion approach worked extremely well, indicating the potential of this approach to real time real world public surveillance applications, a truly next generation of surveillance and security systems. Our future research involves investigating novel approaches for exploiting multimodal complementary information available to enhance the performance of human identification for public video surveillance systems.

Acknowledgments. We are very much pleased and thankful to publicly available tools and databases for this paper. We would like to convey our gratitude to Institute of Automation, Chinese Academy of Sciences, for their excellent Database called "CASIA gait database". We also grateful to Machine Learning Group at University of Waikato for their "Weka" machine learning software. This is really massive software especially in machine learning area.

References

1. Zheng, S.: CASIA Gait Database collected by Institute of Automation, Chinese Academy of Sciences, CASIA Gait Database, http://www.sinobiometrics.com
2. Huang, L.: Person Recognition By Feature Fusion. Dept. of Engineering Technology Metropolitan State College of Denver Denver. IEEE, USA (2011)
3. Bringer, J., Chabanne, H.: Biometric Identification Paradigm Towards Privacy and Confidentiality Protection. In: Nichols, E.R. (ed.) Biometric: Theory, Application and Issues, pp. 123–141 (2011)
4. Jain, A.K.: Next Generation Biometrics, Department of Computer Science & Engineering. Michigan State University, Department of Brain & Cognitive Engineering, Korea University (2009)
5. Yampolskiy, R.V., Govindaraja, V.: Taxonomy of Behavioral Biometrics. Behavioral Biometrics for Human Identification, 1–43 (2010)

6. Meraoumia, A., Chitroub, S., Bouridane, A.: Fusion of Finger-Knuckle-Print and Palmprint for an Efficient Multi-biometric System of Person Recognition. IEEE Communications Society Subject Matter Experts for Publication in the IEEE ICC (2011)
7. Berretti, S., Bimbo, A., Pala, P.: 3D face recognaition using isogeodesic stripes. IEEE Transaction on Pattern Analysis and Machine Intelligence 32(12) (2010)
8. Yuan, L., Mu, Z., Xu, Z.: Using Ear Biometrics for Personal Recognition, School of Information Engineering, Univ. of Science and Technology Beijing, Beijing, 100083 yuanli64@hotmail.com
9. Ross, A., Jain, A.K.: Information fusion in biometrics. Pattern Recognition Letters 24, 2115–2125 (2003)
10. Jain, A.K., Hong, L., Kulkarni, Y.: A multimodal biometric system using fingerprints, face and speech. In: 2nd Int'l Conf. AVBPA, pp. 182–187 (1999)
11. Wang, Y., Tan, T., Jain, A.K.: Combining face and iris biometrics for identity verification. In: Int'l Conf. AVBPA, pp. 805–813 (2003)
12. Chang, K., et al.: Comparison and Combination of Ear and Face Images in Appearance-Based Biometrics. IEEE Trans. PAMI 25, 1160–1165 (2003)
13. Kittler, J., et al.: On combining classifiers. IEEE Trans. Pattern Anal. Mach. Intell. 20, 226–239 (1998)
14. Smith, L.I.: A tutorial on Principal Components Analysis
15. Linear discriminant analysis, Wikipedia, http://www.wikipedia.org
16. MULTI LAYER PERCEPTRON, http://www.neoroph.sourceforge.net
17. Platt, J.C.: Sequential Minimal Optimization: A Fast Algorithm for Training Support Vector Machines, Microsoft Research, Technical Report MSR-TR-98-14, (17) (1998) jplatt@microsoft.com
18. Shlizerman, I.K., Basri, R.: 3D Face Reconstruction from a Single Image Using a Single Reference Face Shape. IEEE Transactions on Pattern Analysis and Machine Intelligence 33(2) (2011)
19. Hossain, E., Chetty, G.: Multimodal Identity Verification Based on Learning Face and Gait Cues. In: Lu, B.-L., Zhang, L., Kwok, J. (eds.) ICONIP 2011, Part III. LNCS, vol. 7064, pp. 1–8. Springer, Heidelberg (2011)
20. Chin, Y.J., Ong, T.S., Teoh, A.B.J., Goh, M.K.O.: Multimodal Biometrics based Bit Extraction Method for Template Security. Faculty of Information Science and Technology, Multimedia University, Malaysia, School of Electrical and Electronic Engineering. Yonsei University, IEEE, Seoul (2011)
21. Multilayer Perceptron Neural Networks, The Multilayer Perceptron Neural Network Model, http://www.dtreg.com

Author Index